Safeguarding
the Nation

Safeguarding the Nation

The Story of the Modern Royal Navy

JOHN ROBERTS

*The Royal Navy is not an assembly of ships.
It is an institution, enduring through centuries
and rich in the experience and skills of the generations
who have made it and which it has made.*

PAUL AND MARGARET McGUIRE, *The Price of Admiralty*

Seaforth
PUBLISHING

DEDICATION

This book is dedicated by the White Ensign Association
to all those men and women who have served in the Royal Navy,
the Royal Marines and their Reserves

This tribute is the story of what the Royal Navy has done and its many great achievements over the last fifty years. It is an account of the numerous operations, actions, engagements and deployments over that period. Time, space and the Official Secrets Act have limited the scope for developing certain aspects of the whole picture and some subjects have perforce had to remain largely outside the coverage of this tribute. Those matters have included covert submarine operations and incidents during the Cold War, the evolution and implementation of tactical doctrine and the deployment of tactical nuclear weapons, the development and integration of certain sophisticated sensors and weapons systems, information technology and data handling, and command, control and communications equipments. Other issues such as funding, budgeting, recruiting, changing shipboard living conditions etc have also not been developed in this tribute.

The views expressed in this book are those of the writer, and many contributors, and do not necessarily represent the views of the Royal Navy or Her Majesty's Government.

The White Ensign Association is especially indebted to the Naval Historical Branch, *Navy News*, the Royal Naval Museum, the Royal Navy Submarine Museum, the Fleet Air Arm Museum, the Fleet Photographic Unit and the Director of Public Relations (Navy).

The White Ensign Association is very grateful to Amlin, a marine insurer at Lloyd's for over one hundred years, for very kindly sponsoring the production and distribution of this book.

 AMLIN

THE WHITE ENSIGN ASSOCIATION LTD
HMS *Belfast*
Tooley Street, London, SE1 2JH
office@whiteensign.co.uk

Half title page: *Ark Royal* on completion of her refit with the third mast (MS)(RC).(Ms Mandy Shepherd. By kind permission of the Commanding Officer, *Ark Royal*, and supplied by www.maritimeprints.com)

Title page: *Triumph* and *Northumberland* – see page 266

First published in Great Britain in 2009 by
Seaforth Publishing,
Pen & Sword Books Ltd,
47 Church Street,
Barnsley S70 2AS

www.seaforthpublishing.com

British Library Cataloguing in Publication Data
A catalogue record for this book is available from the British Library

ISBN 978 1 84832 043 7

Typeset and designed by Roger Daniels
Printed and bound in Thailand

Contents

FOREWORD

Admiral His Royal Highness the Prince of Wales KG, KT, OM, GCB, AK, QSO, ADC
Patron of the White Ensign Association

I am delighted to have the opportunity to write the foreword to this important book, which pays tribute to the Royal Navy on the occasion of the 50th Anniversary of the White Ensign Association. As the Association works so closely with the Royal Navy it is in a unique and privileged position to observe and comment on the many great achievements of the Service over the last half century. This book highlights the impressive record of what the Royal Navy has done and I hope will help to bring awareness to many.

For several hundred years the Royal Navy was the most powerful navy in the world and played a key role in building and defending the British Empire which, in the late nineteenth century, covered a large proportion of the globe. The huge burden of two World Wars, however, led to the end of the British Empire, which then became the British Commonwealth of Nations. It was inevitable after the Second World War that the Armed Forces would face major changes and those finally came with the far-reaching Defence Review of 1957. The consequent reordering of Britain's defences brought large scale reductions in equipment and manpower, and established new priorities. The Royal Navy, along with the other two Services, had to adjust during a difficult period of transformation to meet the requirements of the post imperial era. Throughout those years the Navy had to maintain its key role in the defence of the United Kingdom and her many interests worldwide and was involved in numerous operations, engagements and confrontations, from the Cold War and Cod Wars to the Falklands Campaign and Gulf Wars of this century. The story of how well the Royal Navy coped with those difficult changes and the demanding tasks it was called upon to perform are set out in this record of its service and many achievements. It shows clearly how the Navy has continued to safeguard the nation.

CLARENCE HOUSE

It was the cuts in naval manpower in 1957 which led to the establishment of the White Ensign Association in the City of London by my Great Uncle, Lord Mountbatten, in June 1958. He was the First Sea Lord at that time and was determined to help all those officers and men leaving the Service under the 'Duncan Sandys' Axe'. The 1957 Defence Review had called for very substantial reductions in the Fleet and for Naval Manpower to be cut by 26,000 in four years, which necessitated a redundancy programme. A great many of those leaving needed help and the Association provided much of that necessary assistance. It then became apparent that this unique charity should extend its help to include all those serving, which it duly did.

Over those fifty years the Association has maintained station on the Royal Navy providing faithful support and assisting a huge number of officers, men and women with a whole range of services. The Association serves the entire Naval Community – assessed at around one million in 2005, including all ranks and rates, serving, resettling and retired – and, of course, their families. Although the Royal Navy has reduced in size, particularly over the last twenty years or so, its role is undiminished and there seems to be no reduction in the calls for assistance.

As Patron of the Association, I take a close interest in its many activities and derive much pride from the tremendous support it still provides to all those who serve, particularly in these difficult times. I am also pleased that the Association has used its unique position, close alongside, to provide this tribute to the Royal Navy.

PREFACE

Commodore Sir Donald Gosling KCVO, RNR
President of the White Ensign Association

The White Ensign Association has had the great honour of serving the Royal Navy over the past fifty years, since it was founded by Admiral of the Fleet the Earl Mountbatten of Burma in June 1958. Throughout that time the Association has worked very closely alongside the members of the Naval Services of the Crown and has helped well in excess of 37,000 people as well as briefing over 100,000 of them. The Association has therefore been in a privileged position to observe those men and women carrying out their many tasks and witness the great changes that have taken place in the Service over that time.

The Association has also been in a unique situation to note and appreciate the great contribution made by the Royal Navy during that period. Operating as it does for much of the time over the horizon and thus out of the public eye, a great deal of what the Navy achieves is often unobserved and frequently not acknowledged. Inevitably therefore it goes largely without due recognition.

So it is fitting that on the occasion of the fiftieth anniversary of the Association it should take the opportunity to pay tribute to the Royal Navy. This book is a straightforward account of what the Royal Navy has done over those years and sets out to place on record the tremendous achievements of the Service over the last half-century. It shows just what a debt of gratitude the nation owes the Royal Navy for its unstinting and valiant service in war and peace. It has

been a period during which the White Ensign Association has been proud to play its part in helping to support all those who serve in the naval forces of the Crown.

The past few years have seen a much reduced Navy having to cope with a significantly busier operational tempo, and this has inevitably increased the pressures on those who serve. The consequences of this have led more and more of them to turn to the Association and seek assistance. It is here that the work of the Association comes to the fore, helping and assisting all with the many problems that they face. Each year we are now carrying out over 3,700 tasks, conducting 200 visits to ships, establishments and individuals, and providing over 100 presentations. This is no mean achievement and is a very clear demonstration of the ongoing need for all our services. There is certainly no sign of the pace letting up, and it is therefore the aim and desire of the Association to continue to provide a first-class service to all those who need us.

This book also helps remind us that the many threats, difficulties and problems we face today are just as great as ever they have been, which reinforces the essential requirement for a strong Royal Navy. We overlook that basic lesson at our peril. I commend this book to you, and I am sure you will be impressed by what the Navy has done and the great service it has rendered this nation – a message I would urge you to spread at every opportunity.

Donald Gosling.

24 June 2008
HMS *Belfast*

INTRODUCTION

*"It is upon the Navy, under the Providence
of God that the safety, honour and welfare
of this realm do chiefly attend"*

(KING CHARLES II, FROM THE PREAMBLE TO THE ARTICLES OF WAR)

Admiral the
Lord Boyce
GCB OBE DL

Chief of the
Defence Staff
2001~2003

FOR THE LAST HALF-CENTURY the Royal Navy has continued to act as the 'Safeguard of the Nation', defending Britain and her many interests worldwide. It has proved a turbulent and at times painful period of adjustment as Britain downsized from her status of a leading world empire to that of a medium power, a change driven by economic, industrial, territorial and trade decline, with commensurate political levelling. Over the period the Royal Navy has been hugely reduced, with naval manpower being cut from 121,500 in 1957, to 35,000 by 2008, as well as going through an era of difficult transformation from a very large Fleet of conventional warships to the modern, relatively small, high-tech and highly capable Navy of today.

The Duncan Sandys defence review of 1957, which followed Operation Musketeer and the Suez crisis, resulted in major reductions to the armed forces and introduced a fundamental change in strategy. As well as imposing big cuts in manpower, switching from National Service to leaner, all-volunteer, professional services, it changed the emphasis from large-scale conventional forces to concentrate on nuclear weapons, guided missiles and modern technology. Prior to the defence review Britain had a large powerful Fleet of conventional warships operating worldwide, with three fundamental tasks, namely defending Britain's Empire and interests worldwide, safeguarding her trade and contributing to the defence of the West in the Cold War. The fundamental defence review changed priorities and tasks and in the event was a major turning point for the armed forces and, to a certain extent, for the position of Britain in the world order. Over the following half-century the role, shape and size of the Fleet was to change considerably during a period that can be roughly divided into two distinct eras, with the first covering the time of the Cold War up to the ultimate triumph of the West in 1990, and the second being the period dominated by operations against rogue or failing states and by the war on international terrorism.

In the earlier part, during the Cold War stand-off between the two superpowers until the collapse of the Warsaw Pact, the Royal Navy with its ASW expertise was able to play an important role in the North Atlantic, where it underpinned NATO's ability to ensure the reinforcement of Europe that was crucial to NATO's defence strategy. The prime threat to the vital resupply convoys across the North Atlantic came from the Warsaw Pact's vast submarine fleet, which needed access through the GRIUK (Greenland–Iceland–Faeroes–UK) Gap to the open sea, and Royal Navy escorts and submarines were regularly deployed forward to mount a barrier across this strategic piece of water and prepare to interdict the Soviet Northern Fleet and submarines as they attempted to gain access to the Atlantic. The Royal Navy also had a key part to play in protecting the northern flank of NATO with regular deployments and exercises off Norway.

On 30 April 1969 the Royal Navy took over responsibility from the RAF V-bomber force for maintaining the nation's strategic nuclear deterrent, and at least one SSBN (ballistic missile nuclear submarine) has been continuously at sea on deterrent patrol ever since. At the other end of the spectrum, the Royal Navy in the sixties had to cover, and where necessary defend, the retreat from empire as Britain steadily shed her colonies and withdrew from her many possessions and responsibilities overseas. Then in 1982, almost out of the blue, the Royal Navy had to mount an expedition to retake the Falkland Islands, nearly 8,000 miles away, as part of Operation Corporate.

In more recent years, following the collapse of the Warsaw Pact, a very different defence posture has been required as the UK has adjusted to diverse threats, in particular the need to combat international terrorism and maintain stability in key areas of the world, including along the vital sea lines of communication – with the most obvious example of this being the First Gulf War, very soon after the fall of the Iron Curtain – just as the liberal democracies of NATO were seeking to run down their forces to provide a 'Peace Dividend'. Since that event the rapid pace and escalating costs of technology and ever more complex defence systems have all added to the burdens of governments seeking to provide security for their people. As for the Royal Navy, it has had to change from a primarily blue-water ASW (anti-submarine warfare) force in the Atlantic to a littoral expeditionary force capable of power projection far inland, as typified by operations in Afghanistan, where at times more than 50 per cent of the personnel in theatre have been from the Naval Service.

Over this period of changing strategic and military requirements Britain suffered an inexorable industrial and economic decline and went through an extremely painful period of adjustment. The country had to come to terms with her new position in the world order as a medium power, which was not an easy adjustment with all her residual commitments flowing from running the biggest empire in the world as a super-power. The decline inevitably caused a ceaseless round of defence reviews and cuts in the armed forces as successive governments had little alternative but to seek every possible means of reducing overall expenditure and commitments. The Royal Navy, the smallest and least visible of the three services, has certainly had to bear her

Silver Jubilee Fleet Review, 28 June 1977

share, with the Fleet and naval manpower being steadily cut back. At the same time the Navy has been busily engaged in many operations and confrontations around the globe, from Cod Wars in the extreme north to the Falklands War in the far south, with wars in the Middle East as well as the Far East. So despite the reduction in the size of the Fleet, the magnitude and range of the tasks confronting the Royal Navy have remained largely the same and the Service has met all of its many commitments with great distinction. Britain may no longer have a world empire to defend, but it still has its vital world trade, on which it depends for survival, to protect.

Throughout these fifty years the White Ensign Association has been helping to support all those who serve in the naval forces of the Crown and it has witnessed how the Royal Navy has continued to discharge its important tasks with fewer and fewer resources as the defence budget has inexorably shrunk. As the President has pointed out, the Association has noted that a consequence has been to increase the pressures on those who serve, leading an increasing number of them to turn to the Association and seek assistance. Those who serve today tend to be better educated and more aware of what is available to help them, and they also are inclined to be less inhibited about requesting assistance when they need it. For these reasons the assistance being provided by the Association now actually appears to be greater than when the Fleet was much larger.

The story of what the Royal Navy has achieved over the last fifty years is both a fascinating and a proud one. The Navy, known as the 'Silent Service' and usually seen only at Fleet Reviews such as the Silver Jubilee Review in 1977, has not been fully successful in gaining due recognition for all its many achievements. Much of what it has done and achieved is not as widely known as it should be, particularly amongst those who have every reason to be deeply grateful, and hence it has not been accorded the full recognition that it so justly deserves. The White Ensign Association is therefore pleased to be able to play some small part in helping to put this right by producing this Golden Jubilee commemorative book. The book is a straightforward account of the many operations and deployments of the Royal Navy over the last fifty years and serves to remind us of just how important the Service has been to the survival and safety of Britain, and the protection of her many interests throughout the world.

Mike Boyce

Chairman
24 June 2008 HMS *Belfast*

CHAPTER 1

Genesis of the Modern Navy 1957–1959

At dawn on a clear day in the western Mediterranean two warships, a US cruiser and a British destroyer, were on a converging course some sixty miles south-east of Gibraltar. The sea was flat calm with the early morning sun rising over the eastern horizon. The ships were approaching each other at a combined speed of over twenty-eight knots. When they had closed to within visual range a challenge was flashed from the signal deck of the larger warship, a US heavy cruiser of the 6th Fleet. A short while later, on receipt of the correct identification signal, a brief further message was flashed from the US cruiser: 'Greetings to the second biggest navy in the world!' She then courteously dipped her ensign in the traditional salute to the Royal Navy.

An equally brief reply was flashed back from the bridge of the Royal Navy destroyer as she hove to on the cruiser's starboard bow: 'Greetings to the SECOND BEST navy in the world!!' The destroyer then dipped her ensign, acknowledging the salute from the US cruiser.[2]

This story of the exchange of signals between the Royal Navy and the United States Navy in the Mediterranean, some time after the end of World War II, poignantly summed up the dramatic change of status of the Royal Navy. For nearly 200 years, from the Seven Years War (1756–63) to World War II , the Royal Navy had been the supreme maritime power, exercising command of the sea and dominating the world's oceans. She had played the key role in supporting and defending the British Empire. At the end of World War II the Royal Navy had 8,940 ships and vessels of all types in commission and 864,000 people in uniform, yet the United States Navy was even bigger. Despite this the traditions, expertise and standards set and maintained by the 'Senior Service' of the world's leading maritime nation remained second to none.

Although the United States Navy had overtaken the Royal Navy in terms of size, Britain still held her position as the world's greatest maritime nation. The Royal Navy and Merchant Navy combined outnumbered the total number of warships and registered merchant ships belonging to the United States. Britain's merchant fleet was to remain the world's largest until well into the 1960s.[3] Britain clearly remained a great maritime trading nation dependent on the sea. Over forty years later, in 2001, the First Sea Lord, Admiral Sir Alan West, stated that 'The Royal Navy was still the second most powerful Navy in the world and certainly the best.'[4]

The early post-war years were overshadowed by Britain's rapid economic, industrial and political decline as she

FIRST SEA LORDS
Admiral of the
Fleet the
Earl Mountbatten
of Burma
and
Admiral Lambe

SECOND SEA LORDS
Admirals
Lambe and
Holland-Martin

NAVAL MANPOWER
121,500

MERCANTILE MARINE
5,508
merchant ships[1]

A traditional challenge being flashed from a Royal Navy destroyer
(NN)

struggled to shoulder the crippling burden of paying the cost of the war and rebuilding her shattered industries and infrastructure. The national debt had soared to a record level and Britain was unable to pay the 'Lend-Lease' debt to America at the end of World War II. Britain was forced to take on a further loan of $3,750 million to be repaid in fifty equal payments until 2001.

In step with the huge economic and political decline was the continued break-up of the British Empire. By the mid-1950s only a relatively small number of colonies and protectorates were left of an empire which at its peak, in 1921, had covered a quarter of the surface of the globe, and included a quarter of the world's population. It was known as 'the empire on which the sun never set'.

Britain's true place in the new world order was finally recognised in the Defence White Paper of 1957 (Cmnd. 230), which resulted from a fundamental defence review ordered in response to Britain's rapidly declining economic situation. It was a defining moment for the armed forces of the United Kingdom marking the major shift in defence policy from large expensive conventional forces to smaller specialised forces more reliant on nuclear weapons and missiles. It was a watershed for the Royal Navy, being the turning point from the old traditional imperial navy towards the modern Royal Navy of the nuclear age.

NATO, NUCLEAR DEFENCE POLICY AND NAVAL STRATEGY

At the end of the fifties the government of the United Kingdom had four prime requirements for their naval and military planners to meet: defence of the realm, maintenance of defence commitments to NATO and the mainland of Europe, support of the colonies and overseas interests, and finally the protection of Britain's worldwide trade. Whilst the first two requirements were met in conjunction with allies, the last two were covered solely by the armed forces of the UK, primarily the Royal Navy.

The Cold War By 1957 the 'Third World War', commonly known as the 'Cold War', had reached its eighth year. Predominantly a political and economic war of force deployment, manoeuvre and military technology, it was fought slowly and with much less intensity than its two immediate predecessors between 1914 and 1945. Nevertheless it was a perilous and dangerous confrontation, which seriously

HMS *Vanguard*

The Last of the *Vanguard* Class Battleships

The *Vanguard* was the very last of the battleships and had been replaced by the aircraft carrier as the capital ship of the fleet.

Launched:	30 November 1944
Commissioned:	9 August 1946
Displacement:	46,000 tonnes
Length:	246.8m
Propulsion:	8 Admiralty 3-drum water-tube boilers, 4 Parsons single reduction steam turbines, 4 shafts
Armament:	8 BL 15 in guns in 4 twin mountings,
	16 QF 5.25 in guns in 8 twin mountings,
	54 40mm Bofors AA guns in 9 sextuple mountings,
	2 40mm Bofors AA guns in twin mounting,
	11 40mm Bofors AA guns in single mountings and
	4 QF 47mm saluting guns
Complement:	1,500
No. in class:	1

threatened the Western world with catastrophic destruction. It dominated all defence planning and expenditure, and nuclear weapons became the key components of the overall strategy.

NATO As the political situation in Europe had steadily deteriorated and the threat from the Soviet Union had relentlessly increased, the Western allies explored their common defence needs. The Washington Treaty of 1949, built on the 'Western Union' Brussels Treaty of 1948, established NATO as the security alliance for the collective self-defence of the West. By the end of that year NATO had formulated its defence strategy (the Strategic Concept for the Defence of the North Atlantic Treaty Area – DC 6). DC 6 set out the basic principles of military co-operation and force co-ordination to provide collective defence in the event of an attack against any member state.

Military Strategy DC 6 was then refined and modified to respond to the growing might of the Soviet armed forces,

The battleship *Vanguard*, flagship of the Reserve Fleet
(RNM)

MAIN PICTURE:
The Royal Yacht *Britannia* leading the Fleet
(RNM)

BELOW LEFT:
Cruisers firing the traditional royal salute
(OJ) (CH) (RC)

RIGHT:
Operation Steadfast
(NN)

mostly land and air forces. The NATO Military Committee set out the allied military planning framework in Plan MC 14, and the detailed military strategy (MC 14/1) was finally approved in December 1952.

Nuclear Strategy By the mid-fifties the West had become thoroughly alarmed by the massive build-up of Soviet and Warsaw Pact conventional forces and realised it would have little alternative but to depend on nuclear weapons in order to counter them. Fears of Warsaw Pact aggression and expansionism were further fuelled by Soviet intervention in Hungary and the Lebanon in 1956. Consequently in 1957 the Allies formulated the fundamental NATO strategy of 'massive retaliation', known as the 'trip wire' strategy, whereby the Alliance would use nuclear weapons to respond to any major Soviet attack. By concentrating on nuclear weapons the NATO Allies reduced the need to inflate their defence spending on expensive conventional forces in order to try

and match the huge Soviet arms build-up. As regards naval strategy, the effect of a short war scenario was to reduce the reliance of NATO and Europe on resupply across the Atlantic and hence lessen the importance of ASW (anti-submarine-warfare) ships. The NATO strategy was however inherently dangerous, as the Soviets had already developed a hydrogen bomb, and in 1957 they successfully launched their first satellite, 'Sputnik', with an SS-6 Sapwood ICBM (intercontinental ballistic missile).

In 1958 Khrushchev demanded the withdrawal of all Western occupying forces from Berlin. Next, after the Cuban Revolution in 1959, he formed an alliance with Fidel Castro and was in a position to start deploying forces in close proximity to the United States. East–West tension was steadily rising by the turn of the decade.

UK Defence Review 1957 In the Suez Crisis of 1956 Britain and France had launched Operation Musketeer against Egypt

The cruiser *Bermuda* at Malta, April 1958 (RNM)

in response to President Nasser's nationalisation of the Suez Canal. The military operation had been a success but severe economic pressure from the USA had forced a cease-fire and an embarrassing climb-down by Britain and France. Anthony Eden, the British Prime Minister, resigned on 9 January 1957 and was replaced by Harold Macmillan. One of Macmillan's early actions was to order Duncan Sandys, his new Defence Minister, to carry out a fundamental defence review. The main driver of the review was the need to achieve huge savings in the defence budget in order to ease the many pressures on the failing British economy. The result was the Defence White Paper (Cmnd. 230), published in April 1957 and entitled 'Defence: Outline of Future Policy'. The White Paper set out huge cuts in equipment and reductions in uniformed manpower across all three armed services, with the Royal Navy taking the brunt.

Defence policy was reordered to concentrate on the immediate requirements of defence of the homeland and

commitments to NATO, with reliance on nuclear deterrence and modern military technology. This shifted the emphasis from large conventional forces deployed worldwide to smaller more professional forces based much closer to home. National Service was to be phased out, regiments and air squadrons scrapped, and big reductions imposed on the Fleet and naval manpower. Most of the Reserve Fleet, of over 500 ships, was to be paid off and ultimately scrapped or sold. Over 100 shore establishments were to be closed.

Sandys was certainly no friend of the Royal Navy and was very much opposed to the concept of big expensive fleets. He saw the Royal Navy as ripe for yielding the greatest savings of the three armed forces and added to his Defence White Paper the infamous phrase 'The role of naval forces in total war is uncertain'. The phrase was based on the perception that total war would rapidly resort to crippling nuclear strikes and thus all be over within a matter of a few weeks at the most, before naval forces would have any opportunity to participate. The White Paper did accept however that a nuclear exchange might not prove conclusive, in which case it would be vital to defend reinforcement convoys across the Atlantic against Soviet submarines.

Desmond Wettern stated that the defence review of 1957 'set a precedent that would be followed by successive governments in that it established the paramountcy of the economy over national security'.[5]

Defence Review 1958 (ASW) Following on from the 1957 White Paper, the 1958 Defence White Paper provided some clarity on the role of naval forces, stating that the priority in home waters would be ASW, as well as an effective contribution to the combined naval forces of the Western Alliance. This would be at the expense of balanced forces, and outside the NATO area the prime role would be the protection of shipping in peace and limited war. Even the two operational aircraft carriers, one deployed with the Mediterranean Fleet and one with the Home Fleet, would have ASW as their primary role.

THE FLEET

At the very end of 1956, when the last ships of Operation Musketeer had been withdrawn from the eastern Mediterranean, the Royal Navy still possessed a massive fleet, deployed in four operational fleets – Home, Mediterranean, Far East and East Indies – and supported by a huge Reserve Fleet. As well as five large naval bases in home waters the Royal Navy maintained overseas naval bases in Gibraltar, Malta, Simonstown, Trincomalee, Singapore and Hong Kong.

Operation Steadfast The Home Fleet, including the aircraft carriers *Ark Royal*, *Albion* and *Ocean*, was reviewed by HM the Queen on board the Royal Yacht *Britannia* in the Cromarty Firth on 27–9 May 1957. The impressive review was codenamed Operation Steadfast.

During that year, however, a large number of warships, many from the Reserve Fleet, were scrapped as a result of

The aircraft carrier *Victorious* leaving New York on 3 August 1959 (RNM)

the Duncan Sandys' defence review. Six aircraft carriers, including *Ocean* and *Theseus*, which had only just been converted to improvised helicopter carriers and deployed to Suez, were scrapped. The other aircraft carriers, *Perseus, Glory, Illustrious* and *Unicorn*, which had already been laid up in reserve, were also consigned to the scrapyard.

The great *King George V* class battleships, *Anson, Duke of York, Howe* and *King George V*, were all finally scrapped, leaving *Vanguard*, flagship of the Reserve Fleet, as the sole remaining battleship, the very last of the mighty super-Dreadnoughts. The cruisers *Liverpool, Glasgow, Bellona, Cleopatra, Dido, Euryalus,* and *Cumberland* also went to the breakers' yards.

In addition six destroyers, forty frigates, twenty ocean minesweepers and a whole range of other ships, submarines and vessels were scrapped. Some warships were sold to other countries, including the aircraft carrier *Warrior*, which had been fitted with an angled flight deck and was sold to Argentina.

Strength of the Fleet Despite the large-scale reductions the strength of the fleet at the end of 1957 was still impressive. Officially the Navy had nearly 800 ships and vessels on its books in 1957. The backbone of the fleet, the capital ships, included seven aircraft carriers, the 43,000-ton fleet carriers *Ark Royal* and *Eagle*, the newly, and extensively, rebuilt *Victorious* (30,000 tons), the three *Centaur* class light fleet carriers, *Albion, Bulwark* and *Centaur* (22,000 tons), and *Magnificent* (15,700 tons), just returned from loan to the Royal Canadian Navy. In addition the fourth and final *Centaur* class light fleet carrier *Hermes* was nearing completion. The *Bulwark* was being converted for her modern commando carrier role as a result of lessons learnt during the amphibious phase of Operation Musketeer, and work started on converting the light fleet aircraft carrier *Triumph* to a repair ship.

The cruiser squadrons comprised thirteen cruisers including *Superb*, *Swiftsure* and *Belfast*, three *Southampton* class, five *Mauritius* class and two *Ceylon* class. In addition work was being continued on the three *Tiger* class cruisers, *Blake*, *Lion* and *Tiger*, which had been laid down at the end of World War II but never completed. The rest of the fleet consisted of fifty-six destroyers, 107 frigates, forty-eight submarines, 200 minesweepers, fifty-two coastal and landing craft and eighty-eight support ships as well as large numbers of auxiliaries.

HMS *Ark Royal*

Audacious Class Aircraft Carrier

Ark Royal and *Eagle* were the two largest fixed-wing fleet carriers in the Royal Navy and served up until the mid-seventies (*Eagle* to 1972 and *Ark Royal* to 1978). They operated nuclear strike capable aircraft and were the backbone of the fleet. The fleet carriers were the capital ships of the Royal Navy until the 1970s.

Launched:	3 May 1950
Commissioned:	25 February 1955
Displacement:	36,800 tonnes
Length:	245m
Propulsion:	8 Admiralty 3-drum boilers in 4 boiler rooms, 4 sets of Parsons geared turbines, 4 shafts
Armament:	As built 16 4.5 in gun (8 2)
	52 40mm (6 6, 2 2, 12 1)
	All fixed armament removed in 1969
	Carrier air group – when embarked
	Carrier air group 1970:
	12 Phantom FG Mk 1,
	14 Buccaneer S Mk 2,
	4 Gannet AEW Mk 3,
	6 Sea King HAS Mk 1,
	2 Wessex HAR Mk 1,
	1 Gannet COD Mk 4
Complement:	2,250 (2,640 with embarked air staff)
No. in class:	2: *Ark Royal* and *Eagle*

***Ark Royal*'s Visit to New York** In June 1957 the aircraft carrier *Ark Royal*, escorted by the destroyers *Diamond* and *Duchess*, crossed the Atlantic and visited New York before taking part in the US Navy's International Naval Review and 'Fleet Week'. The naval review, which marked the 350th anniversary of the founding of the first colony at Jamestown, included 103 warships from seventeen nations and, at the time, was the largest naval review in history. The US Navy was impressed with *Ark Royal* and her escorts, stating, 'The Royal Navy was still an efficient, modern and powerful fighting force'.

Follow-Up Visit to New York by *Victorious* Two years later the aircraft carrier *Victorious* carried out a further successful visit to New York, where her ship's company received a great welcome.

FIRST SEA LORDS

Admiral the Earl Mountbatten had been appointed First Sea Lord on 18 April 1955 and right from the start had tackled his important task with energy and relish reminiscent of the great Admiral Jackie Fisher. He was full of enthusiasm and ideas, which were essential at such a difficult time for the Royal Navy facing decline and huge cut-backs in ships and manpower. He foresaw the cuts of the Sandys defence review and had already formed a 'Way Ahead Committee' to identify economies and savings and to modernise and streamline the Royal Navy. The committee selected many shore establishments to be closed and also ships to be taken out of the Fleet.

Admiral Mountbatten Mountbatten was born on 25 June 1900 and joined the Royal Navy as a cadet in 1913. He served on board Admiral Beatty's flagship *Lion* and also in the battleship *Queen Elizabeth* during World War I. Between the wars he served in the battleships *Revenge* and *Centurion* and the battlecruisers *Renown* and *Repulse* before being given command of the destroyers *Daring* and *Wishart*.

In World War II Mountbatten commanded the destroyer *Kelly* and the 5th Destroyer Flotilla until the *Kelly* was sunk off Crete in 1941. He was subsequently appointed Chief of Combined Operations and then Supreme Allied Commander South-East Asia as an admiral. After the war he became Viceroy and Governor-General of India, and he had to deal with Indian independence and the partition of the Indian Empire in 1947.

In 1948 Mountbatten commanded the 1st Cruiser Squadron, and two years later he was the Fourth Sea Lord. He then commanded the Mediterranean Fleet in 1952, being promoted full Admiral the following year. In April 1955 he was appointed First Sea Lord, in which post he was to remain for four years until Admiral Sir Charles Lambe relieved him in July 1959. Mountbatten was then appointed Chief of the Defence Staff and continued sadly to witness the decline of his great Service. He was passionate about everything that concerned the Royal Navy and proved to be one of the most important and influential of the post-war senior admirals. Many of his ideas and innovations had significant and lasting effects on the future of the Royal Navy.

Admiral Lambe Charles Lambe was born in December 1900 and joined the Royal Navy as a cadet in 1914, going to sea in the battleship *Empress of India* at the end of World War I. At the outbreak of World War II he was in command of the cruiser *Dunedin*, but he spent most of the war in the Naval Plans Division at the Admiralty. In 1944 he commanded the aircraft carrier *Illustrious* in the Pacific. He then returned to the Admiralty in charge of flying training before commanding the 3rd Aircraft Carrier Squadron. He was promoted Vice Admiral in 1950 and was Flag Officer Air (Home) before being appointed Commander in Chief Far East Station. He served as Second Sea Lord for three years from 1954 and then became Commander in Chief

Mediterranean Fleet before relieving Lord Mountbatten as First Sea Lord in 1959.

Admiral Lambe suffered a heart attack six months after taking over and had to be relieved on 10 May 1960. He died three months later aged fifty-nine.

OPERATIONS AND DEPLOYMENTS, 1957–1959

In 1957 the Royal Navy was deployed on a range of operational peace-keeping tasks around the world. Ships and squadrons were maintained on station as guardships in key strategic bases on the main shipping routes and SLOCs (sea lines of communication). At home, in early 1958, the Home Fleet sailed for its last deployment as a fleet. The aircraft carrier *Bulwark*, escorted by cruisers and destroyers, led the Home Fleet for its spring cruise, which was to be its last regular one. In the future ships of the Home Fleet would be deployed in task groups for specific operations, deployments, tasks or exercises.

The Persian Gulf In the Persian Gulf a squadron of four Loch class frigates (*Loch Fada, Loch Fyne, Loch Killisport* and *Loch Ruthven*) was stationed at Jufair, the naval station in Bahrain. The frigates conducted extensive patrols, searching dhows, intercepting arms and slave trafficking and preventing smuggling, piracy and rebel infiltration. They also had

to carry out policing actions ashore, protecting British nationals and property and quelling local riots and disturbances.

The East Indies Station was disbanded in 1958 and replaced by the Arabian Seas and Persian Gulf Station, covering the Persian Gulf, Straits of Hormuz, Arabian Sea and north-east Indian Ocean.

The Far East The Malayan Emergency was continuing, and Royal Navy ships and naval aircraft were employed in support of British troops, carrying out coastal patrols, aerial reconnaissance and naval gunfire support, as well as resupply and reinforcement tasks. In one incident, in early December 1957, the cruiser *Newcastle* carried out an intensive shore bombardment of terrorist positions with her main armament of 6-inch guns, having sailed up the Kota Tinggi River in Malaya. Further south, Indonesian gunboats were interfering with British merchant vessels and had to be deterred by British frigate patrols. Piracy continued to be a problem in the area and naval ships were needed to conduct regular deterrent patrols.

Hong Kong In Hong Kong the six inshore minesweepers of the 120th Minesweeping Squadron took over guardship duties from the hard-worked HDML (harbour defence motor launch) squadrons.

The Crown Colony of Cyprus By the middle of the 1950s Cyprus had become an important UK strategic base, dominating the eastern Mediterranean. Cyprus lacked a deep-water port for the Royal Navy, though ships could use the port at Famagusta, but Nicosia provided a vital airfield to counter Soviet encroachment in the Middle East. It had also proved crucial for the mounting of Operation Musketeer during the Suez crisis in 1956.

Sadly the local Greek and Turkish Cypriots were at each other's throats, each wanting independence from the UK and alignment with their mother country. In 1955 the rebel EOKA (Ethniki Organosis Kuprion Agoniston) guerrillas of General Grivas started their terrorist campaign of attacks, bombings and shootings. It became necessary for more and more UK troops, including Royal Marines, to be deployed to try and maintain the peace. For two years 40 and 45 Commandos were continually engaged on a rotational basis from Malta in anti-terrorist operations in Cyprus. A lot of the offensive operations were conducted in the inhospitable Troodos Mountains, used as hideouts by various local terrorist groups.

45 Commando was deployed to Kyrenia, one of the main strongholds of the EOKA guerrillas, and within three months established complete dominance over the area, severely limiting EOKA operations throughout the rest of Cyprus.

Throughout the period ships of the Mediterranean Fleet were required to conduct coastal patrols on a regular basis

in order to prevent the smuggling of arms and ammunition as well as supporting operations being conducted by security forces ashore.

Jordan In early 1957 Britain was pulling all her forces out of Jordan, as decided by mutual agreement in March, following the expiry of the original Anglo-Jordanian Treaty. Considerable unrest remained in Jordan, which threatened to break out in violence against British nationals. On 15 April the frigate *Opossum*, which was lying at Port Sudan, was brought to immediate notice to proceed to Aqaba and evacuate British personnel, but on 25 April King Hussein of Jordan declared martial law. As martial law restored security, the situation eased and the frigate was stood down a week later. On 6 July the ss *Devonshire*, escorted by the destroyer *Modeste*, evacuated the last British troops from Jordan.

Cyprus Emergency The situation in Cyprus steadily worsened, and in April 1958 it was decided to reinforce the security forces with 45 Commando, Royal Marines from Malta. The cruiser *Bermuda* embarked 45 Commando and helicopters from 728 NAS (Naval Air Squadron) and sailed from Malta on 16 April, bound for Cyprus.

Two days later *Bermuda* arrived off Akrotiri and landed 45 Commando and the naval helicopters ashore in Cyprus. The following month, on 23 May, a state of emergency was declared.

Aden Trouble was also being experienced in Aden and reinforcements were needed to deal with the internal unrest. On 18 April 1958 the cruiser *Gambia*, escorted by the frigate *Loch Fyne*, arrived in the Port of Aden with the first echelon of British troops.

Crisis in the Middle East

Formation of the Arab Federation Following the formation of the United Arab Republic by President Nasser of Egypt in 1958, much of the Middle East had become very unstable with the rapid rise of Arab nationalism. Jordan and Iraq were forming the Arab Federation, and 'Nasser's' call was being spread to other Arab countries. There were problems from increased agitation in Lebanon, Libya, Jordan, Aden and Cyprus.

Lebanon On 13 May 1958 Lebanon requested military assistance following clashes between Muslims and Christians. On 14 May the Amphibious Warfare Squadron sailed from Malta and headed east for the coast of Lebanon. The aircraft carrier *Ark Royal*, conducting exercise Medflexfort, was put on alert to evacuate British subjects from Lebanon. On 22 May *Ark Royal* completed the exercise and headed east but was ordered to remain on stand by off the coast of Cyprus. Whilst off Cyprus *Ark Royal*, with her air squadrons, supported British troops engaged in security operations ashore, where EOKA was continuing to wage a violent terrorist campaign. The UN Assembly reviewed the whole

situation, and plans for joint British and US operations, including landings by US Marines were drawn up.

Cyprus On 10 June the aircraft carrier *Eagle* arrived off the coast of Cyprus. She sailed into the Bay of Akrotiri and came to anchor a short distance from *Ark Royal*. As soon as she had anchored, the helicopters of 820 NAS together with all their equipment and stores from *Ark Royal* were transferred to *Eagle*.

The next day *Ark Royal*, having handed over patrol duties to *Eagle*, weighed anchor and headed west en route for Malta, Gibraltar and ultimately Devonport for refit. *Eagle* maintained operational support to the Royal Marines and British troops ashore engaged in anti-terrorist patrols and internal security operations. At the same time *Eagle* was on standby to deploy to the Lebanon.

Jordan The problems in the Middle East were made worse by a revolution in Iraq and the murder of King Feisal on 14 July 1958. Both President Chamoun of Lebanon and King Hussein of Jordan appealed to the West for military

The cruiser *Gambia* en route to the Middle East (NN)

assistance to maintain order. It was agreed internationally that the US 6th Fleet would respond over Lebanon's request, whilst Britain would assist over Jordan and also a subsequent request from Libya.

On 16 July *Eagle*, escorted by the cruiser *Sheffield*, sailed from Cyprus, heading south-east at speed to join the rest of the Mediterranean Fleet, which was deployed off the coast of Israel. The carrier *Albion* sailed from Rosyth and embarked 42 Commando Royal Marines at Portsmouth before heading south and making a fast passage to Malta.

Meanwhile the cruiser *Bermuda* and her escorts were detached to Malta to transport units of 45 Commando Royal Marines to the Libyan ports of Tobruk and Benghazi. 45 Commando held the Libyan ports until relieved by the 1st Battalion of the Royal Sussex Regiment, transported from Gibraltar by the old heavy cruiser *Cumberland*. On being relieved, 45 Commando was transported to Cyprus on board the cruiser *Bermuda* to take over from 40 Commando. *Sheffield* was detached to take 40 Commando back to Malta. In parallel the US 6th Fleet conducted operations in Lebanon.

Operation Fortitude, July 1958 After a swift passage from Cyprus *Eagle* arrived off the coast of Israel, joining the destroyers *Dunkirk* and *Cavendish* and the frigates *Salisbury* and *Torquay* for Operation Fortitude. The operation was for the reinforcement of Jordan. *Eagle*'s aircraft provided support and cover for the major airlift of British troops to the Jordanian capital, Amman. On 17 July two battalions of the 16th Independent Parachute Brigade were airlifted to the city. During the operation *Eagle*'s air group flew 500 sorties and 136 combat missions. Operation Fortitude was successfully completed on 23 July with the loss of only one Sea Venom aircraft, a considerable achievement.

Ships from the East Indies Fleet, including the carrier *Bulwark*, escorted by the frigate *Ulysses*, were despatched west across the Indian Ocean to assist with the crisis. The ships called into Mombasa, where, on 7 August, Cameron Highlanders were embarked on board *Bulwark* to reinforce the troops deployed in Jordan. She then transported the troops up the Red Sea, escorted by the frigates *Ulysses* and *Bigbury Bay*, and landed the Cameron Highlanders at Aqaba in the Gulf of Sinai. Meanwhile, in the Persian Gulf, a frigate was stationed up the Shatt al-Arab waterway in Iraq.

With the situation in Jordan stabilised *Eagle* returned to Cyprus and resumed support operations off the coast for a month. She was then relieved by *Albion*, which had transported 42 Commando from the UK. Only then could *Eagle* sail for Malta and some well-deserved rest and recreation for her hard-worked ship's company and air group.

The following month *Bulwark* returned through the Gulf of Aden and was deployed further east off the coast of Muscat, where she operated her aircraft in a series of strikes against rebels in the Jebel Akhdar Mountains from 12 to 21 September.

By late October the crisis in Jordan had eased sufficiently for British troops to be withdrawn. On 2 November the troops embarked on board the cruiser *Ceylon* and the frigates *Chichester* and *Loch Fyne*. King Hussein of Jordan flew down from Amman to Aqaba to review and thank the departing British troops. The swift and positive action taken by British and US forces in the eastern Mediterranean had undoubtedly managed to restore order in a volatile region at a particularly dangerous time.

———————•———————

Cyprus On 3 October *Eagle* left Malta and returned to Cyprus, where, on arrival, she relieved *Bulwark*. Having handed over responsibility, *Bulwark* departed from Cyprus and sailed west across the Mediterranean on passage to the UK, where she was due to commence important dockyard work to be converted to a commando carrier.

On 18 October the Ton class minesweeper *Burnaston* intercepted the Turkish vessel MV *Denil* and, having boarded her, discovered she was carrying a considerable quantity of arms and ammunition to Cyprus. After the crew were evacuated and arrested the MV *Denil* and her cargo of arms were scuttled.

A short while later, the aircraft carrier *Victorious* joined *Eagle*, and the two carriers conducted a series of joint flying exercises off the coast of Cyprus. On their completion *Victorious* took over responsibility for support of counter-terrorist operations ashore in Cyprus, enabling *Eagle* to sail for the UK to arrive in Devonport in time for Christmas.

The situation ashore eased in late 1959 with the Zurich Agreement, which renounced union with Greece and partitioned the island into separate Greek and Turkish enclaves. Naval patrols were reduced as the situation improved in the period running up to independence.

The Persian Gulf The Royal Marines were involved in minor operations conducted in the Persian Gulf in 1957. In the summer the frigate *Loch Alvie* was en route to Abadan, with Royal Marines embarked, when she received an immediate signal to divert to the Shatt al-Arab waterway at best speed. A mutiny had broken out on board a British tanker loaded with aviation fuel. On arrival off the coast *Loch Alvie* ran up her battle ensign and increased speed to full ahead. The Royal Marines boarded the tanker, and after a brief action the mutiny was quickly quashed.[6]

Two months later the Royal Marines were in action again further south. A revolt had broken out against the Sultan of Oman, who appealed to Britain for help. The Loch class frigate squadron on station in Bahrain quickly sailed and headed south at full speed. Ashore in Oman the Royal Marines were soon in action. They were supported by the frigates, which provided further supplies of ammunition and equipment and acted as the communications link with area command HQ at Bahrain. The frigates also blockaded the coast to prevent any arms and reinforcements from reaching the rebels on shore. The Royal Marines quickly and efficiently suppressed the revolt.

North Borneo At the beginning of March 1958 British merchant vessels were being attacked by Indonesian gunboats off Tawau and appealed for help. On 8 March the frigate *Modeste* was despatched to the area and immediately deterred the Indonesian gunboats from any further attempts to interfere with British ships in the area. On 12 March *Modeste* patrolled off the coast of Mendao, North Celebes, for several more days and then departed from the area when order had been restored.

The First Cod War,
1 September 1958 – 11 March 1961

Extension of Territorial Limit On 1 September 1958 Iceland unilaterally extended the limits of her territorial waters from three miles to twelve miles to protect her fishing grounds from over-fishing. This had been announced earlier in May, and despite the declaration being condemned in The Hague on 14 July the Icelandic government was determined to go ahead to conserve 'her' fish stocks, which were so vital to her economy.

Operation Whippet The Royal Navy was prepared, and the Captain of the Fishery Protection Squadron ('Captain Fish') had issued orders for Operation Whippet in June. The frigates *Eastbourne*, *Russell* and *Palliser* and the ocean minesweeper *Hound* were on patrol off Iceland on 1 September when the Icelandic gunboats *Aegir*, *Albert*, *Odinn*, *Thor* and *Maria Julia* appeared and started harassing British trawlers, threatening and trying to arrest them. There then followed a series of confrontations, hostile manoeuvrings at close quarters and opposed boardings. In most incidents Royal Navy frigates managed to defend the trawlers. In the first skirmishes *Eastbourne* managed to free several trawlers and capture two Icelandic boarding parties. The *Aegir* rammed several trawlers and also attempted to ram *Russell*, which was manoeuvring to protect the trawlers. *Russell* threatened to open fire and sink the *Aegir* before she finally backed off.

On 5 September the destroyer *Lagos* was sent to the area as the gunboats continued their attempts to arrest British trawlers, and eight days later the destroyer *Hogue* arrived. On 18 September *Aegir* attempted to arrest the trawler *Valafell*, which then in response tried to ram the gunboat.

On 20 September the powerful *Daring* class destroyers *Diana* and *Decoy* arrived in the disputed area. Nine days later the gunboat *Maria Julia* fired warning shots when attempting to arrest the trawler *Kingston Emerald*. Both *Odinn* and *Thor* then fired warning shots when trying to arrest other trawlers.

Hostile engagements between gunboats, trawlers and defending destroyers and frigates continued throughout the rest of the year, by which time twenty-two Royal Navy warships, supported by five RFA (Royal Fleet Auxiliary) tankers, had been involved. In several engagements the Icelandic gunboats had opened fire with solid shot. There had been some thirty unsuccessful attempts to arrest trawlers. Although incidents had eased over the winter months, encounters continued in the spring of the following year as the trawlers returned to the fishing grounds and Icelandic gunboats maintained their persistent attempts to arrest trawlers in the disputed waters. As incidents continued the Royal Navy sent more warships to patrol closer into the

The Cod War: a trawler astern of the frigate *Eastbourne*
(RNM)

The destroyer *Trafalgar* in the Cod War, August 1959
(RNM)

disputed areas. In encounters in April both *Odinn* and *Thor* fired warning shots at trawlers. Then in May *Thor* fired on the trawler *Arctic Viking*, first with warning shots and then directly at her masts to knock out her radio and prevent her calling for help. The destroyer *Contest* arrived on the scene and opened fire with star shell, which was sufficient to prevent *Thor* from continuing and persuade her to break off the action. A little while later the destroyer *Chaplet* was involved in a collision with *Odinn*, though fortunately the damage was not too serious.[7] In July *Maria Julia*, *Thor* and *Aegir* all fired shots in separate incidents. Throughout the rest of the year sporadic incidents continued, with the warships on patrol managing to thwart attempts by the Icelandic gunboats to arrest British trawlers.

Many of the incidents were very confused, with differing accounts resulting in claim and counter-claim. Different reports from commanding officers made it difficult for accurate assessments to be made of many of the dangerous incidents. The fact that no lives had been lost was down to the great ship-handling skills and seamanship on both sides.

All political attempts to resolve the dispute failed, and the 'Cod War', as it had become named, dragged on for a further fifteen months, involving thirty-seven warships and six Royal Fleet Auxiliaries. It was not until midnight on 14 May 1960 that British trawlers were finally withdrawn from Iceland's extended territorial waters and Operation Whippet was suspended. The Royal Navy had protected the British fishing fleet for eighteen months, enabling the trawler men to fish almost normally, despite continuous harassment and some seventy attempted arrests as well as a great many hostile encounters.

Trouble in the Indian Ocean, August 1959 On 6 August 1959 trouble broke out on the important strategic island of Gan in the Maldives. Gan was a key island in the Indian Ocean that acted as a staging post to the Far East, which made it essential to restore order and protect the British military and airfield installations. The destroyer *Cavalier* was immediately despatched to the island and a company of soldiers was flown in from Singapore.

The presence of a powerful British warship in the harbour and a company of soldiers was sufficient to protect the vital RAF installations. Order was eventually restored and *Cavalier* remained at Gan until the end of the month. The destroyer *Caprice* arrived off Gan on 29 August and took over from *Cavalier*.

OTHER DUTIES

Operation Grapple Between March and June 1957 the Royal Navy formed a special task group known as the Grapple Squadron, to assist in the thermo-nuclear weapon tests being conducted on Malden Island under the codename Operation Grapple. In early January 1957 the light fleet carrier *Warrior* sailed with the armament stores ship RFA *Fort Rosalie*, bound for the Pacific Ocean.

The Commodore of the Grapple Squadron was embarked in *Warrior*, and the rest of the squadron comprised two landing ships (tanks), nine smaller landing craft (tanks), a survey vessel, a salvage vessel, a despatch vessel and two Royal New Zealand Navy frigates. An additional landing ship (tanks) and various support vessels remained at Christmas Island some 400 nautical miles north-north-east of Malden Island. The ships of the squadron performed a range of tasks associated with the tests. After the final test on 19 June *Warrior* and most of the Grapple Squadron returned to the UK.

'Showing the Flag' In addition to operations, deployments and security patrols, the Royal Navy was engaged in a great many other duties, not the least of which was the traditional 'showing the flag'. Goodwill visits were an important element of British foreign policy and were considered to be 'one of the best ways of maintaining British prestige and influence abroad'. In 1959 Royal Navy ships and submarines paid over 300 foreign visits. Ships were often 'dressed overall', with signal

flags, and open to visitors. Ships of the Fleet also visited home ports regularly and conducted 'Meet the Navy' programmes.

Naval Exercises As well as 'showing the flag' the Royal Navy was also heavily involved in joint naval exercises all round the world. In 1957 a massive NATO exercise, Operation Strikeback, was conducted in the North Sea, involving the carriers *Ark Royal, Bulwark,* and the US Navy carriers *Forrestal* and *Essex* and the missile cruiser USS *Canberra.* In 1959 the Royal Navy took part in seven major NATO exercises in the Atlantic, Channel and Mediterranean, Commonwealth naval exercises in the Indian Ocean and South Atlantic, a SEATO (South East Asia Treaty Organisation) exercise in the South China Sea and a CENTO (Central Treaty Organisation) naval exercise in the northern Gulf.

Rescue and Relief Operations

Fishery Protection On 20 April 1957 the ocean minesweeper *Bramble* was ordered into Norwegian waters, where there was a dispute over Russian interference with fishing on the

The light fleet carrier *Warrior* (RNM)

Viking Bank. Russian vessels had damaged British fishing gear. By swift action *Bramble* was able to resolve the dispute without provoking an international incident.

The following year on 17 April there was further Russian interference with British fishing vessels some 250 miles north-east of Aberdeen. The coastal minesweeper *Belton* was sent to the area and the dispute was quickly resolved. As a result of intervention by the Royal Navy, the Russian trawlers agreed to pay compensation for damage to the nets of British trawlers.

Earthquake Relief Work In the Mediterranean the *Daring* class destroyer *Dainty* was sent to Fethiye following an earthquake in Turkey on 25 April 1957. On arrival the destroyer was able to provide important emergency relief aid in the wake of the disaster.

Sea Rescue On 20 August 1957 the tanker ss *World Splendour* caught fire after a major explosion on board. She was off Gibraltar, and the *Daring* class destroyer *Delight* was

immediately sailed to attempt a rescue. The destroyer managed to rescue forty survivors and assist the disabled tanker, which was taken in tow. Sadly the tanker sank the next day but the Admiralty tug *Confident* arrived from Gibraltar and rescued the remaining survivors.

Dubai In the Persian Gulf the frigate *Loch Ruthven* sailed for Dubai on 24 November 1957 with emergency medical and food supplies following a severe storm, which had devastated the area. On arrival the frigate was able to carry out emergency relief operations.

West Indies Violence broke out on the island of Nassau in the Bahamas following a strike on 18 January 1958. The frigate *Ulster* was summoned to the island at full speed and arrived shortly afterwards. Immediately a naval party was landed from the frigate and took over the power station to safeguard emergency services during the disturbances. The presence of the British frigate helped to calm the situation and order was soon restored.

Mediterranean Whilst the aircraft carrier *Eagle* was operating in the western Mediterranean she was off the port of Hyeres on 8 March 1958 when she received an urgent order to sail due south at full speed. Two French naval aircraft had collided in mid-air and crashed into the sea sixty miles north of Cape Bon, Tunisia, and both pilots were missing. *Eagle* arrived in the area several hours later but after an intensive search only one pilot was recovered.[8]

Indian Ocean On 1 April 1958 the Norwegian tanker ss *Skaubrun* was on fire in the Indian Ocean. The frigate *Loch Fada* hastened to assist the tanker, which was abandoned as the fires raged. Merchant ships in the vicinity had taken off most of the survivors but the frigate was able to assist in extinguishing the fire and then took the tanker in tow.

West Indies A strike in Grenada on 21 August 1958 caused severe problems, and the frigate *Troubridge* was sent at speed to the island. An emergency relief party was quickly landed from the frigate. Once ashore the relief party managed to restore power and run the power station, maintaining emergency supplies during the strike. Five days later the strike was over and *Troubridge* was able to hand over to the local authorities, sailing from the island on 26 August.

Persian Gulf On 13 September 1958 the French tanker *Fernand Gilbert* collided with a 21,000-ton Liberian-registered tanker, the *Melika*. Both tankers were on fire and the aircraft carrier *Bulwark*, escorted by the frigate, *Loch Killisport*, was ordered to the area. The frigates *Puma* and *St Brides Bay* were also in the vicinity and quickly arrived on the scene. Survivors were rescued by helicopter from *Bulwark*, and helicopters were also used to convey fire-fighting parties to the blazing French ship. The fires were brought under control and *Bulwark*, assisted by *Puma*, towed

A Royal Navy cruiser open to visitors on a port visit
(TT)

the *Melika* to Muscat, arriving on 20 September, whilst *Loch Killisport* towed the *Fernand Gilbert* to Karachi.

Libya Severe floods struck Libya at the beginning of October 1959, and 40 Commando Royal Marines was quickly sent to provide emergency relief work. The Royal Marines provided much valuable assistance, helping to restore essential services and distribute emergency food and medical supplies.

Philippines On 23 November 1959 the ss *Szefeng* was in distress in the Sulu Sea, and the destroyer *Solebay* was immediately diverted to the area to render assistance. The destroyer managed to secure a tow and then towed the ss *Szefeng* to Pujada Bay in south-east Mindanao.

SHIPS, SUBMARINES, WEAPONS AND AIRCRAFT

The late 1950s saw the Royal Navy taking major steps forward into the era of nuclear technology and missile warfare. Research and development of naval gunnery was discontinued whilst missile and ASW technology were allocated high priority. Development of 'afloat support' (fleet tankers and replenishment ships) was also undertaken to reduce the Fleet's reliance on shore base support, which could be vulnerable in the event of nuclear war.

The Royal Navy still possessed a large fleet of aging conventional warships, the majority of World War II design or construction, though large numbers were assigned to the Reserve Fleet (over 400) and a great many were laid up. Much of the design work for new construction was still based on revised and improved conventional ship classes.

Nuclear Weapons Between 1956 and 1958 Britain conducted a series of hydrogen bomb tests at Malden Island and Christmas Island in order to become a thermo-nuclear power. Britain's first megaton H-bomb was detonated on 8

November 1957. These tests, carried out under the codename Operation Grapple, mentioned above, were successful. They impressed the Americans, and in 1958 the US–UK Mutual Defence Agreement was signed, bringing in an era of US–UK nuclear co-operation and development. The agreement was to prove crucial to the development of Britain's submarine-based strategic nuclear deterrent in the future.

As regards strategic weapons, Britain's deterrent force was, from 1956, the responsibility of the RAF operating the 'Quick Reaction Alert' V-Bomber squadrons of Valiant, Vulcan and Victor manned bombers, armed with 'Blue Danube' free-fall bombs.

First RN Nuclear Weapons The Royal Navy took delivery of its first nuclear weapons in 1959. These were free-fall tactical nuclear bombs, designated Red Beard and carried in the Supermarine Scimitar, and later the Buccaneer, aircraft of the Fleet Air Arm operating from aircraft carriers. The initial main tactical role for these weapons was ship strike in the north-east Atlantic, though clearance for aircraft to take off with the weapons armed for this role was not finally approved until August 1960.

Aircraft Carriers and Naval Aircraft Although the aircraft carriers of the Royal Navy were of World War II design and construction, naval jet aircraft had become progressively heavier and faster, making deck operations much more difficult and dangerous. In 1958 two new fast and powerful naval strike fighters, the Supermarine Scimitar and the de Havilland Sea Venom, joined the Fleet Air Arm. Fortunately many advances had been pioneered by Britain to improve the operating of modern heavy jet aircraft from aircraft carriers. These included the angled flight deck, steam catapults, improved radar and data control and deck landing sights. The angled flight deck and steam catapult were great innovations, allowing much of the flight deck to be used during both launching and recovery operations. These innovations were quickly taken up by the US Navy, which found them a huge help in operating modern heavy US naval aircraft.

Aircraft Carrier Refits *Ark Royal* was refitted in 1959, and at the end of the year *Eagle* commenced a major four-year modernisation and update refit in Devonport. The £30m refit provided her with an 8½° angled flight deck, steam catapults and the large state-of-the-art 984 radar.

Commando Carriers Operation Musketeer, during the Suez crisis, had proved the effectiveness of launching airborne assault waves using helicopters embarked in carriers, and the concept of the commando carrier had then been accepted. The Naval Staff decided to convert the light fleet carriers *Albion* and *Bulwark* to the commando role. In December 1959 *Bulwark* was commissioned as the Royal Navy's first commando carrier with 848 Naval Air Squadron.

Nuclear Submarines The Royal Navy commissioned two experimental HTP (high test hydrogen peroxide) submarines, *Excalibur* in 1956 and *Explorer* in 1958. They were based on a German HTP U-boat, *U 1407*, which had been scuttled

Bulwark as a commando carrier
(NN)

Trials of the commando helicopter carrier concept (RNM)

The British nuclear submarine programme, however, made very slow progress. The Dreadnought Project did not get properly underway until 1957, and then there were problems with her UK-designed gas coolant propulsion system. It was not until March 1958, when Admiral Rickover visited the UK, that a deal was made to install a US Skipjack propulsion unit (a water-cooled Westinghouse S5W power plant) into the UK's first nuclear submarine. The deal was entirely due to the close personal relationship between Mountbatten and Rickover and was part of the emerging special relationship between the UK and the USA.

The Mutual Defence Agreement Behind the veil of national security the Macmillan government was embarking on wide-reaching agreements with the United States of America, which fundamentally altered the structure and modus operandi of the Royal Navy Submarine Service for decades to come. The major agreement came on 4 August 1958 with a document entitled 'Cooperation on the Uses of Atomic Energy for Mutual Defence Purposes'. This laid the foundations for the exchange between the USA and UK of controlled nuclear information, sensitive nuclear technology and materials. For the submarine service this meant the transfer of submarine nuclear propulsion plant and other materials to enable the Royal Navy to play a major role in the Cold War.

In August 1958 the USS *Nautilus* completed her famous voyage under the polar ice cap (Operation Sunshine),[9] arriving at Portland on 12 August. When she arrived in the Channel the Royal Navy was given operational control of her for a week's operational evaluation in exercise Rum Tub. The exercises were conducted in the South-Western Approaches (SWAPS), with the carrier *Bulwark,* ASW escorts, aircraft and submarines. Post-operational analysis by the naval staff confirmed the enormous tactical advantages of the SSN (nuclear fleet submarine), which were due to her high underwater speed.

Guided Missiles Although the guided missile trials ship, *Girdle Ness*, was coming to the end of her time she had achieved her purpose, and two surface-to-air guided missiles (SAMs) were shortly to join the Fleet; the short-range, wire-guided Seacat missile and the medium-range, beam-riding Seaslug missile. The Seaslug system was also to have a limited surface-to-surface (SSM) capability. Both missile systems were to serve in the Falklands War some twenty-five years later. The Seacat was to be credited with destroying a number of Argentinean aircraft. *Girdle Ness* was paid off as a guided missile trials ship in December 1961 and was reclassified as an accommodation ship in the following year.

Guided Missile Destroyers The Royal Navy's first class of guided missile destroyers (GMDs), the County class, had been ordered, and the first of class, *Devonshire*, was laid down in March 1959. These 6,000-ton ships were, to all intents and purposes, light cruisers but were officially categorised as DLGs (destroyer leader guided). They were designed to

at the end of the war. *U 1407* was salvaged and then commissioned into the Royal Navy as *Meteorite* for trials and evaluation.

Excalibur and *Explorer* were both assigned to the 3rd Submarine Squadron but spent little time at sea. The fuel was highly unstable and very dangerous. *Explorer* was known as '*Exploder*' as a result of several serious accidents, and *Excalibur* was known as '*Excruciator*'. Although they achieved an impressive twenty-five knots submerged, the project was not a success and it was clear from the US Navy nuclear submarine programme that nuclear propulsion was the only way forward. Thanks to the relentless drive of Admiral Hyman Rickover the US Navy had made great progress with nuclear propulsion and submarine design, culminating in the first nuclear submarine, the 4,040-ton USS *Nautilus* (SSN 571), commissioned in September 1954. The USSR was not far behind and had built its first ballistic missile nuclear submarine (SSBN) by the following year.

When the USS *Nautilus* made an official visit to Portsmouth in October 1957, the Defence Minister, Sandys, and Lord Mountbatten went aboard and were greatly impressed by all they saw. Sandys said, 'The nuclear submarine represents, in the sphere of naval warfare a revolutionary advance as great as the change from sail to steam'.

provide area defence for aircraft carriers and high-value assets and were to be equipped with both Seaslug and Seacat missile systems.

Gas Turbines The DLGs were to be constructed with a new propulsion system, a combination of steam and gas turbines known as COSAG (combined steam and gas). The Royal Navy had been experimenting since the end of World War II with the use of gas turbines for ship propulsion. Trials had started with a converted steam gunboat (*Grey Goose*) and gas turbines had then been fitted in fast torpedo boats. A developed marine gas turbine (G6) was installed in a frigate (*Ashanti*, the first of the Tribal class general-purpose frigates), and was next fitted to the DLGs.

The first batch of DLGs was under construction in 1958, with the ships (*Devonshire*, *Hampshire*, *Kent* and *London*) scheduled to join the Fleet in the early 1960s.

Devonshire, the first Royal Navy guided missile destroyer (CC)

Kent, one of the first batch of guided missile destroyers (RNM)

A Wasp ASW helicopter landing on the deck of a Type 12 frigate, *Falmouth* (JAR)

The Wasp Helicopter and ASW As anti-submarine tactics evolved helicopters were considered as a possible ASW weapon platform. In 1957 trials were conducted with the frigate *Grenville* to investigate the concept of operating light helicopters from small ships. This led to the development of the small anti-submarine warfare Wasp helicopter, armed with depth charges and homing torpedoes, being deployed to sea in frigates. The quick-reaction Wasp helicopter could be rapidly vectored (directed) out to a distant target and thus greatly extended the operational tactical range of ASW frigates.

Propulsion and Ship Design In 1958 the great majority of the Royal Navy's major warships were steam-driven, as they had been throughout World War II. Most had main boilers of standard, war-proven and reliable Admiralty three-drum design, burning viscous furnace fuel oil (FFO) to supply main steam turbines designed for greatest fuel efficiency at

high speed. The smaller war-construction escorts were propelled by reciprocating steam engines. In all steam ships, however, the need for adequate supplies of high quality 'feed' water for the boilers, as well as large quantities of fresh water for the crews from inefficient seawater distillation plants, was a constant problem. Electricity supply was direct current from steam-driven turbo-generators.

Modern Design By the late 1950s, fast modern *Daring* class destroyers had begun to join the Fleet. These were designed and built with lighter, more compact boilers working at higher pressure and greater efficiency with superheated temperatures. The *Darings* also confirmed the use of all-welded construction for warship hulls. A start was also made in using alternating current electrical supplies, with significant advantages in terms of weight, space and ease of transmission.

Anti-Submarine Frigates The *Daring* class destroyers were overlapped by modern frigate designs; the *Whitby* class (Type 12), the *Rothesay* class (Type 12M) and the smaller, less capable single-shaft *Blackwood* class (Type 14). All were designed for fast anti-submarine warfare in the North Atlantic, with innovative hull shape and relatively light and compact propulsion machinery. They had all welded hulls and better sea-keeping abilities as well as enclosed bridges. Steam was still generated from FFO, but at higher pressure and temperature to turbines designed for greatest fuel

The destroyer *Daring* (RNM)

The Type 14 *Blackwood* class frigate *Russell* (TT)

efficiency at cruising speeds, a lesson learnt from World War II operations with the US Navy over large ocean distances in the Pacific.

***Leander* Class Frigates** Through the 1960s, these post-war designs evolved into the three variants (batches) of the *Leander* class of general-purpose frigate, of similar hull form and main machinery but specially designed to operate the small anti-submarine Wasp helicopter. The earlier *Rothesay* class was later modified so as to operate the Wasp helicopter as well. The later, Batch 3, broad-beam *Leander* frigates remained in service right up until the early 1990s.

The Type 12 frigate *Whitby*, seen here refuelling from the light fleet carrier *Centaur*
(RNM)

The second rate anti-aircraft frigate *Morecambe Bay*
(RNM)

Anti-Aircraft Frigates Over a similar period two classes of specialist frigate, the *Salisbury* class (Type 61) for aircraft direction, and the *Leopard* class (Type 41) for anti-aircraft roles, were introduced with a hull form similar to that of the *Whitby* class but propelled by four Admiralty-design diesels on each of two shafts. These provided much greater fuel endurance and introduced remote engine controls, but had limited top speed and required controllable pitch propellers for astern manoeuvring. The new machinery design introduced diesel oil ('Dieso') as a major warship propulsion fuel in the surface fleet.

Bay and Loch class frigates Whilst the new frigate classes were joining the fleet, some older frigates were retained in commission as second-rate frigates to cover general duties serving all over the world. The three prime classes of World War II frigates retained in service were the Bay class (anti-aircraft escorts), the Loch class (anti-submarine escorts) and the smaller Castle class (anti-submarine). The Loch class provided valuable service in the Persian Gulf and Arabian Sea.

Conventional Submarines Between 1959 and 1964, thirteen all diesel-electric *Oberon* class submarines were built. The

first of class, *Oberon*, was launched at Chatham on 18 July 1959. The submarines were capable of high underwater speeds of up to seventeen knots and carried the latest technology in detection equipment and weapon systems. The most significant of the improvements came from the designed soundproofing of all internal machinery, making them the quietest diesel submarines of their time. They were designed to conduct continuous submerged patrols conducting 'Indicators and Warning' missions vital to countering the emerging Soviet Cold War threat. As a class of submarine they were workhorses, operating primarily in arctic Europe, but saw service all over the world. In 1982 they saw service in the Falklands, and in 1991 they played a significant part in Operation Desert Storm. They also made a valuable contribution as a modern submarine to train the

Oberon class submarines of the 1st Submarine Squadron (NP)

future commanding officers of the nuclear submarine fleet.

NBCD (Nuclear, Biological and Chemical Defence) In the late 1950s the Royal Navy developed new defensive measures and procedures against the very real threat of modern nuclear, biological and chemical weapons. Ships were designed and built with isolation 'citadels' and upper-deck spray systems enabling them to close down and continue to operate whilst under attack from NBC weapons. NBCD exercises became an important element of general training.

NAVAL PERSONNEL

In 1957 the Royal Navy was manned by 121,500 officers and men, a considerable reduction from the 865,000 in uniform only twelve years earlier in 1945. Various personnel changes had been introduced in the late fifties to improve professionalism and conditions of service. The 1956 Armed Forces Pay Code increased pay, allowances and pensions. The naval estimates in the same year announced a new regular nine-year engagement, though it remained at twelve years for artificers. Centralised drafting from the shore establishment *Centurion* was introduced with shorter foreign drafts. As it became clear that more of those serving were married, measures were introduced to curtail long periods of separation and long foreign drafts.

Officer Structure Two main changes affected the officer structure and resulted from the COST committee (Committee on Officer Structure and Training) set up in 1954. First was the formation of the single 'General List' of officers on 1 January 1957; this had been set out in AFO 1/56 (Admiralty Fleet Order No 1 of 1956). The new General List consolidated into a single list the four separate professional branches of the Navy, namely: X, or Executive Branch; E, or Marine Engineering Branch; L, or Electrical Engineering Branch; and S, or Supply and Secretariat Branch. The aim was to foster an 'all of one company' concept with a period of common training on entry, all exercising equal powers of military command ashore, and the old distinctive coloured cloth worn between the gold stripes by non-executive officers since 1863 was abolished. The basic idea was not new, having been one of the aims of the great Admiral Jackie Fisher at the beginning of the century. Fisher's plan was known as the Selbourne–Fisher reform after the recommendations of the Selbourne Committee, but its inception was delayed by the outbreak of World War I and then by some considerable resistance from members of the Executive Branch.

Post and General Lists The smaller fleet meant a reduced number of sea commands, which caused problems with the rationing of the important command appointments, so essential for qualification for future promotion. This problem was resolved by introducing a split list for seaman specialist commanders and captains, dividing them between the categories of Post List, known as 'Wet', for those who would be appointed to sea command, and General List, known as 'Dry', for those who would not but nevertheless would be eligible for promotion for staff and general shore appointments.

Manpower Reductions The most far-reaching effects on both manpower and morale throughout the Fleet, however, were caused by the drastic cuts of the Duncan Sandys defence review. The whole emphasis of defence policy, on high-tech modern weapon systems and nuclear deterrence, encompassed a move away from large manpower-intensive conventional forces to smaller highly trained armed forces.

Accordingly National Service was phased out and a large redundancy programme was introduced. In the Royal Navy the aim was to reduce manpower to about 95,000 by 1959. Over 2,000 naval officers and 1,000 naval ratings were compulsorily retired in the first phase.

Naval Engineering Training In 1958 the Duke of Edinburgh opened the wardroom at the new RNEC (Royal Naval Engineering College) at Manadon on the northern outskirts of Plymouth. For many years engineers had been trained at Keyham College, but that site was transferred to the Dockyard Technical College in 1959. All engineering training was then consolidated at RNEC Manadon, where facilities and courses existed for all engineer officers, including those studying for university degrees.

Over the next thirty-five years engineering training was developed to deliver nationally accredited university degree courses in mechanical and electrical engineering. Four-year courses were tailored to meet the Royal Navy's ever-changing demands on naval constructors as well as seagoing officers of the Marine, Electrical, Weapons and Air engineering sub-specialisations in response to rapid technological change throughout the second half of the century. Courses were also developed in marine engineering at MSc level for newly commissioned Special Duties List engineer officers as well as for engineering management training of junior engineer officers. Courses were also established for improving the engineering knowledge and awareness of junior warfare officers. RNEC Manadon was to educate several generations of engineer officers until its closure in 1995.

THE WHITE ENSIGN ASSOCIATION

The 'Sandys Axe' was not the first time the Royal Navy had been savagely cut back, and bitter memories recalled the

---

Steaming the Fleet (The Men Who Made the Fleet Go)

In 1958 men of ships' Engine Room Departments had been 'going down below' to their steam machinery for well over 100 years: the Stoker Petty Officer (properly known as a P. O. Mechanic (E)) in his steam-faded blue overalls, some 4 hours before sailing time, to the Boiler Room to 'flash up' and begin to 'raise steam', followed some 2 hours later by the Engine Room Artificer 1st Class, in his battered, oily 'steaming cap', to the main engine throttle control position in the Engine Room, there to supervise draining and 'opening out' of the steam systems and start-up of auxiliary machines such as turbo-generators and pumps. Qualified to control one Boiler Room and one Engine Room 'Unit' he was rated Chief Petty Officer and in larger ships, such as cruisers and aircraft carriers with more than one Unit, was followed 'below' by the 'Chief Tiff' (Chief ERA), and the Engineer Officer of the Watch; both 'Charge' qualified to control several Units or take sole charge of a small ship's machinery.

Cruising at sea these men normally followed a 1 in 4 watchkeeping routine of 4 hour watches in physically arduous conditions, standing on the 'plates' throughout or climbing ladders on endless 'rounds' of machinery inspection and always in mind-numbing noise, without protection. In the Boiler Room the POM (E) hung from his handwheel controlling the boiler fans, one eye always on the boiler water 'gauge glass' level, especially when manoeuvring and at high power, whilst he foot-adjusted fuel oil pump speed and hand-signalled his Mechanics (E) how many fuel oil 'sprayers' to 'flash up' or shut down at the boiler front, anticipating the brusque order from the Bridge – 'stop making black smoke'. He might respond by requesting to 'blow soot' – a frequent routine in the 50s and 60s, when thick black Furnace Fuel Oil (FFO) fired boilers. In the Tropics, even under Engine Room ventilation fans, they all sweated the last of the daily tot of rum from their bodies helped by pints of lime juice, supplemented with salt tablets. In the North and South Atlantic winters they froze, especially at high power in an aircraft carrier's Boiler Room, wrapped in layers of warm clothing against rushing icy air, and all longing for bubbling hot kye (Navy cocoa) at midnight. These working conditions endured until most steam ships decommissioned, notably HMS *Ark Royal* in 1978 and early *Leander* class frigates in the mid 1990s.

Machinery Control Rooms (MCR) first appeared in Diesel-engined Ton Class minesweepers and Type 41 and Type 61 frigates in the 1950s, then installed in steam-propelled *Tiger* Class cruisers to provide control of machinery when engine and boiler rooms were vacated and closed down to minimise nuclear, biological or chemical contamination. But it was the MCRs of the COmbined Steam And Gas turbine (COSAG) Type 81 frigates and GMDs of the early 1960s which most dramatically changed the working conditions of a 'steaming watch', providing them with primary control positions whilst sitting in air-conditioned, relatively quiet comfort. Key changes were: the introduction of air-driven controls to automatically adjust boiler output and remotely control main steam and gas turbines, as well as the start-up and shut-down of auxiliary machinery; and specialised clutches allowing the synchronous engagement of main turbines to a rotating main gearbox. But the greater complexity of engine combinations via remote control threw greater emphasis on correct operating procedures and their frequent practice. However, watchkeeping life outside the MCR in any steam ship – including the LPDs of the mid-'60s and *Leanders* of the late '60s – remained physically demanding, especially to complete extensive 'rounds' both to monitor machinery and to counter the ever-present threat of fire from fuel and oil in large machinery spaces. Indeed these remained manned only by some of the most junior and youngest men, on their own, though backed-up by a relatively large engineering crew.

Captain Jock Morrison RN

'Geddes Axe' between the wars. In 1921 the Royal Navy had been forced to carry out major manpower reductions when the country was facing a severe economic crisis. The former First Lord of the Admiralty, Sir Eric Geddes, presided over a committee, which recommended drastic reductions in naval expenditure and manpower. This became known as the infamous 'Geddes Axe' and was described by a senior officer: 'the Geddes' Axe, surely the most cruel and unjust instrument ever used on a splendidly loyal service, descended with brutal force. None of us who saw those days can ever forget the stunning effect of that monstrous measure.' A great deal of distress and suffering was caused, and the

The White Ensign Association
(WEA)

name of Geddes was reviled by a generation of naval officers.

Thus when the Sandys' axe cut naval manpower by some 26,000, to be achieved by 1962, there was a determination to avoid some of the worse suffering caused by the 'Geddes Axe'. At the instigation of Lord Mountbatten, the First Sea Lord, an association was set up to help all those leaving the Service. This was the White Ensign Association, founded in the City of London on 24 June 1958 under the chairmanship of Admiral Sir John Eccles GCB, KCVO, CBE.

The reason for setting up the Association was stated by Admiral Eccles as follows:

'The present day "Axe" [The Duncan Sandys Defence cuts] is the second in this century. After the first there was much distress and waste, particularly amongst ex-naval officers who, because they had spent the majority of their adult life afloat, were comparatively unversed in financial and commercial matters. The object of the Association is to avoid this in future.'

He added; 'The Association is a measure of the goodwill felt for the Royal Navy by many prominent men in the City of London and elsewhere.' The establishment of the Association was promulgated by Admiralty Fleet Order.[12]

The Admiralty officially recognised the White Ensign Association, and welcomed its formation as a valuable addition to the existing Regular Forces Resettlement Service under the Minister of Labour, which embraced the Officers' Association and the Regular Forces Employment Association.

The Association was not a profit-making organisation. Funds, sufficient to cover its expenses for a limited period, would be donated by the business institutions which sponsored its formation.[13]

The Council and Staff A Council of Management was formed of thirteen leading people, chairmen, managing directors and senior partners drawn from the City, commerce and industry under the presidency of David Robarts, Chairman of the National Provincial Bank. An office was established in the City, and Commander Charles Lamb DSO, DSC, RN was appointed as the first Manager.

Commander Charles Lamb Commander Lamb was a naval Swordfish pilot who had an illustrious career in the Fleet Air Arm. He had survived the sinking of the aircraft carrier *Courageous*, flown at the Battle of Taranto, escaped as a prisoner of war and been seriously wounded in the Pacific campaign whilst serving in the aircraft carrier *Implacable*. He was to serve as Chief Executive of the White Ensign Association for fifteen years.

Work In its first two years of operation the White Ensign Association directly assisted 1,453 officers and men. Financial advice and guidance was provided on gratuities and redundancy lump sums and, with the help of financial expertise in the City of London, an investment trust, the Sheet Anchor Investment Company, was formed on 11 September 1959, open to all qualified to use the services of the Association.

The Royal Naval Reserve and Minesweeping, 1958

The Royal Naval Reserve had Sea Training Centres (STCs) round Britain, as well as Headquarters Units. The STCs trained crews for minesweeping operations, as well as reinforcing the RN when necessary in many Branches.

The HQ Units were tied to specific RN Headquarters such as Northwood near London, Pitreavie near Edinburgh and Faslane, near Glasgow and in times of emergency or war would be called up for work in their HQs. Pitreavie was the official war alternative HQ to Northwood.

Depending on their background, officers and men came from several lists, with differing levels of training. List 3 for example was for professional Merchant Naval officers and men, and many were to prove their value in the Falklands War. The RNR [Royal Naval Reserve] also provided a means of introducing the RN to men and women who would not otherwise have had anything to do with the Navy. Even if they only joined up for short periods, their experiences and influence was most important in educating the British public as a whole, on Naval matters.

The Korean War had shown that the Russians were experts in laying mines in very large numbers, and over 100 wooden hulled Ton class Minesweepers were subsequently built. Each STC was allocated a minesweeper, and practised sweeping regularly alone or team sweeping with other RN and RNR MCMVs [mine counter-measures vessels], at weekends and on fortnightly training cruises.

Many minefields remained extant or only partially swept after World War II.

The Germans used contact mines – the ones with spike triggers, often still seen at seaside resorts as RNLI collecting boxes; influence mines, which were set off by the magnetic influence of steel hulled ships, and acoustic mines which listened to engines. There were combination mines, and some that had been fitted with ship counts – they would not be activated until several ships (including minesweepers) had passed over them. These would sometimes activate themselves years after the end of World War II.

NEMEDRI[10] routes had been produced for merchant shipping and telephone cables, which were deemed safe, but these were checked, and gradually the other sea areas cleared to allow fishing (and eventually oil rigs).

The RNR in the 50s had plenty of ex RN officers and senior rates, but were sometimes short of junior rates; Trinity Sea Cadet Unit at the shore establishment *Claverhouse* in Granton, Edinburgh, allowed Sea Cadets to go to sea regularly, including live minesweeping. (As a Sea Cadet aged 12 and a half I was allowed to shoot a short butt Lee-Enfield at the mines we'd swept). Detonating the mines allowed the crewmembers – and Cadets – to take home fresh fish.[11]

The RNR STCs provided a naval presence all over Britain and support of all sorts. Sadly many have been closed down for reasons of economy, and training is now concentrated on relatively few areas, including Logistics and Medical.

Lieutenant Commander Ken Napier MBE, RN

CHAPTER 2
Post-Imperial Peace-Keeping 1960–1964

EAST–WEST TENSIONS (CUBAN MISSILE CRISIS) – NASSAU AGREEMENT (POLARIS DETERRENT) – COD WAR – KUWAIT (OPERATION
VANTAGE) – BRUNEI INSURRECTION – INDONESIAN CONFRONTATION – EAST AFRICAN MUTINIES – RADFAN OPERATIONS

'One of the most efficient uses of military force in the history of the world' [1]

1960 heralded the very last of the 'old' and the first of the 'new'. The Royal Navy's sole remaining battleship, the mighty 44,500-ton *Vanguard*, last of the line of super-Dreadnoughts, was sold for scrap for £500,000. She was Britain's last and biggest battleship, and on 4 August 1960 she was towed from Portsmouth, where the first Dreadnought had been built some fifty-six years earlier. In a final act of defiance, *Vanguard* broke from her tow and was temporarily grounded, wedged solid across the harbour mouth, blocking Portsmouth for several hours. Fortunately tugs managed to free her before the tide dropped and she was towed away to Faslane, arriving safely five days later for scrapping.

Just over two months later, HM Queen Elizabeth II launched Britain's first nuclear submarine at Vickers Armstrong's yard in Barrow-in-Furness on 21 October, Trafalgar Day, 1960. She was the first in a formidable line of revolutionary new war vessels, which would include nuclear ballistic missile submarines (SSBNs), each with infinitely more fire power than all the Dreadnought battleships put together. She was the ninth *Dreadnought* to serve in the Royal Navy, and what name could be more appropriate than that? Meanwhile on the world stage the situation was becoming ever more dangerous, with a very real threat of Armageddon approaching.

The Cold War Comes to the Boil, 1960–1962

The Berlin Crisis and the Iron Curtain East–West tensions escalated through a series of crises during the early sixties, bringing the Cold War to boiling point. In the spring of 1960 the Berlin crisis had deteriorated to a critical level and a top-level summit in Paris of Eisenhower, Khrushchev and Macmillan was set for May to try and avert all-out war. Fate intervened, however, and just days before the world leaders met, a US U-2 spy plane, piloted by Gary Powers, was shot down over the Soviet Union. The pilot was captured and paraded to the world's media. Arriving in Paris, Khrushchev demanded an apology from the USA. Eisenhower refused, the summit collapsed, and the Berlin crisis took a turn for the worse with growing numbers of East German refugees fleeing to the West from the Soviet side.

By the following year, over 30,000 East Germans were 'escaping' to the West each month, and on 16 August 1961 East Germany began constructing the infamous Berlin Wall to stem the flow. In October British and US tanks confronted

FIRST SEA LORDS
Admirals John and Luce

SECOND SEA LORD
Admiral Tyrwhitt

MANPOWER
102,000

MERCANTILE MARINE
5,395
merchant ships

Soviet tanks along the wall, most notoriously at checkpoint 'Charlie', and the Soviets began constructing tank traps.

The Space Race Earlier in April, Yuri Gagarin became the first person to travel into space. This was a great coup for the Soviets and alarmed NATO intelligence, making the West apprehensive over Warsaw Pact advances in missile and military technology. President J F Kennedy, having recently taken over from Eisenhower, made a firm undertaking to overtake the Soviets and be the first to land a man on the moon.

The Bay of Pigs Fidel Castro had come to power in Cuba in 1959 following a Communist revolution the year before. The USA became alarmed when Castro and Khrushchev met in September 1960 and decided to try and topple this dangerous Communist regime on their doorstep by training and arming Cuban exiles. A band of 1,500 armed exiles were then landed in the Bay of Pigs on the southern coast of Cuba on 17 April 1961, but within three days they were ignominiously defeated and the USA humiliated.

The Cuban Missile Crisis In September 1962 US U-2 spy plane flights over Cuba detected a build-up of missile sites and military aircraft. Further flights revealed the probable existence of nuclear missiles, capable of striking the US mainland, and on 22 October Kennedy publicly announced the presence of the missile threat to the USA. More Soviet missiles were detected being shipped to Cuba, and Kennedy promptly responded by setting up a blockade of the island. US forces worldwide went to alert state DEFCON-3 (preparations for nuclear war) whilst in the UK the V-bomber force was put on high alert. The Soviets responded by bringing all their nuclear forces to full alert. The Soviet ships carrying missiles to Cuba maintained their course and Kennedy ordered a fleet of 180 US warships to the Caribbean to intercept them and sink any Soviet ships attempting to break the blockade. All US forces were then ordered to alert state DEFCON-2, and the B-52 strategic bombers, armed with nuclear weapons, were scrambled into the air.

The world was on the brink of nuclear war. The tense stand-off dragged on for six long days whilst the world held its breath. On 26 September a US plane was shot down over Cuba and the world tensed for a nuclear exchange! Finally, on 28 September Kennedy and Khrushchev agreed a deal: the Soviets would remove their missiles from Cuba, whilst Kennedy promised not to invade Cuba and also to remove

US Jupiter intermediate-range missiles from Turkey. The world had stepped back from nuclear Armageddon.

Vanguard, the last battleship in the Royal Navy
(NN)

A US Navy destroyer intercepts a Soviet merchant vessel in the Caribbean
(USN)

The Polaris Agreement A consequence of the Cuban missile crisis was to move the threat of total war and nuclear deterrence to the very top of the agenda. The shooting down of the U-2 aircraft had shown the vulnerability of manned aircraft, and consequently the UK had been developing the Blue Streak (land-based) and Blue Steel (air-launched) missile systems to replace the strategic V-bomber force. Unfortunately the costs of both systems spiralled out of control and the UK switched to buying the much cheaper US Skybolt missile system. At the same time, Britain agreed to let the US Navy use Holy Loch in Scotland for its Polaris missile submarines as well as building a missile early warning system (the 'Three Minute Warning') at Fylingdales in Yorkshire.

The USA then cancelled Skybolt, leaving Britain with no real replacement for its V-bomber force. In December 1962 Macmillan and Kennedy discussed the problem during talks in the Bahamas. After three days of intense negotiations a deal was finally struck. The USA would provide Britain with Polaris missiles, but Britain would build her own nuclear missile submarines and also the nuclear warheads for the missiles. It was a most important deal for the Royal Navy and the future long-term defence of the United Kingdom. The Royal Air Force realised that responsibility for the country's strategic nuclear deterrent would pass to the Royal Navy and was less than totally enthusiastic about the deal.

———•———

The Board of Admiralty On 1 April 1964 the new unified Ministry of Defence was established, replacing the Board of Admiralty. The office of First Lord of the Admiralty, held by George, Second Earl Jellicoe at the time and formerly a

Firing a Royal Navy
Polaris missile
(RNSM)

Cabinet post, was abolished with it, and HM Queen Elizabeth II became her own Lord High Admiral. It was a historic moment ending 336 years of service by the Board, which had been formed in 1628 under King Charles I. The role of the Board of Admiralty was taken over by the Ministry of Defence under the Secretary of State for Defence, Peter Thornycroft. Commenting on the rapid run-down of the Royal Navy, Andrew Marr later wrote of the demise of the Board of Admiralty, 'It was the last act in the ruthless liquidation of

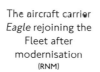

The new
amphibious assault
ship *Fearless*
(RNM)

The aircraft carrier
Eagle rejoining the
Fleet after
modernisation
(RNM)

the organisation that had been central to British identity for as long as Britain had been a single nation.'[2]

THE FLEET

Despite the substantial cuts in ships and submarines ordered by the 1957 defence review, the Royal Navy remained a powerful fighting force with a large fleet in the early 1960s.

Aircraft Carriers The capital ships forming the backbone of the Fleet were the aircraft carriers, which comprised the fleet carriers *Ark Royal, Eagle* and *Victorious* and the smaller carriers *Centaur* and *Hermes. Ark Royal* had just been commissioned in December 1959 on completion of an extensive refit. In her place, *Eagle* was taken to Devonport dockyard in 1959 for an extensive refit and full modernisation. She was eventually recommissioned in May 1964. In July 1963 it was announced that a new 50,000-ton aircraft carrier would be built to replace *Victorious*. The project for the new-generation fixed-wing strike carrier was named CVA-01. Naval plans were based on maintaining one operational aircraft carrier deployed east of Suez, as well as two in home waters.

The *Tiger* class
cruiser *Blake*
(RNM)

Amphibious Ships The light fleet carriers *Albion* and *Bulwark* were being converted to the commando role and two new 12,000-ton purpose-built assault ships, *Fearless* and *Intrepid*, were being ordered to reinforce the amphibious capability of the Royal Navy. *Fearless* was launched in 1963, and *Intrepid* the following year.

Cruisers Although most of the great classic cruisers (the *Southampton*, *Ceylon* and *Mauritius* classes, plus the cruisers *Superb* and *Swiftsure*) were being scrapped, the 10,000-ton *Tiger* class cruisers with modern automatic guns were being completed to replace them: *Tiger* in 1959, *Lion* in 1960 and *Blake* in 1961.

New Missile Destroyers The new 6,000-ton County class guided missile destroyers (officially 'destroyer leader guided' or DLG) were being built with Seaslug and Seacat guided missile systems. *Devonshire*, the first of class, was launched on 10 June 1960. A class of eight ships was to be ordered, with four (*Devonshire*, *Hampshire*, *Kent* and *London*) to be completed by 1963.

Destroyers and Frigates Large numbers of the old World War II destroyers and frigates which had been mostly placed in reserve were being scrapped, but in response to a growing threat of Soviet submarines and long-range maritime strike aircraft, quite a number had been converted to fast anti-submarine (AS) and anti-aircraft (AA) frigates. These were being supplemented by newer purpose-built destroyers and frigates.

The Type 14 *Blackwood* class utility AS frigates were all in service with the fleet whilst the rest of the more modern Type 12 *Whitby* class AS frigates were being completed. The *Salisbury* class and *Leopard* class (the 'Cathedrals' and 'Cats') AA frigates had already joined the Fleet.

Prominence of ASW ASW (anti-submarine warfare) was seen as the prime role of the escort fleet, particularly the frigates. At the beginning of 1960 there were approximately fifty-four older converted AS frigates and twenty-four modern AS frigates, as against seventeen older AA frigates and four new AA frigates, as well as five new aircraft-direction (AD) frigates.

The new Type 12 frigate *Rothesay* operating ASW helicopters (RNM)

A new general-purpose frigate, the Type 81 Tribal class, designed primarily for service in the Gulf (fully air-conditioned), was being built, and all seven ships would join the Fleet by 1964.

Leander Class Frigates The most important of all the general-purpose frigates, the *Leander* class, were under construction. They would become the basic workhorse escorts of the Royal Navy through to the late 1980s. The *Leander* class frigates were derived from the successful Type 12 frigates and had excellent sea-keeping capabilities; they would turn out to be the best frigates ever to serve with the Royal Navy. A total of twenty-six would be built, with the first completed and joining the Fleet in 1963.

The Rest of the Fleet In addition, the Fleet included fifty-six submarines, thirteen minelayers, 217 minesweepers, thirty-four patrol vessels and gunboats, thirty-three landing ships and eighty landing craft.

Support Ninety transport ships, supply ships and tankers, manned by the RFA (Royal Fleet Auxiliary), supported the Fleet.

Fleet Air Arm In 1960 the Fleet Air Arm operated fixed-wing aircraft in three basic roles, fighter, strike and ASW. The Sea Vixens and Scimitars were the modern fighters, replacing the older Sea Venoms and Sea Hawks. Whilst the Scimitar had a limited strike role, the new Buccaneer long-range strike aircraft were joining the Fleet by 1962.

The Buccaneer also had a nuclear strike role. The prime ASW aircraft was the Gannet, which was also developing an airborne early-warning role. Helicopters were also taking over the ASW role as well as developing their other tasks such as transport, evacuation and airborne assault. The new Wessex helicopter was replacing the Whirlwind, which had in its turn replaced the older Dragonfly helicopters.

Royal Marines The Royal Marines provided the permanent amphibious force of 3 Commando Brigade, comprising 40, 42 and 45 Commandos, with two further Commandos, 41 and 43, authorised. The Royal Marines also provided detachments in most major surface ships. Admiral Mountbatten, when First Sea Lord, had planned to raise a new brigade of commandos for quick reaction to limited wars, but the plan was shelved.

Naval Hovercraft In 1961 a hovercraft trials unit was established at RNAS (Royal Naval Air Station) Daedalus at Lee on Solent. Initially trials were conducted to establish the suitability of hovercraft for ASW. Subsequently they were considered for amphibious warfare, and it was decided to use them in the Far East. The Hovercraft Unit (Far East) was then formed in August 1964. Two hovercraft were armed and sent to Singapore in January 1965; two months later they were deployed to Tawau in North Borneo for use in the river delta areas during the Indonesian Confrontation.

FIRST SEA LORDS

Admiral Sir Caspar John In 1960 the Vice Chief of the Naval Staff (VCNS), Admiral Sir Caspar John, was appointed First Sea Lord, relieving Admiral Sir Charles Lambe, who was not well. Caspar John went to Osborne and Dartmouth before being appointed to the battleship *Centurion* as a Midshipman

in 1921. After service with the Mediterranean Fleet he switched to the Fleet Air Arm and qualified as a pilot in 1926. During World War II he served in the heavy cruiser *York* and commanded *Pretoria Castle*, an emergency light carrier conversion. Later he commanded the aircraft carrier *Ocean* and the 3rd Aircraft Carrier Squadron. He was a tough admiral with piercing eyes and a fierce reputation.

As First Sea Lord, he was forced by defence cuts to disband the Mediterranean Fleet, but he did manage to achieve government agreement to build a new 50,000-ton aircraft carrier.

Admiral Sir David Luce Admiral Luce was appointed First Sea Lord in 1963 but, ironically for a submariner, he had to resign in 1966 when the new carrier project CVA-01, won by his predecessor, was scrapped as part of the 1966 defence review.

David Luce joined the Royal Navy at the end of World War I and served in a number of submarines, commanding H44 in 1936. During World War II he commanded the submarines *Rainbow* and *Cachalot*, and

after the war he commanded the cruisers *Liverpool* and *Birmingham*. He was appointed Naval Secretary to the First Sea Lord in 1954 and then Flag Officer Flotillas, Home Fleet in 1956. From 1960 to 1962 he was the Commander in Chief Far East Station, and he went on to become Commander in Chief British Forces, Far East. He was appointed First Sea Lord in 1963 but resigned in protest against the carrier decision in 1966. He was not then promoted to Admiral of the Fleet in retirement. Admiral Luce was popular in the Service and was known as a man of strong principles.

OPERATIONS AND DEPLOYMENTS, 1960–1964

Throughout the early sixties the Royal Navy kept up its important peace-keeping duties around the world, often in dependent territories or former possessions, maintaining order and security

and protecting British citizens, interests and trade. General Sir William Jackson has commented: 'Though many of the crises involving British forces in the 1960s were to appear totally unexpected, it was remarkable how often the Naval Staff had made far-sighted anticipatory deployments and had appropriate forces in the right place at the right time.'[3]

Persian Gulf Frigates continued to patrol the Persian Gulf searching dhows and other shipping to prevent arms running, drug smuggling, slaving, piracy and insurgent infiltration as well as helpng civil powers to quell local riots and disturbances. The frigates *Loch Fada* and *Loch Lomond* intercepted an enormous haul of arms and ammunition being smuggled from Saudi Arabia to Omani rebels in July 1960.

In 1962 the four minesweepers of the 9th Minesweeping Squadron, *Appleton*, *Flockton*, *Kemerton* and *Chilcompton*, were deployed to the Gulf (based in Bahrain) to assist the frigates with Gulf patrol duties.

Aden Aden provided a key base facility on the main route to the Far East, and British forces maintained a garrison in the base (Britain had been in Aden for over 120 years). In April 1960, 45 Commando Royal Marines was deployed to

The new 'general-purpose' frigate *Gurkha* (RNM)

The *Leander* class
frigate *Achilles*
(RNM)

Admiral Sir David
Luce
(GI)

Aden to assist with internal security operations.

Hong Kong In the Far East a squadron of six inshore minesweepers carried out guardship duties in the Hong Kong area. They were replaced by three coastal minesweepers (the Ton class minesweepers *Woolaston*, *Wilkieston* and *Fiskerton*) in 1962, though these were deployed for patrols in Malaysian waters from time to time during the period of Indonesian Confrontation.

Malayan Emergency Further south, ships of the Far East Fleet, operating from Singapore, were engaged in the ongoing Malayan Emergency in support of British forces waging a campaign in the jungles of Malaya against Communist terrorists. The Royal Navy carried out coastal patrols, naval gunfire support, aerial reconnaissance and reinforcement and resupply right up until a successful end to the emergency was finally achieved on 31 July 1960.

West Indies Frigates and destroyers were regularly deployed to the West Indies. The frigates of the Dartmouth Training Squadron were deployed to the West Indies for three or four months every year. In 1964 a permanent guardship was stationed in the Bahamas, largely to counter the activities of the anti-Castro exiles in the area.

Royal Marine Deployments In 1960 the Royal Marines were primarily deployed east of Suez. 40 Commando was already in the Far East, and on 14 March 42 Commando embarked on board the commando carrier *Bulwark* and sailed from the UK, bound for the Far East. 45 Commando was deployed to Aden the following month. 41 Commando was reforming in the UK and plans were set in hand to raise a fifth commando, 43 Commando.

Submarine Surveillance Operations Britain and America were intensely concerned with developments in the Soviet Submarine Fleet and ran a regular programme of covert surveillance operations. These consisted of intelligence gathering patrols off the main Russian naval bases and fleet training grounds in the Barents Sea.

The Royal Navy shouldered its share of the burden and

deployed conventional 'A' and 'T' class submarines, adapted for surveillance with special intelligence intercept equipment, on a series of missions in the Barents Sea, off the Murmansk naval base and in the Kola Inlet. These were dangerous operations and submarine commanders knew what to expect if they were detected. On 19 August 1957 the USS *Gudgeon* had been detected lying off the naval base of Vladivostok and was immediately attacked by the Soviet Navy. The submarine had been repeatedly depth-charged and was lucky to escape after a forty-eight-hour ordeal.

The information brought back was immensely valuable in developing tactics and equipment to counter Soviet submarines.

The First Cod War (Continued)

Operation Whippet, 1959–1961 Meanwhile in the Arctic waters off Iceland, the First Cod War continued, with Royal

A Buccaneer long-range strike aircraft (RNM)

Navy destroyers and frigates endeavouring to protect British trawlers fishing legitimately in the disputed fishing grounds. Britain eased back on operations in the run-up to the Second UN Conference on the Law of the Sea on 16 March 1960 to ease tension. There were few incidents, though on 21 February the Icelandic gunboat *Albert* fired warning shots across the bow of the trawler *James Barrie*. When the *Albert* then attempted to arrest the trawler, the frigate *Palliser* was forced to intervene to prevent any such action. Eight days later the gunboat *Thor* fired warning shots at the *Camilla*, and on 1 March the gunboat *Albert* fired warning shots at the trawler *Bengali* and then attempted to arrest her.

So as not to aggravate the situation and compromise the British negotiating position, all British trawlers and the frigates *Paladin* and *Undine* were withdrawn from the disputed area on 14 March. Although the UN conference failed to resolve the issue, British trawlers and Royal Navy warships remained outside the twelve-mile limit for a further three months.

Operation Mint At the end of April the destroyers *Delight* and *Battleaxe* and the frigate *Palliser*, supported by RFA *Wave Ruler*, were back on station off Iceland as part of Operation Mint. The ships patrolled in different sectors and were ordered to protect trawlers but to avoid incidents as far as possible. Gradually more and more British trawlers resumed fishing inside the twelve-mile limit, and Icelandic gunboats resumed operations against them. On 22 June the gunboat *Albert* fired warning shots at the trawler *Thuringia*, and the *Thor* attempted to arrest the trawler *Northern Sceptre*. These incidents were followed by other attempts to arrest trawlers. Six days later the gunboat *Thor* boarded the *Northern Queen* and the trawler had to be rescued by the frigate *Duncan*. Two days after that *Thor* fired warning shots at *Lifeguard* and

Naval hovercraft at the Interservice Trials Unit at HMS *Daedalus* (RNM)

attempted to arrest her, whilst the gunboat *Odinn* tried to arrest the *Kingston Jade*.

On 10 July *Odinn*, which had been nearly rammed by the trawler *Grimsby Town*, opened fire, hitting the trawler's superstructure. In response *Palliser* closed at full speed and chased off the gunboat. Four days later the gunboat *Albert* fired warning shots at the *Hull City* and tried, unsuccessfully, to arrest her.

Despite every attempt being made to avoid any further incident, harassment of trawlers continued. On 13 November an unidentified gunboat opened fire on the *William Wilberforce* but swiftly retired when *Duncan* arrived to defend the trawler. The rest of the year was relatively quiet with only one attempt to arrest the trawler *Red Knight*.

One incident provoked a good deal of press attention. The Danish frigate *Neils Ebbesen* attempted to arrest the trawler *Red Crusader* south of the Faeroes and opened fire, hitting the trawler three times. The trawler departed at full speed and had to be escorted into Aberdeen by the frigate *Troubridge* and the Ton class coastal minesweeper *Wotton*.

Talks resumed between Britain and Iceland during the winter and, though the talks dragged on for several months, they ended in a compromise agreement being brokered between the two governments, and the Cod War was finally over on 11 March 1961. The frigates *Rhyl* and *Malcolm*, supported by RFA *Tidepool*, remained on patrol to ensure that there were no further incidents.

During the First Cod War Icelandic authorities had made eighty-four serious attempts to arrest British trawlers but thanks to the protection provided by the Royal Navy

Landing a Royal Marine Landrover on the Malaysian coast at Usukan in early 1960
(RNM)

none had been successful. The Royal Navy had deployed sixty-three warships and ten RFA support ships to the area, enabling the British fishing fleet to bring home 85 per cent of its normal catch during the course of the dispute.[4]

Southern Arabia British forces continued to be employed against tribal factions in Southern Arabia in an effort to keep the peace. In April 1960 naval aircraft from the carrier *Centaur*, escorted by the destroyer *Lagos*, participated in operations against dissident elements of the Burbakr tribe. Air strikes were also carried out jointly with RAF strike aircraft operating from Khormaksar airfield in Aden.

Kuwait Emergency

Operation Vantage, June–August 1961 In June 1961, Kuwait was released from the Anglo-Kuwaiti Treaty of 1899 and granted independence with agreed defence support from the UK if attacked. Towards the end of the month Iraq, which had long claimed possession of Kuwait, threatened to revive her claim and prepared her forces to invade. On 25 June President Kassem of Iraq announced his intention to annex Kuwait. A great proportion of the UK's oil supplies came from the oilfields of Kuwait, and if they were to be taken over by the Iraqis that vital supply would be seriously threatened.

On 27 June the British Embassy in Baghdad reported large columns of Iraqi armour and troops moving south-east, in the direction of Basra and towards the border with Kuwait. The Amir of Kuwait called upon Britain to defend his country, and British forces, which had been gathering in the region, were put on high alert.

Operation Vantage was initiated straight away and the commando carrier *Bulwark*, with 42 Commando Royal Marines embarked, was sailed from Karachi with orders to head to the northern Gulf at best possible speed. *Bulwark* maintained a speed of twenty-four knots, arriving off Kuwait on 1 July, and started landing 42 Commando by helicopter in the middle of a sand storm. Despite the adverse weather, 750 Royal Marines were landed by the helicopters of 848 NAS (Naval Air Squadron). RAF Britannias, Beverleys and Hastings flew in 45 Commando from Aden the next day. The Royal Marines dug in ashore and were backed up by further troops and armoured units from the Amphibious Warfare Squadron, including Centurion tanks landed from the LST (landing ship tank) *Striker*. By 11 July there were nearly 6,000 troops ashore as well as various armoured units. The aircraft carriers *Victorious* and *Centaur* quickly arrived in the area, *Victorious* having sailed at full speed from the Far East, escorted by the destroyer *Cassandra* and the frigate *Lincoln*. Once the aircraft carriers arrived in the Gulf their aircraft provided continuous air cover.

The British forces ashore were well deployed to defend Kuwait, and the Iraqis were surprised at the considerable show of force gathered by the Royal Navy in the waters of the northern Gulf. Ultimately forty-five RN warships were deployed to the area, with the amphibious ship *Meon* acting as the command and control ship for the operation.

The frigate *Hardy* in Icelandic waters
(RNM)

Victorious in the Gulf
(MH)

The tension eased, and by mid-August it was clear that Iraq had abandoned her plans to invade Kuwait. Gradually the forces were stood down and reduced. The carriers *Victorious* and *Centaur* sailed south and resumed their deployments, and the various other naval units were dispersed. The whole region then remained relatively quiet, though towards the end of the year there was an incident in the Indian Ocean when Goa was threatened by invasion from India and the frigate *Rhyl* had to be sent there to prevent an attack and restore peace in the area.

HM **Ships and Units Engaged in Operation Vantage**	
Aircraft carriers:	*Victorious* and *Centaur*
Commando carrier:	*Bulwark*
Amphibious ships:	*Meon, Messina* and *Striker*
Destroyers and frigates:	*Camperdown, Finisterre, Saintes, Cassandra, Yarmouth, Llandaff, Lincoln, Loch Ruthven, Loch Fyne* and *Loch Alvie*
Minesweepers:	*Ashton* and *Rodington*
42 and 45 Commandos	
Tanker:	RFA *Olna*

Further Threat to Kuwait In early January the following year there was a further threat of invasion of Kuwait by Iraqi forces. Immediately operations were set in train and a task force consisting of the Far East Fleet aircraft carrier *Centaur*, escorted by the frigates *Plymouth* and *Eastbourne*, was ordered to the area to stand by to intervene. The Task Force steamed at full speed across the Indian Ocean and transited the Straits of Hormuz straight into the Gulf. Once in the northern Gulf the Task Force stood by off Masirah Island as a precautionary measure. The speedy show of force was sufficient to deter Iraqi forces. Eventually the situation on the border eased sufficiently for the Task Force to be withdrawn from the Gulf.

The Far East

On 27 March 1962 the aircraft carrier *Ark Royal* arrived in Aden, having sailed from the UK at the end of the previous year. In Aden she relieved *Centaur* as the 'East of Suez' operational aircraft carrier. *Centaur* then headed home to the UK and *Ark Royal* proceeded to the Far East Station, arriving in Singapore on 12 April.

Laos The following month Communist forces on the border of Laos threatened Thailand, and the US 7th Fleet was sent into the South China Sea. The Far East Fleet, with the newly arrived *Ark Royal*, prepared to reinforce the US fleet but in the event only RAF Hunter jet fighters from RAF Tengah at Singapore supported the US operations.

Exercise Fotex 62 Two months later in July, after exercising with the US Navy, including the major SEATO exercise codenamed Sea Devil, the Far East Fleet made an impressive display of force in the South China Sea by conducting exercise Fotex 62. *Ark Royal* (with Admiral Sir David Luce, Commander in Chief Far East Station, embarked), *Bulwark*, *Tiger*, *Cavalier*, *Cassandra*, *Carysfort*, *Plymouth* and *Eastbourne*, HMAS *Parramatta* and HMAS *Yarra* and HMNZS *Tarranaki* steamed in column off the island of Pulau Tioman. The exercise provided a good photographic and press opportunity.

***Ark Royal* leaves the Far East** By October *Ark Royal* had completed her commission in the Far East and it was time to return home. At the same time guns were needed in Aden, and so it was decided that *Ark Royal* should transport the 34th Artillery Regiment from Singapore. The regiment, with its guns and vehicles, was embarked, and on 25 October *Ark Royal* sailed from Singapore and headed west across the Indian Ocean. After landing the artillery regiment at Aden and paying a final call to Mombasa she headed for the Suez Canal and home.

Borneo

In May 1961 the Prime Minister of Malaya, Tunku Abdul Rahman, had proposed the formation of an economic and political union of Malaysia, comprising Malaya, Singapore, North Borneo, Brunei and Sarawak. President Sukarno of

Indonesia was totally opposed to the idea as he had his own plan for the region, which was to bring the whole area into a confederation of Indonesian states. The stage was set for confrontation between the two protagonists.

Insurrection in Brunei, 8 December 1962 – April 1963
On 8 December 1962 the Indonesian-backed North Kalimantan National Army (TKNU) revolted. The rebel force of some 4,000, led by Yassin Affendi, attacked the Sultan of Brunei as well as the main towns and oilfields. The rebels seized the British Resident and staff at Limbang in Sarawak, as well as taking control of Tutong, Seria, Bangar and other smaller settlements. The British commander in the area was Major General Walter Walker, who responded by flying Gurkhas from Singapore to Brunei Town where they immediately engaged the rebels, taking some 800 prisoners during the first night of fighting. One Gurkha officer was killed and seven Gurkhas were wounded.

HQ 3 Commando Brigade Royal Marines was in Singapore, and reacted instantly, flying 'L' Company, from 42 Commando in *Bulwark*, across to Brunei, where it arrived on 10 December. Captain Jeremy Moore, commanding 'L' Company was ordered up river in Sarawak to rescue British hostages being held in Limbang.

The coastal minesweepers *Fiskerton* and *Chawton* from the 6th Minesweeping Squadron in Singapore had already sailed to Brunei. Men from the minesweepers, under the command of Lieutenant Commander Jeremy Black, commandeered two flat-bottomed 'Z' lighters to transport the Royal Marines ten miles up river to Limbang. The force arrived close to Limbang late on 12 December and lay up out of sight, in a curve of the river, for the night.

At first light the next day the 'Z' craft sailed round the bend in the river and very quickly came under fire as they approached the waterfront of Limbang. Three Royal Marines were shot dead and several wounded in the leading 'Z' craft as they were beached on the riverbank. Immediately the rest of the Royal Marines leapt ashore and stormed up the main street under heavy fire. After a fierce gun battle they managed to rescue all the hostages alive. In the fighting thirty-five rebels were killed and a great many more were captured or wounded, whilst five Royal Marines were killed and seven wounded. Captain Moore was awarded a bar to his Military Cross.[5] (Jeremy Moore and Jeremy Black were to serve together, again in key appointments, in the Falklands War twenty years later.)

The destroyer *Cavalier*, on passage back from Australia, was ordered with all haste to Singapore, where she embarked troops from the Queen's Own Highlanders and headed out again at full speed to land her troops at Labuan. The Queen's Own Highlanders then swiftly retook Seria. The coastal minesweepers *Wilkieston* and *Woolaston*, supported by the modified Loch class frigate *Woodbridge Haven*, were ordered to reinforce Kuching in Sarawak, whilst RFAs *Gold Ranger* and *Wave Sovereign* were sent to reinforce Labuan.

The remaining companies of 42 Commando then liberated Bangar from the rebels, sadly not before six hostages

Ark Royal with the 34th Artillery Regiment embarked sailing from Singapore on 25 October 1962 (RNM)

had been beheaded. A battalion of Green Jackets was landed from the cruiser *Tiger* to secure Miri and arrived just in time to forestall an attack by rebel forces. Other reinforcements on board the despatch vessel *Alert* and *Woodbridge Haven* arrived in support of the Royal Marines. Other successful actions took place at Bekenu and Anduki, fortunately with relatively few casualties.

The commando carrier *Albion*, with 40 Commando and 845 and 846 Naval Helicopter Squadrons on board, had sailed from Mombasa on 5 December and was on passage across the Indian Ocean to join the Far East Fleet at Singapore. She then received orders to proceed at best speed and headed as fast as she could for Singapore. After a very short stop to embark additional troops, equipment and ammunition *Albion* sailed swiftly from Singapore to land her Royal Marines and helicopters at Kuching, Sarawak, by 14 December. Once ashore the Royal Marines were able to assist in flushing out the last pockets of resistance. By the

end of December over forty rebels had been killed and some 3,500 had been captured.

The versatility of the helicopters was to prove one of the key factors in success in the war in the jungle. General Walker was appointed Commander British Forces Borneo, and the swift, resolute action taken broke the back of the rebellion although it was to be a number of months before the last of the rebels were finally accounted for in April 1963. Gurkhas discovered the leader's secret hideout near Limbang on 18 May, and Affendi was captured. Malaysia came into being on 16 September, but without Brunei.

Indonesian Confrontation, 20 January 1963 – 11 August 1966

On 20 January 1963 Indonesia announced a policy of 'Confrontation' against Malaysia, and from April Indonesian forces began raids into Sarawak and Sabah in North Borneo. *Albion* returned from Borneo to Singapore at the beginning

Midshipmen from *Albion* on patrol in the Borneo jungle (KR)

Royal Marines of 40 and 42 Commandos, one of which was always present throughout the whole campaign. Officers and ratings from the ships at sea were often landed to assist the patrols ashore in Borneo.

It was in the Confrontation that *Albion*, which had a habit of appearing out of the grey morning mist off the Borneo coast, acquired the title of 'The Old Grey Ghost of the Borneo Coast'! Ton class minesweepers and patrol vessels carried out patrols close inshore and in the main rivers.

There was a steady build-up of forces engaged in the area. Forts and observation posts were constructed along the border and British forces settled down to a drawn-out war of infiltration, patrol and ambush in the hostile environment of the jungle. The Indonesians regularly attacked the British bases and frontier posts. In April an Indonesian force invaded Sarawak, captured Tebedu, close to Kuching, the capital, and murdered the police in the local police station. In June the Indonesians took a frontier post and killed the five Gurkhas they caught.

General Walker was appointed Director of Borneo Operations in April and was allocated six coastal minesweepers and two squadrons of naval helicopters to support his three battalions of troops on the ground. It was decided to reinforce the Far East Fleet with warships being diverted to the area. The aircraft carriers *Ark Royal* and *Centaur* were sent from UK to the Far East to reinforce the carrier *Hermes*. The County class DLG *Hampshire* was sent to relieve the cruiser *Lion*, which had been damaged by an explosion in one of her boilers. Submarines were also sent and painted with camouflage for operations close to shore.

Ark Royal arrived in the Far East in July, and shortly after arriving took part in an impressive exercise Fotex off the coast of Malaya. Fotex 63 was the largest gathering of ships in the Far East for many years. At the end of it *Ark Royal* unfortunately suffered a breakdown of her main engines. The damage required dockyard assistance and so it was decided to send the aircraft carrier *Victorious* to the Far East to relieve her. *Victorious* arrived in the Malacca Strait in September.

Despite the ongoing war in Borneo, the London Agreement, setting up the Federation of Malaya, was signed in July 1963, and the Federation was established, without Brunei, on 16 September. There was then an escalation in the fighting as the political situation deteriorated. Indonesian mobs attacked British citizens in Indonesia, the British embassy in Jakarta was burned to the ground, and the Indonesians launched attacks against the mainland of Malaya. Western aid to Indonesia was suspended and President Sukarno turned to Communist China for assistance.

Fighting in North Borneo and on the border intensified. The helicopters of 845 NAS and 846 NAS were regularly operating in rotation to bases ashore set up in Sarawak and Sabah at Sibu and Nanga Gaat. By June they had completed 3,500 operational sorties.

In August and September the Indonesians launched raids on Malaysia by sea and air. The seaborne raids were nearly

of April to embark a battalion of Gurkha Rifles (2/10th). On 18 April she sailed from Singapore and headed for the coast of Sarawak, where the helicopters of 845 NAS landed the Gurkhas ashore. Indonesian attacks along the border intensified and the Whirlwind helicopters of 846 NAS, which had been operating in Brunei, were flown west to Kuching to assist with deploying Royal Marines and Gurkhas inland.

The Gurkhas and Royal Marines deployed on the borders of Borneo clashed with Indonesian troops and guerrillas in the jungle. Other army units assisted, including the SAS, but the brunt of the fighting fell to the Gurkhas and the

The submarine *Alliance* operating off the Borneo coast with camouflage paint (RNSM)

The commando carrier *Bulwark* in the Far East
(CC)

Bulwark, when they rendezvoused in Aden. *Bulwark* then sailed east for Singapore and was soon patrolling off the coast of Sarawak.

Naval Party 'Kilo' Early in 1964 it was decided to set up an inshore patrol of small converted patrol craft fitted out with radios and mounted machine guns. The twelve craft were based on Kuching and conducted regular inshore patrols of up to ten days. The patrol craft were camouflaged and flew the international code flag 'Kilo', meaning 'stop instantly', hence the name of the naval party. The patrol craft each carried an interpreter, and they regularly stopped and searched local craft. Minesweepers and frigates provided cover off shore as guardships. The guardships also provided support to 846 NAS ashore.

During the summer the attacks against the patrol craft increased, and in August the Ton class minesweeper *Maryton* came under heavy fire from enemy howitzers whilst patrolling off Tawau.

Passage of the Lombok Strait, 12 September 1964 In September a small task force consisting of the fleet carrier *Victorious*, escorted by the destroyers *Cavendish* and *Caesar*, was on passage back to Singapore after a goodwill visit to Western Australia. After sailing from Fremantle they set course north-north-west for the Sunda Strait. As they approached Indonesian waters there was widespread panic in the Indonesian capital, Jakarta, and many people started to flee the capital fearing air strikes and bombing raids. South of Java the Task Force rendezvoused with the guided missile destroyer *Hampshire* and the frigates *Dido* and *Berwick*.

To obstruct the transit of the powerful Task Force the Indonesians closed the Sunda Strait, declaring it an area for Indonesian naval exercises. Not daunted by the closure of the Sunda Strait, on 12 September the Task Force sailed through the narrow Lombok Strait, east of Bali, in Indonesian waters and asserted the continued right of innocent passage in international waters. The ships closed up at action stations, with all guns manned, and stood by to repel attacks from Indonesian warships or the Indonesian Air Force as they passed through the narrow straits. At one stage an Indonesian submarine was spotted on the surface and the ships prepared to open fire on the submarine if she displayed any hostile intent. In the event the Indonesian forces decided it was wiser to leave the Task Force unchallenged in Indonesian waters and the submarine sent messages of good wishes. The Task Force emerged, unscathed, from the Lombok Strait in to the Java Sea, where the ships then altered course west for Singapore.[6]

all intercepted and driven off whilst the troops parachuted into Malaysia were rounded up and captured.

In response it was considered necessary to increase force levels in the region, and a further build-up of naval forces was set in hand. Additional helicopters were also needed, and in November 1963 *Albion* made a fast passage west across the Indian Ocean to the Mediterranean to embark RAF Whirlwind and Belvedere heavy-lift helicopters in Tobruck. 'The Old Grey Ghost of the Borneo Coast' was renamed 'The Old Grey Gharrie of Tobruck Alley'.

The Attack on Long Jawi *Albion* made a fast passage back to Singapore, and as the helicopters were being landed in the naval base, reports of a major Indonesian attack on Long Jawi in Sarawak were received. *Albion* immediately sailed and headed east to Sarawak at full speed. The helicopters of 845 NAS were launched as soon as they were in range of the coast. On landing at Sibu 845 NAS embarked several units of Gurkhas and swiftly ferried them on to Long Jawi. The Gurkhas caught the Indonesians by surprise and defeated them, killing some forty enemy soldiers. At the same time Gurkhas transported by the helicopters of 846 NAS defeated an Indonesian attack on Simanggang. By November 846 NAS had flown 3,184 sorties during its year in the Far East.

In December the carrier *Centaur* was sailed early from the UK to strengthen the fleet in the Far East. A short while later the commando carrier *Bulwark* also sailed for the Far East to relieve her sister ship *Albion*. In February 1964 *Albion* completed her commission in the Far East and sailed from Singapore bound for the UK. She left some of her helicopters deployed in Borneo and transferred the rest to her relief,

In November a small Indonesian craft attacked the Ton class minesweeper *Fiskerton* with grenades off Singapore. In the ensuing action the Indonesian crew of three were all killed, and though several grenades exploded on board *Fiskerton* no casualties were sustained. The following month the *Leander* class frigate *Ajax* foiled an Indonesian incursion by six craft in Kuala Lumpur. When she approached the Indonesian craft in the Malacca Strait she was attacked, but after opening accurate fire on the leading craft all sped off at high speed for the safety of Indonesian territorial waters. Later in the month the Australian minesweeper HMAS *Teal* was attacked by two Indonesian craft in the approaches to Singapore. In the attack one Indonesian was killed and six captured.

By the end of 1964 the fleet in Indonesian waters of nearly eighty ships was the biggest since the Korean War and consisted of three aircraft carriers, *Victorious*, *Centaur* and *Bulwark*, two guided missile destroyers, *Kent* and *Hampshire*, seventeen destroyers and frigates, twelve minesweepers, five submarines and a whole host of supporting craft, as well as ships from Commonwealth navies.

Operation Claret Towards the end of the year the strength of the Indonesian forces on the border was estimated at over 22,000. General Walker obtained clearance to launch operations in hot pursuit behind Indonesian lines under the top-secret codename Operation Claret. These raids took the Indonesians by surprise and started to turn the tables against the Indonesian forces.

By the end of 1964 the British forces were well deployed in, and around, Borneo, and though the campaign was far from over, the end, with the defeat of Indonesia, was inevitable. At the end of the campaign the Secretary of State for Defence, Denis Healey, said, 'When [one] thinks of the tragedy that could have fallen on a whole corner of a Continent if we had not been able to hold the situation and bring it to a successful termination, it will be appreciated that in the history books it will be recorded as one of the most efficient uses of military force in the history of the world.'[7]

The Loss of HMAS *Voyager* In February 1964 a tragic accident befell the Royal Australian Navy, which had been operating with the Royal Navy during the Indonesian campaign. At 2100 on the night of 10 February the aircraft carrier HMAS *Melbourne* (ex HMS *Majestic*) was conducting night flying operations off Jervis Bay in the Tasman Sea. The plane guard (safety ship) was the modern *Daring* class destroyer HMAS *Voyager*.

Having found the right course to obtain the necessary wind speed over the deck for aircraft launch, HMAS *Melbourne* signalled to *Voyager*, stationed on *Melbourne*'s starboard bow, 'Flying course 020, speed twenty-two knots.' To take up plane guard station *Voyager* needed to position herself on the port quarter of the aircraft carrier, which was in a diagonally opposite position to where she was steaming on the starboard bow of the carrier. Instead of turning away from the carrier and passing astern of her to take up her new position, the destroyer turned in and attempted to pass ahead. In doing so the destroyer came under the bows of the 22,000-ton aircraft carrier steaming at twenty-two knots. The carrier crashed straight through her, cutting her in half, with the tragic loss of eighty-two officers and men, including the Captain and officers on her bridge.[8]

(Note: HMAS *Voyager* was replaced by the *Daring* class destroyer *Duchess*. In 1965, as HMAS *Duchess*, she was able to take thirty-eight Indonesian prisoners on a single patrol during the Indonesian Confrontation. By then almost 70 per cent of the Royal Australian Navy was deployed in and around Indonesian waters on Confrontation operations.[9])

Tanganyika and East African Mutinies, 12 January – 19 March 1964

The aircraft carrier *Centaur* was operating off Aden in early 1964. She entered harbour on 20 January to recover a damaged Gannet aircraft, which had been landed at Khormaksar airfield, when she received immediate orders to embark 45 Commando Royal Marines and a squadron of two RAF Belvedere helicopters and proceed to sea.

On 12 January the Sultan of Zanzibar had been overthrown by the native African population of the island and hundreds of Arabs and Indians had been massacred. The Prime Minister, Julius Nyerere, had fled for his life and appealed to Britain for help. In response the frigate *Rhyl* embarked a company of 1st Staffords at Mombasa and sailed for Zanzibar to provide protection for the British community. The massacres in Zanzibar were followed by uprisings and mutinies in the newly independent Tanganyika, Uganda and Kenya on the mainland. In Tanganyika (now Tanzania) the Tanganyikan Army mutinied on 18 January and was attempting to take over the country, with much killing and looting. 41 Commando from the Strategic Reserve was quickly flown to Kenya from the UK. The British government then mounted an operation, putting together an intervention force, using *Centaur* and the Royal Marines of 45 Commando, to quell the mutinies and restore order.

HM Ships and Units Engaged in the Indonesian Campaign	
Aircraft carriers:	*Ark Royal*, *Victorious*, *Hermes* and *Centaur*
Commando carriers:	*Albion* and *Bulwark*
Cruisers:	*Tiger* and *London*
Guided missile destroyers:	*Devonshire*, *Hampshire* and *Kent*
Destroyers:	*Agincourt*, *Aisne*, *Barossa*, *Cavalier*, *Caesar*, *Cambrian*, *Carysfort*, *Delight*, *Diana* and *Duchess*
Frigates:	*Ajax*, *Blackpool*, *Brighton*, *Chichester*, *Crane*, *Dido*, *Euryalus*, *Lincoln*, *Llandaff*, *Loch Fada*, *Loch Killisport*, *Loch Lomond*, *Plymouth*, *Salisbury*, *Whitby* and *Zest*
Minesweepers:	*Chawton*, *Dartington*, *Dufton*, *Fiskerton*, *Houghton* (MSM 6), *Hubberston*, *Invermoriston*, *Kildarton*, *Lanton*, *Maryton*, *Penston*, *Picton*, *Plaston*, *Puncheston*, *Sheraton*, *Thankerton*, *Wilkieston*, *Woolaston* and *Ickford*
Support ships:	*Manxman*, *Woodbridge Haven*, *Alert* and LCT *Reginald Kerr*
Submarines:	*Alliance*, *Ambush*, *Amphion*, *Anchorite*, *Andrew*, *Auriga* and *Oberon*
Naval Air Squadrons:	845 (Wessex helicopters, embarked in *Albion*), 846 (Whirlwind helicopters, embarked in *Albion* and *Bulwark*), 848 (Wessex helicopters), 849 (Fairey Gannet AEW (airborne early warning) aircraft from *Victorious*)

It took *Centaur* less than twelve hours to load 45 Commando with all their equipment, including vehicles and Ferret armoured cars, and she sailed from Aden at 0100 during the night of 21 January. Once at sea, she was ordered to proceed south for the coast of Tanganyika at full speed. *Centaur* was very soon underway, and increasing her speed to twenty-five knots she steamed south-south-west, escorted by the destroyer *Cambrian*, for Dar es Salaam on the east coast of Africa.

Owen, *Hebe* and *Rhyl* had previously been ordered to Zanzibar and had arrived there on 12 January to evacuate British nationals. The ships remained in the area to cover the safety of those still on shore.

Centaur arrived off Dar es Salaam in the Zanzibar Channel in the evening of 23 January and embarked senior members of the local government and army, loyal to the President. The Tanganyikan Army had taken over the main garrisons at Dar es Salaam, Tabora and Nachingwea. It was decided to take immediate action by launching an airborne assault on Dar es Salaam at dawn.

A force of 350 Royal Marines was landed by stripped-out Wessex helicopters at first light and advanced on the main army barracks at Colito. The frigate *Rhyl* was close inshore in the Bay of Msasani in support, whilst *Cambrian* provided NGS (naval gunfire support). The destroyer opened fire with anti-aircraft shells set to explode in the air over the army barracks and intimidate the mutineers. Despite the fact that the rounds had all been accurately fused causing no casualties, Somalia Radio reported that a British battleship had opened indiscriminate fire on the capital butchering many innocent civilians.

Meanwhile the Royal Marines approached the barracks, where they challenged the soldiers on guard, demanding an immediate and unconditional surrender. Only light opposition was encountered and after a brief exchange of fire, including the use of a 3.5in rocket to take out the main guard post, the rebel units surrendered. It had been an easy engagement with light casualties, and only three soldiers had been killed with six more wounded.

On entering the barracks the Royal Marines discovered that many of the rebel soldiers were suffering hangovers following heavy drunken celebrations the night before. More men and equipment were landed during the morning, and the Royal Marines quickly took over the town, airport and bridges.

The Royal Marines followed up the success in Dar es Salaam by commandeering transport aircraft to fly them to the Tabora garrison nearly 400 miles away. On board *Centaur* a flight of six Sea Vixens of 892 Naval Air Squadron were armed with two-inch rockets and drop tanks of fuel for maximum range. The aircraft, under the command of Lieutenant Commander Ian Blake, were launched and after a circuit of the aircraft carrier headed west for Tabora.

On arrival at Tabora the Sea Vixens dived down and roared over the garrison in a series of threatening low-level passes, whilst under cover of the deafening noise the Royal Marines closed in quickly. They soon overpowered the disorganised and terrified rebel soldiers with minimum casualties.

The Sea Vixens were at extreme range, and to conserve fuel on the return flight they resorted to turning off their jet engines and gliding down to low level before flashing up engines again and flying in to recover on board *Centaur*, with the bare minimum of reserve fuel remaining.

Two days later the final garrison at Nachingwea surrendered to the Royal Marines, and the attempted revolution in Tanganyika was over. The government was restored to power, and law and order was quickly re-established.

At the same time army units, including the 1st Staffords and Scots Guards, put down mutinies in Uganda at Jinja (1st Uganda Rifles) and in Kenya at Nanyuki (3rd Kenya Rifles). News of the prompt action spread rapidly and no further mutinies took place.

The aircraft carrier *Victorious* arrived in the area on 29 January to relieve *Centaur*, whilst 41 Commando, which had been flown in to prevent an uprising in Uganda, took over the policing of the main towns from 45 Commando.

The Royal Navy and army units carried out the whole operation so quickly and efficiently that the rebellions were quashed with the absolute minimum of casualties before many were aware that they had actually taken place. It was a splendid example of the efficient use of military force in a distant part of the world.

HM Ships and Units Engaged in Suppression of the East African Mutinies

Aircraft carriers:	*Victorious*, *Albion* and *Centaur*
Destroyers:	*Diana* and *Cambrian*
Frigates:	*Eskimo*, *Rhyl* and *Salisbury*
Naval Air Squadrons:	892 (Sea Vixens embarked in *Centaur*)
Commandos:	41 and 45

Operations in the Radfan, 1963–1964

Royal Marines of 45 Commando had been deployed to Aden since April 1960 and had become engaged up in the mountains of the Radfan in operations against rebel Yemeni tribesmen, who were being supported by Egyptian forces. 45 Commando was stationed in Little Aden and was part of the British forces backing up the local Federal Regular Army (FRA).

The main troubles started towards the end of 1963, with a civil war in the Yemen and a terrorist campaign in Aden. On 10 December 1963 terrorists attacked the British High Commissioner, Sir Kennedy Trevaskis, and a state of emergency was declared. The terrorists aimed to lead a rebellion with the tribes in the Radfan. The main Dhala road through the Radfan was regularly attacked by terrorists.

Operation Nutcracker A powerful force was formed to advance into the Radfan on 4 January 1964, codenamed Operation Nutcracker. The column included Centurion

Commando, entitled Radforce, was formed. 45 Commando had just returned from action in East Africa. The operation started on 30 April, and the Royal Marines moved up into the mountains of the Radfan in a combined operation with 3 Para. The plan was to take the ridges further to the north of the Bakri Ridge. B Company of 3 Para, consisting of only ten men, was parachuted into the mountains in a key advanced position but was cut off by hundreds of rebel tribesmen. In a desperate fight, supported by RAF Hunter strike jets, the company managed to extricate itself, but not before sadly losing the officer in command and a trooper. The heads of the officer and trooper were later displayed on spikes in Sa'ana, the Yemeni capital.

At the same time that night three rifle companies of Royal Marines scaled one of the dominant peaks in the Radfan to command a strategic position. By daylight 250 Royal Marines were safely on the top of the peak overlooking and commanding the Danaba basin. Five days later the Royal Marines moved on to scale the highest peak, which involved another dangerous night climb, and before daylight they were again on top of the mountain. By 5 May, for the loss of only twelve men, the expedition had managed to occupy the key strategic positions. Under top cover, units of Radforce were then able to move in and engage the rebel forces in a series of running gun battles, supported as necessary by air strikes from RAF Hunter jets. The highest peak in the Radfan, Jebel Huriyah, was cleared of rebels by 11 June. The Royal Marines deployed artillery in the mountains, but the most difficult targets were the snipers concealed in small stone-roofed trench positions. When the Danaba valley and surrounding area were cleared of rebel tribesmen the Royal Marines, supported by 3 Para, scaled the Bakri Ridge and after a four-day battle cleared it of all insurgents. Various units of the British Army moved up in the final phases of the operation to clear the remaining areas of dissident tribesmen.[11]

Having won a number of successes by October and having finally completed the operation, Radforce continued policing the Radfan Mountains and the main Dhala road up into the mountains with regular security patrols.

tanks as well as armoured cars and pack howitzers. The RAF provided two Belvedere helicopters, and *Centaur* sent six Wessex helicopters to support the column.

The column advanced up the Dhala road and was regularly shot at and attacked by tribesmen. Despite heavy opposition, the column forced its way up into the hills of the Radfan, supported by the naval and RAF helicopters. The helicopters transported 105mm guns up on top of overlooking ridges to defend the flanks.

The column took all its objectives, including the strategically important Bakri Ridge, with only seventeen casualties, five of them fatal. It was a most successful combined operation, demonstrating the value of using RAF and naval helicopters. The leader of the column, Brigadier Lunt, was awarded a sword, inscribed 'Hero of the Radfan', by the Emir of Dhala.[10]

The column was eventually withdrawn, and it did not take long for dissident tribesmen to start causing trouble again. It became clear that it would be necessary to plan another, bigger expedition to clear the Radfan.

On 14 April 1964 a second expeditionary column with 45

A Naval Wessex helicopter transporting a 105mm gun to a ridge top in the Radfan
(BSF)

South Arabian Operations In May the Royal Navy was required to provide further support to army operations ashore in southern Arabia. On 13 May the aircraft carrier *Centaur* was in Singapore where she embarked a Royal Artillery battery of 5.5in guns. The guns were required for use against some of the strong forts in the Radfan. The next day, escorted by the destroyer *Cavendish*, she sailed from Singapore and steamed west across the Indian Ocean. Arriving off the coast of Aden, *Centaur* landed the guns and the helicopters of 815 NAS. She then commenced flying operations in support of the forces deployed ashore; and over a period of eleven days 560 sorties were flown. The helicopters from *Centaur* proved invaluable, transporting supplies, men and ammunition in support of forward operations by the army.

Centaur continued to conduct flying operations off the coast of Aden, and in June her Sea Vixen aircraft of 892 NAS carried out strikes against various Yemen rebel positions and forts in the Radfan area of operations.

The Falkland Islands The 3,000 ton converted Royal Navy net-layer *Protector*, with a Royal Marine detachment embarked, was regularly deployed to the South Atlantic during the Antarctic summer to protect British interests in the Falkland Islands Dependencies and the Antarctic region.

In 1963 the Argentine government gave way to popular sentiment for the return of the Falkland Islands to Argentina and introduced a 'Malvinas Day' national holiday. In 1964 Argentina raised the issue of the Falkland Islands with the United Nations.

In September an Argentine aircraft landed illegally on the Port Stanley Racecourse and planted an Argentine flag. The frigate *Lynx*, which was part of a task group off the coast of South America, was immediately detached from the group and ordered to proceed south. *Lynx* arrived in the Falkland Islands on 14 October and remained in the area until 11 November.

OTHER FLEET ACTIVITIES

Humanitarian Assistance Operations On 3 January 1960 the Ton class minesweeper *Fiskerton* sailed to support a stricken US freighter, the *Valley Forge*, which was sinking in the Singapore Strait, and managed to rescue twenty-two of the crew. At the end of the month the cruiser *Gambia* took emergency relief stores to Mauritius in the Indian Ocean after a cyclone struck the island on 29 January. The frigate *Leopard* stood by in Durban, but in the event the assistance from *Gambia* was sufficient. On 5 March *Tyne* and *Darlaston* arrived at Agadir on the Moroccan coast to provide emergency humanitarian relief following a major earthquake. In June the frigate *Torquay* went to the assistance of the ss *Shanlee*, which had run aground on the Pratas Reef in the South China Sea on 10 June, and rescued the crew.

In the West Indies the frigate *Ulster* went to provide relief assistance in the Leeward and Virgin Islands following the devastation caused by Hurricane 'Donna' on 5 September.

On 23 October the Norwegian tanker *Polyana* caught fire in the Persian Gulf, and *Loch Ruthven* and *Dampier* closed the tanker and fought the fires. *Bastion* and *Redoubt* also assisted in the operation. Eventually the fires were brought under control and the tanker was towed into Bahrain.

On 7 February the following year the Norwegian tanker *Bergehus*, in the Mediterranean, suffered an explosion in her engine room. The Ton class minesweeper *Stubbington* was quickly on the spot to render assistance and helped tow the tanker into Malta.

The ss *Dara* On 8 April 1961 the frigates *Loch Alvie*, *Loch Ruthven* and *Loch Fyne* attempted to assist the 5,000-ton British India line passenger-cargo ship ss *Dara* in the Persian Gulf. The *Dara* was en route to Bombay from Basra when

she was hove to riding out a storm off Dubai. A bomb went off in the hold, and a fire broke out which quickly engulfed the ship. Eight minutes later the order to abandon ship was given. *Loch Ruthven* attempted to tow the stricken *Dara* but eventually she sank. The frigates helped to rescue survivors but 238 of the 700 passengers perished.

On 10 October the frigate *Leopard* helped in the evacuation of the inhabitants of Tristan da Cunha after a volcanic eruption. At the end of the month the frigates *Troubridge*, *Londonderry* and *Vidal* provided emergency relief in Belize following the passage of Hurricane 'Hattie'.

Victorious and *Striker* with 3 Assault Squadron Royal

A *Leander* class frigate
(JAR)

Marines were deployed to Kenya on 15 November to provide emergency assistance after major flooding. Helicopters from 825 NAS were landed to deliver emergency supplies, and on 3 December helicopters from 824 NAS, from the carrier *Centaur*, relieved them. *Striker* remained until the relief work was completed in January 1962.

On 27 January 1962 *Centaur* and RFA *Tidesurge* went to the aid of a Greek tanker, the *Stanvek Sumatra*, in the South China Sea. The tanker had broken in half in a gale and the British ships rescued the survivors. At the end of 1963 the destroyer *Duchess* and the boom defence vessels *Barbain* and *Barfoil*, together with the tug *Nimble*, helped salvage the ss *Woodburn*, which had run aground on the Horsburgh Reef in the Singapore Straits.

On 22 December 1963 the Greek cruise liner ss *Lakonia* caught fire off the Azores. The aircraft carrier *Centaur* had sailed from the UK the day before, on passage to the Far East, and she was quickly on the spot to co-ordinate the rescue operations. Damage control parties from *Centaur* were the first on board and fought the fires, but sadly the *Lakonia* sank under tow. A total of 128 people perished, and two

Developments in Steam Propulsion and Ship Design

Back in the 1930s, development of steam propulsion by the Admiralty had been modest, partly due to funding constraints, with general reversion for high power requirements, after vibration failures with Curtis Brown turbines, to the heavy but reliable Parsons impulse reaction designs, cross compounded with separate HP and LP turbines and sometimes with a de-clutchable cruising turbine. Boiler steam conditions were conservative at a maximum of about 400 psi and 700° F, which meant that plant efficiency was moderate with consequent implications for endurance and fuel storage capacity. In contrast in the US, radical advances had been made in the 1930s with the adoption of much higher steam conditions and smaller, more flexible and efficient all impulse turbines yielding major gains in efficiency and endurance. Joint operations in the Pacific in the Second World War showed the superiority of the US Navy ships in this regard, over their Royal Navy counterparts.

After the War, the Admiralty endeavoured to correct the shortcomings in endurance and boiler and turbine designs produced for the post war construction of frigates and destroyers were based closely on US practice. All welded hull construction, reduced weight and improved hydrodynamic design also contributed to better fuel economy with the result that about a 25% improvement was achieved compared to the wartime vessels. Ironically, it was not until the advent of the wide beam *Leander* class of frigates that the full endurance benefit of the improved efficiency was realised for escorts, when fuel storage capacity was increased to a similar level to that in the later wartime destroyers.

The steam plant in the County class destroyers represented the culmination of surface warship steam plant development in the Royal Navy with higher steam conditions than in the *Leander* class of 700 psi and 950° F, giving a relative thermal efficiency improvement of about 6%. The cancelled CVA-01 aircraft carrier plants would have offered further efficiency improvement with a higher steam pressure of 1000 psi. The *Olwen* class fleet tankers introduced in the 1960s had a steam plant with similar conditions and efficiency to the County class; they gave stalwart service for over 30 years and were the last surface steam ships in the Fleet.

Captain Bill Harris RN

days later *Centaur* landed eighty-eight bodies at Gibraltar.

In May 1964 the frigate *Loch Fada* sailed to the assistance of the Kenyan authorities. A Kenyan police company, which had been carrying out anti-terrorist operations, had been cut off, and the Kenyan government requested assistance from Britain. *Loch Fada* arrived off the coast and rescued the company of sixty-nine officers and men, taking them safely to Mombasa.

SHIPS, SUBMARINES, AIRCRAFT AND EQUIPMENT

Leander **Class Frigates** In 1960 the Admiralty announced that three updated Type 12 *Rothesay* class frigates under construction would be completed as the first general-purpose *Leander* class frigates, *Leander*, *Ajax* and *Dido*. A *Salisbury* class frigate also under construction would be completed as a *Leander*, named *Penelope*, and the following year orders for three more, *Aurora*, *Euryalus* and *Galatea*, were placed.

In 1962 three more *Leanders* were ordered, *Arethusa*, *Naiad* and *Cleopatra*, and shortly afterwards a further six *Leanders* were ordered, taking the class to a total of sixteen ordered or under construction. The *Leander* class frigates started to join the Fleet from 1963, and a total of twenty-six would be built.

The 2,500-ton *Leanders* were initially armed with a Mk 6 4.5in gun, a Seacat surface-to-air missile, a Mk 10 Limbo ASW mortar and a Westland Wasp helicopter. More advanced weapon systems would be added later during refits and conversions.

The *Leanders* had excellent sea-keeping qualities, and for the next three decades they proved to be the most successful frigates in the Fleet.

Nuclear Submarines VALIANT AND CHURCHILL CLASS: Once the potential of nuclear power had been demonstrated with the nuclear submarine *Dreadnought*, a more robust and enduring design was sought to harness the power of the nuclear plant and enabling great stealth under water. The nuclear submarine *Valiant* was launched on 3 December 1963 and showed her endurance in April 1967 with a submerged transit of 12,000 nautical miles from the UK to Singapore. The nuclear submarine *Warspite*, launched by Mrs Wilson, wife of the Prime Minister, joined her in 1965. The 1962 Polaris Sales Agreement then influenced submarine building, and the priority of effort was placed on building the four *Resolution* class submarines to deploy Britain's independent nuclear deterrent. As the *Resolution* class neared completion, work restarted on the *Churchill* class, incorporating evolving design improvements from *Valiant* and *Warspite*. Three were ordered, *Churchill*, *Courageous* and *Conqueror*, and they were an evolutionary improvement on their predecessors. The submarines saw considerable service worldwide and were to demonstrate their presence with devastating effect in the Falklands in 1982.

RESOLUTION CLASS (SSBNs): For nuclear deterrence to be effective, a potential enemy had to be given real cause to pause and think very carefully indeed before initiating an attack with nuclear weapons. The adversary had to understand that if it attacked it would in turn face a devastating response that would destroy its strategic

HMS Dreadnought
The *Dreadnought* Class SSN

Dreadnought was Britain's very first nuclear submarine and served from 1963 to 1982. Armed with torpedoes and able to achieve a fast underwater speed, she had the role of hunting other submarines, and was designated a 'hunter-killer' submarine.

Launched:	21 October 1960
Commissioned:	17 April 1963
Displacement:	4,000 tonnes
Length:	81m
Propulsion:	1 Westinghouse S5W nuclear reactor, two geared Westinghouse steam turbines, one shaft
Armament:	6 bow tubes, 30 Mk 8 Torpedoes (later Mk 23)
Complement:	113
No. in class:	1

infrastructure. The submarine-launched nuclear deterrent provided a nuclear weapons battery that was hidden, was virtually invulnerable, could be launched from almost anywhere and thereby constituted a guaranteed nuclear response to any aggression from the Soviet Bloc, or indeed any other major enemy. With the advances in noise quietening techniques, submarines were almost undetectable.

Five submarines of the *Resolution* class were planned – *Resolution*, *Repulse*, *Renown*, *Revenge* and *Ramillies*. These were names of former battleships and battlecruisers, signifying that the nuclear submarine was now the capital ship. The Labour government reviewed the Polaris programme on coming to power and cancelled the fifth boat, with the savings being used to continue the hunter-killer submarine fleet. Vickers, at Barrow in Furness, was the lead yard and built *Resolution* and *Repulse*, while Cammell Laird at Birkenhead built *Renown* and *Revenge*. Displacing 7,600 tons and 130 metres in length, *Resolution* was launched in 1964 and after a long period first of class sea trials she fired her first test missile at 1115 on 15 February 1968. On 15 June 1968 she set 'Quick Reaction Alert (Nuclear)' for the first time, beginning the process towards maintaining 'Continuous At Sea Deterrence' which was to begin in 1969. From that time the Royal Navy Submarine Service would always have an SSBN at sea ready to launch strategic missiles. The *Daily Telegraph* was to comment later, 'The Resolution in making her first dive of her patrol into the waters of a troubled world will be taking out on behalf of the nation the best insurance policy it has ever had'.

AEW In 1960 the Royal Navy received the much needed AEW Mk 3 Fairey Gannet turboprop aircraft, fitted with the APS-20 radar, which had been adapted from the basic ASW Gannet. This considerably improved the organic AEW capability of the Fleet. AEW had been a point of weakness in the fleet owing to the limited 'over the horizon' capability of the converted radar picket Battle and Weapon class destroyers.

The AEW Mk 3 Gannet was first deployed at sea on board the carrier *Hermes* and flew operationally for the first time

in July 1960. The AEW Mk 3 Gannet subsequently served with the Royal Navy right up to the decommissioning of *Ark Royal* in 1978.

PERSONNEL MATTERS

Manpower In the early 1960s the Navy was struggling to come to terms with the post-Sandys reductions and changes in manpower. Although the Service had contracted from 125,000 to 105,000 by 1960 it still had to reduce to 97,000 by the end of 1964. The Navy was also adjusting to the phasing-out of National Service and switching to an all-volunteer service, with the last National Service man leaving the Service in 1961.

Officer Structure SD List: More fundamental changes were being introduced into the officer structure with increased promotions from the lower deck. A special branch, the SD List (Special Duties List), was established for ratings promoted within their own specialist areas of employment.

SL List: In 1961 another measure was introduced to supplement the officer structure, and this was the introduction of short service commissions to fill certain shortage categories such as aircrew. These officers were entered on to the SL List (Supplementary List) as serving for a short commission, but with the possibility of being offered a transfer to the main stream General List of officers, depending on their performance in their rank.

Engineers: Following the recommendations of the Carlill Committee in 1961 the engineering and electrical specialisations were amalgamated into a single Engineering Branch.

Murray Scheme: Sir Keith Murray chaired a committee on officer training which recommended higher educational standards for officer entry and the restoration of sea time for midshipmen in the Fleet. The recommendations were accepted and introduced in 1961, with the first officers joining under the Murray Scheme in that year. Officer entry level was based on that for university entry, with an absolute minimum of two high-grade 'A' level GCEs being required.

HM submarine
Repulse
(RNM)

Pay and Conditions of Service As part of the process of moving the armed forces to all-volunteer services, a tri-service committee was set up under Sir James Grigg, known as the Grigg Committee, to examine pay, pensions, promotion prospects and general conditions of service. The committee recommended many improvements, including a biennial review of pay which would consider comparisons with the wages of similar civilian jobs. New rates of pay were then introduced from April 1960.

Messing A new style of messing (feeding arrangements) on board ship was introduced. Instead of the traditional eating in individual mess decks, a centralised multi-choice 'cafeteria

AEW Mk 3 Fairey
Gannet
(PD)

A Battle class radar
picket destroyer
(RNM)

HMS **Devonshire**
County Class Destroyer

Devonshire was the lead ship of the Royal Navy's first class of guided missile destroyers, which were officially termed 'DLGs' (destroyer leader guided missile). They were classified as 'leaders' owing to their size, which was as big as that of earlier cruisers. They were the new generation of warships for the missile age. The *Devonshires* were smart ships with excellent command facilities and were often used as flagships of small squadrons and task forces. Unfortunately their initial missile systems were not as effective as their design specification, particularly the later surface-to-surface capability of the modified Sea Slug system.

Launched:	10 June 1960
Commissioned:	15 November 1962
Displacement:	5,440 tonnes
Length:	158.6m
Propulsion:	COSAG (combined steam and gas) turbines, 2 shafts
Armament:	1 2 Sea Slug Mk 2 SAM (26 missiles),
	2 4 Sea Cat GWS21 SAM (60 missiles),
	4 4.5in /45 DP (2 2),
	2 20mm AA,
	6 12 in torpedo tubes (2 3) ASW,
	1 Lynx or Wessex helicopter
Complement:	470
No. in class:	8 (*Devonshire, Hampshire, Kent, London, Glamorgan, Fife, Antrim* and *Norfolk*)

---

style' was established to improve standards. After initial resentment by die-hard traditionalists the new system was accepted.

Flag Officer Sea Training To improve standards of training and efficiency in the Fleet, flag officer sea training was established at Portland. Ships on commissioning were required to pass four weeks of realistic and tough training at Portland before being accepted into the Fleet.

Public Relations To raise awareness of the Royal Navy and

improve the public image of the Service the appointment of DPR (N) (Director of Public Relations, Navy) was introduced in 1964.

The White Ensign Association Throughout the early 1960s the Association went from strength to strength, providing ever more assistance to the Fleet as its important network of specialist contacts grew. In 1960 the Association conducted 520 interviews and brought to a total of 2,351 the number of cases where assistance had been provided.

The reputation of the Association was growing, and by 1963 some 3,000 officers and men had applied to it for assistance. The following year the total had grown to 3,475 officers and men. Assistance was provided on a range of matters, with 1,886 being assisted with employment, 777 with investment and 649 with insurance; 402 mortgages had been arranged, and 282 officers and men had been assisted to set up their own businesses.

Association staff visited twenty-one establishments during 1964 and gave forty lectures. It was encouraging to note that the proportion of serving officers and men using the services of the Association was steadily growing.

CHAPTER 3

The Strategic Nuclear Deterrent and Beira Patrol 1965–1969

WITHDRAWAL FROM EAST OF SUEZ – CVA-01 CANCELLED – ROYAL NAVY TAKES OVER THE NUCLEAR DETERRENT –
INDONESIAN CONFRONTATION – TIGER TALKS – BEIRA PATROL – ADEN EVACUATION

The passing of the imperial era was marked on 24 January 1965 when Sir Winston Churchill, the last great icon of the British Empire, died. An ex-First Lord of the Admiralty and Prime Minister, he had steered Britain to ultimate victory in World War II and remained the symbol of Britain's greatness. It was fitting that the Royal Navy had the honour of providing the gun carriage for the state funeral and leading the procession on 30 January.

In the Far East the USA was being drawn into the war in Vietnam with bombing of the North starting in February 1965, followed by the landing of Marines in the South at Da Nang on 8 March. By the end of the year there were over 184,000 US troops in Vietnam, and the war was to drag on for ten years.

MAJOR CHANGES FOR UK NAVAL STRATEGY

New NATO Strategy In 1967 NATO strategy underwent a fundamental revision. Awareness of the dangers of the 'Trip Wire' (immediate nuclear response) strategy and the growing ability of the Warsaw Pact to respond with strategic nuclear weapons necessitated a major revaluation by the West. As a consequence NATO evolved a new military strategy set out in Military Committee Paper 14/3, known as 'Flexible Response'. The essence of the new strategy was an escalating series of graduated military responses to any Warsaw Pact aggression, rather than an immediate all out nuclear strike.[1]

Naval Strategy and Anti-Submarine Warfare (ASW) The new military strategy was to have a fundamental impact on naval strategy and planning for the Royal Navy. The old strategy envisaged a short war scenario with no time for reinforcement or resupply convoys, whereas the new strategy saw the probability of a much longer campaign where reinforcement of Europe would be essential to success.

The reinforcement of Europe depended on resupply across the Atlantic with large convoys. ASW and the defence of NATO convoys transporting vast quantities of troops, arms, ammunition, equipment and supplies would be a prime requirement of NATO navies. Equally the destruction of those convoys would be crucial to the strategy of the Warsaw Pact and thus the main target of the Soviet Northern Fleet. It was in this area that the Royal Navy, with its expertise in ASW, would be required to play a leading role against the threat from the huge Soviet submarine fleet. The expertise

FIRST SEA LORDS
*Admirals Begg
and Le Fanu*

SECOND SEA LORD
Admiral Dreyer

MANPOWER
97,000

MERCANTILE MARINE
*4,538
merchant ships*

of the Royal Navy in ASW was second to none and was one of its most important contributions to NATO. During the Cold War the Royal Navy was to build over 120 ocean escorts.

The UK At the same time political changes in the UK and the USSR were to have a profound effect on UK defence policy in the second half of the sixties. In 1964 a Labour government under Harold Wilson had been elected to power in Britain, and on the same day Khrushchev had been ousted in the Kremlin to be replaced by the hard-liner Leonid Brezhnev.

The Labour government went on to seek an election in March 1966 and was returned with an increased majority of ninety-seven.

Defence Review The new Labour government faced a massive balance of payments deficit and a collapsing currency. Denis Healey, the new Secretary of State for Defence, initiated a fundamental defence review in 1965, based on the new government's political priorities and the growing economic crisis.

The overriding factor was the need to drive down public spending, and defence was again the prime target. Healey saw the answer in placing full reliance on nuclear deterrence to prevent war in the European area, whilst at the same time maintaining just sufficient conventional forces to cover commitments outside the NATO area. In addition, he saw that progressively reducing those commitments beyond the NATO area would enable the supporting conventional forces to be cut back even further, yielding greater savings. In his 1965 Statement on Defence Healey stated: 'it was neither wise nor economical to use military force to seek to protect national economic interests in the modern world'.[2]

The Defence White Paper, setting out the findings of the fundamental defence review, was published on 22 February 1966 and, as expected, entailed major defence cuts.[3] The review, which came to be known as the 'Healey Axe', called for the withdrawal of British forces from East of Suez and an end to British commitments in the Far East.

Abolition of the Carriers For the Royal Navy the review set out to abolish the Fleet Air Arm and the aircraft carriers. The new aircraft carrier was to be cancelled and the existing aircraft carriers all phased out by 1977. All air defence would become the responsibility of the Royal Air Force, operating from the United Kingdom and overseas island bases. The air

Hermes as converted to a commando carrier (RNM)

defence of the Fleet was to be based on guided missiles, whilst other fixed-wing airborne tasks, such as AEW (airborne early warning), ASW, screening and strike, were to be assigned to naval helicopters.

It was considered that aircraft carriers were too vulnerable to long-range missiles and too costly to build, man and maintain. Approaches had been made to the US government to investigate the possibility of buying or leasing a US aircraft carrier but to no avail. The Royal Air Force had suggested to the Treasury that the BAC TSR-2 tactical strike aircraft be procured in place of new aircraft carriers. In the event the Treasury cancelled both the TSR-2 and the new aircraft carrier.

Cancellation of CVA-01 The tragedy for the Royal Navy was the cancellation of the new-generation 50,000-ton fixed-wing strike aircraft carrier CVA-01, announced in July 1963 (see Chapter 2). Much of the money saved was to be devoted to the purchase of fifty US General Dynamics F-111A strike aircraft and some McDonnell Douglas Phantoms for the Royal Air Force. The pro-carrier lobby rightly protested that the RAF would not be able to provide proper air cover for the

Fleet or for Atlantic convoys in any major war with the Warsaw Pact. Mr Christopher Mayhew, the Minister for the Navy, and Admiral Sir David Luce, the First Sea Lord, resigned, as they had threatened to do if such a policy was imposed.

The distress felt throughout the Navy was profound and the new First Sea Lord, Admiral Sir Varyl Begg, appointed in April 1966, had a major task to rebuild confidence and morale throughout the Fleet. He set up a project team to plan the future navy without the backbone of the new carrier. Rear Admiral Adams headed the project in the newly formed post of Assistant Chief of Naval Staff (Policy) (ACNS (P)).

THE FLEET

In 1965 the Royal Navy continued to be cut back, and although it still possessed a powerful fleet, decisions in 1968 were to impose far-reaching cuts in its size and capability.

Aircraft Carriers The capital ships of the Fleet comprised the remaining aircraft carriers *Ark Royal*, *Eagle* and *Hermes* (*Centaur* was paid off in 1965 and was used as a depot ship, whilst *Victorious* was scrapped in 1968 after a fire on board).

Eagle had just been commissioned in May 1964 following a four-year major refit and modernisation. In 1967 *Ark Royal* commenced her major three-year modernisation refit, to enable her to operate the new heavy Phantom strike-fighter aircraft. Later it was decided to convert *Hermes* to a commando carrier in 1970.

The new capital ships of the Navy, the nuclear-powered submarines, were about to join the Fleet, with the first four SSBNs (nuclear ballistic missile submarines) of the *Resolution* class being completed between 1967 and 1969. By 1969 three nuclear fleet submarines (SSNs) were in service, with five more under construction.

The assault ships *Fearless* and *Intrepid* were completed between 1965 and 1966. The *Tiger* class cruisers *Tiger* and *Blake* were converted to ASW command cruisers and equipped to carry four Sea King helicopters between 1965 and 1973. In 1968, however, the decision was taken not to convert the third cruiser, *Lion*.

The rest of the Fleet included thirty-eight destroyers, eighty-nine frigates, forty-two conventional diesel-electric submarines and several hundred minesweepers and smaller patrol boats and craft. The Fleet was well supported by the survey ships of the Survey Flotilla and by the supply ships and tankers of the Royal Fleet Auxiliary (RFA).

Western Fleet In 1967 the fleet structure of the Royal Navy was reordered to reflect the reduced number of ships. The fleets were rationalised into two fleets, and the Home Fleet became the 'Western' Fleet.

FIRST SEA LORDS

Admiral Sir Varyl Begg Varyl Begg was born on 1 October 1908 and joined the Royal Navy in 1926. In 1931 he joined the cruiser *Shropshire* as a lieutenant, and after specialising in gunnery he served as Gunnery Officer of the battleship *Nelson*. During World War II he served in the cruiser *Glasgow* and the battleship *Warspite*, and was awarded the DSC for his part in the Battle of Matapan.

After the war he commanded the Gunnery School in the rank of Captain before commanding the 8th Destroyer Squadron during the Korean War and being awarded the DSO. He then commanded the aircraft carrier *Triumph*, and subsequently, as a rear admiral, he commanded the 5th Cruiser Squadron. He served as Assistant Chief of the Naval Staff from 1961 to 1963, and then as a full admiral he was Commander in Chief Far East during the Indonesian Confrontation.

In 1965 he was appointed Commander in Chief Portsmouth, but when the First Sea Lord, Admiral Luce, resigned over the decision to phase out the aircraft carriers Admiral Begg relieved him. He remained as First Sea Lord until his retirement in August 1968.

Admiral Sir Michael Le Fanu Michael Le Fanu was born on 2 August 1913 and joined the Royal Navy in 1926. As a junior officer he served in the *Dorsetshire*, *York*, *Whitshed* and *Bulldog*, and during World War II he served in the cruiser

Aurora, taking part in the Bismarck campaign. Later he was awarded a DSC for his part in a night engagement whilst serving with Force 'K' in the Mediterranean. He also served in the battleship *Duke of York*, and after the war he served in the cruiser *Superb*, before commanding the 3rd Frigate Squadron.

He commanded the training establishment HMS *Ganges* and then served as Flag Captain in the aircraft carrier *Eagle*. As a rear admiral he was Second in Command Far East, flying his flag in the carrier *Hermes*, before being appointed Controller of the Navy as a vice admiral in 1961. As Controller he was credited with the hugely successful *Leander* class frigate programme.

In 1965 he was appointed Commander in Chief Middle East, and in this post he oversaw the withdrawal from Aden in 1967. He was appointed First Sea Lord in August 1968 and faced the difficult task of rebuilding the spirit of the Navy after the damaging cuts and reductions of the Healey defence review.

OPERATIONS AND DEPLOYMENTS, 1965–1969

Throughout the second half of the sixties the Royal Navy continued to be engaged on a whole range of operational deployments and important peace-keeping tasks around the world. First and foremost was the national strategic deterrent.

The Nuclear Deterrent On 14 June 1968 the SSBN *Resolution* sailed from Faslane to carry out the first submarine nuclear deterrent patrol in the vast depths of the ocean. She carried her full load of sixteen Polaris ICBMs (intercontinental ballistic missiles).

The following year, with sufficient SSBNs in service to maintain the deterrent patrol cycle, the Royal Navy assumed responsibility on 1 July for the national strategic nuclear deterrent from the V-bomber force of the Royal Air Force: 'to ensure a submarine deterrent remained totally credible at all times, it required that, for week upon week when at sea, the crews were in all respects equivalent to being on patrol under conditions of war. Likewise to keep the submarines at sea on a schedule permitting not the slightest variation required a similar approach from all those who worked ashore.'[4]

'Delousing' Operations The location of the British Polaris deterrent base was not secret, and so it was easy for the USSR to send submarines to lie in wait outside the Firth of Clyde to try and trail a Polaris submarine as it deployed to its patrol area. To guarantee the strategic deterrent, it was essential for deterrent patrols to remain undetected and thus invulnerable. This meant that it was necessary to deploy submarine escorts and ASW surface ships in 'delousing' operations to protect Polaris submarines and ensure they were not tailed.

Covert Submarine Operations Britain and the USA continued to monitor closely the rapidly expanding Soviet

Submarine Fleet. In 1963 the USSR had twenty-six nuclear submarines, and by late 1969 they had forty-three SSBNs and seventeen SSNs. The first of the powerful 9,600-ton *Yankee* class SSBNs was commissioned in May 1967 and was rated by NATO as good as the Polaris SSBNs. In addition the USSR had fifty missile-armed diesel-electric submarines and 263 other conventional submarines.

US and British submarines maintained a demanding series of covert surveillance operations. These consisted of 'close-in' intelligence-gathering patrols off the main Russian naval bases and fleet training grounds in the Barents Sea.

The Royal Navy carried out its share of the important task and continued to deploy conventional diesel-electric submarines, adapted for surveillance with top-secret intelligence intercept equipment, on missions in the Barents Sea off the Murmansk naval base and in the Kola Inlet.

These were dangerous operations, and submarine commanders were fully aware of the difficulties and huge risks if they were detected. One Royal Navy submarine was apparently detected in 1966 in the Barents Sea off Murmansk

The Grand Harbour, Malta, In the mid-1960s (RNM)

but managed to elude her pursuers. There were other cases when submarines were attacked and depth-charged.

The following year a Soviet submarine hit a US Polaris submarine in the Mediterranean. In 1968 the USSR claimed that a NATO surveillance submarine, British or American, was involved in a collision with a Soviet nuclear submarine in the Barents Sea, but were not able to determine which navy was responsible. Towards the end of the next year there was yet another collision, this time between a US SSN and a Soviet *Hotel* class SSBN.

One of the tasks of the surveillance operations was to detect any sudden surge (deployment of a large number of Soviet submarines), which could be a precursor to imminent hostilities, and provide valuable warning time. Towards the end of the 1960s SSNs started being assigned to the surveillance operations. The introduction of SINS (the Ship Inertial Navigation System) made possible much more accurate navigation. In April 1967 the nuclear fleet submarine *Valiant* returned to the UK from Singapore, carrying out the entire 12,000-mile passage under water.

Other Operations and Deployments In Hong Kong the three Ton class minesweepers of the 8th Minesweeping Squadron (*Fiskerton, Woolaston* and *Wilkieston*) carried out guardship duties and were periodically deployed south to assist with defensive patrols off the east coast of Malaysia. In the Persian Gulf the four Ton class minesweepers of the 9th Mine-sweeping Squadron (*Appleton, Flockton, Kemerton* and *Chilcompton*) carried out security patrols against arms smuggling, piracy, slaving and insurgent infiltration. The minesweepers were based in Bahrain (Jufair, which was the headquarters of 'SNOPG', the Senior Naval Officer Persian Gulf, was the shore base at Bahrain). Frigates supported the minesweepers on a regular basis. In May 1966 the Tribal class frigate *Gurkha* embarked a company of troops and sailed

for Abu Dhabi. Arriving on 7 May, she stood by during an important oil dispute and her presence was sufficient to bring the dispute to an end after only two days.

Further south in Aden, a garrison unit of Royal Marines from 45 Commando was deployed for anti-rebel operations in both east and west Aden and for internal security duties.

In the Mediterranean, Malta, which had been the base of the Mediterranean Fleet for a great many years, experienced a considerable run-down. By 1965 the only ships permanently based in Malta consisted of a squadron of destroyers or frigates and a minesweeping squadron of six Ton class minesweepers, including *Walkerton, Leverton, Shavington, Crofton, Ashton* and *Stubbington*. In June 1967, with the formation of the Western Fleet, the flag of the then Commander in Chief

Mediterranean (Admiral Sir John Hamilton) was hauled down for the very last time. Then in 1969 the minesweepers were withdrawn and mothballed in Gibraltar.

The 6th Minesweeping Squadron was based in Singapore for guardship duties. Singapore was of great strategic importance and its dockyard was a large fully operational naval base, with a drydock, built for the largest ships, and a floating dock. *Triumph*, the fleet repair ship, was based there, and the Inshore Flotilla was run from the fast minelayer *Manxman*, converted as a minesweeper support ship. The air station at Changi, took disembarked NAS (naval air squadrons) and included a large wireless station, a hospital, gunnery ranges, a fuel tank farm, stores and ammunition depots, a barracks (HMS *Terror*) and extensive supporting

STANAVFORLANT
(MH)

facilities. The Commander Far East Fleet was Vice Admiral Sir Frank Twiss.[5]

In the Antarctic *Protector* was deployed for service in the Falkland Islands Dependencies during the Antarctic summer. *Protector* was a converted netlayer fitted out for guardship and Antarctic survey duties. In 1968 *Endurance*, with a Royal Marine detachment embarked, took over responsibility from *Protector* for the protection of British interests in the Antarctic.

NATO Naval Squadrons In January 1968 a permanent NATO Naval Squadron was established with the UK, the USA, Canada, West Germany and the Netherlands each contributing a destroyer or a frigate. The forerunner of the squadron had been the British annual exercise codenamed

Matchmaker which combined destroyers and frigates from NATO countries to deploy together as a joint squadron. The Royal Navy allocated the frigate *Brighton* to join the permanent NATO Squadron when it was formed at Portland under the command of Commodore G C Mitchell RN. *Brighton* was relieved later in 1968 by the new *Leander* class frigate *Dido*. The squadron became the Standing Naval Force Atlantic (STANAVFORLANT, or SNFL for short), and each nation took it in turn to command the squadron on an annual basis. Norway, Denmark, Belgium and Portugal assigned ships to join the squadron from time to time. SNFL enabled NATO ships to develop and improve joint tactics and operating procedures and regularly took part in joint maritime exercises.

The following year a second NATO squadron was formed to cover the Mediterranean, but on an 'on call' basis to respond as required, the Naval On Call Force Mediterranean (NAVOCFORMED). The force was regularly activated to participate in NATO maritime exercises.

NATO Flanks Towards the end of the sixties the Commando Brigade reduced its commitment to the Southern Flank of NATO and took over a more important role in the defence of the Northern Flank in Norway. It was on the Northern Flank that highly trained and hardened amphibious forces would be essential. The strategic objective would be to deny the Warsaw Pact access to the airfields of northern Norway, where their strike aircraft would be able to extend their range

The commando carrier Bulwark embarking Royal Marines of 45 Commando for deployment to exercise Polar Express off Norway (RNM)

far out in the Atlantic. As a consequence of the change of role, 45 Commando, recently returned from Hong Kong, was to be based in Arbroath in Scotland, and in 1970 it was assigned to NATO specifically for the Northern Flank. The Royal Marines specialised in winter and mountain warfare, with regular deployments to the Northern Flank such as the annual reinforcement exercise Polar Express. The commando carrier *Bulwark* was deployed to Norway in Polar Express for the first time in June 1968 with twenty Wessex V helicopters of 845 NAS and 650 Royal Marines of 45 Commando embarked.

Indonesian Confrontation, December 1962 – 11 August 1966

In the Far East in 1965 the Royal Navy remained very heavily involved in the Indonesian Confrontation, defending Malaysia, including Singapore and North Borneo, against attacks from Indonesian forces. Indonesia continued to launch attacks across the Malacca Strait to infiltrate the mainland of Malaysia in an attempt to destabilise the local population. Ships of the Far East Fleet, reinforced by units of the Royal Australian Navy and Royal New Zealand Navy, provided the regular security patrols off the coast. The struggle was to continue until the signing of the Bangkok Agreement in August 1966.

On 8 January a bomb, planted by Indonesian raiders, exploded on board the merchant ship *Oceanic Pride* in Singapore. That night the Ton class minesweeper *Wilkieston*

Ton class wooden minesweeper *Woolaston* (RNM)

intercepted a small Indonesian craft trying to escape from the harbour. One Indonesian was captured and another was seen to leap overboard. It was subsequently discovered that they had been part of the attack team which had planted the bomb on board the *Oceanic Pride*. The economy of Singapore was totally dependent on seaborne trade, and threats to shipping in the harbour were taken very seriously. The security authorities imposed a night curfew in Singapore harbour and the small Malaysian Navy was involved in various incidents with Indonesian raiders along the coast.

In March 1965 General Suharto took over from Sukarno, but the attacks against Malaysia and Singapore continued. At the same time General Waite-Walker, in command of British forces in Borneo, handed over to General Lea.

On 28 March there was a sharp engagement between two heavily armed Indonesian landing craft and the Ton class minesweepers *Maryton*, *Invermoriston* and *Puncheston*. The landing craft were trying to land soldiers on the south coast of Malaya. The gun battle lasted over an hour before one of the landing craft was sunk. Three ratings were wounded in the action, with seven Indonesians killed and nineteen captured. A little while later the Ton class minesweeper *Lullington* captured another Indonesian raiding party. In a further engagement with Indonesian raiders *Maryton* sustained fifty bullet holes. In one incident Midshipman Michael Finch, from the minesweeper *Woolaston*, was killed when trying to rescue an injured Indonesian from a captured Indonesian patrol craft. The craft had been booby-trapped

Naval helicopters from the County class destroyer *Kent* in Borneo (RNM)

and blew up. Midshipman Finch and Midshipman Michael O'Driscoll, killed in *Invermoriston*, were given posthumous mentions in despatches.

In April the Malaysian Navy took over responsibility for inshore coastal patrolling and naval party 'Kilo' (see Chapter 2), based at Kuching, was disbanded.

The Indonesian Navy was headed by *Irian*, an ex-Russian *Sverdlov* class cruiser, and included numerous ex-Russian destroyers and frigates, as well as modern European-built

The commando carrier *Albion*, 'The Old Grey Ghost of the Borneo Coast' (RNM)

escorts, scores of patrol craft including modern German-built fast patrol boats (FPBs) and twelve ex-Russian 'W' class submarines. The potential threat was therefore very serious.[6] On the Indonesian border with North Borneo several Indonesian battalions were deployed with artillery, notably at the western and eastern coasts of Borneo (Kalimantan). Attacks on Malaysian civilians by land continued, and it was necessary to deploy British battalions all along the mountainous jungle-covered border, in places up to 2,400 metres high. Forward-deployed Royal Navy helicopters, operating seven days a week in very trying conditions, supported them. In many cases helicopter support, in and out, was the only practical means of transport, as the fighting patrols on the border were up to a month's march from the coast.

Throughout the Confrontation the commando carriers *Albion* and *Bulwark* played a major role and clearly validated the new commando carrier concept. They alternated on station off the coast of North Borneo and in the Strait of Malacca acting as offshore bases operating helicopters to take Royal Marines, army units and supplies to forward bases and patrols deep into the jungle.

During the Confrontation, between April 1965 and July 1966, *Albion*'s eighteen Wessex and two Whirlwind helicopters of 848 NAS flew 5,000 hours, transporting 12,000 men and 5,000,000 pounds of freight in Sarawak.[7]

In December 1965, *Albion* was going back to Singapore after a roulement to Labuan when an Indonesian patrol boat attacked her. The gunboat opened fire with 40mm guns at close range. *Albion*, which was commanded by Captain Godfrey Place VC (decorated for his attack on the German battleship *Tirpitz* during World War II), promptly rammed and sank the gunboat. Sadly the action damaged the bow of the commando carrier and she had to go into the drydock in Singapore for repairs, which put her out of action for a few months.[8]

In the summer two Royal Navy SR.N5 hovercraft arrived in Borneo, where they operated in the rivers and swamps (see Chapter 2). They carried out valuable work over a period of six months, demonstrating the reliability of such craft,

Wessex helicopters operating from the commando carrier *Albion* off Borneo (NN)

which were later to be used in large numbers by the United States Navy in Vietnam.

'Hearts and minds' operations were critical, and the local villagers (many of whom had only recently given up head-hunting) welcomed the visits from the Royal Navy minesweepers on patrol from Kuching, or Tawau, with medical and other support. Rigid raiders were used to penetrate up the many rivers to reach distant villages. The Indonesians were not the only enemy as there had been frequent pirate raids from both the Philippines and Indonesia before the Royal Navy patrols commenced.[9]

Minesweepers, operating close inshore and up to the border, were within easy gunnery range of the Indonesian heavy artillery. Heavier support in the form of a frigate or destroyer on patrol further off shore was usually available. The wooden minesweepers were vulnerable to modern weapons, and several had many bullet holes, frequently running right through from side to side. Many of the Ton class minesweepers had their after 20mm gun replaced by a second 40mm Bofors gun and carried Vickers fixed machine

guns, Bren guns, mortars and small arms.[10] Searching small craft such as fishing kotaks or slightly larger kumpits was risky, and in at least one case a kotak blew up alongside a minesweeper that was searching it, killing members of the boarding party.[11]

By night off Singapore and in the nearby Malacca Strait, up to fifteen ships were deployed, reducing to two by day; most were minesweepers and patrol craft supported by frigates and destroyers.

Royal Fleet Auxiliaries were present in strength, in varying sizes, from the new fleet tanker RFA *Tidespring* down to the small Eddy class support tankers. Other support ships included the British and Indian Steam Navigation Company's *Empire Kittiwake*, a converted army tank landing ship, which was used to ferry wheeled 40mm Bofors guns to and from Borneo. The civilian crews were paid a 30 per cent bonus to man their four 20mm Oerlikon guns.

Fotex 65: Far East Fleet, March 1965 The heavier fleet carriers reinforced the ships deployed off Borneo and in the

Malacca Strait from time to time. In February 1965 the carrier *Eagle* sailed from Hong Kong to Singapore, where she operated with units of the Far East Fleet. The high point was an impressive show of force when she took part with the aircraft carriers *Victorious, Bulwark* and HMAS *Melbourne* in exercise Showpiece and Fotex 65 in March. The fleet manoeuvres were witnessed by Tungku Abdul Rahman, Prime Minister of Malaysia, and served as a useful high-profile demonstration of sea power and the strength of Britain's commitment to defending Malaysian interests. *Eagle* then sailed for home and refit in the UK.

The End of the Confrontation By the end of 1965 the Royal Navy had notched up 500 days of patrols during the Confrontation. In that time it had killed or captured over 1,400 Indonesian raiders for the loss of two officers and eleven ratings.[12] The Confrontation continued into the following year, and in January the Ton class minesweeper *Dartington* came under heavy fire from shore batteries whilst escorting Malaysian vessels. The following month the minesweeper *Puncheston* and a Malaysian patrol boat came under fire from shore batteries on the Rhio islands in the Malacca Strait (over a hundred shells were fired by the shore batteries). Then in March the minesweeper *Picton* was attacked but fortunately was not seriously damaged. The Navy was deploying more submarines to the area, as they were proving most useful in conducting covert coastal patrols. To support them the submarine depot ship *Forth* was being prepared for the Far East.

Frigates on Beira
Patrol
(JAR)

Indonesia and Malaysia held serious negotiations in the summer, which were to lead to the Bangkok Agreement and the eventual end of the conflict. The last Borneo patrol was conducted by *Dartington* in September, and the following month the naval helicopters were withdrawn from Sarawak.

The Secretary for Defence, Denis Healey, announced in Parliament that the Royal Navy had successfully intercepted over 90 per cent of the Indonesian attempts to invade western Malaysia.[13]

The Royal Marines, who were highly skilled in jungle warfare, fought with great distinction throughout the Confrontation. There was always a Commando, usually 40 or 42 Commando, deployed in Borneo during the entire campaign. Not only had the Royal Marines been the first forces engaged but they were also amongst the last to leave. They were extremely effective and suffered only thirty-six casualties (sixteen of them fatal).

Aden and the Radfan

The Radfan Operations by British forces against rebel Yemeni tribesmen continued in the mountains of the Radfan in southern Arabia. On 4 June 1965 a flight of four Wessex was disembarked from *Albion* and flown up to provide additional forward support. It was during this period that the Royal Marines in Aden and the Yemen were instructed to stop using the expression 'Wogs' to avoid causing offence to local people. The Royal Marines readily complied and thereafter referred to local people as 'Gollies'.[14]

Aden Whilst in Aden itself the internal security situation deteriorated further and the Governor, Turnbull, was forced to declare a state of emergency. The National Liberation Front (NLF), which was behind much of the agitation and violence, was proscribed. In August the police superintendent and the Speaker of the Assembly were murdered, and then

---

HMS *Maryton* during the Indonesian Confrontation

When I joined the Ton class minesweeper *Maryton* in early 1965, she had over 300 varied bullet holes in her – some double, i.e. in one wooden side and out the other. My Chinese cook and steward were unimpressed, as their 'action station' was the Wardroom Flat – with bullets coming in one side and out the other.

The Captain, Lieutenant Commander Doug Holder, was awarded a DSO and the Leading Seaman gunner, a DSM; the ship had fought a successful engagement against several Indonesian fast craft with huge outboards.

The job of my men was to carry ammunition to the various gun positions: we had two 40mm Bofors (one had replaced the normal twin 20mm Oerlikon aft), six Vickers machine guns (two twins and two singles), three Bren Guns, a couple of rocket flare launchers and a mortar on the bridge roof. Everyone not involved with those had Sterling sub-machine guns, or in my case as prisoner reception, a 9mm Browning pistol. When we opened fire at night it was spectacular.

As prisoner reception, I had two very large sailors who swung the prisoner from the jumping ladder (only a few feet above sea-level) onto the engine room bulkhead where he was thoroughly searched – they had a trick of hiding hand grenades on their person. On a number of occasions I had to swim out with a grapnel to the stopped Indonesian craft, or perhaps a kumpit, a slower and larger goods carrying boat, as the outboards and cargo were valuable. Sometimes the boats were also carrying contraband like cigarettes. We would then tow the boat back to base.

The swim was OK by day but dangerous at night, as the lights of the action could attract sea snakes and large stinging jellyfish which were of course very difficult to see at night.

Lieutenant Commander Ken Napier MBE,
RN

---

on 23 September schoolchildren were attacked with grenades. Turnbull dismissed President Mackawee and direct rule was imposed.[15]

In view of the serious political situation Britain decided to send the aircraft carrier *Eagle* to Aden. 45 Commando was already in Aden and could be embarked on board *Eagle* if necessary. *Eagle* was in Malta in September having completed an ASW exercise with the US 6th Fleet, exercise Quick Draw. Accordingly *Eagle* sailed from Malta, escorted by the frigate *Lowestoft* and the RFAS *Tidesurge* and *Reliant*, and headed east for the Suez Canal en route for Aden.

After a fast passage *Eagle* anchored off Aden on 1 October and commenced supporting the British forces engaged in maintaining defensive patrols ashore. Her helicopters greatly assisted in internal security operations for a busy period of nine days before she was released to sail to Mombasa for a maintenance and rest period.

Gannet Rescue, 12 October It was a short while later, whilst *Eagle* was conducting flying operations in the Indian Ocean, that a remarkable recovery occurred. A Gannet aircraft

The carrier Eagle sails from Malta heading east at speed
(NN)

crashed into the sea on launch, and sank dead ahead of the aircraft carrier. *Eagle* thundered straight over the top of the sinking Gannet at full speed. Amazingly the three members of the crew came to the surface astern of the aircraft carrier clear of the propellers and were picked up safely by the plane guard helicopter, hovering on the port quarter. After leaving Mombasa on 23 October *Eagle* steamed east, arriving in Singapore on 3 November.

Zambia and UDI, 11 November – 7 December 1965 On 11 November 1965 Ian Smith, the Prime Minister of Southern Rhodesia, made a unilateral declaration of Rhodesian Independence (UDI). This action was condemned by the United Nations, but the international community expected Britain to deal with the problem.

President Kaunda of Zambia appealed to the UK for support and in particular for air defence protection. He wished to ensure the safety of the vital Kariba Dam. The aircraft carrier *Eagle* was by this time in Singapore preparing for a visit to Hong Kong, and was sent an immediate signal

on 18 November to prepare for sea. Two days later she sailed from Singapore, escorted by the frigate *Brighton*, and embarked her aircraft as she steamed through the Malacca Strait. The ships headed west across the Indian Ocean, passing Gan four days later. *Eagle* then arrived off the coast of Tanzania on 28 November and was fully ready to operate her aircraft in defence of Zambia. She was by this time supported by four frigates.

At the same time arrangements were being made to fly ten RAF Javelin aircraft to the region from Cyprus, but problems were being experienced in obtaining over-flight

clearance. Eventually the RAF Javelins arrived in Ndola on 3 December and *Eagle* was able to stand down from her operational state and leave the area. Four days later she sailed north for a break in Mombasa and then on to Aden to resume flying operations. The incident clearly demonstrated the flexibility of naval air power. The *Times* reported, 'the sudden appearance of the aircraft carrier *Eagle* cruising off Tanzania emphasises the advantages and flexibility held by a carrier in the Indian Ocean'.[16]

The Beira Patrol, 1 March 1966 – 25 June 1975 On 20 November 1965 the Security Council of the United Nations instituted a regime of voluntary sanctions against Rhodesia. The Security Council Resolution (UNSCR 217) called for an international embargo on all shipments of oil to Rhodesia. Britain was unwilling to use direct force to intervene in its own colony but nevertheless was fully aware of the need to be seen to be doing something in the eyes of the rest of the world. The government of Prime Minister Harold Wilson hoped that sanctions would work, but it became clear that

The frigate *Zulu* returning from for the Beira Patrol. In 1967 she spent more than 120 days on the patrol, intercepting only four ships
(NJBM)

The 'Tiger Talks': Prime Minister Harold Wilson on the quarterdeck of the cruiser *Tiger*
(JAR)

oil was reaching Rhodesia. In February 1966 the Chiefs of Staff considered that tankers could be arriving in the port of Beira unobserved and recommended a maritime surveillance plan. The Rhodesian Minister of Commerce and Industry even announced that tankers would be arriving in Beira and that in consequence they would have managed to defy the international community and achieve their goal of white rule in the face of economic sanctions.

On 1 March 1966 Britain instituted the Beira Patrol, and the frigate *Lowestoft* was ordered to head for the port of Beira and to be prepared to intercept suspect tankers. On 3 March the carrier *Ark Royal*, escorted by the frigate *Rhyl*, sailed from Mombasa but instead of heading for Singapore she was ordered to operate her Gannet AEW aircraft to search the Mozambique Channel for tankers. Intelligence indicated that the tankers *Joanna V* and *Manuela* were en route to Beira and that oil tanks were being constructed in the port of Beira. On 15 March *Eagle* arrived off the Mozambique Channel to release *Ark Royal* to continue en route to Singapore. *Eagle* had to launch AEW surveillance aircraft straight away, as the RAF Shackletons (maritime patrol aircraft), ordered to Mombasa for the surveillance task, had not arrived.

Once again aircraft carriers had to meet a task that the RAF had been given but had not managed to carry out in time. By the 19 March, however, the Shackletons were

flying regular surveillance patrols from Majunga in Madagascar. Ironically newspapers in the UK had been showing photographs of aircraft flying patrols in the Mozambique Channel, and claimed they were RAF aircraft even though they were AEW Gannets from *Eagle*, clearly marked 'Royal Navy'.

The destroyer *Cambrian* and the frigate *Plymouth* were patrolling close inshore monitoring all shipping approaching the port of Beira, whilst RFAs *Reliant*, *Resurgent* and *Tidepool* were further out to sea in support of the patrol. On 17 March the fully laden tanker MV *Enterprise* was intercepted by *Eagle* approaching Beira, but on being challenged claimed that she was bound for South America instead and sailed away. The tanker MV *Joanna V* was intercepted by *Plymouth*, but as the

Royal Navy had not been authorised to use force the *Joanna V* was able to break away and sail into territorial waters at Beira. Eventually the United Nations authorised the Royal Navy to use force if necessary (UNSCR 221) and also authorised the Royal Navy to arrest the *Joanna V* if she departed from Beira having discharged any oil.

Various tankers were intercepted. On 8 April the frigate *Berwick* intercepted the tanker *Manuella* and escorted her well clear of the Mozambique Channel; however, after *Berwick* had departed to refuel, the *Manuella* reversed her course and made a run for Beira again. This time the frigate *Puma* intercepted and prevented the tanker reaching Beira.

On 30 April *Eagle* was authorised to leave the area and proceed to Singapore for a maintenance period. During her time off Beira she had identified 116 tankers and 651 other ships in the area. *Ark Royal* arrived in the Mozambique Channel on 7 May to resume the Beira Patrol before finally leaving the area on 25 May to head north for the Suez Canal and return to the UK. The Beira Patrol was to continue for over nine years.

———•———

The 'Tiger Talks', 1–3 December 1966 On 30 November 1966 the cruiser *Tiger* was carrying out an official visit to Casablanca in Morocco when she received an 'immediate' signal ordering her to sail forthwith and head north for Gibraltar. At the same time the guided missile destroyer *Fife* was ordered to sail from Madeira and head immediately for Gibraltar. Once in Gibraltar high-level political delegations from Britain and Rhodesia including both Prime Ministers, Harold Wilson and Ian Smith, were embarked on board *Tiger*. Both ships then sailed east into the Mediterranean whilst intensive talks to resolve the problems of Rhodesia and UDI were conducted on board *Tiger*. The top-level meetings were dubbed the 'Tiger Talks'. Unfortunately after two days of exhaustive discussions no solution was achieved and the ships returned to Gibraltar to disembark both groups.

With no agreement reached it was necessary to continue the Beira Patrol, and so the patrol was maintained throughout the year, mostly by two ships, frigates or destroyers, supported by RFA ships and tankers. Many ships were intercepted and escorted away from Beira. The extent of the 'rules of engagement' (ROE) used by the Royal Navy were tested in a difficult incident on 19 December 1967 when the frigate *Minerva* intercepted the French tanker *Artois* making for Beira. *Minerva* ordered the *Artois* to stop but the *Artois* refused to comply and *Minerva* fired warning shots across her bow, before the MoD signalled that the *Artois* could legitimately enter Beira. The *Artois* incident led to a revision of the ROE and an increased authorisation for the Royal Navy to 'open fire and continue until the ship does stop'. The revised ROE were sufficient as no further attempts were made to evade interception by the Royal Navy.

A further attempt was made to resolve the problem of UDI by a high-level conference at sea in October 1968. Under the codename Operation Diogenes, the assault ship *Fearless* and the guided missile destroyer *Kent* arrived in Gibraltar on 8 October and embarked British and Rhodesian delegations. The ships put to sea but no progress was made in the meetings and eventually the talks were called off, with the ships returning to Gibraltar on 14 October. At the end of March 1969 a final round of talks, codenamed Operation Estimate, were held at Lagos with *Fearless*, sailing from Malta on 15 March. The talks were held from 27 to 31 March, but yet again without a successful outcome.

Aden, September 1966 – May 1967

The situation in and around Aden in 1966 remained tense, with attacks and incidents continuing to take place. In September disturbances occurred in Mural in the East Aden Protectorate, and on 14 September the Ton class minesweeper *Kildarton* was sent to Mural to restore order. Armed units were also sent to Riyadh to demonstrate a show of force.

Operation Fate The brand new assault ship *Fearless*, which had successfully completed her trials, sailed from Portsmouth on 13 September bound for Aden. She made a fast passage, via the Suez Canal, to the Gulf of Aden, arriving off the port on 29 September. Seventeen days later she carried out her first operational task, landing a troop of scout cars some seventy miles west of Aden in a surprise operation to catch rebel tribesmen inland. The mission provided experience for Operation Fate two weeks later. On 25 October *Fearless* departed from Aden and steamed 500 miles east to conduct a surprise 'cordon and search' operation (Operation Fate) against rebel tribesmen in the Hauf region. The area was being used as a training ground for members of the Dhofar Liberation Front, and the plan was to surround and capture the rebels. The two-day operation, which was conducted with the Irish Guards and 78 Squadron RAF, was a total success. Twenty-two terrorists were captured and a vast haul of weapons confiscated.[17]

In the spring of 1967 the situation in Aden continued to cause much concern, and at the end of April the Chiefs of Staff determined to mount a show of force. It was decided to use naval aircraft to carry out the demonstration of power, and the aircraft carriers *Hermes* and *Victorious* were ordered to proceed to Aden.

Hermes, which had been on her way to the Far East, was in the eastern Mediterranean standing by off Athens following the army coup (the 'colonels' coup d'état') in Greece on 21 April. *Hermes* then operated off Cyprus for a week before being released to continue to Aden. She transited the Suez Canal on 3 May and arrived off the port of Aden three days later. On 15 May *Victorious*, having sailed from the Far East escorted by the frigate *Brighton*, joined *Hermes* off Aden.

On 16 May there was an attack by bazooka rockets on the British Residency at Mural. *Brighton* and the minesweeper *Puncheston* immediately proceeded to the area and provided a naval presence off the East Aden Protectorate, in case of any further violence.

On 17 May the two aircraft carriers carried out an impressive show of force, with squadrons of jet aircraft roaring

The assault ship
Fearless
(RNM)

Fearless
Landing Platform Dock
The assault ships (officially landing platform docks or LPDs) were extremely versatile amphibious ships and provided sterling service with the Royal Navy to the end of the nineties, with *Fearless* remaining in service until 2001.

Launched:	19 December 1962
Commissioned:	25 November 1965
Displacement:	12,120 tonnes
Length:	160m
Propulsion:	2 English Electric 2 shaft geared steam turbines
Armament:	2 BMARC GAM B01 20mm single mounted guns, 2 x Phalanx CIWS, up to 5 Sea King helicopters
Complement:	580
No. in class:	2: *Fearless* and *Intrepid*

in low over Aden and the south Arabian territories. Over fifty aircraft took part, including Buccaneers and Sea Vixens as well as RAF Hunters. With the powerful demonstration completed the aircraft carriers sailed from Aden on 20 May. *Hermes* continued on her way to Singapore via Gan, whilst *Victorious* headed for the Red Sea on passage back to the UK. Within two weeks both aircraft carriers would reverse course and head back to a fresh crisis in the Middle East.

The Six-Day War, 23 May – 10 June 1967 Earlier in April 1967 Israeli troops and aircraft clashed with Syrian forces close to their northern border. Then in May, Egyptian troops moved into the Sinai and on 23 May announced a blockade of the Straits of Tiran. It became clear to the Israelis that their neighbours were preparing to invade. UN forces were ordered out of the Sinai by Egypt, and Egypt, Syria and Israel then mobilised for war. On 1 June Jordan was persuaded to join Egypt and Syria and even accepted the deployment of Iraqi troops across her territory.

Victorious and *Hermes* off Aden
(NN)

Although the Western powers had a policy of non-intervention, the UK took steps to prepare for any eventuality and even considered trying to force a passage through the Straits of Tiran to demonstrate the international right of law to transit the strait, but without immediate air cover planning was discontinued. The aircraft carrier *Victorious*, which was in the Mediterranean homeward bound for the UK, was held at Malta together with five frigates, four minesweepers and a submarine as the basis of a Western task force. At the same time the carrier *Hermes*, which was off Gan, was ordered west at full speed for Aden and the Red Sea. *Hermes* made a high-speed passage to Aden and there, together with four frigates, *Nubian*, *Ashanti*, *Brighton* and *Leopard*, and four minesweepers, formed the elements of an Eastern task force. *Hermes* started to work up her group straight away with a series of exercises conducted away from the port, which, with its large Arab population, was increasingly hostile to Western forces.

At dawn on 5 June Israel launched all-out pre-emptive air

strikes against Egypt, Syria and Jordan, striking initially to cripple their air forces on the ground. Having achieved air superiority these attacks were followed up with further strikes against secondary targets, preparing the ground for swift advances by armoured columns and mechanised infantry.

The Israeli Navy was already at sea and attacked Port Said and Alexandria harbour on the night of 5 June. After a gun battle with Egyptian missile-armed Osa attack craft off Port Said, the Egyptian Navy was forced to withdraw, leaving the Israeli Navy to blockade Egypt and protect the northern flank. By bottling up the Egyptian Navy it prevented Egyptian Osa and Komar missile craft from launching strikes against Tel Aviv.

In the second phase of the war Israeli ground forces moved fast, penetrating enemy defences and pushing on deep into enemy territory. Within two days the Israelis had pushed Jordanian forces back to the East Bank, taken over the Gaza Strip and captured all the key passes in the Sinai. After a further two days of hard fighting in the south-west the

Israelis overran the whole of Sinai and reached the Suez Canal, whilst in the north they took the strategically vital Golan Heights.

Demonstration of naval air power over Aden
(JAR)

On 10 June a cease-fire was declared and the war was halted, with the Israelis occupying the Sinai Peninsula, the whole of the west bank of the Jordan and the Golan Heights. It was an enormous humiliation for Egypt and the Arab nations, which indulged in many recriminations including the belief that the British had assisted the Israelis with their key air strikes in the opening phases of the war. Questions were raised in Parliament about the involvement of the British aircraft carriers and the aircraft of the Fleet Air Arm. The Prime Minister, Harold Wilson, had to explain where the carriers were and deny any involvement of the Royal Navy in the war.[18]

One important consequence of the war was the closure of the Suez Canal, which was to have a considerable effect on ships travelling to and from the Middle and Far East.

With the cease-fire holding, it was considered safe to disperse the two task forces, and *Hermes* was released to return east to Singapore, via Gan. Similarly *Victorious* was permitted to continue with her homeward passage from Malta to the UK.

Incidents continued after the cease-fire, however, and on 12 July the Israeli destroyer *Eilat*, together with Israeli fast attack craft, engaged Egyptian attack craft at sea off the northern coast of Sinai and sank two. The Soviet Navy, just fifteen miles away to the north, closely monitored the engagement. Three months later, on 21 October, the Egyptian Navy retaliated, firing Soviet-made Styx missiles from attack craft sheltering inside Alexandria harbour, and sank the *Eilat*.

Hong Kong, May–October 1967 In the Far East, the Cultural Revolution in China in 1967 had a dramatic effect in the region, with thousands fleeing from China. It thus put pressure on Hong Kong, and when serious riots broke out in the colony in May it became necessary to reinforce the garrison. The commando carrier *Bulwark*, with 40 Commando Royal Marines embarked, and a frigate were immediately sent to Hong Kong. The Royal Marines carried out a high-profile rapid landing by helicopter in the New Territories, which served as a powerful demonstration. The Royal Marines then stood by to restore order until the tension eased at the beginning of June, and on 12 June the Royal Marines were withdrawn.

Rioting broke out again the following month and problems were experienced on the border where the frontier guards were attacked. The police on the border had to be replaced by troops, and again it became necessary to reinforce the garrison. This time the carrier *Hermes* was ordered to Hong Kong. She arrived in early August and assisted the Royal Hong Kong Police, deploying them by helicopters in successful anti-Communist raids. At one stage it had been discovered that heavily armed Communists had established bases on the rooftops of blocks of flats and tall buildings. The helicopters of 826 NAS were able to deploy units of the Royal Hong Kong Police supported by British troops in a series of daring rooftop raids. The raids were entirely successful and resulted in many arrests as well as the recovery of considerable quantities of arms and ammunition.

In October 1967 the 8th Minesweeping Squadron handed over responsibility for guardship duties to the 6th Minesweeping Squadron, which was on regular deployments from Singapore. The minesweeper *Fiskerton* left Hong Kong that month, en route for the UK to pay off, and *Woolaston* and *Wilkieston* left the station shortly afterwards. In September 1968 five specially converted minehunters formed the Hong Kong Squadron.

Nigerian Civil War, June 1967 Onwards The commando carrier *Albion*, with 41 Commando embarked, sailed from Devonport on 31 May and headed south at speed. Her mission was to protect and evacuate, if necessary, British nationals from Nigeria, which was ravaged by civil war. A

Hermes off Aden
(NN)

The commando
carrier *Albion* off
Aden
(NN)

short while later four RFA support ships sailed to assist the commando carrier. *Albion* arrived in the Gulf of Guinea and closed the Nigerian coast on 9 June. The RFA support ships arrived eight days later. The Task Force operated off the coast in protection of British nationals for three weeks. *Albion* then departed from the area on 23 June, arriving back in Devonport on 5 July. RFA support ships remained in the area for a further week before being withdrawn.

The Evacuation of Aden:
Operation Magister (Task Force 318),
11 October 1967 – 25 January 1968

Terrorist attacks and civil disturbances continued in Aden in 1967 and the situation rapidly deteriorated as British forces were steadily pulled back to a series of defence lines. As they slowly withdrew heavy fighting for control broke out in the abandoned areas. By 24 September all British forces were withdrawn behind a Victorian defence works just to the north of RAF Khormaksar, known as the 'Scrubber Line'. It was decided to bring forward the date of evacuation from Aden to the end of November 1967. The detailed

The carrier *Eagle* on her way to Aden
(NN)

planning for the formation of Task Force 318 for Operation Magister, to cover the final stages of the withdrawal, was speeded up and the ships began to assemble off Aden at the beginning of October 1967. It was to be a very powerful force, including four aircraft carriers and two assault ships, commanded by Rear Admiral Edward Ashmore.

The commando carrier *Albion* had departed from the UK on 7 September and after participating in Operation Last Fling with 41 Commando steamed south. She rounded the Cape and after a five-day visit to Durban headed north to Aden, arriving on 12 October. As soon as *Albion* anchored in Aden air staff from 78 Squadron RAF, based at Khormaksar, commenced briefing 848 NAS on joint RN–RAF security operations. The Wessex helicopters were landed ashore and after being fitted with armour plating and GPMGs (general purpose machine guns) started patrols controlled by the operations cell at Khormaksar.

On 23 October the aircraft carrier *Eagle*, with 820 NAS embarked, sailed from Singapore, bound for Aden. After working up her aircraft in the Malacca Strait she steamed west across the Indian Ocean and joined the Task Force off the coast of Aden at the beginning of November. With the arrival of *Eagle*, eight RAF Wessex 2 helicopters were transported on board the assault ship *Fearless* to Sharga. As the last fighter aircraft of the RAF left their base at Khormaksar, on 7 November, responsibility for area air defence was taken over by *Eagle*. Her Buccaneers and Sea Vixens flew air patrols whilst, with her 984 radar, she provided early warning as well as co-ordination and control of all air operations.

As a powerful demonstration of force the twenty-four ships of Task Force 318, including the new assault ships *Fearless* and *Intrepid*, were formed in four lines, just off the entrance to Aden harbour, on 25 November. After a seventeen-gun salute, the Task Force was formally reviewed by Sir Humphrey Trevelyan, the Governor of Aden, embarked on board the minesweeper *Appleton*.

On completion of the review twenty-four helicopters from 848 and 820 NAS formed up and conducted a fly-past. The helicopter squadrons were followed by the fixed-wing aircraft, Buccaneers, Sea Vixens and Gannets, flying overhead in a final show of power.

The task of evacuating British forces began at dawn on 26 November in three phases. Crater City, Steamer Point and Ma'alla were quickly evacuated whilst a huge airlift was under way. The garrison was evacuated in an orderly manner, with 45 Commando being the last of the garrison to be pulled out. 45 Commando were not, however, the last British forces to leave Aden, as Royal Marines from 42 Commando had been landed from *Albion* to help cover the final withdrawal phase. So on 28 November at 1500 the last units of 42 Commando Royal Marines were lifted off by helicopter and flown out to *Albion*, thus gaining the distinction of being the very last British forces to leave Aden.

The Task Force remained just off Aden until midnight, when independence was officially recognised, and then began to disperse, with *Eagle* heading east for Singapore. On 7

Bulwark with RFA *Tidereach* and the destroyer *Barrosa*
(RNM)

The powerful Task Force formed in the Arabian Sea, including the carriers *Eagle* and *Albion*
(NN)

The commando carrier *Bulwark* in the Far East
(CC)

HM Ships and Royal Marine Units Engaged in the Aden Evacuation

Aircraft carriers:	*Eagle* and *Hermes*
Commando carriers:	*Albion* and *Bulwark*
Assault ships:	*Fearless* (responsible for co-ordinating the withdrawal operation) and *Intrepid*
Guided missile destroyers:	*London* and *Devonshire*
Submarine:	*Auriga*
Destroyer:	*Barrosa*
Frigates:	*Ajax, Phoebe* and *Minerva*
Minesweeper	*Appleton*
RFA support ships:	*Dewdale, Appleleaf, Olna, Retainer, Stromness, Reliant, Resurgent, Fort Sandusky, Tidespring* and *Tideflow*
Landing ship (logistic):	*Sir Galahad*
	42 and 45 Royal Marine Commandos

December the commando carrier *Bulwark* arrived to relieve her sister ship *Albion*, and three days later *Bulwark*, escorted by *Devonshire* and *Barrosa*, sailed north-east for Masirah. A small naval task force remained in the area for several months to provide cover for the British nationals still employed in the BP oil refinery at Little Aden and for the British Embassy staff.

In 1967 there were over 3,000 terrorist incidents in Aden; fifty-seven British servicemen were killed and 325 wounded. There were also over a hundred British civilian casualties, eighteen of them fatal.[19].

Aden, which had been a British colony for 128 years, was bankrupted by Britain's withdrawal and the closure of the Suez Canal. After the British left, it became a breeding ground for terrorists and also, for a time, a base for the Soviet Navy. Much later an Al-Qaeda cell was to be established in Aden, and this attacked Western shipping including the destroyer USS *Cole*, which was severely damaged with many casualties.

In February 1968 political trials were held in Aden, and government officials who had been pro-British were put on trial. In view of the situation *Bulwark*, with 40 Commando embarked, was deployed to the area on 14 February, escorted by the frigates *Llandaff* and *Eskimo*, as a standby force. The ships were withdrawn on 20 March. The following month, however, another standby force was required during acrimonious finance talks with the Aden government over the sensitive subject of financial compensation. At the beginning of April the aircraft carrier *Eagle*, exercising with the US Navy off Subic Bay, was ordered west at speed to form a naval task force secretly in the Arabian Sea. *Albion*, with 40 Commando embarked, together with supporting frigates and RFA vessels, joined the Task Force, which remained within close range of Aden until 28 May. *Eagle* was then released to return to UK via Cape Town, as the Suez Canal remained closed.

Gibraltar, 13 October 1967 Onwards Continuous harassment by the Spanish government increased the pressure on Gibraltar. Tactics included closings and restrictions on movements across the border and anchoring Spanish warships in Gibraltar waters. The Spanish had closed the border on 3 February 1965 and maintained a limited blockade ever since. In 1967 a Spanish minesweeper sailed into the bay and refused to leave territorial waters when ordered to do so by the guardship, the frigate *Grenville*. Eventually, after considerable pressure had been applied, the sweeper was escorted out of the bay. To reassure the people of Gibraltar it was decided to deploy a permanent guardship, and on 13 October 1967 the frigate *Brighton* arrived to start the first tour of duty on station. A permanent guardship, reinforced from time to time, was to remain in Gibraltar waters for many years, right on into the next century.

Cyprus, 23 November – 2 December 1967 In September 1967, Greek terrorists of EOKA (Ethniki Organosis Kuprion Agoniston) incited violence against Turks in Cyprus, and in an attack against a Turkish village twenty-seven Turks were slaughtered. Turkey then announced its intention to invade Cyprus. On 23 November the minesweepers *Walkerton, Leverton, Shavington* and *Stubbington*, supported by *Layburn*, were deployed from Malta to Cyprus as a standby force to cover immediate emergencies. In the event the Turks were dissuaded from intervening by President Johnson of America, who threatened to expel Turkey from NATO if the invasion took place. President Johnson also insisted that Greek troops be withdrawn from the island and 10,000 were evacuated. The situation eased and the Royal Navy ships returned to Malta on 2 December.

Persian Gulf At the end of March 1968 Iran threatened to invade and occupy the Tunb Islands in the Persian Gulf. On 29 March the assault ship *Intrepid* and the frigate *Tartar*, acting as escort, steamed to the islands and spent two days sailing in close proximity, which served as sufficient deterrent to protect the islands from invasion.

Philippines, September 1968 In September 1968, when the Philippine government refused ships the right of innocent passage, the Far East Fleet formed a task group to provide a powerful show of force. The group assembled on 23 September and consisted of the carriers *Hermes* and *Albion*, the converted maintenance carrier *Triumph*, the assault ship *Intrepid* and the guided missile destroyers *Glamorgan* and *Fife*, escorted by four frigates and destroyers. The Task Group then passed through the Sulu Sea, without any interference at all, and dispersed on 24 September.

Anguilla: Operation Sheepskin, 14 March – 5 May 1969 Severe political problems and civil disturbances broke out in Anguilla following its break away from St Kitts-Nevis in March 1969. The frigates *Minerva*, *Rothesay* and *Rhyl* were deployed to the island on 14 March on Operation Sheepskin to restore sovereignty and order. Paratroops, RAF units and civil police assisted the Task Force. Operation Sheepskin was maintained until order was completely restored by 5 May.

Northern Ireland: Operation Banner, 14 August 1969 Onwards

The bitter 'troubles' in Ireland and Northern Ireland had endured for hundreds of years and had been a constant intractable problem for the UK. After partition between the Irish Free State and Ulster (Northern Ireland) in 1921, hatred and hostility continued, and ultimately in 1969 serious civil disorder was triggered by Catholic civil rights marches. The marches provoked violent clashes with the largely Protestant authorities, police and 'B Specials' (auxiliary police).

On 12 August 1969 the Battle of the Bogside was fought in Londonderry when riots broke out at a parade of Orange Apprentice Boys. This was followed by violent street fighting and rioting in Belfast as well. Two days later it became necessary for the armed forces of the UK to intervene to restore law and order, and two battalions of infantry were sent in as an 'aid to civil power'. The following month the British army started to erect the 'peace wall' between the Falls Road and the Shankill Road in Belfast. On 28 September, 41 Commando Royal Marines, as 'Spearhead Battalion' (the duty battalion on standby to deploy anywhere

in the world at immediate notice), was deployed to the Divis Street area of Belfast on internal security duties; it was to remain there until 10 November.

Intelligence reports indicated that arms were being smuggled into Northern Ireland by the Ulster Volunteer Force (UVF), and the GOC NI (General Officer Commanding, Northern Ireland) requested assistance from the Royal Navy. He asked for anti-smuggling patrols to be conducted off the coast of Northern Ireland to intercept arms shipments. The Ton class minesweepers *Kellington*, *Wasperton* and *Wotton* carried out a series of patrols from 25 to 29 October, from 30 October to 17 November and from 17 to 24 November. In addition the Ton class minesweeper *Kedleston*, which was engaged on fishery protection duties, was put on standby from 11 to 28 December.

FLEET REVIEWS

The NATO Review off Spithead, 16 May 1969 On Friday 16 May 1969 a fleet review was held off Spithead to celebrate the twentieth anniversary of NATO. At 1200 the Royal Yacht *Britannia*, preceded by the Trinity House vessel *Patricia*, sailed from Portsmouth harbour and headed out to Spithead.

British Warships Present at the NATO Review	
Helicopter cruiser:	*Blake*
Guided missile destroyer:	*Glamorgan*
Frigates:	*Dido, Phoebe, Eastbourne, Puma, Wakeful, Tenby* and *Torquay*
Submarines:	*Tiptoe* and *Olympus*
Ships:	*Shoulton, Alcide* and *Letterston*
	RFA *Olmeda*

HM the Queen, accompanied by HRH the Duke of Edinburgh, the Secretary General of NATO, Signor Manlio Brosio, Admiral of the Fleet Earl Mountbatten of Burma, NATO representatives and other dignitaries, were embarked on board the Royal Yacht. The Royal Navy was represented by fifteen ships, though the aircraft carrier *Eagle*, in Portsmouth at the time, did not take part in the review. The Commander in Chief Western Fleet (also NATO Commander in Chief Channel, or CINCHAN), Admiral Sir John Bush, flew his flag in the guided missile destroyer *Glamorgan*.

At 1210 the NATO ships at Spithead fired a royal salute. Then, following a reception, the reviewing ships sailed up and down the lines of sixty-three NATO ships from eleven countries. The following day the NATO ships were open to the public in Portsmouth dockyard.

HM Ships and Royal Marine Units Engaged at the Start of Operation Banner
Minesweepers *Kellington, Wasperton, Wotton* and *Kedleston*
41 Commando Royal Marines

The Western Fleet
steam past on
29 July 1969
(NN)

Royal Review of the Western Fleet, 29 July 1969 Two months later a further review was held in Torbay. This was the Royal Review of the Western Fleet on 29 July, with HM the Queen and the Duke of Edinburgh embarked on board the Royal Yacht *Britannia*.

It was a cloudy day with strong winds blowing when the fleet put to sea, led by *Eagle* flying the flag of the Commander in Chief, Admiral Sir John Bush. First there was a fly-past of ninety Fleet Air Arm aircraft, and that was followed by an impressive steam-past of two columns of over forty warships, submarines and RFA support ships. Earlier in the day the Queen had presented new colours to the fleet on board *Eagle*.

OTHER DUTIES

Quelling a Mutiny On 15 January 1966 a mutiny broke out on board the British ship ss *Sudbury Hill* in the Gulf of Aden. The *Leander* frigate *Dido*, on her way back from Indonesian waters, was quickly on the spot and an armed boarding party was put on board the cargo ship. The mutiny was quelled with no serious casualties.

Aberfan Disaster On 21 October 1966 a disaster occurred in South Wales when a slagheap collapsed, engulfing the small mining town of Aberfan and killing 144 people. The cruiser *Tiger*, flying the flag of Admiral Pollock (Flag Officer Second in Command, Home Fleet), arrived in Cardiff the next day and 380 of the ship's company were immediately landed to assist in the search for survivors and carry out emergency disaster relief work.

East Malaysia In January 1967 east Malaysia suffered severe flooding and *Bulwark*, en route to Singapore from Hong Kong, was diverted to provide emergency aid. The commando carrier arrived on 8 January and was able to carry out essential relief work, restoring basic services.

Tasmania At the beginning of February 1967 Tasmania was devastated by bush fires. The submarines *Tabard* and *Trump* were in New Zealand at the time, and they immediately sailed on 7 February for Tasmania, where they landed working parties, which provided much valuable relief work ashore. The submarines were withdrawn on 15 February.

Operation 'Mop Up': The *Torrey Canyon* Disaster On 18 March 1967 the tanker *Torrey Canyon* ran on to rocks off the coast of Cornwall and started to spill vast quantities of crude oil. The destroyer *Barrosa* and the minesweeper *Clarbeston*, at Plymouth, were immediately sailed with large quantities of detergent on board, which they used on the spreading oil slick. Gradually more ships arrived to assist, including the destroyer *Delight*. Eventually on 30 March it was decided to bomb the stricken tanker, and naval Buccaneer aircraft were used, with aircraft from 800, 809, 890 and 899 NAS taking part.

The *Essberger Chemist* On 24 June 1967 the submarine *Dreadnought* was ordered to sink the 13,000-ton German tanker *Essberger Chemist*, which was a hazard to shipping off the Azores. *Dreadnought*, commanded by Commander Peter Cobb, had sailed from Gibraltar at thirty knots, and when she arrived in the area fired four torpedoes. Three torpedoes struck the stricken vessel, though eventually she had to be finished off by gunfire from the frigate *Salisbury*.

Sicilian Earthquake An earthquake occurred in north-west Sicily on 15 January 1968, and the minesweepers *Walkerton*, *Stubbington*, *Crofton* and *Ashton* immediately sailed from Malta to render emergency assistance. The ships provided valuable relief work over the course of five days before returning to Malta on 21 January.

SHIPS, SUBMARINES, AIRCRAFT AND WEAPONS

Nuclear-Powered Ballistic Missile Submarines Britain's first SSBN, the 8,000-ton *Resolution*, was launched on 15 September 1966 and commissioned one year later in October 1967. She fired her first Polaris test missile at Cape Canaveral (Cape Kennedy) on 15 February 1968 and was deployed on her first deterrent patrol in June. She was built on time and to budget, which, for a project of such magnitude and immense complexity, was an incredible achievement. Together with her sister SSBNs, *Repulse*, *Renown* and *Revenge*, she maintained deterrent patrols until finally handing over to the next generation Trident SSBNs in 1995.

The *Swiftsure* Class Submarines By 1969 there was, effectively, a nuclear submarine arms race between the Western Powers and the Soviet bloc. The submarine design bureaus and their associated yards in the Soviet Union were turning out nuclear submarine classes at an alarming rate. Soviet technology was evolving and was fast matching the advantages the West had, greatly assisted by espionage. Technology stolen from the West was being incorporated into the designs in the Soviet Union. Against this backdrop a new class of submarine, the *Swiftsure* class, was procured, and whilst it was a follow-on from the *Valiant* class it marked a step change in design and stealth underwater, providing greater speed, a quieter platform and greater diving depths. Displacing 5,000 tons, it incorporated a change in hull shape with a more streamlined design. Its sonar was very advanced, providing greater detection ranges and giving a true range advantage on the enemy. Its weapon outfit had also developed: armed initially with the Tigerfish homing torpedo the submarines were also fitted with the Royal Navy Sub-Harpoon (a sub-surface-to-surface anti-ship missile) and,

A Royal Navy Phantom fighter by LA Wilcox (LW) (RC) (DD)

Swiftsure class SSN (NN)

latterly, the Spearfish torpedo (the successor to the Tigerfish) and the Tomahawk cruise missile. Six were ordered, and one, *Sceptre*, remained in service in 2008.

Gas Turbine Engines The Royal Navy had spent over twenty years researching into gas propulsion for warships. As an experiment the Type 14 *Blackwood* class frigate *Exmouth* was converted to gas turbine power with a Rolls Royce Olympus engine for full power and two Rolls Royce Proteus engines for cruising. She began sea trials in 1968 and was the first major NATO warship to be propelled by gas turbine engines. The Soviet Navy had launched the first all-gas turbine major warship in the world with the *Kashin* class destroyers, launched in 1962.

Phantom Fighters for the Fleet Air Arm Despite the decision to phase out the carriers and naval fixed-wing aircraft, procurement of the US-built McDonnell Douglas F-4K Phantom II naval fighters, ordered in 1964, continued. The original order of fifty for the Royal Navy was cut back to twenty-eight. Phantoms were also ordered for the RAF. A Flying Trials Unit was formed at RNAS (Royal Naval Air Station) Yeovilton in May 1968, and one year later the navy won the *Daily Mail* trans-Atlantic Air Race with a flight of three Phantoms.

ASW The development of ASW sensors, weapons and tactics remained a high priority for the Royal Navy throughout the sixties. As well as submarines being used in the ASW hunter-killer role and ship-borne ASW helicopters, surface ships were improving their ASW weapons and sensors. Considerable advances in submarine detection and prosecution ranges were achieved by the introduction of the VDS (variable depth sonar) and Ikara ASW missile. Sonars mounted on the hulls of ships had many limitations owing to hull water noise and the warmer surface layers of the sea, which could cause sonar beams to be refracted or reflected, allowing submarines to avoid detection. The Canadians pioneered the use of a VDS, which could be towed astern of a ship and be lowered beneath the warm surface layer of the sea to detect submarines hiding in colder layers below. The Australians then developed the ship-launched rocket-propelled Ikara ASW missile, which could be guided to the approximate position of a submarine. On entering the water Ikara homed in on the target submarine. The Ikara ASW system was to be fitted to the *Leander* class frigates from the beginning of the seventies.

PERSONNEL MATTERS

In 1965 the strength of the Royal Navy stood at 97,000, and by the end of 1969 that had reduced by 9,500 to 87,500. The five-year period was dominated by the devastating decision cancelling the new generation of aircraft carriers. It was a severe blow, and cast doubts over the long-term future of the Service and caused many to wonder whether they should perhaps consider a career outside the Navy.

Leander
Leander Class Frigate

Leander was the lead ship of the most successful frigates to serve with the modern Royal Navy. The *Leanders* were developed from the basic hull form of the earlier *Rothesay* class frigates, which were highly manoeuvrable at speed with excellent sea-keeping qualities. They had high bows that kept them relatively dry in heavy weather, and they provided a very stable platform for modern sensors and weapon systems. The numbers built and the long period of time for which they remained in service were testimony to their success.

Launched:	28 June 1961
Commissioned:	27 March 1963
Displacement:	2,860 tonnes
Length:	113.38m
Propulsion:	2 boilers, 2 steam turbines on 2 shafts
Armament:	1 twin 4.5in gun (later replaced by Ikara ASW missile launcher),
	2 x 40mm Bofors,
	2 Oerlikon 20mm cannon,
	Seacat missiles,
	Mk 10 Limbo mortar and Westland Wasp helicopter.
	Many armament changes were to be made in all three batches of ships.
Complement:	257
No. in class:	26

The White Ensign Association Throughout the period the White Ensign Association continued to provide valuable advice and guidance to the large numbers that were still leaving the Service. The Association was also building up its many useful networking contacts, extending the areas where it was able to offer help and finding more job opportunities. It also provided key investment advice and arranged mortgages for the increasing numbers of men who wished to purchase property using their lump sums as a deposit.

Home Ownership The idea of house purchase was starting to spread in the Navy, and more and more of those serving were turning to the Association to arrange mortgages. The incidence of home ownership in the Royal Navy was to be much greater than in the other two services and was to provide a number of significant advantages. Firstly it provided a wise capital investment, and secondly it invested money which otherwise would have been spent and sunk on rent. Thirdly it provided an element of stability for the married family whilst the husband was away at sea, and finally it meant that a man already had a home when he came to leave the Service.

The frigate *Rothesay*
(RNM)

CHAPTER 4

Evacuations, Withdrawals and the Group Deployment Concept 1970–1974

In the early 1970s the world remained under the dark shadow of the Cold War, though there were the first few glimmers of a possible future thaw. The Strategic Arms Limitation Talks (SALT) between the superpowers had started, but there was to be a long slow process before finally Nixon and Brezhnev signed the first Strategic Arms Limitation Treaty (SALT 1) on 26 May 1972. The Soviet Union had been catching up with the USA in terms of strategic inter-continental ballistic missiles (ICBMs), whilst the USA had been pressing ahead with an anti-ballistic missile defence shield (ABM system). SALT 1 placed limits on the numbers of both nuclear strike and defensive missiles. It was greatly welcomed on both sides, which were faced with the crippling costs of nuclear missile technology, development and procurement.

The world remained a very dangerous place, and the Royal Navy, which had taken over responsibility for Britain's vital nuclear deterrent role on 1 July 1969, maintained its contribution to the deterrent posture of the West, with at least one Polaris SSBN constantly on patrol, hidden deep in the oceans of the world.

Despite the nuclear stalemate between the superpowers, conflicts continued around the world. US involvement in the Vietnam War, following the devastating Tet Offensive of 1968, was winding down, with the 475,200 men deployed in 1969 reducing to 157,800 by 1971, and after the signing of the armistice in January 1973 only 23,500 US troops remained. Britain had steadfastly managed to avoid being involved in Vietnam.

Elsewhere Biafra surrendered in 1970, bringing to an end the bloody Nigerian civil war in Africa, whilst in 1971 civil war in Pakistan ended with East Pakistan gaining independence as Bangladesh. In 1973 the Arab oil-producing countries caused a world economic crisis by restricting supplies to demonstrate their collective power.

This was followed by a coalition of Arab states, led by Egypt in the south and Syria in the north, launching an all-out attack on Israel on 6 October 1973 (the day of the holiest Jewish festival), starting the 'Yom Kippur' War. The war pitted Soviet-backed Egyptian and Syrian forces against Israel supported by the West, thus threatening rapid escalation. Within three days the USSR was resupplying Egyptian forces with a whole range of weapons and two days later the USA was supplying arms to Israel. On 14 October the biggest tank battle since World War II was fought out in the Sinai Desert, with the Israelis gaining a great victory, wiping out the Egyptian 2nd Army and advancing across the Suez Canal.

FIRST SEA LORDS
Admirals Hill-Norton and Pollock

SECOND SEA LORDS
Admirals Lewis and Empson

MANPOWER
87,500

MERCANTILE MARINE
3,858
merchant ships

'Gone is the traditional method of operating single ships over a wide area, and in its place is the Task Force.'

(MOD, 1974)

The UN Security Council brought about a cease-fire on 22 October. This led indirectly to NATO and Warsaw Pact countries embarking on discussions to consider 'mutual force reductions'.

In the UK a new Conservative government under Edward Heath had come to power on 19 June 1970 in a surprising election with the lowest turn-out of voters since the war. The new government was confronted with declining production and industrial output combined with rapidly rising inflation and an ever-worsening balance of trade deficit. Industrial relations broke down, and Heath had to deal with major problems over Northern Ireland, rising unemployment, immigration, Rhodesia and negotiations for Britain to join the EEC (European Economic Community). In January 1973 the UK did finally achieve full membership of the EEC, along with Denmark and Ireland, thus completing yet another important step in Britain's painful journey from global empire to a medium-power European country.

Negotiations with the miners and the unions broke down and led to the declaration of a state of emergency and introduction of the three-day working week on 2 January 1974. The state of emergency ended with a General Election in March 1974 and the return to power of a Labour government under Harold Wilson, but it was a minority government in an extremely difficult position, facing an economic crisis.

Defence Policy In 1970 the new Conservative government reviewed the previous Labour Party defence policy of reducing Britain's armed forces, and in October 1970 published a supplementary statement on defence policy (Cmnd. 4521), prepared by the new Defence Secretary, Lord Carrington. The policy stated: 'The Government is determined to restore Britain's security to the high place it must take among national priorities and to make good as far as possible the damage of successive defence reviews.' Its first objective was 'to enable Britain to resume, within her resources, a proper share of responsibility for the preservation of peace and stability in the world'.[1]

The Navy had high hopes that the unfortunate Labour decisions to phase out aircraft carriers and withdraw from east of Suez within three years would be reversed, but sadly that did not happen, though the government did agree to maintain a military presence east of Suez. The 1972 defence estimates reinforced the UK's commitment to NATO and to Europe, but the government also considered Britain's interests in the Middle East and Far East. To replace the Far East Fleet, which was disbanded in October 1971, and the Anglo-Malaysian Defence Agreement, a five-power Commonwealth defence agreement was set up with Australia, New Zealand, Singapore, Malaysia and the UK known as the Five-Power Defence Arrangement (FPDA). A squadron of ships was formed under the FPDA in the Far East, referred to as the ANZUK Squadron, and the UK agreed to contribute destroyers and frigates. The first ANZUK Squadron consisted of the frigates *Gurkha* and *Jaguar* with HMAS *Swan* and HMNZS *Otago*.

HMS *Blake* is a helicopter cruiser. She is 565 feet long, has a beam of 64 feet and a standard displacement of 12,300 tons. She has 900 officers and ratings. She is armed with two 6-inch guns, two 3-inch guns and two Seacat missile launchers. Aft is a hanger for four Sea King anti-submarine helicopters.

The Group Deployment Concept Financial and political circumstances were putting immense pressures on the Royal Navy to abandon its key responsibilities in critical parts of the world east of Suez, particularly the hot spots of the Middle East and Far East. In a remarkably short-sighted way the government was forcing the Navy to limit itself to concentrating solely on its prime anti-submarine warfare commitment to NATO in the eastern Atlantic. The Naval Staff, however, were fully aware of just what an important instrument of national policy the Navy could provide in the Middle and Far East, and were reluctant to abrogate these important responsibilities. Naval forces could easily be deployed abroad in areas where a squadron of aircraft or a battalion of soldiers could not.

Accordingly the Naval Staff evolved the important strategic concept of out-of-area group deployments. This entailed assembling a powerful naval task force, or 'group', and deploying it out of the NATO area to carry out a series of high-level visits in politically sensitive and important areas. It would help enable the Royal Navy to protect Britain's

interests worldwide. The group would conduct exercises, both together and with other allied navies, and would gain valuable experience of operating on its own, without support, in different parts of the world.

More importantly this policy would enable Britain to exercise considerable power, reach and influence as well as providing an excellent platform on which to demonstrate modern technology and generate sales of defence equipment. It was probably the prospect of lucrative export orders that persuaded the government to approve the policy, albeit reluctantly.

The MoD press release for the Second Group Deployment stated: 'The Royal Navy is now meeting its commitments east of the Cape of Good Hope, in South Africa, in a different way. Gone is the traditional method of operating single ships over a wide area, and in its place is the Task Force idea. This system provides a much more economical and flexible method of operating in distant waters … greater efficiency and a much higher level of training.'[2]

It was a brilliant concept, masterminded by Admiral Lewin as VCNS (Vice Chief of the Naval Staff) and was to set the basic pattern of naval deployments for at least several decades. The first group was planned to sail from the UK in May 1973.

The CVS Concept The other major problem faced by the Royal Navy was the phasing-out of the carriers, and the Naval Staff had been hard at work to find a solution. The ingenious compromise that emerged was the concept of the 'through deck' cruiser operating VSTOL (vertical short take off and landing) jet aircraft.

Experiments with VSTOL aircraft had been taking place for nearly a decade, with the first vertical landings and take-offs being conducted on board the aircraft carrier *Ark Royal* in the Channel by a P.1127 VTOL (vertical take off and landing) jet aircraft in February 1963. It had been intended that the new carrier CVA-01 would be able to operate VTOL aircraft, but when the new carrier project was cancelled it was inevitable that means of getting VTOL aircraft to sea would be thoroughly explored. The result was the *Invincible* class CVS, the first of which, the *Invincible,* would be at sea in time to take part in the Falklands Campaign.

THE FLEET

In 1970 the Fleet still retained two fixed-wing aircraft carriers, *Ark Royal* and *Eagle*. *Ark Royal* had just been recommissioned on 25 February after being refitted with a new strengthened flight deck, catapults and arrester gear to operate her air group of heavy Phantom strike-fighter aircraft.

The light fleet carrier *Centaur* was being used as a depot ship but was disposed of in 1971, and *Victorious* had been scrapped in 1968, following a fire in refit. The light fleet carrier *Hermes* was taken in hand in Devonport on 1 March 1971 for conversion to a commando ship. In 1973 the first of the new 'through deck' cruisers, the future ASW (anti-submarine warfare) command carriers, *Invincible*, was laid down.

The group deployment concept (JAR)

Amphibious Element The amphibious component included the commando ships *Albion* and *Bulwark*, plus *Hermes*, under conversion, as well as the new assault ships, *Fearless* and *Intrepid*. In addition there were six landing ships (logistic) operated by the RFA (Royal Fleet Auxiliary).

Helicopter Cruisers The cruisers *Blake* and *Tiger* had been converted to helicopter cruisers with the third, *Lion*, being held for spares before being scrapped in 1975.

The Escort Fleet The escort fleet included nine missile destroyers with a new class, the Type 42 *Sheffield* class, under construction (*Sheffield* was launched in June 1971). The twenty-six ships of the *Leander* class provided the backbone of the frigate squadrons, which totalled sixty-four ships.

The Submarine Fleet The submarine squadrons were made up of the four SSBNs (the Polaris strategic deterrent ballistic missile nuclear submarines) and seven SSNs (nuclear hunter-killer fleet submarines), with two more, *Sovereign* and *Superb*, having been launched. The Navy also had twenty-three conventional SSKs (diesel-electric submarines).

The Minesweeping Ships The minesweeping squadrons included thirty-nine coastal sweepers and twenty-four inshore minesweepers.

The aircraft carrier *Ark Royal* with her Phantom strike-fighter aircraft embarked
(NN)

The new Type 42 destroyer *Newcastle*
(RNM)

Patrol Vessels A range of patrol vessels was employed on various tasks from coastal protection to fleet training. A squadron of fast patrol boats (FPBs) was maintained at Portland for training ships in defensive tactics against FPB attack.

Fleet Air Arm The front-line aircraft operated by the Fleet Air Arm included twenty-four F-4K Phantom IIs and twenty-four Buccaneer S.2s as well as some Sea Vixen interceptors, Scimitar tankers and AEW (airborne early warning) Gannets. The helicopters included sixty Sea King ASW helicopters, 150 Wessex helicopters and ninety Wasp general-purpose helicopters.

Hermes	
Centaur Class Aircraft Carrier	

Hermes was the last conventional fixed-wing aircraft carrier built for the Royal Navy and served until she was sold to the Indian Navy after the Falklands Campaign. She served initially as a light fixed-wing aircraft carrier and was then converted to a commando carrier in 1971–3. She was subsequently converted to an ASW carrier in 1976 and then later adapted to operate Sea Harriers.

Launched:	16 February 1953
Commissioned:	25 November 1959
Displacement:	23,000 tonnes
Length:	236.14m
Propulsion:	4 Admiralty 3-drum boilers,
	2 shafts, Parsons geared turbines
Armament:	5 twin Bofors 40mm;
	4 single 3 pdr saluting guns
Carrier air group up to 1970:	12 Sea Vixen FAW2s,
	Buccaneer S2s,
	4 Gannet AEW3s,
	1 Gannet COD4,
	5 Wessex HAS3s,
	1 Wessex HAS1
Carrier air group from 1980:	Up to 28 Sea Harriers
Complement:	2,100
No. in class:	4: *Centaur*, *Albion*, *Bulwark* and *Hermes*

The Royal Marines The corps of the Royal Marines consisted of 3 Commando Brigade with 40, 41, 42 and 45 Commandos, supported by artillery, engineering and logistic units.

Support The Fleet was supported by the tankers and supply ships of the Royal Fleet Auxiliary, as well as various other repair, maintenance, survey and support ships.

Fleet Command The Commander in Chief Western Fleet in 1970 was Admiral Sir William O'Brien; Admiral Sir Edward Ashmore relieved him in September the following year. Admiral Sir Terence Lewin was subsequently appointed Commander in Chief in December 1973.

With the demise of the Far East Fleet at the end of October 1971, following the government policy of withdrawal from east of Suez, the Commander of the Western Fleet took overall command, becoming the 'Commander in Chief Fleet'. On 1 November 1971 Admiral Ashmore was appointed as the first Commander in Chief Fleet (CINCFLEET), commanding the entire fleet from his headquarters at Northwood, Middlesex.

Below the Commander in Chief the Fleet was divided into three flotillas of surface ships (the 1st Flotilla at Portsmouth and the 2nd Flotilla at Devonport, with the 3rd Flotilla comprising the aircraft carriers and amphibious ships). There were also two separate commands for submarines and sea training.

NATO Commands: The Commander in Chief Fleet was also the NATO Commander in Chief Channel (CINCHAN) and

The Ton class minesweeper *Wolverton* (TT)

The Portland Fast Patrol Boat Squadron (NJBM)

Eastern Atlantic Area (CINCEASTLANT). As CINCHAN he was one of the three Major NATO Commanders (MNCs), the others being SACEUR (Supreme Allied Commander Europe) and SACLANT (Supreme Allied Commander Atlantic); both the latter posts were held by senior US four-star officers.

FIRST SEA LORDS

Admiral Sir Peter Hill-Norton Admiral Hill-Norton was appointed First Sea Lord in succession to Admiral Le Fanu, who was suffering from leukaemia, in July 1970. It had become, in rotation, the turn of the Navy to take the position of Chief of the Defence Staff (CDS), and the plan had been for Admiral Le Fanu to take up that appointment. Instead

Admiral Hill-Norton became CDS in April 1971 having spent only nine months as First Sea Lord. He served a full three years as CDS before being appointed chairman of the Military Committee of NATO in April 1974. He then served three years with NATO before finally retiring as Baron Hill-Norton of South Nutfield in 1977. He had a reputation throughout the Navy of not being the most approachable of admirals but he certainly appears to have been in the right place at the right time.

Admiral Sir Michael Pollock Admiral Pollock, Controller of the Navy in 1971, relieved Admiral Hill-Norton in March and served in the appointment for three years. Michael Pollock, born in October 1916, was a gunnery specialist who had been the gunnery officer of the heavy cruiser *Norfolk* at the Battle of North Cape and the sinking of the German battlecruiser *Scharnhorst*. He was awarded the DSC for his part in the battle.

In the 1950s he commanded the cruiser *Newcastle* and saw action in the Malayan Emergency, where his ship provided gunfire support. He then commanded in turn *Vigo*, *Blake* and *Ark Royal* before being appointed Assistant Chief of the Naval Staff as a rear admiral in July 1964.

He was appointed Flag Officer Submarines in December 1967 after serving as Flag Officer Second in Command Western Fleet. At the beginning of 1970 he was appointed Controller of the Navy and promoted to Admiral, but after barely a year in post he moved to relieve Admiral Hill-Norton as First Sea Lord in March 1971. He served three years before being relieved by Admiral Ashmore.

OPERATIONS AND DEPLOYMENTS, 1970–1974

In the early seventies the Royal Navy was heavily committed, maintaining defensive and deterrent patrols in key areas of the world as well as conducting major operations and deployments.

Strategic Nuclear Deterrent First and foremost the Royal Navy operated Britain's strategic deterrent force, which consisted of the four 7,000-ton Polaris ballistic missile submarines of the *Resolution* class, *Resolution*, *Renown*, *Repulse* and *Revenge*. Each submarine carried sixteen Polaris missiles, with a range of 2,500 nautical miles. The SSBNs operated from their base in Faslane, on the west coast of Scotland, and deployed out on patrol into the oceans of the world to remain undetected, for months on end, within missile range of predetermined strategic targets. The submarines were assigned to NATO and controlled by CTF (Commander Task Force) 345 deep in underground bunkers below the headquarters of the Commander in Chief at Northwood outside London.

Submarine Operations in the Cold War: Operation Holystone Throughout much of the Cold War the submarine squadrons conducted many covert, dangerous and top-secret

STANAVFORCHAN
(RNM)

Resolution
Resolution Class SSBN

The *Resolution* class SSBNs with their Polaris missiles took over Britain's strategic nuclear deterrent from the RAF in 1969 and maintained ceaseless deterrent patrols undetected in the world's oceans until they were replaced by the Trident submarines in the mid-1990s.

Launched:	15 September 1966
Commissioned:	10 February 1967
Displacement:	8,400 tonnes
Length:	129.5m
Propulsion:	1 Vickers/Rolls-Royce PWR.1 pressurised-water nuclear reactor, single shaft
Armament:	16 Polaris A3 missiles, 6 21in torpedo tubes, Marconi Tigerfish Mk24
Complement:	143 (two crews)
No. in class:	4: *Renown*, *Revenge*, *Repulse* and *Resolution*

operations in the north-east Atlantic and Barents Sea as well as some missions in the Baltic and also the Mediterranean on the southern flank of NATO. Operations Holystone and Barnacle were joint US–UK intelligence-gathering missions. The Royal Navy, for its part, deployed covert missions to the Barents Sea in both the spring and the autumn each year. The British submarines on theses missions were controlled by CTF 311 operating close to CTF 345 (responsible for SSBN deployments) at the Commander in Chief's headquarters at Northwood. For reasons of national security, nearly all of these operations are very firmly subject to the Official Secrets Act and must remain so.

Beira Patrol In the Indian Ocean the ongoing Beira Patrol, implementing the UN embargo on oil for Rhodesia, was carried out constantly by two frigates, supported by an RFA tanker on station, until March 1971, when it was reduced to one frigate or destroyer. By March forty-seven interceptions had been carried out since the patrol started in 1966.

Gibraltar One frigate remained on station inside the Straits of Gibraltar to deter any moves by Spanish authorities against the naval base and the local community.

Northern Ireland Off the coast of Northern Ireland regular surveillance and anti-smuggling patrols were maintained by MCMVs (mine counter-measures vessels) whilst Royal Marines of 42 and 45 Commandos carried out internal security duties.

Antarctica *Endurance* with Naval Parties 8901 and 8902 protected British interests in the Falkland Islands and South Georgia.

Persian Gulf In the Persian Gulf patrols were maintained by

frigates and by the seven Ton class minesweepers of the 9th MCM (Mine Counter-Measures) Squadron. Duties involved stopping and searching dhows and vessels to deter arms smuggling, slavery, piracy and infiltration by subversive elements. In 1971 it was decided to withdraw the 9th MCM Squadron from the Persian Gulf, and in September ships of the squadron began to return to the UK.

Hong Kong In Hong Kong the five MCMVs of the 6th MCM Squadron, which had been formed in September 1969, maintained guardship duties. They were reinforced by frigates and destroyers deployed from Singapore from time to time. The ships were replaced in October 1971 by five converted Ton class minesweepers, *Wolverton*, *Beachampton*, *Wasperton*, *Yarnton* and *Monkton*, specially adapted for patrol duties in Hong Kong.

At the beginning of September 1970 the Hong Kong garrison was reinforced by 40 Commando for a period of two weeks until political tension eased. On 24 April 1973 the Cathedral class air direction frigate *Chichester* was deployed to Hong Kong as the permanent guardship, supporting the patrol craft of the Hong Kong Squadron.

West Indies The frigates *Jupiter* and *Sirius* were operating in the Caribbean at the beginning of 1970 and on 21 April they were ordered to Trinidad when riots broke out following an army mutiny. At the same time the ocean liner ss *Orsova* was chartered by the MoD to evacuate refugees from the area.

The frigate *Chichester* converted as the Hong Kong Guardship (NN)

Kotlin Class Soviet destroyer shadowing a carrier (NN)

Jupiter stood by, liaising with the US COMPHIBRON 12 (Commander Amphibious Squadron 12) whilst *Sirius* was diverted to help quell an uprising in the Cayman Islands. By the end of the month order had been restored and the frigates stood down, although they were required in the following month to rescue kidnapped fishermen from Cuba (the fishermen had been kidnapped by Communist activists).

Whilst the rest of the year remained calm, the following year the frigate *Bacchante* was on station and was required to intervene in brief cases of public disorder in Antigua in February and in Bermuda in March. In January of that year Royal Marines from 41 Commando had to be deployed to the Bahamas on exercise Fettle for three weeks to counter Cuban terrorists on the islands of William and Billy. Later in the year *Glamorgan* and *Phoebe* provided conference facilities in Bermuda for talks between the Prime Minister and the President of the USA. In 1972 Royal Marines from 40 Commando had to be sent to the Bahamas to combat terrorist attacks.

NATO Assignments The Royal Navy continued to assign ships to the standing NATO naval squadrons. A frigate or destroyer was permanently assigned to the Standing Naval Force Atlantic (SNFL), and also, as required, to the new NAVOCFORMED (Naval on Call Force Mediterranean). In addition, on 11 May 1973 a new standing naval force was established in the Channel as STANAVFORCHAN, which was formed from MCMVs under the command of CINCHAN (the UK major NATO commander at Northwood). Initially the squadron consisted of three MCMVs, from the UK, the Netherlands and Belgium.

The Dangerous *Ark Royal* Incident, 9 November 1970 A dangerous Cold War incident occurred at sea in the Mediterranean on 9 November 1970. The aircraft carrier *Ark Royal* was taking part in the major two-week exercise Lime Jug 70.

Whilst she was conducting flying operations, as part of the exercise, she was being closely shadowed by a Soviet *Kotlin* class SAM (surface-to-air missile) destroyer, the *Bravyy*. At that stage of the Cold War it was normal for Soviet warships and Elint intelligence ships to monitor NATO naval activity at dangerously close ranges.

At one stage in the early evening, during flying operations, the Soviet destroyer suddenly closed in at speed and attempted to cut straight across the bows of *Ark Royal*. The carrier sent emergency warning signals and went full astern in a desperate attempt to avoid the Russian warship. The two ships collided and the bows of *Ark Royal* struck the Russian destroyer astern, rolling it over and wrecking the whole of the after section of the ship.

The destroyer managed to right itself, but seven Russian seamen were washed overboard. The frigate *Yarmouth* conducted a search for the missing Russian sailors and four were saved. It was a serious incident but fortunately not as fatal as the loss of the *Voyager* in a similar accident some six years earlier.

The dangerous incident led to a high-level meeting with Admiral Gorshkov in Moscow to consider means of reducing such risks. At first Gorshkov was silent, listening to the complaints about dangerous manoeuvres performed by Soviet forces. He is then reputed to have produced a photograph of a Royal Navy Buccaneer jet aircraft passing

under the anchor cable of a Soviet *Don* class submarine tender, anchored in the Bay of Sirte. It was then agreed that in future, signals would be exchanged before close-quarters manoeuvres were attempted.[3]

The Nuclear Submarine *Dreadnought* at the North Pole, 3 March 1971 The Royal Navy achieved a notable success on 3 March 1971 when the nuclear submarine *Dreadnought* became the first RN submarine to surface at the North Pole. On reaching the Pole she had to search for nine hours using sonar, periscope, upward-looking echo sounder and flood-lights before she could break through the ice, which was fifteen feet thick when she emerged. Spending seven days under the ice and surfacing six times, she sustained only minor damage during her 1,500-mile voyage under the Arctic.[4]

The Persian Gulf: Operation Bracken and Task Force 318, November 1971 On 1 November 1971 Task Force 318 was established for Operation Bracken to protect British interests and ensure a safe evacuation of British bases in the Persian Gulf. The powerful Task Force consisted of the aircraft carrier *Eagle* and the commando carrier *Albion* with 40 Royal Marine Commando embarked, escorted by the guided missile destroyer *Glamorgan* and the frigates *Scylla, Arethusa, Achilles, Argonaut* and *Gurkha* with RFA support ships and tankers.

Most of the ships, including *Eagle*, had been in the Far East. The air squadrons from *Eagle* had performed a fly-past off Singapore to commemorate the withdrawal of British

A powerful carrier task force (NN)

forces from the naval base and the carrier had then participated in exercise Curtain Call in the Malacca Strait. On completion of that exercise the ships of the Task Force assembled to form Task Force 318 and to carry out training off Penang. The Task Force then steamed west across the Indian Ocean, via Gan, through the Straits of Hormuz and into the Gulf. *Glamorgan* was detached from Task Force 318 on 25 November and departed for Bermuda to provide

---

Submarine Concept of Operations

In the early 1970s, when the Soviets were launching one new nuclear submarine every three weeks, Flag Officer Submarines (FOSM) began to develop a concept of operations that was to revolutionise the way in which our own submarines were programmed and operated.

In essence, instead of almost exclusively playing the "loyal opposition" in national and NATO exercises, the aim was to give all our nuclear and diesel attack submarines frequent time in contact with their potential adversaries in order to enhance our own capabilities and to provide that essential but undefined element of threat that is inherent in submarine operations – so that an enemy, when considering options for action in any given scenario, would always have to consider the possibility that a Royal Navy submarine might be in close contact, possibly with a firing solution on its attack computer.

To establish and support these operations, a centre was set up in the 'bunker' at the Northwood Fleet Headquarters, where all the essentials for successful control of submarine operations were available – access to real-time all-source intelligence, secure communications between the headquarters and individual boats, water management (rather akin to air traffic control), proximity to political decision making and not least submarine watch keeping expertise on a 24/7 basis. Thus, in 1977, Flag Officer (Submarines) moved most of his staff from what had been its traditional home at Fort Blockhouse at Gosport and set up shop at Northwood.

The starting point of the concept was to define the contributions to be made by our submarines in all the various scenarios ranging from 'peacetime' up to all-out nuclear war. From this, it was possible to develop training and equipment

procurement priorities and to measure the effectiveness of our submarine force. Recognising that the only RN platforms capable of detecting, classifying and tracking Soviet submarines were our own submarines, and that the major threat to NATO and the UK was that posed by them, our submarines were routinely programmed to intercept and 'trail' Soviet submarines, including ballistic missile firers, en route to their Atlantic and Mediterranean patrol areas. Also, to monitor Soviet surface forces on their deployments out of area. And in addition covertly to gather intelligence, a task for which submarines are uniquely suited, close to the Barents Sea bases of the Northern Fleet as well as in the open oceans.

Occasional judicious 'leaks' of results of operations against the Soviets resulted in them developing general awareness of the Royal

Navy's superiority, but without ever having details of exact capabilities, or times and locations when they had been under surveillance. Intelligence gathering patrols were conducted in the close approaches to the Soviet Northern Fleet bases in the Barents Sea and provided unique data, often gathered at very close quarters – yet undetected – on the latest Soviet platforms and weaponry, unobtainable from any other collection source. Trails and surveillance of Soviet forces out of area could last for weeks, even months, so that 'in-contact' time – one of the prime objectives of the Submarine Concept of Operations – became almost routine for our crews, enhancing their expertise and confidence across the board and making the Royal Navy's most significant single contribution to the successful outcome of the Cold War.

Captain John Speller OBE, RN

Withdrawal from
Malta with *Bulwark*
in Grand Harbour,
Malta
(NN)

facilities for a high-level conference between Britain and the USA. The remaining ships of the Task Force supported Operation Bracken, and the aircraft from *Eagle* provided air cover. The operation continued throughout December.

Third Indo-Pakistan War, 23 November – 17 December 1971
In October 1971 Pakistan and India continued hostilities and engaged in artillery exchanges across the border. On 21 November India launched a major offensive to destroy the Pakistani guns, and two days later the Third Indo-Pakistan War began.

A state of emergency was declared and Britain prepared naval contingency plans at the beginning of December for the evacuation of British nationals from East Pakistan. *Albion*, escorted by *Gurkha* and *Arethusa*, was detached from Task Force 318, and the three formed a powerful naval task group. *Albion* embarked Sea King helicopters of 826 NAS (Naval Air Squadron) from *Eagle*, and the squadron was then ordered to head for the Bay of Bengal.

On 3 December the Pakistani Air Force launched air strikes on Indian air bases, copying the Israeli tactics in the Six-Day War, but failed to destroy the Indian Air Force. The next day the Indian Army attacked East Pakistan.

On 11 December *Albion*, flying large white ensigns, with a big Union Jack painted on the flight deck, and supported by the frigates *Arethusa* and *Gurkha*, steamed north into the Bay of Bengal closing into the coast of East Pakistan. *Gurkha* detached and headed further north into the East Bay of Bengal whilst *Albion* and *Arethusa* then sailed south-west, standing off the coast. Then on 16 December East Pakistan surrendered and the new state of Bangladesh was proclaimed.

As the security situation eased the Task Group was withdrawn from the Bay of Bengal and headed back to the Gulf to rejoin Operation Bracken.

Withdrawal from Malta, 21 December 1971 – 28 March 1972 On 24 December 1971 the Prime Minister of Malta,

Dom Mintoff, issued an ultimatum for the withdrawal of all British forces from the island. A small naval task force was quickly formed off the coast consisting of the helicopter cruiser *Blake* and the commando carrier *Bulwark* with an escort of frigates, including *Euryalus*, *Bacchante* and *Ashanti*. 41 Commando was deployed ashore guarding key points. The Task Force remained off the island during the winter and then withdrew at the end of March. *Bulwark*, with 41 Commando embarked, had to return to Malta on 6 July to standby for further disturbances, but fortunately the situation eased without the necessity of landing the Royal Marines ashore.

British Honduras, 26 January – 7 February 1972 In January 1972 British Honduras was threatened with invasion by Guatemalan troops massed on her border. At the time the aircraft carrier *Ark Royal* was out in the Atlantic en route to rendezvous with ships of the US Navy for joint exercises. She was promptly diverted and ordered south-west to the area. The guided missile destroyer *London* and the frigates *Dido* and *Phoebe* were also ordered to the Caribbean at speed.

On 26 January *Ark Royal* launched a pair of Buccaneer strike aircraft from 809 Naval Air Squadron, at extreme range. The jets closed into the coast and then roared in very low over the Honduran capital in a most powerful display of force before returning 1,250 miles to *Ark Royal*. It was a very effective demonstration of force projection by the Royal Navy and served to reduce the threat of invasion. Nevertheless *Phoebe* was ordered to remain on stand by off the coast of British Honduras for a further week and was then withdrawn on 7 February.

The Second Cod War, 1 September 1972 – 8 November 1973

On 1 September 1972 the Icelandic government started to enforce a new fifty-mile fishing limit, extended from the twelve-mile territorial limit. Despite this, British and German trawlers continued to fish in the disputed waters. Icelandic gunboats started to harass trawlers inside the new fifty-mile limit, and on 2 September the gunboat Aegir chased sixteen trawlers out of the disputed waters. On 7 September the Royal Navy instituted a special patrol with a frigate, *Aurora*, and RFA *Blue Rover* on the edge of the disputed waters, just outside the fifty-mile limit, in readiness to protect British trawlers.

Warp Cutters This time the Icelandic gunboats started to use special warp cutters designed to sever the trawlers' warps (trawling lines). These cutters had been developed but not used during the First Cod War. On 12 September the gunboat *Aegir* cut the warps of the trawlers *Lucinda* and *Wyre Victory*. Seven days later *Aurora* entered the zone, but it was on a rescue mission to assist an Icelandic fishing boat, *Jon Eiriksson*, which was on fire. *Aurora* managed to rescue the crew, though the trawler sank whilst under tow. A short while later the gunboat *Odinn* cut the warps of the trawlers *Kennedy* and *Wyre Captain*.

In October the frigates *Palliser* and *Achilles* were on patrol on the edge of the area and further incidents took place. In one incident the gunboat *Odinn* opened fire on the *Wyre Vanguard*. From the end of October and into November the frigates *Phoebe*, *Berwick*, *Falmouth* and *Juno* took turns on patrol. Then in December the frigates *Jaguar*, *Apollo* and *Rhyl* were deployed, in turn, to the area. Over the course of the year there were eleven incidents, but none involved Royal Navy warships, which remained outside the disputed waters.

In January 1973 the frigates *Lowestoft*, *Yarmouth* and *Berwick* took turns on patrol. The gunboats cut more warps, and on 18 January eighteen warps were cut. In response to requests from the fishermen for close support a large fast defence tug, the *Statesman*, was chartered and sent to the

Refuelling during the Second Cod War
(NN)

Trawlers under the protection of Royal Navy frigates in the Second Cod War
(NN)

area, arriving on station on 22 January. The following day the volcano Eldfell, on the island of Heimaey, erupted and the Icelandic gunboats withdrew to assist in evacuating the island. They were away until 5 March, when they returned to harass trawlers and resume warp cutting (twenty warps were cut in March). The frigates continued to patrol outside the fifty-mile limit, leaving the chartered defence tugs in direct support of the trawlers. At the end of March there were two shooting incidents when the gunboat *Aegir* opened fire on the trawlers *Brucella* and *St Leger* in separate actions.

In April and May the number of shooting incidents increased, with eight in April and four at the beginning of May. By this time many trawlers had had warps cut, and on 17 May British trawlers withdrew from the disputed area. They refused to fish in the area unless they were given direct support in the disputed waters by frigates. Up to 17 May there had been fifty-nine incidents but none involved Royal Navy warships, which showed the remarkable restraint exercised by the British government at that stage.

The Royal Navy Goes In On 19 May the British government gave way to pressure to send warships into the disputed area, deploying the frigates *Plymouth*, *Cleopatra*, *Lincoln*, *Jupiter* and *Scylla* at various times in the vicinity. The three defence vessels in the disputed area, *Statesman*, *Irishman* and *Englishman*, came under naval command. The British trawlers returned inside the fifty-mile limit to fish. Action was not long in coming, and on 26 May the gunboat *Aegir* opened fire on the trawler *Everton*. After firing blanks the *Aegir* switched to firing shells into the hull of the trawler. With some of the shots hitting below the waterline, the *Everton* started to sink. The frigate *Jupiter* (commanded by Commander Slater) was soon on the scene to render assistance, sending over engineers and salvage equipment including powerful pumps. Fortunately *Jupiter* was able to save the sinking trawler.

In June and July the frigates *Scylla*, *Jaguar*, *Ashanti*, *Leopard*, *Charybdis*, *Falmouth*, *Lincoln*, *Gurkha*, *Arethusa*, *Berwick*, *Argonaut* and *Andromeda* took turns in the area. The first collision with a frigate occurred on 1 June when the gunboat *Aegir* collided with *Scylla*. Incidents with warp cutting and the firing of warning shots continued throughout the summer, with the frigates frequently frustrating the attempts by the gunboats to arrest British trawlers.

On 17 July *Aegir* collided with *Lincoln*, and two days later *Odinn* collided with *Arethusa*. Then in August the gunboat *Albert* collided with the defence vessel *Lloydsman*, and a week later *Odinn* collided with *Andromeda*. At the end of the month *Aegir* collided with *Apollo*, with one fatality on board the gunboat. In September incidents continued, with warps being cut, and on 10 September *Thor* collided with *Jaguar*.

NATO Pressure In September the Secretary-General of NATO, Joseph Lunns, went to Reykjavik to heal a growing rift between NATO and Iceland. Iceland was a vital link in the strategic GRIUK gap (Greenland–Iceland–Faeroes–UK gap), straddling the Soviet Northern Fleet's route into the

The frigate *Jupiter* (Commander Slater) stands by a trawler (JCKS)

The frigate *Falmouth* (Commander Giles) refuelling (NN)

Defence vessels on
patrol in the
disputed area
(NN)

North Atlantic. Whilst talks took place in NATO, incidents at sea continued with warp cutting and harassment. On 22 September *Aegir* collided with *Lincoln*, and an Icelandic television crew filmed the event. Following the incident the Icelandic government threatened to break off diplomatic relations with Britain if warships and defence vessels were not withdrawn from the fifty-mile limit by 3 October. The UK decided to pull back, and the frigates and defence vessels were withdrawn from the disputed area on that day.

Frigates and the defence vessels continued to patrol outside the fifty-mile limit until finally on 13 November an agreement was signed between Britain and Iceland. The agreement limited British fishing by small trawlers to an annual quota of 130,000 tons whilst large trawlers would remain outside the fifty-mile limit for a period of two years.[5]

Submarine 'Intruder' Incident in the Clyde Area, December 1972 At the end of December 1972 a Soviet submarine was believed to be in the sensitive Clyde area. Indications had been picked up by SOSUS[6] intercepts, and the nuclear submarine *Conqueror* was sailed to search for the intruder. *Conqueror* hunted in the area, listening with her sonar in the passive mode, and picked up the Soviet submarine, which she then identified as a *Victor* class nuclear fleet submarine. *Conqueror* was able to track the Soviet submarine until finally it withdrew from the area. It was the first known penetration of the Clyde area by a Soviet submarine, and following the incident procedures were developed to deal with any future intruders.[7]

Sea Day 'Sally Forth 73', 24 July 1973 At the beginning of July 1973 ships gathered off the coast of Scotland for the annual two week Joint Maritime Course exercise (JMC 168). On its completion the ships, including *Ark Royal*, *Devonshire*, *Fife*, *Kent*, *Bristol* and a host of destroyers, frigates and MCMVs, gathered at Rosyth and off the Forth estuary for a 'sea day', Operation Sally Forth 73, on 24 July. The Secretary General of NATO, Dr Lunns, and Lord Carrington witnessed the event. They also watched a Harrier VTOL demonstration. Several Soviet warships and intelligence gatherers shadowed the exercises and watched the sea day manoeuvres at very close quarters.

First Group Deployment (TG 317.1), 8 June – 21 December 1973

Early in May 1973 ships for Task Group 317.1 gathered in Portsmouth to prepare for an out-of-area deployment to the Far East. This was to be the first of the new concept of out-of-area group deployments by the Royal Navy. The Task Group was under the command of Rear Admiral Dick Clayton, FOF2 (Flag Officer 2nd Flotilla), flying his flag in the helicopter cruiser *Tiger*, with the Sea King helicopters of 826 NAS embarked. The escorts included the *Leander* class frigates *Hermione* and *Dido* and the Type 12 frigate *Rhyl*. The fleet tanker RFA *Tidespring* and the replenishment ship RFA *Regent* supported the group. The nuclear submarine *Dreadnought* also accompanied the group for part of the deployment.

The Task Group Sails Task Group 317.1 sailed from Portsmouth on 8 June 1973 and formed up in the Channel before proceeding west for Portland. A Dutch frigate also accompanied the group as it continued west out into the Atlantic, altering course south to head for Gibraltar. The Task Group conducted shake-down exercises in the Bay of Biscay and then called into Gibraltar for a brief three-day visit.

On to Cape Town The group sailed from Gibraltar on 18 June and continued south, bound for Cape Town. During the passage south the opportunity was taken to conduct ASW exercises with *Dreadnought* and the Sea King helicopters. Arriving in Cape Town on 2 July, the group spent a week preparing for the next leg and a heavy exercise programme. Finally it headed back out to sea on 9 July and shaped course, round the Cape of Good Hope and on into the Indian Ocean.

The Far East Once at sea the group conducted exercise Sanex with units of the South African Navy, mostly a series of ASW exercises over three days, before saying farewell to their South African hosts and steaming north-east across the Indian Ocean. Ten days later the Task Group arrived off the coast of Malaysia and took part in exercise Penangex, a five-day joint maritime exercise in the Andaman Sea.

Singapore On completion of the exercise the group transited through the Malacca Strait and entered Singapore on 27 July

The Task Group takes part in close-quarters exercises (JAR)

Tiger leading the group deployment (JAR)

for a two-week period of maintenance in the naval base. The opportunity was also taken for rest and recreation before the next exercise schedule.

Exercise Greenlight The Task Group sailed from Singapore on 13 August and rendezvoused with the US Navy for the Anglo-US naval exercise Greenlight. It was a fairly intense exercise programme, with most ships closed up at action stations for long periods of time, as the main force was under almost continuous air, surface and sub-surface threat. After the exercise the squadron proceeded to Olongapo for post-exercise briefing and analysis as well as a short break.

Guam The group then sailed on to Manila for a short break in the Philippines before steaming on east to the US naval base at Guam in the Marianas. A serious engine-room breakdown in the flagship meant that *Tiger* remained in Guam whilst other ships of the group carried out visits to other ports, including Rabaul and Manus Island. Finally, with her defects rectified, *Tiger* sailed from Guam on

24 September and headed south-west for Singapore. The passage schedule was devoted to a series of exercises, including ASW exercises with *Dreadnought*, culminating in exercise Grass Snake, a nuclear submarine hunting and tracking exercise.

Singapore The ships of the group arrived in Singapore naval base on 5 October for a two-week maintenance period prior to the home leg of the deployment. Finally on 23 October the Task Force Group sailed out of Singapore naval base for the long return passage back to the UK.

Diego Garcia The group steamed west across the Indian Ocean, stopping briefly at Diego Garcia, a small atoll in the Chagos Islands, on 30 October. Lieutenant Commander Richard Baker RNR, the BBC newscaster, was serving in *Tiger* for his annual reserve training, and he took the opportunity to fly in a Sea King to the small, uninhabited Danger Island and claim it for the British Crown. The Task Group then steamed west-south-west to Mauritius arriving on 6 November for three days before heading on down to Cape Town.

Cape Town After a week in Cape Town the group sailed on 24 November for exercise Capex, a four-day ASW exercise with the South African Navy. The start of the exercise was delayed as two South African Buccaneer aircraft, due to conduct air strikes on the group, crashed into the sea, and an exhaustive search recovered only one body. The exercise was resumed and provided useful experience in hunting the small French-built Daphne class submarines of the South African Navy. On completion of the exercise the ships sailed into the naval base at Simonstown on 30 November for the post-exercise 'wash up' (debrief).

Homeward Bound After a final weekend in Cape Town the Task Group bade farewell and sailed on 3 December for the three-week homeward passage to the UK. Whilst in South Africa the group had heard dramatic stories about life in the UK with power cuts and petrol rationing, and wondered what they would find on their return. The group sailed steadily north through the warm waters of the South Atlantic and finally, after crossing the Bay of Biscay, arrived in the Channel. On altering course east *Tiger* disembarked the helicopters of 826 NAS on 20 December to return to their base at RNAS (Royal Naval Air Station) Culdrose in Cornwall. The ships of the Task Group sailed on and entered Portsmouth naval base the next day to complete their seven-month deployment to the Far East. The success of the First Group Deployment validated the concept and encouraged the Naval Staff to plan subsequent deployments.

———— • ————

The Fleet Assembly, 15 February 1974 In the middle of February 1974 ships of the fleet started to arrive in the Caribbean and headed for the British Virgin Islands. FOF1, Vice Admiral Raikes, flew his flag in the helicopter cruiser

Blake, and she led other ships of the flotilla in to anchor off Virgin Gorda. The guided missile destroyers *Kent* and *Devonshire* followed her in.

The commando carrier *Bulwark* and the amphibious assault ship *Fearless*, with an escort of frigates and destroyers, arrived and anchored close by. Within the space of two days there were fourteen ships anchored off Virgin Gorda, including *Bacchante*, *Brighton*, *Whitby*, *Nubian* and *Torquay* and RFAs *Resource*, *Tidepool* and *Orangeleaf*. The submarine *Narwhal* also joined the ships at anchor.

On Friday 15 February the First Sea Lord, Admiral Sir Michael Pollock, arrived and flew his flag in *Bulwark*. Shortly afterwards the ships weighed anchor and sailed out to sea before forming up into divisions. The fleet, led by *Narwhal*, then steamed past *Bulwark* with decks lined to cheer Admiral Pollock, the outgoing First Sea Lord. On completion the ships formed up in their divisions and turned to pass down on either side of *Bulwark* followed by a fly-past of Sea King, Wessex and Wasp helicopters.

It was an impressive sight, and on completion of the assembly Admiral Pollock sent a personal message to the fleet: 'Thank you for a most marvellous send off.'

Task Group 317.1: Deployment to the Far East, January–October 1974

Task Group 317.1 On 17 December 1973 the guided missile destroyer *Fife* in the naval base at Portsmouth, was transferred to the 2nd Flotilla at Devonport. She prepared to deploy to the Far East as the flagship of Rear Admiral Dick Clayton, FOF2. Admiral Clayton was to lead Task Group 317.1 on a nine-month out-of-area deployment to Australia and the Far East. The Task Group consisted of the ships of the Second Frigate Squadron, the *Leander* class frigates *Scylla*, *Apollo*, *Ariadne*, *Danae* and *Argonaut* and the *Rothesay* class frigate *Londonderry*. The store support ship RFA *Tarbatness* accompanied the group.

Outward Leg The ships sailed from the UK early in the New Year and headed south for the warmer weather. After a brief call at Gibraltar the group set course for South Africa and sailed on down to the Cape, conducting exercise training en route. The ships of the Task Group enjoyed a very welcome break in Simonstown and Durban before sailing into the Indian Ocean and setting course north-east. A visit was paid to Mombasa, and several frigates carried out turns on Beira Patrol, whilst other frigates headed for the Gulf and a visit to Bandar Abbas.

ADEX On 20 February *Fife* accompanied by several frigates arrived in Gan, where Admiral Clayton transferred his flag to the guided missile destroyer *Norfolk*. The group then sailed for Singapore for a two-day visit before departing on 28 February for Hong Kong. Out at sea the group conducted a series of 'ADEX' (air defence exercises) where they were subjected to repeated fast attacks from low-flying Hunter jets flown by the Singapore Air Force.

AMP On arrival in Hong Kong at the beginning of March the group had a three-week AMP (assisted maintenance period) assisted by the base staff HMS *Tamar*. *Fife* left Hong Kong on 27 March and sailed for Subic Bay in the Philippines prior to carrying out live Sea Slug missile firings on the US Navy range facilities.

Exercise Spring Board After an Easter break in Singapore the group took part in exercise Spring Board, in which they were subjected to attacks from Exocet missile-armed Malaysian FPBs (fast patrol boats). It provided a useful demonstration of the Exocet weapon system. The missile system was eventually to be fitted to a number of the *Leander* class frigates including *Danae* and *Argonaut*. Having returned to Singapore in April, Admiral Clayton transferred his flag back to *Fife*.

Australia The Task Group sailed from Singapore on 19 April and headed south-east for a series of visits to Australia and New Zealand and to carry out an ambitious programme of exercises with the Royal Australian Navy and the Royal New Zealand Navy. On 24 June *Scylla* visited Possession Island and took part in the commemoration ceremonies marking the 200th Anniversary of the original landing by Captain James Cook. Towards the end of June the Task Group steamed back north, splitting up for a round of visits to various countries. *Fife* returned to Singapore, where Admiral Clayton transferred his flag to the *Juno* on 2 July, whilst *Scylla* proceeded to Hong Kong for a brief refit in the dockyard.

Exercises *Fife* sailed two weeks later bound for Djakarta for a five-day visit before commencing exercises with the Indonesian Navy, again testing defence measures against attacks from missile-armed fast patrol boats. On completion of the exercise *Fife*, escorted by *Argonaut* and *Onslow*, sailed through the Malacca Strait for Penang and entered Penang harbour. On departing from Penang on 6 August *Fife* and her escorts rendezvoused with the rest of the Task Group to take part in exercise Penangex, a series of air-defence and anti-submarine exercises.

Homeward Leg On completion of the exercises *Fife* detached from the group and sailed west to Diego Garcia to embark Admiral Clayton on 14 August. The rest of the Task Group also set course west across the Indian Ocean for the return leg of the deployment. On the return passage, visits were paid to Gan, Diego Garcia, Mauritius and the Seychelles before the Task Group called into Cape Town and Durban at the end of August. On departing from South Africa on 12 September the Task Group set course north for the homeward passage and after a brief call into Gibraltar finally arrived back in Plymouth on 4 October.

———•———

Operation Rheostat I, 7 April – 31 October 1974 At the beginning of 1974 the Egyptian government requested

assistance in clearing the Suez Canal of war debris. Operation Rheostat I was initiated, and on 20 March 1974 an MCM task group of *Wilton*, *Bossington* and *Maxton*, supported by *Abdiel*, sailed from the UK. The MCM Squadron transited the Mediterranean and arrived in the canal region on 7 April. The MCM group joined with US and French MCMVs in the area, and commenced clearance operations. It was a slow task, but eventually the canal was cleared by the end of October. *Bossington* had left earlier for Gibraltar, and the rest of the MCM Squadron returned to the UK on 22 November.

Cyprus Emergency, 15 July – 30 September 1974 On 15 July 1974 the Cypriot government of Archbishop Makarios was overthrown by EOKA (Ethniki Organosis Kuprion Agoniston), a radical terrorist group of Greek Cypriots backed by the Athens military junta in mainland Greece. Britain had to rescue Archbishop Makarios. Five days later Turkish forces invaded Cyprus, establishing beachheads in the north to protect the Turkish Cypriots, and as they penetrated further south severe fighting broke out between Greek and Turkish forces. The Turks then occupied Nicosia. Britain convened a conference in Geneva to resolve the crisis but without success, and on 13 August Turkish reinforcements landed and partitioned the island.

Britain assembled a powerful task force in the eastern

Royal Marines prepare to evacuate personnel from Cyprus
(NN)

Mediterranean, with the aircraft carrier *Hermes* and the guided missile destroyers *Devonshire* and *Hampshire*. *Hermes* embarked 41 Commando from Malta and sailed directly to Cyprus. The Task Force was escorted by the frigates *Andromeda*, *Brighton* and *Rhyl* and supported by RFAS *Regent* and *Olwen* with RFAS *Gold Rover* and *Olna* standing by. The submarine *Onslaught* was also deployed to the area. The frigate *Ajax* was sent out to the eastern Mediterranean to relieve *Devonshire* and was soon hard at work with *Rhyl* evacuating 250 British passport holders stranded in the occupied port of Famagusta.

Ships and Units Engaged in the Cyprus Evacuation

HM ships *Hermes, Devonshire, Hampshire, Andromeda, Argonaut, Brighton, Rhyl, Ajax, Onslaught*
RFAS *Regent,* and *Olwen*
40 and 41 Commandos Royal Marines

Group deployment exercises in the South Atlantic
(JAR)

Arriving off the coast of Cyprus, *Hermes* landed the Royal Marines of 41 Commando. 40 Commando, which was the 'Spearhead Battalion', standing by for rapid deployment from the UK, was flown out direct to the Sovereign Base Area of Cyprus to reinforce 41 Commando. Its presence helped contain the violence, preventing the mass migration of Cypriots, fleeing north and south, from turning into a massacre. Over 200,000 families were displaced, most of them Greek. The British forces were also able to rescue and evacuate refugees and British nationals. The Task Force was finally withdrawn from the eastern Mediterranean at the end of September.

Second Group Deployment, 17 September 1974 – 11 June 1975

The ships of the Second Group Deployment, Task Group 317.2 (TG 317.2), assembled in Portsmouth in early September 1974 for a deployment to the Far East via the Cape of Good Hope.[8] They were under the command of Rear Admiral Henry Leach, FOF1, flying his flag on board the helicopter cruiser *Blake.* The group consisted of five frigates, *Diomede, Leander, Achilles, Falmouth* and *Lowestoft.* An SSN, *Warspite,* and *Stromness, Olna* and *Green Rover* RFA support ships were attached to the Task Group.

The Task Group Sails After a brief period of weapon trials in the Channel with *Blake* embarking the Sea King helicopters of 820 NAS, the Task Group sailed from Portsmouth on 17 September 1974. It headed down the Channel and then set course south-west across the Bay of Biscay, conducting shake-down exercises en route.

Cape Town The ships called in at Gibraltar for a brief two-day visit before sailing again on 23 September and heading due south. Whilst on passage south the group conducted a series of ASW exercises with *Warspite* before arriving off the Cape on 14 October.

The squadron then called into the South African naval base at Simonstown, close to Cape Town, and fired a national salute. In harbour the ships spent a week carrying out maintenance and repairs whilst the ships' companies took the opportunity to visit South Africa and enjoy the lavish hospitality that was offered.

Media Attention Unfortunately the visit generated a certain amount of unfavourable media attention at a time when relations with South Africa were strained over her support for Rhodesia. The Naval Staff attempted to brief the press on the difference between an 'operational visit' (such as the Group Deployment) and a 'good will' diplomatic visit, with

Warspite surfaces during an ASW exercise with Task Group 317.2
(JAR)

political overtones, which the Task Group visit was most certainly not. The front-page photographs of ratings on the beaches of South Africa with young bikini-clad girls had also not been well received by families and girlfriends in the UK.

End of Visits to South Africa When the group sailed on 21 October the government decided that for political reasons there would be no more visits to South Africa by the Royal Navy for the foreseeable future. With the Suez Canal still closed this created a severe strategic handicap for the deployment of naval forces to the Middle East and Far East.

Exercise Midlink After rounding the Cape of Good Hope, the Task Group steamed into the Indian Ocean and set course north-east for a rendezvous with the Indian Navy for the major maritime exercise in the Middle East, exercise Midlink. En route ships reinforced the Beira Patrol and visited Mombasa at the beginning of November, before sailing on towards Karachi.

In the middle of the Indian Ocean the frigate *Falmouth* caught fire, as a result of an electrical defect, and very quickly

The frigate
Falmouth
(Commander Giles)
(JAR)

the blaze spread, engulfing the whole centre section of the ship in a raging fire. The nearest frigates closed in spraying the ship whilst fire-fighting parties on board fought bravely to bring the fires under control. When the fires were extinguished it became clear that the central section of the ship had been severely damaged, but nevertheless the ship was able to proceed under her own steam and participate in the various exercises. Whilst the frigate continued with the planned programme, arrangements were made for her repair in the Far East.

Ships of the group then rendezvoused off Karachi and took part in exercise Midlink from 19 to 29 November. Midlink was the annual exercise of CENTO (the Central Treaty Organisation, an alliance established in 1955 and comprising the UK, USA, Pakistan, Turkey, Iraq and Iran). It was a large-scale exercise involving fifty ships, and the Commander in Chief Fleet, Admiral Lewin, took the opportunity to visit the Task Group during the exercise.

Base Visits On completion of the exercise the ships visited Karachi for a post-exercise debrief before sailing on east, some to the naval base at Singapore for a week's maintenance and some to Hong Kong, arriving on 21 December for Christmas and the end of the year. *Falmouth* was taken in hand in Hong Kong for extensive repairs to her fire damage.

War in Dhofar, 1965–1975

For nearly ten years a little-known war was fought in the Dhofar, a region of Oman, bordering the Yemen. It was between Communist-backed guerrillas and the forces of the Sultan of Oman, the SAF (Sultan's Armed Forces). It was a war of strategic importance as the coast of Oman bordered the vital oil route from the Gulf. Other dissident groups in neighbouring Arab countries also watched it closely. During the war Royal Marine officers as well as British army officers were regularly loaned or seconded to the Sultan of Oman to command SAF troops. Naval officers were also seconded to command positions in the Sultan of Oman's Navy (SON). Fast patrol boats of the SON guarded the coast.

It was a hard struggle and it was not until 1970, as the Sultan was losing, that the British government decided to provide arms and equipment, including helicopters and artillery. The fighting was hard but two successful operations, Jaguar and Leopard, were mounted in 1972. These were followed by a hard-fought battle at Marbat on 19 July 1972. A small SAS (Special Air Service) team managed to defend the town and fort at Marbat against hordes of tribesmen, just long enough for relief forces to be flown in by helicopter. It was a heroic defence and proved a turning point in the war.[9]

Operation Simba In an operation in June 1973 two RFA vessels, *Sir Lancelot* and *Stromness*, provided assistance to the SAF in support of Operation Simba. The SAF had taken a strategic position at Sarfait in Operation Simba but were hard pressed, being surrounded by rebel forces and under heavy fire from repeated rocket and mortar attacks. RFA *Stromness* provided a helicopter base as relief supplies and ammunition were flown in to Sarfait, enabling the SAF to consolidate their position.

The war dragged on for five years before the SAF finally won. It was a vicious war with numerous skirmishes and hard-fought engagements, but it provided many Royal Marines with invaluable experience that they were able to put to good use in subsequent campaigns. Five Royal Marines were killed during the war.

Northern Ireland

Operation Banner At the beginning of 1970 British forces, with the Royal Navy and Royal Marines in support, continued to be deployed in Northern Ireland under Operation Banner. Anti-smuggling patrols were maintained constantly off the coast of Northern Ireland to intercept arms shipments.

Operation Grenada Seven patrols were conducted during 1970, and the following year it became necessary to establish a permanent patrol under the codename Operation Grenada. The Ton class minesweeper *Nurton* carried out the first patrol, with the task of intercepting and stopping all smuggling of arms and personnel into or from Northern Ireland.

Operation Interknit At the end of the year it was necessary to establish a permanent patrol in Carlingford Lough, codenamed Operation Interknit, to prevent terrorist activities in the area. The vessels *Alert* (*A510*) and *Vigilant* (*A382*) carried out the patrol. In the course of 1973 thirty-five patrols were conducted under Operation Grenada, and in 1974 this total increased to forty-five plus a further two patrols conducted by RFA vessels.

On 1 June 1970 45 Commando, Royal Marines, part of Britain's Strategic Reserve, was deployed from its base at Stonehouse Barracks, Plymouth, to Belfast for internal security duties; this was to be the first of many tours of duty in the Province.

On 31 August they were relieved by 41 Commando, Royal Marines, but they were to be back again for a month in August 1971. Then again they were back in Belfast on 17 October and stayed this time until 18 February 1972, though during that time 42 Commando reinforced them from 28 October to 18 January.

'Bloody Sunday' It was on Sunday 30 January 1972 that a disastrous shooting outbreak at an illegal civil rights demonstration in Londonderry resulted in the deaths of thirteen people and the wounding of a further thirteen. In

Painting of *Wotton* and *A510* on Carlingford Lough, Royal Yacht passes to port, by L A Wilcox (RC)

the confused situation British troops, deployed on riot control duties, believed they had been fired on and returned fire with deadly effect, causing the casualties. The incident became known as 'Bloody Sunday' and put back the slender hopes of any easy peaceful solution being found to the troubles in Northern Ireland. The incident became the subject of various protracted enquiries without any clear firm findings being forthcoming. Four months later 45 Commando were back in the Province from 10 June to 28 July. 40 Commando arrived on 14 June and 42 Commando on 27 July.

Operation Motorman, 31 July 1972 On 31 July 1972 a major operation, codenamed Operation Motorman, was launched in a concerted drive to clean up the dangerous 'no-go' areas in Londonderry and West Belfast. West Belfast was completely controlled by the Provisional Irish Republican Army and had become known as the 'Wild West'. Nearly 22,000 British troops, including two armoured battalions, were engaged in the operation, which was a complete success with minimum casualties. Four landing craft manned by Royal Naval personnel and Royal Marines were used to convey British Army units, and bulldozers, up the River Foyle and deep into Londonderry. Rapid action by determined forces defeated the terrorists, and by the end of the day there were no 'no-go' areas left anywhere in Northern Ireland. The Royal Marines sustained twenty-one casualties, including two killed.

40, 42 and 45 Commandos continued to deploy to Northern Ireland for internal security duties, gaining valuable anti-terrorist experience. In 1973 40 and 42 Commandos sustained fourteen casualties, including three killed, and in 1974 42 and 45 Commandos took ten casualties, with three being killed.

The ex-submarine depot ship *Maidstone* was deployed to Belfast as a prison ship and base. Eventually she was withdrawn, and the Royal Naval detachment, under SNONI (Senior Naval Officer Northern Ireland), was based in Moscow Camp, Belfast, with a jetty and workshop.

Humanitarian Operations

Channel Rescue On 8 September 1970 the MV *St Brenden* caught fire in the Bristol Channel. The destroyer *Cavalier* was sent to help and on arrival managed to bring the fires under control. The next day the destroyer took the *St Brenden* under tow and managed to tow her safely to Milford Haven.

St Kitts Ferry Disaster In 1970 there was a disaster in St Kitts when the ferry foundered. The frigate *Sirius* was very quickly on the scene and managed to rescue a hundred people. For her swift action in saving so many lives *Sirius* was awarded the Wilkinson Sword of Peace.

Operation Burlap In the wake of violent cyclones in East Pakistan a task group of ships comprising the maintenance and repair ship *Triumph*, the assault ship *Intrepid*, the survey ship *Hydra* and the landing ship (logistic) RFA *Sir Galahad*, with 3 Commando Brigade, was formed on 19 November 1970. The Task Group provided a great deal of humanitarian assistance and relief work as part of Operation Burlap. After three weeks of extensive emergency relief work the operation was completed on 11 December.

Mount Soufriere In November and December 1971 the frigates *Berwick* and *Phoebe* provided emergency relief work in St Vincent following a minor eruption of Mount Soufriere. The relief operation was completed on 8 December.

Rescue Operation off Durban On 21 April 1972 the Liberian tanker SS *Silver Castle* was on fire off Durban. The frigate *Lowestoft* was en route from Simonstown and immediately proceeded at full speed to assist the stricken tanker. The frigate fought the blaze and managed to bring the fires under control before towing her to safety.

The Rescue of Crew from the *Carnation* On passage to Penang, between 22 and 27 July 1973, the nuclear submarine *Dreadnought* rescued thirty-five crewmen from the stricken merchant vessel *Carnation*, which had been in a collision with the *Anchor Ansen*.[10]

Rescue On 19 September 1972 the frigate *Aurora* went to the aid of an Icelandic fishing boat, the MV *Jon Eiriksson*, which was on fire. *Aurora* managed to rescue the crew of five successfully from the blazing ship.

SHIPS, SUBMARINES, AIRCRAFT AND WEAPONS

Chevaline Project Towards the end of the 1960s Britain was concerned with the threat to the Polaris deterrent posed by advances in ABM (anti-ballistic missile) defence systems. The superpowers were developing systems which could threaten the technical credibility of a limited Polaris missile strike.

Instead of purchasing the new US Poseidon strategic missile system Britain worked on a project, codenamed Antelope, to improve the penetrative capability of the existing Polaris system. Politically it was less sensitive to develop an existing weapons programme rather than seek Parliamentary approval to purchase a whole new expensive weapon system from the USA.

AWRE (the Atomic Weapons Research Establishment) developed the project in great secrecy, and in 1972 the government agreed the 'Super Antelope' programme. The Royal Navy would have preferred to move to the next-generation Poseidon system rather than modifying the older Polaris system. The modifications to Polaris would make the missile heavier, thus reducing its range. With a reduced range British SSBNs would have to operate closer to the Soviet coast, making them more vulnerable to Soviet submarines and ASW forces. AWRE estimated that the 'Super Antelope' programme would be considerably cheaper than procuring Poseidon from the USA. In 1972 the superpowers agreed to limit ABM systems, thus reducing the threat to Polaris. At the same time President Nixon was pushing ahead with the Trident missile system, the third-generation nuclear deterrent, and it was thought that Britain might be able to skip a generation by keeping an updated Polaris system operational in the meantime. Super Antelope, renamed Chevaline, was then refined and accepted by the government in early 1974.

The government also set up a study to review the options for replacing the Polaris submarine force when it came to the end of its scheduled life in the mid-1990s. This study pleased the RAF with the prospect of possibly wresting back the responsibility for the nation's strategic deterrent force, but disappointed it by very firmly recommending a submarine-launched ballistic missile system as by far the best means of maintaining the strategic deterrent. When Labour came to power in the same year it initiated a defence review but agreed to stand by the Chevaline decision and maintain the nuclear deterrent.

***Swiftsure* Class** It was found that using nuclear submarines was the best means of hunting and destroying other submarines, particularly SSBNs, and in 1973 the first of the new *Swiftsure* SSKNs (nuclear hunter-killer submarines) were under construction, with *Swiftsure* being completed that year and *Sovereign* the following year. They were an updated and much improved *Valiant* class. Although at 4,500 tons dived they were very slightly smaller than the *Valiant* class and with one torpedo tube fewer, they were faster and quieter and could dive to greater depths. They also had a much improved sonar fit.

Firing an Exocet surface-to-surface missile from a frigate
(NP)

Towed Array Sonar

The introduction of towed-array (TA) sonar in the mid 1970s revolutionised anti-submarine warfare against the Soviets. First fitted to SSBNs for self-protection it was successively fitted to SSNs and then ASW frigates. The TA not only enhanced detection ranges by several factors of magnitude because of a dramatic reduction in self-noise of the searching platform, its wide aperture allowed exploitation of the lower frequency (narrowband) noises emanating from opposition submarines' pumps and other rotating machinery. In order to exploit the greater ranges being achieved, there was an explosion of R&D investment in Target Motion Analysis (TMA), beam-forming and signal processing techniques.

Commander Jeff Tall OBE, RN
Director of the Royal Naval Submarine Museum

The system was fitted in place of the second 4.5in gun turret. *Glamorgan*, *Antrim* and *Fife* were to be fitted in turn with the Exocet system.

Exocet Missile System In 1970 it was planned to procure the French Exocet surface-to-surface missile system to help cover the reduction in the Navy's surface capability, consequent on the decision to phase out the carriers. The system was ordered in 1972 and was to be fitted in four of the County class guided missile destroyers, as mentioned above, and frigates.

Sea King Helicopter In 1970 the Westland Sea King all-weather ASW helicopter entered service with the Royal Navy. It was the British built version of the robust Sikorsky helicopter, which had been in service with the US Navy for nearly ten years, and was powered by two Rolls Royce engines. It was an extremely successful helicopter and would serve the navy for well over three decades.

The County Class Anti-Surface Missile System The County class guided missile destroyers did not prove quite as effective as they were designed to be. The four later ships were fitted with the improved Seaslug II missile system but it gave them only a limited anti-surface role and it was decided not to fit the four earlier County class ships with the system. Seaslug was a beam-riding system, with the missile riding up a radar beam locked on to the target. The main problems with Seaslug II as an anti-surface system were due to ground clutter, with wave interference impeding the missile guidance radar at low level.

During the maritime air defence exercise Highwood, in December 1971, three of the County class missile destroyers were 'sunk' or severely 'damaged' by ships acting as Russian missile destroyers. In 1973 *Norfolk* was fitted with the much more effective Exocet anti-surface missile system (see below).

An ASW Sea King
(DD)

PERSONNEL MATTERS

End of the 'Tot' The traditional daily 'tot' of rum, 'up spirits', was finally abolished in August 1970. It was considered that with modern complex high-technology equipment and weapon systems to be operated it made no sense to give men strong spirits at midday. In compensation, bars for senior rates were introduced, though these were supervised. A sailors' fund (the 'Tot' Fund) was set up with a grant of £2.7 million to provide amenities, which were not a proper charge to the defence vote and therefore had to be purchased with non-public funds. The abolition of the 'Tot' was a sensitive subject and was even debated in Parliament but its demise was inevitable.

Two Dolphins In 1970 approval was granted for qualified

officers and men of the Submarine Service to wear the distinctive two dolphins badge on the left breast of their uniforms.

Constrain The concept of centralising and consolidating training into fewer and more efficient training establishments, known as Project Constrain, was introduced in 1970. Training was rationalised into three main branch groups, Operations, Weapons Engineering, and Marine and Hull Engineering. A fourth group covered the rest, including Supply and Secretariat, Regulating, Divisional and Leadership, and Seamanship. The project achieved efficiencies but resulted in the closing of some of the old long-established schools, including HMS *Vernon* (the TAS school) and Whale Island (the home of naval gunnery).

Iveston **Incident** In July 1970 an embarrassing incident occurred on board the minesweeper *Iveston* in Ullapool, which attracted a lot of unfavourable media attention. Five ratings conducted a 'sit-down protest' and had to be arrested. They were eventually dismissed from the Service but the incident acted as a reminder in the fleet of the need to preserve good order and discipline.

Prince Charles In 1971 HRH the Prince of Wales joined the Royal Navy at Britannia Royal Naval College, Dartmouth, as Acting Sub Lieutenant Wales RN. His first appointment was to the *Leander* class frigate *Minerva* in the West Indies. Thirty years later he was to become Patron of the White Ensign Association as a vice admiral.

The PWO Concept By the late 1960s it was apparent that operations officers, with their individual specialist area (gunnery, communications, navigation, TAS (torpedo and anti-submarine warfare), etc), were too narrowly specialised for the conduct of modern naval warfare. This was particularly true in a fast-moving multi-threat environment. In 1968 Admiral Ashmore proposed that seamen officers should discontinue their specialist training in favour of a broader warfare specialisation. Against much opposition from traditionalist officers the concept, known as the PWO (Principal Warfare Officer), was introduced in April 1972.

THE WHITE ENSIGN ASSOCIATION

The demand for the services of the White Ensign Association continued to grow in the 1970s. In April 1970 new pay codes for the Navy were announced, and the Commander Far East Fleet, concerned that all his ratings were then paying income tax and should be saving about £10 a month, invited the Association to visit the Far East and tour the ships providing presentations and advice. A programme of fifteen lectures was carried out.

In 1971 the Association was invited to provide regular lectures for the Staff Course and for the Senior Rates Leadership Course. Association presentations were also added to the curriculum of the Royal Naval College at Dartmouth.

In 1972 the World War II veteran cruiser *Belfast* was gifted

The last Rum Issue on board the assault ship *Intrepid* in the Far East in 1970 (RNM)

Sub Lieutenant Wales RN joins the *Leander* class frigate *Minerva* (NN)

to the Imperial War Museum and moved to a berth in the Pool of London adjacent to the Tower of London. The following year it was agreed that the offices of the White Ensign Association would be moved on board from their offices in the City. This was a most appropriate move as *Belfast* was granted the right to continue to fly the White Ensign. The Royal Marine Band of the Commander in Chief played at a reception onboard, which the Association held in June.

In 1973 Sir John Prideaux succeeded Mr David Robarts as President of the Association and Captain Henry relieved Commander Lamb as the Manager.

The White Ensign

In the early 17th Century the Fleet was divided into three squadrons, Red, Blue and White in that order of seniority, sailing under English ensigns of each colour. By 1653 squadron seniority had become Red, White and Blue, and in 1702 a large red cross was placed on the White Ensign to differentiate it from the plain white French ensign of that time. After British political union in 1707, the Union Flag replaced St George's Cross in the canton of the three ensigns. Following the union with Ireland in 1801 the red diagonals of St Patrick's cross were added to the Union Flag and the three ensigns took their modern form.

At the Battle of Trafalgar in 1805 Nelson, Vice Admiral of the White Squadron, ordered all his fleet to wear the White Ensign, including ships from other squadrons. In 1864 the long outdated squadron system was abandoned and the entire Royal Navy adopted the White Ensign. The Merchant Navy was given the Red Ensign and the Blue Ensign was reserved for civilian manned government ships. In the late 1960s the Royal Australian Navy, Royal New Zealand Navy and Fijian Naval Forces each adopted their own version of the RN's White Ensign. In the 21st century the Royal Navy and Royal Marines continue to sail and to serve under the White Ensign.

Captain Malcolm Farrow OBE, RN
President of the Flag Institute

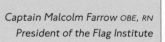

NATO Maritime Strategy in the North Atlantic and Out-of-Area Group Deployments 1975–1979

RISE OF SOVIET NAVAL CHALLENGE – DEFENCE CUTS – THIRD COD WAR – END OF BEIRA PATROL – QUEEN'S JUBILEE FLEET REVIEW – WITHDRAWAL FROM MALTA – OPERATION JOURNEYMAN (FALKLAND ISLANDS)

The war in Vietnam finally ended in 1975 after the fall of Da Nang to the Viet Minh and the surrender of the South to the North. The end of the war was dramatically symbolised by the rescue of the US Ambassador by helicopter from the roof of the US Embassy in Saigon, late in the evening of 29 April. The very last of the Marines evacuated the embassy grounds the following morning. The conflict in Vietnam had been a very long war of attrition, costing the USA many thousands of lives and billions of dollars (US casualties alone amounted to well over 56,000 dead and over 300,000 wounded). Britain had been very wise to avoid involvement despite repeated requests from the USA for allies and support. The Royal Navy, notwithstanding its emphasis on ASW (anti-submarine warfare) in the north-east Atlantic, still possessed deployable forces capable of force projection in the Gulf of Tonkin and the South China Sea and would undoubtedly have been able to play much more than a token role.

The US military had evolved and matured greatly during the course of the eleven-year war. Fundamental errors of defence policy, strategy and tactics were shown up, addressed and in many cases corrected.

The conflict clearly demonstrated the acute lack of modern strike fleet carriers from the outset. This serious handicap was a situation partly engineered by the US Air Force, which had always pressed the case for long-range land-based bombers to the detriment of the US Navy carrier programme. The US Air Force fought several successful congressional campaigns to gain the exclusive right to the strategic bomber role and for the diversion of carrier funds to the development of air force bombers. It used its powerful lobby to undermine the case for expensive modern nuclear strike carriers, which would have consumed a large share of the defence budget and enhanced the strategic value of the US Navy.[1]

Interestingly there were valuable lessons for the British defence establishment, as it was a situation not unlike that to which the Royal Navy was subjected to at a similar time in the early 1960s.

Other Wars and Conflicts Whilst the war in Vietnam was ending in 1975 other conflicts were starting in other parts of the world. Civil war broke out in the Lebanon between Christians and Muslims, as well as in Cambodia as the Khmer Rouge under Pol Pot captured Phnom Penh and seized power. It was to be three years before Vietnam invaded Cambodia to throw out the Khmer Rouge, which had

FIRST SEA LORDS
Admirals Ashmore and Lewin

SECOND SEA LORDS
Admirals Williams and Tait

MANPOWER
77,100

MERCANTILE MARINE
3,628 merchant ships

slaughtered between two and three million people. Whilst in Argentina the ineffectual President Isabel Peron was deposed by the military in 1976. She was replaced by a repressive regime under a junta, composed of the Chiefs of Staff of the armed forces, who commenced the internal 'Dirty War', which was to lead, ultimately, to the Falklands War in 1982.

In the Middle East important changes took place in 1979, with an Islamic revolution in Iran. The Shah of Iran was forced into exile and replaced by Ayatollah Khomeini, who introduced a fundamentalist Islamic state. Across the Iranian border in Iraq, Saddam Hussein became President and was supported by the West. In the same year the Soviet Army invaded Afghanistan, seized Kabul and killed the President, Halizullah Amin, thus starting the long, bloody and ultimately fruitless Russo-Afghan War.

Northern Ireland Nearer home the IRA (Irish Republican Army) started up its campaign of violence again in 1975 with bombings and killings on the mainland, including London and Manchester, as well as in Northern Ireland. The violence and killings escalated with high-profile murders, including that of the British Ambassador to Eire, the British Ambassador to the Netherlands, the senior politician Airey Neave, and on 27 August 1979 Admiral of the Fleet Lord Mountbatten. On the same day the IRA killed eighteen British soldiers at Warrenpoint. Lieutenant Colonel David Blair, responsible for that area, was immediately flown to Warrenpoint by helicopter, and as he went forward to investigate he too was killed by the IRA, taking the total of British servicemen killed in Northern Ireland over the period of ten years to 316.[2]

UK Defence Policy In 1975 the Labour government of Harold Wilson was facing an economic crisis with a collapse in the value of sterling. On 15 April Denis Healey, the Chancellor of the Exchequer, introduced an extremely tight and ambitious budget which he himself described as 'tight and tough'. As well as raising income tax and introducing a wage restraint policy, he aimed to cut back public spending by £900 million. Inevitably defence spending was to bear the brunt, and yet again the Royal Navy was in the front line. The cuts imposed on the Navy were savage. The Defence White Paper of 1976 announced major reductions in the surface fleet. The large amphibious ships *Hermes*, *Bulwark*, *Fearless* and *Intrepid* were not to be replaced, and thus

Britain's vital amphibious warfare capability would be completely phased out. The Royal Marines were to be reduced by one Commando.[3]

The number of destroyers, frigates and mine warfare vessels was to be reduced by one-seventh. This, combined with the decision to cancel the building plans for nine destroyers and frigates, would severely restrict the ASW capability of the Royal Navy in the Atlantic, one of the key components of NATO's maritime strategy. The Royal Navy contributed the largest part of NATO's available maritime forces in the eastern Atlantic and the Channel. To maximise the assignment of the remaining units of the surface fleet to the eastern Atlantic, all destroyers and frigates were to be withdrawn from the West Indies and the Mediterranean. The number of submarines was to be cut by 25 per cent. Refitting was to be concentrated in the royal dockyards.

These cuts were in the face of the stark fact that Britain, still with the largest merchant navy in the world, was completely dependent on its trade with Europe and the rest of the world. Sea lines of communication were crucial to Britain, with 95 per cent of her trade being transported by sea.

The Soviet Navy

As the Royal Navy was being steadily cut back both in size and role, the Soviet Navy in contrast was being built up into a major 'blue water' navy and being increasingly deployed worldwide.

Okean 75 In 1975 the Soviet Navy carried out a major naval deployment, exercise Okean 75, deploying 220 ships and submarines operating with a large number of aircraft. The exercise was widespread, taking place in the Atlantic, Baltic, Mediterranean, Pacific and Indian Ocean, and even involved sending some units into the Gulf of Mexico.

The *Kiev* The following year the Northern Fleet sailed from Murmansk for the annual exercise, which included exercises in the North Sea followed by a passage through the Skagerrak into the Baltic. The great point of interest, however, was the brand new 44,000-ton STOVL (short take off and vertical landing) aircraft carrier *Kiev*, which deployed from the Baltic, sailing through the Bosphorus on 18 July. The ship was classified as a Cruiser to try and avoid infringing the Montreux Convention. The *Kiev* then sailed to Murmansk, closely tailed and observed by NATO ships including the frigate *Torquay*, which shadowed her closely in the Mediterranean.

At the end of May that year the Soviet *Kashin* class guided missile destroyer *Obraztsovj*, bristling with missiles, visited Portsmouth naval base. In 1977 the Soviet Navy did suffer a setback when another *Kashin* class guided missile destroyer *Orel* blew up and sank in the Black Sea.

The huge Soviet submarine fleet was formidably powerful and was already operating in all oceans of the world. When handing over as Chairman of the Military Committee of NATO in 1975, General Johannes Steinhoff claimed he was almost more alarmed by Soviet power politics at sea than

The passing of an era: *Ark Royal* sails past the decommissioned *Eagle* at Devonport shortly before *Eagle* is scrapped (CC)

by the confrontation in central Europe. Certainly Admiral Gorshkov regarded the rapidly expanding Soviet Fleet as the main political instrument to further state interests by dominating the key maritime areas of the world.

The 'Iron Lady' In 1976 Margaret Thatcher spoke out against the Soviet regime and in particular against the unprecedented expansion of the Soviet Navy. She stated, 'The first duty of any Government is to safeguard its people against external aggression. To guarantee the survival of our way of life.' She went on to say: 'A largely land based country like Russia does not need to build the most powerful Navy in the world just to guard its frontiers. No, the Russians are bent on world domination and they are rapidly acquiring the means to become the most powerful imperial nation in the world.'[4] In response the Soviet media bestowed on her the title of 'Iron Lady', a label that was to stick with her.

———•———

Increased NATO Spending In view of the steady increase in Soviet and Warsaw Pact armed forces, in both quantity and quality, the USA urged the UK and European members of NATO to increase defence expenditure. An increase of 3 per cent a year in real terms was finally agreed, with a commitment to bring in a long-term defence programme. As part of this the UK agreed to retain the Royal Marine Commando, which was about to be disbanded, and to retain the commando carrier *Bulwark*.

In 1979, when a Conservative government took over, it approved a necessary, but huge, increase in the pay of the armed forces, which had fallen seriously behind. The increased cost to the defence budget enabled the UK to claim it was meeting the 3 per cent NATO increase in defence expenditure.

The USA also maintained its Strategic Arms Limitation Talks (SALT 2) with the Soviet Union, and there was a hope that success might just enable defence spending to be reduced in the future.

THE FLEET

The fleet of 1975 was changing from its worldwide versatile role to one centred on ASW in conjunction with NATO allies in the eastern Atlantic and European waters. The Navy had the strategic role of providing the UK's nuclear deterrent with its squadron of Polaris submarines (SSBNs), *Resolution, Renown, Repulse* and *Revenge.* There were nine hunter-killer nuclear powered fleet submarines (SSNs) with three more building, and twenty conventional patrol submarines.

Carriers and Cruisers The aircraft carrier *Ark Royal* was still in service but was due to be decommissioned by 1978, and her fixed-wing aircraft, Phantoms and Buccaneers, transferred to the RAF. She was eventually withdrawn from service in 1979.

The old converted helicopter cruisers *Blake* and *Tiger* were equipped with four ASW Sea King helicopters and fitted out

with full command and control facilities. Due to manpower shortages *Blake* would be decommissioned in 1979. The small 'jump jet' (VSTOL) carriers of the *Invincible* class, known for political reasons as the 'through deck cruisers', were planned to join the Fleet from the end of the seventies. They were designed primarily for ASW and command and control duties in the eastern Atlantic, and HM the Queen launched the first of class, *Invincible*, on 3 May 1977 at Vickers Yard at Barrow. *Illustrious*, the second of class, was launched the following year, and *Invincible* was commissioned in 1979.

Amphibious Capability The Royal Navy still retained a powerful amphibious squadron in 1975, which included the

Invincible on trials
(NN)

commando carrier *Hermes*. It was decided however to convert *Hermes* to an anti-submarine helicopter carrier, and the conversion was carried out during her refit in 1976, though she still retained an amphibious capability. The rest of the amphibious squadron included the commando carrier *Bulwark* and the assault ships *Fearless* and *Intrepid*, backed up by six logistic landing ships of the *Knight* class, operated by the Royal Fleet Auxiliary. *Bulwark* was relegated to the Reserve Fleet in 1976 but brought out and prepared for operational service again in 1978 to cover the delay over *Invincible*'s entry into service.

Rest of the Fleet The Royal Navy also possessed a strong fleet of destroyers and frigates, with nine guided missile destroyers, plus seven more building, and sixty-one frigates. The mainstay of the escort fleet consisted of the twenty frigates of the very successful *Leander* class. In addition there were some forty-nine mine counter-measures vessels, fifty-four fleet support ships and just under 400 other minor support vessels.

FIRST SEA LORDS

Admiral Sir Edward Ashmore Edward Beckwith Ashmore was born in County Cork in 1919 and joined the Royal Navy in 1933. During World War II he served in the destroyers *Jupiter* and *Middleton*, the battleship *Duke of York*, the cruisers *Swiftsure* and *Newfoundland* and the aircraft carrier *Implacable* and was awarded the DSC. Later he commanded the frigate *Alert* and was promoted Captain in 1955 (the youngest captain since Beatty). He was Director of the Naval Plans Division in 1960 and was then appointed Director of Plans on the defence staff under Lord Mountbatten.

He was promoted Admiral in 1965 and Assistant Chief of the Defence Staff (Signals) in the MoD. In 1968 he was appointed Vice Chief of the Naval Staff, and in 1971 he became Commander in Chief of the Fleet. After his appointment as First Sea Lord in 1974 he had to implement the cuts in the Royal Navy resulting from the Labour government's defence review. Admiral Lewin relieved him at the beginning of 1977. He had a rather chilly austere presence and a reputation of being a severe admiral.

Admiral Sir Terence Lewin Terry Lewin was born in 1920 and joined the Navy in 1939. During World War II he served in the destroyers *Highlander* and *Ashanti*, where he won the DSC, the cruiser *Belfast* and the battleship *Valiant*. He was a gunnery specialist and commanded the destroyer *Corunna*, the Royal Yacht *Britannia* and the aircraft carrier *Hermes*. Lewin was promoted Rear Admiral in 1968 and appointed Assistant Chief of the Naval Staff (Policy); in that position he had the unenviable task of reducing training and support, which entailed the closing of many shore establishments.

In 1971 he became Vice Chief of the Naval Staff, where he masterminded the introduction of the carrier-borne version of the VTOL (vertical take off and landing) Harrier aircraft, which was eventually to join the Fleet as the Sea

Harrier (SHAR). He also formulated and introduced the system of group deployments for the Fleet whereby powerful task groups were deployed to the Middle East and Far East, a brave move after the Labour government had decided to hasten the withdrawal of all British forces from east of Suez.

He was appointed First Sea Lord in 1977 and served until he became Chief of the Defence Staff in 1979.[5] He had great personal charm and was extremely popular throughout the Fleet. He was elected to the Council of the White Ensign Association and became Chairman in 1983.

OPERATIONS AND DEPLOYMENTS, 1975–1979

Although the whole focus of the Royal Navy was centred on the NATO area and in particular anti-submarine warfare in the eastern Atlantic, there was still an important range of defence commitments around the world to be met.

Hong Kong In Hong Kong, guardship and policing duties were maintained by the Hong Kong Patrol Craft Squadron, consisting of five converted Ton class minesweepers, *Yarnton, Beachampton, Monkton, Wasperton* and *Wolverton*, supported by the converted frigate *Chichester* on station. However a new Hong Kong Defence Agreement was signed on 18 December 1975, and as a result *Chichester* was no longer required. She sailed for the UK on 31 March the following year, leaving the patrol craft of the Hong Kong Squadron to carry out all guardship duties on their own. They carried out sterling work and in 1976 the squadron was awarded the Wilkinson Sword of Peace. It was not until 13 March 1979 that the squadron was reinforced with an ex harbour tug, *Clare*, brought into service as an additional patrol craft.

Antarctic In the Antarctic the ice patrol ship *Endurance* and Naval Party 8901 maintained patrols to protect British interests in the area during the Antarctic summer. She also acted as a survey ship, working closely with the British Antarctic Survey Team.

Gibraltar Gibraltar remained a politically sensitive problem requiring constant and close monitoring. The Royal Navy was obliged to retain a permanent presence in the area to deter Spanish interference, encroachment and general harassment as well as to reassure the Gibraltarians of Britain's continued commitment to Gibraltar. As well as frequent visits by passing warships, there was a frigate kept on station as the Gibraltar Guardship.

Cyprus Following the partitioning of Cyprus in 1974 the United Nations had established a peace-keeping force (UNFICYP), to which Britain was obliged to contribute forces. At the beginning of the year the Royal Marines of 41 Commando formed the backbone of UNFICYP.

In February 1975 the situation in Cyprus deteriorated, and on 6 February the helicopter cruiser *Tiger*, in Gibraltar, was despatched east across the Mediterranean. At the same

Admiral the Lord Lewin (WEA)

time the frigate *Charybdis* was withdrawn from exercises off Lisbon and sent at best speed to join *Tiger* east of Malta. Both ships were supported by the tanker RFA *Olmeda* and closed the coast of Cyprus. The frigate *Ajax* was diverted to Gibraltar to replace *Tiger* for a flag visit to Morocco. On 13 February the Turkish Cypriots declared the northern part of the island a separate state. By the next day the situation had eased sufficiently for the ships to be withdrawn from Cyprus. On 14 April the Royal Marines of 41 Commando left Cyprus and returned to the UK.

The Strategic Nuclear Deterrent Throughout the period the four 7,000-ton Polaris submarines of the *Resolution* class maintained the nation's strategic nuclear deterrent with continuous operational patrols hidden in the depths of the oceans of the world.

Submarine Operations Also throughout the period the patrol submarines and the nuclear fleet submarines conducted many important and dangerous covert operations in northern waters monitoring the Soviet Navy. Such highly classified operations remain shrouded by the Official Secrets Act and cannot be revealed in unclassified documents.

Fishery Protection Squadron Eight converted Ton class patrol vessels of the 'Fish' Squadron, *Bickington, Brinton, Crichton, Cuxton, Hodgeston, Pollington, Shavington* and *Wotton*, carried out the important offshore policing duties. The squadron also safeguarded the gas and oilfield installations when North Sea oil came on stream in 1975. Valuable North Sea oil and gas supplies were to last until the end of the century, and protection of the installations was an important task for the squadron. The Fishery Protection Squadron was awarded the Wilkinson Sword of Peace in 1978.

In view of the increasing importance of British offshore

interests it had been decided to build five new specialist vessels for distant patrols in offshore waters. *Jersey*, completed in 1976, was the first of the new Island class purpose-built offshore patrol vessels (OPVs). The OPVs *Guernsey*, *Shetland*, *Orkney* and *Lindisfarne* joined the Fleet by the end of 1978. Two additional Island class ships, *Anglesey* and *Alderney*, were due to join by the end of 1979.

Suez Canal Mine Clearance: Operation Rheostat II, 8 March – 9 July 1975 In March 1975 the Egyptian government requested further assistance from the UK in clearing mines and war debris from the Suez Canal zone. In compliance the Royal Navy set up Operation Rheostat II, with the minehunter *Hubberston* sailing from the UK on the 8 March. The support ship *Abdiel* and minehunter *Sheraton* followed, sailing for the Mediterranean on 1 April. Clearance work in the Suez Canal started on 4 April and continued through to the 1 June before the canal was rendered safe. Then on 10 June the ships departed and returned to the UK, arriving a month later on 9 July.

Second Group Deployment, Continued: 17 September 1974 – 11 June 1975

At the beginning of 1975 the Second Group Deployment, Task Group (TG) 317.2, consisting of the helicopter cruiser *Blake* (Captain Herbert) the flagship of Vice Admiral Henry Leach, FOF1 (Flag Officer 1st Flotilla), the nuclear-powered fleet submarine *Warspite* and five frigates, *Leander*, *Achilles*, *Diomede*, *Falmouth* and *Lowestoft*, supported by three RFA supply ships and tankers, had dispersed around the Far East. *Falmouth* had been detached to Hong Kong, where her extensive fire damage was being repaired. The Task Group had recovered well from exercise Midlink in the Indian Ocean and the diplomatic furore following its visit to Cape Town. In February the flagship, *Blake*, sailed from Manila and rendezvoused with SEATO (South East Asia Treaty Organisation) ships for exercise Sea Fox, off the Philippines.

Cambodia: Operation Faldage, 10–11 March 1975 In the middle of the work-up phase of exercise Sea Fox, on 10 March an immediate operational signal was received on board *Blake*. She was detached from the exercise, together with the support tanker RFA *Olna*, to proceed at best speed to the Gulf of Siam to stand by off the coast of Cambodia. Her task, codenamed Operation Faldage, was to rescue British nationals following the outbreak of civil war and the reign of terror of the Khmer Rouge there. Admiral Leach was immediately transferred from his flagship to *Leander* by jackstay to continue with exercise Sea Fox. *Blake* then departed from the exercise and steamed at full speed, achieving twenty-eight knots, for the port of Sihanoukville on the coast of Cambodia. She arrived two days later off Kong Pong Som. *Blake* and her helicopters of 820 NAS (Naval Air Squadron) were able to assist in the protection of British nationals and Commonwealth personnel, most of whom were eventually evacuated by RAF Hercules aircraft. It was a timely rescue as a short while later the Khmer Rouge

captured Phnom Penh and took over the whole country, slaughtering hundreds of thousands indiscriminately. On completion of Operation Faldage *Blake* sailed south for Singapore, arriving ahead of the ships returning there from exercise Sea Fox.

Vietnam: Operation Stella, 29 March – 26 April 1975 At the end of the March 1975 Viet Minh captured Da Nang, and it was necessary to launch Operation Stella to rescue thousands of British and Commonwealth personnel from Vietnam. The frigates *Lowestoft* and *Achilles*, joined by the frigate *Mermaid* from Singapore and supported by the tanker RFA *Green Rover*, steamed north for the coast of Vietnam and Cambodia. Off the coast they were in dangerous waters and were constantly overflown by Mig jet aircraft. Over a period of almost thirty days they steamed up and down the coast as refugees went from port to port in chaos. Finally Saigon fell on 29 April, when the US Ambassador was dramatically rescued by helicopter, and the following day South Vietnam surrendered. On completion of Operation Stella the British ships left Cambodian waters and returned to Singapore.

Return Leg *Blake* and her consorts sailed from Singapore on 3 April and after conducting exercise Penangex headed west across the Indian Ocean. The return leg posed a problem, as the Suez Canal remained closed, whilst on the other hand there was absolutely no possibility of using any South African port en route following the political debacle on the outward leg. After a brief visit to the Seychelles, the group steamed south to round the Cape of Good Hope and head up into the South Atlantic. It was a long three-and-a-half-week passage with no port visits whilst rounding the Cape.

Task Group ships on passage home
(JAR)

BRAZEX   19th May 1975

End of the Beira Patrol, 25 June 1975 In the Indian Ocean the Beira Patrol, which had become intermittent, was still endeavouring to enforce the UN embargo on oil to Rhodesia. The frigates from TG 317.2 had taken their turns to carry out spells on the patrol, watching for ships attempting to evade the embargo. After they had departed from the area other ships resumed the patrol. It was continued until finally, on the day Mozambique became independent and agreed not to allow the shipment of oil to Rhodesia, the government decided to end the patrol. On 25 June 1975 the frigate *Salisbury* was ordered to discontinue the patrol and withdraw from the Mozambique Channel.

Thus ended a ten-year patrol carried out by seventy-six ships of the Royal Navy, including aircraft carriers, at a cost well in excess of £100 million. The success or value of the patrol was much debated, with few firm conclusions. The highly visible naval blockade carried out by the Royal Navy, assisted by the RAF, did however save the UK from being forced to take direct military action in Rhodesia, which would have been a hugely difficult and controversial mission.

Exercise Brazex 75, May 1975 After sailing north-west into the South Atlantic the group rendezvoused with the aircraft carrier *Ark Royal* and her escorts, including the guided missile destroyer *Hampshire* and RFA *Resource*, off the coast of Brazil in May. The *Ark Royal* group had just completed a Westlant Deployment where together with the assault ship *Fearless* they had carried out live weapon firings on the American Atlantic Fleet weapon range. After both groups had rendezvoused they conducted joint exercises, codenamed Brazex 75, with the Brazilian Navy.

On completion of the exercises most of the ships put into Rio de Janeiro, with some being detached to Salvador and Santos. On sailing from Brazilian ports the whole group assembled and, following further exercises with the Brazilian Navy, headed north.

After the major exercise Last Chance (simulating an escalating war situation) on 1 June, the ships visited Gibraltar before finally returning to the UK later in the month to complete a busy nine-month deployment.

Exercise Brazex 75 in the South Atlantic: formation review
(JAR)

The combined Westlant and Group Deployment Task Force heads for the UK
(NN)

Frigates receiving a mail delivery on the Beira Patrol
(JAR)

The Beira bucket, handed from ship to ship on taking up the patrol and painted with ships' crests
(RNM)

Northern Ireland

The IRA's bombing and murdering campaign in Northern Ireland resumed on 16 January 1975, and the security operations Operation Grenada and Operation Interknit continued. In the course of 1975 the Royal Navy carried out forty-seven patrols off the coast of Northern Ireland: most were conducted by the MCMVs (mine counter-measures vessels) of the Northern Ireland Squadron, but there were also some by the submarine tender *Wakeful* as well as four patrols conducted by RFA vessels. In addition submarines conducted covert surveillance operations from time to time. Meanwhile on Carlingford Lough the auxiliary tenders *Alert* and *Vigilant* maintained their constant anti-terrorist patrols.

The Royal Marines continued to fulfil their share of internal security duties. 40 Commando was deployed from 24 February to 24 June and then, when Protestant revenge killings escalated, 42 Commando carried out a short spell of reinforcement from 6 October to 5 November.

In 1976 the Royal Navy carried out forty-one patrols off the coast of Northern Ireland. *Abdiel* and RNR (Royal Naval Reserve) units backed up the MCMVs on patrol. On Carlingford Lough *Tenacity* supported the patrol vessels *Alert* and *Vigilant*, and three patrols were carried out by MCMVs.

42 Commando returned to Northern Ireland on 27 February 1976 and resumed security operations in South Armagh. On 11 June the Provisional IRA launched a mortar attack on the Royal Marine base in Andersontown; fortunately there were no casualties and little damage was done. 42 Commando remained in the Province until 24 June.

Operation Shoveller On 16 June 1976 a security operation, codenamed Shoveller, was commenced in Londonderry with a detachment of Royal Marines providing river patrols in the area. This replaced the security cover previously provided by *Rame Head*, which had been withdrawn from Northern Ireland.

40 Commando returned to south Armagh on 16 August and resumed security patrols until 15 December. Over that year (1976) the Royal Marines suffered eight casualties on security duties in Northern Ireland.

Belize, 1975–1976 Belize remained an area of concern, and Britain, fully aware of her responsibilities to the small vulnerable country, maintained a frigate on the West Indies station on standby as Belize Guardship throughout the year. In November 1975 additional Guatemalan troops carried out manoeuvres close to the border and a threat of invasion prompted an increase in the defensive posture. On 11 November additional army and RAF units reinforced the garrison and a second frigate on the West Indies station was brought to five days' alert status. Although the threat remained for some time, the reinforcements were sufficient to deter invasion. Slowly, as tension reduced, the reinforcements were withdrawn, and by March 1976 only one frigate remained on standby, to be within five days' steaming of Belize.

Third Group Deployment (Task Group 317.3), 22 July 1975 – 14 April 1976

Building on the success of the first two Group Deployments, the Third Group Deployment (TG 317.3) was planned as an ambitious circumnavigation of the globe. Rear Admiral John Fieldhouse, FOF2, flying his flag in the guided missile destroyer *Glamorgan*, commanded the Third Group Deployment. The frigates *Ajax*, *Berwick*, *Plymouth* and *Rothesay* escorted her. A fifth frigate, *Llandaff*, was scheduled to join in Gibraltar. The tankers RFAs *Tidespring* and *Gold Rover* and the supply ship RFA *Tarbatness* supported the group.

The Task Group left the UK on 22 July 1975, and sailed south for Gibraltar. The group, without *Glamorgan*, then departed from Gibraltar on 28 July heading east for Malta. *Glamorgan* had suffered from gearbox trouble and was delayed in Gibraltar for repairs. When the problem was rectified the flagship sailed and rejoined the group off Malta. After exercising with units of the US Navy 6th Fleet, including the strike carrier USS *John F Kennedy*, ships of the

The Third Group Deployment sails from the UK (NN)

group were able to shadow and observe Soviet warships including the carrier *Leningrad* off the Libyan coast.

The Suez Canal had been opened, thanks to the clearance work by the Royal Navy, but as a precautionary measure *Ajax* was sent on ahead, followed a short while later by the rest of the group, clearing into the Red Sea by 17 August. In the Arabian Sea, the group exercised with the US Navy 7th Fleet and also took part in the important CENTO (Central Treaty Organisation) exercise Midlink. On completion of the exercises the Task Group sailed on to Singapore before dispersing about the Far East for various port visits and exercises with other navies.

Exercise Tasmanex In October the group joined up with the Royal Australian Navy, and the combined group conducted joint exercises as they transited the Torres Strait and Great Barrier Reef on their way to Australia. The US Navy, Royal Canadian Navy and Royal New Zealand Navy then joined them for the major eleven-day exercise Tasmanex, which lasted into January 1976.

Exercise Valiant Heritage, March 1976 After Tasmanex and a round of port visits the group headed north-east for Hawaii. They then exercised in and around Pearl Harbor working up, mostly with US Navy submarines and aircraft in preparation for the major exercise with the US Navy. Exercise Valiant Heritage, involving over forty ships from the US Navy, Royal Navy, Royal Australian Navy and Royal Canadian Navy, started on 2 March. The US nuclear strike carrier uss *Enterprise* was the largest ship involved.

A notable success was achieved on the very first day when, much to the surprise of the USA, *Glamorgan* engaged and shot down a distant drone target with a Sea Slug missile (the Americans were to be equally surprised, and very grateful to the Royal Navy, some fifteen years later when in another incident a British destroyer was to save a US battleship by shooting down an incoming enemy missile). The exercise was a total success, with the US Navy being very favourably impressed with the professionalism of the Royal Naval operational procedures and tactics. Following debriefing in San Diego the group steamed south-east for the Panama Canal, which was transited on 24 March. After various very enjoyable visits in the West Indies the group headed east-north-east across the Atlantic, arriving back in the UK on 14 April 1976.[6]

The Third Cod War,
15 November 1975 – 1 June 1976

In November 1975 Iceland unilaterally extended her fishing limits out to 200 miles, thus starting the Third Cod War. Britain immediately took steps to protect her fishing vessels in the area, and defensive operations were set in hand. The support vessel *Lloydsman* arrived in the area on 19 November. Two days later the gunboat *Tyr* started cutting the warps of British trawlers, and three days after that an RAF Nimrod maritime patrol aircraft (MPA) undertook the first aerial surveillance sorties over the area. Meanwhile the frigate *Leopard* stood by to enter the disputed waters.

Operation Dewey Following the harassment of several British trawlers by Icelandic gunboats, the Royal Navy launched Operation Dewey on 25 November, and later that day the gunboat *Aegir* cut the warps of the trawler *William Wilberforce*. Four days later the frigates *Falmouth* and *Brighton*, supported by RFA *Tidepool* and chartered defence tugs, arrived in the area and relieved the frigate *Leopard*. The weather deteriorated and no fishing took place for several days. Then on 2 December the *Arvakur* cut the warps of the *Port Vale*, and the next day the *Aegir* cut the warps of the *Boston Comanche*. Three days later Icelandic gunboats

An Icelandic gunboat attempts to ram the frigate *Bacchante* (Captain Dunn)
(NN)

The Icelandic gunboat sheers off
(NN)

Heading off an Icelandic gunboat
(KR)

The frigate *Scylla* (Captain Checksfield) manoeuvres to shield a trawler
(NN)

attempted flanking attacks on many of the fifty British trawlers fishing in the disputed waters. The gunboat *Thor* managed to cut a warp of the *Ross Ramilles* and engaged in dangerous manoeuvres with *Brighton* before colliding with the defence tug *Euroman*. *Thor* then threatened to open fire on any British vessels within range. When she started to uncover her guns, *Brighton* warned *Thor* that she would return fire with her much heavier guns.

The *Thor* Incident Other attacks took place during the day and a number of warps were cut. On 11 December *Thor* had a run-in with three British vessels and after colliding with the defence tug *Lloydsman* fired a shot across her bow. A short while later, after a further collision, *Thor* fired more shots, and the newly arrived frigate *Galatea* hastened to the area. *Thor* returned to base for repairs to her collision damage.

On 12 December the Icelandic government raised the issue with the UN and with NATO, but the incident was not considered to be a threat to international peace. In the disputed waters the frigates *Leander* and *Lowestoft* relieved *Falmouth* and *Galatea*. Whilst the three frigates on station did their best to protect the many trawlers, the gunboats still managed to elude them from time to time and cut the trawlers' warps. On 20 December the frigate *Andromeda* arrived in the area, relieving *Leander* and *Brighton* to return to UK for Christmas.

After a quiet period over Christmas the Icelandic gunboats were out at sea again harassing British trawlers. In an incident on 28 December, *Andromeda* was protecting two trawlers when the gunboat *Tyr* rammed her. On 3 January *Aegir* managed to cut the warps of two trawlers, and four days later three gunboats closed in to attack more trawlers. This time *Thor* rammed *Andromeda* but, owing to skilful ship handling, serious damage was averted. *Leander* then relieved *Andromeda*, and on 9 January *Leander* and the damaged *Thor* collided. *Thor* was further damaged by the second incident and needed repairs, which prevented her from attacking more trawlers for a while.

Hostilities Recommenced in 1976 Incidents at sea quietened down for a short period during diplomatic negotiations within NATO, and HM ships were withdrawn from the area on 20 January. The talks continued through to 5 February, when they broke up without resolution, and defensive operations were resumed in Icelandic waters. Despite the negotiations, Icelandic gunboats had continued to harass British trawlers and several had their warps cut. Accordingly *Juno* and *Diomede*, supported by RFA *Olwen*, resumed protection duties on 6 February. Almost immediately *Juno* and *Tyr* were involved in a collision whilst *Tyr* was attempting to cut the warps of the *Ross Altair*.

For the next few weeks the frigates and defence tugs were hard pressed to foil concerted attacks by up to four Icelandic gunboats at a time, including the powerful new gunboat *Baldur*. On 11 February the *Baldur* outmanoeuvred the frigate *Lowestoft* and managed to cut the warps of several trawlers, but the next day the *Baldur* collided with *Diomede*.

The frigate *Falmouth* (Commander Plumer) with her damaged bow
(KR)

The damaged frigate *Diomede* (Captain McQueen)
(NN)

The frigates *Scylla* and *Bacchante* relieved *Juno* and *Diomede* in the middle of February and were then involved in a run of attacks, warp cuttings and minor collisions.

On 18 February *Thor* deliberately rammed *Lowestoft*, and the next day *Aegir* cut the warps of the trawler *Royal Lincs*. The frigate *Yarmouth* arrived to relieve the damaged *Lowestoft* and entered straight into a period of intensive harassment by Icelandic gunboats with many collisions, mostly minor but some very dangerous. On 24 February *Yarmouth* collided with *Thor* and substantially damaged her. The remaining gunboats continued to harass the trawlers and cut their warps whenever they got a chance.

The next significant collision occurred on 24 February when *Baldur* and *Yarmouth* collided, causing damage to the bow of the frigate, which necessitated her return to the UK for repairs in a drydock. The frigate *Naiad* sailed to take her place. Other ships, including the frigates *Lincoln* and *Jaguar*, were prepared for operations with strengthened bows and fore sections. The frigates *Mermaid*, *Juno*, *Diomede* and *Galatea* arrived in early March to relieve the ships on station. The frigates were all soon in action, shielding trawlers from repeated attacks from four Icelandic gunboats, and collisions became commonplace as ships tried to outmanoeuvre each other. Most collisions were minor but in some cases damage inflicted on the frigates required extensive repairs. In a collision with *Baldur*, *Diomede* sustained a twelve-foot gash down her port side, fortunately well above the waterline.

Talks Continued in the Spring At the end of March the frigates *Scylla*, *Bacchante*, *Tartar* and *Salisbury* arrived to relieve the ships still on duty in the area. Special tactics were evolved to fend off attacks from *Baldur*. On 1 April *Tyr* was involved in seven collisions with *Salisbury* and *Tartar*, and on the next day *Andromeda* arrived back in the area.

Throughout the rest of April and May the relentless game of cat and mouse continued, with the Icelandic gunboats seeking every opportunity to slip past the defending frigates and attack the British trawlers. Whilst a great many attacks were successfully fended off, quite a few trawlers had their warps cut, but the gunboats did not manage to board or arrest any of them, despite an attempt by *Aegir* to arrest the *Primella*. Inevitably collisions continued to take place, though with few deliberate ramming attacks.

A number of serious collisions happened on 6 May and *Tyr* and *Falmouth* both sustained serious damage, *Mermaid* was badly damaged by *Baldur*, and *Odinn* and the frigate *Gurkha* collided four times. The last collision occurred between *Aegir* and *Tartar* on 26 May.

End of the Third Cod War Finally agreement was reached between the two governments on 31 May. The dispute ended on 1 June 1976 and Operation Dewey was suspended.

The Third Cod War had been the most hazardous, and during the dispute there had been fifty collisions, some highly dangerous. Forty-one warps had been cut, though trawling gear had been recovered on eighteen occasions. Twenty-one frigates had been deployed and fifteen of those had been involved in collisions.[7]

1976 Westlant Deployment On 9 January 1976 *Bulwark* embarked 40 Commando by 848 NAS helicopter transfer off Plymouth, and set course west across the Atlantic for the annual major Westlant Deployment. It was to be her final deployment.

The following month *Ark Royal* sailed from Devonport to follow her across the Atlantic. First, though, *Ark Royal*, accompanied by *Blake* and two RFA support ships, steamed south for the regular exercise Springtrain before heading across the Atlantic to the US naval base at Roosevelt Roads in Puerto Rico. Embarked on board was a BBC TV film crew preparing a documentary series entitled *Sailor*.

Bulwark on her last deployment
(RNM)

USS *Nimitz* and *Argonaut* during exercise Safe Pass
(NN)

Bicentenary display on the flight deck of *Ark Royal*
(CC)

On 3 March *Ark Royal* sailed for the major NATO exercise Safe Pass and joined the US carriers USS *Nimitz*, *America* and *Franklin D. Roosevelt* using the Rodman bombing ranges. *Bulwark* in the meantime took part in exercise Rum Punch on the island of Vieques, close to Puerto Rico. On completion of the exercises the aircraft carriers headed for a break and a maintenance period in Mayport. After Mayport, *Ark Royal* visited Norfolk, Virginia, before sailing south to Fort Lauderdale for the 4 July celebrations. 1976 was the bicentenary of American Independence, and the Americans laid on a great deal of lavish entertainment for their British guests. To commemorate the occasion *Ark Royal* prepared a '1776–1976' flight deck display. On completion the carrier set course east for the return passage

The aircraft carrier *Ark Royal* in the Atlantic
(RNM)

across the Atlantic, arriving back in Devonport on 16 July.

Following her return home to the UK, *Bulwark* was paid off and placed in the Reserve Squadron. She was however, to be brought out of reserve two years later and prepared for operational service to cover the delay in commissioning *Invincible*.

South Atlantic Deterrent Operation, 25 February – 4 April 1976 Following intelligence of Argentine naval and military deployments, and the severing of diplomatic relations at ambassadorial level between Argentina and Britain, plans were considered for reinforcing the Falkland Islands. On 17 February the Argentine destroyer *Admiral Storni* intercepted and opened fire on the British

research ship ss *Shackleton* in Antarctic waters eighty miles south of the Falkland Islands. The frigate *Eskimo* was then despatched south from the West Indies station, and after refuelling from the fleet tanker RFA *Tidesurge* she steamed south at full speed for the Falkland Islands. The frigate *Chichester*, returning to the UK from Hong Kong, was diverted west in the South Atlantic towards the Falkland Islands. On 24 March Isabel Peron was ousted by a military coup in Argentina and replaced by a military junta. *Eskimo* remained in the area until 4 April, when it became clear that the situation had stabilised and there was no longer a direct threat against the Falkland Islands. *Eskimo* was then withdrawn from the area and steamed north back to the West Indies station.

The 1976 Group Deployment The Fourth Group Deployment was planned for April 1976, to be led to the Far East by FOF1. In the event the deployment had to be shelved owing to the pressure of other fleet and NATO commitments, not least the requirement to provide escorts for the Third Cod War as well as the need to repair the frigates damaged in Icelandic waters. Instead the Naval Staff planned to send a short thirteen-week deployment to the Middle East in the autumn to coincide with the principal annual CENTO exercise Midlink.

The Lebanon, 17–22 June 1976 Civil war broke out in the Lebanon on 13 April 1976 after a massacre of Palestinians by the Phalange extremists. The war escalated in violence, with Beirut being steadily torn apart in street battles. The following month Syrian troops crossed the border, and at the beginning of June they joined in the war attacking Palestinians. On 16 June the US Ambassador in Beirut was kidnapped and murdered and foreign nationals started to panic. Two British frigates, *Exmouth* and *Mermaid*, were immediately ordered to the area to stand by to evacuate British nationals. RFAs *Grey Rover* and *Stromness* supported the frigates, whilst RFA *Engadine*, which was in Gibraltar with 826 Naval Air Squadron embarked, was brought to immediate readiness to reinforce the group. The situation then eased and the ships were withdrawn on 22 June.

The Loss of HMS *Fittleton*, **20 September 1976** A relatively minor though none the less tragic event happened in the North Sea on 20 September 1976. The incident occurred during the major NATO naval exercise Teamwork, which involved 300 warships. Part of the Royal Navy's contribution included the 10th MCM Squadron, consisting of seven Ton class minesweepers manned by members of the Royal Naval Reserve. The minesweepers rendezvoused with the Admiral Commanding Reserves (ACR), embarked in the frigate *Mermaid*, and executed a series of manoeuvres.

At one stage the Ton class minesweeper *Fittleton* closed on *Mermaid* for a jackstay transfer, but before transfer lines were secured she suddenly surged ahead and almost immediately swung sharply to starboard right under the bows of *Mermaid*. The impact when *Mermaid* struck her rolled *Fittleton* completely over, and she sank with a loss of twelve lives.[8]

Reduced Group Deployment (Task Group 317.4), 25 September – 21 December 1976

Following the cancellation of the main Group Deployment to the Far East in the spring of 1976, the Naval Staff deployed a smaller task force (TG 317.4) to the Middle East in the autumn. The Task Group was led by FOF1, Rear Admiral Morton, flying his flag in the guided missile destroyer *Antrim* accompanied by her sister ship *Devonshire* and the frigates *Naiad, Bacchante, Charybdis* and *Yarmouth*, supported by RFAs *Olna* and *Stromness*.

Lisbon The Task Group sailed from Portsmouth on 25 September 1976 and headed out to rendezvous with the carrier *Ark Royal* on her completion of the major NATO exercise Teamwork. The group of ships then set course south down to Lisbon for a three-day visit, before transiting through the Straits of Gibraltar into the Mediterranean. On sailing from Lisbon, *Devonshire* had been suffering problems with her boilers and so was detached from the group and returned to the UK for repairs.

Exercise Display Determination Once in the Mediterranean the group took part in exercise Display Determination. This was a major NATO exercise involving over sixty ships including four aircraft carriers, *Ark Royal*, USS *Nimitz*, USS *America* and FS *Clemenceau*.

Into the Indian Ocean The exercise was completed on 10 October and the group, with RFA *Black Rover* and *Devonshire* having rejoined, headed east for the Suez Canal. After transiting through the canal, the Task Group divided into two task units as they steamed south: the main Task Unit arrived in Mombasa on 22 October whilst *Antrim* and *Naiad* and RFA *Black Rover* visited the Seychelles.

Exercise Midlink The ships sailed at the beginning of November and rendezvoused with the submarine *Osiris* on 7 November. After a brief pre-exercise briefing in Karachi, the Task Group participated with ships of the US and Pakistani navies in the second phase of the important

Exercise Locked Gate On arrival in the approaches to the Straits of Gibraltar on 9 February the group carried out exercise Locked Gate, an exercise designed to close the entrance to the Mediterranean in the event of war and prevent Soviet ships and submarines from breaking out into the Atlantic. On completion of the exercise the ships sailed into Gibraltar for a short break.

Across the Atlantic On sailing from Gibraltar on 14 February the group set course west across the Atlantic. The ships arrived in Roosevelt Roads and West Palm Beach at the end of February for a short two-day break.

Weapon Training The ships then had an intensive period of exercises and live weapon firing on the ranges of the US Atlantic Fleet Weapon Training Facility. After six days of weapon training, the ships returned to Roosevelt Roads on 5 March for a two-week AMP (assisted maintenance period). On completion of the AMP, the ships sailed on 21 March for a second session on the Weapon Training Facility.

Various Port Visits At the end of March the ships dispersed for visits to different ports including Barbados, St Lucia, Trinidad and Martinique before heading south for Rio de Janeiro and Buenos Aires.

Exercise Brazex On 18 April the group sailed for exercise Brazex with the Brazilian Navy. On completion of the exercise *Tiger* and escorts returned briefly to Rio de Janeiro.

Return Leg On sailing from Rio de Janeiro on 29 April, *Tiger* and the main group set course east across the South Atlantic for Dakar. At the same time the detached frigates left South America and transited the Atlantic via Funchal for a brief refuelling stop. After a four-day visit to Dakar the Task Group sailed on 14 May for passage back to UK. The ships of the Task Group arrived back in Devonport on 23 May, in plenty of time to prepare for the Silver Jubilee Fleet Review at Spithead the following month.

Tiger leads the Fourth Group Deployment across the Atlantic
(RNM)

CENTO naval exercise Midlink. The exercise ended on 19 November and the ships returned to Karachi two days later for post-exercise briefing.

Passage Home The Task Group departed from Karachi on 23 November and split up for visits, with *Antrim* and the main group sailing for Bandar Abbas, whilst other ships visited Muscat and ports in the Gulf. *Antrim* left Bandar Abbas at the end of November and the group transited through the Suez Canal before visiting Alexandria on 8 December. On leaving Alexandria two days later, the Task Group headed straight for home with just a brief stop in Gibraltar before arriving back in the UK on 21 December.

Fourth Major Group Deployment (Task Group 317.5), 25 January – 23 May 1977

The fourth major Group Deployment (TG 317.5) was commanded by Rear Admiral Martyn Wemyss, FOF2, flying his flag in the helicopter cruiser *Tiger*, escorted by the frigates *Antelope*, *Aurora*, *Jupiter* (Captain 7th Frigate Squadron), *Euryalus*, *Ariadne* and *Danae*. The group included the nuclear fleet submarine *Churchill* and was supported by the tankers RFAS *Tidepool* and *Green Rover* and the store ship RFA *Tarbatness*.

Departure The group sailed from Devonport on 25 January 1977 and headed through the Bay of Biscay, conducting three days of 'shake-down' weapon training in heavy seas as they made their way south.

> **Submarines Operations, 1977: The SSN *Swiftsure***
>
> *Swiftsure* (Commander John Speller OBE, RN) was the first of this very successful class of nuclear attack submarines (SSNs) and was specially equipped for intelligence gathering in 1976.
>
> In 1977 she took part in three ground-breaking intelligence gathering patrols, the results of which provided an invaluable insight into the operational capability of the Soviet Navy.
>
> She was the first Royal Navy submarine to deploy a new tactical towed sonar array; she provided outstanding acoustic intelligence data, unobtainable by any other platform.
>
> These long patrols – without support and at long range from friendly bases – proved the ability of the *Swiftsure* class to operate successfully, undetected in a hostile environment, in close contact with enemy maritime forces, and to bring back a wealth of unique intelligence.

Silver Jubilee Fleet Review: Spithead, 28 June 1977 The Queen's Silver Jubilee Fleet Review was held in the Solent off Spithead on Tuesday 28 June 1977. The big ships present consisted of the aircraft carriers *Ark Royal* (flagship of the Commander in Chief, Admiral Sir Henry Leach), *Hermes* (flagship of Rear Admiral Staveley) and the Australian carrier HMAS *Melbourne*. The helicopter cruisers *Tiger* and *Blake* were also there. Many other warships arrived in the Solent and anchored in set lines for the review. It was the biggest Fleet Review since the Coronation Review in 1953.

Her Majesty the Queen arrived in the evening of 27 June and embarked in the Royal Yacht *Britannia*. The next day, after a twenty-one-gun salute, the Royal Yacht, with Her Majesty on board, sailed out of Portsmouth harbour led by the Trinity House vessel THV *Patricia*. Then, on a cold blustery day, Her Majesty spent two hours reviewing the assembled warships, sailing slowly up and down the lines of 180 ships drawn up in the Solent.

Sadly the planned fly-past of 150 aircraft, including over 100 from the Fleet Air Arm, had to be cancelled because of the low cloud cover. Instead a much reduced fly-past of ninety helicopters took place.

The following day the fleet weighed anchor and sailed out into the Channel. The fleet flagship, *Ark Royal*, then led a steam-past of sixty warships, to cheer and bid farewell to Admiral Sir Edward Ashmore, the outgoing Chief of the

The fly-past of
ninety helicopters
(RNM)

The ship's company
of *Glamorgan*
stands to attention
as the Royal Yacht
passes to starboard
(NN)

The public watching
the Silver Jubilee
Fleet Review at
Spithead, 28 June
1977
(RNM)

Defence Staff, who was embarked in the destroyer *Birmingham*.

The Silver Jubilee Fleet Review was a great success and despite the weather proved to be a very popular event, drawing many crowds of spectators to Portsmouth and the Solent.

Group Deployment Task Group 317.6, 5 September 1977 – 20 April 1978

The next planned Group Deployment was for a seven-and-a-half-month voyage to the Far East and Australia. TG 317.6 was led by Rear Admiral Wemyss, FOF2, flying his flag in the helicopter cruiser *Tiger* with the Sea King helicopters of 826 NAS embarked. The rest of the group included the frigates of the 4th Frigate Squadron, *Cleopatra*, *Amazon*, *Mohawk*, *Zulu* and *Rhyl*, and the nuclear submarine *Dreadnought*. The tankers RFAS *Tidepool* and *Grey Rover* and the replenishment ships RFAS *Regent* and *Tarbatness* supported the group.

Departure *Tiger*, *Rhyl* and the RFA vessels sailed from Portsmouth on 5 September 1977 and headed down the Channel to rendezvous with the other frigates sailing from Devonport later the same day. After a period of shake-down weapon training in the Bay of Biscay the Task Group headed south, arriving in Gibraltar on 15 September.

Exercise Display Determination On sailing from Gibraltar the group took part in the important exercise on NATO's southern flank, Display Determination. On completion of the exercise on 5 October the group dispersed for various port visits. *Tiger*, escorted by *Amazon*, visited Istanbul, whilst *Cleopatra* and *Mohawk* visited Varna, and *Zulu* and *Rhyl* visited Piraeus.

Passage through the Canal The Task Group headed for the Suez Canal, but *Dreadnought* was refused permission to pass down it and had to be withdrawn from the group. *Tiger* and *Amazon* transited through the Canal on 17 October, with the other ships coming through several days later. Once in the Red Sea the ships of the group dispersed for different port visits in the Gulf before sailing on to Karachi.

Exercise Midlink *Tiger* sailed from Karachi on 7 November, and the whole Task Group took part in the annual exercise Midlink. The exercises lasted for twelve days, and on their completion FOF2 returned to the UK. The group went on to participate in exercise Compass 77 with the US Navy, including the carrier USS *Midway*, followed by exercise Sindex 77 with the Royal Australian Navy.

Far East Visits Exercise Sindex 77 was completed on 9 December and the group dispersed for individual port visits. *Tiger* proceeded to Fremantle for four days before going on to Sydney for an AMP. FOF2 rejoined his flagship on 21 January, and two days later *Tiger* sailed for Brisbane. *Cleopatra* had an AMP in Hong Kong whilst *Amazon* had her AMP in Singapore. Other ships visited Geraldton, Adelaide, Melbourne, Bunbury, Geelong, Albany, Cairns, Tokyo, Yok, Pusan, Kagoshima and Shimoneski.

Return Leg The Task Group assembled at Manila on 17 February and five days later sailed for Hong Kong, with *Cleopatra* and *Rhyl* detaching to Subic Bay. After Hong Kong the group arrived in Singapore on 3 March for a self-maintenance period (SMP), whilst the detached frigates visited Bangkok. The ships then set course west across the Indian Ocean for the homeward passage, calling in at Bombay en route.

The group transited through the Canal on 6 April and after a brief two-day visit to Malta continued the passage home, arriving in the Channel on 19 April, when *Zulu* detached for Rosyth. The ships of the 4th Frigate Squadron entered Devonport and the rest of the group continued to Portsmouth, entering harbour the next day, 20 April.

South Atlantic Operation: Operation Journeyman, 25 November – 19 December 1977 On 6 January 1977 an Argentine camp was discovered on South Thule by the ice patrol ship *Endurance*. The discovery was reported and monitored by *Endurance* with Naval Party 8901 embarked. Further talks over the Falkland Islands were initiated with the Argentine government, as there were real concerns for the future safety of those remote islands. In September the Argentine Navy started to harass fishing vessels in the waters off the Falkland Islands, claiming that they were fishing in Argentine waters. In one incident an Argentine warship opened fire on a Bulgarian fishing vessel, causing one casualty. The next move by the Argentine Navy was to cut off the fuel supply to the Falkland Islands, as well as refusing to fly the British flag when in Falkland waters. In November the Argentine Navy was preparing for naval exercises in the area, and in the UK the JIC (Joint Intelligence Committee) advised the government of a direct threat to the islands. In response the government approved Operation Journeyman, authorising the First Sea Lord, Admiral Sir Terence Lewin, to reinforce the Falkland Islands.

The Commander in Chief, Admiral Sir Henry Leach, ordered a small naval task force of two frigates, *Alacrity* and *Phoebe*, and a nuclear-powered submarine, *Dreadnought*, for operations in the South Atlantic. On 21 November *Dreadnought* was deployed to patrol the approaches to Port Stanley and the Falkland Islands. The two frigates, supported by a tanker, RFA *Olwen* and a replenishment ship, RFA *Resurgent*, sailed in secret from Devonport on 25 November and reached a holding position some 1,000 miles north-east of the Falklands (40° south, 40° west) on 13 December. In this position they were able to provide an efficient communications link for *Dreadnought*, which was deployed forward in the Falklands area.

By 19 December it was considered that the immediate threat had reduced and it was safe to withdraw the Task Force from its holding position. The squadron was ordered to return covertly to the UK, and the frigates headed back via Funchal whilst the nuclear submarine returned directly, calling in only briefly at Gibraltar on the way. The whole deployment was kept secret. (Five years later the two

Exercise Fleetex The Task Group arrived in Bermuda on 24 June and four days later sailed for Cartagena, with *Hermione* and *Leander* visiting St Domingo and Curaçao. It then transited through the Panama Canal on 9 July, with *Juno* and *Birmingham* following on two days later. Out in the Pacific the Task Group headed for an AMP in San Diego before joining the US Navy for exercise Fleetex. After the exercise the ships headed for Long Beach and then on to Esquimault, where FOF1 disembarked and returned to the UK on 8 September.

Exercise Marcot The group participated in the multi-national naval exercise Marcot, then on completion headed for Vancouver, where they arrived on 16 September. Nine days later the group set sail for visits to San Francisco and Acapulco before returning through the Panama Canal on 21 October.

Port Visits *Blake*, escorted by *Birmingham*, visited Port Everglades for an SMP, with FOF1 rejoining his flagship on 4 November. The rest of the group dispersed for visits to Barbados, San Juan, Chagaramus and Mayport, where *Nubian* joined the group. All ships of the group sailed for weapon training from 8 to 16 November before taking part in exercise Computex.

Return to the UK The exercise was completed on 22 November, and the ships of the group then visited St Kitts before finally leaving harbour and setting course east across the Atlantic on 30 November. On arrival in the Channel *Nubian* detached from the group for Rosyth, whilst *Hermione*, *Leander* and *Ambuscade* returned to Devonport, leaving *Blake* and the rest of the ships to enter Portsmouth on 12 December.

admirals, Leach and Lewin, would be respectively First Sea Lord and Chief of the Defence Staff, responsible for the conduct of the Falklands War.)

Phoebe sails for the South Atlantic (NN)

Defence of Belize, 1977–1979 In February 1977 the frigate *Tartar* completed her deployment in the West Indies, and on her departure for the UK it was decided to extend the notice to reinforce Belize to fourteen days. Security threats to Belize continued, however, and these became acute in June. The carrier *Hermes*, with 40 Commando embarked, was put on alert to deploy to the area on 7 June, and on 27 June, after talks broke down, the frigate *Achilles* was sent to lie off Belize. The situation eased but notice to reinforce was brought back to five days. Guatemalan pressure continued, and at one stage in 1978 *Ark Royal* was put on standby to cross the Atlantic and reinforce Belize. In another incident in July a Guatemalan gunboat ran aground in Belize waters.

Group Deployment TG 317.7, 31 May – 12 December 1978

The next planned out-of-area Group Deployment was Task Group 317.7. FOF1, Rear Admiral Hallifax, flying his flag in the helicopter cruiser *Blake*, led the Task Group.

Departure *Blake*, escorted by the frigate *Juno* and supported by RFAs *Tidespring*, *Stromness* and *Green Rover*, sailed from Portsmouth on 31 May 1978 and headed down the Channel to rendezvous with the frigates *Hermione*, *Leander* and *Ambuscade*, sailing from Devonport. The rest of the group included the nuclear fleet submarine *Conqueror* and the destroyer *Birmingham*, which was due to join it later.

Exercise Suroit After calling into Brest the group sailed for exercise Suroit with the French Navy. On completion of the exercise the ships returned to Brest for a second visit and for post-exercise debriefing. The group then sailed from Brest on 14 June and set course west across the Atlantic.

Withdrawal from Malta, 31 March 1979 British forces were finally withdrawn from Malta in March 1979. On 22 March the last Royal Marines in Malta, Salerno Company, marched from RAF Luqa and embarked on board RFA *Sir Lancelot*. RFAs *Olna* and *Tarbatness* arrived in Valletta to embark the final British forces, stores and equipment before sailing out of Grand Harbour on 30 March.[9] The British flag was hauled down over Fort St Angelo at midnight on 31 March for the very last time.[10] Rear Admiral Cecil sailed out of Grand Harbour in his flagship, the guided missile destroyer *London*, the next day, ending 178 years of British naval presence at Malta. One of the ratings on board *London* said, 'It was the most incredible thing. Thousands and thousands of people lined the ramparts, screaming, 'We love the British!' The ordinary people did not want the Royal Navy to go.'[11]

Atlantic Deployment (Task Group 316.1), March–May 1979 In March 1979 Rear Admiral Hallifax, FOF1, led a naval task group (TG 316.1). Accompanying his flagship, the guided missile destroyer *Kent*, were the destroyer *Newcastle*, the frigates *Naiad*, *Ashanti* and *Eskimo* and the nuclear fleet submarine *Warspite*, supported by three RFA vessels.

The Task Group sailed at the beginning of March and headed for the west coast of Africa before crossing the South Atlantic for Rio de Janeiro. Off the coast of South America the group participated in exercise Brazex with the Brazilian Navy.

In the course of the deployment, ships of the Task Group visited Dakar, Freetown, Banjul, Abidjan, Lagos, Ascension Island, St Helena, Fortelaya, Recife and Port Stanley before returning to the UK at the end of May.

Group Deployment (Task Group 317.8), 8 May – 14 December 1979

The next Group Deployment, TG 317.8, was led by FOF2, Rear Admiral Stanford, flying his flag in the guided missile destroyer *Norfolk*. The Task Group included the frigates *Arethusa*, *Achilles*, *Falmouth*, *Arrow* and *Dido*, the RFAS *Olmeda*, *Black Rover* and *Regent* and the nuclear fleet submarine *Courageous*.

Exercise Dawn Patrol The group sailed from Portsmouth on 8 May 1979, with the frigates *Arrow* and *Dido* having joined from Devonport. It headed straight down to Gibraltar and after a brief three-day visit took part in the major NATO exercise Dawn Patrol. The exercise ended on 24 May, and the group dispersed for visits to Izmir, Akrotiri, Corfu and Latakia, before reuniting on 1 June for exercise Exahoy.

Australia The Task Group transited through the Suez Canal on 7 June and headed for a two-day visit to the Seychelles before sailing on to Diego Garcia. On leaving Diego Garcia the group set course south-east for Australia with *Norfolk*, *Falmouth* and *Dido* visiting Fremantle on 4 July, whilst the rest of the group visited Bunbury, Albany and Geraldton. The group then continued to Hobart and Sydney for an AMP from 21 July to 7 August before visiting Auckland. On sailing from Auckland on 17 August the group participated in exercises Tasmanex and JUC 101 with the Australian Navy, before conducting visits to Suva, Lautoka, Nukualofa, Brisbane and Jakarta.

AMP in Singapore All ships returned to Singapore on 19 October for a two-week AMP. On leaving Singapore for the last time on 3 November the group visited Cochin and then set course for the return passage to the UK. Various exercises, including exercise Passex, were conducted en route as the ships headed west.

Return Leg *Norfolk* and most of the Task Group transited through the Suez Canal on 28 November and visited Athens, whilst *Arethusa* and *Arrow* visited the port of Elat in the Gulf of Aqaba before transiting through the Suez Canal on 3 December. The group then sailed to the UK, with *Arrow*, *Arethusa* and *Dido* entering Devonport on 14 December and the rest arriving in Portsmouth later the same day, except for *Achilles*, which proceeded to Chatham.

Northern Ireland, 1977–1979 In 1977 the internal security situation in Northern Ireland continued with operations Grenada, Interknit and Shoveller being reinforced with additional units on an opportunity basis. More submarine patrols were conducted off the coast, and Fleet Air Arm helicopters were used for reconnaissance operations. 45 Commando was deployed from 22 June to 19 October, suffering eleven casualties, one fatal. The IRA bombing campaign on the mainland continued, with seven bomb attacks in London in January 1977.

On the night of 19 March 1977 the patrol vessel *Vigilant* scored a significant success on Carlingford Lough, using special tactics to co-ordinate Royal Marine patrols in small rigid raider craft. Having picked up a high-speed target on radar she was able to position rigid raiders to intercept, then, after a short gun battle including an exchange of fire with terrorists on the south bank, the terrorist craft was captured together with a band of terrorists and a large haul of weapons and explosives. These were the first IRA bombers caught red-handed at sea.[12]

In 1978 it became necessary to increase security force dispositions in the area. A detachment of four helicopters from 845 Naval Air Squadron was deployed to Northern Ireland on a permanent basis. The Bird class patrol boats *Cygnet* and *Kingfisher* were deployed on Operation Grenada, with *Alert* and *Vigilant* continuing Operation Interknit on Carlingford Lough. Naval ships made additional visits to the area, and the RNR manned Ton class minesweepers, also conducting Operation Grenada patrols, augmented by professional members of SNONI (Senior Naval Officer Northern Ireland) staff. Clever and deceptive arms smuggling took place, with ingenious means of concealment being used. In one incident a shipment was discovered hidden inside an entirely hollow diesel engine. Two small craft were permanently available for operations on Lough Neagh, where aircraft landing at Aldergrove were under missile threat. The submarines *Osiris* and *Finwhale* conducted covert patrols off the coast, whilst units from the MCMVs *Bronington*, *Shoulton* and *Glasserton* reinforced patrols in Carlingford Lough.

41 Commando carried out a tour of duty from 27 February to 21 June 1978 and was replaced by 42 Commando from 16 July to 14 November. 45 Commando carried out special operations from 6 to 14 August, and during the year the Royal Marines suffered fifteen casualties, two of them fatal.

In 1979 the coastal patrols of Operation Grenada were conducted by MCMVs and patrol craft, supported by *Abdiel* and occasionally reinforced by frigates. RAF craft also carried out patrols, and the submarines *Walrus* and *Opportune* conducted covert coastal surveillance. In Carlingford Lough the auxiliary patrol vessels *Alert* and *Vigilant* were supported by additional patrols conducted by the Ton class minesweepers *Gavinton*, *Bildeston* and *Iveston*.

On 5 March 1979 40 Commando was deployed to Northern Ireland as the 'Resident Battalion' and served a full tour of one year, suffering two casualties. On 27 August

Admiral of the Fleet the Lord Mountbatten was murdered when fishing at Mullaghmore in County Sligo. The IRA blew up his fishing boat *Shadow V*, killing four people on board. The IRA also murdered eighteen soldiers on the same day when their lorry was blown up at Warrenpoint.

In 1977 the Royal Navy joined the other services in providing fire-fighting cover in Northern Ireland during a firemen's strike. The Navy had fully trained fire-fighters available, and manned 'Green Goddesses'. There was a continuing security risk, as some fires appeared to be started by the IRA deliberately to draw in the service teams, who would then be attacked. One team arrived before its escort, and coming under fire, the senior rate in charge had to order his team to take cover inside the burning building.[13]

Iran: The Fall of the Shah, 7 December 1978 – 21 February 1979 In October 1978 a revolutionary group led by the Ayatollah Khomeini threatened an uprising against the Shah of Iran, and on 6 November the Shah imposed military law. Mass demonstrations against the Shah were held at the beginning of December and civil unrest escalated. The situation became dangerous for foreign nationals, and ships of Task Group 321.1, which were on passage in the Arabian Sea from Karachi to the Seychelles, were ordered to close the coast of Iran and prepare to evacuate British nationals. The frigates *Sirius* and *Ardent* together with the fleet tanker RFA *Grey Rover* altered course north-west and headed for the Gulf. In the event the situation eased and the ships of the Task Group were able to resume their deployment on 9 December.

By the end of December, however, it became essential to evacuate British and Commonwealth personnel from the region, and on 2 January 1979 the frigate *Active* and the survey ships and vessels *Hydra*, *Herald*, *Fawn* and *Fox* were sent into Gulf ports to carry out the evacuation. On 16 January the Shah fled into exile, and at the end of the month the Ayatollah entered Iran. Eleven days later Ayatollah Khomeini took power and established a fundamentalist Islamic republic in Iran. The evacuation of British and Commonwealth personnel was completed with the assistance of chartered aircraft and RAF flights by 21 February. The necessity to evacuate all foreign nationals was proved on 14 February when the US embassy was attacked and many hostages taken. An attempt by the USA to rescue the hostages by helicopter on 24 April, Operation Eagle Claw, ended up a disastrous failure and a high-profile humiliation for the West.

Hong Kong, July 1979 Onwards From the summer of 1979 the flow of illegal immigrants into Hong Kong reached unacceptable levels, and Operation Culex was initiated to reinforce the Hong Kong garrison and the Hong Kong Patrol Squadron. A Sea King helicopter was transported to Hong Kong on board RFA *Fort Grange* from Task Group 317.8, arriving on 16 July. 42 Commando, Royal Marines was deployed for an emergency tour to the colony on 10 September. Two hovercraft were conveyed in RFA *Bacchus*, and the fast patrol boat *Scimitar* was transported from the UK on board MV *Happy Pioneer*, arriving in Hong Kong on 20 September.

Whilst in Hong Kong the Royal Marines of 42 Commando assisted the Royal Hong Kong Police and pioneered the use of fast raiding craft for seaborne anti-illegal immigrant patrols. The Royal Marines were extremely effective and apprehended large numbers of illegal immigrants attempting to infiltrate by sea, earning much praise from the Hong Kong government.

Following the deployment of the hovercraft and *Scimitar*, the Sea King helicopter was released for return to the UK on 17 October and the Royal Marines returned on 9 November.

Humanitarian Operations

***Amoco Cadiz* Disaster** In April 1978 the supertanker *Amoco Cadiz* ran aground off Ushant, spilling her vast cargo of oil. The frigate *Yarmouth* was quickly in the area and took charge, organising the clean-up operation. She was relieved a short while later by the frigate *Nubian*.

Hurricane 'David' At the end of August 1979 Hurricane 'David' struck Dominica. The guided missile destroyer *Fife* was ordered there at speed, arriving on 30 August. It was the most devastating hurricane of the century. The capital, Roseau, was flattened; there were many casualties and over 100,000 were made homeless. *Fife* immediately provided a great deal of emergency relief, restoring water and power supplies, finding missing women and children, and opening roads and hospitals. In one week of hard work *Fife* did much to restore order and basic services.

SHIPS, SUBMARINES, AIRCRAFT AND WEAPONS

Farewell the Fleet Carrier In December 1978 the fleet carrier *Ark Royal* returned to Devonport for the very last time. Just days before she arrived off the naval base the carrier *Eagle* had been towed away to be scrapped. *Ark Royal* was therefore the last fleet carrier, and she was finally decommissioned early the following year. It was a sad day for the Fleet Air Arm and the Royal Navy, ending a fine tradition of service by the fleet carriers.

Sea King Helicopter	
The Sea King helicopter was an extremely versatile all-weather twin-engined helicopter, which served with the fleet in all roles to the end of the century and beyond.	
First flight:	7 May 1969
Introduced to service:	August 1970
Weight:	6201kg
Length:	22m
Propulsion:	2 Rolls-Royce Gnome H 1400 IT turboshafts mounted side by side
Armament:	Torpedoes or depth bombs
Crew:	2 pilots and 1 aircrewman
No. completed:	56

Farewell the Cruiser In 1979 it was decided to lay up the helicopter cruiser *Blake*, as well as several frigates, as the manpower shortages in the Fleet had become acute. In June the new Conservative government announced that *Blake* would be decommissioned, though that did not actually take place until the following year. *Blake* was the last cruiser in the Royal Navy, and her passing marked the end of that major class of warship. Cruisers had served in the Royal Navy for well over a hundred years and played an important part in nearly all aspects of naval warfare. They had been central to safeguarding the sea lanes and maintaining peace and security in the far-flung areas of the British Empire.

New Destroyers and Frigates Although the fleet carriers and the cruisers had gone, new ships were still being ordered, and in 1979 the Labour government ordered three new Batch III Type 42 destroyers and two new Type 22 frigates.

A Sub-Harpoon missile (RNSM)

circumnavigated the globe via both Panama and Suez covering an impressive 38,452 nautical miles, almost all of them submerged. *Trafalgar* class submarines were to contribute later to the Afghanistan Campaign by firing Tomahawk missiles at strategic and tactical targets.

Sub-Harpoon Missile System In 1979 the US submarine-launched anti-ship Sub-Harpoon missile was ordered. The missile had a range of sixty miles. After trials in the submarine *Churchill* in 1980, the missile system entered service in 1982.

HMS *Southampton*	
Type 42 Destroyer	
The Type 42 air defence destroyers were the successors to the *Hampshire* class guided missile destroyers. They were designed to provide area defence for task group operations and were quickly to prove themselves in the Falklands Conflict. They provided excellent service for well over thirty years.	
Launched:	29 January 1979
Commissioned:	31 October 1981
Displacement:	3,560 tonnes
Length:	125m
Propulsion:	COGAG 2 Rolls-Royce Olympus TM3B gas turbines, 2 Rolls-Royce Tyne RM1C gas turbines, 2 shafts
Armament:	Sea Dart missiles, 1 4.5 /55 Mk 8, 2 or 4 Oerlikon/BMARC 20mm, 6 STWS Mk 3 torpedoes, Lynx HMA8 helicopter
Complement:	266
No. in class:	14 (built in 3 batch types) – 8 still in service

---

Trafalgar **Class Submarines** By 1977 expenditure by Western governments on submarine technology had greatly increased and was being countered by the Soviet Union at the expense of all other programmes. To keep up and maintain the advantage in the Cold War, below the surface of the oceans, the UK embarked on building a state-of-the-art nuclear hunter-killer submarine, the *Trafalgar* class. Combining all the lessons learnt from its predecessors, it was, and still is in 2009, a major achievement in underwater stealth. The *Trafalgar* class submarines were to be faster and quieter than any previous submarines and were to be fitted with state-of-the-art equipment and weaponry, which included Tigerfish, Spearfish, the Royal Navy Sub-Harpoon system and Tomahawk missiles. They were deployed throughout the latter stages of the Cold War, fulfilling the role they were designed for: operating up-threat and close to the enemy. After the end of the Cold War they contributed to important deployments and operations worldwide. In 1997 *Trafalgar*

PERSONNEL MATTERS

In 1975 naval manpower stood at just under 79,000, and over the next five years it was to reduce by 6,000 to 73,000.

Naval Training The 'Constrain' plan, introduced in the early 1970s, had streamlined naval training and reduced the number of shore establishments. The training establishment HMS *Ganges* at Shotley, near Ipswich, was finally closed in 1976 after a long career, having trained over 100,000 boys. Three hundred veteran Ganges men attended an emotional farewell ceremony for the decommissioning when the final intake graduated in June.

Operations Branch A fundamental change brought about by Constrain was the introduction of the Operations Branch on 1 January 1975. The Principal Warfare Officer (PWO) concept had already been introduced in 1972, when it was recognised that specialist officers were too narrow in their expertise to fight efficiently in the multi-threat environment of modern naval warfare. Specialist weapons long courses for officers were replaced by PWO courses with sub-specialisations of 'Above Water' and 'Under Water' warfare courses. Courses were organised and run by SMOPS (the School of Maritime Operations) at HMS *Dryad* at Southwick in Hampshire. For ratings two main groups were introduced: the Communications Branch and the Seaman Branch.

Engineering Branch Changes Fundamental changes were also achieved in the engineering branches. The Engineering

Branch Working Group reported its findings in 1975, and the main recommendations entailed a reallocation of responsibilities, with the establishment of two sub-branches. The first was the Marine Engineering sub-branch, with responsibility for all hull systems and accommodation services ('hotel services'), including electrical generation and maintenance and, increasingly, machinery electronic control systems. The second was the Weapons Engineering sub-branch, with responsibility for all weapons, sensors and communications systems, including navigational, IT and internal communications systems. The change was fully implemented on 1 September 1979, when over 2,500 ratings transferred from the old Weapons Electrical Branch to the new Marine Engineering Branch. The Royal Naval Engineering College (RNEC) at Manadon, in Plymouth, started to award its own internal degrees.

Instructor Branch As regards officers, the 'General List' concept of a common body of officers was working well, and in 1978 the Instructor Branch was absorbed into the General List.

Major Naval Pay Increase Rates of service pay had steadily decreased during the 1970s and had fallen seriously behind civilian rates, so much so that they were a major cause of the outflow of people from the armed services in the mid-seventies. By the late seventies there was a 21 per cent shortfall in rating recruitment. The outflow of people had caused reduced manning standards in the Fleet and was a cause of great concern to the Admiralty Board. In 1979 the incoming Conservative government of Margaret Thatcher agreed the recommendations of the Armed Forces Pay Review Body (AFPRB) and approved a huge pay rise of 32 per cent as well as agreeing to keep pay at a fair and proper level in the future. Recruitment and retention measures then began to improve, but of course, the big

Ark Royal at the Silver Jubilee Fleet Review
(NN)

increase in the pay bill put yet further pressure on the defence budget.

Sailor The Royal Navy received a fair amount of good public visibility from a popular television documentary programme made by the BBC. The programme was entitled *Sailor* and was filmed on board the fleet carrier *Ark Royal* during a deployment across the Atlantic to Florida and was reported to have been watched by 10 million people. The series of ten episodes had an attractive signature tune called 'I am Sailing' by Rod Stewart, which added to the popularity of the programme.

The White Ensign Association By 1976 over 9,360 officers and men had been assisted by the Association. Nevertheless it was clear that large numbers of officers and men were not aware of the facilities it offered. Many applications came from those who had already entered into unsound business ventures or other financial contracts in connection with assurance or house purchase which could well have been avoided had the advice of the Association been sought in the first instance. In many cases the damage was done and financial losses to the individual could not be avoided.

To help improve the situation, the Association increased its lecture programme to ships and establishments and made a series of recordings for ships to include in their onboard news broadcasts. To launch the new programme, the Association gave live TV talks and discussions on board *Hermes*, *Norfolk* and *Bristol*.

In 1977 the Council of the Association was given a privileged preview of the Silver Jubilee Fleet Review and on completion hosted a reception on board the fleet flagship, the carrier *Ark Royal*. During the year Admiral Sir John Treacher, a former commanding officer of the fleet carrier *Eagle* and Commander in Chief Fleet, was elected to the Council.

CHAPTER 6

Operation Corporate:
The Falklands Campaign 1980–1982

NEW NAVAL STRATEGY – NOTT AND 'THE WAY FORWARD' – TRIDENT – ARMILLA PATROL –
FALKLAND ISLANDS CONFLICT: OPERATION CORPORATE

The early 1980s encompassed many changes on the world scene, but the most significant of all for the UK was the conflict in the South Atlantic, fought to recover the Falkland Islands. The Falklands Campaign provided a clear example of the dangers and severe penalties of ignoring warning signs, however minor, distant or remote they might be.

In 1980 President Tito of Yugoslavia died, and within a decade blood would flow all over the former Yugoslavia (just such a scenario had been a standard exercise setting for NATO for many years). In Poland an independent trade union movement named 'Solidarity' was formed, which in due course would contribute to the fermentation of ideas and ultimate break-up of the Soviet Union. In the USA Ronald Reagan was elected President and would remain in office to see the end of the Cold War. In the Soviet Union in 1982 Yuri Andropov replaced Leonid Brezhnev as head of the Communist Party.

Soviet troops had invaded Afghanistan on Christmas Day 1979, and by the end of January 1980 (despite condemnation by the President of the USA) there were well over 80,000 Russian forces assisting the Afghan Army in its war against the Mujahideen. The numbers were to rise steadily to over 100,000, but even with their modern weapon systems and control of the cities and main lines of communications they could not wipe out the Mujahideen in their mountain strongholds. The West provided a covert supply of arms and ammunition to the Mujahideen fighters, including Stinger and Blowpipe anti-aircraft missiles and Oerlikon anti-aircraft guns.

New Naval Strategy In 1981 the Reagan administration announced a bold new strategy for the US Navy. The strategy involved changing the posture of the Navy from a defensive role, protecting the main SLOCs (sea lines of communication) and carrier battle groups (CBGs) in the Atlantic, assisted by the Royal Navy with its expertise in ASW (anti-submarine warfare), to a more aggressive forward deployment. Under the new forward strategy the US CBGs would be deployed forward into higher-threat areas, from the Norwegian Sea on NATO's northern flank to the eastern Mediterranean on NATO's southern flank. The strategy would drive the Soviet Navy back towards its home waters, where it represented less of a direct threat to the mainland of America. The new strategy was reflected in changed naval

FIRST SEA LORD
Admiral Leach

SECOND SEA LORD
Admiral Cassidi

MANPOWER
74,500

MERCANTILE MARINE
3,211
merchant ships

'Operation Corporate was a brilliant success in which the Royal Navy and Royal Marines played the major part ... it was an extraordinary record of achievement at every level of the Naval Service.'

(MOD, JULY 1982)

exercises, and towards the end of 1981 a major British and US naval exercise was conducted in the Norwegian Sea instead of in the Atlantic as usual. Three US carriers and two Royal Navy ASW carrier groups were deployed to the north of Norway, carrying out simulated air strikes in the Barents Sea and on the Kola Peninsula. The new forward strategy would, however, entail a significant shipbuilding effort to expand the US Navy to a force of 600 ships with fifteen CBGs, an increase of two CBGs. The Royal Navy studied the new American naval strategy very closely to evaluate changes for NATO and particularly the naval plans of the UK. Unfortunately political and economic factors were dragging the Royal Navy in the opposite direction.

The UK In the UK the continued severe economic decline forced the newly elected Conservative government under Margaret Thatcher to seek out all possible savings and financial efficiencies. As had happened so often in the past this led the government to look for the apparently easier short-term options, such as cutting the armed forces, and inevitably a defence review was initiated to enable it to find the huge savings it desperately needed.

Consequently the early 1980s saw a great step change in the fortunes of the Royal Navy and marked the final changes from broad capability and size to a highly professional, specialised and versatile Service, though it very nearly did not happen. It was the lessons learnt from the Falklands Campaign in 1982 which were to reverse the drastic cuts of the 1981 defence review.

UK Defence Policy: 'The Way Forward' (Cmnd. 8288)
In 1980 the government stated: 'It is the fundamental duty of Government to ensure the nation's security and keep it free to pursue, by just and peaceful means, its legitimate interests and activities both at home and abroad. It is a duty which the Government takes very seriously.'[1] The statement went on to explain how collective security was entirely dependent on the Atlantic Alliance, which was the cornerstone of Britain's defence policy, adding; 'The United Kingdom's defence resources must be concentrated on our key NATO tasks, but our defence policy should also be designed to help protect, wherever possible, our own and more general Western interests over a wider area, including those outside the NATO area.' It was ironic that less than

two years later the UK would find itself fighting a war on its own, with no single ally, NATO, WEU (Western European Union) or otherwise.

Nuclear Deterrent: Trident In July 1980 the government did announce that it had decided to procure the US Trident long-range nuclear ballistic missile system to replace the Polaris nuclear deterrent system in the 1990s. The previous year the Prime Minister had agreed the replacement with President Carter.

The Trident I (C4) missile had a range of nearly 4,000 nautical miles as against the Polaris's 2,500 nautical miles. The Trident II (D5) missile had a range of 6,000 nautical miles, and it was decided in March 1982 to procure that system. The blow for the Navy was the decision that the total cost of the new Trident system (£7,500m) was to be contained within the Navy programme. This meant that it would be acquired at the expense of other important items of equipment in the long term costed and approved programme. The decision that the Navy should carry the full cost of the nation's nuclear deterrent was not well received in some quarters. Some in the Royal Navy had not been totally committed to the Polaris nuclear deterrent system, even when part of the costs were met from other areas of the defence budget.

NATO Increase in Defence Expenditure Earlier in 1977 NATO had decided to increase defence budgets by 3 per cent a year in real terms to compete with the military expansionist policies of the Soviet Union and the Warsaw Pact. From 1979 the UK planned to increase defence spending 'year on year' for the next ten years, with the greatest increases being allocated to the equipment programme.

Unfortunately the increased defence spending coincided with a continued severe decline in the British economy. In her first budget in 1980, Mrs Thatcher, the Prime Minister of the newly elected Conservative government, stated that the UK would actually meet the increased NATO commitment of 3 per cent, but that it would not be at all easy. As events were to show, she was not wrong. One of her first decisions was to increase the pay of the armed forces by 32 per cent, which was inevitably well received by the Royal Navy though it greatly increased the pressures on the defence budget.

To meet the now huge pressures on the defence programme the new Defence Secretary, Mr John Nott, was invited to conduct a fundamental review and take a very hard look at the escalating equipment programme.

Command 8288: 'The Way Forward' The results of the 1981 defence review were set out in the government's second defence statement, 'The United Kingdom Defence Programme: The Way Forward' (the infamous 'Cmnd. 8288') on 25 June 1981. The review did not actually change the defence roles of the United Kingdom, but in their reinstatement emphasis was placed on the roles where ground and air forces, which had cheaper long-term

equipment programmes, were the prime components, leaving the Royal Navy to face the main impact of the consequent reductions. The excuse used by Nott to reduce the Royal Navy was that a smaller more specialised and flexible fleet would, he claimed, provide a more effective contribution to NATO!

He also chose to place his faith in the specious and previously dishonoured argument that land-based aircraft could cover all the roles of carrier-based aircraft. It was all very convenient as it pleased the Air Staff and at the same time achieved major savings in the cost of aircraft carriers. It was almost as if he had taken the simplest of approaches, identifying the most expensive single item in the long-term defence programme, other than the deterrent, and then selectively giving prominence to all the arguments against it to make its being cut such an obvious and logical choice.

Cuts in the Fleet The consequences for the future of the Royal Navy were drastic. First the big ships were to go, with the new carrier *Invincible* (CVS: the new-generation multi-purpose small aircraft carrier) being sold to Australia and the carrier *Hermes* being phased out. The two remaining amphibious assault ships, *Fearless* and *Intrepid*, were to be withdrawn earlier than planned without any replacements. At the same time there was to be a 30 per cent reduction in frigates and destroyers, with the scrapping of all the *Rothesay* and *Leander* class frigates. Also the ice patrol ship *Endurance* was to be withdrawn from Antarctica and scrapped, a decision which was to have an enormous political consequence out of all proportion to any financial savings. There was the added advantage that a much smaller fleet would require many fewer people to man it, with consequent further savings on the manpower bill for the Royal Navy. It was also decided therefore to introduce a phased redundancy programme.

THE FLEET

At the beginning of 1980, despite her economic and industrial decline, the UK still possessed the largest navy of the 'medium powers'. The strength of the Fleet, as set out in the 'Statement on the Defence Estimates 1980' (Cmnd. 7826), included the following:

Major Warships One ASW carrier (*Invincible*), two ASW/commando carriers (*Bulwark* and *Hermes*), two amphibious assault ships (*Intrepid* and *Fearless*) and one converted helicopter cruiser (*Blake*, though she was already laid up and about to be decommissioned).

Escort Ships The escort fleet consisted of sixty-seven frigates and destroyers, namely: five County class guided missile destroyers, one Type 82 destroyer, seven new Type 42 destroyers, twenty-six *Leander* class frigates, seven Tribal class frigates, eight *Rothesay* class frigates, eight Type 21 frigates, two new Type 22 frigates and three other older frigates. In addition three new Type 42 destroyers and two new Type 22 frigates had been ordered.

Submarines Four Polaris ballistic missile nuclear submarines (SSBNs) (*Repulse, Resolution, Revenge* and *Renown*), twelve nuclear fleet submarines, thirteen conventional *Oberon* class submarines and three remaining *Porpoise* class conventional submarines.

Mine Counter-Measures Vessels (MCMVs) Thirty of the old Ton class coastal minesweepers and minehunters, one new Hunt class and five old inshore minesweepers.

Other Vessels In addition there were various patrol craft, survey ships, training and trials ships, a Royal Yacht and a fleet of twenty-one support ships, mostly manned by the Royal Fleet Auxiliary.

Naval Aircraft The Fleet Air Arm consisted of two squadrons of Sea Harriers, six squadrons of Sea King Mk 2 ASW helicopters, eighteen Lynx Mk 2 and twenty-five Wasp ASW helicopter flights, as well as seven Wessex Mk 3 helicopter squadrons for training and commando assault work.

Royal Marines The Royal Marine commando forces were made up of four Commandos, with supporting brigade headquarters, artillery, engineers, logistics and a brigade air squadron. In addition there were the SBS (Special Boat Service) and two raiding squadrons.

Assigned to NATO All the major ships, escorts and submarines, plus three coastal minehunters and ten offshore patrol vessels, were assigned to NATO, whilst all other ships and vessels were under national control, but available for the support of NATO operations. Despite this and its concentration on its prime role of ASW in the North Atlantic, the Royal Navy still possessed a powerful, fairly balanced and relatively flexible fleet capable of projecting power around the world in 1980. But John Nott was about to bring forward radical plans to change all that and drastically cut the Fleet.

FIRST SEA LORD

Admiral Sir Henry Leach Henry Leach was born in 1923 and joined the Royal Navy in 1937. During the war he served in the battleship *Rodney* and the cruisers *Mauritius* and *Edinburgh.* After serving in the destroyer *Sardonyx,* he joined the flagship of the Home Fleet, the battleship *Duke of York,* and took part in the Battle of North Cape and the sinking of the German battlecruiser *Scharnhorst.*

After the war Leach served in destroyers and went on to become a gunnery specialist. He served in the cruiser *Newcastle* during the Korean War and was on the staff of the Flag Officer Far East Fleet during the Indonesian Confrontation. He commanded the commando carrier *Albion* before being promoted Rear Admiral in 1971. Three years later he was appointed FOF1 (Flag Officer 1st Flotilla) and led the second out-of-area major group deployment to the Far East in his flagship, the cruiser *Blake.*

Admiral Sir Henry Leach with his secretary, Captain Ian Sutherland (JAR)

He was promoted Vice Admiral and then in 1976 became VCDS (Vice Chief of the Defence Staff) before being appointed CINCFLEET (Commander in Chief Fleet) as a full admiral.

Leach relieved Admiral Lewin as First Sea Lord in July 1979 and had a very hard time fighting to try and save the Royal Navy from the extremely severe cuts being imposed by the new Conservative government. When Nott relieved Pym as Defence Minister the fight got harder, and although Leach had the full support of the Navy Minister, Keith Speed, he was fighting a losing battle trying to preserve an 'out-of-area capability'. Keith Speed did his best to protect the Navy but ultimately was sacked.

In an ironic twist of fate the nation suddenly found itself in dire need of mounting an out-of-area major naval task force in the spring of 1982. Admiral Leach is credited with being the strong voice which helped persuade Margaret Thatcher to take firm action to recover the Falkland Islands. He then presided over the magnificent achievement of the Royal Navy for its fundamental role in the great success of Operation Corporate. When the war was over he found that he had to fight hard once again to ensure that the ships lost in the conflict were properly replaced. He was well aware that promises made in war can easily be overlooked when the immediate crisis passes. Admiral Fieldhouse relieved him in December 1982.

OPERATIONS AND DEPLOYMENTS, 1980–1982

The Royal Navy continued to deploy forces around the world in the defence of dependent territories as well as in support of various other defence commitments. These included the following:

Gibraltar A frigate or destroyer was permanently held on standby to assist in the defence of Gibraltar, and 650 Royal Navy personnel manned the naval base and assisted in running the dockyard.

Belize A frigate or destroyer, supported by an RFA (Royal Fleet Auxiliary) tanker, was deployed to the Caribbean as the WIGS (West Indies Guardship) and was maintained on call to assist in the defence of Belize at short notice if required. Army and RAF forces were stationed on shore.

The Falkland Islands A detachment of forty Royal Marines provided the garrison on shore to defend the Falklands, and the ice patrol ship *Endurance* patrolled the waters around South Georgia and the Falkland Islands.

Hong Kong The Royal Navy maintained the Hong Kong Squadron of five converted Ton class MCMVs. In addition there were two Sea Kings and a special Royal Marine raiding unit with raiding craft working in close conjunction with the Royal Hong Kong Police. 42 Commando Royal Marines had been deployed to the colony in the autumn of the previous year but had returned to the UK, and in April 1980 3 Raiding Squadron (3 RSRM) was formed, equipped with Avon Searider rigid inflatable boats (RIBs).

Cyprus Britain continued to provide forces to Cyprus, both to defend the Sovereign Base Area and to contribute to UNFICYP (the United Nations Force in Cyprus). The Royal Marines took their turn to provide regular reinforcements as necessary.

Nuclear Deterrent The Polaris SSBNs of the *Resolution* class maintained the nation's ceaseless strategic nuclear deterrent.

Submarine Operations Fleet and patrol submarines continued their vital covert patrols in northern waters, shadowing and monitoring the Soviet Navy. The missions were very dangerous, and a number of 'incidents' occurred. Most were not revealed, and the exact details remain highly classified to this day.

Fishery Protection Squadron The Coastal Division of the 'Fish' Squadron consisted of eight Ton class MCMVs, and the Offshore Division comprised the new purpose-built Island class patrol vessels. As well as fishery protection the Offshore Division policed the vital oil and gas installations.

The Armilla Patrol, 7 October 1980 Onwards In the Middle East, Iraq, concerned about the radical changes on her border, seized the initiative and launched a full-scale invasion of Iran on 22 September 1980 to take the all-important strategic area of the Shatt al-Arab waterway. Iraqi forces poured over the border and both sides became locked in a grim war of attrition.

The war which developed posed a serious threat to one of the world's most important oil supply routes through the waters of the Gulf. To protect British and international tankers and shipping in the region during the war the UK decided to introduce defensive patrols in the Gulf of Oman and the Straits of Hormuz. The first patrol, codenamed Armilla Patrol, started on 7 October 1980 and was undertaken by the destroyer *Coventry* supported by the frigate *Naiad*, with the frigate *Alacrity* joining them on 23 October. All three ships had been detached from the group deployment TG (Task Group) 318.0 (see below). At the same time the destroyer *Birmingham* and the frigate *Avenger* sailed from the UK to take their turn on the patrol.

The Middle East remained an area of extreme sensitivity with bombings, murders and political assassinations. In Iran, bombs in Tehran killed the President, the Prime Minister, religious leaders and top government officials.

Operation Babylon On 7 June 1981 Israel initiated Operation Babylon, launching an attack by eight F-16s, into Iraq, against the nuclear reactor plant at Osirak. The aim of Operation Babylon was to prevent Iraq from developing a nuclear weapon. It was a daring raid as the facility was heavily defended, following an attack by Iranian Air Force Phantoms

the previous year. The attack was a success, and the nuclear plant at Osirak was destroyed. In Egypt President Sadat was assassinated on 6 October.

Group Deployments

The out-of-area group deployment (outside the NATO area) planned for Task Group 317.9 in 1980 was cancelled. The next major group deployment was planned for Task Group 318.0 as a seven-month out-of-area deployment to the Far East.

Task Group 318.0 Task Group 318.0 was led by FOF1, Rear Admiral Jenkins, in his flagship, the guided missile destroyer *Antrim*. The group included the ships of the 1st Frigate Squadron, *Galatea*, *Alacrity*, *Naiad* and the destroyer *Coventry*, supported by the RFAS *Olwen*, *Stromness* and *Blue Rover*. It was to be joined by RFA *Resource* in the Far East.

Departure The group sailed from Portsmouth on 19 May 1980 and headed across the Bay of Biscay for Gibraltar. After four days in Gibraltar it sailed on 27 May for a period of weapon training in the Mediterranean before a port visit to Istanbul.

Ships of Task Group 318.0 follow astern of *Antrim* in the Mediterranean (JAR)

Middle East The group departed from Istanbul on 10 June and transited through the Suez Canal four days later. Emerging from the Gulf of Aden, the group sailed south for a six-day visit to Mombasa and then on 30 June headed for Karachi for a brief four-day visit.

The Far East The group departed from Karachi on 14 July and set course due east for Singapore, where it arrived on 25 July. After just three days the group proceeded to Hong Kong for an AMP (assisted maintenance period), followed by weapon training with the US Navy and a short visit to Manila. The group visited Shanghai at the beginning of September and then continued with short visits to Tokyo, Kagoshima and Hong Kong before returning to Singapore on 3 October for an AMP. On departing from Singapore the Task Group participated in the major exercise Beacon Compass, which lasted two weeks.

Armilla Patrol At the beginning of October *Coventry* and *Naiad*, supported by RFA *Olwen*, were in the Gulf, and on 7 October *Coventry* was ordered to commence the first Armilla

Patrol. A week later *Alacrity* in Hong Kong was detached from the group and ordered to the Gulf at best speed to join *Coventry* and *Naiad* for the Armilla Patrol. *Alacrity* sailed from Hong Kong and after making a fast passage across the Indian Ocean passed through the Straits of Hormuz. On 23 October *Alacrity* rendezvoused with *Coventry* and RFA *Olwen*, and then on 3 November *Coventry* sailed from the Gulf.

Return Leg On completion of exercise Beacon Compass on 4 November the group visited Bombay for four days. On sailing from Bombay on 10 November it transited through the Straits of Hormuz and joined *Alacrity* and *Naiad* in the Gulf. *Antrim* relieved *Alacrity* on 12 November to return home with *Galatea*. The frigates then set course for return direct to the UK, passing through the Suez Canal on 21 November and arriving home on 8 December. The remainder of the group, *Antrim* and *Naiad*, with RFA support, carried out a patrol in the Gulf before heading for home, passing through the Suez Canal on 9 December. After calling in at Gibraltar on the way, the group finally arrived in Portsmouth on 19 December, with *Naiad* having detached earlier in the day to return to Devonport.

Task Group 316.5 Early in September 1980, frigates of the 7th Frigate Squadron, *Argonaut*, *Aurora* and *Apollo*, supported by RFAs *Regent* and *Tidepool*, formed Task Group 316.5 and prepared for a deployment to the Mediterranean.

The squadron departed from Devonport on 23 September and, after a short three-day visit to Lisbon, sailed through the Straits of Gibraltar to participate in the major NATO naval exercise Display Determination in the Mediterranean. The exercise terminated on 14 October and the ships dispersed for port visits to Athens, Taranto, Palermo, Naples, Tunis, Algeria and Casablanca. The ships then gathered at Gibraltar on 24 October and three days later sailed for Devonport arriving on 31 October.

Group Deployment 1981 Owing to the need to minimise fuel consumption to ease the enormous pressure on the defence budget, it was decided not to deploy a major naval task group out of area during 1981.[2]

Task Group 323.1 On 30 March 1981 FOF2, in his flagship, the guided missile destroyer *Antrim*, sailed from Portsmouth leading Task Group 323.1 for the Mediterranean. The guided missile destroyer *London* joined the group for the important exercise Springtrain off Gibraltar. The exercise was completed on 16 April and the nine destroyers and frigates of the squadron dispersed.

Exercise Springtrain 82 On 17 March 1982 the ships of the regular Springtrain exercise group sailed from the UK and headed south for the warmer waters of the Mediterranean. In command was Rear Admiral Sandy Woodward, FOF1, flying his flag in the 6,200-ton guided missile destroyer *Antrim*.

The first week, as they sailed south, was spent in working-up exercises in preparation for the more demanding exercises to come. The ships steamed through the Straits of Gibraltar on 26 March and sailed into the harbour for a period of rest and relaxation in the warmth of the 'Rock'. On the same day the fleet replenishment ship RFA *Fort Austin*, under the command of Commodore Dunlop, sailed quietly out of harbour and headed south for the South Atlantic at best speed. The group was also due to join up with other ships which would be taking part in the forthcoming exercises. But it was not to be. On 29 March Admiral Woodward ordered all the ships under his command to report their readiness for war!

THE FALKLAND ISLANDS CONFLICT: OPERATION CORPORATE, 2 APRIL – 14 JUNE 1982

The Falklands crisis came almost out of the blue, and while there had been a few warning signs, very few of them had been serious. It was an indicator of the decline in Britain's status and position of influence in the world, as well as a consequence of the dramatic run-down of the nation's naval forces. Argentina would never have dared consider taking any such action when Britain had a world empire with an unchallengeable navy.[3]

The Lead-Up President Galtieri of Argentina and his Junta were facing an economic, social and political crisis, and were fully aware that they had to do something drastic to have any prospect of saving their regime. With Britain appearing to lose all interest in the Falkland Islands, and running down the very forces that would have been needed to protect them at such a distance from the UK, it seemed that a crusade to recover the islands would be a realistic possibility. Certainly it would be an extremely popular expedition, which would unite the country and divert attention away from the political crisis at home. Planning had been conducted in great secrecy, and even practice amphibious manoeuvres held on 19 March 1982 had escaped attention.

Opening Moves On 9 March the British Embassy was informed that forty-one men would be employed on salvage work on the derelict whaling machinery in South Georgia, for which a contract had been let. The men would sail on board the 3,000-ton naval transport ship *Bahia Buen Suceso* and work for a number of months in South Georgia. The ship sailed on 11 March and arrived at South Georgia eight days later. When the men landed on 19 March they promptly raised the Argentine flag, and in response *Endurance* (Captain Nick Barker), with twenty Royal Marines on board, promptly sailed from Port Stanley the next day to investigate. *Endurance* arrived at South Georgia on 23 March but was ordered not to take any action which could provoke an international incident. She was merely to observe and provide a military presence.

The Argentine Navy Proceeds to Sea The Argentine Navy despatched a corvette to South Georgia on 24 March, and the next day the 6,000-ton naval transport *Bahia Paraiso* arrived in the area. On 26 March a powerful task group of the Argentine Navy, including the flagship, the aircraft carrier *Veintecinco De Mayo* and the modern Exocet missile-armed Type 42 destroyers *Hercules* and *Santissima Trinidad* as well as the corvettes *Drummond* and *Granville*, sailed for unscheduled anti-submarine training exercises with the Uruguayan Navy off the Plate estuary. Rather surprisingly for anti-submarine exercises, the group included the 4,300-ton amphibious landing ship *Cabo San Antonio* with a marine infantry battalion embarked. Naval Special Forces were also embarked on board the destroyers, and it appears that the Junta had finally made the decision to invade the Falklands on that day, 26 March. Intelligence of the planned invasion did not finally reach the UK until 31 March, though contingency plans were already being considered at high level several days before.

Invasion of the Falklands: Operation Rosario

Argentine Task Forces 20, 40 and 60 On 28 March, just two days after the 'Springtrain' ships arrived in Gibraltar, the Argentine task forces sailed for Operation Rosario to take the Falkland Islands. The planned date was 1 April, but because of adverse weather conditions the invasion date was delayed by twenty-four hours (reminiscent of the twenty-four-hour delay to Operation Neptune, the invasion of Europe, due to adverse weather conditions, some thirty-eight years earlier!).

The main invasion force, Task Force 40, headed east for the Falkland Islands, and the smaller task unit, Task Force 60, headed south-east for South Georgia. The powerful covering force, Task Force 20, consisting of the flagship, the aircraft carrier *Veintecinco De Mayo*, escorted by the destroyers *Comodor Py*, *Hipolito Bouchard*, *Piedra Buena* and *Segui*, was cruising some 500 miles to the north.

The Invasion Force Task Force 40 was the main amphibious assault force, consisting of the large landing ship (tanks) *Cabo San Antonio*, with 2nd Marine Infantry Battalion embarked. Other troops, including Special Forces, were embarked in the ice breaker *Almirante Irizar*, escorted by the powerful Type 42 destroyers *Santissima Trinidad* and *Hercules* and the corvettes *Drummond* and *Granville*. Also attached to Task Force 40 was the diesel-electric submarine *Santa Fe*. Sailing south-east was Task Force 60, comprising one corvette, the *Guerrico*, supported by a naval supply ship and heading for a rendezvous with the naval transport ship the *Bahia Paraiso*.

The Invasion of East Falkland, 2 April 1982 Task Force 40 arrived off the coast of East Falkland during the night of 1 April. The Argentine Special Forces unit of seventy men on board the *Santissima Trinidad* was put ashore by boat transfer five miles south of Port Stanley and set off north, in two separate units, one to attack Government House and one to attack the Royal Marine barracks at Moody Brook to the west of Port Stanley. At the same time frogmen had come

ashore from the submarine *Santa Fe* to secure the airfield, and having achieved that they moved on swiftly to occupy the eastern point of the narrows leading into Port Stanley. A small garrison of forty Royal Marines, which was rotated each year, defended the Falklands, and fortuitously the new garrison had just arrived on 30 March, on board the research ship *John Biscoe*. Instead of leaving the following day the outgoing garrison was retained by the governor, thus doubling the size of the Royal Marine force defending the islands. The Royal Marines manned various observation posts and stationed themselves so as to best defend Port Stanley.

Just after six on the morning of 2 April the first Argentine Special Forces unit attacked Moody Barracks, opening fire with small arms and grenades. Fortunately the barracks were empty. Ten minutes later the second unit attacked Government House, but the Argentine officer in charge was shot dead and his men retreated under fire. A three-hour gun battle then ensued, and although casualties were mounting on the Argentine side, many more Argentine troops were pouring ashore from the *Cabo San Antonio*. The amphibious armoured carriers formed up into columns and advanced on Port Stanley but were checked when they ran into a Royal Marine ambush. The Royal Marines scored direct hits on the leading vehicles with rockets and Carl Gustav anti-tank weapons. The sheer numbers of Argentine soldiers returning fire forced the Royal Marines to fall back. Throughout the engagement more troops were coming ashore by helicopter and landing craft, forcing the Royal Marines back.

Having captured and secured the airfield, Argentine C-130 Hercules transport aircraft started to arrive bringing more troops and equipment. Eventually the Royal Marine officer in command, Major Norman, advised the Governor, Rex Hunt, that in view of the overwhelming numbers of Argentine troops surrounding Port Stanley and Government House, further resistance would serve little purpose and would endanger the lives of the civilian population. After negotiating terms the Governor surrendered. It is greatly to the credit of the Royal Marines that, despite being hopelessly outnumbered, they had resisted for so long without sustaining a single casualty and also that no civilian had been injured. The occupying forces hoisted Argentine flags everywhere, disarmed the Royal Marines and forced them to lie down for the cameras. That evening the Governor and Royal Marines were flown out to Argentina and then on to the UK, where they arrived on 5 April. Meanwhile the Argentine occupying forces set about securing and fortifying the islands. Reinforcements were flown in and eventually some 13,000 Argentine troops were deployed to defend the Falklands against recapture.

Invasion of South Georgia, 3 April

The very small Royal Marine detachment at Grytviken, South Georgia, became aware of the Argentine invasion and prepared their defences as best they could for the inevitable arrival of Argentine forces. Task Force 60 duly arrived off South Georgia late on 2 April in stormy weather, and the *Bahia Paraiso* entered Cumberland Bay. *Endurance*, which had originally been sailing to Port Stanley, reversed course and headed for Grytviken to assist the Royal Marine detachment but she was still some way off to the north-west.

The *Bahia Paraiso* The Argentinians on board *Bahia Paraiso* demanded that the Royal Marines surrender and started landing troops by helicopter. The Royal Marines refused and opened fire, shooting down one of the helicopters and damaging the second, with heavy casualties. The Argentinians returned fire, and the damaged helicopter managed to land reinforcements at a healthy distance from the Royal Marines' deadly fire. *Endurance*, which had been closing South Georgia at full speed, launched one of its two Wasp helicopters as soon as it was in range, to observe and report on the battle ashore.

The *Guerrico* At this stage the powerfully armed *Guerrico*, with Exocet missiles and 100mm, 40mm and 20mm guns, entered the bay and opened fire at almost point-blank range with her 40mm guns. In the restricted waters of the bay there was little room for the *Guerrico* to manoeuvre as she came under heavy return fire from the Royal Marines. At close range the Royal Marines scored many hits with rockets and heavy anti-tank rounds from the Carl Gustav launcher, as well as raking the decks with rifle and machine gun fire. The *Guerrico*, with over 1,000 bullet holes in her, steamed back out to sea to open the range and engage with her 100mm main armament. Fortunately the main gun had been damaged by rocket fire and was not able to engage accurately. There then followed a stand-off, with the Royal Marines heavily outnumbered and surrounded but the Argentinians not able to press home their attacks. Eventually, following negotiations, the Royal Marines surrendered and were taken aboard the *Bahia Paraiso*, which then sailed for Argentina.

The Wasp helicopter from *Endurance* returned on board but the ship was not equipped to tackle Task Force 60. *Endurance* could do nothing and eventually had to head north to rendezvous with the support ship RFA *Fort Austin*.

The 'Task Force': Task Force 317

Preparations When the news of the invasion broke in the UK there was an uproar of protest throughout the country. The Royal Navy had already set swift action in hand, and on 1 April the aircraft carriers had been put on alert to be ready to proceed to sea within forty-eight hours.

View of the First Sea Lord Reputedly, the Prime Minister had sought the counsel of her key ministers at a meeting in 10 Downing Street on the evening of 31 March. The First Sea Lord, Admiral Leach, had just returned from an engagement, and even though he was still in uniform he had gone straight across to 'No 10' as he was fully aware that the Chief of the Defence Staff, Admiral Lewin, was

out of the country at the time. When the Prime Minister was informed that the First Sea Lord had arrived she invited him to join the discussion on the options that could be taken if the Falkland Islands were invaded. He is said to have briefed the Prime Minister that he could mobilise a task force by the weekend and that, in his opinion, if there was an Argentine invasion the Navy could 'and should be used'. It is thought that his confident and uncompromising views helped to strengthen the Prime Minister in her resolve to take a firm line over any Argentine attack. The Fleet was then put on standby. The 'Springtrain' group of ships in Gibraltar had already been charged with preparing for war, and in the UK the dockyards were set to work to repair, mend, supply, store, ammunition and refuel as many ships as possible with utmost speed for operations in the South Atlantic.

Submarines On 1 April two nuclear-powered fleet submarines, having embarked torpedoes, covertly put to sea and headed south at speed: *Splendid* (Commander Lane-Nott) from Faslane and *Spartan* (Commander Taylor) from Gibraltar. The nuclear-powered fleet submarine *Conqueror* (Commander Wreford-Brown) sailed from Faslane three days later and also headed fast for the South Atlantic.

The Submarine HMS *Superb* The SSN (nuclear fleet submarine) *Superb* (Commander Perowne) had previously been operating with the 'Springtrain' group and had been in Gibraltar towards the end of March when she was ordered to put to sea immediately for a secret mission. Her hurried, early sailing did not go unnoticed and, according to intelligence channels, was reported to President Galtieri. The *Daily Telegraph* reported that *Superb* had gone down to the Falklands.

US intelligence sources later considered that the threat of *Superb* had persuaded President Galtieri to bring forward his invasion plans. Had the invasion taken place later in the year, as was thought to have been originally planned, when the hostile winter weather conditions had set in and Britain had decommissioned her two aircraft carriers, then the result of Operation Corporate could have been very different indeed.

In fact *Superb* had been sailed to head in the opposite direction and investigate two Soviet *Victor* class nuclear fleet submarines detected in the Western Approaches. At the time *Superb* was commanded by Commander James Perowne, who was later to serve as a senior admiral with the US Naval Staff. It was when he was serving as Deputy Supreme Allied Commander Atlantic that he was able to substantiate the intelligence story of the part his submarine had played in the ultimate success of Operation Corporate.[4]

Gibraltar Rear Admiral Woodward in his flagship, *Antrim*, ordered the seven frigates and destroyers of his task group that were designated to sail south to take on board as many supplies, stores, spares, fuel and ammunition as possible from the ships due to return to the UK. Fortunately there were ships of different classes in both groups to cover most requirements. The group sailed from Gibraltar and continued VERTREPS (transfers by helicopter, known as 'vertical replenishment') as they headed out into the Atlantic and set course south. At that stage the group consisted of the County class guided missile destroyers *Antrim* (Captain Young) and *Glamorgan* (Captain Barrow), the new Type 42 destroyers *Coventry* (Captain Hart-Dyke), *Glasgow* (Captain Hoddinot) and *Sheffield* (Captain Salt), and the frigates *Arrow* (Commander Bootherstone), *Plymouth* (Captain Pentreath) and *Brilliant* (Captain Coward). The first surface ship to head south, RFA *Fort Austin* (Commodore Dunlop), was well ahead of the group.

The 'Task Force' On 3 April the Prime Minister announced to Parliament that a 'Task Force' (Task Force 317) under the command of Admiral Fieldhouse, the Commander in Chief Fleet, from his headquarters at Northwood outside London, was to be sent to the South Atlantic to recover the Falkland Islands. Two days later on the morning of 5 April the aircraft carrier *Invincible* (Captain Jeremy Black), closely followed by *Hermes* (Captain Lyn Middleton), sailed out of Portsmouth harbour to the rapturous applause of huge crowds, bands playing 'We are Sailing' and the attention of the world's press. The fact that the carriers had sailed on time on the 5 April represented an absolutely amazing achievement by the naval services. The air groups had been hurriedly improvised to provide a total of twenty Sea Harriers, with 800 NAS in *Hermes* and 801 NAS in *Invincible*. Spare aircraft from training and trials had been used to make up the complements of the squadrons.

The frigates *Alacrity* (Commander Craig) and *Antelope* (Commander Tobin) sailed from Devonport and escorted the LSLs (landing ships, logistic) RFAS *Sir Geraint* (Captain Lawrence), *Sir Galahad* (Captain Roberts), *Sir Lancelot* (Captain Purtcher-Wydenbruck) and *Sir Percivale* (Captain Pitt) south. The LSLs had embarked Royal Marines, stores, weapons and ammunition.

The frigates *Broadsword* (Captain Canning) and *Yarmouth* (Commander Morton) had sailed from Gibraltar on 5 April and set a course towards the eastern Mediterranean en route for the Canal and the Gulf, but after twelve hours steaming it was realised that they would be needed and they were recalled to Gibraltar to prepare for deployment to the South Atlantic.

On 6 April the amphibious assault ship *Fearless* (Captain Larken) sailed from Portsmouth laden with vehicles, three Sea King helicopters of 846 NAS (Naval Air Squadron) and heavy equipment for 3 Commando Brigade. The next day the last of the first wave of ships, the fleet replenishment ship RFA *Stromness* (Captain Dickinson), sailed fully stored and with 350 Royal Marines on board.

Follow-On Ships After the first wave of ships had set off for the South Atlantic the dockyards set to work to prepare ships in refit and repair, and to bring forward ships from the Standby Squadron. At the same time the many merchant ships being commandeered to support the campaign, known as STUFT (ships taken up from trade), were being adapted and converted for deployment south. More famous were the passenger liners, such as the *Queen Elizabeth II* (Captain Jackson), the *Canberra* (Captain Scott-Masson) and the *Uganda* (Captain Clark); all were all rapidly converted to troop ships. In Portsmouth dockyard the assault ship *Intrepid* (Captain Dingemans) was very quickly overhauled, restored and recommissioned in just twenty-two days. On 26 April *Intrepid* sailed from the UK and headed south at full speed.

Ascension Island Ascension Island was situated 3,700 nautical miles from the UK and 3,300 from the Falkland Islands, and thus nearly midway between the two, and with its airfield (at Wideawake) and its naval base it had been selected as the forwarding operating base (FOB) for the Task Force. On 2 April RAF C-130 Hercules transport aircraft started to fly stores, personnel and equipment down to Ascension Island to prepare the base to receive the Task Force.

Passage to Ascension Island Once clear of the Channel the various groups of ships headed south at their best cruising speed, using the valuable time to restore the large quantities of hastily stocked supplies, provisions, spares, fuel, equipment and ammunition. At the same time the opportunity was taken to make plans and preparations as well as exercise equipment and drills. There was a feeling that high-level political discussions and negotiations would resolve the situation long before the Task Force arrived off the Falkland Islands.

Diplomatic Negotiations and the United Nations There were a great many who hoped and assumed that, with the UK refusing to accept the Argentine invasion of the Falklands and sending a much publicised task force south, a diplomatic solution would be found to resolve the crisis. An intense round of negotiations was embarked on and various plans and formulas put forward at all levels. A resolution of the United Nations Security Council (Resolution 502) on 3 April demanded an immediate cessation of hostilities and an immediate withdrawal of Argentine forces from the Falkland Islands. The United Nations also directed Argentina and the UK to seek a diplomatic solution to the crisis by peaceful means. On 10 April the EEC (European Economic Community) introduced trade sanctions against Argentina. Both sides exerted much pressure on the Americans, who found themselves in a difficult position, being intent on preserving good relations with both key allies. Some plans offered glimmers of hope but in the end were not fully acceptable to both sides. All the time the intense round of negotiations was taking place, the various task units were making their way steadily south and time was running out.

Arrival at Ascension Island A small task group (Task Group 317.9) consisting of *Antrim*, supported by *Plymouth* and RFA *Tidespring* (Captain Redmond), was detached and sent on ahead at speed, arriving at Ascension Island on 10 April.

Hermes sails for the
South Atlantic
(RNM)

After embarking equipment and men the group left the next day, heading south at speed for a rendezvous with *Endurance* (Captain Barker). *Glamorgan*, flying the flag of Admiral Woodward, and the rest of his group (Task Group 317.8) arrived the next day at Ascension Island and set to work embarking more stores, spares and ammunition. From then on a constant stream of ships and vessels arrived at Ascension Island and were quickly readied for the final leg south.

The Recapture of South Georgia, Operation Paraquet, 25 April

The *Antrim* group (TG 317.9), under the command of Captain Brian Young, steamed fast towards South Georgia after leaving Ascension Island. Whilst diplomacy continued, no final decisions were made, but gradually it became evident that an acceptable political solution was not going to be found to the crisis and it became necessary to decide on action. On 20 April, when *Antrim* was less than 200 miles from South Georgia, the government authorised TG 317.9 to proceed with Operation Paraquet, the recapture of South Georgia.

Rescue on the Fortuna Glacier, 21 April At first light the next day *Antrim* launched SAS (Special Air Service) and SBS reconnaissance teams by helicopter to land on the Fortuna Glacier overlooking Grytviken and Leith. Three Wessex helicopters from *Antrim* and *Tidespring* arrived above the glacier in a driving snowstorm but managed, with great difficulty, to land the twenty men and their equipment and return to their ships. The weather deteriorated to blizzard conditions during the night and it became necessary to rescue the reconnaissance teams. The three helicopters returned to the glacier the next day and embarked their men in driving snow but, in attempting to take off in blind 'white-out' conditions, two of the helicopters careered on to their sides and had to be abandoned. The third helicopter, after landing its load, returned to attempt a rescue of the other crews stranded on the glacier. After numerous attempts, and in appalling conditions, a rescue was finally effected which saved the lives of the men, as they would not have survived a further night on the glacier. For his extreme bravery in rescuing all the remaining crews and flying a heavily overloaded helicopter in such conditions the pilot, Lieutenant Commander Ian Stanley was awarded the DSO (Distinguished Service Order). To replace the lost helicopters *Brilliant*, with two Lynx helicopters, was detached from the main Task Group (TG 317.8) to head south and join the group off South Georgia, subsequently arriving on 24 April.

The Submarine *Santa Fe* The following day Gemini boats landed parties of SAS and SBS covertly from *Antrim* and *Endurance* in positions around Grytviken and Leith. The group was informed that an Argentine submarine, the *Santa Fe*, was in the area of South Georgia and so, after sailing away from the islands, ASW helicopters were launched. The *Santa Fe* landed twenty Argentine marines at Grytviken and then proceeded back out to sea on the surface, when she was

spotted by *Antrim*'s Wessex helicopter. The helicopter, piloted again by Lieutenant Commander Stanley, attacked with depth charges (it was the first attack on a submarine by a British naval aircraft since World War II), one exploding close alongside the port casing and causing enough damage to prevent the submarine from diving. The submarine reversed course and tried to escape back in to the harbour but was then attacked by helicopters from *Plymouth* and *Endurance*. The *Santa Fe* fought back but was struck by missiles and strafed by machine guns. Eventually on fire and listing heavily, the submarine came alongside a pier so that the crew could escape.

The Recapture of Grytviken At this stage Captain Young decided to press on and launched an assault on Grytviken. *Plymouth* opened fire with her main armament of 4.5in guns, clearing the landing area and then blasting Argentine troops and other targets to cover the landing party.

The first wave of assault troops were landed by helicopter and, though heavily outnumbered, stormed into Grytviken. It was not long before the Argentine forces surrendered.

The Recapture of Leith *Plymouth* and *Endurance* then sailed into Stromness Bay to engage the detachment of Argentine marines ashore there in Leith. The Argentine Commander, Lieutenant Commander Astiz, tried to persuade the Captain

of *Endurance* to land by helicopter on the local football pitch, which they had packed with explosives, to accept the Argentine surrender! Fortunately Captain Barker of *Endurance* came ashore by boat and took the surrender peacefully.

At 1730 on 25 April Captain Young sent a signal: 'Be pleased to inform her Majesty that the WHITE ENSIGN flies alongside the Union Flag at Grytviken. Argentina was not immediately aware of the surrender and a squadron of Canberra bombers took off from Tierra del Fuego on 26 April to attack TG 317.9. On arrival off South Georgia the ships were spotted, but the weather had clamped down, preventing a bombing attack and forcing the aircraft to return to base. The 137 Argentine troops and the fifty-one scrap metal workers were rounded up and, after clearing the many booby trap mines, working with Royal Marines, were taken off South Georgia and embarked on board RFA *Tidespring*.

———————•———————

The Total Exclusion Zone (TEZ) The main Task Group (TG 317.8) had sailed from Ascension Island during the recapture of South Georgia. The ships of the Task Group were closed up in 'defence watches' with an ASW screen of three Sea King Mk 5 helicopters out ahead. The Sea King Mk 5s were to fly 2,253 sorties, an indication of their extremely good reliability record. A Boeing 707 of the Argentine Air Force sighted the Task Force on 21 April. It was quickly intercepted, but not shot down, by two Sea Harriers from 800 NAS. Argentine 707s continued to shadow the Task Force but were careful to remain well out of range. With the Argentine forces aware of the precise location of the Task Force, Nimrod surveillance patrols were flown from Ascension Island to detect any Argentine moves to attack the Task Force.

On 7 April the UK had announced a 200-mile maritime exclusion zone around the Falklands, effective from 12 April. Calculating that the Task Force would be in position to enforce any exclusion zone from 28 April, the UK informed the Argentine government that a 200-mile 'total exclusion zone' (TEZ) would be imposed from 30 April and that any

Harriers strike
Port Stanley
(DC)

Argentine ships or aircraft, civilian or military, would be liable to attack within that zone.[5] On 29 April *Brilliant* and *Plymouth* rejoined the group, and in the evening of the next day ships of the Task Force started to patrol inside the TEZ. The carriers were deployed some way to the east of the Falklands, out in the South Atlantic and well 'down-threat'. Additional ships were on their way to reinforce the Task Force, with the frigates *Argonaut* (Captain Layman) and *Ardent* (Commander West) arriving at Ascension Island with RFAS *Regent* (Captain Logan) and *Plumleaf* (Captain Wallace) on 29 April.

Operation Black Buck, 1 May

As the Task Force entered the TEZ, two Vulcan bombers, supported by eleven Victor tankers, took off from Ascension Island and headed south-west. The RAF were keen to demonstrate their contribution to the UK's ability to project power in the South Atlantic by launching Operation Black Buck, the longest bombing mission ever flown by any air force at that time. One of the Vulcans had to turn back, but in the very early hours of 1 May the remaining bomber took the Argentinians by surprise and dropped its load of twenty-one 1,000lb bombs across the Port Stanley airfield. As the Argentine gunners opened fire the Vulcan was already streaking away out of range and heading back to Ascension

Island. As the bomber had completed a 7,860-mile trip, achieved total surprise and bombed the airfield with precision it was certainly a great achievement by the RAF. Although the damage to the airfield was not great, the attack had a significant psychological impact on the Argentinians.

Harrier Strike, 1 May Just before dawn on 1 May *Hermes* launched her twelve Sea Harriers of 800 NAS, which sped in to attack Port Stanley and Goose Green carrying twelve 1,000lb bombs and twelve cluster bombs. Coming in low and fast, the Sea Harriers carried out their attacks under heavy fire. Having caused a certain amount of damage and casualties the Harriers then turned and headed back out to *Hermes*, the rearmost aircraft being hit but managing nevertheless to keep in the air. The Harriers landed back on deck with the BBC reporter Brian Hanrahan who had been told not to report actual numbers, making his famous comment 'I counted them all out and I counted them all back!'

Argentine Air Attacks Meanwhile the Harriers of 801 NAS were maintaining protective CAPs (combat air patrols) above the Task Force and were engaged by incoming raids of attacking aircraft. Only by violent manoeuvres, releasing chaff and applying their air brakes did the Harriers manage to evade the Argentine missile attacks. Several waves of attacks were fought off, but the enemy aircraft had managed to establish the position of the aircraft carriers.

Later in the afternoon a large force of forty-six enemy aircraft (A-4s, Canberras and Mirage Daggers) took off to attack the Task Force. As the aircraft approached the Task Force more Harriers were launched and the CAPs were vectored in to intercept the enemy bombers and turn them away. A Sea Harrier from 801 NAS shot down a Mirage with a Sidewinder missile, which was the first 'kill' by a Sea Harrier, and another Mirage, damaged by a Sidewinder missile, was shot down as it tried to land at Port Stanley. In further engagements a Canberra and a Dagger were shot down.

During the air battles *Glamorgan*, supported by the frigates *Arrow* and *Alacrity*, had closed Port Stanley and carried out a shore bombardment of the airfield with her main armament. In that position she was attacked by four Daggers, but survived with 500lb bombs bursting on both sides of her quarterdeck. *Arrow* also came under attack and suffered some damage and casualties. This was the first air attack on Royal Navy ships since World War II. The ships then returned to complete their shore bombardment.

By evening the Task Force had survived the onslaught of the Argentine Air Force, but the next day it would face the Argentine Navy.

The Sinking of the General Belgrano, 2 May

Disposition of Argentine Task Forces The next day, 2 May, the bulk of the Argentine Navy forming Task Force 79, commanded by Admiral Lombardo, the Fleet Commander, was at sea, heading for the Falklands. The strategy of the

Argentine Navy was to split the Fleet into four separate task groups, which would close on the Falklands to deliver a series of blows. The two main task groups were to execute a classic 'pincer' manoeuvre, with one to the north of the Falklands and one to the south to close and attack the Royal Navy Task Force. The manoeuvre was referred to as 'Lombardo's Fork'.

Task Group 79.1 to the North-West The most powerful force, which was to the north, TG 79.1, consisted of the fleet flagship, the carrier *Veintecinco De Mayo*, escorted by the powerful modern Type 42 destroyers, and was closing for a dawn strike with her Skyhawk jets to destroy the *Hermes* and *Invincible*. Further to the north was TG 79.4, of three Exocet-armed fast corvettes, *Drummond*, *Granville* and the damaged *Guerrico*. TG 79.4 had been sighted the previous day by the SSN *Splendid*, providing important intelligence of the build-up of Argentine naval forces.[6]

Task Group 79.3 to the South Some 300 miles to the south-east of Port Stanley, and much closer to the UK Task Force, was the powerful TG 79.3, commanded by Captain Bonzo, consisting of the big 11,000-ton, 6in-gun cruiser *General Belgrano*, escorted by Exocet-armed destroyers. TG 79.3 was heading east, outside the southern edge of the TEZ.

Contact At 1130 on 1 May a tracker aircraft from the Argentine aircraft carrier spotted the Task Force and began shadowing it. At this stage Admiral Woodward was aware of the Argentine dispositions but his submarines to the north, under the control of Northwood, had not managed to make contact with the Argentine carrier group, TG 79.1. Admiral Lombardo, being informed of the exact position of the Task Force, headed south-east. He prepared his Skyhawks for an attack at first light, but as the wind was light and the Skyhawks were heavy, being fully loaded with bombs and maximum fuel, he held back from launching them. Admiral Woodward meanwhile had been heading south-east to increase the distance from the Argentine carrier. Two Argentine Exocet-armed Super Etendards of the Argentine Navy took off to attack the Task Force but their attempt at in-flight refuelling failed and they had to return to base.

As Admiral Woodward made ground to the south-east he became increasingly concerned by the threat from the *Belgrano* Task Group (TG 79.3) on the southern edge of the TEZ, which was being tracked by the submarine *Conqueror*.

The *Belgrano* group was only 300 miles away from the Task Force and, although it was heading slowly west at the time, could easily turn north-east during the night and be in a position to attack the Task Force with Exocets and the cruiser's fifteen big 6in guns in the morning. Furthermore the *Belgrano* group was close to the comparatively shallow water of the Burdwood Bank, where it would be relatively easy to shake off any submarines and extremely difficult for *Conqueror* to operate. The group represented a clear and present danger to the Task Force. Aware of his vulnerability to the pincer attack, Admiral Woodward recognised the

The fleet submarine
Conqueror
(NN)

necessity of neutralising the southern threat whilst he had a chance of doing so.

Rules of Engagement Owing to the strict rules of engagement, however, Admiral Woodward needed authority to engage the *Belgrano* group, as it was thirty miles outside the southern limit of the TEZ. The Chief of the Defence Staff, Admiral Lewin, took up his request for a change to his rules of engagement and raised it with the Cabinet. Finally the rules were amended to authorise *Conqueror* to engage the cruiser, and accordingly she closed in on the *Belgrano* group, which was zig-zagging in a defensive manoeuvre against any possible submarine attack.

The Sinking Commander Wreford-Brown, the commander of the *Conqueror*, manoeuvred his submarine with great skill. The cruiser was sailing on a defensive course and closely screened by her two destroyer escorts. Eventually *Conqueror* was in a position 1,400 yards on the cruiser's port bow and Commander Wreford-Brown fired a salvo of three old Mk 8 torpedoes. Two torpedoes struck the *General Belgrano* and she sank very rapidly, in under fifteen minutes, with the loss of 321 of her crew. The destroyers then hunted for the submarine, dropping patterns of depth charges, and although some were close, *Conqueror* was able to escape.

The sinking of the *General Belgrano* was undoubtedly a turning point in the war, and although it caused a tragic loss of life it was a tactical masterstroke from which the Argentine Navy was never to recover. Woodward's position remained extremely tenuous but at least there were now fewer of the many cards stacked against him. The Argentine fleet was effectively paralysed by the shock and took no further part in the war, but Woodward still faced the full force and violence of the Argentine Air Force as well as the Argentine Naval Air Arm, and he did not have to wait long for their response.

There were conspiracy theorists who claimed that the sinking of the *Belgrano* was deliberately contrived by the British in order to scupper peace negotiations, which were still going on at the time.[7] Such claims do not take into account the realities of the situation. The British Task Force, nearly 8,000 miles from UK with very slender resources, particularly in surveillance assets, and in hostile weather with winter fast approaching, was under serious threat from surface, sub-surface and air attack. It was in a fairly desperate situation, facing an extremely difficult task, and had to take every chance it possibly could. The government, having put the Task Force in that difficult situation, decided to support it and acquiesced with the requested change in the rules of engagement.

Success with Sea Skua Missiles That night a Sea King helicopter investigated an unidentified ship to the north of the Falklands and came under fire. Immediately two Lynx helicopters armed with Sea Skua missiles were scrambled from *Coventry* and *Glasgow*. On closing the ship the first Lynx came under heavy fire but managed to launch both its missiles. The radar-guided missiles both struck the target, which blew up and sank. Half an hour later the second Lynx came under fire from another unidentified ship and responded with her two Sea Skua missiles, one of which hit the target, destroying the bridge structure. The target turned out to be the 700-ton corvette *Alferez Sobral*. The corvette was severely damaged by the attack, and the Captain and seven of his crew were killed. Nevertheless the ship remained afloat and two days later just managed to make port.

The Sinking of HMS Sheffield, 4–11 May
Withdrawal of the Argentine Fleet On 3 May the wind was too strong for the Argentine carrier to operate her aircraft, and when news of the sinking of the *Belgrano* was received, the fleet was ordered home. The fleet duly turned west and headed back to the coast of Argentina, where it would be in shallow water safe from attack by nuclear submarines.

Position of the Task Force During the night the Task Force sailed west towards the Falklands, and in the morning of 4 May an RAF Vulcan bomber attack was carried out on Port Stanley airfield. By the middle of the morning the Task Force was approximately a hundred miles to the east of the islands. Regular CAPs were flown and the Task Force was protected by a picket line of three modern Type 42 anti-aircraft destroyers, *Sheffield*, *Glasgow* and *Coventry*, deployed 'up-threat' twenty miles to the west of the group.

Super Etendard Attack Just after midday a Neptune reconnaissance aircraft of the Argentine Naval Air Arm picked up and reported a number of large radar contacts to the east of the Falklands, evidently the three destroyers on the picket line. Thirty minutes later a pair of Exocet-armed Super Etendards of the Argentine Naval Air Arm took off from their base at Rio Grande. They refuelled after 130 miles and pressed on due east with their radars switched off to avoid giving any warning of their approach. As they closed their targets, the picket line destroyers, the Super Etendards flew very close to the sea so that they would be below radar

coverage from the Task Force. *Glasgow*, to the south, only became aware of a possible attack when the aircraft were just twenty-five miles away, and a CAP was ordered to investigate. Meanwhile *Sheffield* was using her satellite communications system and had her 'air-guard' warning radar switched off to avoid interfering with her satellite transmissions. *Sheffield* immediately terminated her satellite transmissions and picked up the Super Etendards, which had climbed to 120 feet to make target acquisition height and switched on their Agave radars to lock on their AM-39 Exocet missiles. The Super Etendards then dropped back to sea level and at a range of twelve miles launched their missiles before peeling off in opposite directions to escape back west.

HMS *Sheffield* is Struck, 1414 on 4 May The Exocet missiles took about one minute flying at six feet above the water to reach their target, *Sheffield*. One missile struck the destroyer amidships on the starboard side whilst the other missed and flew on before ditching into the sea close to *Yarmouth*. It was assessed that the 370lb warhead failed to explode but the kinetic energy ignited the rest of the missile's fuel, causing an intense conflagration throughout the centre of the ship and killing twenty-one men.

The ship's company fought valiantly to stop the raging fires and save the ship, but without power, communications, water and pumps it was a desperate battle which they had little chance of winning. Helicopters and ships from the Task Force rendered immediate assistance. *Arrow* came alongside on the port side and provided fire-fighters and equipment.

Yarmouth came close alongside on the damaged starboard side to help but a short while later had to break away when a torpedo track was reported. After four hours of desperate fire-fighting the Captain, Captain Sam Salt, realised that the fires were reaching the Sea Dart missile magazine and ordered the ship's company to abandon ship.

HMS *Sheffield* Sinks, 11 May The ship remained afloat, drifting for several days, and an attempt was made to tow her out of the TEZ in heavy seas, but early in the morning of 11 May she rolled over and sank. *Sheffield* was the first Royal Navy warship to be lost to air attack since World War II.

———— • ————

Reinforcements To replace *Sheffield*, the Type 42 destroyer *Exeter* (Captain Balfour), off Belize, was ordered south to join the Task Force on 5 May. On 10 May a further group sailed from Portsmouth and Devonport for the South Atlantic. The group consisted of the 6,000-ton Type 82 destroyer *Bristol* (Captain Grose), two Type 21 frigates, *Avenger* (Captain White) and *Active* (Commander Canter), and three *Leander* frigates, *Minerva* (Commander Johnston), *Penelope* (Commander Rickard) and *Andromeda* (Captain Weatherall) supported by the fleet tanker RFA *Olna* (Captain Bailey). The Type 42 destroyer, *Cardiff* (Captain Harris), on her way home from the Gulf, was ordered to store in Gibraltar and then head out and join the group en route to the Falklands.

Sheffield struck by Exocet missiles
(NN)

Arrow on the port side of the stricken *Sheffield*
(NN)

The fires on board *Sheffield* rage out of control
(NN)

Loss of the First Sea Harrier Whilst the fires were raging in *Sheffield* in the afternoon of 4 May, three Sea Harriers from 800 NAS were carrying out a strike on enemy aircraft based at Goose Green. As the Harriers came in low to attack, the second Harrier was hit by anti-aircraft fire and burst into flames, crashing into the ground and killing the pilot, Lieutenant Nick Taylor. The remaining Harriers dropped their bombs and returned safely to *Hermes*.

Capture of the *Narwal*, 9 May The weather deteriorated and the next few days were subject to very low cloud, fog and poor visibility, which severely handicapped operations on both sides. On 9 May the 1,400-ton Argentine vessel *Narwal*, which had been spying on the Task Force and reporting movements, was attacked and damaged by a CAP, and then captured by an SBS unit which abseiled on to the deck from a Sea King 4. When the *Narwal* was captured, a prize crew from *Invincible* took over the vessel, which later sank. Later on the same day *Coventry* shot down an Argentine helicopter over Port Stanley with a Sea Dart missile.

22/42 Combo Admiral Woodward introduced a new defence tactic by pairing ships with different missile systems, predominantly by combining a Type 22 frigate carrying a short-range Sea Wolf missile system with a Type 42 destroyer equipped with a longer-range Sea Dart missile system. The term '22/42 Combo' was used to describe the new defence tactic, which proved to be an effective measure with the ships providing mutual anti-aircraft support.

Falkland Sound, 10–11 May In the afternoon of 10 May Admiral Woodward detached the Type 21 frigates *Arrow* and *Alacrity* to explore the Falklands, *Arrow* to investigate the north coast and *Alacrity* to explore Falkland Sound. During the night *Alacrity* made the dangerous passage through the Sound from south to north. Fortunately she did not run into any mines, but at about 0100 an unlit ship was detected underway close to Swan Island. The ship was the *Isla de los Estados*, and *Alacrity* opened fire with her main armament. After scoring a number of direct hits with high-explosive shells the ship, which was carrying nearly 90,000 gallons of highly inflammable aviation fuel, blew up in a massive fireball. *Alacrity* completed her exploration of the Sound and exited to the north to meet up with *Arrow*, and both ships then headed east at speed to rejoin the Task Force. As they sailed east an Argentine submarine, the *San Luis*, attacked them firing a torpedo at a range of 5,000 yards. A small explosion was heard but it was not until *Arrow* retrieved her towed torpedo decoy that she discovered it was badly damaged. When the Commander of the *San Luis* reported his attack, the Argentine press hyped the story as a successful attack on *Invincible* by torpedoes which failed to explode.

First Sea Wolf Kills, 12 May On 12 May an Argentine Skyhawk was shot down over Goose Green by gunfire. A little later in the day a '22/42 Combo' of *Brilliant* and *Glasgow*

The weather deteriorated and hampered flying operations (NN)

was close into Port Stanley when a force of three Skyhawks attacked the ships, coming in low. *Brilliant* fired three Sea Wolf missiles in rapid succession, shooting down two Skyhawks, and the third, flying just above the waves, crashed into the sea whilst manoeuvring to evade the third Sea Wolf missile (these were the first 'kills' by Sea Wolf missiles). During the engagement *Glasgow* was struck by a 1,000lb bomb, which fortunately failed to explode.

Raid on Pebble Island, 15 May After dark on 14 May *Hermes*, escorted by *Broadsword* and *Glamorgan*, left the Task Force and closed to the north of East Falkland. Shortly before midnight, when she was in range, *Hermes* flew off four Sea Kings with a raiding force of forty-five SAS men. The men landed on the north coast of Pebble Island and crossed the three miles to the Argentine airfield undetected. The SAS then attached demolition charges to eleven aircraft, fuel and ammunition dumps and the centre of the runway. When the charges were detonated the Argentine troops were roused and opened fire as well as setting off defensive mines. *Glamorgan* then carried out a shore bombardment to cover the SAS troops, who escaped back to the north of the island, where they were rescued and brought back to *Hermes*. It was a very successful raid and only two minor casualties were sustained.

Bristol heads for the South Atlantic (RNM)

The Landings at San Carlos: Operation Sutton, 21 May

By 16 May the units of the Amphibious Task Group had all arrived in position well to the north-east of the Falkland Islands and joined elements of the Task Force. The Amphibious Task Group (Task Group 317.0), under the command of Commodore Mike Clapp, included the LPD assault ships (landing platform (dock)) *Fearless* and *Intrepid* and fifteen RFA vessels and STUFT, escorted by *Antrim*, *Plymouth*, *Ardent* and *Argonaut*.

The next day was Argentina's 'Navy Day', and the Task Force

Fearless and *Invincible* refuel (NN)

braced itself for an attack by Exocet-armed Super Etendards. Constant CAPs by Harriers were maintained over the Task Force throughout the day. A Super Etendard raid was launched, but as the Argentine Neptune reconnaissance aircraft were unserviceable no hard information was available to the pilots. When the Super Etendards climbed to search for targets they failed to find any and returned to base. In the late afternoon the converted 'roll on/roll off' ship *Atlantic Conveyor* arrived in the area with much needed transport helicopters and fourteen Harriers, including RAF GR3 Harriers. The Harriers of 809 NAS were transferred to *Hermes*, but the helicopters were retained on board to await the arrival of their ground crews embarked in the *Europic Ferry*.

That evening the two groups (Task Groups 317.8 and 317.0) finally rendezvoused some 300 miles east-north-east of the Falklands, making an armada of some thirty-two ships gathered together in close company. The next day, 19 May, the amphibious group carried out a series of transfers to ensure that all the right forces were embarked in the correct ships.

Approach By dark in the evening of 20 May the amphibious group, heavily protected by screening warships, moved into position to the north of the Falklands and prepared to move in for the landings. The landing force commander was Brigadier Julian Thompson, embarked in the LPD *Fearless*, with his staff, Brigade HQ and 40 Commando. 45 Commando was embarked in RFAs *Stromness* and *Fort Austin*. Half an hour before midnight the amphibious group divided into three columns. The LPDs *Fearless* and *Intrepid* were in the first column, escorted by *Yarmouth. Plymouth* led the next group of *Canberra, Norland* and RFA *Stromness.* The third wave included the six LSLs and *Europic Ferry,* escorted by *Broadsword* and *Argonaut.* The three columns followed *Antrim* and *Ardent,* which were some way ahead, on a course south-west into Falkland Sound to execute Operation Sutton – the amphibious landings. Fortunately it was a dark night and good progress was made. SBS teams were landed to take care of the Argentinians on the headland at Fanning Head overlooking the approach to San Carlos Bay.

The Landings *Ardent,* commanded by Commander Alan West, entered the Sound at 2000, and sped south at thirty knots to provide gunfire support for a diversionary raid by the SAS. The first column sailed into the Sound shortly before midnight and anchored at the entrance to San Carlos Water. Commodore Clapp, the Commander of the Amphibious Task Group, wanted a 4.5in gun frigate available in San Carlos 'for local and instant Naval Gunfire Support', so *Plymouth* led the way in, prepared to assist the attack on Fanning Head close by if necessary. She was followed by the landing craft and eventually the rest of the Amphibious Task Group including *Canberra,* a very prominent all-white target. Just two and half hours later they were landing their troops as the second wave was entering the narrows. Although the sky was clearing, the amphibious group was not spotted by the Argentinians. The landings progressed very well, and by 0900 on 21 May the landing areas were well secured and the first phase of troops were all safely ashore. The destroyers and frigates positioned themselves in a 'gun-line' across the entrance to San Carlos. It was not until 1000 that an Argentine reconnaissance aircraft spotted the landings and reported them.

The First Air Attacks Within little more than five minutes an Argentine naval Macchi MB339 swooped into the bay, flying low across the water, and fired rockets and 30mm cannon at *Argonaut,* causing damage to the upper works and several casualties.

A quarter of an hour later a pair of Pucaras dived into attack but were beaten off by *Ardent.* Half an hour later six Dagger fighter-bombers arrived and attacked low in formations of three aircraft. The ships in the Sound opened fire and a Seacat missile brought down one Dagger. In the next attack two 1,000lb bombs narrowly missed *Broadsword,* but the 30mm cannon ripped into the ship, wounding fourteen men. At the same time a Dagger managed to bomb *Antrim* with a 1,000lb bomb, which tore through the centre of the ship, setting it on fire, but fortunately failed to explode. One Dagger attacked RFA *Fort Austin* but was destroyed by a Sea Wolf missile from *Broadsword* before it could release its bombs. *Broadsword* herself was strafed and just managed to escape several near misses from 1,000lb bombs.

Follow-On Air Attacks There was a short lull whilst the Daggers returned to base and briefed on the dispositions of the British forces and ships. The landings went on feverishly,

Cross-deck transfers to ensure that the right forces were in the correct ships (DC)

Fearless in San Carlos Bay (RNM)

'First Light San Carlos Water': SS *Canberra* lies quietly to anchor. Having disembarked 40 Commando the helicopters begin lifting supplies ashore
(DH)

'Time to go amigo!'
Lieut. Commander
Sharky Ward holds
back to allow his
victim to eject
safely, which he did
(DH)

'First Contact': *Argonaut* is attacked on 21
May off Fanning Head
(DH)

Air attacks in
San Carlos Bay
(DC)

consolidating the position ashore and establishing anti-aircraft defences during the lull. At about 1045 three Pucaras jumped *Ardent* but three Sea Harriers of 801 NAS were vectored on to the Pucaras, shooting one down and chasing the remaining pair.

Next to attack *Ardent* was a Skyhawk A-4B, coming in from dead ahead and so low that she hit the 992 radar. Immediately a Sea Harrier CAP was vectored on to the attack. As the two Sea Harriers closed in they engaged four Skyhawks. The Sea Harriers each fired Sidewinder missiles, both scoring direct hits, shooting down two Skyhawks and breaking up the raid.

HMS *Argonaut* No sooner had the raid been broken up than another six Skyhawks screamed in to attack from the north, pouncing on *Argonaut*. The frigate was momentarily lost in clouds of smoke and spray as bombs exploded close alongside, whilst two 1,000lb bombs hit the frigate and penetrated deep inside. One bomb hit a magazine and set off Seacat missiles whilst another in the engine room severed all power and steering apparatus. Only by swiftly letting go the anchor was the frigate saved from colliding with Fanning Head. A CAP by a Sea Harrier from 800 NAS in turn attacked the Skyhawks, and a Sidewinder missile destroyed one Skyhawk.

During the afternoon successive raids of Mirages, Skyhawks and Daggers swept down on the ships in the Sound and San Carlos Bay. The ships had little warning as the Fleet

'Splash one Dagger': *Broadsword*'s Sea Wolf downs one Argentine Air Force Dagger. Damaged *Argonaut* in the foreground with *Antrim* in the background
(DH)

'Vengeance is ours': two SHARS of 801 NAS bounce *Ardent*'s attackers as they flee. All three were splashed
(DH)

BAe Sea Harrier FRS.1
Naval VTOL/STOVL Jet Fighter
The Sea Harrier (SHAR) enabled the Royal Navy to maintain an
airborne air-defence and strike capability after the demise of
the big fixed-wing aircraft carriers in 1978. The fighters very
quickly proved themselves during the Falklands Conflict,
where they were a great success, defending the Task Force and
destroying thirty-one Argentine aircraft.

First flight:	20 August 1978
Entered service:	April 1980
Withdrawn from service:	March 2006
Span:	7.7m
Length:	14.5m
Powerplant:	Single 21,500lb Pegasus 104 vectored thrust turbofan
Max speed:	740mph
Armament:	Twin 30mm cannon with 5 pylons carrying an 8,000lb mix of weapons
Crew:	1 pilot
Number produced:	57, followed by 18 FA.2 variant

lacked adequate AEW (airborne early warning) and the ship's radars were 'boxed in' by the surrounding high ground. The Argentine pilots pressed home repeated raids with much courage. Fortunately most of the attacks were concentrated on the defending frigates and destroyers rather than the more vulnerable STUFT and large amphibious shipping in San Carlos Water, which would have presented much bigger and easier targets. A considerable barrage of missiles and anti-aircraft fire was put up from the ships, and it was difficult to credit individual ships with aircraft shot down. 30mm cannon shells from the attacking aircraft hit many of the ships. Most of the Argentine pilots came in so low that their bombs did not have sufficient time to arm before striking their targets and so failed to explode on impact.

Loss of HMS Ardent, 22 May Ardent was isolated to the south and, being under the flight path of incoming raids, came under repeated attacks and sustained substantial damage. A formation of three Skyhawk A-4Qs attacked in quick succession, scoring three hits with 500lb bombs, two exploding in the hangar area and igniting fires and the third

'He isn't heavy': Surgeon Commander Rick Jolly clutches a survivor from the burning Ardent as both are winched to safety by a Wessex 5 of 845 NAS (DH)

lodging in a machinery room. At the same time, to the north, a raid of three Daggers was completely destroyed by two Sea Harriers of 801 NAS with their Sidewinder missiles.

Back with *Ardent* yet another formation of three Skyhawks came in to attack, dropping their bombs on the frigate, which was already on fire. At least three bombs hit and two exploded. The Skyhawks did not escape as a 800 NAS CAP caught them and all were shot down.

By this time *Ardent* was seriously damaged, listing to starboard with raging fires, and so, having dropped anchor, *Yarmouth* came alongside her to evacuate the surviving ship's company, including thirty-seven wounded men. Twenty-two officers and men of *Ardent* were already dead. *Yarmouth* then pulled away, abandoning the blazing frigate, which later sank during the night with just the top of the main mast remaining visible, sticking out of the water.

In the course of the day the Argentinians claimed to have launched sixty-three bombing raids. It was also calculated that as many as fifteen of their aircraft had probably been destroyed on that first day. Eventually, as the dark descended, the air raids ceased and the battered escorts could concentrate on putting out fires, pumping out water, defusing unexploded bombs and making emergency repairs. It had been an exhausting day but at least the landings had been carried out successfully and the forces were well established, with 3,000 men securely ashore. It was considered too dangerous to leave the vulnerable *Canberra* and the rest of the STUFT in the enclosed bay, so it was decided to evacuate them that night, and at 2230 they sailed from San Carlos Water, escorted by the damaged *Antrim*.

———————•———————

The Loss of HMS ***Antelope*, 23 May** During the remainder of 22 May there were only sporadic attacks and incidents, including a Sea Harrier attack on a patrol craft, the *Rio Iguazu*, which was heavily damaged and beached. The next day, however, after a brief respite, saw a resumption of heavy air attacks. The first raid of four Skyhawks came in to attack

Ardent on fire and listing heavily to starboard, with *Yarmouth* alongside
(NN)

compartment exploded, and although the ship's company attempted to fight the fire, which had become a raging inferno, it was decided to abandon the ship. Only ten minutes after the last man was evacuated, the Seacat and torpedo magazine blew up, destroying the ship.

Heavy Air Attacks, 24 May At dawn on 24 May *Coventry* and *Broadsword* had sailed to the north of West Falkland to establish a forward '22/42 Combo' picket to break up incoming air raids. The Argentinians, however, had decided to try different tactics, with raids coming in up Falkland Sound from the south. The first raid of five Skyhawk A-4Bs took the Task Group by surprise and scored direct hits with 1,000 bombs on RFAS *Sir Lancelot*, *Sir Galahad* and *Sir Bedivere*. Two bombs failed to explode but ignited fires, whilst a third bomb penetrated right through *Sir Bedivere* before exploding. As the ships' companies attempted to fight the fires another raid of four Daggers swung in to attack, but this time they were met by a barrage of anti-aircraft fire. The Daggers pressed home their attacks, bombing and shooting up *Fearless*, *Sir Galahad*, *Fort Austin*, *Norland* and *Stromness*.

All four Daggers were badly damaged but managed to make it back to base. A Sea Harrier CAP from 800 NAS attacked a raid by four Daggers from the north and shot down three of the enemy aircraft.

At the same time a raid of three Skyhawk A-4Cs came in from the south and attacked *Fearless* and other amphibious shipping. The attack was carried out under intense anti-aircraft fire, and all Skyhawks missed their targets. All three aircraft were badly shot up, and only one managed to struggle back to base. No further raids were mounted that day, and the ships could continue to fight fires, defuse unexploded bombs and make emergency repairs, with *Sir Galahad* being beached.

Argentine air and naval air forces had sustained very heavy losses, and even those that had managed to return to base were mostly damaged and out of action. The Task Force was immensely lucky that so many of the bombs had failed to explode owing to the height at which they were released. The bombs had a small propeller fuse, which had to rotate a set number of times before the bomb armed. This time delay was to protect the pilot from his own bomb exploding too soon underneath him. Because the Argentine pilots were courageously dropping their bombs at the very last minute, after pressing home their attacks to ensure hits at the closest range, the bombs did not have time to arm. Unfortunately the BBC World Service decided to announce that information, which was invaluable to the Argentinians and seriously endangered men of the Task Force.

The attacking aircraft had a major advantage over the CAP as they did not have to use their radars, which would have been detected, as they approached over West Falkland. Flying low, they could navigate easily, and they knew that their main targets were going to be in San Carlos. This meant that only short-range anti-aircraft weapons could be used.

The helicopters continued to operate despite the raids,

shortly after midday and singled out *Antelope* and *Broadsword*. One Skyhawk scored a direct hit with a 1,000lb bomb on *Antelope* which failed to explode. The pilot had flown so low that he hit the mast at almost the same moment as his aircraft was blown apart by a Sea Wolf missile. Seconds later another raid arrived and a Skyhawk scored a direct hit with another 1,000lb bomb on *Antelope*'s port side.

Ongoing Air Attacks Yet another formation of Skyhawks came in to attack *Broadsword*, *Antelope* and *Yarmouth* from a different direction, but all the bombs missed their targets. Several raids from formations of Daggers came in to attack the escorts. They came under heavy fire, with an 800 NAS CAP managing to shoot down one Dagger with a Sidewinder missile. Super Etendards were launched to attack but failed to find suitable targets and returned to base.

Once again the raids ceased as the daylight disappeared and the opportunity was taken to try and defuse the bombs lodged in *Antelope*. At 1715 the bomb in a machinery

Antelope under attack
(DC)

(Top) *Antelope* blows up in San Carlos Water
(Martin Cleaver, Associated Press)

Bombs land close alongside RFA *Stromness* (*Stromness* had 200 tons of ammunition in her forward hold) (NN)

A Sea Harrier CAP from 800 NAS attacks a raid of Daggers (DC)

Antelope burns in San Carlos Bay (NN)

Coventry listing to port (NN)

withdrawing into the valleys on either side of San Carlos Water while the air raids passed through. *Antelope* continued to burn in San Carlos Bay.

'Veintecinco de Mayo': Argentine National Day, 25 May

The Task Force braced itself for major attacks on 25 May, the Argentine National Day, and TG 317.8, the Carrier Battle Group, closed East Falkland during the night to be in a position closer to Port Stanley. From this position Sea Harriers could quickly react to incoming raids and spend more time on task. The depleted air assets available to the Argentine high command reduced their options, and only twenty-two air raids, with a maximum of six aircraft in any one raid, were planned for that day.

The Sinking of HMS *Coventry* The first raid dived in at 0830, and a Sea Dart missile from *Coventry* shot down one of the Skyhawks. Several more raids were mounted by Daggers and

Skyhawks, with *Yarmouth* managing to shoot down a Skyhawk A-4C before it could release its bombs against *Fearless*. A little while later a further attack by three Skyhawks was engaged by *Coventry*, with one being shot down with a Sea Dart and a second being severely damaged but managing to struggle back to base.

In the early afternoon a raid of six Skyhawk A-4Bs closed the Falklands to the north and was monitored. A CAP was preparing to intercept but the '22/42 Combo', which was working well, was tracking the raid and ordered the CAP to disengage. The leading pair of A-4Bs zoomed in on the 'Combo', which prepared to engage them. Despite the heavy anti-aircraft fire the Skyhawks pressed home their attack and scored a direct hit on *Broadsword* with a 1,000lb bomb, which penetrated right through the ship but failed to explode.

As two more Skyhawks roared in to attack, *Coventry* tried to engage with her Sea Dart but the system failed to acquire either of the incoming aircraft. The system may have been confused by having two separate targets in such close proximity to each other. *Coventry* then desperately tried to manoeuvre so that *Broadsword* could engage with her Sea Wolf system, but as the two ships turned at speed *Coventry* passed in front of *Broadsword*, obscuring her Sea Wolf weapon system. Three bombs tore into *Coventry* and exploded, killing nineteen of her men. The ship heeled over with smoke pouring from her. In less than ten minutes *Coventry* was on her beam end. The ship had to be abandoned, and shortly afterwards she rolled over and sank.

The Sinking of the *Atlantic Conveyor* Argentine reconnaissance picked up the Carrier Battle Group, which was only some sixty miles to the north-east of East Falkland, and later in the afternoon it was decided to attack it with Exocet missiles. Two Exocet-armed Super Etendards were launched and flew to an in-flight refuelling point 120 miles to the north of the Falklands. The aircraft then altered course south-east to close the Task Group from an unexpected direction. As they approached to within forty miles of the group they transmitted briefly on their Agave radar and picked up a large radar echo which they assumed to be from one of the two carriers. The Agave transmissions were detected and identified by the group, which immediately took defensive action.

At 1538 both Super Etendard pilots launched their Exocet missiles at the same large radar contact on their screens. The group detected the launch and ships immediately turned towards the threat to present minimum radar profiles and fired Chaff patterns to decoy the missiles away from them.

One Exocet was successfully deflected away but the second struck the *Atlantic Conveyor*, which had been turning hard to port. The missile penetrated the port quarter ten feet above the waterline and ignited a raging fire. 'Only twenty minutes after being hit it was clear that our ship was doomed and all our attempts to quell the fires were to no avail.'[8] The master, Captain Ian North, and the Senior Naval Officer, Captain Mike Layard, agreed there was no chance of saving the ship, and as the fires rapidly approached the magazines orders were given to abandon ship. Twelve men including

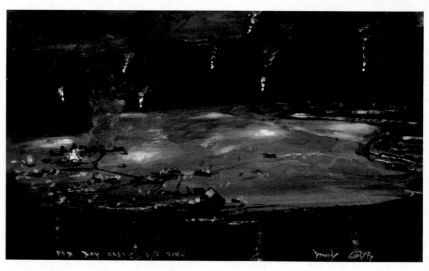

the master perished. Although the ship remained afloat for several days she was a burned-out wreck and nothing could be salvaged from her. Lost with the *Atlantic Conveyor* were three valuable Chinook helicopters and six Wessex 5 helicopters, which meant that progress across East Falkland would have to be by foot.

It had been a desperate day, but on land there were now 5,500 troops well established with some 5,000 tons of ammunition and equipment. Brigadier Thompson decided there was no time to lose and on 26 May gave orders for the advance across West Falkland. The amphibious group still came under air attack but at a much-reduced intensity so that unloading operations were able to continue with minimum disruption. Several attacks were carried out on shore positions, causing some casualties.

The Advance

The break-out from the beachhead at San Carlos started on 27 May, with 45 Commando and 3 Para setting out due east to advance on Teal Inlet.

Goose Green 2 Para meanwhile advanced on Darwin and were undetected as they prepared to attack Argentine forces at Goose Green. Unfortunately the BBC World Service announced the impending attack on Goose Green, and during the night Argentine reinforcements were flown in from Port Stanley. Sea Harriers attacked Goose Green in the morning and one was shot down by anti-aircraft fire, but bad visibility prevented more sorties, and 2 Para, with only three 105mm guns, had to attack the Argentine garrison at Goose Green without the benefit of air support. *Arrow* however provided NGS (naval gunfire support) and fired twenty-two rounds of starshell and 135 rounds of 4.5in, which were placed with great accuracy from a range of over ten miles.

The NGS had a devastating effect on the Argentine defenders. In the opinion of 3 Commando Brigade staff officers, the accurate NGS was the decisive factor in the rapid advance of the Paras.[9] At one stage shells were arriving only fifty metres in front of the advancing troops. However, *Arrow* had to withdraw to be back in San Carlos, two hours away, by daylight.

It was a very hard-fought battle during the course of which the commanding officer of 2 Para, Lieutenant Colonel H Jones, was killed (he was posthumously awarded a Victoria Cross). Reinforcements were flown in by Sea Kings and eventually the Argentinians capitulated on 29 May.

The British forces were further reinforced by the arrival of the *Queen Elizabeth II* with the Guards and the Gurkhas of 5th Infantry Brigade. The marines and soldiers advancing across East Falkland continued to make good if slow progress. All the while the naval forces continued to bombard Argentine positions in range of the sea and to use Sea Harriers to mount strikes on targets inland.

The Last AM.39 Exocet Attack, 30 May Whilst the campaign advanced steadily on shore, the Argentinians remained

Royal Marines advance across West Falkland towards Port Stanley
(NN)

Star shell being fired by naval guns at night
(DC)

determined to sink one of the carriers. On 30 May a raid was planned using two Super Etendards, one armed with the last remaining AM.39 Exocet missile. They were to be supported by four Skyhawks armed with three 500lb bombs each. The plan was to use in-flight refuelling to fly some hundred miles south of the Falklands to a position below the Task Group and then turn north and attack from the south. The aircraft flew out to a position 300 miles to the south-east of Port Stanley and then, undetected, they turned north to commence their run-in, flying very low below the group's radar cover. When they were close in, the Super Etendards climbed, making height for a quick burst transmission on their Agave radars. The Task Group detected the transmission and the action warning of 'Handbrake!' was immediately given. The lead Super Etendard fired its Exocet at a range of twenty-one miles and the ships of the Task Group immediately took evasive action.

Whilst the Super Etendards headed for home, the Skyhawks followed the Exocet missile in towards the Task Force. *Exeter* engaged the incoming Skyhawks with Sea Dart missiles, shooting down one as the remaining three pressed on to attack the frigate *Avenger* ahead of them. *Avenger* shot down one Skyhawk but the other two released their bombs, which fell all round the frigate, two very close on either side of the bow, but miraculously with no direct hit. The Skyhawks turned to port and headed south-west to escape. The Exocet missile meanwhile disappeared, though *Avenger* claimed to have shot it down with a 4.5in shell.

The surviving Skyhawk pilots claimed they had hit *Invincible*, which had also, supposedly, been struck by the Exocet missile and was on fire. The Argentine media made it front-page headline news, with lurid artists' impressions of the burning *Invincible*!

Although Argentine attacks on the forces at sea had gradually reduced and more ships had arrived to reinforce the Task Force, the land campaign slogged slowly on with no sign of the Argentinians surrendering as Paras, Guards and Royal Marines slowly and determinedly closed in on Port Stanley.

On 7 June two unarmed Learjets approached at 40,000 feet on a high-altitude reconnaissance mission. *Exeter* acquired them, and when they came within range, engaged with Sea Dart missiles. One Learjet was shot down, which crashed over Pebble Island, killing all five of its crew.[10] The second Learjet was not re-engaged but was deliberately allowed to return to report that San Carlos remained well defended.

The Attack at Bluff Cove, 8 June In an attempt to speed up the capture of Port Stanley the Welsh Guards were embarked in the LSLs *Sir Galahad* and *Sir Tristram* and sailed round at night to the east coast close to Fitzroy, some miles to the south of Port Stanley. The LSLs were spotted and the Argentine Air Force planned to attack them, as they appeared to be undefended. Raids were also mounted against the ships in Falkland Sound.

Plymouth had gone out from San Carlos into the open Sound to bombard Argentine spotters on Mount Rosalie, on

RFA *Sir Galahad* on fire at Bluff Cove (NN)

West Falkland, which had a clear view of the mouth of San Carlos Water. Just after midday five Daggers, on their way to Fitzroy, spotted *Plymouth* and dived down to attack her.

Four 1,000 lb bombs hit the frigate, although two of the Daggers were shot down (one by Seacat missile and one by 20mm Oerlikon). Three bombs caused considerable damage without detonating, but the fourth hit a depth charge, which exploded with the bomb, causing a major fire. Many rounds of 30mm cannon shell also hit *Plymouth*.

As the remaining Daggers were escaping to the west, five Skyhawks were flying round the south coast of East Falkland and up the coast towards Fitzroy. One of the aircraft spotted the two LSLs in Fitzroy Cove, and the leader then led the Skyhawks in to attack from the sea at low level. The LSLs were taken completely by surprise and had no time to prepare any defence. Being at anchor, they were sitting ducks, and each was hit by at least two 500lb bombs, as well as being strafed by 20mm cannon fire. Not all the bombs exploded but both ships were set on fire, with heavy casualties. The Master of *Sir Galahad* immediately gave the order to abandon ship. *Sir Tristram* was not quite so badly damaged but eventually she had to be abandoned as well. Fifty men were killed and another fifty-seven were wounded, many being badly burned. 8 June was a tragic day for the Task Force.

Exocet Strike on HMS *Glamorgan*, 12 June By 11 June the Royal Marines and Paras were attacking the Argentine forces in the hills around Port Stanley. As the land forces closed in, the naval bombardment of the Argentine defenders was intensified. The pattern of operations was for bombarding ships to close the land and open fire at night, withdrawing before daylight. On 12 June *Glamorgan* and *Yarmouth* had been providing naval gunfire support and shelling Argentine positions on Two Sisters, Mount Harriet and Mount Tumbledown. *Avenger* had been shelling Mount Longdon. After firing 428 high-explosive shells *Glamorgan* and *Yarmouth* turned east and commenced their withdrawal shortly after 0200.

When *Glamorgan* was approximately seventeen miles south-west of Port Stanley, a small contact approaching fast from well astern was detected on her radar. It was assumed to be a shell but it continued beyond the range of any gun and was quickly identified by *Avenger* as an Exocet missile (a ground-launched Exocet missile dismounted from a frigate and fired from the back of a lorry). *Glamorgan* held fire until the missile was within one mile and then launched a Seacat, which burst close to the Exocet, deflecting its flight but not sufficiently to cause it to miss *Glamorgan*. It hit the upper deck and tore into the hangar before exploding. The explosion ignited the aviation fuel, creating a fireball which devastated the stern of the ship. Fires raged in the galley, hangar and after machinery spaces. Thirteen men were killed and fourteen wounded. Listing heavily, and with smoke pouring from her, the ship managed to make eighteen knots and continued on course to rejoin the Task Group. By 1100 the next day *Glamorgan* had rejoined the group and brought her fires under control.

Ashore the Paras and Royal Marines were pressing home their attacks and by 0800 had secured all their objectives on the high ground overlooking Port Stanley. Later that morning an air raid of seven Skyhawk A-4Bs flew up the east coast of East Falkland and then turned in to attack the tactical headquarters of 3 Commando Brigade, Royal Marines on Mount Kent. Fortunately most of the bombs dropped failed to explode, though two helicopters were wrecked. Three of the Skyhawks were severely damaged by anti-aircraft fire but managed to return to their base.

Aircraft Attrition By 14 June the Argentinians had very few serviceable aircraft left: they had lost seventy and many more were severely damaged. It showed the courage of the Argentine pilots that they had continued to fly missions in the face of such a high attrition rate. Losses for the Task Force were thirty-four aircraft, twenty-four being helicopters (including the ten which were lost on board *Atlantic Conveyor*). The air battles also demonstrated the success of Sidewinder and Sea Dart missile systems, which had accounted for twenty-four aircraft between them. The reliability, availability and operational effectiveness of the Harriers had also been very clearly demonstrated. Meanwhile the ships of the Task Force continued to patrol the waters around the islands, fully ready to repulse any further air attacks.

The Final Advance and Cease-Fire, 14 June

In the late evening of 13 June the British forces commenced a heavy artillery and mortar barrage, supplemented by naval gunfire support. At approximately 2200 two major assaults were launched, supported by covering fire from frigates, close to the coast. 2 Para, supported by *Yarmouth* and *Ambuscade* (Commander Mosse), advanced to capture the western part of Wireless Ridge, whilst the Scots Guards advanced to take Mount Tumbledown, to be followed by the Gurkhas in their assault on Mount William. *Active* supported the assault on Mount Tumbledown firing starshell as well as high-explosive shells. The Argentine forces put up a determined resistance, and it was not until the early hours of the morning of 14 June that they were finally dislodged from Mount Tumbledown.

The British forces were now in possession of all the high ground overlooking Port Stanley, with the exception of Sapper Hill. Naval helicopters were then used to transport

The Task Force off the Falkland Islands, led by *Andromeda* (NN)

assault teams from 40 Commando to attack the hill. At that stage the Argentine forces were completely surrounded and General Menendez was negotiating for a cease-fire. At 1105 white flags were flying over Port Stanley and the fighting ceased. There was no guarantee that the Junta would accept the cease-fire, and constant vigilance was required in case of any further attacks from the mainland.

Operations were still required to mop up outlying Argentine positions on West Falkland and other islands. There was also the enormous logistics challenge of processing 10,254 prisoners, caring for the many wounded on both sides and starting the long slow work of clearing up. The weather deteriorated rapidly, impeding transport and replenishment, and there were many other matters to be dealt with including the problems of large quantities of landmines and other unexploded ordnance.

HM the Queen Mother greets *Queen Elizabeth II* on her arrival in the Solent on 11 June
(KR)

Invincible arrives home in Portsmouth on 17 September
(NN)

Crowds greet
Hermes
(NN)

Hermes sails into
Portsmouth harbour
on 21 July
(NN)

Operation Keyhole 19–20 June The very last operation of the Falklands Campaign was Operation Keyhole, the recapture of Southern Thule. On 15 June *Yarmouth* was ordered to detach from the Task Force and proceed to South Georgia to rendezvous with *Endurance*. *Yarmouth*, supported by the tanker RFA *Olmeda*, sailed south-east into heavy seas and arrived at Grytviken on 17 June. The Task Unit, under the command of Captain Barker of *Endurance*, embarked two rifle troops of 42 Commando and with six helicopters between them sailed for South Thule, 450 miles south-east of South Georgia.

HMS *Invincible*

Invincible Class Aircraft Carrier

The *Invincible* class VSTOL (vertical short take off and landing) light aircraft carriers, designed for ASW in the North Atlantic, arrived just in time to enable the Royal Navy to retain a crucial element of organic air power, in both air-defence and strike. *Invincible* played a key role in the Falklands Campaign and with her sister ships provided the backbone of the surface fleet, operating all over the world for more than three decades.

Launched:	3 May 1977
Commissioned:	11 July 1980
Displacement:	20,000 tonnes
Length:	210m
Propulsion:	COGAG 4 Rolls-Royce Olympus TM3B gas turbines, 2 shafts
Armament:	Sea Dart missiles,
	3 Goalkeeper CIWS,
	2 Oerlikon/BMARC 20mm GAM BO1
Typical air group:	6 Harrier GR7,
	6 Merlin Mk 1,
	3 Sea King
Complement:	682 plus 366 air group plus up to 600 Royal Marines
No. in class:	3: *Invincible*, *Illustrious* and *Ark Royal*

Arriving off South Thule two days later, *Endurance* used her helicopters to land sections of Royal Marines, whilst flights were made by other helicopters to confuse the Argentinians. In the morning of 20 June *Yarmouth* was ordered to conduct a gunfire demonstration as the Royal Marines advanced on the Argentine positions. Fortunately, as the Royal Marines prepared to advance and *Yarmouth* prepared to open fire, the Argentinians decided to surrender. The very last act of the campaign was for the Royal Marines to hoist the Union Jack over South Thule. It was both right and appropriate that the Royal Marines should play the first and last part in the Falklands War.

The Happy Return On 17 June General Galtieri and the Junta resigned. Then on 21 June General Bignone, the new interim President of Argentina, finally ratified the ceasefire negotiated on 14 June and the threat of hostilities was at last lifted. The British government decided nevertheless that it would retain sufficient forces in the area to safeguard the Falkland Islands for the time being.

It was then time for all those ships not involved in the logistics and recovery work in the Falkland Islands to make the welcome passage back to the United Kingdom. One of the first ships to return home was the *Queen Elizabeth II*, transporting the survivors of *Ardent*, *Antelope* and *Coventry*. She arrived back in the Solent on 11 June and was greeted by HM Queen Elizabeth the Queen Mother on board the Royal Yacht. A gun salute was fired by *Lowestoft*. The rest of the ships arrived back to rapturous welcomes and celebrations in Devonport, Portsmouth, Portland, Faslane and Rosyth from 21 June onwards. In the South Atlantic, Rear Admiral Reffell relieved Rear Admiral Woodward on 1 July, and *Hermes* then returned to Portsmouth on 21 July.

Change of Command The brand new carrier *Illustrious*, completed well ahead of time by Swan Hunters on Tyneside, quickly completed her sea trials and, commanded by Captain Jock Slater, sailed south. She arrived in the South Atlantic on 27 August and the following day relieved *Invincible* (Captain Jeremy Black) to return to Portsmouth.

***Invincible* Returns Home** On being relieved *Invincible*, escorted by *Bristol*, set course for the UK. Both ships finally arrived in Portsmouth on 17 September.

In Conclusion

Operation Corporate and the retaking of the Falkland Islands constituted the biggest naval campaign of the eighties. It was a relatively short, sharp, unexpected conflict fought nearly 8,000 miles away and the Royal Navy bore the brunt of it. It was 'short' in the sense that there were only seventy-four days from the Argentinean invasion to their subsequent capitulation. It was 'sharp' because British forces suffered over 1,000 casualties (Argentina's exact casualties are unknown, but the total number was certainly more than double the number of British casualties and well exceeded the Falklands Islands' population of 1,800). Over 57,000 tons of shipping were sunk. The British Task Force lost six major ships, including two modern Type 42 destroyers and two Type 21 frigates, and had ten others severely damaged. The Argentineans lost well over a hundred aircraft, and the cost to the British taxpayer has been estimated at over £2 billion.

The conflict was remarkable in many ways, a war which was certainly not anticipated and for which the Royal Navy was not well prepared owing to severe cuts in the defence budget and changes in government defence policy. At the time the Royal Navy was fully committed to NATO in an ASW role in the North Atlantic. The Fleet was reliant on land-based air cover, the last fleet carrier, *Ark Royal*, having been scrapped just two years earlier. Then suddenly the Navy found itself fighting a war in the distant South Atlantic facing air, surface and sub-surface threats with no allies and no land-based air cover. Of necessity it became an excellent proving ground for the Sea Harrier.

'Operation CORPORATE became necessary because deterrence failed, but in its execution it represented a triumph of military capability backed by resolute political will. The difficulties of short notice, extreme range and appalling weather under which this operation was mounted were all overcome by a single factor, the quality of our people.' Falklands despatch by John Fieldhouse, Commander in Chief Fleet.

OTHER ACTIVITIES

Operation Agila In January 1980 Britain despatched forces to Rhodesia to monitor the cease-fire prior to elections. Royal Marines and naval personnel were included as well as naval doctors and medical assistants. The forces were withdrawn on 15 March.

Bahamas On 12 May 1980 Cuban MiG fighter aircraft attacked the Bahamian Defence Force ship *Flamingo*, which was attempting to arrest Cuban fishing vessels fishing illegally. The Bahamian government appealed to the UK and the frigate *Eskimo*, with RFA *Black Rover*, sailed immediately from St Vincent. By the time they arrived the *Flamingo* had already sunk but they were able to rescue the crew.

Operation Titan In June 1980, units of 42 Commando flew out to the New Hebrides to assist French troops with Operation 'Titan'. The forces restored order during the run-up to Independence, and the Commander in Chief Fleet's band flew out to perform during the celebrations on 10 July. The Royal Marines remained until 19 August.

Fastnet Race Disaster In August 1980 the Fastnet Race in the Atlantic was devastated by a hurricane, with many yachts swamped and sunk. The frigate *Broadsword* was quickly on the scene and was able to supervise and co-ordinate all the difficult rescue operations.

Hurricane 'Allen' When Hurricane 'Allen' struck St Lucia and the Cayman Islands on 5 August 1980 the destroyer *Glasgow* and the frigate *Scylla* were quickly in the area, providing emergency relief aid.

Algeria On 24 June 1981, Algerian gunboats stopped a Shell tanker off Oran in the Mediterranean. The gunboats were attempting to divert the tanker, which appealed for help. The frigate *Dido* was ordered to the area at full speed to assist. As she closed the area the gunboats broke off and the incident was cleared up.

Operation Lesser Renewed violence in the Lebanon in June 1982 led to the UK launching Operation Lesser to protect and evacuate British nationals. The frigate *Leander* was detached from NAVOCFORMED (the Naval On Call Force Mediterranean) on 14 June and sent east to stand by off Akrotiri. MV *Royal Prince* with Royal Marines and naval personnel on board was sent in to Jounich to evacuate British nationals. The evacuation was completed by 24 June.

PERSONNEL MATTERS

The Redundancy Programme The infamous 1981 defence review, Cmnd. 8288 ('The Way Forward'), set out reductions in the manpower of all three armed services. The Royal Navy was to be reduced to 46,000 by 1990, in proportion to the reductions in the Fleet. Although it was not specifically mentioned, there was fear for the future of the Royal Marine Corps, with the decision to phase out and not replace the main amphibious ships. A redundancy programme was needed to remove such a large number of personnel, and the first phase of 500 redundancies was carried out before the Falklands Campaign took place. After the completion of Operation Corporate all plans were placed on hold, pending a fundamental re-evaluation of defence policy.

Recruiting Officer recruiting was becoming a problem, owing primarily to the publicity given to manpower cuts and redundancies. Studies were underway to consider the structure of the officer corps. Rating recruiting was very strong, with only 4,000 being accepted from the 30,761 applicants in 1982. The only problem was over a slight lack of sufficient high-calibre candidates for Artificer places.

New Open Engagement A new Open Engagement (contract of service) was introduced in September 1982, the aim being to simplify the nine different forms of engagement and encourage more senior rates to sign on for a full twenty-two-year pensionable engagement. There was also a revised bonus scheme, with an Open Engagement Bonus replacing the previous committal pay. The new scheme entailed ratings being paid £1,000 on completion of four and a half years' service and the same amount after seven and a half years' service for all those who had not given notice.

White Ensign Association Throughout the Falklands Campaign many people contributed and did their bit to help. Looking back through the records of the White Ensign Association it is noted that the Association also played its part in assisting all those involved. The Association organised life insurance for those sailing to the South Atlantic and also provided much help to the dependants of those killed or crippled during the campaign.

CHAPTER 7

Reprieve, Consolidation and Orient Express 1983–1985

INVINCIBLE REPRIEVED – SSN OPERATIONS AND SOVIET NAVAL BASTIONS – GRENADA – ORIENT EXPRESS DEPLOYMENT – OPERATION HARLING – OPERATION OFFCUT (THE LEBANON)

Within the space of three years from 1983, the main influential world leaders who would see the end of the Cold War were elected or re-elected. Following on from her great triumph in winning the Falklands War, Margaret Thatcher won a huge majority of 144 in the UK in May 1983, whilst the following year Ronald Reagan was re-elected President of the USA, and in 1985 Mikhail Gorbachev was elected Soviet party leader, reflecting the changes stirring in the Soviet Union. Gorbachev was to push for *perestroika* (restructuring) and *glasnost* (openness), though the nuclear disaster at Chernobyl in April 1986 was to test *glasnost*. He also called for nuclear disarmament and reinvigorated strategic arms reduction negotiations.

The year after Margaret Thatcher was re-elected she survived a bomb attack in Brighton when the Provisional Irish Republican Army tried to blow up her Cabinet, gathered together in the Grand Hotel for the annual party conference. The vulnerability of world leaders was demonstrated at the same time when Sikh extremists in India assassinated the Prime Minister, Indira Gandhi.

The Iran–Iraq War continued in the Middle East, posing a constant threat to international shipping and the crucial oil supply routes in the Gulf. In the Lebanon a huge car bomb was detonated by a suicide bomber on 23 October 1983, killing 241 US Marines, part of the UN peace-keeping force. A second car bomb on the same day killed a further fifty-eight French UN peace-keepers. A short while later the USA withdrew its forces from the Lebanon.

Defence Policy Following her re-election Margaret Thatcher appointed Michael Heseltine to replace John Nott as Secretary for Defence, and the main lessons learnt from the conflict were digested to reform defence policy. The Franks Committee, set up under Lord Franks to examine events leading up to the Falklands War, reported at the beginning of 1983,[1] whilst the MoD's internal review of the conflict reported at the end of 1982.[2]

Despite the Falklands War being fought without the assistance of NATO, the NATO alliance remained the cornerstone of Britain's defence policy in 1983, with some 95 per cent of the defence budget devoted directly or indirectly to the alliance. The main threat to the United Kingdom was still seen to come from the nuclear and conventional forces of the Soviet Union and the Warsaw Pact. The four principal roles of Britain's contribution to NATO remained as laid down by the infamous 1982

FIRST SEA LORDS
Admirals
Fieldhouse and
Staveley

SECOND SEA LORD
Admiral Cassels

MANPOWER
71,300

MERCANTILE MARINE
2,826 merchant
ships

statement of defence requirements, Cmnd. 8288, 'The Way Forward':

> The provision of independent strategic and theatre nuclear forces.
>
> The direct defence of the United Kingdom.
>
> A major land and air contribution to the European mainland.
>
> The deployment of substantial maritime capability in the eastern Atlantic and Channel.

Nevertheless the Falklands War and the many lessons learnt from Operation Corporate inevitably led to a reappraisal of Britain's defence requirements and a recognition by the government of the crucial importance of the Royal Navy. The First Sea Lord stated, 'It is a time of consolidation for the Royal Navy after a turbulent post-Falklands phase; for re-appraisal of our overheads, and for review of the country's overseas commitments and national interests, both within and beyond the NATO area.'[3]

Unfortunately the importance of the naval case did not appear to be fully recognised by the general public, as was stated by the Naval Staff: 'Although the Falklands Campaign should have underlined the importance of sea power the degree of public understanding of the naval contribution has in fact been disappointing. Perhaps the brilliance of the success of the Task Force has blinded the public eye to what is needed to preserve a naval capability.'[4] It was nevertheless acknowledged that Britain's amphibious capability with assault ships and 3 Commando Brigade provided an essential ability to respond to any unexpected crisis in a flexible way. This therefore necessitated the retention of the assault ships *Fearless* and *Intrepid* and the LSLs (landing ships, logistic).

The importance of retaining the availability of two operational aircraft carriers was also clearly demonstrated, and so it was decided to retain *Invincible*. Her sale to Australia was not progressed, ensuring that the Royal Navy possessed three *Invincible* class carriers. With three carriers two could be maintained at operational readiness with one in refit, maintenance or modernisation. The wisdom of this decision was to be proved many times over the next two decades. It was also agreed that the numbers of frigates and destroyers would be kept at about fifty-five instead of having four in the Standby Squadron.

The government also agreed to make good all war losses, and so the ships sunk were to be replaced. The two Type 42 destroyers *Sheffield* and *Coventry* and the two Type 21 frigates *Ardent* and *Antelope* were to be replaced by four large Type 22 anti-submarine frigates, three being the new improved 4,600-ton Batch 3 ships. The LSL *Sir Galahad* was to be replaced by a new and larger ship, and the seriously damaged LSL *Sir Tristram* was to be rebuilt. The aging ice patrol ship *Endurance*, which was to be withdrawn, was retained and a successor was planned for her.

THE FLEET

In 1983 the Royal Navy consisted of sixty-five major surface ships. The carriers included the dual-role anti-submarine commando carrier *Hermes*, and the two anti-submarine warfare carriers *Invincible* and *Illustrious*, about to be joined by the third, *Ark Royal*. To man *Ark Royal*, with both *Invincible* and *Illustrious* operational in 1984, it was necessary to run down *Hermes* to provide sufficient manpower. *Hermes* was put into dockyard maintenance and was employed on training tasks, though she retained the capability of being brought forward for operational deployment if required.

The rest of the Fleet included the two assault ships *Fearless* and *Intrepid*, the 6,000-ton Type 82 destroyer *Bristol* and the three remaining County class guided missile destroyers. In addition there were nine Type 42 destroyers and forty-seven frigates, including five of the new Type 22s, the six remaining Type 21s, twenty-four *Leander* class, three Tribal class and the nine remaining Type 12s. The Fleet included four SSBN Polaris deterrent submarines, twelve SSN nuclear fleet submarines and fifteen conventional patrol submarines. There were thirty-seven mine counter-measures vessels and twenty-one fishery protection and offshore patrol vessels.

The Royal Marine Corps consisted of 3 Commando Brigade with 40, 42 and 45 Commandos, together with artillery, logistics, engineering and communications support. The corps included the Special Boat Service (SBS). In 1983 the Royal Marines increased the specialist Protection Group, which had been formed in 1980 at HM Naval Base Clyde, to become 'Comacchio' Group.

Command of the Fleet The Fleet was commanded in 1983 by Admiral Sir William Staveley, who was relieved in June 1985 by Admiral Sir Nicholas Hunt. FOF1 (Flag Officer 1st Flotilla) was Rear Admiral Hogg, FOF2 was Rear Admiral Bathurst, and FOF3 was Vice Admiral Fitch. Flag Officer Naval Air Command was Rear Admiral Middleton, Flag Officer Submarines was Rear Admiral Heaslip, and Commandant General Royal Marines was Lieutenant General Wilkins.

FIRST SEA LORD

Admiral Sir John Fieldhouse Admiral Sir John Fieldhouse, fresh from his great success directing Operation Corporate

as CINCFLEET (Commander in Chief Fleet), relieved Admiral Sir Henry Leach as First Sea Lord in December 1982.

John Fieldhouse was born in 1928 and joined the Royal Navy as a cadet at the end of World War II. In 1948 he volunteered for the submarine service, in which he commanded the submarines *Subtle*, *Acheron*, *Tiptoe* and *Walrus*. Then from 1964 to 1966 he commanded the nuclear-powered submarine SSN *Dreadnought*. After serving as the Commander of the carrier *Hermes* he was promoted to Captain and commanded the nuclear deterrent Polaris

The new *Illustrious*
(JCKS)

submarines of the 3rd Submarine Squadron from 1967 to 1970. He then commanded the frigate *Diomede*, being at one stage Commodore of STANAVFORLANT (the Standing Naval Force Atlantic), before becoming Director Naval Warfare on the Naval Staff.

In 1975 he was appointed FOF1 as a rear admiral and led the Third Group Deployment to the Pacific, before being appointed FOSM (Flag Officer Submarines). From 1979 to 1981 he was the Controller of the Navy as a vice admiral. As Controller he had an important role in supporting the case for the Trident project and helping to persuade the government to push it through Parliament.

He became CINCFLEET in 1981 and was thus at the helm for the Falklands War, which he directed from his headquarters at Northwood. Following the great success of Operation Corporate he was appointed First Sea Lord in December 1982. As First Sea Lord he was in a position to oversee the reprieve and consolidation of the Fleet, ensuring that progress was made in achieving a balanced and flexible force mix for the Royal Navy. It was important work which later was to prove of great value.

When the post of CDS (Chief of the Defence Staff) was due to rotate to the RAF in 1985 the Prime Minister intervened so that Fieldhouse, with his great experience of directing a successful war, was given the top job. Accordingly he was appointed CDS, out of turn, in August 1985 and promoted Admiral of the Fleet. He finally retired in 1989 and was created Baron Fieldhouse of Gosport. He also became Chairman of the White Ensign Association but tragically died in 1992.

OPERATIONS AND DEPLOYMENTS, 1983–1985

In 1983 ships and units of the Royal Navy continued to be deployed around the world, with ships and vessels on station in Hong Kong, Gibraltar, Belize, the West Indies (the West Indies Guardship, or WIGS) and Northern Ireland as well as the Fishery Protection Squadron. Ships were also assigned to NATO and deployed with STANAVFORLANT as well as on short assignments to on-call forces in the Channel and Mediterranean.

Nuclear Deterrent Patrols Throughout the period nuclear deterrent patrols were constantly maintained in the depths of the oceans by the Polaris SSBNs of the *Resolution* class, *Renown*, *Repulse* and *Revenge*, with *Resolution* undergoing a two-year refit. *Resolution* completed her refit and shakedown period off Cape Canaveral before rejoining the operational cycle at the end of 1985.

Submarine Operations The fleet submarines and patrol submarines continued their vital intelligence-gathering missions in the Barents Sea. The secret patrols, observing and monitoring the Soviet Navy's Northern Fleet, were highly dangerous but essential for the West to maintain its supremacy in anti-submarine warfare. Similar covert missions were conducted in the Mediterranean. Secret intelligence was also essential to detect any sudden large-scale deployments of Soviet naval forces, which could indicate the opening moves of a pre-emptive strike.

Soviet Naval Bastions From 1983 the Soviet Navy developed a strategy of operating their ballistic missile submarines in heavily defended 'naval bastions' relatively close to their main naval bases or under the Polar ice cap. This became possible when their strategic missiles had developed sufficient range to be able to strike targets in America without having to be deployed close to the North American coast, as had been necessary with shorter-range missiles. It was also a response to the interdictory tactic of the emerging NATO maritime strategy of forward deployment. The Soviet Northern Fleet operating out of Murmansk deployed to a bastion in the Barents Sea, whilst the Soviet Pacific Fleet established a bastion in the Sea of Okhotsk. Whilst the US Navy covered the Okhotsk bastion, the Royal Navy was concerned with the Barents Sea bastion. It was essential to detect and mark the Soviet Navy missile submarines so as to be able to neutralise them in the event of hostilities. Collisions and accidents happened from time to time within the bastions, but for the most part these were kept secret. The Soviet submarines were steadily improved by using all the submarine information and technology provided to the Russians by the notorious Walker spy ring. This enabled them to build faster, quieter submarines as well as giving them operational data concerning US submarines and tactics.[5]

Admiral Fieldhouse
(WEA)

The Falkland Islands and Antarctic The protection of British interests in the aftermath of the Falklands War, and a deterrent posture against any possibility of revenge operations, remained a high-priority task for the Royal Navy. Three destroyers or frigates and three patrol vessels, under the command of the Senior Naval Officer Falkland Islands (SNOFI), were maintained on station in the waters around the Falkland Islands. The ice patrol ship *Endurance* and the survey ship *Herald* as well as RFA replenishment ships, tankers and other maintenance vessels supported them. The security position was kept under close surveillance and contingency plans had been prepared for rapid reinforcement by other ships and submarines if the situation ever warranted it. D Company of 40 Commando, Royal Marines was deployed for an operational tour of the islands in support of the garrison from 27 March to 2 August 1983.

In 1984 the new Falkland Islands patrol vessels, *Protector*, *Guardian* and *Sentinel*, arrived on station. They were specially converted 1,000-ton offshore oilrig support tugs (*Sentinel* was 1,700 tons) and were armed with two 40/60mm Bofors guns and three GPMGs (general-purpose machine guns).

In November Operation Okehampton, to salvage the Argentine submarine *Santa Fe*, was carried out by a RMAS (Royal Maritime Auxiliary Service) salvage vessel and tug. The submarine, which had been sunk during the Falklands War, was recovered from South Georgia and then scuttled in deep water.

At the end of 1985 the number of frigates and destroyers required on station was being reduced to two following the opening of the Mount Pleasant airfield. The helicopter support ship RFA *Reliant* was also deployed to the area with two Sea King helicopters.

The Armilla Patrol The Royal Navy continued to maintain the Armilla Patrol, with two frigates or destroyers, supported by an RFA tanker, deployed in the Gulf region to provide a visible British presence in the Gulf of Oman and the Straits of Hormuz during the Iran–Iraq War. Iraq, following the example of Britain in the Falklands War, had declared the northern Gulf an exclusion zone, warning that any ships in the area would be liable to attack from air-launched missiles. In retaliation Iran had threatened to close the Straits of Hormuz; it was a very serious threat as nearly a hundred tankers a day sailed through the straits.

Ships of the Royal New Zealand Navy had been sent to the Gulf in 1982 to release British frigates and destroyers to join the Task Force in the South Atlantic. The Royal New Zealand Navy continued to assist the Royal Navy, and between 1982 and 1983 the *Leander* class frigates HMNZSS *Canterbury* and *Waikato* carried out alternate patrols alongside British frigates in the Gulf. The last ship, HMNZS *Waikato*, was finally withdrawn in September 1983.

The Group Deployment Concept The success of the Falklands Campaign fully validated the concept of group deployments by the Royal Navy outside the NATO area. Not only did the deployments provide invaluable operating and

and steamed east back across the Atlantic to Gibraltar.

On arrival off Gibraltar the group joined up with other warships and submarines to take part in the regular major exercise Springtrain, involving missile firings in both the Atlantic and the Mediterranean. On completion of the exercise the group returned to Portsmouth, arriving at the end of April.

Sea Days, July 1983 In 1983 it was decided to reintroduce the showpiece exercise Staff College Sea Days, after a break of four years. Five frigates, *Ariadne*, *Torquay*, *Apollo*, *Liverpool* and *Alacrity*, sailed out of Portsmouth in July with over 800 VIPs, senior military spectators and staff college students embarked. The ships performed an impressive series of manoeuvres and weapon firings culminating in a spectacular 'gun line' firepower demonstration.

logistical support experience, but they also fulfilled an important high-profile role in maintaining Britain's status and prestige, being a clear outward sign of Britain's influence and ability to project power around the world. As well as being an excellent demonstration of the flexibility of maritime forces they provided a powerful overseas showcase to enhance sales and orders for British products and defence equipment.

Invincible Group Deployment for Caribtrain 83 (NN)

The Falklands Campaign unquestionably boosted Britain's status, but it was acknowledged that it would be important to maintain that position. and that it was therefore necessary to continue the policy of sending naval task groups on deployments outside the NATO area. The decision to continue with group deployments would pay great dividends in the years ahead. A major group deployment to the Far East was planned for later in the year, but first a shake-down deployment to the Caribbean was organised.

Group Deployment Caribtrain 83, 1 February – April 1983
On 1 February 1983 the carrier *Invincible*, flying the flag of Rear Admiral Gerken, FOF2, sailed out of Portsmouth for a deployment to the USA and Caribbean. The 6,750-ton Type 82 destroyer *Bristol* and the frigates *Battleaxe*, *Arethusa*, *Zulu* and *Euryalus* escorted her, and the group was supported by the fleet tanker RFA *Olwen* and the fleet replenishment ship RFA *Resource*.

The group headed west down the Channel, and *Invincible* embarked the Sea Harriers of 801 NAS. The group then weathered atrocious heavy seas and storms, which hampered the work-up exercises as it sailed out into the Bay of Biscay and altered course south-west. After flying exercises off the coast of Portugal the group headed across the Atlantic for the Caribbean. The ships used the US weapon range facilities off the Bahamas for missile firing exercises, including ASW (anti-submarine warfare) exercises with the nuclear fleet submarine *Splendid*. On completion *Invincible*, escorted by *Bristol* with RFA support, headed for Belize, where her Sea Harriers were able to exercise with RAF GR3 Harriers in the skies over Belize, whilst the frigates visited the eastern Caribbean. After visits and exercises the group rendezvoused

Grenada On 19 October 1983 a violent revolution in the former British colony of Grenada overthrew the government and killed Maurice Bishop, the Prime Minister. Many loyal Grenadians were massacred by the rebel soldiers. Anxious to divert attention from the crisis in the Lebanon, President Reagan ordered an invasion of Grenada. He diverted a powerful CBG (carrier battle group) of US warships with the strike carrier USS *Independence* and a marine amphibious unit with USS *Guam*, which had just sailed for the Lebanon, to reverse course and head for Grenada. Vice Admiral Metcalfe commanded the force, with Major General Schwarzkopf added to his staff to co-ordinate elite Air Force and army units supplementing the amphibious forces. Urgent discussions took place between Britain and the USA at high level over the planned invasion of this independent state within the Commonwealth.

The British government immediately ordered the guided missile destroyer *Antrim* to head for the area at full speed and stand by during the crisis. *Antrim* arrived off Grenada on 23 October. Two days later the US forces, with Commonwealth Caribbean assistance, invaded the island and conducted Operation Urgent Fury to restore order. Within two days the invasion forces had defeated the rebel forces, killing over seventy, for the loss of eighteen US servicemen. It was a powerful show of force, and peace and democracy were rapidly restored to Grenada. By 7 November the situation on the island had stabilised and *Antrim* was withdrawn from the area.

Major Group Deployment Orient Express (Task Group 318.3), 1 September 1983 – 18 April 1984

At the beginning of September 1983 *Invincible*, flying the flag of Rear Admiral Jeremy Black, FOF1, led a task group, codenamed Orient Express (TG 318.3), bound for the Far East. The ships of the group included the Type 42 destroyer *Nottingham*, the *Leander* class frigates *Achilles* and *Aurora* and the older Type 12 frigate *Rothesay*, as well as the older diesel-electric submarine *Opossum*. The fleet tanker RFA *Olmeda* and the freighting tanker RFA *Appleleaf* supported the group.

Ships on the gun
line at Sea Days 83
(NN)

Invincible arrives
in Sydney for
Christmas
(NN)

The carrier
Illustrious inspects
a Soviet carrier in
the western
Mediterranean
(JCKS)

Departure The ships sailed from Portsmouth on 1 September and headed west down the Channel, embarking the new Secretary of State for Defence, Michael Heseltine, en route. After watching flying displays off the Cornish coast, the Secretary of State was landed and the group continued out into the Atlantic, altering course south for Gibraltar.

The Lebanon The group transited through the Straits of Gibraltar and after a brief visit sailed east across the Mediterranean towards the Lebanon, where the situation was tense. At the very end of August, UN troops in the Lebanon had come under fire and been engaged in gun battles. On 3 September Israel had begun to withdraw her troops from Lebanon, and at the end of September a cease-fire was agreed. The way was then clear for the group to transit through the Suez Canal, particularly as the carriers *Illustrious* and *Hermes* were already in the western Mediterranean to take part in the major NATO naval exercise Display Determination.

In the Indian Ocean After transiting through the Canal and Red Sea the group headed east into the Indian Ocean and rendezvoused with a powerful US carrier battle group based on the 61,000-ton carrier USS *Ranger*. The group then conducted a series of exercises with the US ships before continuing east. The ships divided for port visits, with *Invincible* visiting Bombay and providing extensive displays

173

of her Sea Harriers and Sea King helicopters for the Indian Navy. The Indian Navy was suitably impressed with both aircraft and eventually would order them, together with the carrier *Hermes*. On completion of the highly successful Indian visit, *Invincible* and the frigates *Aurora* and *Rothesay*, with RFA support tankers, headed for Singapore.

Diplomatic Incident in Australia Following a period of maintenance the group proceeded to sea and steamed south-east for Australia, passing through the Java Sea and islands of Indonesia. The ships then rendezvoused with US and Australian ships for joint amphibious exercises off the west coast of Australia before visiting Fremantle. On sailing from Fremantle *Invincible* experienced excessive vibration on her port shaft bearings, which unfortunately was serious enough to warrant her needing to be drydocked. The decision was taken for her to be drydocked in the Australian naval yard at Sydney after her visits to Wellington and Auckland on North Island, New Zealand. *Invincible* then arrived in Sydney in time for Christmas.

A diplomatic incident then arose when the Australian government denied access to the drydock facility following the British government's policy of refusing to 'confirm or deny' whether *Invincible* had nuclear weapons embarked. The same problem had already led to the earlier cancellation of the planned visit to Japan. Sadly that left no alternative but for *Invincible* to use the Sembawang docking facilities in Singapore. On 29 December she sailed from Sydney and headed for Singapore Island. *Invincible* arrived back in Singapore on 9 January 1984 for a month of inspection and repairs in the King George VI graving dock.

The temporary work on the port shaft bearings had been completed by the beginning of February, and *Invincible* was able to sail for exercises with the US Navy in the South China Sea. During the course of the exercises further problems were experienced with the bearings on the port shaft. Knocking was heard at certain shaft speeds and *Invincible* had to return to Singapore.

The rest of the Task Force continued with exercises and then split up for various port visits. *Aurora*, on passage to Okinawa to pick up Rear Admiral Jeremy Black (FOF1), ran into a force 7 monsoon and experienced great difficulty in refuelling from RFA *Olmeda*. She was at sea for several weeks before finally making her way into Okinawa.

When *Invincible* arrived in Singapore further checks were carried out in the dockyard but without success, and it became obvious that it would be necessary for the ship to return to the UK for full investigation and repairs during her programmed DED (docking and essential defect repair).

Exercise Team Spirit The US Navy continued joint exercises, including exercise Team Spirit, with the South Korean Navy, without *Invincible* participating. Exercise Team Spirit was to be marred by an extremely dangerous Cold War incident when the carrier USS *Kitty Hawk* collided with a Soviet *Victor* class nuclear submarine on 23 March. The Soviet SSN had been tailing close astern of the *Kitty Hawk* at speeds up to almost

thirty knots whilst the carrier had been conducting flying operations. When the carrier suddenly reduced speed for a RAS (replenishment at sea) the submarine appeared not to notice the reduction in speed and passed directly underneath, overtaking her. Then, having realised the carrier was no longer ahead, the SSN stopped. At that stage she was dead ahead, lying in the direct path of the *Kitty Hawk*. The submarine came up to periscope depth to look for the *Kitty Hawk* and as she did so she was run down by the 84,000-ton aircraft carrier. The severely crippled Soviet nuclear submarine survived the collision and was eventually towed to the Soviet naval base at Vladivostok.

Return to the UK The planned visit to Pusan in South Korea was cancelled, and the group began the return passage to the UK. *Invincible*, accompanied by *Olmeda*, headed west across the Indian Ocean for the Gulf of Aden. In the Gulf of Aden exercises were conducted with the French Navy, very closely observed by a Soviet *Krivak* class guided missile destroyer. *Invincible* then steamed up the Red Sea and transited through the Suez Canal. Once in the Mediterranean and just south of Cyprus, the Sea Harriers of 801 NAS (Naval

Aurora refuelling from RFA *Olmeda* in heavy seas
(NN)

Air Squadron) were launched to fly on ahead to the UK. The Harriers staged home via the NATO training facility of Decimomanu on the island of Sardinia, and on via Istres, eventually reaching Yeovilton.

Meanwhile 820 NAS Sea Kings flew covert surveillance missions over the Soviet naval base in the Gulf of Solum, managing to photograph various units including a previously undetected Soviet *Tango* class, long-range hunter-killer, submarine. *Invincible* then sailed on to Gibraltar, arriving on 13 March for a brief visit before heading on across the Bay of Biscay and up the Channel. Finally she arrived back in Portsmouth on 20 March 1984. The remaining ships of the Orient Express deployment arrived back in the UK in April. Having de-ammunitioned, *Invincible* sailed down the Channel to Devonport for her DED. Fortunately the problem with the port shaft main bearing was solved and successfully repaired during the DED without causing any delay to the ship's operational programme.[6]

The Lebanon: Operation Offcut, 18 November 1983 – 31 March 1984

During the Orient Express deployment a serious situation had arisen in the eastern Mediterranean. In 1982 Israel launched Operation Peace in Galilee and invaded the Lebanon. The invasion was ostensibly an attempt to establish a demilitarised zone to protect Israel from continued rocket attacks; however, the Israeli forces then advanced on Beirut and laid siege to the city. In the fierce fighting with the Syrian Army some 10,000 people were killed. Israeli aircraft wiped

out the Syrian air force, and then launched air strikes on Beirut, doing great damage. The repeated bombing attacks were televised by the world media, prompting an international outcry. Eventually the USA managed to arrange a cease-fire monitored by US and European peace-keepers, but when the peace-keepers left a short while later, Lebanese forces massacred over 1,000 Palestinian refugees in camps

The County class guided missile destroyer *Glamorgan* (NN)

Enter the Gas Turbine (The Men who Made the Fleet Go)

The mix of old and modern propulsion systems in ships fighting in the Falklands Campaign illustrates well their evolution in the Royal Navy. Commissioning of the gas turbine propelled Type 21 frigates and Type 42 destroyers in the mid-1970s, followed by the similar Type 22 frigates, was as great a leap forward as the change from coal to fuel oil. More capable air-conditioned Ship Control Centres (SCCs) and absence of large steam systems made life not only more comfortable for Marine Engineering watchkeepers, but also safer. The threat of massive high-pressure steam leakage due to action damage, and consequent deadly scalding of many men was finally removed; the old steam-drench fire-fighting systems being simply replaced by inert gas drench systems. Central control and analysis of machinery performance from the SCC, was extended and much improved by introduction of transistorised electronic control systems, but with significantly smaller numbers of men now available careful training in routine operation and practice of emergency

procedures gained significance: whilst the risk of fire and flood in several very large machinery spaces, now routinely unmanned, required ever more careful 'rounds' routines with each man more alert and competent, assisted by remote detection equipment.

Systems for formal planning of maintenance had been introduced to Engineering Departments in the early 1960s, replacing the less formal 'Chief Tiff's Notebook', and supplemented by a flood of Books of Reference, notably Marine Engineering administrative and technical instructions in BRs 3000 and 3001, replacing the old BR16 Steam Manual. Gradually Marine Engineers of the steam generation edged away from 'open up and inspect' to Repair by Replacement (RxR), later known as Upkeep by Exchange (UxE), and the adoption of Non-Destructive Testing (NDT) procedures, such as Vibration Analysis (VA) and more comprehensive on-board oil and water testing. With aero-derived gas turbines fitted in ships, air engineering standards and techniques, such as spectrographic

analysis of lubricating oil and magnetic chip detection, also diffused into ME procedures, to give better prediction of problems, and their repair or replacement, helping realise the aim of increased ship availability.

As these all-gas turbine ships were commissioned responsibility for electrical and electronic equipment, upon which the Marine Engineers depended, lay with the Weapon and Electrical Engineering Branch, formed from the Weapons and Radio Branch, itself expanded from the Electrical Branch of 1946. But in 1979, Engineering Branch Development (EBD) returned responsibility for electrical power generation and ship-wide distribution to the Marine Engineers, as well as responsibility for electronic equipment in their own systems. To these were added computer software-driven control systems, first introduced in the Hunt Class MCMVs in 1980, allowing much greater degrees of machinery control and analysis. From the Hunt Class to the Type 23 frigates, to the latest LPDs and Type 45 destroyers of 2008, Marine Engineers must now

be masters of a very wide range of technologies, including the latest high-voltage Integrated Electric Propulsion systems. Yet properly organized, rigorous 'rounds' by a reduced number of people must continue under all conditions: including war, when they must still be able to control and survive action damage.

As ever, a ship's Marine Engineers can never sleep. If the 'iron mistress' is unable to leave harbour, or to 'obey telegraphs', or won't steer: or the lights go out, or the air's too warm, or the water too cold, or there's no ice for drinks: someone, sometimes everyone, will notice. When everything works, nobody notices. Marine Engineers experience their own excitements, but unlike the orchestrated drama of firing a gun or launching a missile these are usually unplanned, sudden and unwelcome. Perhaps even the most modern watchkeeper, as he leaves the SCC at the end of his watch in 2008, still utters the old Engineers' blessing – 'Keep it steady'.

Captain Jock Morrison RN

at Sabra and Shatila. A multi-national force of US Marines and European troops, including a contingent from the UK (British Forces Lebanon, or BRITFORLEB), was quickly sent to Beirut to protect the remaining refugees.

Repeated bomb attacks were launched against US- and Israeli- occupied buildings. During the summer of 1983 there was a build-up of US naval forces off the coast, and the battleship USS *New Jersey* engaged in shelling terrorist positions. On 23 October 1983 a suicide bomber in Beirut detonated a massive car bomb outside the building where the US Marines of the UN peace-keeping forces were accommodated, killing 241 US Marines. At the same time fifty-eight French peace-keepers were killed in their barracks by another car bomb, and on 4 November forty Israeli soldiers were killed in another suicide attack.

Britain promptly launched Operation Offcut, sending naval forces to the area to protect British troops deployed with the multi-national forces in Lebanon. On 18 November the guided missile destroyer *Glamorgan* and the frigate *Brazen*, together with the fleet tanker RFA *Blue Rover*, were ordered to stand off the Lebanese coast. Two days later the assault ship *Fearless* was ordered to sail from the UK for the eastern Mediterranean, with the tanker RFA *Brambleleaf* in support. *Fearless* arrived off Lebanon on 28 November and relieved *Glamorgan*. At the beginning of December the *Leander* class frigates *Andromeda* and *Achilles* were returning to the UK having been relieved in the Gulf on Armilla Patrol. Having transited through the Suez Canal the frigates, supported by the fleet tanker RFA *Grey Rover*, were ordered to Cyprus to stand by in readiness to reinforce *Fearless*. On 4 December US carriers launched waves of aircraft to attack Syrian anti-aircraft missile sites in Lebanon, with two of their own aircraft being shot down.

On 8 December it was decided that *Andromeda* and RFA *Grey Rover* could be detached to continue their return passage to the UK, with *Achilles* being retained off the east coast of Cyprus. Then a week later it was decided that *Achilles* should also continue her passage back to the UK, leaving *Fearless* and *Brambleleaf* in close support of British troops ashore in the Lebanon.

RFA Reliant At the beginning of January the new 28,000-ton helicopter support ship RFA *Reliant* was working up at Portland. RFA *Reliant* was a converted container ship (the ex MV *Astronomer*), specially adapted as an aviation support ship to carry four Sea King helicopters and with a naval party of 150 on board. She was converted using the 'Arapaho' concept used by the USA to convert merchant ships into helicopter operating bases, which involved bolting on a specially designed flight deck and hangar kit. She was ordered to sail to the eastern Mediterranean with three Sea King helicopters of 846 NAS and Naval Party 2240 embarked. RFA *Reliant* immediately proceeded from Portland and headed for Gibraltar and the Mediterranean. She made a fast passage and arrived off the coast of Lebanon to relieve *Fearless* on 11 January.

Local militia forces steadily took over most of Beirut,

leaving the peace-keepers exposed and in considerable danger. On 3 February President Reagan ordered the evacuation of the US Marines to the ships of the 6th Fleet, and on 7 February the international peace-keeping force began pulling out. The following day the decision was taken to evacuate BRITFORLEB. The 115 British troops were quickly withdrawn by helicopter to RFA *Reliant*, and fifty military trucks and armoured vehicles were also embarked. Some 5,000 British nationals and refugees were also evacuated. The last US Marines were pulled out on 26 February, leaving just a few French observers ashore. RFA *Reliant* transported the evacuated personnel to the safety of Cyprus, and having landed them remained in the area with elements of BRITFORLEB still embarked and standing by for any international emergency operations. Finally on 23 March Operation Offcut was terminated and RFA *Reliant* was withdrawn from the eastern Mediterranean.

Operations Harling and Armilla Accomplice
Operation Armilla Accomplice On 26 March 1984, an MCM (mine counter-measures) force was formed for deployment to the Mediterranean. The force consisted of the Ton class MCMVs (mine counter-measures vessels) *Brinton* and *Gavinton*, from the 3rd MCM Squadron based at Rosyth,

The MCMV *Kirkliston* departs for Operation Armilla Accomplice (TT)

and *Kirkliston* and *Wilton*, from the 2nd MCM Squadron based at Portsmouth. *Wilton* was the world's first warship to be built of glass reinforced plastics, which made her ideal for mine counter-measures operations.

The MCM force, supported by MV *Oil Endeavour* (chartered from trade), was ordered to sail from the UK for the Mediterranean as part of Operation Armilla Accomplice. Its task was to stand by in the eastern Mediterranean in readiness to deploy to the Gulf of Oman and Straits of Hormuz to assist with mine clearance in the vital oil tanker routes to and from the oil terminals in the northern Gulf. The ships of the squadron remained at readiness, constantly exercising in the eastern Mediterranean off Cyprus. In July a further MCMV, *Bossington*, from the 2nd MCM Squadron, was ordered to sail from Portsmouth to the eastern Mediterranean to join them. Meanwhile, despite the fact that tankers were being harassed and attacked in the Gulf, with some eighty ships being attacked during the year, no evidence of a mining threat emerged.

REPRIEVE, CONSOLIDATION AND ORIENT EXPRESS 1983–1985

Operation Harling, 15 August – 14 October 1984 On 15 August the Egyptian authorities requested assistance with mine clearance in the Gulf of Suez, following mine damage to several merchant ships at the northern end of the Red Sea. The British government agreed to reactivate Operation Harling and send the Armilla Accomplice MCMV squadron south through the canal to the Gulf of Suez to embark on mine clearance work. The squadron joined other MCMVs from the French, Italian and US navies, but all ships operated independently, remaining under national control. A number of mines were located and destroyed, and a Russian mine was also recovered, which was taken back to the UK for analysis. Eventually the area was declared cleared on 14 October.

The MCMV squadron was withdrawn, transiting the Canal to the eastern Mediterranean, where it was eventually decided that the vessels should return to the UK, though they were to remain on standby for mine clearance operations in the Gulf. The squadron of four MCMVs was held in UK waters at thirty-two hours' notice to deploy, and it was not until June 1985 that the notice to deploy was finally extended to forty-two days.

———•———

Hong Kong In 1983 the Hong Kong Squadron consisted of the five converted Ton class MCMVs, *Beachampton*, *Monkton*, *Wasperton*, *Wolverton* and *Yarnton*. They had been converted to patrol craft specifically for operations in the waters around Hong Kong. They were assisted by 3 RSRM (the 3rd Raiding Squadron Royal Marines), which was equipped with Avon Searider RIBs (rigid inflatable boats). The Royal Marines had been deployed to Hong Kong a few years earlier in response to an emergency but had proved so successful in stopping large numbers of illegal immigrants attempting to cross by sea that the Hong Kong government had requested that they remain in the colony.

By 1984 the Royal Marines found themselves being outmanoeuvred and outrun by the faster speedboats being used by illegal immigrants, and in September it was decided to re-equip them with the much faster FPCs (fast pursuit craft). These modern fast craft were highly effective, and twenty-one 'Snakeheads' (illegal immigrant smugglers) were captured in the first six months of operations.

In November 1984 *Yarnton* and *Wasperton* were replaced by the first of the new purpose-built 700-ton *Peacock* class OPVs (offshore patrol vessels). The first two new patrol vessels, *Peacock* and *Plover*, arrived in Hong Kong in November. The remaining three OPVs, *Starling*, *Swallow* and *Swift* arrived and replaced the last three of the Ton class by 1 October 1985.

Gibraltar In 1983 a frigate or destroyer was maintained permanently on standby to carry out guardship duties for Gibraltar. In January 1984, when the political pressure being exerted by Spain appeared to ease, the notice for the guardship was extended to ninety-six hours, but in the following year it was decided to maintain a permanent squadron of patrol craft at Gibraltar. Accordingly in August

two ex-RAF fast auxiliary craft were commissioned as *Cormorant* and *Hart* and assembled as the new Gibraltar Squadron on 29 August 1985.

Canada In June 1985 a small force consisting of the frigates *Brilliant* (serving with STANAVFORLANT) and *Alacrity*, the patrol submarine *Sealion* and a squadron of MCMVs, *Waveney*, *Carron* and *Dovey*, manned by RNR (Royal Naval Reserve) personnel, sailed across the Atlantic to Canada. They arrived in Halifax and joined the Atlantic Assembly gathered to celebrate the seventy-fifth anniversary of the Naval Service of Canada, from 26 June to 2 July. The ships were reviewed by the Governor General of Canada on board the Canadian armed forces vessel *Quest*.

HMS *Valiant*: Anti-Soviet Operations, 14 July – 8 August 1985 Periodically the USSR deployed significant numbers of submarines into the Atlantic to probe the West's ASW capability and validate the vital submarine intelligence it had obtained from the US Whitworth–Walker spy ring. In response to one of these surges into the Atlantic in 1985, the Royal Navy SSNs *Valiant*, *Churchill* and *Trafalgar* were deployed to detect and track the Soviet submarines.[7]

In July 1985 the SSN *Valiant* was at sea in the North-West

HMS *Trafalgar*
***Trafalgar* Class Submarine**

The *Trafalgar* class nuclear fleet submarines started to join the Fleet in 1983. They were a considerable improvement on the *Swiftsure* class, being faster and much quieter. They also had a much greater endurance than their predecessors. They would eventually be fitted with land-attack cruise missiles from 1999, which they would fire in anger.

Launched:	1 July 1981
Commissioned:	27 May 1983
Displacement:	5,208 tonnes
Length:	85.4m
Propulsion:	1 Rolls-Royce pressurised water-cooled nuclear reactor supplying steam to two sets of General Electric geared turbines, 1 shaft
Armament:	5 533mm (21in) tubes for 20 Mk 24 Tigerfish wire-guided and Mk 8 anti-ship torpedoes, up to 50 Mk 5 Stonefish or Mk 6 Sea Urchin mines instead of torpedoes, 5 UGM-84A Sub-Harpoon missiles
Complement:	110
No. in class:	7: *Trafalgar*, *Turbulent*, *Tireless*, *Torbay*, *Trenchant*, *Talent* and *Triumph*

Approaches taking part in a sonar trial when a Soviet submarine build-up became evident. In view of the potential threat to the UK Polaris SSBN on patrol, *Valiant* was ordered at full speed to Faslane to embark a towed array and deploy to the west of the UK to hunt the Soviet submarines. The SSN *Churchill* in the same areas was already trailing a *Victor* class SSN, but was being withdrawn.

With her towed array embarked, *Valiant* proceeded fast to the area and soon was in contact with a *Victor* class SSN (a special fit unit) and proceeded to trail him; this was a challenging situation as he was frequently manoeuvring. On the fourth day of trailing the *Victor* a second, much quieter submarine was detected and *Valiant* commenced the trail of both. Unfortunately *Valiant* then encountered a problem with her propulsion system, and her nuclear plant had to be shut down, but she continued tracking the Soviets in battery drive. By this stage the SSN *Trafalgar* had joined in the hunt, but was not in contact. It was a tense time as engineers investigated, though fortunately it turned out to be a false alarm, and *Valiant* was soon able to take up the hunt again.

Both Soviet submarines were tracked as they headed for the Shetland/Faeroes Gap, but the following day strong sonar transmissions were detected to the south-west from a Soviet *Udaloy* class destroyer. Multiple ship noise on the sonar transmission bearings indicated the presence of a Russian surface force. At periscope depth *Valiant* sighted the *Udaloy* on the horizon with the masts of other ships. Right ahead of the force *Valiant* dived deep and headed for its northern flank, avoiding the approaching *Udaloy*, but holding the *Victor*. As the ships passed, *Valiant* crossed to the southern flank and on turning to parallel the most southerly ship, she regained contact with the second Soviet submarine. It was evident that the Soviet submarines were carrying out exercise attacks on the surface ships, simulating a NATO convoy, and the *Valiant* sonar and control room teams had a real challenge in maintaining the overall tactical picture. Meanwhile in the air the Soviets were carrying out simulated air attacks.

The next day, whilst continuing to shadow the Soviet ships, *Valiant* sighted two Soviet auxiliaries and one escorting *Kotlin* class destroyer. The *Victor* submarine ahead suddenly went deep and fast, crossing at close range, carrying out an attacking exercise on the surface ships. A short while later a probable diesel submarine was detected at close range astern of the ships, and a good tracking solution was achieved on him.

A day later *Valiant* was north of the Shetland Islands and had lost contact with the two Soviet SSNs but had detected two new distant Soviet nuclear submarines. However, her priority was to hunt for any submarines lurking off the North-West Approaches, and therefore she headed back south.

Whilst conducting a search of the Rockall Trough area, *Valiant* received a report of two closing *Delta* class SSBNs, and moved to intercept. In due course the first of the *Deltas* was detected and trailed heading north. When it was established that the *Delta* clearly was heading home, *Valiant* broke off and headed south to continue the hunt for diesel submarines. The second *Delta* was detected at range to the north-west later the same day.

Valiant then headed to the north-west of Scotland to hunt an outbound *Victor II* SSN, which appeared to be heading for the Mediterranean. The *Victor II* was assessed to have slipped past by transiting in shallower and noisier water, as by the time *Valiant* detected him he was well past heading south. After a few more days' searching, *Valiant* managed to intercept and track a homeward-bound *Charlie II* class missile submarine returning from the Mediterranean.

Type 22 frigate
(NN)

On completion of the successful three-week operation *Valiant* headed home having gained a great deal of valuable intelligence of Soviet submarine operations.

Joint Operation in the Mediterranean, 8 October 1985 In October 1985 a group of terrorists, led by Abdul Nidal, took over the cruise ship *Achille Lauro* as she was cruising in the Mediterranean, and murdered one of the passengers, a disabled US citizen. The aircraft carrier *Invincible* was immediately ordered to the eastern Mediterranean at full speed on 7 October to intercept and board the ship. The plan was to insert a Royal Marine assault team swiftly from astern by low-flying helicopter, which would give a strong possibility of boarding swiftly without detection.

Invincible headed east at full speed to track the *Achille Lauro*. She steadily closed on the ship with the assault team standing by to board, but unfortunately before she arrived the *Achille Lauro* altered course away and diverted to Alexandria.

The *Achille Lauro* arrived safely in the port of Alexandria and the terrorists, holding hostages, managed to take a flight for Libya. All was not lost, however, as the National Security Council in the USA, including Marine Colonel Oliver North, persuaded President Reagan to authorise an 'in-flight interception' of the terrorists by the 6th Fleet. A US Navy E-2C tracker aircraft located and monitored the Libyan flight. As soon as authorised four US Navy F-14 Tomcat jet

---

HMS *Broadsword*

Type 22 *Broadsword* Class Frigate

The Type 22 frigates were designed for the primary role of ASW in the North Atlantic and were built to carry two Lynx ASW helicopters. They were big potent frigates, as large as earlier light cruisers, and carried a range of weapons to provide defence against air and surface threats. Additional Type 22s were built to replace the ships lost in the Falklands.

Launched:	12 May 1976
Commissioned:	3 May 1979
Displacement:	Batch 1: 4,400 tonnes, Batch 2: 4,800 tonnes, Batch 3: 4,600 tonnes
Length:	Batch 1: 131.2m,
	Batch 2: 146.5 m,
	Batch 3: 148.1m
Propulsion:	Batches 1 and 2: 2 shaft COGOG,
	2 Rolls-Royce Olympus TM3B high-speed gas turbines,
	2 Rolls-Royce Tyne RM1C cruise gas turbines
	Batch 3: 2 shaft COGAG,
	2 Rolls-Royce Spey SM1A boost gas turbines,
	2 Rolls-Royce Tyne RM1C cruise gas turbines
Typical armament:	Surface-to-surface missiles (SSM)
(variations in batch)	8 Harpoon (130 km range),
	surface-to-air missiles (SAM) Sea Wolf (6km range),
	1 4.5in gun (25 rounds/min 22km range),
	1 Goalkeeper 30mm close-in weapon system,
	2 20mm twin guns (10km range), Lynx/Merlin helicopter
Complement:	Batch 1: 222,
	Batch 2: 273,
	Batch 3: 259
No. in class:	14, built in 3 batches. Only 4 Batch 3s remained in service by 2009

fighter interceptors were scrambled from their aircraft carrier. The US E-2C Hawkeye vectored the Tomcat jets to intercept the civil airliner. Having found the airliner the F-14s then appeared alongside the airliner, on each side, and forced it to land at the NATO airfield of Sigonella. Once on the ground all the terrorists were promptly arrested by the Italian authorities and the hostages released. It was a successful conclusion to a joint operation.[8]

Northern Ireland: Operations Grenada and Interknit, 1983–1985

Operation Grenada Throughout the period 1983 to 1985 the Royal Navy was committed to Northern Ireland security operations and patrols. The vessels of the Northern Ireland Squadron, the Bird class patrol boats *Kingfisher* and *Cygnet*, maintained the patrols of Operation Grenada off the coast of Ireland to prevent the smuggling of arms and personnel. A few additional patrols were carried out briefly by *Bronington* and *Wakeful* in support.

Operation Interknit Operation Interknit, policing the waters of Carlingford Lough to prevent terrorist activities in the area, was carried out by the patrol craft *Alert* and *Vigilant*, with a Royal Marine detachment. On two occasions of heightened alert additional patrols were carried out by the patrol boat *Kingfisher*.

Internal Security Deployments Meanwhile on shore, the Royal Marines of 40 Commando, less 'D' Company (which was deployed to the Falkland Islands), carried out internal security duties in southern Armagh from 3 January to 6 June 1983. Their patrols were conducted in the dangerous 'bandit country' with great skill, and during that time only one Royal Marine was killed in action. From 3 July to 12 November the following year 42 Commando was deployed to the area for routine security operations, whilst 40 Commando was sent to Cyprus as the UK's contribution to the UN peace-keeping force.

Helicopter Support In 1984 helicopters from 815 NAS and 819 NAS were deployed to Northern Ireland for additional reconnaissance and insertion operations, and they continued operations on into the following year.

SHIPS, WEAPONS AND AIRCRAFT

New Frigates The Falklands War had a profound effect on the design, construction and deployment of frigates. Hitherto the predominant requirement had been for ASW frigates operating in the North Atlantic, supported by AAW (anti-aircraft warfare) destroyers of the new Type 42 *Southampton* class. One of the prime lessons from the Falklands was a reinforcement of the need for all-round 'general purpose' ships.

Type 22 Frigate The first result was the modification of the Type 22 *Broadsword* class large ASW frigates. These 3,556-

---

The Perisher (The Submarine Command Course)

This world famous course seems to have been put on a formal footing during World War II and is certainly mentioned in books written by such eminent wartime submarine commanding officers as Arthur Hezlett and Edward Young. Given its epithet, as failing the course meant your career had effectively ended, its format has changed over the years (especially with the introduction of an all-nuclear submarine flotilla), in essence, however, the aim is very simple; to pass, each member of the course has to prove that he can operate a submarine safely and then effectively in a tactical setting, through a mixture of training at sea and ashore. Standards remain absolute and are entirely at the discretion of the course officer (known as 'Teacher').Shore training was conducted originally in the Rothesay Attack Trainer and then from the mid 70s onwards at Faslane, Plymouth and HMS *Dolphin* in Gosport. At sea the two key training periods are known as 'Cockex' and 'Cockfight'. 'Cockex' owes its origins to short range torpedo attack tactics and was vividly captured in Jonathan Crane's acclaimed 1980's BBC documentary. This practical hands-on test for would-be submarine COs of keeping their submarine safe in the Firth of Clyde whilst trying to press home an attack on a 'Heavy' protected by up to four escorts could become almost a Control Room ballet as student and Teacher operated their periscopes independently but with undoubted synchronicity, until the limits of safety were reached and the submarine had to 'go deep' to stay clear of trouble whilst trying to regain the initiative.

On 'Cockfight', initially in the open ocean and then on the West Coast of Scotland and in the Clyde, each student is placed in command for extended periods and with a number of tactical serials to complete – against a task force, other submarines, to gather intelligence or to land members of the SBS – the complete spectrum of submarine activity is covered. After several weeks at sea and growing more and more tired (and with Teacher deliberately increasing stress levels) there is no doubt that if the student passes he has earned the right to be a member of a particularly exclusive club.

Vice Admiral Peter Wilkinson CVO

---

ton Batch 1 and 4,160-ton Batch 2 ships, though originally described as the *Leander* class replacement frigates, were in fact highly specialised 'hi-tech' ASW frigates designed specifically for the North Atlantic, with the Batch 2s being fitted with the new Type 2031Z 'towed-array' sonar. The replacements for the destroyers and frigates lost in the Falklands were to be a further Batch 2 Type 22 frigate and three modified and extended new 4,300-ton Batch 3 Type 22 frigates. The Batch 3 ships were fitted with the automatic 4.5in gun, the Goalkeeper rapid-fire gun system for close range anti-missile defence and the longer-range Harpoon anti-ship missile in place of the Exocet missile system.

Type 23 Frigate The Type 23 Duke class frigate was originally announced in 1980 as the future replacement of the *Leander* class frigate. The design had been subjected to an intense debate between those advocating a 'short fat' ship and the traditionalists who campaigned for a 'long thin' narrow-hulled ship. There was also considerable discussion on the optimum weapon fit. In the end it was decided to continue with the more conventional long slim hull.

Prior to the Falklands the new Type 23 had been intended as a smaller ASW frigate with the Type 2031Z 'towed array', which was much cheaper than the larger Type 22 frigate. The design of the Type 23 was then redrawn to provide a much more potent all-round ship, still with a prime ASW role but with an enhanced general-purpose capability with the Sea Wolf missile system. The Type 23 was also designed to be 'lean-manned' with a complement of only 146, compared with the complement of 296 required for the Batch 3 Type 22 frigate.

The order for the first ship, *Norfolk*, was awarded on 24 October 1984. She was laid down in 1985 and launched two years later.

CIWS (Close-In Weapon System) In 1983 it was announced that the Dutch Goalkeeper fast-firing seven-barrelled Gatling gun system was to be procured for the Royal Navy's inner layer of defence against anti-ship missiles. The system was known as the CIWS.

Stingray Torpedo Following successful development the Stingray Advanced Lightweight Torpedo entered service in the Royal Navy in 1983. The torpedo was designed to be launched from fixed-wing aircraft as well as helicopters and surface ships.

Spearfish Torpedo By 1985 the principal anti-surface weapon deployed in all Royal Navy submarines was the highly successful Sub-Harpoon long-range anti-ship missile. The submarines also carried the Tigerfish torpedo, and trials were well advanced with the new advanced heavyweight torpedo Spearfish, which was designed to be the main anti-submarine and anti-surface ship torpedo weapon system in the 1990s. The *Oberon* class submarines were still equipped with the veteran Mk 8 torpedo (as used by the SSN *Conqueror* to sink the Argentine cruiser *Belgrano*).

MANPOWER MATTERS

Redundancy Programme The Falklands Campaign caused a review of manpower requirements, and one of the results was to halt the second phase of the redundancy programme. The 500 officers and men who had been selected for the first phase all left the Service by March 1984. The second phase, of 2,000 redundancies, was put on hold whilst further studies were carried out on the revised manning requirements. The new stable manpower plan was announced in the 1984 Defence White Paper with a projected requirement of 63,500 by the early 1990s.

The New Open Engagement The new Open Engagement scheme introduced at the end of 1982 was encouraging ratings to stay on for a full twenty-two-year pensionable engagement. The aim had been to prevent trained and experienced men from leaving on completion of a shorter engagement.

Artificers One of the results of far-reaching important studies into the future of the Engineering Branch, known as EBD (the Engineering Branch Development Study), was the abolition of the title 'mechanician'. It was considered that mechanicians, first introduced in the Royal Navy in 1903 to relieve artificers of some of their watch-keeping duties, had

White Ensign Association: twenty-fifth anniversary banquet with HRH the Princess Anne, October 1983
(WEA)

The White Ensign Association: anniversary banquet, 25 June 1985, with HRH the Duke of Edinburgh and Admiral the Lord Lewin
(WEA)

become interchangeable with artificers. From 1 April 1983 all skilled engineering personnel, whether entered as apprentices or mechanics, were called artificers.

Seamanship Training A working party, set up in 1979, had identified shortcomings in standards of seamanship in the Service, and so a Seamanship sub-branch at senior rate level was introduced. Greater emphasis was placed on basic seamanship during training courses to redress the problem.

The White Ensign Association The White Ensign Association continued to provide a great deal of help and assistance to the naval community and assisted those being made redundant. The Association had been gearing up to assist

with the second phase of the redundancy programme when fortunately that did not occur.

On 31 October 1983 the Association celebrated its twenty-five years of service to the Royal Navy with an anniversary banquet in the Guildhall in London, at which the guest of honour was HRH the Princess Anne, Commandant of the WRNS. 650 people attended the banquet, and many representatives of the ships and units which fought in the Falklands were invited.

In November that year, Lord Kingsdown (then Sir Robin Leigh-Pemberton) stepped down as President of the Association to take up his appointment as Governor of the Bank of England. Lord Boardman, President of the National Westminster Bank, succeeded him. The following year Admiral of the Fleet the Lord Lewin relieved Sir Donald Gosling, the Chairman, and a new system, whereby the chairmanship of the Association would alternate between representing Business and Navy, was introduced. To strengthen the Association, the post of Deputy Chairman, recruited from either business or Navy to complement the Chairman, was also introduced.

On 25 June 1985 the Association held a twenty-seventh anniversary banquet for over 800 guests at Hampton Court Palace. The guest of honour on this occasion was HRH the Duke of Edinburgh.

CHAPTER 8

Forward Maritime Strategy and the End of the Cold War 1986–1989

FORWARD MARITIME STRATEGY AND ASW – GLOBAL 86 AND OUTBACK 88 DEPLOYMENTS – OPERATION BALSAC (ADEN EVACUATION) – GULF OPERATIONS AND END OF IRAN–IRAQ WAR – FALL OF THE BERLIN WALL AND END OF THE COLD WAR

By 1986 the naval forces of the Warsaw Pact were approaching their zenith with immensely powerful fleets and real global reach. But with the election of Gorbachev the world was already changing, and the late 1980s were to see a fundamental shift in world politics, with the decline and eventual break-up of the Soviet Union, resulting in the end of the Cold War and ultimate victory in the West. The end of the Cold War was symbolised by the breaching of the Berlin Wall on the night of 9 November 1989, with dramatic pictures of that defining moment being flashed around the world.

The increasing power of the Soviet Navy had been underpinning the increased involvement of Soviet forces and influence in the affairs of the Third World, apart from Afghanistan, where Soviet forces were to withdraw in 1987 after a long and costly campaign. The spread of Soviet domination greatly concerned NATO leaders and was behind the shift in focus towards the evolving NATO defence strategy of 'out of area' and 'rapid deployment'. In its application to naval strategy this was to evolve into the full policy of 'Forward Maritime Strategy' for the navies of the NATO countries.

In 1986 the USA advocated the doctrine of early and forward deployment of naval forces, set out in a policy document entitled 'The Maritime Strategy'.[1] This represented a quantum change from its previous defensive maritime posture to a much more aggressive forward deployment. The new offensive strategy was pushed hard by the Reagan administration, and John Lehman, the Secretary of the US Navy, was one of its chief proponents.[2]

Defence Policy In 1986 the UK government was desperate to trim money from the defence budget but, at the same instant, anxious to avoid all mention of a defence review at a time when the West was facing an extremely powerful Warsaw Pact. All three services had expensive major equipment programmes. The Defence White Paper stated: 'We shall need to balance the preservation of the front line against the requirement to invest in expensive new equipment to strengthen the fighting power of our armed forces in the 1990s. Some difficult decisions will have to be taken.'[3]

Michael Heseltine, who was to be succeeded by George Younger as the Defence Secretary after a high-profile row over the future of Westlands, was a supporter of European collaboration for defence projects. He was keen on the NATO frigate replacement and the EH 101 naval ASW (anti-submarine warfare) helicopter projects. ASW remained an important cornerstone of NATO naval strategy.

FIRST SEA LORD
Admiral Staveley

SECOND SEA LORDS
*Admirals Fitch
and Brown*

MANPOWER
68,200

MERCANTILE MARINE
*2,378
merchant ships*

The Type 22 frigate *London* trailing a Soviet submarine (NN)

Anti Submarine Warfare (ASW) In 1986 the menace of the Soviet submarine threat had never been greater. The huge 25,000-ton *Typhoon* class SSBNs (ballistic missile-carrying nuclear submarines) were already at sea, and the ultra-modern *Delta IV* class SSBNs were just entering service. The 7,550-ton *Sierra* class and 10,000-ton *Akula* class SSKNs (hunter-killer nuclear submarines) were already on patrol, and the 16,000-ton *Oscar II* class and 8,500-ton *Mike* class submarines started joining the fleet in 1986. NATO defence planners were most concerned about the threat posed by the huge Soviet submarine fleet.[4] ASW had moved centre stage in the Cold War.

THE FLEET

In 1986 the Fleet was still recovering from the setbacks of the Nott defence cuts and the Falklands Campaign, though the government had agreed to replace all the ships lost in Operation Corporate and to reverse the most drastic of the Nott Fleet reductions. With the new carrier *Ark Royal* having been completed in 1985, all three of the new CVSs (18,000-ton small anti-submarine, VSTOL (vertical short take off and landing) aircraft carriers) were in service. Though the carrier *Hermes* was still sold to India in 1986, both of the elderly assault ships *Fearless* and *Intrepid* were retained, and new destroyers and frigates were entering service. *Invincible* had just completed a two-year modernisation programme and had been fitted with a 12° ski jump ramp to extend the range of the Harriers.

Major Surface Ships The Fleet, then, consisted of the three light fleet carriers, *Invincible*, *Illustrious* and *Ark Royal*, two assault ships and forty-two escorts (twelve Type 42 and one Type 82 destroyers, six Type 21, seven Type 22, and sixteen *Leander* class frigates). Four more Type 22 frigates would join the Fleet by 1988, with a further three building.

Type 23 Frigates In addition the first of the brand new 3,500-ton Type 23 Duke class frigates with the 2031Z towed-array sonar were being laid down. Following a considerable debate over the optimum hull shape for the new frigate, between those who favoured a short fat hull and the traditionalists who preferred a long slim ship, sixteen of the new frigates were planned, with a long and relatively narrow hull.

The Submarine Fleet The submarine fleet consisted of the

four *Resolution* class Polaris strategic deterrent nuclear submarines, with their replacement, *Vanguard* class Trident missile SSBNs building. The fourteen nuclear fleet submarines (SSNs) of the *Valiant*, *Churchill*, *Swiftsure* and *Trafalgar* classes would be joined by the last four of the *Trafalgar* class. In addition the Navy still had eleven diesel-electric patrol submarines (SSKs) of the *Oberon* class, half of which had been completely modernised. Four SSKs of the new Type 2400 *Upholder* class diesel-electric submarines had been ordered in 1983 and were under construction.

Smaller Vessels The MCM (mine counter-measures) and offshore patrol squadrons consisted of fourteen of the old Ton class, ten of the advanced glass-reinforced-plastic-built Hunt class MCMVs (mine counter-measures vessels) with three more building, and twelve modern River class MCMVs, and also twenty-one patrol vessels. Two patrol vessels, *Swallow* and *Swift*, were sold to Ireland in 1988. In addition there were ten survey ships and vessels.

Support Ships Fourteen tankers, with six replenishment ships, six LSLs (landing ships, logistic) and three support ships manned by the RFA (Royal Fleet Auxiliary), supported the Fleet.

Fleet Air Arm The Fleet Air Arm consisted of the Sea Harrier STOVL (short take off and vertical landing) jets (three squadrons: 800, 801 and 899), the Sea King ASW, AEW, SAR and Commando helicopters (nine squadrons: 810, 814, 819, 820, 824, 826, 845, 846 and 849) and the advanced high-speed multi-purpose Lynx helicopters (two squadrons: 815 and 829), as well as various support and training aircraft. A new helicopter, the EH 101, Merlin, was planned to enter service from the early to mid-1990s.

Royal Marines The Royal Marine Corps consisted of 3 Commando Brigade with 40, 42 and 45 Commandos, together with artillery, logistics, engineering and communications support. The Corps also included the Special Boat Service (SBS).

Command Admiral Sir Julian Oswald commanded the Fleet from his shore headquarters at Northwood, Middlesex (HMS *Warrior*). The fleet was divided into three flotillas. Rear Admiral John Kerr commanded the 1st Flotilla, with a shore-side office in Portsmouth naval base, whilst Rear Admiral Guy Liardet commanded the 2nd Flotilla, with an office in Devonport. Rear Admiral Hugo White commanded the 3rd Flotilla, which consisted of the aircraft carriers, and he also carried the appointment of Commander Anti-Submarine Striking Force.

FIRST SEA LORD

Admiral Sir William Staveley William Staveley was the son of Admiral Staveley and a grandson of Admiral Sir Doveton Sturdee, victor of the Battle of the Falkland Islands (1914).

He was born in November 1928 and joined the Royal Navy in 1942. He served as Flag Lieutenant to the Commander in Chief Home Fleet in the battleship *Vanguard* and then in the Royal Yacht before commanding the minesweeper *Houghton* during the Borneo Campaign and Indonesian Confrontation in 1962–4.

After commanding the Tribal class frigate *Zulu* he was promoted Captain and became Assistant Director of Naval Plans. In 1972 he took command of the commando carrier *Albion*, and after appointment as Director Naval Plans he became Flag Officer 2nd Flotilla and then FOCAS (Flag Officer Carriers and Amphibious Ships).

He was appointed Vice Chief of the Naval Staff in 1980 and was thus in the MoD for the Falklands Campaign. He then served as Commander in Chief Fleet from 1982 and spoke out against reductions in defence expenditure at a time when the forces of the Warsaw Pact were greater than ever. He became First Sea Lord in 1985, enabling Admiral Fieldhouse to take up the appointment of Chief of the Defence Staff. He retired in 1989 and died of a heart attack eight years later in October 1997, aged sixty-eight.

OPERATIONS AND DEPLOYMENTS, 1986–1989

In 1986 the Royal Navy continued to be fully involved with a range of important commitments around the world, among which the protection of British interests in the Falkland Islands and Antarctica remained a high priority.

The Falkland Islands and Antarctica The protection of British interests in the aftermath of the Falklands War, and the maintenance of a deterrent posture against any possibility of revenge operations, remained high-priority tasks for the Royal Navy. Two destroyers or frigates and three patrol vessels, under the command of the Senior Naval Officer Falkland Islands (SNOFI), had been maintained on station in the waters around the islands.

The ice patrol ship *Endurance* and the survey ship *Herald*

Admiral Staveley (left) with HRH the Duke of Edinburgh at a White Ensign Association reception (WEA)

as well as RFA replenishment ships and tankers and other smaller vessels supported them. The security position was kept under close surveillance, and contingency plans had been prepared for rapid reinforcement by other ships and submarines if the situation ever warranted it.

In 1986 the new military airfield at Mount Pleasant on the Falkland Islands had just been opened, making possible a reduction in naval forces by one destroyer or frigate and the Sea King helicopters of 826 Naval Air Squadron, which returned to the UK. Other ships, including the support ships RFAS *Reliant* and *Diligence*, also returned to the UK.

Hong Kong In the Far East the Hong Kong Squadron, based at HMS *Tamar*, consisted of the five new purpose-built 700-ton *Peacock* class offshore patrol craft, *Peacock*, *Plover*, *Starling*, *Swallow* and *Swift* but was reduced to three ships in July 1988 when *Swallow* and *Swift* returned to the UK. It carried out guardship duties, including the prevention of smuggling and mass illegal immigration, in conjunction with the Hong Kong Police as part of the Hong Kong garrison.

The 3rd Raiding Squadron Royal Marines (3 RSRM), operating FPCs (fast pursuit craft), reinforced the squadron. It was eventually disbanded on 1 July 1988. Whilst it had been in Hong Kong 3 RSRM had carried out 1,800 patrols, conducted 4,200 boardings, captured sixty-five speedboats, and arrested 954 illegal immigrants and thirty-six criminals.

Gibraltar: Start of Operations Clover and Kingpin Gibraltar Guardship duties were carried out by a small squadron consisting of two patrol craft, *Cormorant* and *Hart*, reinforced by a frigate or destroyer as necessary. Frequent incursions into Gibraltar territorial waters by Spanish vessels led to the activation of Operation Clover on 17 April 1986. This was a reinforcement operation carried out by the Type 42 destroyer *Exeter*, which was deployed in the area until the situation eased, and the operation was terminated on 2 May. On 9 June an MCMV was placed on seven days' notice to proceed to the area and RAF Phantoms were forward-based in Gibraltar. Operation Clover was re-titled Operation Kingpin on 28 January 1987.

Cyprus Elements of all three services were maintained in Cyprus, as the Sovereign Base Area was essential for the support of peace-keeping operations in the eastern Mediterranean and for support of UN forces in Cyprus and the Lebanon. Support facilities were maintained for warships transiting to and from the Suez Canal.

West Indies and Belize A frigate or destroyer, supported by an RFA tanker, was maintained on station in the Caribbean as the West Indies Guardship (WIGS). The WIGS carried out guardship duties and continued to work closely with the US Coast Guard on anti-drug trafficking operations. She also supported the Belize garrison.

Operation Eschew Civil unrest broke out in the Turks and Caicos Islands in January 1986, and the WIGS frigate,

Ariadne, was sent there. She conducted Operation Eschew to provide stability with security patrols in the area from 22 January through to 30 July.

Fishery Protection The Fishery Protection Squadron of thirteen vessels was fully engaged in coastal and offshore policing duties around the United Kingdom.

Armilla Patrol Since the beginning of the Iran–Iraq War the Royal Navy had deployed ships to the region to protect British tankers and international shipping in the Gulf and the Straits of Hormuz. The operation was codenamed Armilla, and the operational patrol was maintained with two ships, destroyers or frigates, constantly on station, supported by an RFA tanker. It was a dangerous task as tankers were frequently attacked by both Iraq and Iran.

Armilla Accomplice In support of Armilla operations a squadron of MCMVs was retained in UK waters at forty-two days' notice to deploy to the Gulf. They were on standby for mine clearance operations, codenamed Armilla Accomplice, in the vital shipping routes in the Gulf, the Straits of Hormuz and the northern area of the Arabian Sea. It was essential to keep those important international shipping lanes, carrying 42 per cent of the West's oil supplies, open, and the Royal Navy was still the foremost navy in terms of skill and experience in mine clearance.

Strategic Nuclear Deterrent Throughout the period the Royal Navy maintained the strategic nuclear deterrent, with at least one of the four Polaris SSBNs always on patrol, hidden in the depths of the oceans. In 1987 the submarines *Revenge* and *Repulse* completed their refits and, after conducting successful test missile firings, rejoined the deterrent patrol cycle.

Forward ASW Operations With the new emphasis on forward maritime strategy, the Navy's role was to operate her ASW task groups north of the GRIUK (Greenland–Iceland–Faeroes–UK) Gap, well up into the northern Norwegian Sea, in advance of the main US CBGs (carrier battle groups). Type 42 destroyers and SSNs were deployed even further north, ahead of the ASW task groups. Britain was continuing to provide 70 per cent of the NATO maritime forces in the eastern Atlantic area.[5]

The Falklands War had demonstrated the importance of distant operational logistics, from tactical support from tankers, and provision of stores and ammunition, to defect rectification and major forward repair, to enable ships to be retained forward-deployed in the area of operations, rather than having to return, possibly through hundreds of miles, to home bases. Previously NATO exercises had concentrated on tactics and joint operational matters rather than logistics.

Forward logistic sites (FLSs) were planned, where helicopters would support deployed ships, and anchorages and alongside berths were available for repair, from Shetland in the UK to the far north at Evenes and Tromso in Norway

Anti-submarine
warfare hunting
group
(RNM)

Air crew prepare
for a NATO NBCD
exercise
(DD)

(a NATO FLS was to be used at Grottaglie in Italy during operations in the Adriatic in 1993).

The Navy's four annual advanced operational training exercises, Joint Maritime Courses (JMCs), became more and more complex, with raids of up to a hundred aircraft a day and eight or nine 'enemy' submarines, surface attacks and onboard damage control exercises. Nuclear, biological, chemical and defence incidents thoroughly tested the Royal Navy and increasing numbers of NATO ships and aircraft.[6]

STANAVFORLANT The Royal Navy continued to assign ships to the Standing Naval Force Atlantic of NATO, STANAVFORLANT (or SNFL). With up to eight nations represented, this acted as a tripwire group in times of increasing tension, as all nations participating would be involved if it was attacked. SNFL was regularly deployed far forward during increasing tension, frequently off northern Norway.

Operation Balsac: Aden Evacuation, 15–28 January 1986
On 13 January 1986, in a bid for tribal dominance, most of the members of the Cabinet of South Yemen were massacred on the orders of the President, Nasser el Hassam. A few managed to escape and immediately a civil war erupted between the different tribal factions. The fighting in the city

of Aden was ferocious, with over 13,000 casualties and 60,000 refugees fleeing to North Yemen. Foreign nationals were also forced to flee the fighting. Soviet diplomats and military advisers took refuge in a Soviet freighter in the harbour whilst Western nationals fled to the beaches.

The Royal Navy then mounted a dramatic rescue, codenamed Operation Balsac. The Royal Yacht, *Britannia*, which had been sailing down the Red Sea en route to New Zealand to join HM the Queen, was diverted on 14 January to head at best speed for Aden. In Mombasa the *Leander* class frigate *Jupiter*, the Type 42 destroyer *Newcastle* and the tanker RFA *Brambleleaf* were ordered to sail for Aden at full speed. The survey vessel *Hydra*, surveying off the coast of east Africa, and the chartered merchant ship MV *Diamond Princess* were also ordered to join the group heading for the Gulf of Aden.

On arrival off Aden on 16 January it was clear that serious fighting was taking place in the port, which was under fire from heavy artillery. The airport was also under attack, so evacuation would have to be from the beach at Khormaksar. Communication with the Ambassador in Aden was made through a French destroyer, the FNS *De Grasse*. As the ships

Operation Balsac: Aden under attack (NN)

Operation Balsac: Evacuation from Aden beaches (NN)

arrived off Aden they immediately started rescuing the large numbers of refugees gathering on the beaches. Dramatic pictures were taken of the evacuation from the beaches, with large columns of smoke rising from the burning city in the background[7].

At several stages the evacuation had to be suspended as tanks and artillery fought close by with shells landing on the beach and sea close to rescue boats. 1,082 refugees were eventually rescued by *Britannia*, and as they were brought to safety the Royal Marine band on board played music to

calm them. The refugees were then transported to the port of Djibouti. In total 1,379 civilians of fifty-five nations were rescued by Operation Balsac.[8]

The Gulf of Sidra and Operation Cert, 21–25 April 1986

In the spring of 1986 the eastern Mediterranean had become more dangerous as a result of increasing terrorist activity, which Western intelligence firmly indicated was supported by the Libyan regime of Colonel Gaddafi. Libyan terrorists were also found to be assisting the IRA (Irish Republican Army). Against international law, Gaddafi had earlier laid claim to the entire Gulf of Sidra (formerly the Gulf of Sirte), which for many years had been the area used by the American 6th Fleet for training and live firings, as it was well clear of the main shipping and air routes across the Mediterranean. Under orders from President Carter the US Navy had withdrawn from the Gulf of Sidra at the time, but later, following the election of Ronald Reagan as President on 20 January 1981, US defence policy changed and it was decided to stand up to Gaddafi.

The 'Gulf of Sirte Incident' The American 6th Fleet then returned to the Gulf of Sidra in 1981, and several clashes took place between US naval aircraft and the Libyan Air Force.[9] An early incident occurred on 19 August 1981 when two Libyan Air Force Su-22 fighters attacked two F-14 Tomcat fighters from the American carrier uss *Nimitz*. The Libyan aircraft launched Soviet AA-2 heat-seeking air-to-air missiles and were then shot down by the F-14s using AIM-9L Sidewinder missiles. The brief 'dogfight', a dangerous 'hot moment' in the Cold War, became known as the 'Gulf of Sirte Incident' and formed the background to a popular American film about naval fighter pilots entitled *Top Gun*.[10]

US Operation Attain Document III, 22 March 1986 Following a series of terrorist attacks on US citizens in Germany, Egypt, Rome and Vienna the 6th Fleet, commanded by Vice Admiral Frank Keslo on board his flagship the uss *Coranado*, entered the Gulf of Sidra on 22 March 1986 for Operation Attain Document III.[11] The operation involved the US carriers *Coral Sea*, *America* and *Saratoga*, escorted by the Aegis cruisers *Ticonderoga* and *Yorktown*, for fleet manoeuvres and exercises. The Libyan Air Force of over 500 Soviet- and French-built aircraft was brought to alert, but following experience with previous naval exercises when all attempted air strikes were repulsed, Gaddafi ordered his aircraft to remain out of range of the US Navy. Instead, as soon as US aircraft came within range of his land-based surface-to-air missile sites he ordered them to engage. The Aegis-equipped cruisers tracked the SA-5 missiles and all were evaded by counter-measures. US A-7 Corsair aircraft struck back and knocked out the Libyan SAM (surface-to-air missile) sites.

The final attack that day came from three missile-armed fast-attack craft of the Libyan Navy. These were quickly destroyed by A-6 Intruder attack aircraft from the US

HMS *Archer*	
P2000 *Archer* Class Fast Patrol Boat	
The versatile *Archer* class fast patrol boats were built primarily for training with Royal Naval and Royal Marine Reserve and university units, but they are also used as search and rescue craft and for other fleet tasks. Some have been armed and deployed as patrol craft and guard boats to Gibraltar and Cyprus.	
Launched:	25 June 1985
Commissioned:	1985
Displacement:	40 tonnes
Length:	20m
Propulsion:	2 Perkins CVM 800T diesels, 2 shafts
Armament:	Can be fitted with 1 20mm AA gun and a number of 7.62mm GPMGs
Complement:	13
No. in class:	18

carriers. On 27 March the Pentagon called off the operation and ordered the fleet out of the Gulf of Sidra, thus allowing Gaddafi to declare victory and recommence terrorist attacks.

US Operation El Dorado Canyon, 15 April 1986 After the retreat of the US 6th Fleet, terrorist attacks against Western targets intensified. Thanks to intelligence intercepts many attacks were defeated, but on 5 April a nightclub in West Berlin was bombed, killing US servicemen, and three days later a US TWA flight from Rome was blown up, killing more Americans.

The United States retaliated on 15 April with Operation El Dorado Canyon,[12] in which it launched bombing strikes on five military targets (terrorist training centres, military airfields and intelligence centres) in Tripoli and Benghazi. The raids were carried out by fifteen A-6 Intruder all-weather attack aircraft from the US carriers *America* and *Coral Sea* bombing the Benghazi targets, and by eighteen US Air Force F-111 attack aircraft bombing the Tripoli targets. The F-111s from the 48th Tactical Fighter Wing flew from their Lakenheath RAF base in Suffolk in the UK, but as most European countries did not wish to become involved and denied authority for them to enter their air space the bombers had to fly out over the Atlantic and then via Gibraltar into the Mediterranean.

The USA had requested assistance from Europe, but all countries except for the UK refused. After Britain was approached the Prime Minister, Margaret Thatcher, declared, 'It was inconceivable to me that we should refuse United States aircraft and pilots the opportunity to defend their people ... it would be ridiculous to refuse it.' The assistance rendered by the Americans during the Falklands crisis and the fact that Libyan terrorists were aiding the IRA may have helped influence the decision taken by the British government.

The F-111s had to fly 2,800 miles with four in-flight refuelling stages during their seven-hour flights, which were modelled on the RAF Black Buck operations during the Falklands Campaign. The Libyan targets were heavily defended, with over 3,000 Soviet air defence technicians manning the air defence radars and missile sites, but the 6th Fleet, with its advanced and highly sophisticated electronic warfare suppression equipment, managed to neutralise them and only one F-111 was lost.

The Lockerbie Bomb Although the raid was a total success from a military point of view in the fight against terrorism, politically it was highly controversial, and Britain, because of her direct involvement, came under a certain amount of international criticism. It was probably a contributory factor in the Lockerbie bombing on 21 December 1988, when a Pan American World Airways airliner en route from Britain to the United States was blown up over Scotland by a terrorist bomb. All 258 passengers on board Pan Am Flight 103 were killed, and a further eleven people on the ground also died. It was Britain's worst air disaster. A Libyan, Abdel Basset Ali al-Megrahi, was eventually convicted for perpetrating the atrocity.

Operation Cert, 21–25 April 1986 Shortly after the attack on Libya the Royal Yacht *Britannia*, which was on passage back to the UK after the royal tour of New Zealand, was approaching the Mediterranean and there were fears for her safety. She transited through the Suez Canal and entered the Mediterranean on 19 April, sailing north-west for Crete with RAF Phantoms flying CAPs (combat air patrols) overhead. It was a very sensitive time for a high-profile and vulnerable target to be passing within striking range of the Libyan coast, particularly after the involvement of the UK in providing bases for the US bombing raid. Some thirteen years earlier Gaddafi had ordered a submarine in the Libyan Navy to attack the liner *Queen Elizabeth II* when it was in the Mediterranean on a chartered cruise to Israel to commemorate Israel's twenty-fifth anniversary. Fortunately the submarine, which was commanded by Egyptian officers, refused to carry out the attack and promptly sailed to Alexandria to report to President Sadat.

On 21 April the Royal Navy, taking no chances, implemented Operation Cert to protect the Royal Yacht. Close escort was provided by the destroyer *Southampton* and the frigates *Brazen* and *Aurora*. RAF aircraft from Cyprus provided air cover and, for part of the westbound transit, US naval aircraft operating from the carrier USS *America* provided additional fighter cover.

The ships sailed steadily west with air-defence watches closed up in the operations rooms, reminiscent of the Malta convoy escorts in World War II. By 25 April the group was well clear of any threat from Libya and air-defence watches were stood down. Operation Cert was successfully completed.[13]

The Global 86 Deployment (Task Group 318.4), 3 April – 18 December 1986

In 1986 Rear Admiral Robin Hogg, FOF2 (Flag Officer 2nd Flotilla), led a task group on a deployment to the Far East on an eight-month 'westabout circumnavigation' named Global 86. His flagship was the carrier *Illustrious*, and the rest of Task Group 318.4 consisted of the Type 42 destroyer *Manchester*, the Type 22 frigate *Beaver* and the Type 21 frigate *Amazon*. The fleet tanker RFA *Olmeda*, the support tanker RFA *Bayleaf* and the fleet replenishment ship RFA *Fort Grange* supported the Task Group. Attached to the group for the initial stages of the deployment and ASW exercises in the Pacific was the nuclear-powered fleet submarine *Swiftsure*.

Fire in *Illustrious* The Task Group sailed from Portsmouth on 3 April but sadly, on the first night out, *Illustrious* suffered a serious fire in her forward gearing room and the group was forced to return to Portsmouth. Inspection of the damage revealed that it would take quite some time to repair, and the decision was taken for the rest of the Task Group to sail on without her.

Flag Transfer to *Beaver* Admiral Hogg decided to transfer his flag to *Beaver* and the frigate was manoeuvred alongside *Illustrious*. It was not an easy operation, but when *Beaver* was firmly secured alongside the carrier the staff of FOF1 and all the staff baggage were transferred across to the new flagship. *Beaver* was a 4,200-ton 'stretched' Batch 2 Type 22 frigate with a more advanced weapon fit and a sophisticated towed-array sonar system. She was well equipped to act as flagship for the deployment. The group was then divided into Task Unit 318.4.1 (*Illustrious* and RFA *Olmeda*) and Task Unit 318.4.2, which consisted of the remainder of the group.

The Task Group Sails The Global 86 Task Group then finally sailed from Portsmouth, together with the outgoing Gulf patrol ships, the destroyer *Southampton* and the frigate *Brazen*, supported by the tanker RFA *Brambleleaf*. The ships sailed in company on 14 April and, having rounded the Isle of Wight, headed west down the Channel, with the rest of the group joining from Devonport en route. When the ships arrived off the Portuguese coast they parted company, with the Gulf Squadron heading for Gibraltar and the Mediterranean whilst the Global 86 Task Group altered course to the south-west, sailing across the Atlantic.

The West Indies After a brief visit to St Lucia the ships sailed on to La Guaira, the port of Caracas, arriving on 28 April. On sailing from La Guaira it made for the Panama Canal, transiting through the canal on 6 May.

In the Pacific Once in the Pacific the group rendezvoused with RFA *Olmeda* and the submarine *Swiftsure*, which had rounded Cape Horn the previous month. The opportunity was taken to conduct important ASW exercises with the fleet submarine, the ASW Sea King helicopters of 814 NAS (Naval Air Squadron) in RFA *Fort Grange* and the excellent towed-array sonar system in *Beaver*.

Defence Sales On completion of the ASW exercises the group split into two units, with Captain Richard Hastilow in *Manchester* leading *Amazon* and RFA *Bayleaf* first to San

Francisco and then on to Vancouver, where he conducted receptions and defence sales open days. Meanwhile the other ships headed for Acapulco on the Mexican coast and then went on to San Diego in southern California for similar receptions and defence sales exhibitions. After successful and enjoyable visits the ships prepared for the important RIMPAC exercise.

Exercise RIMPAC The major Pacific naval exercise codenamed RIMPAC was an important multi-national exercise involving five nations, the UK, USA, Canada, Japan and Australia. Starting at the end of May, it lasted three weeks and involved 50,000 men, fifty ships and over 250 aircraft. One of the strong points of the exercise was the fact that it was unscripted, allowing free play so that ships had to be fully alert, testing equipment under real-time conditions.

Dominance in ASW An important element of the exercise was ASW, and it was in that area that the Royal Navy was able to demonstrate that in its procedures and experience it was way ahead of the other navies. It was also an opportunity for the Royal Navy to show that its sophisticated towed-array sonar system in *Beaver* was a world-beater and certainly well in advance of any of the US Navy sonar systems.

Pearl Harbor After three weeks of constant exercises the ships sailed into Pearl Harbor for exercise debriefing and staff analysis, which allowed the ships' companies to take some well-earned rest and recreation. Having completed the ASW phase of the deployment, *Swiftsure* detached from the group and sailed for the return passage to the UK. The group then sailed on 17 June for live missile firings on the weapon ranges of the US Navy's Pacific Fleet.

The Type 21 frigate *Amazon*, uncharacteristically making smoke (NP)

swift passage across the Indian Ocean to Singapore to meet up with the Task Group.

Across the Pacific into Typhoon 'Peggy' After completing all exercises with the US Navy, the group set off on the long voyage west across the vast Pacific Ocean. As the ships headed west they ran straight into Typhoon 'Peggy' and for several days could make very little headway into the huge seas and winds created by it. Eventually the ships arrived on the other side of the Pacific and split up for port visits, with *Beaver* and RFAS *Fort Grange* and *Olmeda* sailing north-west to Pusan in South Korea and *Manchester* and *Amazon* sailing due west to Shanghai.

Defence Sales Delegates from sixteen leading UK export industries joined the ships in Shanghai for a major sales exhibition promoting British goods. It was a popular event well attended by regional buyers and clearly showed the interest in British export goods.

Hong Kong The ships then sailed to rendezvous together in Hong Kong, with the first ships, the *Manchester* group, arriving on 13 July. En route RFA *Bayleaf* diverted to rescue the crew of a cargo ship, the ss *Hwai Lie*, which was sinking in heavy seas. The rest of the group, with *Beaver*, conducted a night exercise with the Hong Kong Squadron before entering harbour on 18 July.

Singapore On sailing from Hong Kong the group steamed south, with *Beaver* making for Brunei for another defence exports day. The group then arrived in Singapore for a mid-deployment maintenance period. FMGs (fleet maintenance groups) from Portsmouth and Devonport flew out to Singapore to carry out the necessary defect rectification and maintenance schedules. On 18 August *Illustrious* sailed up Johore Strait and into Singapore naval base after her twenty-five-day 'dash' from Portsmouth. The next day the 'flag' was transferred from *Beaver* back to the flagship, *Illustrious*.

Exercise Starfish On 21 August the Task Group sailed from Singapore to take part in the FPDA (Five Power Defence Arrangement) exercise Starfish off the coast of Malaysia. The exercise involved the navies of Malaysia, New Zealand, Australia, the UK and Singapore and was carried out in the sea area above the war graves of the World War II capital ships *Prince of Wales* and *Repulse*. The Sea Harriers of 800 NAS made a valuable contribution to the success of the exercise.

Illustrious Meanwhile back in the UK *Illustrious* had, at long last, completed her repairs and after satisfactory trials and testing was preparing to sail. Finally on 21 July she sailed from Portsmouth and headed out to join the Global 86 Task Group. After completing weapons trials on her run south, the carrier called into Gibraltar for a brief two-day visit. She sailed on 28 July and transited east across the Mediterranean before passing down the Suez Canal on 4 August. Turning out into the Gulf of Aden, *Illustrious* headed due east for a

Global 86 in the Pacific (NN)

Australian Fleet Review, 4 October 1986 After exercise Starfish the group sailed for visits to Port Kelang in Malaysia, Jakarta, Fiji and Tonga before heading south for Australian waters. The ships then split up to carry out a series of twelve individual Australian port visits as part of the Australian seventy-fifth anniversary celebrations. The culmination of the celebrations was to be a Fleet Review, and on 29 September *Illustrious*, leading the entire Task Group, entered Sydney harbour. In Sydney the group joined up with twenty-two other warships from six navies, and all sailed for the Australian Fleet Review on 4 October. HRH the Duke of Edinburgh was embarked on board *Illustrious* for the review.

The Return West After the review and the many celebrations, which formed the highlight of the Global 86 deployment, the ships prepared for the final exercises and port visits before the long voyage back to the UK. They left Sydney on 13 October to take part in exercise Croweater, which lasted a week. Then after a final visit to Fremantle at the end of October the group steamed west across the Indian Ocean before passing the Maldives and sailing up into the Arabian Sea for Mumbai (Bombay).

Exercise Saif Sareea, 16 November – 8 December 1986 After a brief two-day visit to Mumbai the Task Group sailed on 16 November to join up with the Omani Navy and take part in exercise 'Saif Sareea' ('Shining Sword') off the coast of Oman. This was a large-scale rapid amphibious deployment exercise outside the NATO area, for which the Task Group was joined by an amphibious task group (ATG) including the assault ship *Intrepid* with 40 Commando Royal Marines embarked, escorted by the destroyer *Nottingham* and the frigate *Andromeda* and supported by RFAS *Orangeleaf* and *Olmeda*. The exercise ended at the beginning of December and the group sailed for the Red Sea.

Back to the UK, 18 December 1986 The ships transited through the Suez Canal on 7 December and after a short stop in Gibraltar sailed for the last leg of the deployment. Finally the group arrived back in the Channel, with the Devonport ships sailing into Plymouth on 18 December and the rest of the group sailing back into Portsmouth the next day. It had been a very successful deployment during which the Task Force had covered over 42,000 miles and visited twenty-five countries, building many contacts and sales opportunities as well as promoting British standing and interests in the Far East.

Exercise Autumn Train, October–November 1986 On 13 October 1986 FOF2, Rear Admiral Liardet, in his flagship, the aircraft carrier *Ark Royal*, led a powerful task group out into the South-West Approaches. The group consisted of the destroyer *Bristol*, the frigates *Broadsword*, *Ambuscade*, *Arethusa* and *Andromeda*, the nuclear submarine *Superb* and the patrol submarine *Onyx*, and was supported by RFAS *Green Rover* and *Black Rover*. The Task Group deployed for the major maritime exercise Autumn Train, conducting a series of live weapon firings as the ships headed south in the Atlantic. On completion of the exercise the ships steamed into Gibraltar for a break before sailing for a visit to Lisbon and then returning to the UK.

Cold War Submarine Incidents

Towards the end of 1986 several dangerous and dramatic incidents at sea, involving nuclear submarines, served as

Global 86 Task Group at sea (NN

reminders of the extreme dangers faced by submarines during the Cold War.

Nuclear Missile Accident: SSBN K-219, October 1986 On 3 October the Soviet *Yankee* class SSBN K-219 was on patrol in the north-west Atlantic off Bermuda when she suffered an explosion in her missile compartment caused by igniting missile fuel and a serious fire broke out. The situation was extremely dangerous, as nuclear missiles could have 'cooked off' and been launched against targets on the US mainland.

submarine event occurred during June 1987 when the nuclear fleet submarine *Superb*, commanded by Commander Jeff Collins, was conducting special operations with US submarines beneath the Arctic ice cap. The submarines were testing new underwater tactics and equipment.

Submarine operations and tactics beneath the polar ice cap were important, as submarines were safe there from being detected by aircraft, surface ships or seabed surveillance systems. They also had protection against detection from other submarines thanks to the considerable underwater noise generated by the movement of the pack ice as well as the mixing layers of salt and fresh water, which impeded sonar sensors. This made the Pole an ideal area for Soviet ballistic missile submarines to deploy and hide in, hence the importance of developing Polar anti-submarine tactics.

At one stage during the joint US–UK operations *Superb* surfaced through the ice together with two US submarines, the *Billfish* and the *Sea Devil*. It was the first time that British and US submarines had surfaced together through the ice cap and provided an excellent photo opportunity.

1987 Caribtrain Deployment, 12 January – 9 April 1987 On 12 January Rear Admiral Liardet (FOF2) in his flagship, the carrier *Ark Royal*, led a powerful task group across the Atlantic for a three-month Caribtrain deployment to the West Indies. The Task Group included the Type 82 destroyer *Bristol* and the Type 42 destroyers *Southampton* and *Liverpool*. It joined the US Navy for fleet exercises on the US fleet's weapon ranges. The Sea Harriers from *Ark Royal* carried out live bombing missions on the Puerto Rico ranges and the ships carried out live missile firings. The Task Group used the new Petrel target missile, which performed well under live firing conditions and impressed the US Navy. The Task Group then participated in exercise Punish before returning east across the Atlantic, arriving back in the UK on 9 April.

The Ongoing Iran–Iraq War in the Gulf

Changes to the Armilla Patrol in 1987 The protection of shipping in the Gulf during the Iran–Iraq war was a constant and at times dangerous task for the ships of the Armilla Patrol. In view of the increasing dangers to international shipping it was decided at the beginning of 1987 that the two ships on Armilla Patrol duties would spend more time in the Gulf, west of the Straits of Hormuz, to reassure British merchant shipping in the area. Every week many British merchant ships were escorted through the Straits of Hormuz. Both the Iranians and the Iraqis frequently launched anti-ship missiles as well as carrying out air strikes. According to US assessments the Iraqis had carried out over 130 attacks on shipping by the beginning of the year, whilst the Iranians had launched some seventy attacks.

To release the Armilla ships to spend more time on task in the Gulf it was decided to send a third ship to the Indian Ocean. This commitment took up a total of six destroyers or frigates either in the Gulf region or en route to, or from,

Many major towns and cities were well within the missile range of K-219. An SSN of the US Navy, the USS *Augusta*, which was tailing the Soviet submarine at the time, witnessed events. Eventually the fires were brought under control, though not before three of the Soviet crew had perished. The K-219 finally sank off Bermuda on 6 October. (The incident was later portrayed in an American film, *Hostile Waters*.[14])

Submarine Operations at the Pole, June 1987 A happier

the Gulf. Both British ship owners and unions expressed their gratitude to the Royal Navy for the tremendous reassurance and assistance they provided in the region.

Attack on the USS *Stark*, 17 May 1987 The Royal Navy worked closely with the US 5th Fleet, never knowing when they might be on the receiving end of indiscriminate attacks mounted on shipping by both sides. The attack on the US frigate USS *Stark* was a 'stark' reminder of the dangers which the ships faced.

On 17 May 1987 the USS *Stark* was underway some eighty miles north-east of Bahrain when she picked up an incoming aircraft on her radar and interrogated it. The aircraft was an Iranian Exocet-armed Mirage F-1 searching for a tanker to attack. Having identified a surface contact, the F-1 launched two Exocet missiles at a range of twenty miles. Both missiles, similar to those which sank *Sheffield* in the Falklands Campaign, hit the USS *Stark*, one exploding. The frigate was severely damaged and thirty-seven of her crew were killed instantly. The *Stark* was given a lot of assistance from allied ships in the area, including the frigates *Broadsword* and *Active*. Eventually the raging fires were brought under control and the badly damaged frigate was able to sail back to the USA. Following the air attack it was decided to reinforce the air-defence equipment of the Armilla Patrol ships with additional close-range surface-to-air missiles.

The situation in the Gulf now became more dangerous, and on 20 July 1987 the United Nations Security Council demanded that Iraq and Iran agree to a cease-fire. This was not acceptable to Iran, which as well as making more progress in the war than Iraq demanded recognition as the aggrieved party.

Operation Cimnel, 12 August 1987 The mines laid haphazardly at sea by Iran and Iraq posed a serious hazard to international shipping, and in late July a 400,000-ton tanker, the *Bridgeton*, struck a mine in the northern Gulf. The US authorities requested assistance from the Royal Navy in mine-clearing operations in the Gulf. The 4th MCMV Squadron had been held on standby in the UK for deployment to the Gulf for just such an eventuality under Operation Armilla Accomplice.

Initially Britain refused the request, being anxious to avoid becoming too closely involved with either side in the Gulf War, but eventually it was decided that the increased threat posed by mines to British shipping justified a response. Accordingly the decision was taken to activate Operation Armilla Accomplice, now renamed Operation Cimnel, and deploy the 4th MCMV Squadron to the Gulf as quickly as possible.

The squadron of four Hunt class MCMVs, *Brecon*, *Brocklesby*, *Bicester* and *Hurworth*, supported by *Abdiel* and the fleet replenishment ship RFA *Regent*, sailed from Rosyth on 12 August. The next day the forward repair ship RFA *Diligence*, off the Falkland Islands, was ordered to sail for the Gulf to support the operation.

The Operation Cimnel Squadron arrived in Oman on 14 September and began its mine-hunting tasks in the Gulf of Oman and the Persian Gulf. It did not take the MCMVs long to find and start clearing mines; in one operation in October *Brecon* discovered a mine 300 feet down on the sea bed, and after destroying it found four more, which she also destroyed. By the end of November the Royal Navy had cleared five mines off Fujayrah and a further five off Qatar.

In September 1987 both the Royal Navy and the US Navy deployed more warships to the Gulf. The two navies continued to work very closely together over the important and highly dangerous task of escorting ships through the Straits of Hormuz and in the Gulf. Particularly vulnerable were tankers carrying oil, and the Iranians were using every means possible to interdict any tankers thought to be carrying oil from Iraq or Kuwait. The Iraqis responded and in one incident destroyed a 75,000-ton tanker anchored in Bandar Abbas.

On 21 September an Iranian gunboat in the Gulf of Kuwait attacked the British tanker *Gentle Breeze*. A few hours later the Americans caught an Iranian landing craft, the INS *Iran Ajr*, laying mines further south and attacked her. The US frigate USS *Jarret* then closed in and sank her with gunfire.

On 8 October the US Navy sank three Iranian patrol boats which had fired on US aircraft. The Iranians retaliated eight days later by attacking the tanker *Sea Isle City* with a shore-launched Silk Worm missile. The Americans responded in turn on 19 October, attacking two sea platforms that were being used to co-ordinate Iranian attacks. The US Navy destroyers *John Young*, *Leftwich*, *Hoel* and *Kidd* destroyed the platforms with gunfire. Three days later the Iranians launched an attack on Kuwait's Sea Island oil terminal.

Royal Navy warships accompanied merchant shipping transiting through the Straits of Hormuz whenever possible, with up to three transits a day being accompanied by a frigate or destroyer. Transits by US shipping were normally confined to a weekly US national convoy, which was usually escorted by two or three warships. Iranian aircraft were especially dangerous: armed Iranian aircraft were taking off from Bandar Abbas and flying attack profiles directly against allied warships, breaking off only when acquired by Sea Dart search radar and air-defence systems. All ships passing through the Straits of Hormuz were at most four minutes away from several Iranian anti-ship missile sites. This situation necessitated ships remaining closed up at action stations albeit slightly relaxed, for sixteen to eighteen hours a day, reverting to defence watches only when well clear of the straits. It was also necessary for ships to be prepared for chemical attack, as both Iran and Iraq had chemical weapons, and Iraq had already used hers. British-built Iranian corvettes also took part in attacks on shipping.

Attacks on shipping continued throughout the rest of the year, and official UN statistics showed eighty-seven Iranian strikes on ships in the Gulf and seventy-six Iraqi ship attacks. Meanwhile on land the war was turning in favour of the Iranians as their troops pushed further into Iraqi territory north of Basra.[15]

Under-Ice Torpedo Firings

Soviet submarines, particularly SSBNs, could exploit the Arctic ice cap as a sanctuary and thus for the first time the Royal Navy conducted a series of test torpedo firings under the ice of the Beaufort Sea to the north of Alaska. *Turbulent* (Commander Ian Richards) and *Superb* (Commander John Tuckett) participated. The firings took place about 120 miles north-east of Prudhoe Bay at an ice station and tracking range set up by the University of Washington State – the Applied Physics Laboratory Ice Station (APLIS). The firings were part of a series of joint US–UK tests involving the participation of two other SSNs, uss *Lapon* and uss *Silversides*.

APLIS had been set up on first year ice on a frozen polyna (stretch of open water), which offered both a flat area as a landing strip and uniform ice thickness to recover the torpedoes through. Its tracking range, fixed onto the ice, had the complexity of drift of up to four miles a day and a slow anti-clockwise rotation. During the tests there was a bit of excitement with the formation of a large polyna, which took a chunk out of the end of the landing strip.

After being fired the torpedoes were recovered from under the ice by a combination of divers and helicopter. They were then shipped by light aircraft to Prudhoe airfield where a team of Coulport Depot civilians undertook post-firing routines before the weapons were airlifted back to Anchorage by RAF Hercules.

Never before had RN SSNs penetrated so far under the Arctic pack. To reach APLIS they had undertaken a passage of over 1,500 miles under the ice but it was somewhat daunting that their only exit route to reach open water was the same passage back. With their limited under ice sonar capability there was no prospect of our SSNs making transit to the closest open

Under-Ice Torpedo Firings HMS *Turbulent* (March 1988)

water down through the narrow and shallow Bering Straits, with the likely presence of ice canyons, which reached to the seabed.

Any serious propulsion or engineering problem deep under the ice pack would, of course be compounded by the inability to surface without the delay incurred in locating thin ice or open water. In event of an SSN losing propulsion under the ice, the contingency plan to dig it out presumed that it was able to successfully send a distress signal and that it could be located.

On its arrival at APLIS *Turbulent* reported a serious problem with its oxygen making electrolysers and having had to fall back to burning oxygen candles, needed a replenishment of these urgently. Indeed having penetrated the pack ice, *Turbulent*'s CO had made the courageous decision to press on to APLIS past the point of no return in terms of having enough oxygen candles to return south out of the ice. The oxygen candle replenishment was organised with some degree of ingenuity and arguably the most unconventional replenishment at sea (RAS) ever, took place with *Turbulent*

undertaking an unprogrammed surfacing in a polyna. However, this was the only serious problem on the part of our SSNs in what was to be an almost flawless series of firings and evaluations.

On reaching APLIS from the Pacific through the Bering Strait, the San Diego based uss *Lapon* conducted a number of under ice surfacing tests. A few minutes after the SSN made its first surfacing it was overflown by two Soviet 'Bear' reconnaissance aircraft at very low altitude pursued by two USAF F-15s, very much emphasising the Cold War environment the operation was taking place in.

Turbulent and *Superb* fired a total of 16 Tigerfish weapons, all of which were successfully recovered. Most of the firings were conducted with each submarine alternating as targets although some weapon runs were against static targets. The weapons performed extremely well in the Arctic conditions and American observers were impressed by both their solid performance and their precision guidance, which enabled them to be parked under suitable flat, thin ice at the end of their run.

At about 1,000 feet or more the underwater visibility was exceptional, thus aiding weapon recovery. The recovery routine consisted of creating two plugs in the ice, one for a diver the other for the torpedo. Once the diver had attached a harness to the weapon it was pulled out of the ice by helicopter. Perhaps surprisingly no weapon was seriously damaged although at least one had to be recovered from underneath ice rubble about 20 feet thick.

The 1988 under ice Tigerfish firings were in many ways a very remarkable achievement and firmly demonstrated the RN SSN's capability to successfully engage submarines under the Arctic ice pack. In particular the crews of *Turbulent* and *Superb* performed exceptionally well in the very challenging environment of the deep ice pack, demonstrating great professionalism in very competently conducting an especially unique series of torpedo firings which firmly put the Royal Navy on a par with the USN in terms of under-ice warfare.

Captain Dan Couley OBE RN

Interception of the *Eksund*, 30 October 1987 In 1987 Libya had resumed supplying arms to the IRA, and various surveillance operations had been undertaken to stop the arms smugglers. Assistance was received from the French Navy in late October when it carried out an operation tracking a Panamanian-flagged ship, the *Eksund*, from the Mediterranean and across the Bay of Biscay. On 30 October, when the ship was off the coast of Brittany, the French Navy intercepted it and discovered that the cargo contained 150 tons of arms destined for the IRA. These included twenty surface-to-air missiles, machine guns, anti-tank grenade launchers, over 1,000 Kalashnikov AK-47s and large quantities of explosives; all of which were impounded. The successful operation was a tribute to the co-operation and good relations between the Royal Navy and the French Navy. The loss was a blow to the IRA but did not stop its campaign of violence: on 8 November an IRA bomb in Enniskillen slaughtered eleven people at a Remembrance Day parade. Four months later an IRA active service unit planned to attack a military band in Gibraltar by detonating a car bomb. The band was due to play at the weekly changing of the guard ceremony at the residence of the Governor, Air Chief Marshal Sir Peter Terry, on 6 March 1988. An SAS (Special Air Service) team carried out Operation Flavius, shooting the IRA unit, which it believed to be on the point of detonating the bomb, and preventing the attack.

Operation Purple Warrior, November 1987 In November the Royal Navy mounted Operation Purple Warrior, the biggest single maritime operation conducted by British forces since the Falklands Campaign. The exercise involved thirty-nine ships, including the aircraft carriers *Illustrious* and *Ark Royal*, and the assault ship *Intrepid*. The basic scenario involved the evacuation of refugees from Scottish islands, including the Mulls of Kintyre and Galloway and the Isle of Arran, and embodied many of the ideas derived from Operation Corporate. The evacuation was followed by a phase of amphibious operations as well as other elements designed to test various aspects of maritime warfare.

Under-Ice Torpedo Firings

HMS *Turbulent*, March 1988 Early in 1988 the nuclear-powered fleet submarines *Turbulent* and *Superb* sailed across the North Atlantic on a secret mission to the Beaufort Sea to test the capability of the Royal Navy's Tigerfish ASW torpedo in an under-ice environment(see opposite).[16]

End of the Iran–Iraq War, August 1988

At the beginning of 1988 the Iranians still had the upper hand in the Iran–Iraq War. The Iranian Army was besieging and shelling Basra in the south, pushing through the mountains towards Kirkuk and mounting an offensive further north, which advanced as far as Dukan, capturing 4,000 Iraqi troops. At sea the war against shipping by both sides, continued to necessitate constant protection by British and US warships. In the second half of 1987 the Royal Navy

had deployed the Type 42 destroyer *Edinburgh*, the Type 22 frigate *Brazen* and the *Leander* class frigate *Andromeda* in the region, maintaining the Armilla Patrol in the Gulf, Straits of Hormuz and Arabian Sea. Almost all British-flagged tankers had to be accompanied by a frigate or destroyer in the more dangerous stretches of the main shipping routes.

RFA *Diligence* In 1988 the forward repair ship RFA *Diligence* was based in Djebel Ali, one of the largest man-made harbours in the world. A guarded section of the jetty was used as a depot. RFA *Diligence* acted as a logistics and forward operating base for three Hunt class minehunters, *Middleton*, *Atherstone* and *Dulverton*, a Belgian and a Netherlands minehunter and *Herald*. A naval party (NP 1600) of up to ninety technical rates and others lived in basic accommodation on board *Diligence* and provided the necessary maintenance and support for coalition forces.[17]

The Iraqi Offensive and Chemical Warfare In February Iraq commenced missile attacks on Iranian cities in the north, and when the Iranians responded with attacks on Baghdad the Iraqis launched long-range Soviet-made Scud missiles at Tehran (Iraq fired over 200 missiles at Iranian cities). The following month the Iraqis launched chemical weapons against Halabla, killing over 4,000 people, and on 16 April the Iraqis used chemical weapons again to drive the Iranians back across the Shatt al Arab waterway and recapture the strategically important Al Faw Peninsula. They also engaged Iranian naval units, sinking several warships.

Mines in the Gulf On 14 April the US frigate USS *Samuel B Roberts*, escorting a tanker in the northern Gulf, suffered severe damage when she ran into a minefield on the Shal Allum Shoal. The crew just managed to keep the crippled frigate afloat, and after emergency repairs she was transported back to America on a heavy-lift ship. The MCMVs of Operation Cimnel were quickly deployed to the Shal Allum Shoal and cleared the area of mines, rendering it safe for continued use by shipping.

Operation Praying Mantis Two days later the Joint Task Force Middle East launched an offensive against the Iranian Navy in the northern Gulf, codenamed Operation Praying Mantis. Three naval task units were formed, of which two carried out attacks on two Iranian command platforms whilst the third Task Unit sought to engage the Iranian missile-armed frigate the *Sabalan*. The naval task units managed to destroy the command platforms, with the loss of one Cobra attack helicopter. An Iranian fast attack craft, the *Joshan*, armed with Harpoon anti-shipping missiles, attacked one of the task units and was then sunk with forty-four casualties. The Iranians next launched air attacks on the task units with Phantom strike aircraft and made further attacks with fast attack craft, all of which were fought off. The Iranians followed up the attacks with surface-to-surface missiles launched from the frigates *Sahand* and *Sabalan*. US ships and aircraft from the strike carrier USS *Enterprise* promptly engaged both frigates and knocked them out.[18] The Iranian losses did not appear to deter the Iranian Navy, which continued its attacks on shipping. The day after the Iranian frigates were knocked out another Iranian warship opened fire on a British tanker, the 113,000-ton *York Marine*, though fortunately it inflicted little damage. In May the frigate *Boxer* went to the aid of a Danish supertanker, the *Karame Maersk*, which had been attacked by an Iranian gunboat in the Straits of Hormuz and set on fire.[19]

Operation Calendar II, 1 July 1988 The MCMVs of Operation Cimnel had continued their important work of clearing mines in the Gulf throughout the hostilities. The ocean survey ship *Herald* had relieved *Abdiel* as the support ship, with *Abdiel* returning to the UK to pay off after twenty-one years of service. Following the success of combined clearance operations with Dutch and Belgian MCMVs, the Cimnel operation was revised to incorporate the valuable experience and a joint MCM task unit was formed under British command on 1 July 1988. The codename of the operation was changed to Operation Calendar II (Operation Calendar having been the name of the allied minesweeping force in the Scheldt during World War II).

Chemical Warfare On land the Iraqis intensified their chemical weapon attacks, launching fresh offensives across all fronts at the end of May. Using chemical munitions, bombs and shells, the Iraqis captured town after town, regaining all the areas they had previously lost and advancing well into Iranian territory.

The USS *Vincennes* Incident, 3 July 1988 A tragic event occurred on 3 July when a US AEGIS cruiser (AEGIS being a modern sophisticated air-defence system), the USS *Vincennes*, was attacked by Iranian fast attack craft. As she was manoeuvring to evade the Iranian gunboats the *Vincennes* picked up an incoming fast jet on her radar, which had taken off from Bandar Abbas. When challenged the aircraft did not respond, and immediately the *Vincennes* launched two surface-to-air missiles, destroying the aircraft, which turned out to be an Iranian airliner on Iranair Flight 655. All 290 people on board were killed. The Commanding Officer of the USS *Vincennes* must have remembered the incident a year earlier when the Commanding Officer of the USS *Stark* held back from shooting down an incoming unidentified jet aircraft which subsequently launched its Exocet missiles, killing thirty-seven members of her crew.

Cease-Fire Having previously rejected UN Resolution 598, calling for a cease-fire in the Iran–Iraq War, the Iranians at last announced on 18 July that they would accept the resolution, and on 20 August the cease-fire finally came into effect. Both sides were war-weary after eight years of fighting in which nearly a million Iranians were killed and over 100,000 Iraqis perished.

HMS *Southampton* Despite the cease-fire, British and US warships continued to protect tankers in the dangerous waters of the Gulf region. There was a threat that either side might try and take advantage of the cease-fire to launch a surprise attack. On 4 September the destroyer *Southampton* was providing close escort to a British tanker when the two ships collided. *Southampton* was extensively damaged and eventually had to be transported back to the UK on a heavy-lift ship.[20]

Operation Team Sweep Although the war was over there were still many mines to be found and rendered safe in the hazardous waters of the Gulf. In October a major multi-national mine-clearance operation, Operation Team Sweep, was established, involving US, French and Italian MCMVs as well as the MCMVs of Operation Calendar II. This important operation carried on for the rest of the year, and it was not until the end of the year that it was deemed safe to withdraw the Royal Navy MCMVs from the Gulf. The last two British MCMVs finally left the area on 27 February 1989 for passage back to the UK.

Outback 88 Deployment: Task Group 318.1, 13 June – 15 December 1988

In June 1988 FOF2, Rear Admiral Peter Woodhead, led the Outback 88 Group Deployment (Task Group 318.1) to the Far East. The aircraft carrier *Ark Royal* was the flagship, and the Task Group also included the escorts, the Type 42 destroyer *Edinburgh* and the *Leander* class frigate *Sirius*. The fleet tanker RFA *Olwen*, the support tanker RFA *Orangeleaf* and the fleet replenishment ship RFA *Fort Grange* supported the Task Group. The powerful air group embarked in *Ark Royal* included nine Sea King ASW helicopters, three Sea King AEW helicopters, eight Sea Harriers and two Sea King commando helicopters.

The Task Group Sails, 13 June 1988 The Task Group sailed out of Portsmouth on 13 June and headed west down the Channel. Once clear of the Channel it altered course south-west across the Bay of Biscay to take part in exercise Jolly Roger, a combined three-day exercise with the French Navy and also with the RAF. On completion of the exercise the group headed for the Mediterranean. Having transited through the Straits of Gibraltar the group rendezvoused with an Italian task group led by the aircraft carrier IS *Giuseppe Garibaldi*. A short while later the group met a Soviet naval unit with the aircraft carrier *Baku* operating the Soviet VTOL aircraft, which were codenamed 'Forger'.

Malta *Ark Royal*, escorted by *Edinburgh*, sailed on to Malta for a port visit, whilst *Sirius* headed straight for the Suez Canal. Unfortunately, when *Ark Royal* arrived on the 25 June she found Grand Harbour blocked by anti-nuclear demonstrators. The protesters had blocked the harbour entrance with a tanker, the MV *Olympic Rainbow*, and so the ships proceeded up the coast to St Paul's Bay and then, after anchoring in the bay, managed to enjoy four days in Malta. The ships sailed from

The three sisters *Ark Royal*, *Illustrious*
and *Invincible* together in the Channel
(*Ark Royal* in the foreground)
(NP)

Malta on 29 June, as *Sirius* transited through the Canal, and headed east for Port Said. En route they exercised with a US submarine, the USS *Cincinnati*, and carried out air defence exercises with RAF aircraft from Cyprus.

Exercise Starfish *Ark Royal* passed through the Canal on 2 July and headed down the Red Sea to conduct live firings en route to the Far East for exercise Starfish. Having crossed the Indian Ocean and arrived in the Far East, the group prepared for exercise Starfish. This important multi-national maritime exercise involved the navies from the FPDA, Australia, the UK, New Zealand, Malaysia and Singapore. There was also a major air component, to which the Sea Harriers made an important contribution.

Singapore, 23 July – 8 August On completion of the exercise the group sailed for Singapore, where it arrived on 23 July to be met by an FMU (fleet maintenance unit) flown out from Portsmouth. At the end of the month the Prime Minister, Margaret Thatcher, flew out to Singapore and held meetings with the Singapore Defence Minister on board *Ark Royal*. The group hosted a successful defence equipment sales day on 5 August, and three days later, after sailing from Singapore, it hosted a defence export sea day on the first day out at sea. The group then set course north-east for Subic Bay, the US naval base in the Philippines, where it arrived on 13 August.

Exercises with the US Navy After a brief four-day visit to Subic Bay the Task Group proceeded to sea for joint exercises with the US Navy, including the mighty veteran battleship USS *New Jersey*. Whilst at sea the USS *New Jersey* gave an awesome firepower display from her main armament of nine sixteen-inch guns. The Task Group also conducted a high seas firing before sailing on to Hong Kong, where it arrived on 23 August. *Sirius*, having already detached from the group, proceeded on her way for a visit to Bangkok.

Exercises Setia Kewan and Lima Bersatu On sailing from Hong Kong on 28 August the group took part in the short exercise Setia Kewan with the Brunei armed forces. Exercise Setia Kewan was followed by a bigger joint exercise, entitled exercise Lima Bersatu, with armed forces from Malaysia and Singapore. The Secretary for Defence flew out to Singapore and hosted a defence sales day, which was followed on by a defence equipment sea day on 11 September for Indonesian naval staff.

Australia The Task Group then sailed south for Australia, arriving in Brisbane on 21 September. The city was hosting Expo 88, and the ships' companies of the group enjoyed four days of celebrations. On 25 September the group sailed for Sydney, where it arrived two days later to be received by welcoming crowds. *Ark Royal* was given pride of place, being berthed at the 'Overseas Passenger Terminal'.

Fleet Review On 1 August the group, with HRH the Duke of York embarked in *Ark Royal*, sailed for the International Fleet Review, which formed the centrepiece of Australia's bicentennial celebrations. The review was completed with a fly-past with Sea Harriers and Sea Kings from *Ark Royal* taking part.

After an enjoyable eleven-day visit the ships sailed for exercises with the Australian Navy before splitting up for a range of port visits. *Ark Royal* headed for Melbourne while other ships carried out visits to Hobart and Adelaide. Sadly anti-nuclear protesters prevented *Ark Royal* from entering Melbourne, and after lying off for several days she sailed for the west coast to visit Fremantle.

Return to the UK Finally the Task Group sailed from Australia at the beginning of November and shaped course across the Indian Ocean for the passage back to the UK. It arrived in Mumbai on 15 September and hosted some defence export sales days before sailing on to rendezvous with the US Navy for exercises in the Arabian Sea. Amongst the US ships taking part in the exercises was the nuclear strike carrier USS *Nimitz*. The group then headed on west, transiting through the Suez Canal on 2 December and conducting operations with the aircraft carriers USS *John F Kennedy* and FNS *Clemenceau* as they crossed the Mediterranean. After a very brief call at Gibraltar the ships set off on the final leg across the Bay of Biscay for a brief rendezvous with *Illustrious* before turning into the Channel and going their separate ways.

'Three Sisters' Whilst *Edinburgh* headed for Rosyth and *Sirius* for Devonport, *Ark Royal* continued east towards Portsmouth. On her way up the Channel *Ark Royal* rendezvoused with the other two CVSs off Portland to provide a unique photo-opportunity of the three sister ships *Ark Royal*, *Illustrious* and *Invincible* at sea together. *Ark Royal* then finally entered Portsmouth on 15 December having spent the traditional last night of a deployment anchored off Spithead.

It had been a most successful global deployment to the Far East, enhancing relationships, promoting sales and advancing British standing and interests in that important region of the world.

The End of the Cold War: 'Triumph in the West', 9 November 1989

The Fall of the 'Wall' By 1989 the economy of the Soviet Union was collapsing and tremendous internal political pressures were driving Gorbachev to seek rapprochement with the West. He visited Bonn in June and signed an agreement with Chancellor Kohl of West Germany, in which the two leaders pledged to work together to seek means of ending the division between East and West Germany and to build economic co-operation. Encouraged by the new mood, East Germans were moving to the West in increasing numbers. The Hungarian government had already dismantled the security fence between Hungary and Austria,

Westland Lynx HAS3

The Lynx was the advanced multi-purpose twin-engined helicopter built to replace the Wasp. It was most effective in the ASW role, particularly when deployed in ships' flights. It was to prove itself in various roles including ship strike in many operations and conflicts.

First flight:	21 March 1971
Entered service:	31 March 1980
Length:	11.92m
Power plant:	2 Rolls-Royce GEM 41-1 turbo shaft engines
Max speed:	144 mph
Armament:	2 Mk 46 or two Sting Ray torpedoes,
	4 Sea Skua missiles,
	Mk 11 depth charges and various door-mounted machine guns
Crew:	2 on flight deck and up to 2 mission crew

allowing Hungarians to escape to the West. On 11 October Poland opened her borders to the West. Seven days later Egon Krenz ousted Erich Honecker, the hard-line leader of East Germany, and then on 9 November Krenz ordered the Berlin Wall to be opened.

The fall of the Berlin Wall was the symbolic end of the Cold War, and was undoubtedly one of the major turning points in the history of the modern world. It heralded the end of the forty-year 'Third World War', which mercifully had remained a 'Cold War'. Fundamentally it had been a precarious period of stand-off between the superpowers with their rival socio-economic ideologies and systems, which divided and polarised the world between them.

It had been a very dangerous period and several times had very nearly 'cooked off' into hot war, terrifying moments when the world had teetered on the brink of the abyss. Many have cited the existence of nuclear weapons as providing the ultimate brake which prevented the slide from localised proxy wars into all-out, catastrophic, total war. The shadow of a strategic nuclear exchange between the superpowers had pervaded and influenced the foreign and defence policies of the developed nations in most of their dealings with the Third World.

The end of the Cold War, which was almost unexpected when it happened, appears to have been brought about primarily by the exhaustive effect of excessive military expenditure, which had ultimately bankrupted the Soviet Union, coupled with huge social and political change in the countries of the Warsaw Pact. Towards the end too many of the USSR's vital resources were being diverted into the Warsaw Pact war machine, with devastating consequences for the Soviet economy. Ultimately it was a victory for the liberal democracies of the West and all the greater for being achieved without the dreadful cost of all-out total war. 'To win one hundred battles is not the acme of skill. To subdue the enemy without fighting is the acme of skill.'[21]

Contribution of the Royal Navy It is not easy to apportion credit for the final triumph on a totally fair and accurate basis, but whatever method is used the Royal Navy, as well as the other armed forces, contributed significantly to the collapse of the Soviet Union. There were three principal areas where the Royal Navy contributed to the final victory.

The Nuclear Deterrent First and foremost, the Royal Navy was responsible for maintaining the UK's strategic nuclear deterrent for twenty years from 1969 with the Polaris Submarine Squadron. The deterrent patrol was kept up undetected without a single break in the ceaseless patrol cycle. As John Craven summed up the importance of the submarine deterrent, 'The Cold War was the first major conflict between superpowers in which victory and defeat were unambiguously determined without the firing of a shot. Without the shield of a strong silent deterrent beneath the sea, that war could not have been won.'[22]

The Cold War 'Battle of the Atlantic' Secondly, and largely unknown, the submarine service played a vital role in helping to counter the massive Warsaw Pact submarine threat by waging persistent, highly dangerous, 'in contact' shadowing operations against Soviet submarines. Operations were mounted both to counter Soviet strategic nuclear deterrent submarines and to protect the West's deterrent submarines and high-value assets from any operations by Soviet intruders.

At the end of the Cold War, Admiral Fountain USN stated: 'Whilst our civilian population worried about Armageddon, submarine crews at sea did all they could to stave it off, living on the edge constantly. On the strategic level of this epic struggle, no one did more than our submarine force, the submarines and their crews, to win the Cold War.'[23] The same is of course equally true of the submariners of the Royal Navy who served so courageously, but for reasons of national security very little official information has been released concerning the deadly, silent, 'cat and mouse' battles fought out deep below the surface.

Thirdly, the Royal Navy, with its great expertise in anti-submarine warfare in the north-east Atlantic, led in the protection of the vital Atlantic supply line for the reinforcement and resupply of Western Europe in the event of any Warsaw Pact invasion. The ability of Europe to resist an invasion on the Continent was an essential element of the credibility of the overall NATO strategy.

The Cost of Military Technology Ultimately the soaring cost of military technology must have been one of the decisive factors in the ending of the Cold War. Dr Gary Weir has summed up the effect of the naval and submarine technology race, stating, 'As vital as the human element is in submarine warfare, success, particularly in submarine versus submarine action, ultimately depends upon technological superiority. Fortunately for the West, the United States and the United Kingdom were able to maintain a decisive technological superiority over the Soviet Union. This superiority added immeasurably to the burden of the Soviets. There is no little irony in the fact that the great efforts made by the Soviet Union to catch up in the naval race, as it had done in the aeronautic, missile, and space arenas may well have been the final defence burden straw that broke the economic back of the Soviet Union, plunging it into financial chaos and eventual dissolution.'[24]

OTHER FLEET ACTIVITIES

Operation Care, 27 September–8 October 1987 Naval parties from the shore establishment HMS *Malabar* provided valuable assistance in Bermuda following Hurricane 'Emily'. Under Operation Care from 27 September to 8 October, the Royal Navy repaired generators and restored power and essential services as well as clearing up.

'Piper Alpha' Disaster In July 1988 there was a disastrous explosion on the 'Piper Alpha' oil rig in the North Sea. The frigate *Phoebe* was one of the first on the spot and led the rescue effort.

Hurricane 'Gilbert', September 1988 In September 1988 Hurricane 'Gilbert' struck Grand Cayman and Jamaica. The frigate *Active* and RFA *Oakleaf* hastened to the area on 13 September to provide emergency relief work. Support tasks continued for seven days before the ships sailed on 20 September.

Hurricane 'Dean', August 1989 The next year Hurricane 'Dean' struck Bermuda, and RFA *Fort Austin* was quickly on the scene on 8 August to provide emergency relief work. Fortunately the damage was not as extensive as it could have been and essential services were quickly restored.

THE WHITE ENSIGN ASSOCIATION

In 1986 the Association was delighted to provide 146 corporate members to participate in the 'Global 86' defence export sales days in twenty foreign ports. The Association also hosted a highly successful personnel officers' conference in Portsmouth. In June 1987 the Association held a banquet and a reception for 800 guests on board *Ark Royal* while she was moored in the Thames at Greenwich. Sir Derrick Holden-Brown (Chairman of Allied Lyons) relieved Admiral the Lord Lewin as Chairman, and Admiral Sir Peter Herbert and Mr Michael Bett were elected to the Council in the same year. In 1987 the Association arranged sea days for forty senior and influential people to visit *Apollo, Ariadne, Ark Royal, Birmingham, Coventry, Courageous, Illustrious, Jersey, London* and *Sheffield*. The shock of the investment crisis in October 1987 caused a great deal of concern amongst those serving, and many of them sought advice from the Association.

In 1988 the Association recruited additional companies, bringing the total number of corporate members to over 100. Visits to sea were arranged in *Arethusa, Coventry, Jersey, Scylla, Ark Royal, Dumbarton Castle, Invincible* and *London*.

CHAPTER 9

The Peace Dividend and the First Gulf War 1990–1992

END OF THE COLD WAR – THE PEACE DIVIDEND AND 'OPTIONS FOR CHANGE' – ENDEAVOUR 90 AND ORIENT 92 DEPLOYMENTS – THE FIRST GULF WAR: OPERATIONS GRANBY, DESERT SHIELD AND DESERT STORM

The transformation of the new world order began on 12 January 1990 with the break-up of the Soviet Union for on that day the Baltic states of Estonia, Latvia and Lithuania prepared to break away from Soviet Russia. Also in 1990 East and West Germany were unified, with Helmut Kohl becoming the Chancellor of the new nation. In 1991 the Baltic States declared their independence and Gorbachev resigned, to be succeeded by the more popular and progressive Boris Yeltsin. By the end of the year the USSR ceased to exist.

End of the Warsaw Pact The end of the Warsaw Pact, which was finally dissolved in 1991, brought the Cold War, which had dominated world politics for over forty years, to a close. The threat of total nuclear war had overshadowed the globe for over a generation, and the liberation from that threat sent a ray of hope for the future around the world. It also necessitated a complete rethink of defence and foreign policy by politicians and by the military establishments of the leading nations.

NATO in Europe At Oslo in June 1992 the North Atlantic Council announced that NATO would be prepared to support the peace-keeping activities of the Conference on Security and Cooperation in Europe. This opened the way to use NATO forces in peace-keeping operations in Europe, and indeed they would soon be deployed to the Balkans.

The UK In the UK the government of Margaret Thatcher was becoming increasingly unpopular in 1990, with riots against the poll tax breaking out in London, and on 28 November John Major replaced her. Tom King was the Defence Secretary, having relieved George Younger in the summer of 1989, and was to remain in post until he was relieved by Malcolm Rifkind in the spring of 1992.

UK Defence Policy: 'Options for Change' From early in 1990 the MoD commenced a far-reaching study into future defence requirements and policy entitled 'Options for Change'. The fundamental aim of the study was to find large-scale savings to fund the expected 'Post-Cold War Peace Dividend' whilst preserving as much of the front line as possible. The Treasury wished to save £650 million from the defence budget. The initial findings of the study were announced by Tom King on 25 July, and confirmed, as expected, significant reductions across all three armed services.

FIRST SEA LORD
Admiral Oswald

SECOND SEA LORDS
*Admirals Brown
and Livesay*

MANPOWER
63,200

MERCANTILE MARINE
*2,142
merchant ships*

Admiral Oswald chairing an Admiralty Board meeting as First Sea Lord (left to right, seated: Ken Macdonald, Archie Hamilton, Lord Trefgarne, Admiral Oswald, Tim Sainsbury, Admiral Brown, Admiral Reffell, Admiral Slater, Michael Neubert)
(JCKS)

For the Navy, whilst it was decided that the carriers and amphibious ships would be retained, the escort fleet of frigates and destroyers would be reduced to 'about forty' and the submarine fleet would be reduced to 'about sixteen'. The deterrent force of Trident SSBNs (ballistic missile-carrying nuclear submarines) would, however, be retained in full. Manpower was to be cut by roughly 18 per cent, with the army coming down to about 120,000 and the Navy to around 60,000 by the middle of the 1990s.

Before any further steps could be taken, Saddam Hussein invaded Kuwait on 2 August 1990 and all thoughts of defence reductions were immediately shelved (bringing echoes of the holding back of defence cuts in 1982). The First Gulf War followed, and after the successful completion of Operation Granby the defence planners once more assessed the situation and the 1991 Defence White Paper[1] was announced in July. Instead of this bringing a reprieve, however, the planned reductions were confirmed and even further cuts in manpower were imposed, with the Navy being required to lose a further 5,000, bringing its total manpower down to a total 55,000. The overriding requirement was to deliver the Peace Dividend by whatever means possible.

THE FLEET

Surface Fleet The backbone of the surface fleet in 1990 consisted of the three aircraft carriers, *Invincible*, *Illustrious* and *Ark Royal*, and the two aging amphibious assault ships *Fearless* and *Intrepid*.

The submarines
Trenchant and USS
Spadefish at the
North Pole
(NN)

The escort fleet of forty-eight ships consisted of the large Type 82 destroyer *Bristol* and the twelve Type 42 destroyers, the fourteen Type 22 frigates, the six Type 21 frigates and the remaining fourteen *Leander* class frigates. The first of the new 3,700-ton Type 23 Duke class frigates, *Norfolk*, had just joined the Fleet, with the next three having been launched and six more under construction.

The MCMV (mine counter-measures vessel) squadrons consisted of thirteen of the Hunt class, twelve of the smaller River class and the first of the new *Sandown* class, with four more building and the remaining thirteen of the old Ton class.

There were also seventeen patrol vessels of various classes, three survey ships, and four survey vessels. *Endurance*, the ice patrol ship, was due for an expensive refit, and in the end she was replaced by a Norwegian ship, MV *Polar Circle*, chartered for seven months in 1991 and purchased the following year for service as HMS *Endurance*. The elderly Royal Yacht *Britannia* remained in service.

Submarine Fleet The SSBNs consisted of the four Polaris armed submarines of the *Resolution* class, with the first two of the new Trident missile submarines of the *Vanguard* class under construction.

The nuclear fleet submarines (SSNs) included six of the *Trafalgar* class with the last one building, six of the *Swiftsure* class, two of the *Valiant* class and two of the *Churchill* class. In addition there were nine old *Oberon* class diesel-electric submarines, six of which had been modernised, and the first of the new *Upholder* class diesel-electric submarines, three more of which were building.

Unfortunately, as part of the 'Options for Change' cuts, the patrol submarines *Osiris*, *Ocelot* and *Otter*, and the nuclear submarines *Courageous*, *Swiftsure* and *Revenge* had to be paid off between 1991 and early 1992.

Support The Fleet was supported by eight fleet tankers, three support tankers and four fleet replenishment ships, with the first of the new 'all in one' 32,000 ton Fort class auxiliary oiler replenishment ships fitting out and the second building. In addition there were five landing ships (logistic), a forward repair ship and an aviation training ship, all operated by the RFA (Royal Fleet Auxiliary).

Royal Marines The Royal Marines consisted of HQ 3 Commando Brigade with 40, 42 and 45 Commandos, fully supported by artillery, engineers, logistics and communications as well as a Special Boat Service (SBS).

Naval Aviation The FAA (Fleet Air Arm) operated STOVL (short take off and vertical landing) Sea Harrier maritime fighter/reconnaissance/strike aircraft, with the advanced FRS2 Harrier due to come into service in 1993. The helicopter squadrons included the Mk 6 ASW (anti-submarine warfare), AEW (airborne early warning) Sea Kings and the Mk 4 Commando version of the Sea King. The FAA also operated the Lynx multi-purpose helicopter and the Gazelle light helicopter.

Command In 1990 the Fleet was commanded by the Commander in Chief, Admiral Sir Benjamin Bathurst, from his headquarters at Northwood. He was relieved in January 1991 by Admiral Sir Jock Slater, who in turn was relieved by Admiral Sir Hugo White in December 1992.

Rear Admiral Woodhead commanded the 1st Flotilla at Portsmouth, and Rear Admiral Abbott commanded the 2nd Flotilla at Devonport. Vice Admiral Hill-Norton was FOF3 (Flag Officer 3rd Flotilla) and Commander Anti-Submarine Warfare Striking Force. Rear Admiral Layard was Flag Officer Naval Aviation, Vice Admiral Coward was Flag Officer Submarines, and Lieutenant General Sir Henry Beverley was Commandant General Royal Marines.

In April 1992 the responsibilities for Fleet Flag Officers were rearranged, with Rear Admiral Boyce becoming the Flag Officer Surface Flotilla (FOSF) and Rear Admiral Brigstocke the Commander UK Task Group (COMUKTG).

THE FIRST SEA LORD

Admiral Sir Julian Oswald Julian Oswald was born on 11 August 1933 and joined the Royal Navy in 1947. As a junior officer he served in *Vanguard*, *Verulam*, *Theseus*, *Newfoundland* and *Jewel*, before specialising in gunnery at HMS *Excellent*. He then commanded the minesweeper *Yarnton* and on promotion to Commander served in the Directorate of Naval Plans before commanding the frigate *Bacchante*.

He was promoted Captain in 1973 and commanded the destroyer *Newcastle* before briefly leading the Presentation Team and then becoming Captain of the Britannia Royal Naval College at Dartmouth. In 1982 he was promoted Rear Admiral as Assistant Chief of the Defence Staff, with responsibility first for Programmes and then for Policy and Nuclear.

After serving as FOF3 and Commander Anti-Submarine Group Two, he was appointed Commander in Chief Fleet

---

HMS *Vanguard*

Vanguard Class SSBN

The SSBN *Vanguard* was the first of the new generation of strategic nuclear deterrent submarines designed to take the new Trident missile system to sea and replace the aging shorter-range Polaris SSBNs. The *Vanguard* SSBNs would maintain the nation's nuclear deterrent until well into the twenty-first century.

Launched:	March 1992
Commissioned:	14 August 1993
Displacement:	16,000 tonnes
Length:	149.9 m
Propulsion:	1 Rolls-Royce pressurised water-cooled reactor supplying steam to 2 sets of General Electric geared turbines, 1 shaft
Armament:	4 533mm (21in) torpedo tubes capable of firing Spearfish torpedoes, 16 missile tubes capable of firing Trident II D5 missiles
Complement:	132
No. in class:	4: *Vanguard*, *Victorious*, *Vigilant* and *Vengeance*

HMS *Norfolk*
Type 23 Duke Class Frigate

The Type 23 frigate *Norfolk* was the first of the new generation Duke class general-purpose frigates. Although they were multi-purpose ships they were designed primarily for the ASW role, with the latest towed-array sonar and operating Lynx ASW helicopters. Their versatile weapon and sensor fit provided them with a good all-round capability, and they were built to incorporate the most modern stealth technology, which accounts for the slightly odd angular shape of their superstructure.

Launched:	11 July 1987
Commissioned:	1 June 1990
Displacement:	3,500 tonnes
Length:	133m
Propulsion:	Combined diesel-electric and gas: four 1.3mW Paxman Valenta diesels; two 1.5mW GEC electric DC motors; two 12.75mW Rolls-Royce Spey gas turbines; two GEC double reduction gearboxes; two fixed pitch propellers
Armament:	4.5in Mk 8 Gun Mod 1; eight McDonnell Douglas Harpoon; Sea Skua missiles; vertical launch Seawolf; 2 30mm BMARC cannon; 4 6-barrel Seagnat Chaff dispensers; magazine torpedo launch system with Stingray torpedoes and depth charges; 1 Lynx HMA Mk 3/8 or Merlin
Complement:	173
No. in class:	17 – 4 were subsequently disposed of to meet cuts in the defence programme

in the rank of full Admiral in 1987, relieved Admiral Staveley as First Sea Lord in May 1989 and served until March 1993.

OPERATIONS AND DEPLOYMENTS, 1990–1992

By 1991 the only permanent overseas garrisons maintained by Britain were those in Hong Kong, Gibraltar and the Falkland Islands, plus the Sovereign Base Area of Cyprus and a residual defence commitment to Belize. The Royal Navy deployed ships and vessels to cover guardship duties in each area.

Hong Kong In the Far East the Hong Kong Squadron, consisting of three patrol craft, *Peacock*, *Plover* and *Starling*, was permanently based in Hong Kong for guardship and policing duties in the very busy territorial waters and islands around the British Crown Colony. Much of the work of the squadron, which included anti-smuggling, anti-drug-trafficking and anti-immigration patrols, was carried out in close co-operation with the Hong Kong Police. The tremendous pressure of Chinese immigrants seeking refuge in Hong Kong caused the greatest threat.

The Falkland Islands and Antarctica The protection of British interests in the Falkland Islands and the Antarctic area remained a high priority for the Royal Navy despite the strength of the British garrison and the regular roulement

of British forces through the military airfield. A permanent presence was maintained with the Castle class offshore patrol vessel (OPV) *Leeds Castle* and the ice patrol ship *Endurance*, supported by a destroyer or frigate, a fleet tanker and a heavy repair and maintenance ship, under the command of the Senior Naval Officer Falkland Islands (SNOFI). Both fleet and nuclear submarines were available for rapid deployment to the area should the situation ever warrant it.

The forward repair ship RFA *Diligence* was withdrawn to support Operation Granby in August 1990 and replaced by the repair and maintenance ship *Stena Seaspread*, until the return of *Diligence* on station in May the following year. *Leeds Castle* was relieved by her sister ship *Dumbarton Castle* in September 1991. A short while later *Polar Circle* replaced *Endurance* for the Antarctic summer months, and then on 9 October 1992 she was renamed HMS *Endurance*. The following month *Diligence* sailed for the UK, not returning on station until June the following year.

Gibraltar The patrol craft *Cormorant* and *Hart* maintained Operation Kingpin, providing a British naval presence in Gibraltar, and in June 1991 the patrol vessels *Ranger* and *Trumpeter* relieved them. A destroyer or frigate was maintained in UK waters at notice to deploy to Gibraltar if required.

Cyprus The patrol vessels *Hunter*, *Striker* and *Attacker* were stationed at Cyprus in support of the UK Sovereign Base Area on the south coast. In March 1991 *Hunter* and *Striker* intercepted a drug smuggling vessel off the coast of Cyprus and seized a large quantity of cannabis. A short while later, in the same month, *Attacker* carried out a rescue operation saving the crew from a sinking Lebanese vessel close to the island.

The Caribbean A frigate or destroyer, supported by an RFA tanker, continued to be deployed regularly to the Caribbean to provide a British presence in the islands as the West Indies Guardship (WIGS). The WIGS assisted the US Coast Guard in anti-drug trafficking operations and also supported the Belize garrison.

On 28 March 1990 a detachment of 3 Commando Brigade Air Squadron was deployed to Belize for four months to reinforce the garrison. 605 Tactical Air Control Party Royal Marines joined the detachment on 11 April, returning to the UK on 1 August, and 611 Tactical Air Control Party Royal Marines deployed for a month in October.

In July 1990 the WIGS, the destroyer *Birmingham* and the support tanker RFA *Oakleaf* were ordered to sail immediately from Florida and head south-east for Trinidad at full speed. Islamic fundamentalists had taken over the Parliament and the television station and had also taken hostages. As *Birmingham* arrived the hostages were released and the danger was over.

In July 1991 the frigate *Arrow*, returning from a deployment to the South Atlantic, joined a US Coast Guard patrol boat in the Caribbean and played a major role in a successful operation, which resulted in the capture of 1,500lb of smuggled cocaine.

Operation Citation On 30 September 1991 there was a military coup in Haiti, and the WIGS was immediately sent to the island on Operation Citation to protect British nationals. The guardship arrived on 4 October and evacuation plans were set in hand, but in the event the situation eventually stabilised. Nevertheless the guardship was retained in the area to provide a British presence and was not finally withdrawn until the end of March 1992.

NATO Deployments The Royal Navy continued to contribute ships to the standing NATO maritime forces. At

the beginning of 1990 *Edinburgh* was the British destroyer attached to STANAVFORLANT (the Standing Naval Force Atlantic); she was later relieved by the frigate *Cornwall*. In April it was the turn of the UK to provide the Commodore of the STANAVFORLANT, and Commodore Gretton flew his broad pennant in *Cornwall*, transferring to *Campbeltown* when she relieved *Cornwall* later.

Liverpool and *Penelope* served in turn with NAVOCFORMED (the Naval On Call Force Mediterranean), and the UK provided an MCMV to serve with STANAVFORCHAN (the Standing Naval Force Channel).

The Nuclear Deterrent Throughout the period the four *Resolution* class Polaris submarines continued to deploy the nation's strategic nuclear deterrent to sea with uninterrupted patrols hidden deep and undetected.

Revenge completed her final deterrent patrol in April 1992 and was decommissioned, being the first Polaris submarine to come to the end of her service. The Polaris submarines had provided sterling service, completing an unbroken patrol cycle since taking over complete responsibility for the nation's strategic deterrent on 1 July 1969.

The frigate
Campbeltown
(NN)

The Trident Submarines Meanwhile the first of the next generation nuclear deterrent submarines, *Vanguard*, was under construction and commenced her Contractor Sea Trials in 1992. She was scheduled to join the Fleet with the new Trident II D5 missiles at the end of the year.

Submarine Deployments The submarine flotillas continued to deploy submarines on a range of important missions as far afield as the South Atlantic and the North Pole. The advanced programme of tactical deployments with the US Navy under the Arctic ice cap was maintained.

Spartan was deployed to the Arctic in 1990 spending almost her entire deployment under the permanent pack ice, and *Tireless* was deployed in 1991, exercising with US SSNs. The tradition was for the British and US submarines to surface near the North Pole and play games of baseball and cricket.

Icex 92 In 1992 *Trenchant* deployed to the Arctic to conduct exercise Icex with the US SSN uss *Spadefish*. The submarines engaged in a series of warfare training exercises, but when the submarines surfaced the ice was too thin for them to play the traditional games, though it did provide a splendid photo opportunity (see page 203).

Submarines were regularly deployed to the South Atlantic to reinforce ships stationed in the Falkland Islands. The submarines *Opossum* and *Osiris* were deployed in 1990 and 1991, with *Opossum* carrying out a circumnavigation through the Pacific on her return to the UK. En route she stopped at Pitcairn Island in the Pacific, where she joined the 200th anniversary of the settlement established by the mutineers of the *Bounty*.

A tragic incident occurred on 22 November 1990 when the submarine *Trenchant* was exercising with a submarine training course embarked. At one stage she snagged the nets of the trawler FV *Antares* and dragged the trawler under. The *Antares* sank with the loss of her crew of four. Following the Board of Inquiry measures were set in hand to prevent a recurrence of such a tragic incident.

Armilla Patrol In 1990 the Royal Navy was continuing to maintain the vital Armilla Patrol in the Gulf, Straits of Hormuz and Arabian Sea to protect British tankers. Two ships, frigates or destroyers, usually carried out the patrol. With the time needed to prepare and travel out to the Gulf, maintaining the patrol cycle required a heavy commitment of ships. The patrol had been running for ten years, and in recognition of the valuable work the Board of Shipping presented a red ensign, embroidered with the names of British merchant ships protected in the Gulf, to the Royal Navy. Sir Jeffrey Sterling, President of the Board, presented the ensign to Admiral Sir Jock Slater, the Chief of Fleet Support.

Endeavour 90 Deployment: Task Group 316.1, 15 January – 13 July 1990

In 1990 the DTS (Dartmouth Training Squadron), consisting of the large Type 82 guided missile destroyer *Bristol*, escorted by the *Leander* class frigates *Minerva* and *Ariadne*, sailed on a six-month circumnavigation deployment to the Far East. A total of 160 officers under training and thirty artificers were embarked in the squadron.

Task Group 316.1 sailed from Portsmouth on 15 January 1990 and, after a period of shake-down weapon training at sea off Portland, headed south to Gibraltar. Following a brief three-day visit the group sailed from Gibraltar on 29 January and after crossing the Mediterranean transited through the Suez Canal on 5 February.

Once clear of the Red Sea the ships of the squadron

dispersed for different port visits, with *Bristol* visiting Jeddah and then Cochin, where she arrived on 19 February. *Ariadne* visited Colombo whilst *Minerva* visited Aden before joining *Bristol* in Cochin. The squadron then steamed to Singapore, arriving on 28 February for a five-day visit.

Change-Over in Hong Kong The squadron then headed for Hong Kong, visiting Surabaya en route. Once in Hong Kong the Task Group had an assisted maintenance period before sailing on 9 April for weapon training. After successful exercises the ships returned to Hong Kong for a mid-deployment change-over of officers under training and artificers.

The squadron left Hong Kong on 14 April with *Bristol* and *Minerva* heading for Tokyo and Inchon, whilst *Ariadne* visited Kure and Sasebo. After a visit to Yokosuka the ships steamed across the Pacific to Dutch Harbour, Vancouver and San Francisco, with *Minerva* visiting Seattle and San Diego.

After a four-day visit to Acapulco the squadron sailed on 12 June and transited through the Panama Canal on 16 June with *Minerva* following four days later. The ships of the squadron then separated to pay individual visits to Wilmington, Bermuda and Nassau before sailing east across the Atlantic. The squadron stopped for a day to refuel in Punta Delgada, sailing on 9 July for the final leg back to the UK. *Bristol* and *Ariadne* arrived back in Portsmouth on 13 July, and *Minerva* arrived back in Devonport earlier on the same day.

It was the first time the Training Squadron had been east of Suez, and the deployment was a great success, helping to enhance Britain's reputation abroad.

Westlant 90 Deployment: Task Group 318.1, 18 April – 5 July 1990

Task Group 318.1 In early April 1990 a small task group, TG 318.1, gathered in Portsmouth for the Westlant 90 deployment to North America for exercise Marcot. The Task Group was under the command of Rear Admiral Hill-Norton, FOF3, flying his flag in the aircraft carrier *Ark Royal*, and

Bristol departs for Endeavour 90 (JAR)

comprised the destroyer *Glasgow* and the frigates *Brave* and *Cumberland*. The fleet replenishment ship RFA *Fort Grange* and the fleet tanker RFA *Olna* supported the Task Group.

Exercise Jolly Roger The group sailed from Portsmouth on 18 April without *Glasgow*, and headed west out into the

A Lynx helicopter landing back onboard after carrying out an attack
(NN)

Atlantic for exercise Jolly Roger, an anti-submarine exercise. It then exercised with US and French naval units including the French aircraft carrier FS *Foch*. The exercise included Sea Harrier cross-deck operations from FS *Foch*.

New York A short while later *Glasgow* joined the Task Group, which then entered New York on 9 May for a very popular

Sir Jeffrey Sterling presents the 'Armilla Red Ensign' to Admiral Sir Jock Slater
(JCKS)

four-day visit. On sailing from New York, *Ark Royal* with RFA *Olna* headed south for Mayport, whilst *Cumberland* and *Glasgow* visited Halifax and Toronto and *Brave* visited Hamilton and Ontario. *Ark Royal* arrived in Mayport on 19 May for an eleven-day maintenance period.

Exercise Marcot The Task Group then rendezvoused on 4 June for exercise Marcot, which was conducted by the Canadian Navy. On completion of the exercise *Ark Royal*, escorted by *Glasgow*, sailed for Halifax, arriving on 15 June. Thick fog and anti-nuclear demonstrators hampered the short four-day visit, after which *Ark Royal* sailed on to Boston.

Passage Home Meanwhile the other ships visited St Johns before setting course east across the Atlantic for the passage home, with *Glasgow* arriving in Devonport on 28 June and *Brave* and *Cumberland* arriving in Portsmouth later the same day. *Ark Royal* had been slightly delayed by a problem with one of her gas turbines and arrived back in Portsmouth on 5 July.

———•———

Operation Eldorado In May 1990 the frigate *Broadsword* and fleet tanker RFA *Tidespring* were despatched to stand off Monrovia under Operation Eldorado. The situation ashore during the Liberian Civil War was deteriorating, and the ships were standing by off the coast with a US amphibious task group ready to evacuate refugees and provide protection ashore for British and Commonwealth citizens.

The frigate *Andromeda* then arrived in the area to relieve *Broadsword*, and a little while later the frigate *Phoebe* in turn relieved *Andromeda*. On 25 July nearly 500 people were massacred in a church in Monrovia, showing how dangerous the situation was in Liberia. The ships operated off the coast with US forces as part of the US Operation Sharp Edge. After the evacuation of all those who wished to leave the area had been completed, the forces stood down and withdrew from the area at the end of the month.

The Gulf War: Operation Granby,
2 August 1990 – 12 April 1991

Desert Shield: Build-Up Phase On 2 August 1990 Saddam Hussein, with an Iraqi Army of over half a million men (the fourth largest army in the world), invaded Kuwait. Iraq had long claimed Kuwait but previous attempts to invade in the 1960s had been thwarted by the Royal Navy with the rapid deployment of aircraft carriers, commando carriers, Royal Marines and British troops to the northern Gulf. This time was different, and the world had been caught out despite British and American ships and aircraft being heavily involved in the area monitoring the Iraqi Navy during the Iran–Iraq War and protecting shipping in the Gulf.[2]

The political situation in the area was complex. Iraq had been created by the League of Nations under a British mandate in 1920. Britain had always been fully committed in the area, but sadly British power and influence had steadily declined, this trend coinciding with the rising dependence of the West on the oil-rich states in the Gulf region for the vital supply of oil. The wealth, power and status of the Arab states depended entirely on oil production. Iraq had vast debts following her eight-year inconclusive war of attrition with Iran, while Kuwait, on Iraq's doorstep, was immensely rich, with foreign assets calculated at the time as in excess of £100 billion. Iraq had always claimed that Kuwait belonged to her, and Saddam Hussein decided that it was time to make that so, which at a stroke would solve his problems and make Iraq the wealthiest and greatest power in the region, with him emerging as the natural leader of the Arab states.

Security Council Resolutions Having very quickly overwhelmed Kuwait in six days, Saddam Hussein officially annexed it on 8 August and began massing troops on the border with Saudi Arabia. Saddam Hussein claimed that he had no plans to invade Saudi Arabia, but, seeing what had just happened to Kuwait, the Saudis appealed to America, the UK and the United Nations for help.

The Security Council passed Resolution 661, imposing economic sanctions against Iraq, on 6 August and followed it three days later with Resolution 662, declaring the annexation of Kuwait null and void. Under the United Nations mandate an international coalition of armed forces from thirty nations was formed.

Operation Desert Shield On 9 August President Bush of the USA approved the deployment of US forces to the Gulf and 420,000 were assigned to Operation Desert Shield to defend Saudi Arabia. The UK also wasted no time and on the same day launched Operation Granby (named after the Commander of the British Army at the Battle of Minden in the Seven Years War), sending squadrons of Tornados and Jaguars on ahead to the region.

Air Chief Marshal Sir Patrick Hine was appointed the overall joint Commander of the operation, with the 'Joint Headquarters' being established at his HQ, that of RAF Strike Command at High Wycombe. The Joint HQ staff used a brand new NATO HQ, which had not yet been handed over. Lieutenant General Peter De La Billiere was appointed the 'in theatre' Commander of British Forces in the Gulf at the allied HQ in Riyadh.

The Armilla Patrol The ships of the Armilla Patrol were deployed to assist enforcing the United Nations embargo against Iraq. Saddam Hussein retaliated by increasing his army of occupation to 670,000 and commenced plundering Kuwait. Meanwhile the countries of the coalition started a steady build-up of forces in Saudi Arabia.

The Armilla Patrol at the time when the embargo started on 31 August consisted of the destroyer *York* and the frigates *Battleaxe* and *Jupiter* (designated group 'Whiskey'), supported by the tanker RFA *Orangeleaf*. They were deployed in the northern Gulf, operating closely with ships of the US Navy.

Task Group 321.1 Further ships were being prepared to reinforce Task Group (TG 321.1), but sadly no carrier or assault ship was in a state to be deployed to the Gulf. The carriers *Ark Royal* and *Invincible* were engaged in exercise Teamwork 90 and due to return to Portsmouth naval base on 16 September. *Ark Royal* was brought to thirty days' notice for the Gulf. She sailed for the Mediterranean with a full air group on 15 October but after a brief visit to Gibraltar it was decided to recall her to the UK.

The next group of ships, Group X-Ray, arrived in the Gulf in September and consisted of the destroyers *Gloucester* and *Cardiff* and the frigate *Brazen*. Group X-Ray had worked up with intensive exercises on passage and so arrived in area 'combat ready'. The ships relieved *York*, *Battleaxe* and *Jupiter*, which then returned to the UK.

The Type 22 frigate *London* was quickly equipped with command and control communications equipment and sent to the Gulf to act as the flagship for the Senior Naval Officer Middle East (SNOME), Commodore Paul Haddocks (later relieved by Commodore Chris Craig). *London* arrived on station at the beginning of October. A multinational Maritime Interdiction Force (MIF) was formed of allied warships and aircraft to enforce the United Nations sanctions against Iraq. A short while later, whilst patrolling in the Gulf of Oman with allied destroyers and frigates, *London* intercepted and after opening fire captured an Iraqi ship, which was turned over to the Americans. In the space of under three months over 2,000 ships and vessels had been challenged and twenty-five boardings, mostly by Royal Naval and Royal Marine boarding parties in boats and helicopters, had been carried out.

Support and Sea Train At the end of October the 25,500 ton helicopter support and casualty receiving ship RFA *Argus*, with Sea King helicopters from 846 Naval Air Squadron embarked, sailed from Devonport. She arrived in the Gulf on 15 November. Other ships too were arriving in the Gulf, including the support ship RFA *Fort Grange* and the fleet tanker RFA *Olna*. The MCMVs *Atherstone*, *Hurworth* and *Cattistock* were sent to the region to provide protection from Iraqi mines, and their command ship *Herald* joined them later. The heavy repair ship RFA *Diligence*, having made the long passage from the Falkland Islands, arrived with Naval Party 1600 embarked. The RFA support ships were protected by embarking Royal Marine and Royal Artillery Javelin Air Defence teams.

The might of the US Navy with several carrier battle groups was steadily building up in the Gulf, but the Royal Navy, with the Type 42 Air Defence Destroyers, had the vital role of providing forward air defence 'up-threat' in the dangerous waters of the northern Gulf. A seatrain of ships was formed to transport the units of the British forces assigned to the operation together with all their equipment, supplies and ammunition. The landing ships (logistic) (LSLs) *Sir Percival*, *Sir Bedivere* and *Sir Tristram* played an important role in the seatrain and with the ongoing resupply duties. The fleet replenishment ship RFA *Resource* transported large quantities of ammunition. At the beginning of December

Ark Royal and
Charybdis operating
with USS Virginia
and units of the US
6th Fleet in the
Mediterranean
(NN)

Commodore Chris Craig arrived to relieve Commodore Paul Haddocks as SNOME on board *London*.

Exercise Deep Heat A two-day coalition naval exercise, Deep Heat, was held from 6 to 8 January 1991 with the purpose of conducting a thorough test of operational readiness. Thirteen British ships were involved in the extensive exercise, which was held in a multi-threat environment with simulated attacks by Jaguar aircraft flown by the RAF. The finale of the exercise was an impressive firepower demonstration off the coast of Qatar. On completion the ships of the Royal Navy formed up and performed a steam-past for review by the Prime Minister, John Major, who was embarked in the flagship, *London*.

Task Group 323.2 It was clear that Saddam Hussein was not going to back down, and offensive operations were imminent. *Ark Royal* sailed from Portsmouth on 10 January 1991 with Task Group 323.2, comprising the Type 22 *Sheffield* and the Leander-class frigate *Charybdis* supported by RFAS *Olmeda* and *Regent*. They rendezvoused with the

destroyers *Manchester* and *Exeter* off Portland on 13 January and carried out live weapons firing in the exercise areas.

Manchester and *Exeter* together with the frigates *Brilliant* and *Brave* comprised the next group of Armilla Patrol ships (Group Yankee). Task Group 323.2 accompanied by *Manchester*, sailed south for Gibraltar. A few days later the rest of Group Yankee completed their work up at Portland and with their support tanker RFA *Bayleaf* departed for the Gulf.

Ark Royal arrived off Gibraltar and Admiral Brigstocke, the Task Force Commander, was embarked. *Ark Royal* and the rest of the force then headed east across the Mediterranean and on 22 January arrived off the coast of Cyprus, where *Manchester* was detached to continue south for the Gulf. *Ark Royal* and the rest of the Task Group then operated with units of the US 6th Fleet including USS *Virginia*, USS *Philippine Sea* and USS *Spruance*, guarding the western flank of the coalition forces.

The Deadline The UN had imposed a deadline of midnight on 15 January 1991 for Iraq to withdraw from Kuwait. On 5 January President Bush advised Saddam Hussein to

The battleship USS *Missouri* opens fire (USN)

Closed up at action stations in the Gulf (NN)

comply, but he declined and instead promised 'The Mother of all Battles'. Iraq steadfastly refused to comply, and as the deadline passed the world watched to see what would happen next. It did not have to wait long.

Operation Desert Storm The coalition immediately launched Operation Desert Storm to liberate Kuwait. At 2150 (GMT) on 17 January 1991 allied warships in the Gulf opened hostilities by firing nearly 100 Tomahawk cruise missiles. The cruise missiles were followed by an intensive allied air assault launched from forward air operating bases and US Navy aircraft carriers in the Gulf and the Red Sea to take out key strategic targets, including command and control posts, many in the Iraqi capital Baghdad and the Iraqi airfields. In response the Iraqis launched SCUD missiles at Saudi Arabia and also at Israel in an attempt to widen the conflict and bring in the Arab nations on their side. Fortunately Israel, with the protection of Patriot missiles, was persuaded to hold back. After successful attacks on Iraqi aircraft shelters the coalition finally achieved air supremacy by 29 January, though ships remained closed up for missile attacks.

The Battle of Bubiyan On the same day Iraqi forces launched attacks and captured the Saudi oil town of Khafji. The Lynx helicopter from *Gloucester* was in the vicinity and gained contact with Iraqi Navy surface units just off the coast, close

to Khafji. Seventeen enemy surface craft had sortied to attack coalition forces and help relieve the pressure on Iraqi troops fighting on shore. Lynx helicopters from *Gloucester*, *Cardiff* and *Brazen*, using Sea Skua air-to-surface missiles, engaged the Iraqi naval craft, and eventually all enemy craft were destroyed. Other Iraqi craft arrived, and the battle with Iraqi naval vessels T43, Exocet-armed TNC 45s and *Spasilac* and *Polnochny* craft, armed with Styx missiles continued for two days. As the Iraqi units attempted to get away from Faylakah Island the helicopters of Task Group 321.1 engaged them.

The helicopters from *Gloucester* and *Cardiff* scored seven direct hits with Sea Skua missiles, proving the effectiveness of the missile system. On 3 February the US Navy battleships opened fire with their 16in main armament against Iraqi targets in Kuwait. *Manchester*, first of the next group (Group Yankee), entered the Gulf at the beginning of February, followed a little while later by *Exeter*, *Brilliant* and *Brave*, which together with their support tanker RFA *Bayleaf* formed the rest of the new Armilla Group.

Elimination of the Iraqi Navy Forward-deployed Royal Navy warships were subject to continuous threat and attack from units of the Iraqi Navy, mostly from gunboats and patrol craft. On 8 February the Lynx helicopter from *Cardiff* attacked an enemy *Zhuk* craft and sank it, whilst at the same time the helicopter from *Gloucester* came under fire from coastal anti-aircraft batteries. A short while later, helicopters from *Cardiff* and *Manchester* attacked and scored hits on more Iraqi fast patrol boats. At this stage it was considered that the Iraqi Navy had been effectively neutralised, leaving the coalition naval forces in control of the waters of the northern Gulf.

With the situation easing *Brazen* and *Cardiff* were released from the group, and after exiting the Straits of Hormuz they headed west to return to the UK.

Mine Threat With the elimination of the Iraqi Navy from the area a new threat emerged. On 14 February the US Navy, led by British MCMVs, advanced north-west towards Kuwait. Two days later *Brave* sighted a mine on the surface of the water about a hundred yards off her port bow and manoeuvred carefully to avoid any contact. In the early hours of the morning of 18 February the US Navy was less fortunate and the assault carrier LPH-10, USS *Tripoli*, detonated a mine, blowing a ten-metre hole in her starboard side. Five hours later, as the US ships were manoeuvring out of the danger area, the large *Ticonderoga* class cruiser USS *Princetown* exploded a bottom mine and sustained severe damage. Casualties were airlifted to RFA *Argus* for treatment whilst naval diving teams from RFA *Diligence* helped with temporary repairs to the USS *Tripoli* to keep her afloat. Further mines were detected, and coalition ships were withdrawn south to safety escorted by British Hunt class MCMVs.

The naval forces remained under constant threat from enemy surface-to-surface Silkworm missiles. The Hunt class MCMVs moved north to clear safe forward bombardment boxes for US Navy battleships to deploy to provide gunfire support. The closer to shore the battleships could approach through the minefields, the further inland their guns could reach. However, the closer the MCMVs operated to the shore, the easier it was for Iraqi guns and missiles ashore to engage them. Once the area was cleared the US battleships, led by the USS *Missouri*, moved north into their bombardment boxes. On 23 February the battleship USS *Missouri* opened fire with her main armament of 16in guns and shelled Faylakah Island.

Saving the Battleship USS *Missouri* Early in the morning two days later the British anti-aircraft picket ships deployed up-threat identified two high-speed contacts on their air defence radars. The missiles had been launched without warning, using visual guidance from the tops of apartment blocks in Kuwait, with no need to use radar direction – which would have been detected and hence given advance warning of launch. The battleship's guns were very clearly visible when firing at night. The contacts, picked up on air defence radar, were incoming Silkworm missiles approaching the coalition forces at high speed. The missiles were tracked closing the battleship USS *Missouri*. One missile malfunctioned and dived in to the sea. The Type 42 air defence destroyer *Gloucester* tracked the second, and when lock-on had been achieved two Sea Dart surface-to-air missiles were launched, intercepting and destroying the one remaining Silkworm

The destroyer *Cardiff* returns to Portsmouth from the Gulf
(RNM)

missile. Fragments of the exploding missile fell into the water very close to the allied ships and just astern of the UK flagship, *London*. The incident became the story of how the 'mighty Mo' was saved by the 'little Glo'. The US Navy had every reason to be extremely grateful for the high professional standards of the Royal Navy.

The Flag Officer Submarines (FOSM) committed a number of submarines to support Operation Desert Storm. The submarines operated both close to the theatre of operations in the north-west Gulf, with special paint schemes, and also further afield, where their unique qualities were used to great effect. Their patrols helped ensure that the sea lines of communications were maintained open, safe from interference by states sympathetic to Iraq. The exact details of those operational patrols remain classified.

Operation Desert Sabre At 0400 on 24 February the coalition forces launched Operation Desert Sabre and two armoured invasion columns made swift advances deep into Iraqi held territory. Two days later Iraqi forces were in full flight from Kuwait City. As they fled they were setting on fire the oil wells in revenge. Coalition forces swiftly entered Kuwait City and liberated it on 27 February. The following day the masses of fleeing Iraqi forces were caught on the Basra road, and thousands of Iraqi tanks, guns, trucks and armoured vehicles were destroyed. By that evening the war was virtually over and all hostilities had ceased.

The War is Over, 11 March 1991 A formal cease-fire was agreed between General Schwarzkopf, Commander of the coalition forces, and the Iraqi Chiefs of Staff at Safwan on 3 March. Once it was formally ratified by the United Nations on 11 March the war was over. The Royal Navy had made a very significant contribution to the victory, and HM the Queen sent a congratulatory message to the ships in the Gulf. With the war over it was time for ships to start returning home. The first ships to leave were those of Group 'X' (*Gloucester*, *Cardiff* and *Brazen*), and *London* and *Herald* joined them on passage back to the UK, where they received a rapturous welcome home. Meanwhile a strong task force, comprising *Exeter*, *Brilliant*, *Brave* and *Manchester* together with the MCMVs, *Hecla* and the RFA support ships remained in the Gulf in the waters off Kuwait. The MCMVs were soon busy clearing the many mines laid during the war.

Operation Haven On 20 April 1991 Operation Haven was launched to provide humanitarian assistance to Kurdish refugees against Iraqi aggression. Some 500,000 Kurdish refugees had fled into the mountains and were struggling to survive in the severe winter conditions. The Kurds were driven by fear following atrocities committed by Iraqi forces. In one incident it was reported that Iraqi secret police had forced young Kurds to drink petrol before firing volleys of tracer bullets into them.

The aviation training ship RFA *Argus*, with 845 and 846 NAS (Naval Air Squadron) embarked and supported by the fleet replenishment ship RFA *Resource*, provided the logistic support for the operation. HQ 3 Commando Brigade together with elements of 40 and 45 Commando and air and logistic support were deployed ashore in the Turkey–Iraq frontier area, and MGRM (Major General Royal Marines), Major General Robin Ross, acted as the Joint Force Commander. The British forces deployed were part of the multi-national Task Force provided by thirteen nations.

RFA *Argus* sailed into Iskenderun on 30 April to offload helicopters and equipment. RFA *Resource* was stationed just off Iskenderun from 15 May to 22 July.

Operation Warden As the situation eased Operation Haven was revised with a reduction of force levels. The operation was reclassified as Operation Warden and a company from 40 Commando Royal Marines provided the British contribution to a multi-national battalion. The Royal Marines remained in Turkey until 1 October.

Operation Dervish 91 August 1991 marked the fiftieth anniversary of the Russian convoys, and to commemorate the event the frigate *London* and tanker RFA *Tidespring* were preparing to sail for Murmansk and Archangel for the first exercises with the Russian Navy since World War II. The deployment was codenamed Operation Dervish 91, after the original Operation Dervish fifty years earlier, the first of a series of heroic Arctic convoys carrying vital war material and supplies up round the North Cape to Russia during World War II. The men had faced horrendous conditions of weather and constant attacks from German bombers, U-boats and warships. Many of the ships were sunk and many sailors perished.

Many had been invited to witness the events in Murmansk, but on 19 August there was an attempted coup against Gorbachev by a hard-line Communist junta led by Gennadi Yanaev, with tanks in the streets of Moscow. The coup failed and Boris Yeltsin, President of the Russian Republic, virtually saved Gorbachev.

Operation Dervish 91 had been cancelled when the attempted coup was launched but it now went ahead. *London* sailed from Devonport on 21 August and set course for Murmansk, being joined by RFA *Tidespring* on passage north.

As *London* rounded the North Cape and entered the Barents Sea powerful units of the Russian North Sea Fleet appeared and long-range 'Badger' bombers flew overhead. It was a nervous moment in view of the precarious political situation in Russia. In the event all was peaceful, and exercises were conducted with the Russian Navy for the first time since World War II. During the exercises the 'convoy' of six Russian ships was repeatedly attacked by squadrons of Russian fighters and bombers and bombarded by dummy bombs and torpedoes.

After visiting Murmansk *London* was escorted through the White Sea to Archangel, where she received a great welcome.[3]

Operation Celia Problems in the Adriatic, arising from the Yugoslavian Civil War, necessitated the despatch of a frigate to the area as part of Operation Celia on 22 November 1991. The aim of the operation was to monitor the movement of shipping in the Adriatic. Both the destroyer *Exeter* and the frigate *Arrow* were deployed.

NATO and WEU Operations In January the following year Operation Celia was superseded by the upgraded WEU (Western European Union) and NATO operations Sharp Vigilance and Maritime Monitor. STANAVFORMED was activated for the upgraded operations in the Adriatic, and the Royal Navy assigned a frigate to the force. Then later in the year the operations were changed again from monitoring shipping to enforcing the UN embargo, and the codenames were changed to Operation Sharp Fence and Operation Maritime Guard. Both the STANAVFORLANT and the WEUCONMARFOR (the WEU Maritime Contingency Force) were deployed to the area to reinforce the STANAVFORMED. STANAVFORLANT and STANAVFORMED both continued to include British frigates and destroyers. By 1993 twenty-two NATO and WEU ships were operating in three flotillas in the Adriatic, supported by the first forward logistic site (FLS) at the Italian naval air station, Grottaglie, near Taranto.

Operation Lecturer In January 1992 the Royal Navy and Royal Marines sent personnel (Naval Party 1042) to Cambodia to engage in Operation Lecturer. The naval party joined the UN Naval Squadron (commanded by Commander Leighton of the Royal Navy), as part of the large 20,000 strong UN force assembled to cover the dangerous transition of the country to stability and democracy after many years of bloodshed and civil war. The army and RAF regiment also contributed forces, and operations went on into 1993.

Orient 92 Deployment: Task Group 318.1, 12 May – 26 November 1992

Task Group 318.1 In May 1992 a powerful task group was assembled in Portsmouth for a deployment to the Far East. Codenamed Orient 92, this was the first major deployment to the Far East since Outback 88. It was also the first activation of the newly formed UKTG (United Kingdom On Call Task Group). The prime purpose of the deployment was to demonstrate and maintain the ability of the UK to operate in strength outside the NATO area for a prolonged period.

In command was Rear Admiral John Brigstocke, COMUKTG, flying his flag in the aircraft carrier *Invincible*. The Task Group also included the destroyer *Newcastle*, the frigate *Boxer* and the new Type 23 frigate *Norfolk*, with the fleet replenishment ship RFA *Fort Austin* and the fleet tanker RFA *Olwen* supporting. The Air Group embarked in *Invincible* comprised six Harriers of 800 NAS, seven Sea King helicopters of 814 NAS and three Sea Kings of 'A' Flight 849 NAS.

The Task Group Sails On 12 May *Invincible* and *Newcastle* with RFA *Olwen* sailed out of Portsmouth naval base and headed down the Channel to rendezvous with the rest of the group, which had sailed from Devonport the day before. The group carried out a range of shake-down exercises as they steamed out into the Atlantic. Once out in the Bay of Biscay, the ships altered course south and conducted exercises with the French Navy and the STANAVFORLANT before transiting through the Straits of Gibraltar and sailing into Gibraltar harbour.

Exercise Dragon Hammer After sailing from Gibraltar the group participated in the major NATO exercise Dragon Hammer in the eastern Mediterranean. This was completed on 20 May, and two days later the Task Group sailed into Piraeus for a short four-day break. On sailing from Piraeus the group transited through the Suez Canal and Red Sea conducting ASW exercises and exercise Minibus.

Indian Ocean *Invincible*, escorted by *Boxer*, then steamed to Mombasa, while *Newcastle* visited the Seychelles and *Norfolk* visited Mauritius. On sailing from Mombasa on 22 June *Invincible* rendezvoused with the rest of the group and headed for Diego Garcia for exercise Sea Cobra.

Exercise Sea Cobra The exercise off Diego Garcia was a service-assisted evacuation with an amphibious landing by the Royal Marine Standby Rifle Company from 40 Commando, which flew out from the UK. The group then sailed on to Singapore, arriving on 9 July for four days, before sailing on to Tokyo and visiting Yokosuka prior to exercises with ships of the Japanese Maritime Self Defence Force, south of Tokyo Bay. The destroyer *Edinburgh* was detached from the Armilla Patrol and joined the Task Group for the main exercises in the Far East.

Defence Sales On 27 July *Invincible* sailed with *Newcastle* for a visit to South Korea, arriving in Pusan four days later. The group spent six days in Pusan and hosted a major British trade and defence industries sales exhibition. On sailing from Pusan on 5 August the ships headed south for a visit to Hong Kong for leave and a self-maintenance period.

Exercise Star Fish In September the group took part in the FPDA (Five-Power Defence Arrangement) exercise Star Fish in the South China Sea. It was a major maritime exercise designed to practise the defence of the Malaysian peninsula, involving thirty-six ships and forty-seven aircraft, all commanded by Rear Admiral Brigstocke. The main component of the exercise was followed by a four-day ADEX (air defence exercise), where ships' companies remained in defence watches and quickly closed up at action stations in response to surprise air attacks.

On completion of the ADEX the group joined the US carrier battle group based on the American carrier USS *Independence* for further joint exercises. On completion the ships visited various ports including Sibuyan, Penang, Singapore and Manila, and *Boxer* visited Fremantle.

The Persian Gulf On sailing from Georgetown on the island of Penang on 9 October the group set course west across the Indian Ocean for the return passage back to UK. After sailing up into the Persian Gulf for a visit to Abu Dhabi to host a major British export sales event, the group exercised with the Omani Navy and also with a US carrier battle group based on the USS *Ranger*.

Exercise Sea Griffon After sailing from the Gulf the group set course for the Red Sea and transited through the Suez Canal on 5 November. On arriving in the Mediterranean the ships visited Haifa before sailing, on 10 November, for exercise Sea Griffon, an air defence exercise off the coast of Cyprus. On completion of the exercise the group headed west for an anti-submarine warfare training period in the western Mediterranean before calling into Gibraltar on 20 November.

Home Leg On sailing from Gibraltar two days later, the Task Group set course north for home. Crossing the Bay of Biscay, the ships ran into gale-force winds and heavy seas, and a distress call was received from a Danish ship, MV *Charm*, in trouble to the west. *Invincible* altered course and increased speed to render assistance, but the *Charm* sank before she arrived and all she could do was help rescue the few survivors. The group then sailed into the Channel and on 26 November, when off Plymouth, embarked the Princess Royal, Chief Commandant of the WRNS, on board *Invincible* to witness a fly-past. There was also a steam-past of the ships of the group to give a 'cheer ship' to the royal guest. On completion the ships returned to their home ports, with *Invincible* and *Newcastle* arriving in Portsmouth on 27 November.

It had been a most successful deployment, renewing and

Invincible leading the Orient 92 Group (NN)

building strong relationships as well as establishing trade links and generating valuable UK export sales in the Middle East and Far East. It also demonstrated the role and ability of the UK in helping to maintain peace and security around the world.

———•———

Operation Grapple In October 1992 the aviation training ship RFA *Argus*, with four Sea King helicopters embarked, sailed with the fleet replenishment ship RFA *Resource* and the landing ship (logistic) RFA *Sir Bedivere* and headed for the Adriatic as part of Operation Grapple. The ships' mission was to support the growing number of British forces operating ashore with the United Nations Protection Force in the former Yugoslavia. On arrival in the Adriatic the RFA vessels were based in the port of Split and remained there, with RFA *Argus* returning to the UK in December.

Northern Ireland

In the early 1990s the security problems in Northern Ireland continued and the Royal Navy was required to carry out protection duties and assist in maintaining order in the Province. Problems were also experienced on the mainland, with the IRA (Irish Republican Army) launching a mortar bomb attack on the Prime Minister at a meeting with his Cabinet on 7 February 1991, followed by a bomb attack on Victoria Station, London, eleven days later. Later in the year two IRA bombers killed themselves in St Albans when their bomb, which they were transporting for an attack, exploded prematurely. The following year the IRA carried out several atrocities in Northern Ireland.

Operation Grenada The Royal Navy conducted regular patrols off the coast of Northern Ireland as part of Operation Grenada. The MCMVs and patrol craft of the Northern Ireland Squadron carried out the task to deter arms smuggling.

Operation Interknit Regular deterrent patrols were also maintained on Carlingford Lough by small craft and Royal Marine units. Two small fast patrol boats, *Grey Fox* and *Grey Wolf*, were launched in December 1992 for duty on Lough Neagh.

Operation Banner 45 Commando was deployed to south Armagh from 8 October 1990 to 18 March 1991 to assist with security patrols in support of Operation Banner. The Royal Marines exercised commendable restraint following the murderous IRA attacks on their Commandant General and the slaughter of eleven Royal Marine bandsmen at Deal the previous year.

At the beginning of 1991 a detachment of 3 Commando Brigade Air Squadron was also deployed to Northern Ireland to provide additional support to the security forces, and 42 Commando, together with 79 Commando Battery, was deployed there from November until 4 May 1992.

Other Activities

Operation Orderly In 1990 the Navy continued to provide personnel to man emergency ambulance services during industrial action by members of the Ambulance Service. The operation was concluded on 31 March when the Ambulance Service called off the strike.

Operation Hound On the night of 17–18 November 1990 the destroyer *Glasgow* intercepted and boarded the MV *Sea Ranger* in the sea off the Hebrides. The vessel was found to be carrying one and a half tons of cannabis, and was immediately arrested. The *Sea Ranger* was then brought into port for HM Customs officers to deal with.

On 29 March 1991 the frigate *Brilliant* went to the rescue of the MV *Mercs Horan*, which was on fire off Jubail in the Persian Gulf. After major fire-fighting operations, assisted by the USS *Francis Hammond* and the Spanish warship *Victoria*, the fires were brought under control and *Brilliant* towed her into Bahrain.

Operation Manna In the wake of a major cyclone in Bangladesh on 8 May 1991, the fleet replenishment ship RFA *Fort Grange*, with a naval party and Royal Marines embarked, was despatched to the area under Operation Manna to render emergency humanitarian relief following major flooding, damage and loss of life. Over 200,000 people died in the cyclone and aftermath. RFA *Fort Grange* remained in the area until 3 June.

On 8 April 1992 the frigate *Campbeltown* and the tanker RFA *Gold Rover* sailed to the assistance of the supertanker *World Hitachi Zosen*, which was on fire following a collision off the coast of West Africa. They were able to render valuable assistance and helped contain the fires until a fire-fighting tug arrived on the scene to extinguish the fires.

In Hong Kong *Plover* went to the assistance of MV *Seastar*, which had caught fire after an explosion onboard on 20 April. *Plover* rescued the crew and spent two days fighting the fires before they were finally extinguished on 22 April.

Hurricane 'Andrew' The destroyer *Cardiff*, the frigate *Campbeltown* and the tanker RFA *Orangeleaf* sailed to Eleuthera in the West Indies on 24 August 1992 following the passage of Hurricane 'Andrew'. On arrival the ships were able to render valuable emergency relief, helping to restore vital services over a period of four days.

Major Naval Exercises

Despite the end of the Cold War and the reduced threat of large-scale conflict the Royal Navy continued to maintain an important programme of regular major exercises.

Exercise Cold Winter In March 1990 a powerful task group, including *Invincible*, *Intrepid*, *Alacrity*, *Amazon*, *Hermione* and *Herald* and the RFAs *Olmeda*, *Sir Bedivere*, *Sir Percivale* and *Sir Tristram* with 42 and 45 Commandos, assembled in the Norwegian Sea for the major annual amphibious NATO exercise Cold Winter.

Invincible in exercise Cold Winter
(NN)

Exercise Dragon Hammer A little later in the year *Invincible* took part in the NATO exercise Dragon Hammer in the Mediterranean. Also taking part were the aircraft carriers USS *Eisenhower* and USS *Saipan* and the Spanish and Italian carriers *Principe de Asturias* and *Giuseppe Garibaldi*. In all forty-two warships from seven NATO navies took part.

Exercise Teamwork In September 1990 the Royal Navy made a major contribution, consisting of the aircraft carriers *Ark Royal* and *Invincible*, the assault ship *Intrepid*, ten escorts, submarines and many other ships and vessels, to exercise Teamwork. It was NATO's largest maritime exercise of the year and took place in the Norwegian Sea.

Exercise Westlant Early in 1991 the carrier *Invincible*, escorted by the destroyer *Edinburgh*, sailed to the eastern seaboard of the USA for the important NATO exercise Westlant, visiting various ports in the USA and the West Indies.

Exercise Ocean Safari Later in the year *Ark Royal* participated in the major NATO exercise Ocean Safari in the North Atlantic.

Exercise North Star At the end of September 1991 *Invincible*, flying the flag of Vice Admiral Hill-Norton, led an important NATO exercise, North Star, in the Atlantic. The exercise involved fifty ships and 200 aircraft from six NATO countries.

Mediterranean NATO Exercise Display Determination Following exercise North Star, *Invincible* headed into the Mediterranean for the equally important major NATO exercise Display Determination.

Exercise Westlant In September 1991 *Ark Royal*, escorted by the destroyer *Gloucester* and the frigate *London*, was the flagship for the annual major naval exercise Westlant with NATO navies off the US eastern seaboard. *Ark Royal* visited Bermuda, Port Everglades and Mayport before returning via Gibraltar.

Exercise Teamwork In the spring of 1992 a further and even bigger exercise Teamwork was carried out in the North Atlantic, involving a total of 200 ships and over 300 aircraft. Vice Admiral Hill-Norton led the UK Task Force from his flagship *Invincible* as Commander ASW Strike Force, with COMAW (Commodore Amphibious Warfare) in *Fearless*.

Exercise Westlant 92 Later in the year *Ark Royal* again led the Task Group, which included *Exeter* and *Coventry*, the RFAS *Olmeda* and *Regent* and the submarine *Triumph*. The group, commanded by Vice Admiral Hill-Norton, flying his flag in the aircraft carrier as Commander ASW Strike Force, sailed out of Portsmouth on 2 September. It crossed the Atlantic and conducted exercise Westlant 92 with the US Navy including the US Carrier Battle Group based on the carrier USS *John F Kennedy*. The Task Group visited Norfolk in Virginia, Mayport in Florida and the Bahamas before crossing back across the Atlantic to the UK on 6 November.

JMCs The important JMC (Joint Maritime Course) exercises off the coast of Scotland, supported by NATO navies, were continuing to provide excellent training and command opportunities for senior officers.

Exercise Purple Monarch A joint amphibious exercise in 1992, Purple Monarch, tested command and control in amphibious warfare and exercised the deployment of a joint force HQ to a forward operating base at Gibraltar. COMUKTG conducted the exercise from his flagship *Ark Royal*.

———•———

***Upholder* Class Submarines** *Upholder*, the first of the new Type 2400 class conventional patrol submarines, was launched in 1990.[4] The diesel-electric *Oberon* class submarines were to have been the last conventional submarines operated by the Royal Navy, and by 1990 all new-construction submarines by the leading navies were nuclear-powered. However, a combination of factors, including the need to operate very close to coastlines to insert Special Forces covertly and the requirement to maintain the industrial base with its submarine building skills, which were focused on Trident, caused a change of decision. The 1981 defence review had stated that the MoD 'will proceed as fast as possible with a new and more effective class to replace our aging diesel-powered submarines'.[5] The result was the *Upholder* class submarines, born out of a previously produced private design for foreign navies by Vickers titled the Type 2400 (the design submarines displaced 2,400 tonnes). Four submarines were ordered: *Upholder*, which was to be built by Vickers in Barrow, and *Unseen*, *Unicorn* and *Ursula*, to be built by Cammell Lairds in Birkenhead.

The new submarines included many innovative features drawn from both nuclear and conventional submarines and had a hull similar in shape to the *Trafalgar* class nuclear submarines but smaller. They were so sophisticated that they were considered virtually as capable as a nuclear submarine but lacked the power produced by a nuclear reactor. They did have a design Achilles heel, however: the first of class proved that their 'weapons handling and discharge system was not fully "fit for purpose"'. They could detect and trail other submarines stealthily but they experienced some difficulties when attempting to attack targets. There followed an expensive rectification programme.

In the end the *Upholder* class became victims of the Peace Dividend at the end of the Cold War. In 1993, owing to constraints of funding, the Royal Navy was facing the stark choice of keeping the *Upholder* class and giving up one nuclear attack submarine or losing the *Upholder* class and retaining the full nuclear submarine fleet. It chose to keep all the nuclear submarines. The four *Upholder* class submarines were subsequently sold to Canada, and one of them, the CFS *Chicoutimi*, came to prominence in 2004.[6]

PERSONNEL MATTERS

Manpower By 1990 the strength of the Navy had reduced by 1,800 to 63,200, but with the size of the Fleet remaining fairly constant there was a fair amount of stretch. However, the 'Options for Change' cuts that were imposed to reduce numbers to 55,000 posed very difficult problems for the personnel departments. Inevitably most of the cuts affected the support and training areas, in order to try and preserve the fighting efficiency of the front line. The adjustments created a great deal of turmoil.

Fleetman 90 A study, known as 'Fleetman 90', was conducted in 1990 to consider the optimum organisation for the Fleet, and this resulted in a proposed centralised structure under a single FOSF.

The study was accepted and promulgated to the Fleet by a signal from the Commander in Chief on 5 February 1991. Vice Admiral Hill-Norton was appointed to the new post of FOSF, based in the naval base at Portsmouth, on 5 April 1992.

Warfare Branch Development The need to address the problems of rapidly changing technology, together with the requirement for a more user-maintainer approach to manning, resulted in various studies into the Operations and Weapon Engineering sub-branches.

A Warfare Branch Development Team was formed to examine the various options. Eventually the team recommended the merger of the Operations and Weapon Engineering sub-branches as the most operationally efficient way of solving the problems and also as providing the greatest savings in manpower. The study led to the decision to phase out the two sub-branches and replace them with a new branch of OMs (Operator-Mechanics) at all levels up to Warrant Officer. It was also decided to retain the WE Officer and the WE Artificer levels to maintain a high standard of engineering and technological skills and experience.

WRNS at sea in the destroyer *Manchester*
(NN)

WRNS to Sea In 1990, although the size of the Fleet had remained unchanged, the total strength of the Navy had reduced by some 1,800 on the previous year, which, combined with a higher wastage rate, added to the considerable pressures of stretch. The armed forces, together with other employers, were facing a demographic trough and a tough recruiting challenge.

The wider employment of women at sea was considered as a means of bridging the gap and in February 1990 the Navy Board announced the intention 'to extend the employment of members of the WRNS to include service at sea in surface ships of the Royal Navy', a historic moment. WRNS personnel serving since before 1 September 1990 had the option of whether to serve at sea, but all recruited after that date were liable for sea service. *Invincible, Brilliant, Battleaxe, Juno* and RFA *Argus* were converted for mixed manning.

Redundancy Programme Ironically. having made the controversial decision to employ women at sea to bridge the demographic trough, the Royal Navy had a redundancy programme imposed on it in 1992 to reduce manpower to 55,000 by mid-1990. The redundancy programme was implemented in three phases, with the 400 selected for the first phase leaving the Service before April 1993 and the second phase of 1,150 leaving by November 1993. The third phase was to be completed by 1995.

The White Ensign Association In 1990 Admiral of the Fleet the Lord Fieldhouse relieved Sir Derrick Holden-Brown as Chairman of the White Ensign Association. In June the Association hosted a banquet on board the aircraft carrier *Invincible* in the Thames off Greenwich, which was a great success. The weather initially threatened to ruin the evening but the ship's company worked extremely hard and transformed the hangar into a magnificent banqueting hall, which greatly impressed the many VIPs and guests. During the year *Alacrity, Andromeda, Beaver, Chatham, Gloucester, Invincible* and *Phoebe* took captains of industry to sea, as organised through the Association, to gain first-hand experience of the high quality of naval personnel. The Association also arranged a VIP visit to the Fleet Air Arm at the naval air station HMS *Heron*, near Yeovilton.

The following year the Association noted the increasing number of personnel falling into debt caused by 'low start' and unsuitable mortgages. It took action to alert people to the dangers of these and other risky types of mortgage offer.

During the year the Association was grateful to *Ariadne, Boxer, Brilliant, Chatham, Coventry* and *London* for taking VIPs and senior business people to sea, and in addition the Flag Officer Plymouth, Commodore Clyde and Flag Officer Naval Aviation hosted high-level Association events.

Very sadly, in 1992 Admiral of the Fleet the Lord Fieldhouse, Chairman of the Association, died. Following his death Mr Henry Lambert took over as Chairman. During the year *Invincible, Ark Royal, Boxer, Manchester, Marlborough, London, Norfolk, Broadsword, Juno* and *Argyll* took senior people from industry to sea, as organised by the Association. The Flag Officer Surface Flotilla and the Flag Officer Naval Aviation also hosted important visits organised by the Association.

At the same time the Association geared itself up to provide valuable assistance to all those leaving the Service under the redundancy programme and established regular clinics in the three main naval bases.

Operation Grapple in the Adriatic 1993–1995

UN Operations in Bosnia and Kosovo – Operations Grapple, Hamden and Sharp Guard –
Australasia 95 Deployment – Trident Deployment

At the beginning of January 1993 Bill Clinton became President of the USA, and on 3 January he and President Yeltsin signed the START II Treaty (Strategic Arms Limitation Treaty) formally ending the Cold War.

The Middle East Tension remained high throughout the Middle East. In the Gulf, Iraq continued to defy the coalition, and Saddam Hussein had moved surface-to-air missiles and anti-aircraft weapons south, where they could be used against allied aircraft trying to enforce the 'no fly' zones. There was an attempted assassination of ex-President George Bush when he visited Kuwait, and in response the USA launched cruise missile attacks against the Iraqi intelligence headquarters in Baghdad. In October 1994 there was a renewed Iraqi threat to Kuwait, as a result of which allied forces were required to reinforce the region.

The Palestinian Question The Palestinian troubles continued, though there was a glimmer of hope when Yitzhak Rabin, Prime Minister of Israel, and Yasser Arafat agreed to recognise each other's legitimacy and signed a peace agreement in the USA. This was followed by an agreement for limited Palestinian autonomy in September 1995, though sadly an Israeli fanatic murdered Rabin a month later.

Africa In war-ravaged Somalia, the USA attempted to take action against Aidid, a hugely powerful Somali warlord. In June 1993, following the slaughter of UN peace-keepers by Aidid's militia, the USA launched a combined ground and air assault on Aidid in Mogadishu. Two US Black Hawk helicopter gunships were shot down, and dead US servicemen were dragged through the city in front of the world's news teams. This distressing, high-profile incident led to the USA withdrawing from the critical and unstable Horn of Africa.

Shortly after the USA pulled out, in early 1994, civil war erupted in Rwanda, with thousands being slaughtered. With only a very small UN force in Somalia, and no US forces on hand, the slaughter in Rwanda reached over half a million by the end of May.

Northern Ireland Meanwhile bombings by the IRA (Irish Republican Army) continued on the mainland of Britain as well as in Northern Ireland, with a spectacular bomb attack on Harrods, firebombs in many stores in central London and a mortar attack on Heathrow Airport. Despite the

FIRST SEA LORD
Admiral Bathurst

SECOND SEA LORD
Admiral Layard

MANPOWER
56,000

MERCANTILE MARINE
1,747
merchant ships

bombing campaign, progress towards a resolution of the 'Troubles' was being made at long last. A Loyalist cease-fire was declared on 13 October 1994, followed eighteen days later by the IRA announcing a cessation of operations. Peace talks continued despite the refusal of the IRA to surrender any weapons.

UK Defence Policy On 14 July 1994 the government announced changes in defence policy with particular emphasis on the international dimension. The NATO summit earlier in the year had established a 'Partnership for Peace' initiative with Central and Eastern Europe and endorsed a plan for a Combined Joint Task Force (CJTF).[1] At the same time major reductions continued to be imposed on the armed forces. The decision was also taken not to replace the WE-177 free-fall nuclear bomb, but instead to develop the sub-strategic capability of the new Trident missile system.

The Royal Navy was tasked with three new roles:

> Defence Role One: the defence, protection and security of the UK base and dependent overseas territories.

> Defence Role Two: to help protect the UK and her allies against any major external threat.

> Defence Role Three: to contribute to promoting the wider security interests of the UK through the maintenance of international peace and stability.

In pursuance of the Defence Roles, the Royal Navy developed three key force capabilities concentrated on the submarine fleet, the aircraft carriers and the amphibious group.

THE FLEET

In 1993 the Fleet was adjusting to the new world order following the end of the Cold War and the end of the primacy of ASW (anti-submarine warfare) capability. The backbone of the Fleet consisted of the three *Invincible* class anti-submarine warfare carriers and the two veteran assault ships, *Fearless* and *Intrepid*.

Destroyers and Frigates The escort fleet consisted of twelve Type 42 destroyers together with thirty frigates. The frigates included six Type 21, fourteen Type 22 and the first four of the new Type 23, with the next batch of six under construction and also the last six *Leander* class, which were still in service. Although more of the Type 23 frigates were planned, the *Leanders* and Type 21s were being withdrawn from service. The planned strength of the escort fleet was forty destroyers and frigates.

Mine Counter-Measures Vessels The MCMVs (mine counter-measures vessels) consisted of thirteen of the Hunt class, twelve of the River class (eleven of them manned by the Royal Naval Reserve) and three single-role minehunters of the new *Sandown* class with two more building. In addition there were the last four of the old Ton class MCMVs still in commission. There were eighteen patrol vessels and fifteen small patrol boats.

Submarines The submarine fleet included four Polaris deterrent SSBNs (ballistic nuclear submarines) of the *Resolution* class, seven nuclear fleet submarines of the *Trafalgar* class, five fleet submarines of the *Swiftsure* class and one remaining submarine of the old *Valiant* class. The new Trident missile submarines of the *Vanguard* class were building, with the first of class, *Vanguard*, joining the Fleet in 1994 and departing on her first operational deterrent patrol in December 1994. The remaining submarines of the planned class of four would then join the Fleet at regular intervals as they became operational between 1994 and 1997. The *Valiant* class and two of the *Swiftsure* class were being withdrawn from service.

Aircraft The Fleet Air Arm had forty Sea Harriers in three fighter squadrons, and 130 helicopters, mostly Sea Kings and Lynx, with forty-four Merlin ASW helicopters in production. In addition there was an establishment of training and support, fixed-wing aircraft and helicopters.

Royal Marines 3 Commando Brigade consisted of three Royal Marine Commandos (40, 42, and 45 Commandos),

The Type 23 Duke class frigate *Norfolk* (RNM)

Flag of the Flag Officer Surface Flotilla (RH)

supported by logistics, artillery, engineers, signals and a helicopter squadron.

Support Vessels A well-balanced fleet of naval auxiliaries supported the Royal Navy. The RFA (Royal Fleet Auxiliary) included thirteen tankers, three fleet replenishment ships with more building, a helicopter training ship and a number of other specialised support ships. In addition there was a host of minor support vessels operated by the RMAS (the Royal Maritime Auxiliary Service) and deployed in an around ports and naval bases. In 1994 it was announced that the Royal Yacht, *Britannia*, would be taken out of service after forty-four years with the Royal Navy.

Command The Commander in Chief Fleet, Admiral Sir Hugo White, commanded the Fleet until he was relieved in 1995 by Admiral Sir Peter Abbott. Rear Admiral Boyce was FOSF (Flag Officer Surface Flotilla), and he was relieved in 1995 by Rear Admiral Brigstocke.

Rear Admiral Lane-Nott was Flag Officer Submarines (FOSM), and Rear Admiral Garnett was Flag Officer Naval Aviation (FONA), relieved in 1995 by Rear Admiral Loughran. Lieutenant General Ross was Commandant General Royal Marines.

FIRST SEA LORD

Admiral Sir Benjamin Bathurst Ben Bathurst was born in May 1936 and educated at Eton before joining the Royal Navy in 1953. He qualified as a naval pilot in 1960 and served as the ship's flight commander in the guided missile destroyer *Devonshire*. Following an exchange appointment with the Australian Navy he became senior pilot of 820 NAS (Naval Air Squadron) in the carrier *Eagle* as a Lieutenant Commander.

In 1971 he was appointed to *Norfolk* as Commander and then went to MoD to join the Directorate of Naval Air Warfare, before commanding the frigate *Ariadne* in the rank of Captain. He then served as the Naval Assistant to the First

---

HMS *Sandown*

Sandown Class Minehunter

Sandown was the first of a new generation of single-role minehunters and entered service in 1989. The ships are built of glass-reinforced plastic and were designed to replace the old Ton class minehunters. They are equipped with powerful high-definition minehunting sonars and mine disposal equipment capable of detecting and destroying mines at depths of 200 metres. They also carry two remotely controlled submersible vehicles which are able to destroy mines at depths of 300 metres.

Launched:	16 April 1988
Commissioned:	9 June 1989
Displacement:	450 tonnes
Length:	52.7m
Propulsion:	2 Paxman Valentia 6RPA 200-EM 1500 diesels
Armament:	1 30mm gun (650 rounds/min 10km range)
Complement:	34
No. in class:	12 (8 still in service)

Sea Lord before taking command of the 5th Frigate Squadron in 1978. After attending the Royal College of Defence Studies he was appointed Director of Naval Air Warfare in 1982.

The following year he was appointed Flag Officer 2nd Flotilla (FOF2) as a rear admiral. He became Director General Naval Manpower and Training in 1985 and subsequently Chief of Fleet Support as a vice admiral. In 1989 he was promoted full Admiral and appointed Commander in Chief Fleet, and then in 1991 he became Vice Chief of the Defence Staff.

He was appointed First Sea Lord in March 1993 and was relieved by Admiral Slater in July 1995. On being relieved, he became the last Admiral of the Fleet, as the tradition of such promotions was then discontinued in all three armed services.

Admiral Sir
Benjamin Bathurst
(JAR)

OPERATIONS AND DEPLOYMENTS, 1993–1995

The Royal Navy continued to be fully engaged around the world with regular routine patrol and guardship commitments. On an average day there were some twenty to thirty warships, submarines and RFA vessels routinely deployed away from United Kingdom waters.[2]

Nuclear Deterrent Throughout the period the SSBNs of the Polaris Submarine Squadron maintained their vital deterrent

patrols in fulfilment of Defence Role One. In 1994 they were joined by the first of the new *Vanguard* class of Trident missile SSBNs, the name ship of the class, *Vanguard*. On a dark day in December 1994 *Vanguard* sailed from the waters of the Clyde and silently deployed into the depths of the oceans on her first operational patrol.

Hong Kong In the Far East the Hong Kong Squadron, made up of the three patrol craft, *Peacock*, *Plover* and *Starling*, formed part of the Hong Kong garrison. The ships were heavily committed, being constantly at sea in the waters

Admiral Sir Peter Abbott, CINCFLEET, visits the Hong Kong garrison, with Officer of the Guard, Lieutenant Howell, on the left
(MH)

FIRST PATROL: *Vanguard* – The First Trident Missile Submarine

The 10th ship to bear the name *Vanguard* may not be the largest (16,000 tons displacement v 48,500 tons for the 1940s battleship) but with the ability to remain submerged almost indefinitely thanks to its nuclear reactor and to launch up to 16 Trident D5 missiles armed with nuclear warheads, it is certainly many times more powerful.

Commissioned in 1993 as the first of class, *Vanguard* underwent a full programme of trials and training that culminated in May 1994 with the test firing of a missile off the Florida coast. And so, on a clear crisp winter's evening in December of that year *Vanguard* slipped quietly out of the Clyde on her first operational patrol, precisely in accordance with a timetable declared by the then Prime Minister, Margaret Thatcher, ten years earlier.

Quickly the crew settle into their routine for the patrol. As in any submarine higher speed equals more

noise, so moving around the ocean slowly is vital if the SSBN is to remain undetected by friend and foe alike. Similarly, crew noise can also give away the submarine's position so 'noisy evolutions' are strictly controlled. Days pass in a schedule of watchkeeping, sleeping and mealtimes. For those that wish to remain fit there are a variety of rowing machines, exercise bikes and step machines, inevitably used more at the beginning of patrol than at its end! To keep the ship's company alert, a variety of exercises are also held; damage control and engineering drills and the all-important missile launch exercises initiated from London, during which the submarine demonstrates its remarkable ability to 'hover' at the depth necessary to launch its missiles if it should ever be required to do so.

Submariners on patrol read – anything! They study for GCSEs and A Levels, for Naval exams and for

Open University degrees. They are keen film buffs and with the huge increase in films on DVD the variety available is almost endless. Christmas Day arrives with the traditional meal and all the trimmings; the turkey carved by the Commanding Officer and served to the sailors by the officers in accordance with tradition. Father Christmas moves through the boat giving out small presents and the Carol Service is well attended, led by the Galley Choir with their rather interesting rendition of 'Away in a Manger'.

There is some contact with home but it's all one way! – Daily extracts from the newspapers are received, as are crosswords, sports results and the weekly Lottery numbers ... and there are 'family grams' – weekly messages of 40 words that allow family and loved ones to pass a few thoughts from home and personal news of families – but which never receive a reply due to the

submarine's strict 'no transmission' rules.

And then in a rush, the end of the patrol is in sight; the records and the patrol report are completed, the coveted 'Dolphins' awarded to those who have qualified as fully-fledged submariners during the trip. The submarine is scrubbed (all four decks of it) in preparation for the arrival of the VIP (often a high ranking officer or politician, sometimes a member of the Royal family) as it moves up the River Clyde for an immediate de-brief of the patrol. And of course, by the time the submarine berths alongside in Faslane, its relief is already on patrol, maintaining the nation's strategic deterrence as the RN has done continuously since 1968.

Vice Admiral Peter Wilkinson CVO,
First Commanding Officer of
Vanguard

The MCMV *Hurworth* leads
the STANAVFORCHAN
(NN)

around Hong Kong and the islands, mostly in deterrent patrols to stop illegal immigration, but also against smuggling and other illegal activities. The operations were conducted in close conjunction with the Hong Kong police and resulted in many arrests, often opposed, with the patrol craft regularly coming under fire.

Gibraltar In Gibraltar it was necessary to maintain a constant naval presence, in order to reassure the people of Gibraltar of British support as well as to conduct regular anti-smuggling and anti-drug patrols. Two patrol craft, *Ranger* and *Trumpeter*, were based in Gibraltar and a frigate was kept at notice to deploy to the area as Gibraltar Guardship. In addition there were constant visits by British warships transiting the Mediterranean, en route to and from the Adriatic and the Gulf.

South Atlantic Further south the Royal Navy continued to deploy a powerful force in the Falkland Islands, under the command of SNOFI (Senior Naval Officer Falkland Islands) as part of the British garrison protecting British interests in the area. A destroyer or frigate and an offshore patrol vessel were maintained on station, together with the ice patrol ship *Endurance*, supported by an RFA tanker. The forward repair ship RFA *Diligence* returned to the Falkland Islands in June 1993 for eleven months. She returned again in November the following year before being finally withdrawn on 28 April 1995. From time to time a submarine visited Port Stanley, and for much of the time a submarine was on standby to deploy to the area as required.

Caribbean The Royal Navy continued to maintain a frigate or destroyer as West Indies Guardship (WIGS), supported by an RFA tanker, in the Caribbean. The frigate *Cumberland* was on station as WIGS in 1993. The WIGS conducted regular anti-drug trafficking operations as well as supporting the Belize garrison until the garrison was withdrawn on 20 September 1994.

Fishery Protection Squadron The Fishery Protection Squadron conducted the tasks of fishery protection as well as patrolling Britain's offshore gas and oilfield installations. The squadron was divided into two divisions. The Coastal Division of the four Ton class MCMVs and one fleet minesweeper carried out fishery protection duties off the coast within the twelve-mile coastal limit. The Offshore Division of the seven Island class patrol vessels conducted fishery protection outside the coastal limit and carried out the surveillance patrols of the offshore gas and oilfield installations.

In March 1993 *Brocklesby*, *Jersey*, *Orkney*, *Brinton* and *Blazer* were involved in a fishing dispute with French fishermen over fishing rights on the Schole Bank off Guernsey. After several incidents and the arrest of a French fishing boat, tensions eased, and by July the dispute was over. There was a brief recurrence of the dispute at the beginning of the fishing season the following year, and *Shetland* and *Cattistock* were deployed to the Schole Bank to resolve the situation.

RFA *Fort Victoria*

Fort Victoria Class Fleet Replenishment Ship

RFA *Fort Victoria*, is the first of a new class of 'one stop' replenishment ships manned by the RFA. The ships are designed to provide fuel, stores and armaments and are able to transfer supplies of all at the same time. They also provide helicopter maintenance facilities. The ships are well equipped with defensive armament, including the facility to carry the Sea Wolf missile system, and can operate up to five ASW helicopters. They are thus very versatile ships, able to operate with the Fleet or on their own.

Launched:	4 May 1990
Commissioned:	24 June 1994
Displacement:	36,500 tonnes
Length:	204m
Propulsion:	2 Crossley-Pielstick V16 medium-speed diesels driving 2 fixed propellers
Armament:	2 30mm guns, 2 Phalanx close-in weapon systems, 5 Sea King or Merlin helicopters
Complement:	Ship's crew 134 (95 RFA plus 15 RN plus 24 civilian stores staff) Embarked air group up to 154 personnel (includes 28 officer air crew)
No. in class:	2: *Fort Victoria* and *Fort George*

In August 1994 *Anglesey*, *Alderney*, *Orkney*, *Shetland* and *Lindisfarne* were deployed to the Bay of Biscay to protect British fishing vessels from attacks by Spanish vessels during a dispute in the Tuna fishing season. The dispute continued into September but was resolved by the end of the month.

Standing Naval Forces Despite the end of the Cold War the squadrons of NATO Standing Naval Forces remained heavily committed to busy programmes of training and peace keeping operations. The Royal Navy continued to assign ships to all squadrons as a matter of priority. The STANAVFORLANT (the NATO Standing Naval Force Atlantic) and STANAVFORMED (the NATO Standing Naval Force Mediterranean) were regularly deployed to the Adriatic (see below). The STANAVFORCHAN (Standing Naval Force Channel) conducted many exercises and goodwill port visits in European waters. In May 1993 the MCMV *Hurworth* completed a year's attachment to the squadron during which time she had visited twenty-five European ports.

Security Operations in the Adriatic

NATO and the WEU (Western European Union) maintained their naval operations in the Adriatic to enforce the embargo on shipping during the civil war in the former Yugoslavia. The operations had previously been codenamed Sharp Vigilance and Maritime Monitor when they had entailed monitoring the movement of merchant shipping in the Adriatic. When the scope of the operations was expanded to include interdiction of shipping, towards the end of 1992, the codenames were changed to Sharp Fence and Maritime Guard.

The codenames for the ongoing Royal Navy operations in support of UK forces deployed in the region were Operation Hamden and Operation Grapple.

Operation Sharp Guard, June 1993 – June 1996 The NATO operations were conducted by STANAVFORMED and the operations of the WEU by its Maritime Contingency Force, WEUCONMARFOR. The NATO and WEU forces were combined in June 1993, and the interdiction operation was renamed Operation Sharp Guard. The Royal Navy contributed either a frigate or a destroyer to STANAVFORMED at any one time (in rotation the destroyers *Gloucester*, *York*, *Cardiff* and *Edinburgh*, then in 1994 the frigate *Chatham*), and in addition the frigate or destroyer attached to STANAVFORLANT in the Atlantic (initially the destroyer *Birmingham*, then the frigate *Beaver*, and in 1994 the destroyer *Southampton*) was deployed to the Adriatic from time to time to provide additional support. Royal Marine specialist boarding parties were normally embarked.

Operation Grapple The Royal Navy also provided support forces, which were forward-deployed in Split, consisting of four Sea King Mk 4 helicopters ('B' Flight from 845 NAS), the fleet replenishment ship RFA *Resource* and the landing ship (logistic) *Sir Bedeivere*, later relieved by *Sir Percivale*. RFA *Resource* was alongside in Split for several years providing considerable ammunition and logistic support for all Services, as well as the UK bases ashore, as part of the ongoing Operation Grapple.

Ark Royal **Task Group (TG 612.02)** At the very beginning of 1993 the world was shocked by reports of rape and slaughter by Bosnian Serbs as part of their campaign of 'ethnic cleansing'. UN plans to partition Bosnia were rejected, and further UN peace-keepers were sent to the region. The UK agreed to send reinforcements to support the peace-keeping forces and humanitarian aid workers in Bosnia. A naval task group (TG 612.02) was assembled under Rear Admiral John Brigstocke (Commander UK Task Group), consisting of the flagship, the carrier *Ark Royal*, escorted by the frigates *Coventry* and *Brilliant* and supported by the fleet tanker RFA *Olwen* and the aviation support ship RFA *Argus*. *Ark Royal* embarked her Air Group, comprising eight Commando helicopters (Mk 4 Sea Kings), eight Sea Harriers and three early warning Sea King helicopters.

The Task Group sailed from the UK on 14 January 1993 and, after a short period of shake-down exercises, headed south for the Mediterranean. By the end of the month the group sailed up into the Adriatic and joined two other allied task groups, the US CBG (Carrier Battle Group) formed around the strike carrier USS *John F Kennedy* and the French group based on the French carrier FS *Clemenceau*.

The three task groups operated closely together, co-ordinating patrol areas and flying missions. The US group operated in the northern Adriatic, whilst the UK Task Group was further south, off southern Bosnia. The US CBGs were there for only limited periods, but the Royal Navy operated in the Adriatic for almost the whole time. The US carriers were frequently needed elsewhere, for example off Lebanon or even further afield, sometimes as far as the Gulf. Similarly

Operations in the Adriatic
(NN)

the French carriers, FS *Clemenceau* and FS *Foch*, spent relatively short periods in theatre.

Operation Deny Flight The air operations were conducted as part of Operation Deny Flight over Bosnian territory as well as including search missions off the Yugoslav coast and over the waters of the Adriatic. During breaks in the operation programme, ships of TG 612.02 exercised with the Italian Navy and enjoyed short breaks in Trieste, Piraeus and Naples. A Dutch frigate, the HNLMS *Jan van Brakel*, joined TG 612.02 in March.

In April the UN tightened sanctions against Serbia, and the task forces in the Adriatic were used to support the warships deployed on Operation Sharp Fence. The Italian aircraft carrier IS *Giuseppe Garibaldi* joined the allied naval forces in the Adriatic in the late spring. In response to a deteriorating position in Bosnia, the UK agreed to make the Sea Harriers available to NATO for bombing missions, and *Ark Royal* made use of the Italian weapon training ranges to prepare for precision air strikes by the Sea Harriers of 801 NAS. In June RFA *Argus* returned to the UK without relief.

Invincible **Relieves** *Ark Royal* In the UK the carrier *Invincible*, with the Sea Harriers of 800 NAS embarked, was preparing to relieve *Ark Royal*. After taking part in exercise JMC (Joint Maritime Course) 932, and taking early summer leave, *Invincible* sailed from Portsmouth on 22 July 1993 and headed south for the Mediterranean. A short while later she relieved *Ark Royal* and the Task Group Commander, now Rear Admiral Gretton, transferred his flag to *Invincible*.

Ark Royal then departed for Portsmouth, arriving on 3 August for a period of maintenance. With *Invincible* in the Adriatic, the Task Group consisted of the destroyer *Edinburgh* and the frigates, *Boxer* and *Beaver*, supported by the fleet tanker RFA *Olwen* and the replenishment ship RFA *Fort George*. The Dutch frigate HNLMS *Jan van Brakel* remained with the group until she completed seven months and was relieved by another frigate at the beginning of October.

Failed Peace Talks The group had a fairly intensive period of flying operations but fortunately was able to combine tasking with the French aircraft carrier FS *Clemenceau* to ease the load. Towards the end of September, the frigate *London* joined the Task Group, and a short while later that month a secret peace conference, organised by Lord Owen, was held on board *Invincible*. *Invincible* was able to stand down for short periods and enjoyed breaks in Corfu and Malta. Towards the end of the year, however, hostilities intensified, and Serb separatists were shelling Sarajevo. In December the peace talks, sponsored by the EU, collapsed, and it became apparent that a task group would be needed in the Adriatic for a continuous period. It was clear that *Ark Royal*, which had been carrying out trials of the new FRS2 Sea Harrier and exercising with the French Navy, would be required in the Adriatic.

Ark Royal **Returns** In January 1994 General Sir Michael Rose was appointed to command UN forces in Bosnia, and a few days later Bosnian and Croatian leaders agreed a cease-fire. On 28 January a naval task force (TG 612.02), led by *Ark Royal*, sailed from Portsmouth, and after embarking 801 NAS of Sea Harriers in the South-West Approaches, she headed for Gibraltar. Transiting through the Straits of Gibraltar at the beginning of February, *Ark Royal* flew off her Sea Harriers, which then flew on to the NATO air training range at Decimomannu in Sardinia to practise their aerial combat skills. After she rendezvoused with *Invincible*, *Ark Royal* took over responsibility for the British contribution to Operation Hamden in the Adriatic on 2 February. *Invincible* then commenced the passage home, arriving back in Portsmouth six days later.

On 5 February a mortar attack on Sarajevo had killed sixty-eight people and wounded over 200 more, putting immense pressure on NATO to retaliate with air strikes. *Ark Royal* sailed east at speed, recovering her Sea Harriers as she rounded Sicily, and headed up into the Adriatic. She arrived in the area on 13 February, and immediately her Sea Harriers

Sea Harriers on board *Invincible*
(JAR)

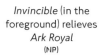

Invincible (in the foreground) relieves *Ark Royal*
(NP)

joined the allied air patrols over the Bosnian theatre of operations. Five days later, under the threat of NATO air strikes, the Serbs besieging Sarajevo started pulling back their heavy armament. NATO maintained its concentrated programme of air missions over Bosnia, all controlled by CAOC (Combined Air Operations Centre) at Vicenza in northern Italy.

On 22 February a UN convoy came under heavy attack and called for help. Two Sea Harriers from 801 NAS buzzed the attackers at high speed; coming in low and fast, they roared over the top, which was sufficient to deter further attacks and save the convoy. The Captain of *Ark Royal* (Captain Loughran) said later of the mission, 'Whilst air strikes were not required, the noise of the jets alone reminded those on the ground of the resolve of NATO and the UN to bring about a ceasefire.'[3] On 28 February four Serb fighter-bomber aircraft, which were launching attacks against Mostar, were shot down. At that time the Sea Harriers of *Ark Royal* were flying up to fourteen sorties a day.

The ships of Operation Sharp Guard were busy enforcing the UN embargo and over the period of a year challenged over 22,000 ships and vessels, with 1,800 being boarded and 400 diverted for inspection. In March the frigate *Chatham* intercepted a ship carrying large quantities of ammunition and escorted it into Taranto, where it was impounded.

Air Strikes In April the Serbs attacked Gorazde, and NATO authorised air strikes, which were carried out by US F-18s. On 16 April the helicopters of 845 NAS flew in to evacuate the wounded from the area, with air cover being provided by 801 NAS Sea Harriers. At one stage, two of the Harriers, piloted by Lieutenants Richardson and Philips, were tasked to take out Serbian tanks engaging UN forces. Whilst pressing home their attacks, the Harrier flown by Lieutenant Richardson was hit by a surface-to-air missile and shot down. Fortunately Lieutenant Richardson managed to eject safely and was later rescued by sympathetic locals and an SAS (Special Air Service) patrol. A few days later he was in the

Invincible in the Adriatic
(NN)

air again flying a Sea Harrier over Mostar.[4] On 22 April the UN agreed to send more troops to Bosnia.

On 1 May the frigates *Chatham* and HNLMS *Van Kinsbergen* tackled the *Lido II*, a large Maltese tanker attempting to break the blockade. In arresting the tanker, which was heading for the Montenegran coast, the frigates had to fend off attacks from small Yugoslavian warships and then escort it into Brindisi to be arrested.

Later in May *Ark Royal* was able to participate in exercise Dynamic Impact, a major NATO amphibious exercise in the western Mediterranean which was in fact the largest NATO maritime exercise since the end of the Cold War. Finally, on 10 June, a cease-fire in Bosnia was brokered in Geneva between all three sides.

FA2 Sea Harriers in Operation In the early summer *Invincible* carried out trials of the new improved FA2 Sea Harriers of 899 NAS. The new updated Sea Harrier Fighter/Attack Mk 2 (FA2) was just entering full operational service; with her new multi-mode pulse doppler radar and the new advanced medium-range air-to-air missile (AMRAAM) giving a 'look down/shoot down' capability, a considerable improvement on the previous Sea Harriers. On 24 August she sailed from Portsmouth, bound for the Adriatic again, but this time, in addition to the Sea Harriers of 800 NAS, she carried the new FA2 Sea Harriers of 899 NAS. She also carried Sea King helicopters of 814 NAS and 'A' Flight of 849 NAS. A week later she relieved *Ark Royal* in the Mediterranean, leaving *Ark Royal* to return home to Portsmouth, where she arrived on 2 September.

After arriving on station in the Adriatic, *Invincible*'s aircraft were soon flying regular missions over Bosnia as part of Operation Deny Flight. Within a few days, two of the new FA2 Sea Harriers were engaged by surface-to-air missiles

Sea Harrier in the Adriatic
(NP)

over Bihac, but managed to avoid being shot down. During this deployment the Task Force included the frigates *Brave*, *Brilliant*, *Campbeltown*, *Coventry* and *Cumberland*, supported by the RFAS *Fort Grange* and *Fort Austin* and the fleet tanker RFA *Olna*. *Invincible* also operated with the Spanish Navy aircraft carrier SNS *Principe de Asturias*, flying US built Harrier-IIs, known as 'Matadors'.

Further NATO air strikes against Serb positions were carried out in November, and towards the end of the month two Sea Harriers managed to evade surface-to-air guided missile attacks over Banja Luka. In December a Sea Harrier was lost in the Adriatic, north-east of Bari, but was recovered in a salvage operation and returned to the UK by road on a low loader. The Harrier was back in the UK within three days, having travelled via the Channel Tunnel.[5]

The frigate *Active* in the Caribbean (NN)

Illustrious Relieves Invincible At the end of February 1995 the carrier *Illustrious* sailed from Portsmouth and headed for the Mediterranean, relieving *Invincible* at the end of the month. *Invincible* returned to Portsmouth for a period of assisted maintenance. After only a comparatively short spell of maintenance, followed by a 'work-up' in May, she was once again heading back out to the Mediterranean for a third deployment to the Adriatic. The war in Bosnia dragged on, with the Croatian capital of Zagreb being attacked by the Serbs. The Serbs also took UN troops as hostages and captured Srebrenica.

On 30 August NATO started retaliating with air strikes against the Bosnian Serbs. The Serbs were again besieging Sarajevo, and Sea Harriers of 800 NAS carried out bombing missions against their attacking positions. During a two-week bombing campaign conducted by NATO aircraft, which included US strike aircraft from the carriers USS *America* and USS *Theodore Roosevelt*, the Sea Harriers carried out twenty-four bombing missions and forty-two CAPs (combat air patrols). The campaign was a success, and the Serbs pulled back their heavy guns and mortars. On 21 November a Bosnian peace settlement was accepted with all armed groups in Bosnia agreeing to disband.

Invincible was able to take part with the US Navy strike carrier USS *America* in the NATO exercise Infinite Courage. Then, at the end of November, she was relieved again, by *Illustrious*, and returned home, arriving in Portsmouth on 9 December in time for Christmas. It had been a very successful deployment, proving the superior operational capability of the new FA2 Sea Harrier and leading to the award to both *Invincible* and *Illustrious* of the Wilkinson Sword of Peace for their role in peace enforcement operations in Bosnia.

Far East Group Deployment: Task Group Australasia 95, May–November 1995 The Naval Staff planned an out-of-area group deployment to the Far East for 1995, codenamed Australasia 95. Sadly the ongoing demand for maritime forces to be deployed to the Adriatic precluded sufficient ships being available for a powerful task group to sail for the Far East. With severe cost constraints any deployment had to be financed within existing budget allocations, and hence only a 'mini-deployment' could be tasked.

The Task Group The Australasia 95 Task Group consisted of two frigates, the Type 22 *Sheffield* and the new Type 23 *Monmouth*, supported by the tanker RFA *Brambleleaf*. It was formed from two components, with *Monmouth* (WIGS) and RFA *Brambleleaf* transiting through the Panama Canal on 15 May on the first leg of the deployment.

On 3 June *Sheffield* was released from Armilla Patrol and headed east to rendezvous with the other component of Australasia 95 via India (Madras), Singapore, Thailand, Brunei, the Philippines and Papua New Guinea.

COMUKTG Joins the Task Group Meanwhile *Monmouth* and RFA *Brambleleaf* were sailing south-west across the Pacific for Pitcairn Island before sailing on to New Zealand. With Rear Admiral Peter Franklin as COMUKTG (Commander UK Task Group) flying his flag in *Monmouth*, the ships visited Wellington before sailing for exercises with HMNZs *Wellington* and *Endeavour*. The ships also visited Fiji, Tonga, Western Samoa, Kiribati, the Solomon Islands and Vanuatu. Whilst the group headed across the South Pacific, *Sheffield* continued her visits and exercises with the Royal Thai Navy.

Fiftieth Anniversary Celebrations *Monmouth* represented the UK at the fiftieth anniversary of the end of World War II commemoration celebrations, whilst *Sheffield*, with COMUKTG embarked, represented the UK at the celebrations held for the fiftieth anniversary of Indonesian Independence in Jakarta, Indonesia. The Task Group also participated in exercise Kangaroo with the Royal Australian Navy and exercise Starfish, the major Five-Power Defence Arrangement maritime exercise off the east coast of Malaysia in September.

End of the Deployment On completion of the exercise the Task Group sailed west across the Indian Ocean. RFA *Brambleleaf* remained in the Gulf region as the Armilla tanker whilst the remaining ships headed for home, arriving back in the UK in early November.

The next out-of-area group deployment to the Far East planned by the Naval Staff was to be Task Group 327.01, codenamed Ocean Wave 97, to deploy two years later.

The Gulf: Armilla Patrol, 7 October 1980 Onwards At the beginning of 1993, the Royal Navy was still maintaining Operation Armilla in the Persian Gulf, the Straits of Hormuz and the Gulf of Oman with two warships, either destroyers or frigates, supported by an RFA tanker. The purpose was to provide a British presence in the region, to protect British interests and shipping and also to contribute to the UN embargo enforcement operations against Iraq following the Gulf War. The area of operations was widened to include the Red Sea.

In 1993 the destroyer *Nottingham* and the frigate *London* were carrying out the patrol. The US Navy maintained a powerful task force in the Gulf which carried out similar duties.

In January Saddam Hussein defied the United Nations by deploying SAMs in the 'no fly' zone of southern Iraq as a direct threat to coalition enforcement aircraft patrols. He then failed to acknowledge an ultimatum from the coalition to remove the missiles, and on 16 January ships of the Task Force launched air raids and missile attacks against Iraqi military targets in southern Iraq. Seven B-52 bombers, flying all the way from the United States, also took part in the strikes. The main targets were Iraqi surface-to-air missile and anti-aircraft sites, but nuclear weapon construction sites were also attacked. The frigate *London* was deployed forward in the northern Gulf and assisted in the raids.

An attempt was made by Iraqi agents to assassinate ex-President Bush when he visited Kuwait in April. The attack failed, but after evidence revealed that the Iraqi intelligence service was behind the attempt, US warships destroyed the Iraqi intelligence headquarters with cruise missiles.

The frigate *Coventry* and the destroyer *Southampton* relieved *London* and *Nottingham* and then, in turn, *Cornwall* and *Liverpool* relieved them. The nuclear fleet submarine *Triumph* also conducted patrols in the Gulf. By the end of the year commercial shipping had begun to use the port of Umm Qasr for the delivery of food and humanitarian aid. In 1994 the submarines *Splendid* and *Unicorn* also carried out patrols in the area as part of deployments to the Indian Ocean and Far East.

Operation Lecturer In 1993 a group of naval personnel and Royal Marines, Naval Party (NP) 1042, continued to be deployed to Cambodia on Operation Lecturer as part of the international stabilisation force covering the transition to peace and democracy in the war-torn region. The UK also provided army and RAF regiment units to assist in the security operations. Operation Lecturer was finally completed in November, and all British forces were withdrawn from Cambodia.

Operation Snowdon, 23 September – 9 December 1993 Haiti had remained a very unstable country since the coup at the end of 1991 which had deposed President Aristide. A desperately poor country, it was struck in 1993 with one of the worst maritime disasters of the century, when a ferry sank off the coast on 18 February with the death of over 1,000 people. During the continuing security problems, the United Nations set up Operation Snowdon, conducting maritime interdiction operations in the waters around Haiti. The United Nations also established a maritime force to conduct Operation Restore Democracy. The frigate *Active*

and the tanker RFA *Oakleaf* were assigned to the international force in September and arrived off the coast on 23 September. *Active* and RFA *Oakleaf* remained in the area for several months, conducting interdiction patrols before being withdrawn on 9 December.

Operation Driver, 9 October – 15 November 1994 In October 1994 Saddam Hussein began a build-up of Iraqi forces on the border with Kuwait in an attempt to coerce the UN into lifting the sanctions, which were crippling Iraq. On 9 October Britain initiated Operation Driver to reinforce British forces in the Gulf region. The frigate *Cornwall* and the destroyer *Liverpool*, supported by the tanker RFA *Bayleaf*, were deployed forward in the northern Gulf. The destroyer *Cardiff* and the nuclear submarine *Splendid* later joined them. RAF aircraft were sent to Kuwait, and Royal Marines of 45 Commando with artillery support were also deployed there, joining US marines as part of the allied build-up in the region. The pressure from the build-up worked, and on 13 October Saddam Hussein withdrew his forces from the border with Kuwait. British forces were relaxed on 22 October, and the Armilla ships resumed their normal patrol duties on 15 November. Finally the Royal Marines returned to UK at the beginning of December.

Operation Triad/United Shield, 1 February – 3 March 1995 In January 1995 the interdiction operations in the Red Sea were suspended, but the Armilla Patrol was maintained, being conducted at the time by the destroyers *Exeter* and *Liverpool*, supported by the tanker RFA *Bayleaf*. Early in the month ships of the patrol intercepted a tanker loaded with illegal oil and escorted her to Kuwait. Then at the end of January, Operation Triad was initiated. *Exeter* was detached from the patrol and sent south to join Operation United Shield, the US-led multi-national operation off the coast of Somalia.

The multi-national Task Force consisted of twenty-three ships from six nations. On 20 February US forces landed ashore to protect the remaining United Nations peace-keeping forces, which were being withdrawn. *Exeter* was given the task of monitoring all shipping approaching and departing from Mogadishu. The operation was completed successfully on 3 March leaving Somalia, tragically, as a failed country abandoned by all UN forces. *Exeter* then departed from the coast of Somalia and resumed her Armilla Patrol duties. The Armilla ships were relieved later by the destroyer *Gloucester* and the frigate *Sheffield*, the patrol still being supported by the tanker RFA *Bayleaf*.

Operation Chantress: Angola, 6 April – 21 August 1995 In early 1995, after the civil war in Angola, the UN decided to deploy nine battalions of troops to help restore peace and stability in the country. In advance of the battalions, however, the UK deployed the LSL (landing ship, logistic) RFA *Sir Galahad* at the beginning of April to Angola on Operation Chantress. *Sir Galahad* was loaded with vehicles, members of the Royal Corps of Transport (RCT) and Royal Engineers.

Their task was to improve infrastructure and to clear roads from mines.

Sir Galahad was an ideal base as she was able to sail up and down the coast unimpeded and land vehicles and equipment as required, without the need to clear roads and landmines ashore first. Her RFA crew and the troops who were embarked worked hard with local orphanages, schools and hospitals, and provided a great deal of relief work.

RFA *Sir Galahad* was duly awarded her second Wilkinson Sword of Peace; this time, however, it was a joint one shared with the engineers and members of the RCT.

Northern Ireland

In Northern Ireland the patrol craft of the Northern Ireland Squadron, *Nurton*, *Cygnet*, *Redpole* and *Kingfisher*, maintained their ceaseless coastal patrols and counter-terrorist operations under Operation Grenada, whilst Royal Marine units patrolled inshore, covering inland waterways and Carlingford Lough under Operation Interknit. Other units and helicopters were deployed to the area in support as necessary. In December 1995 tasking was reviewed, and Operation Interknit was absorbed into Operation Grenada.

Operation Banner 40 Commando Royal Marines deployed to southern Armagh under Operation Banner on 5 November 1993 and remained in the area until 8 May 1994. Then, on 28 September, it was the turn of 42 Commando to deploy to Northern Ireland, where it carried out security operations until 31 March 1995. Two months later 45 Commando arrived in the area and remained until 28 November. 40 Commando returned to the area again on 12 December and remained until the spring of the following year.

Other Activities

The Fiftieth Anniversary of the Battle of the Atlantic In the summer of 1993 forty warships from seventeen different nations gathered together off Liverpool to celebrate the fiftieth anniversary of the Battle of the Atlantic. The ships formed up off Anglesey and were reviewed by HRH the Duke of Edinburgh. The review was followed by various events, including a parade and a thanksgiving service in Liverpool Cathedral attended by HM the Queen and HRH the Prince of Wales.

Operation Harlech, 9–31 August 1995 Early in August 1995 a volcanic eruption caused much damage in Montserrat, and Operation Harlech was initiated. The frigate *Westminster* arrived off the island on 9 August and provided emergency relief aid. The destroyer *Southampton* joined her on 19 August, and both ships provided emergency relief assistance until the end of the month. At the same time the Commando Logistics Regiment was deployed to Antigua to establish reception facilities for refugees.

The following month *Southampton* and RFA *Oakleaf* carried out emergency relief work in Anguilla in the wake of Hurricane 'Luis'.

The destroyer *Southampton* in the Caribbean (NN)

SHIPS, AIRCRAFT AND WEAPONS

The Trident Nuclear Missile System The first of the new generation of nuclear deterrent submarines joined the Fleet in 1994 and deployed with her outfit of the new Trident II D5 ICBM (intercontinental ballistic missile). The Trident missiles were purchased from the USA and, with their extended range (6,500 nautical miles) and improved warheads, provided a greatly enhanced deterrent capability.

The *Vanguard* Class Submarines The *Vanguard* class SSBNs were the most complex submarines the Royal Navy had ever built, and with a displacement of 16,000 tonnes they were twice the size of the previous generation of SSBNs. They were designed with the very latest stealth techniques. Despite a warhead update for Polaris it became clear that to keep up with the advances made in anti-ballistic missiles (ABM) by the Soviet Union, the United Kingdom would have to update its deterrent missile system. It chose the improved Trident II D5 ballistic missile, which because of its large size required a hull of correspondingly greater diameter to house the bigger missile compartment. The result was a submarine with twice the displacement of the previous *Resolution* class and twenty metres longer. The four submarines were built inside the Devonshire dock hall at Barrow in Furness between 1986 and 1999 and were given the names *Vanguard*, *Victorious*, *Vigilant* and *Vengeance*.

The submarines had many advantages over their predecessors, including a more powerful reactor and improved sonar, self-defence and command systems. More importantly, the latest generation of silent stealth technology was incorporated in the design. Not surprisingly, their emergence at sea provoked considerable interest from the Soviets, leading to highly charged spying and intelligence-gathering incidents below the surface. Chillingly, the range of the D5 missile was nominally declared as 4,000 nautical miles (6,400km), which meant there was nowhere on the planet that was out of range of this new-generation deterrent system. Sir Malcolm Rifkind, when Secretary of State for Defence, stated, 'The Cold War has ended but we still live in an uncertain and unstable world. Now more than ever, it is vital to retain Trident.'[6]

Sea Harrier FA2 The new FA2 Sea Harrier had been developed from the FRS1 and represented a considerable improvement in performance. It had been fitted with the Blue Vixen radar, which, combined with the new air-to-air missile, AMRAAM, gave the Harrier a 'look down/shoot down' capability beyond the previous visual range. It had an updated electronics fit and a greatly improved ground attack capability. 899 NAS was equipped with the new FA2, with 801 receiving it shortly afterwards, and by 1995 all Sea Harrier NASs had the FA2.

Project Horizon In 1995 progress was being made with a major collaborative project to procure a common new-generation frigate (CNGF). The aim was to design a general-purpose frigate with a bias towards AAW (anti-aircraft warfare), with a local area air defence capability for the UK, France and Italy. Project Horizon was to replace the failed NATO frigate replacement programme (NFR 90), which had involved eight nations before it collapsed.

PERSONNEL MATTERS

Closure of RNEC Manadon Following extensive study and detailed consideration, the Royal Naval Engineering College (RNEC) at Manadon, Plymouth, was closed in 1995. In the future engineer officers were to be trained at civilian universities as well as at the Navy's specialist establishments in the Portsmouth area. The closure of the college ended 125 years of in-house training of young men, and latterly young women, under naval discipline, in order to develop character and engineering skills to enable them to face the 'dangers of the sea and the violence of the enemy'[7] confident in their individual and collective abilities.

Move of Sea Training to Devonport As part of the restructuring it was decided to close the long-established sea training facilities at Portland in Dorset and move the Flag Officer Sea Training (FOST) and his staff to Devonport. Accordingly, on 21 July 1995, FOST, Rear Admiral John Tolhurst, flying his flag in the frigate *Argyll*, sailed out of the Portland naval base and steamed west to Devonport. The Devonport Sea Training Centre was established ashore in the naval base at HMS *Drake*.

End of Area Flag Officers Following the recommendations of the 'Front Line First' study, it was decided to phase out the posts of Flag Officer Portsmouth and Flag Officer Plymouth and also to merge the post of Flag Officer Scotland, Northern England and Northern Ireland with Commodore Clyde. New responsibilities would be allocated

---

Royal Marine Uniform Clothing

In 1958, Royal Marines were still wearing basic World War II kit. There were 84 pieces of brightwork on training webbing, and boot polish was used to waterproof webbing. Then denims were introduced, jacket/smock, jersey and shirt angora. There were two best blues, one with gold badge, and red stripe on the trouser, the second set red badged, no stripe. Commandos at Eastney were required to remove their commando flashes and were not allowed to wear their green berets!

In 1959 green combat suits with green webbing were introduced which did not require boot polish.

In 1964 Lovats replaced battledress, and the second non-red striped blues. White webbing became plastic, and the white Wolsey pattern pith helmet (named after General Wolsey, the original Modern Major General) was now painted with matt Dulux white paint. At the Coronation, in the rain, the Royals on parade had had long white streaks down their backs, washed off their helmets.

After 1958 green kit came DPM -- Disruptive Pattern Material, 'camouflage', and green Woolly Pullies – and stay bright buttons. DPM also includes an anti-infrared disruptive pattern. Travel in the back of 4 ton trucks was stopped except operationally, because of the lack of seat belts and possibility of rolling.

Finally there have been females in the Band Service for at least 15 years. Pregnant ones have their own General Purpose skirt (maternity).

CSgt SBS John 'Boots' Allistone RM

---

to the one-star naval base commanders. The plans being made were to be implemented by 1 April 1996.

The White Ensign Association In 1994 Sir Donald Gosling relieved Lord Alexander of Weedon as President of the White Ensign Association. Admiral Sir Andrew Lewis, who had served as a member of the Council for over eighteen years and been Chairman for four years from 1974 to 1978, retired and sadly died shortly afterwards. In 1993 the Association was heavily committed, assisting all those being made redundant from the Service under the 'Options for Change' defence review. With recession, unstable house prices, high unemployment and uncertainty it was not an easy time to be leaving the Service. During the year the staff gave lectures and personal interviews to 2,286 officers and ratings. The

The Executive Committee of the White Ensign Association at the Royal Naval College, Greenwich
(WEA)

A Review of Naval Uniform Clothing, 1958–2008

In 1958, naval uniform was more formal than in 2008. Officers and senior ratings wore double-breasted jackets all the time and shirts were worn with stiff starched collars. In the evenings Mess Undress was worn far more frequently than now, and stiff starched shirts, with detached starched wing collars, were worn for balls and the more formal mess dinners. Informal officers' evening dress at sea was and is Red Sea rig: a tropical short sleeved shirt, black trousers and a black cummerbund (many ships had their own pattern of cummerbund). In 1958, No 5 uniform was worn for receptions, now Red Sea rig is worn. Senior rates' evening rig, a tropical shirt with black trousers has not changed.

The risk of damaging the jacket irretrievably was high onboard, as a brush with wet grey paint was only too easy. Woollen navy blue pullovers were introduced for all personnel, with rank epaulettes where appropriate. The snag with the new pullovers was that there was no place for a pen. However, many other navies quickly copied the jumpers, as they were very practical. They were worn by officers and senior rates with collar attached white shirts, at first with black tie, but later with the collar open. Ratings wore the pullovers over Action Working Dress (No 8s).

Shoes were leather or composition soled. They were slippery on wet decks and Boots DMS – with a moulded non-slip sole, and steel

Officers wearing Red Sea rig at sea in the wardroom of the frigate *Falmouth*
(JAR)

toecaps under a leather skin, were introduced, being much safer.

Foul weather gear has seen several changes. Bright orange foul weather jackets and trousers were introduced first, but later a dark blue equivalent replaced the orange. These suits were very waterproof, with a particularly effective peaked hood, and a covering for the mouth in very cold weather.

At sea, when appropriate sailors and officers wore Action Working Dress, dark blue trousers and a lighter blue shirt, usually with rolled up sleeves. These were later replaced by a fireproof equivalent. They were worn in action with a fireproof hood, leaving only the eyes free, and fireproof long sleeved gloves. These had to be specially laundered to retain their fireproofing. Later, fireproof overalls were introduced, worn over the Action Working Dress.

Tropical uniforms also changed:

the formal high collared long sleeved tunic and long trousers are worn only by senior officers on rare occasions, and has been replaced by a short sleeved, open necked bush jacket. Regular tropical wear is still white shorts and open-necked shirt. The material is now much more easy care.

Shoes for sailors were white canvas, and for officers, white doeskin, worn with cotton stockings, which were replaced by much more easy care artificial material stockings. At sea, no stockings were worn, simply leather sandals; these have been replaced by lace up non-slip yachting style shoes.

Female sailors' uniforms changed too, with practical trousers replacing skirts. In 1958, sailors wore 'Square Rig' (a woollen square necked jumper in winter, and a white front, square necked, in summer), with bell bottom trousers. These were turned inside out to be ironed, with the

crease at the side, and seven horizontal folds – originally to allow them to be rolled up easily. The blue detached collar was then tied in place, and the jumper worn over the top. Then a black silk was tied under the collar, and finally a white lanyard tied at the front with a black bow tied tape – (white for weddings!)

Uniform was issued on joining, and then replaced as necessary: ratings had a uniform replacement element with their pay, which was actually sufficient to replace all blue kit in two years. (Officers had tax free pay to cover uniform). Relatively few officers nowadays have their own swords; there are pool swords available for ceremonial purposes. The familiar sailor's hat has stayed the same.

Specialist loan clothing of all sorts is required, and is issued onboard, including action coveralls, divers' kit, flight deck multi-coloured tabards, foul weather gear, disruptive pattern (camouflage) kit for guards, sea survival suits and Arctic (and Antarctic) kit.

Finally, probably the most senior Scottish sailor, Admiral Sir Jock Slater, formally allowed kilts to be worn by officers with Mess Undress jackets and waistcoats. Kilts could be Scots, Irish, Isle of Man, Welsh or Cornish. With local permission, kilts can also be worn with Tropical shirts for evening events when Mess Undress is not being worn.

Lieutenant Commander Ken Napier
MBE, RN – a Scot

Executive Committee held a meeting at the Royal Naval College at Greenwich to review and extend the services being provided by the Association. Over the year the Association arranged visits by senior people in the City to *London, Argyll, Lindisfarne, Ambuscade, York, Amazon, Cornwall* and *Lancaster*. It also hosted a reception by the Royal Navy Presentation Team at St James's Palace in the presence of HRH the Princess Royal.

The following year the third tranche of redundancies was announced and the staff of the Association, now increased to four officers, was heavily engaged with assisting all those leaving the Service at a time when many companies were restricting recruitment and taking all measures to limit expenditure. The Association was able to arrange visits of directors and senior managers to *Ark Royal, Birmingham, Exeter, Ursula, Liverpool, Marlborough, Avenger, Campbeltown* and RFA *Argus*.

In 1995 the last of those being made redundant sought help from the Association. The total reduction in strength of the Navy over the three years had been 15,000 and 1995 had proved the busiest year for the Association on the employment side. During the year Admiral Sir Michael Layard retired as Second Sea Lord and was elected to the Council of the Association.

Ocean Wave 97 Deployment and Operation Bolton 1996–1998

STRATEGIC DEFENCE REVIEW – OPERATION GRAPPLE IN THE ADRIATIC – OCEAN WAVE 97 DEPLOYMENT –
HAND-OVER OF HONG KONG – OPERATION BOLTON IN THE GULF

Many of the seeds of the terrible conflicts which blighted the early years of the twenty-first century were sown, or nurtured, in the second half of the 1990s.

Iraq In Iraq Saddam Hussein continued to obstruct the UN and to hinder the searches for weapons of mass destruction. Sadly it served his purpose, posturing as the leader of the greatest power in the region, to intimidate his neighbours and indeed to let the world believe that he possessed such weapons. In 1997 he stated that he would shoot down UNSCOM (United Nations Special Commission in Iraq) surveillance aircraft, and eventually it was necessary to launch Operation Bolton in the Gulf to counter Saddam Hussein.

Afghanistan In September 1996 the Taliban captured Kabul and seized power in Afghanistan. After executing President Najibullah and imposing strict 'Sharia' law it took savage and ruthless reprisals against all who had hindered or defied it in any way. Osama Bin Laden then fled to Afghanistan having been expelled from the Sudan.

Bosnia and Kosovo In the Balkan Civil War violence continued to ravage the region despite the various official 'cease-fires' brokered by the UN, and eventually it was decided to send a 60,000 NATO stabilisation force to Bosnia to contain hostilities.

Sierra Leone In Sierra Leone troops of the rebel army continued to besiege Freetown, the capital.

The United Kingdom
In the UK the IRA (Irish Republican Army) announced the end of the cease-fire with a bomb in Canary Wharf in London in February 1996. Despite more bombs and killings however, peace talks continued and finally resulted in the 'Good Friday Agreement' in April 1998, celebrated by the award of the Nobel Peace Prize to David Trimble and John Hume six months later.

A Labour government under Tony Blair was elected in 1997, and both Scotland and Wales pushed hard to establish their own parliaments. With the change of government an inevitable full review of defence was commissioned which was to result in the Strategic Defence Review (SDR).

Defence Policy Following 'Options for Change' and the Gulf War, defence policy in the UK was undergoing a radical

FIRST SEA LORD
Admiral Slater

SECOND SEA LORDS
Admirals Brigstocke and Boyce

MANPOWER
48,258

MERCANTILE MARINE
1,454 merchant ships

change to shape up to the new world order. As the First Sea Lord, Admiral Slater, stated, 'The strategic scene is changing fast; sporadic regional conflicts have replaced the monolithic threat. However the need for the versatility and reach of balanced maritime forces, usually within joint and combined operations is clear. The Armed Forces are engaged on a period of reconstruction on an unprecedented scale and the Royal Navy is no exception with radical surgery underway to improve the balance between front line, support and people.'[1]

The Strategic Defence Review (1998) The fundamental defence review set in hand by the new Labour government in 1997 was completed the following year. The results, which revised Britain's defence missions and tasks, were set out in a policy document referred to as SDR (the Strategic Defence Review, entitled 'Modern Forces for the Modern World'). The Defence Secretary, George Robertson, announced the review on 8 July 1998.

Crucially the review recognised the key contribution that maritime forces made to achieving the government's foreign policy and security objectives. The review stated: 'At sea, the emphasis is continuing to move away from large-scale warfare and open-ocean operations in the North Atlantic. In future littoral operations and force projection, for which maritime forces are well suited, will be our primary focus. These tasks, which range from the evacuation of citizens from an overseas crisis to major warfighting operations as part of a joint force, will be highly demanding.'[2]

The new defence policy required the armed forces to be able to respond to a major international crisis requiring military effort and combat operations similar to Operation Granby. They were also to be able to undertake a more extended overseas deployment on a lesser scale while retaining the ability to mount a second substantial deployment if this was made necessary by a second crisis. ('The UK must be prepared to go to the crisis rather than have the crisis come to the UK').

The armed forces were also required to retain the ability to rebuild a bigger force as part of NATO, should a major strategic threat re-emerge. In the meantime the nuclear deterrent and the new Trident SSBNs (ballistic missile-carrying nuclear submarines) of the *Vanguard* class were excluded from the fundamental review. It was decided however to reduce the total stockpile of nuclear warheads from 300 to 200, with a consequent reduction in the warhead load of the SSBNs on patrol, and the outfits of warheads

HMS *Ocean*
Landing Platform Helicopter

The helicopter assault ship *Ocean*, officially an LPH, joined the Fleet in 1998. With a hull built to Merchant Navy standards she is the biggest ship in the Royal Navy. She was designed to operate a powerful air group of twelve Sea King HAS.4 troop lift helicopters and six Lynx attack helicopters. She can carry a full Royal Marine Commando and has complete command and control facilities to act as flagship of the UK Amphibious Task Group.

Launched:	11 October 1995
Commissioned:	30 September 1998
Displacement:	20,500 tonnes
Length:	203.4m
Propulsion:	2 Crossley Pielstick diesel engines,
	1 Kamewa bow thruster
Armament:	3 Vulcan Phalanx Mk 15 close-in weapon systems,
	8 Oerlikon/BMARC 20mm GAM-B03 (4 twin),
	12 Sea King HC4/Merlin helicopters,
	6 Lynx (or navalised variants of WAH-64 Apache)
Complement:	265 + 180 aircrew, up to 830 marines (Marine Commando Group)
No. in class:	1

carried on patrol were being reduced from ninety-six to forty-eight.

The New Aircraft Carriers (CVFs) The major finding for the Royal Navy was the announcement that the three *Invincible* class carriers would be replaced by two new larger and more flexible aircraft carriers, designated CVF (Carrier Vessel Future), to enter service in 2012 and 2015. A new carrier-borne aircraft would also be ordered.

Joint Force Harrier The policy also announced formation of 'Joint Force Harrier': 'Our current *Invincible* Class carriers will be given a wider power projection role by the development of a "Joint Force 2000" combining RN and RAF Harrier aircraft.'[3] The announcement was the result of a historic agreement between the First Sea Lord and the Chief of the Air Staff. It also presaged the phasing out of the Sea Harriers between 2004 and 2006, and their replacement by the RAF GR7 Harriers, which would operate from the *Invincible* class carriers when required.

Reductions The new policy also announced the reductions of three destroyer/frigates, two attack submarines and four mine counter-measure vessels.

THE FLEET

In 1996 the Royal Navy totalled 112 units, comprising fifty-six major warships, eight specialised vessels and forty-eight smaller ships and vessels. It was still a powerful and very capable navy.

Aircraft Carriers The backbone of the Fleet was provided by the three 20,000-ton CVSs, *Invincible*, *Illustrious* and *Ark Royal*. These versatile anti-submarine warfare command ships operated STOVL (short take off and vertical landing) aircraft and were also command ships for air operations. At any one time two carriers were normally operational whilst the third was in refit or standby. *Ark Royal* was on standby in 1996 and due to start a two-year refit in 1997.

Amphibious Ships The two elderly assault ships *Fearless* and *Intrepid* remained in service but were coming to the end of their time, and two replacement amphibious ships were ordered in July 1996. The new 21,500-ton helicopter carrier, the LPH (landing platform helicopter) *Ocean*, which had been launched on 11 October 1995, was due to be commissioned on 30 September 1998.

The 28,000-ton aviation training ship RFA *Argus* was capable of fulfilling various support roles, while the five landing ships (logistic) RFAS *Sir Bedivere*, *Sir Galahad*, *Sir Geraint*, *Sir Percivale* and *Sir Tristram* remained in service, with *Sir Bedivere* due to complete a Ship Life Extension Plan at Rosyth in 1998.

Submarine Flotilla The strategic nuclear deterrent was being taken over by the new SSBNs of the *Vanguard* class with the first two, *Vanguard* and *Victorious*, in service, *Vanguard* having collected her outfit of Trident II D5 missiles in July the previous year.

The last of the Polaris submarines, *Renown*, remained in service to bridge the gap until the last two of the Trident boats, *Vigilant* and *Vengeance*, entered service. *Vigilant* was commissioned in April 1997 and *Vengeance* was launched two months later.

The seven nuclear fleet submarines (SSNs) of the *Trafalgar* class, together with the five older submarines of the *Swiftsure* class, remained in service. The SSBNs and *Swiftsure* class formed the 1st Submarine Squadron, which was based at Faslane, with the *Trafalgar* class forming the 2nd Squadron, based at Devonport.

Destroyers and Frigates The escort fleet consisted of the twelve Type 42 anti-air warfare destroyers, the thirteen large Type 22 frigates and the ten new Type 23 frigates, which, with three more of the class building, would provide a total of thirty-eight ships.

MCMVs and Patrol Vessels The MCMVs (mine counter-measures vessels) comprised the thirteen vessels of the Hunt class and the first four of the smaller, single-role minehunters of the *Sandown* class with five more planned. Five River class remained in service, but these were due to start being withdrawn. The main classes of patrol vessel included the Castle class (two), Island class (six), Bird class (three) and small Archer class (ten).

Survey Fleet The Hydrographic Fleet included two ocean survey ships, *Hecla* and *Herald*, and three coastal survey vessels, *Bulldog*, *Beagle* and *Roebuck*.

Support The Royal Fleet Auxiliary (RFA) of nine tankers, three replenishment ships and two auxiliary oiler replenishment ships supported the Fleet. The RFA also operated a forward repair ship.

Fleet Air Arm The Fleet Air Arm operated some twenty-four Sea Harriers, with the FRS1 being upgraded or replaced by the new FA2. The helicopters included nearly ninety Sea Kings (Mk 6 ASW (anti-submarine warfare), AEW (airborne early warning)and Mk 4 amphibious assault) and forty-four Lynx (Mk 7 and Mk 8). In addition the Fleet Air Arm had a range of support and training helicopters and fixed-wing aircraft.

Royal Marines The Royal Marines Corps of 6,800 consisted of HQ 3 Commando Brigade with 40, 42 and 45 Commandos supported by artillery, engineers, communications and logistics. As well as providing detachments in twelve ships, the Royal Marines had a number of specialist units including the SBS (Special Boat Service).

Command of the Fleet The Fleet was commanded in 1996 by Admiral Sir Peter Abbott, Commander in Chief Fleet

(CINCFLEET), who in the following year was relieved by Admiral Sir Michael Boyce. Vice Admiral John Brigstocke was the Flag Officer Surface Flotilla (FOSF), and Rear Admiral Peter Franklyn subsequently relieved him. Rear Admiral James Perowne was Flag Officer Submarines (FOSM), Rear Admiral Terry Loughran was Flag Officer Naval Aviation, and Major General David Pennefather was Commandant General Royal Marines.

Fleet Headquarters On 1 April 1996 the Secretary of State for Defence opened the new permanent Joint Headquarters at Northwood, and six months later SACLANT (the Supreme Allied Commander Atlantic) opened the Atlantic Building housing the Commander in Chief's eastern Atlantic NATO staff. With the Trident and Tomahawk missile command and targeting facility, Northwood became the greatest focus in Western Europe for 'Power Projection' around the world.

FIRST SEA LORD

Admiral Sir Jock Slater (JCKS)

Admiral Sir Jock Slater Admiral Jock Slater had a distinguished career in the Royal Navy from 1956 to 1998. He was born in 1938 and was educated at Edinburgh Academy and Sedbergh, before joining the Royal Navy. Specialising in navigation, he commanded *Soberton*, *Jupiter* and *Kent* and was the first Captain of the new carrier *Illustrious*. He also commanded the School of Maritime Operations at HMS *Dryad*. He was Equerry to HM the Queen from 1968 to 1971. He was also Assistant Chief of the Defence Staff (Policy and Nuclear), Flag Officer Scotland and Northern Ireland and Chief of Fleet Support.

He was Commander in Chief Fleet from 1991 to 1993 and then became the Vice Chief of the Defence Staff. Sir Jock Slater was appointed First Sea Lord in 1995 and was relieved by Admiral Boyce in 1998. His greatest legacy as First Sea Lord was in ensuring that the UK's next-generation aircraft carriers were firmly established in the Royal Navy's equipment programme.

OPERATIONS AND DEPLOYMENTS, 1996–1998

In 1996 the ships and units of the Royal Navy and Royal Marines continued to be deployed around the world fulfilling the 'Maritime Contribution' to the military strategy of the United Kingdom. The post-Cold War defence policy, set out under 'Options for Change', was developed into three broad overlapping defence roles, with a sub-set of fifty military tasks. Defence Role One was 'To ensure the protection and security of the UK and dependent territories even when there is no external threat', and it was mainly in this essential role that the Royal Navy was committed worldwide. It also played a major part in the contribution to 'the maintenance of peace and stability'. As part of the new policy, the Joint Rapid Deployment Force was established on 1 August 1996.

Standing Commitments Ships and squadrons were

The SSBN *Vanguard*
(NN)

maintained on guardship duties in Hong Kong, the West Indies, the Falkland Islands, Cyprus and Gibraltar. In home waters the Fishery Protection Squadron and fleet contingency ship as well as existing NATO commitments to the standing naval forces in the Atlantic, STANAVFORLANT, the Channel, STANAVFORCHAN and the Mediterranean, STANAVFORMED, were continued.

Trident Takes over from Polaris as the National Deterrent
Throughout the period the ballistic missile nuclear-powered submarines, deploying from their base at Faslane on the Clyde, maintained their ceaseless deterrent patrols hidden deep in the depths of the oceans. In August 1996 the last remaining Polaris submarine, *Repulse*, was decommissioned, and thus the entire responsibility for maintaining the nation's strategic nuclear deterrent passed to the new Trident submarines. Initially *Vanguard*, the first, was deployed on patrol. Then her sister *Victorious*, which had entered service in December 1995, joined her in the deterrent cycle in early 1996.

Hong Kong The three patrol craft of the Hong Kong Squadron, *Peacock*, *Plover* and *Starling*, continued to carry out policing duties in the busy territorial seas of the Square

Boundary around Hong Kong. As well as anti-smuggling and anti-piracy patrols, the main element of their task was conducting deterrent patrols against ever-increasing numbers of illegal immigrants. The squadron worked with the Hong Kong police force, and close co-operation was the key to the high level of success of their many operations. The anti-smuggling patrols were effective, and the task gradually became a lesser priority as smuggling was carried out more and more across land borders. The Hong Kong Squadron was finally withdrawn on 30 June 1997.

Caribbean Frigates and destroyers on detachment fulfilled the role of the West Indies Guardship (WIGS) on station around the islands, carrying out anti-drug smuggling operations and working closely with the US Navy and Coast Guard Law Enforcement Detachments, as well as remaining on call for support of the Belize defence forces. An RFA tanker supported the WIGS. At the beginning of 1996 the WIGS was the Type 22 frigate *Brave*.

On 8 January 1996 *Brave* intercepted a drug runner in the Yucatan Channel, which was forced to jettison its cargo of cocaine valued at over £60 million. Two weeks later *Brave*'s Lynx helicopter detected and assisted in the destruction of marijuana plantations in Belize. Some two months later *Brave* captured a haul of cocaine worth over £30 million in the vicinity of Antilles. The Type 23 frigate *Argyll*, which relieved *Brave* on 24 May, arrested a British registered yacht, MY *Obsession*, with 300kg of cocaine on board. Two weeks later *Argyll* arrested the MV *Cay Trans Caribe*, which was also found to be smuggling cocaine.

Falkland Islands and Antarctica The Royal Navy continued to maintain defensive forces consisting of a destroyer or frigate and a Castle class offshore patrol vessel (OPV) off the Falkland Islands under the command of the Commander British Forces Falkland Islands (CBFFI). There was also the 12,000-ton forward repair ship RFA *Diligence*, on station until 28 April 1995 and again briefly from 18 August to 18 November 1996, when she was replaced by an RFA support tanker. These ships were reinforced by the 5,200-ton ice patrol ship *Endurance* (ex *Polar Circle*) during the Antarctic summer. A nuclear-powered fleet submarine, or later a patrol submarine, was on standby to reinforce the Falklands Squadron should the situation warrant it.

In April 1999 the on-station destroyer or frigate and RFA support tanker were allocated a much wider operational area and reclassified as the Atlantic Patrol Task (South), whilst the OPV remained permanently close to the Falkland Islands.

Gibraltar A destroyer, or frigate, remained based on Gibraltar as the Gibraltar Guardship, supported by two patrol craft, *Ranger* and *Trumpeter*, to protect British interests in the area and carry out anti-smuggling operations.

Cyprus A small unit of patrol craft was maintained in Cyprus to assist in the protection of the Sovereign Base Area on the south coast of the island.

The Adriatic: Operation Grapple Powerful naval forces continued to be needed in the Adriatic in support of the ongoing NATO and UN operations in the former Yugoslavia. A Royal Navy task force, consisting of a carrier and a destroyer supported by an RFA fleet tanker and an RFA replenishment ship, was deployed to the Adriatic as part of Operations Hamden and Grapple. Their task was to provide maritime support for British land forces operating with the UN Protection Force ashore in the former Yugoslavia. The Task Force was placed under NATO operational command, for the first time ever other than for exercises. The replenishment ship RFA *Resource* remained under national command off the Croatian port of Split.

The carrier *Illustrious*, having relieved *Invincible* on 9 December 1995, was flagship of the UK Adriatic Task Force flying the flag of Rear Admiral Franklyn COMUKTG, (or Commander UK Task Group). The Task Force formed part of the NATO maritime force supporting SFOR (the stabilisation force), formerly IFOR (the UN implementation force). It operated alongside the US and French carrier groups as well as the NATO embargo force (Operation Sharp Guard) and the Amphibious Task Group. On 15 February 1996, however, the UK Task Force reverted to national command and, though remaining at twenty-one days' notice to return, was withdrawn from the Adriatic. The fleet replenishment ship RFA *Resource* remained under national command in Split in support of UK forces.

UK Task Groups

With the easing of the situation in the former Yugoslavia it was possible to reduce the major naval commitment to the area. For three years a UK task force, based on the two in-service CVSs (aircraft carriers), had provided a continuous presence in the Adriatic. Such a high level of commitment had reduced the availability of ships for other deployments. With a reduced demand in the Mediterranean it was decided to reactivate a full UK task group for a deployment in the Atlantic area. The Task Group (TG 331.01) was formed in April under COMUKTG, Rear Admiral West. It included the Carrier Task Group based on *Illustrious*, escorted by the destroyers *Glasgow*, *Manchester* and *Southampton*, the frigates *Cumberland*, *Argyll* and *Brave* and the supporting auxiliaries RFAs *Fort George*, *Fort Grange*, *Argus*, *Oakleaf*, *Olna* and *Olwen*. The Amphibious Task Group included the assault ship *Fearless* and the LSLs RFA *Sir Galahad*, *Sir Geraint* and *Sir Tristram* with 3 Commando Brigade embarked, and the on-call MCM (mine counter-measures) force supported by *Hecla*. The Task Group sailed from the UK in early April and headed west across the Atlantic, with two nuclear submarines in company.

Exercise Purple Star When the Task Group arrived off the eastern seaboard of the USA it took part in the major exercise Purple Star with the US Navy. The exercise, a US national exercise, was the largest UK–US bilateral deployment since the end of the Gulf War in 1991 and entailed the UK Task Group being fully integrated as part of the US Carrier Battle Group. On completion of the exercise the Task Group returned across the Atlantic to the UK in June.

Operation Hornpipe In the summer *Invincible* was operating in home waters conducting trials, codenamed Operation Hornpipe, with the RAF's GR7 ground attack Harriers, before deploying north to take part in the JMC (Joint Maritime Course) off the coast of Scotland. At the end of August *Invincible*, escorted by the frigate *Sheffield* and supported by RFAs *Oakleaf* and *Fort Grange* sailed as Task Group TG 333.01 for the Norwegian Sea. Once in the Norwegian Sea the Task Group took part in the major NATO exercise Northern Lights with some fifty allied warships.

Exercise Dynamic Mix On completion of the exercise *Invincible* sailed south heading for the Mediterranean and en route embarked RAF GR7 Harriers to take part in a second major exercise. With the GR7s added to the new FA2 Sea Harriers of NAS (Naval Air Squadron) 800 on board, *Invincible* had a very powerful CAG (carrier air group).

Once in the Mediterranean, after a brief visit to Palma, *Invincible* and escorts took part in the two-week NATO exercise Dynamic Mix, which involved thirty ships and submarines from different NATO nations. Vice Admiral Brigstocke, FOSF, flew his flag in *Invincible* and was the NATO Task Force Commander for the exercise. The exercise included the USS *Enterprise* Carrier Battle Group and was also joined by the ships of the Standing Naval Force Mediterranean. At one stage the Italian and Spanish carriers *Garibaldi* and *Principe de Asturias* took part in the exercise. After completing the exercise the UK Task Group carried out port visits to Piraeus and Izmir before heading east for the Suez Canal. It transited through the canal on 26 October and steamed on to the Gulf, arriving in Dubai on 5 November. Four days later the group sailed for Kuwait and exercises with the Armilla Patrol ships.

The Middle East

Operation Armilla (Ongoing) The important operational patrol codenamed Operation Armilla was maintained in the Gulf of Oman, Straits of Hormuz, North Arabian Sea and Persian Gulf (operations in the Red Sea were discontinued at the end of January 1995). Two ships, destroyers or frigates, supported on station by an RFA support tanker, carried out the patrol. The purpose of the patrol was to protect British interests and shipping as well as contribute to enforcing the UN embargo against Iraq following the Gulf War. The ships conducted regular MIOPS (maritime interdiction operations). MCMVs were also deployed to the Gulf to counter the threat of mines being laid in the vital tanker routes through the Gulf and the Straits of Hormuz.

Tensions in the Gulf region remained high, with Saddam Hussein continuing to seek every opportunity to defy and resist the international community. In the summer Iraq deployed armoured divisions into the sensitive northern areas in contravention of UN directives. In response the area of the 'no fly' zone was increased, and US ships launched

Invincible replenishing at sea from the Dutch support ship *Amsterdam*. The Italian guided missile destroyer *Francesco Mimbelli* is to starboard of the support ship (NN)

land attack missiles against military targets in southern Iraq in September.

Exercise Gulfex 96 When *Invincible* and *Sheffield* arrived in the Gulf at the beginning of November the ships on Armilla Patrol joined them to take part in exercise Gulfex 96 with the US Navy. It was an important joint tactical exercise, with the powerful USS *Enterprise*-led Carrier Battle Group, and provided a joint show of force. It was the first time the Royal Navy had deployed a carrier to the Gulf for many years, and the opportunity was taken to pay a number of visits to ports in the area including Kuwait, Al Jubail and Jebel Ali before departing from the Gulf and heading back to the UK. *Invincible* returned through the Canal on 5 December and steamed west across the Mediterranean. After a brief visit to Gibraltar she sailed on 15 December and headed north-east across the Bay of Biscay for the Channel.

Invincible finally arrived back in Portsmouth on 19 December. At the end of the year the destroyer *Southampton* arrived in the Gulf and relieved *Edinburgh* on Armilla Patrol duties, allowing her to head back home for Portsmouth.

At the beginning of 1997 the ships of the Armilla Patrol joined other navies deployed to the Gulf carrying out MIOPS.

———•———

Operation Helvin On 14 March 1997 the destroyer *Birmingham* was ordered to proceed to the coast of Albania and stand off the port of Durres to evacuate British nationals

The First Sea Lord, Admiral Sir Jock Slater, visiting the MCMV Squadron in the Gulf (JCKS)

as part of Operation Helvin during internal disturbances. The destroyer *Exeter* later relieved her and the operation was completed on 8 April.

Operation Determinant A Royal Marine detachment from 42 Commando formed part of the Joint Service Force deployed to the Congo as part of Operation Determinant to evacuate British nationals during the civil disturbances which erupted at the end of March. The frigate *Chatham* was ordered to the area on 24 March in support. The situation soon eased and *Chatham* withdrew three days later. British forces remained in the area until internal security was restored, and the operation was finally completed on 29 May.

Permanent JHQ, November–December 1996 The Permanent Joint Headquarters was set up at Northwood to replace the two temporary JHQs, at High Wycombe for 'Iraq I', and at Wilton for Yugoslavia and elsewhere. Its first live deployment was a limited one to Entebbe, to assist in the return of Hutu refugees to Rwanda. This was not an easy task, as most Hutus did not want to return. The UK's main contribution was a Canberra photo reconnaissance aircraft, whose vital information was passed by RN staff to the various NGOs involved in assisting the refugees. The majority of refugees made their own way back, but with the logistic support of the NGOs and the information passed to them by the Royal Navy.[4]

Ocean Wave 97 Deployment: Task Group 327.01, January–August 1997

Nearly five years had lapsed since the Orient 92 Task Group had been deployed to the Far East, and it was decided to send a group deployment to the Far East again in 1997. This was a major deployment based on the carrier *Illustrious* under the command of Rear Admiral Alan West, COMUTAG. It was the largest Royal Navy deployment since the Gulf War and was intended to support UK political interests by demonstrating the UK's continuing ability to deploy an operationally effective self-sustainable maritime force out of area for a significant period. As well as exports and defence sales considerations, the aim was a clear demonstration of the Royal Navy's global reach and ability to defend Britain's interests worldwide.

The Task Group, TG 327.01, included an amphibious unit, commanded by COMAW (Commodore Amphibious Warfare) in the assault ship *Fearless* with 40 Commando Group and elements of 3 Commando Brigade Royal Marines embarked, and also the landing ships (logistic) *Sir Galahad*, *Sir Percivale* and *Sir Geraint*. *Southampton*, *Iron Duke*, *Beaver*, *Gloucester* and *Richmond* escorted the group, and the nuclear submarines *Trafalgar* and *Trenchant* with the survey vessel *Herald* accompanied it. In support were the fleet tanker RFA *Olna*, the replenishment ships RFAs *Fort Austin* and *Fort George* and the repair ship RFA *Diligence*. The research vessel RMAS *Newton* also accompanied the group.

Departure The ships of the group sailed from Portsmouth and Plymouth in January, and after rendezvousing in the Western Approaches headed south for Gibraltar, where the Joint Force Headquarters Staff was embarked on board the flagship. Once in the Mediterranean the group steamed east and after port visits headed for the Suez Canal en route for the Gulf and the Far East. The Amphibious Task Unit had already been detached and had gone on ahead through the

Suez Canal, passing down into the Red Sea for the first time in twenty-eight years, and then on across the Indian Ocean to the Far East. After arriving off Brunei at the beginning of March, the Amphibious Task Unit, with 40 Commando embarked, started a progressive series of training exercises with the Royal Bruneian armed forces.

Air operations on board *Invincible* (JAR)

Operation Jural, 7–12 March 1997 Meanwhile the ships of the Carrier Task Group passed through the Suez Canal and arrived in the Gulf, where they joined with the Armilla ships for combined exercises and operations. During March *Illustrious* had RAF GR7 Harriers from 1 Fighter Squadron RAF embarked, and these operated with her FA2 Sea Harriers of 801 NAS. The Harriers flew missions on Operation Jural enforcing the 'no fly' zone over southern Iraq. During the period 7–12 March twenty-eight sorties were flown, eighteen of them directly over Iraqi territory. The FA2 Sea Harriers were armed with AMRAAMs (advanced medium range air-to-air missiles), which greatly enhanced their capability, providing them with a very effective interception ability beyond visual range. The performance of the group, particularly with their flying missions, served to demonstrate to the allied forces operating in the Gulf that the UK still had a strategic role. The RAF GR7 Harrier detachment remained on board *Illustrious* for a month, leaving as the group departed from the region to head further east.

Exercise Setia Kawan II The group next sailed east from the Arabian Sea and transited via Pakistan and India to the China Sea to join the navies of the FPDA (Five-Power Defence Arrangement). In early April, 45 Commando Royal Marines was flown out to join the Amphibious Task Force in the joint warfare exercise Setia Kawan II ('Loyal Friends'), which included the largest amphibious exercise conducted by the Royal Navy in the South China Sea. A balanced force of 1,600

The destroyer *Edinburgh* returns home to Portsmouth
(NN)

Illustrious
(JCKS)

Harriers prepare to enforce the 'no fly' zone
(NN)

maritime exercise codenamed Flying Fish. This combined the regular maritime exercise Starfish and an integrated air defence system exercise, involving forty ships, two submarines and 140 aircraft from the FPDA countries.

The FPDA worked well, and had for over twenty-five years made a major contribution to peace and security in the region. The participation of the Ocean Wave Task Force in the routine annual Starfish exercise provided a big boost to the ongoing success of the 'Arrangement'.

Port Visits On completion of the exercises, ships were dispersed to carry out visits to different ports and countries in the Pacific Rim. Ships of the Ocean Wave Task Force managed to visit over thirty different countries during the deployment. Many visited Singapore, which provided the maintenance support base, and visits were also made as far apart as Vladivostok in the north, visited by *Richmond*, and Australia and New Zealand in the south, where *Gloucester* visited Napier. *Beaver* carried out one of the more unusual visits, to Ho Chi Minh City; it was the first visit by a Royal Navy warship to the Socialist Republic of Vietnam. At the end of June the Task Force headed for Hong Kong.

Hong Kong On 30 June 1997 the Colony of Hong Kong was formally handed back to China, on expiry of the hundred-year lease. At 0930 on that historic day the ships of the Hong Kong Squadron hoisted decommissioning pennants and steamed

Royal Marines was rapidly landed by a combination of landing craft and helicopters, under cover of close air support from the carrier group and NGS (naval gunfire support) from the rest of the ships of the Task Force. The exercise was a great success and a powerful demonstration to all in the region of the UK's strategic reach over 8,000 miles.

Exercise Flying Fish *Illustrious*, escorted by *Beaver*, *Gloucester* and *Richmond* and the submarine *Trenchant*, then joined FPDA ships and aircraft for a two-week multi-national

The destroyer
Gloucester at speed
(NP)

past the Star Ferry Terminal before altering course to starboard and passing the Royal Navy shore base HMS *Tamar*.

The Royal Navy had maintained an operating base in Hong Kong, at Stonecutters Island, since the closure of the naval dockyard in 1959. The Governor of Hong Kong, His Excellency Chris Patten, and the First Sea Lord, Admiral Sir Jock Slater, had already closed the base, at Stonecutters Island, with the White Ensign being hauled down for the last time several weeks earlier.[5]

The ships of the Hong Kong Squadron then completed a circumnavigation of Hong Kong Island, cheered by thousands of well-wishers. At sunset the official ceremonial handover to President Jiang Zemin of China was carried out by Captain HRH the Prince of Wales and the Governor, Mr Chris Patten. The Royal Yacht *Britannia*, escorted by the frigate *Chatham* and RFA *Sir Percival*, was in Hong Kong for the hand-over ceremonies. Meanwhile just over the horizon were the ships of the Task Force of exercise Ocean Wave,

Admiral Sir Jock Slater, the First Sea Lord, arrives in Hong Kong
(JCKS)

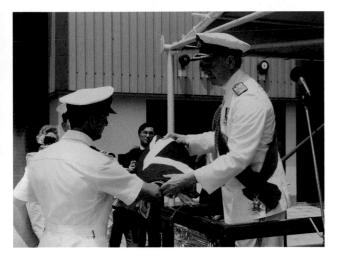

The First Sea Lord receives the White Ensign, hauled down for the last time in Hong Kong
(JCKS)

with the Commander of the force, Rear Admiral West (COMUKTG), flying his flag in *Illustrious*.

Shortly after midnight on the next day, 1 July, HRH the Prince of Wales, in *Britannia*, led the Hong Kong Squadron out of Victoria Harbour to rendezvous with the Ocean Wave Task Force, thus ending over 150 years of British presence in the area. The ships of the Task Force formed up and executed a steam-past in view of the Royal Yacht in traditional salute. The UK having relinquished all responsibilities for the protection of the former colony, the Hong Kong Squadron sailed on for Manila and eventually the UK, for ultimate disposal.

Homeward Bound After the handover of Hong Kong the ships of Ocean Wave sailed south for Singapore and last visits in the area before beginning the homeward voyage west across the Indian Ocean to the UK. They made their way back into the Atlantic and, as they transited the Bay of Biscay, the Sea King helicopters of *Illustrious* carried out two rescue missions.

Finally the ships arrived in the Channel at the end of August and dispersed to Devonport and Portsmouth in time for very well-earned summer leave. The First Sea Lord said of the deployment: 'our major deployment to the Asian-Pacific Rim made a most favourable impression on the international stage'.[6]

———— • ————

The Royal Yacht *Britannia* After the handover of Hong Kong in July, the Royal Yacht *Britannia* made a fast passage back to the UK, arriving in Portsmouth on 1 August. She then remained in home waters and in November visited London to take part in the celebrations to mark HM the Queen's Golden Wedding anniversary. On sailing from London, she headed for Portsmouth, where she arrived on 22 November and made an emotional entry, flying her paying off pennant. Following a ceremony on 11 December in the presence of HM the Queen, the Royal Standards and ensign were lowered for the very last time, completing the yacht's forty-four years of service with the Royal Navy. Four months later it was decided that *Britannia* should go to Edinburgh's port of Leith, where she is now administered by a charitable organisation, the Royal Britannia Trust.

There had been some controversy over the replacement of *Britannia*. Earlier in the year the Conservative government had agreed that the yacht would be replaced, but after the General Election on 1 May, the new Labour government decided that no replacement would be built, in view of the tremendous pressures on the defence budget.

The Adriatic: Operation Alleviate, 23 June – 8 July 1997 The crisis in the former Yugoslavia had spread south towards Albania, and following the collapse of the Albanian government in June, Operation Alleviate was initiated to protect, and where necessary evacuate, British nationals from Albania. The destroyer *Birmingham*, which was assigned to the STANAVFORMED supporting the NATO stabilisation force, was detached and ordered to close the Albanian coast.

Meanwhile the destroyer *Exeter*, which had been conducting gunnery firings off Gibraltar, was ordered east across the Mediterranean to the Adriatic at twenty-eight knots to relieve *Birmingham* off Albania. The frigate *Coventry*, with a force of Royal Marines embarked, was also sent to the area at the end of June to patrol the coast off Durres. *Coventry* had the additional task of assisting observers of the national elections.

The Baltic At the end of May the frigate *Iron Duke* visited the base of the Russian Northern Fleet at Severomorsk and conducted joint anti-submarine exercises. On her way back home *Iron Duke* entered the Baltic and took part in a week-

Harrier on board *Illustrious*, about to patrol the 'no fly' zone (NN)

long 'Partnership for Peace' exercise with forty-eight ships from twelve different nations.

Operation Bolton in the Gulf: Task Group 347.01, 14 November 1997

After leading a successful task force to carry out weapon-firing demonstrations for 'sea days' in the Channel off Portsmouth in July, *Invincible* prepared to deploy to the Mediterranean and Gulf. On 2 September 1997 *Invincible*, supported by the new 32,500-ton one-stop replenishment ship RFA *Fort Victoria*, sailed out of Portsmouth and headed west down the Channel. En route she embarked her CAG, which included the FA2 Sea Harriers of 800 NAS and also five GR7 RAF Harriers from No 1 RAF Fighter Squadron. Mk 6 ASW Sea King helicopters of 814 NAS were also embarked on board.

Exercise Tapon 97, September 1997 The ships sailed south for the major NATO operational exercise Tapon off the Spanish coast. In the exercise *Invincible* joined the Spanish carrier SNS *Principe de Asturias*, operating 'Matadors', EAV-8B Harrier IIs. Intense aircraft exercises were conducted, proving the greatly enhanced capability of *Invincible*'s air group. At the end of the exercise the RAF GR7 Harriers flew back to the UK and *Invincible* headed west across the Atlantic for exercises with US forces. She then carried out a comprehensive training programme with the US Navy and also the US Marine Corps off the eastern seaboard of the USA before heading for Barbados.

The Gulf Crisis In the Gulf a crisis was brewing as Saddam Hussein was continuing to obstruct United Nations weapons inspectors. On 14 November 1997, following Iraq's refusal to comply with the UN Special Council Resolutions concerning weapons of mass destruction, plans were made

Operation Lodestone On sailing from Gibraltar the next day *Invincible* embarked the RAF GR7 Harriers and then proceeded east to work up her aircraft at the NATO weapon range and air training facility at Decimomannu in Sardinia. FRADU (Fleet Requirement and Direction Unit) jets from RNAS (Royal Naval Air Station) Culdrose flew down to assist with the training. Sadly, during flying operations off Sardinia, an RAF GR7 Harrier was lost. At the beginning of December, after a brief visit to Barcelona, *Invincible* sailed north through the Strait of Otranto and entered the Adriatic, where she started to operate her Harrier aircraft. The Harriers reinforced allied aircraft, flying fifty-three operational sorties over the former Republic of Yugoslavia in support of the Operation Deliberate Guard of UNSFOR (the United Nations

Stabilisation Force in the Former Republic of Yugoslavia) and the UK's contribution under Operation Lodestone. On 12 December *Invincible* returned to Gibraltar, but a short while later she was at sea again and headed east for Cyprus. After Christmas, which she spent off Cyprus, *Invincible* sailed back to the Adriatic via Palermo. On 4 January she was back at sea, steaming north into the Adriatic to fly more operational missions, but after only two days of flying operations she was ordered to make a fast transit to the Gulf, where the political situation in the Gulf remained tense.

Operation Jural On 10 January 1998, *Invincible* proceeded south-east to exit the Mediterranean in order to increase political pressure on Saddam Hussein. *Invincible* and RFA *Fort Victoria* transited through the Suez Canal on 18 January and headed down the Red Sea. On 25 January they sailed through the Straits of Hormuz into the Gulf, where they

to enforce those resolutions and Operation Bolton was initiated. The plan was for a rapid-build up of forces in the northern Gulf. The UK planned to deploy RAF Tornados to the area but when it was found to be politically unacceptable to over fly certain countries in the area, it was agreed to send a Royal Naval task force.

Invincible, with RFA *Fort Victoria*, was diverted from Barbados and ordered to make a high-speed passage east across the Atlantic to Gibraltar. Averaging twenty-eight knots, *Invincible* arrived off Gibraltar on 19 November and rendezvoused with COMUKTG, Rear Admiral Forbes, and *Illustrious* to embark additional stores and equipment for hostilities in the Gulf. *Invincible* also prepared to re-embark seven RAF GR7 Harriers from No 1 Fighter Squadron, which were flying down to Gibraltar. *Invincible* was then ordered to deploy to the eastern Mediterranean in support of high-level diplomatic negotiations.

were joined by the ships of the Armilla Patrol, the frigate *Coventry* and the destroyer *Nottingham*.

Once in the Gulf *Invincible* commenced flying operations. Missions were integrated with shore-based aircraft and those of the three US CBGs based on the US carriers USS *Nimitz*, *George Washington* and *Independence*. Patrols were conducted over the southern Iraq 'no fly' zone as part of Operations Southern Watch and Jural. The Harriers also carried out bombing training with US aircraft. Some of the GR7 Harriers were fitted with the latest thermal imaging airborne laser designation pods, which enabled them to attack targets with pinpoint accuracy. They flew 800 hours of missions in theatre, helping to increase the pressure on Iraq to comply with the wishes of the United Nations. A Royal Navy mine counter-measures group consisting of the minehunters *Bridport*, *Inverness* and *Sandown* followed and arrived out in the Gulf on 13 February.

Illustrious **Task Group** On 18 January a second carrier task force, led by the carrier *Illustrious*, with a 'joint air group' of FA2 Sea Harriers of 801 NAS and RAF GR7 Harriers and supported by RFA *Fort George*, was sent to the Mediterranean to work up in case it should be needed to relieve the *Invincible* group. In February Kofi Annan, the Secretary-General of the UN, visited Iraq to persuade Saddam Hussein to back down. Eventually Saddam Hussein agreed to allow arms inspectors access to weapon facilities. Because the situation remained tense, the *Illustrious* group transited

through the Suez Canal and Red Sea to the Gulf, where it joined the *Invincible* group at the beginning of March 1998.

After a short period of operating together, *Invincible* sailed for the UK, arriving back home on 26 March. Meanwhile in the Gulf, the Harriers flying from *Illustrious* were policing the 'no fly' zones in support of Operations Southern Watch and Jural, carrying out various aerial sorties over southern Iraq. Then, when finally the number of RAF Tornados had been increased sufficiently for them to police the zones, the Carrier Task Force was withdrawn, sailing out of the Gulf on 17 April. The ships of Operation Armilla remained on station and continued their important patrol duties. The Mine Counter-Measures Group also remained in the area

The carrier *Invincible* en route to the Gulf (JCKS)

to conduct route surveys during late April before finally leaving the Gulf early in May and returning to the UK.

Operation Desert Fox Towards the end of the year Saddam Hussein was once again resisting the international community and obstructing the arms inspectors. On 16 December the US forces in the northern Gulf launched Operation Desert Fox, firing a barrage of cruise missiles against military and air targets. RAF land-based GR1 Tornados also took part in the bombing raids on southern Iraq.

In view of the escalation of hostilities it was decided to deploy a carrier task group to the Gulf again, and a group,

Harriers commence
flying operations
(NN)

led by the carrier *Invincible*, with the destroyer *Newcastle* and the fleet replenishment ship RFA *Fort Austin*, sailed from Portsmouth on 9 January 1999 to head for the Mediterranean. After transiting through the Suez Canal the group sailed through the Straits of Hormuz into the Gulf area on 30 January 1999 as part of Operation Bolton II. The force was deployed as a precautionary measure in view of Iraq's continuing intransigence in refusing to co-operate over UN Security Council Resolutions concerning weapons of mass destruction. The group again took part in maritime interdiction operations and also air surveillance operations over the 'no fly' zones in southern Iraq. The Task Force finally withdrew from the area on 1 April.

Operation Resilient, 11 February – 20 March 1998 On 11 February 1998 the Type 23 frigate *Monmouth*, supported by the tanker RFA *Orangeleaf*, was ordered to the coast of west Africa to stand by off Sierra Leone as part of Operation Resilient. At the beginning of the year the rebel group, which had deposed the President in a coup in May 1997, was finally ousted from power, and it was now carrying out a savage campaign of reprisals, murdering and looting in revenge. Its aim was to destabilise the government of the newly installed President Ahmad Tejan Kabbah by a war of terror. The mission of Operation Resilient was to prepare to evacuate British nationals and also provide humanitarian aid during the civil war. British forces were assisting the UK High

Commissioner to restore order and democratic government. On 23 February the Type 22 frigate *Cornwall* arrived and after a brief handover relieved *Monmouth*. The ship's company of *Cornwall* worked hard, providing emergency food and medical supplies and helping to rebuild the shattered infrastructure of the country by implementing a range of major engineering projects and rebuilding schools and hospitals. The ship's Sea King helicopter played a crucial role in transporting food supplies and emergency relief teams to remote areas.

After three weeks of hard work President Kabbah came on board *Cornwall* to thank the ship's company personally for their enormous effort in 'kick-starting' the restoration programme. On 20 March Operation Resilient was completed and *Cornwall* sailed for Tenerife for a well-earned break.

Cornwall, supported by the tanker RFA *Orangeleaf*, returned to Sierra Leone as a contingency measure in June, but after two weeks the situation eased and the ships were withdrawn.

NATO Operation Strong Resolve, 7–21 March 1998 The naval exercise Operation Strong Resolve, conducted from 7 to 21 March 1998, was the largest NATO maritime exercise since the end of the Cold War. The aim of the operation was to test the ability of NATO to respond to different crises simultaneously in different locations, primarily the northern NATO area and the Iberian Peninsula. A total of ninety ships in ten different task groups, with over 100 maritime aircraft, took part in the operation, with the UK as the major contributor of forces. Originally the UK had allocated two aircraft carriers to the operation, but with the deepening crisis in the Gulf they were withdrawn, and *Invincible* was sent to the Gulf for Operation Bolton.

The Commander UK Task Group had been designated as the Maritime Component Commander, but in the event he had to sail with his flagship, *Invincible*, for the Gulf. The FOSF then commanded the UK element of the operation. It provided excellent practice in fielding two battle management staffs.

The exercise was a great success and demonstrated the ability of the Royal Navy to respond to two medium-scale operations simultaneously.

Northern Ireland

Despite brief cease-fires and peace talks in Northern Ireland, the requirement for major security operations continued.

Operations Grenada and Lifespan Throughout the period the patrol craft of the Northern Ireland Squadron, consisting of the River class minesweepers *Blackwater*, *Arun*, *Itchen* and *Spey*, maintained their important counter-terrorist patrols around the coast and inland waterways, under Operations Grenada, Interknit and Lifespan. Royal Marine units and Sea King helicopters supported them as required.

Operation Sealion On 19 May 1997 Operations Grenada and Interknit were combined into Operation Sealion, and the River class ships of the Northern Ireland Squadron were replaced by three Hunt class MCMVs from June to August 1998.

Operation Banner 40 Commando Royal Marines, which was deployed on security operations in south Armagh at the beginning of 1996 under Operation Banner, completed its tour and returned to the mainland on 15 June. On 16 September 1998, 42 Commando Royal Marines returned to south Armagh for ongoing security duties. Its tour ended the following year.

Other Fleet Activities

Atlantic On 8 January 1996 the frigate *Northumberland* proceeded at speed to the assistance of the MV *Covasna*, which was sinking 400 miles north-east of the Azores. She arrived in time to evacuate the entire crew to safety.

Adriatic Twenty-two days later the frigate *Brazen* went to the rescue of an Albanian craft sinking in the Adriatic and managed to rescue thirty people.

Irish Sea In the Irish Sea *Cromer* and *Alderney*, with a Sea King helicopter, rescued the crew of a sinking Belgian fishing vessel north-west of Land's End on 6 February 1996.

South Atlantic *Northumberland*, with the fishery protection vessel *Corella*, carried out deterrent operations against illegal fishing vessels off South Georgia between 25 February and 1 March.

Pacific On 25 June *Northumberland* went to the assistance of FV *Lancha Artemisa*, which was sinking off the coast of Chile.

Indonesian Waters The patrol vessel *Plover* went to the assistance of an Indonesian merchant ship in the Makassar Straits on 12 July and then towed her into Tajung Mangkulihat the following day.

Persian Gulf On 6 November the destroyer *Edinburgh* rescued the crew of a sinking vessel in the central Gulf area, using her Lynx to winch the crew to safety.

Operation Caxton The destroyer *Liverpool* and the tanker RFA *Black Rover*, in the Caribbean, went to provide emergency relief work in Montserrat as part of Operation Caxton following major volcanic eruptions at the end of May 1997. Towards the end of August the ships carried out evacuations of areas at greatest risk. Operation Caxton was completed on 29 August.

Atlantic On 5 May the destroyer *York*, working with HM Customs and Excise, boarded MV *Simon De Dancer* off the coast of Portugal and seized cannabis valued at over £10 million. The ship was arrested and escorted back to the UK by the destroyer *Nottingham*.

Operation Kingfisher The frigate *Monmouth* and the tanker RFA *Orangeleaf* were deployed to Pointe Noire, west Africa, on 14 October as part of Operation Kingfisher in the deteriorating political situation in the Democratic Republic of the Congo. The French destroyer FS *Surcouf* joined the ships, and the group stood by to protect foreign nationals. Civil order was restored and, as the situation eased, the ships were withdrawn on 30 October.

Mediterranean On 7 December 1997 *Invincible* sailed to the assistance of MV *Megan*, which was foundering in heavy seas 130 miles east of Sicily. *Invincible*, assisted by the Italian Navy, managed to rescue thirteen members of the crew.

West Indies On 23 January 1998 *Northumberland* went to the aid of a ship sinking at Aruba in the West Indies and managed to rescue four men. A month later the destroyer *Newcastle* went to the aid of MV *Christie* and towed the ship to Basseterre, St Kitts.

Gulf of Aden RFA *Diligence* went to the assistance of MV *Leros Star* in the Gulf of Aden on 6 May. The ship had come under attack off Somalia, and RFA *Diligence* was able to take care of the wounded.

Operation Garrick On 21 May the destroyer *York*, with a Royal Marine detachment embarked, was detached from operation Bolton and sailed for the Far East. Once in Indonesian waters, *York* joined the Australian-led Operation Garrick force, standing by to evacuate foreign nationals and help restore order. Liaison teams worked ashore and the RAF provided transport aircraft. The operation was completed on 20 July, allowing *York* to carry out a series of routine visits in the Far East.

English Channel On 5 September the patrol vessel *Guernsey* went to the aid of the FV *Christina*, which was on fire twenty miles south-east of Brixham. The Torbay lifeboat stood by as *Guernsey* fought the blaze and saved the vessel.

Operation Swanston In the Adriatic the frigate *Cumberland*, with a Royal Marine boat group, was sent to stand off the coast of Albania on 15 September as part of Operation Swanston. The operation was to protect and, if necessary, evacuate British nationals. On 22 September the frigate *London* arrived in the area, having been sailed a week early from the UK, and took over the operation from *Cumberland*. A week later, when the situation eased, the operation was completed and *London* was released to take part in the major NATO exercise Dynamic Mix in the eastern Mediterranean.

Mediterranean The destroyer *Cardiff* went to assist the Maltese ship MV *Beluga* on fire north-west of Crete on 9 October. *Cardiff* brought the fires under control, and the ship was then taken under tow by a tug.

Baltic On 26 October the MCMV *Atherstone* joined a multi-national mine clearance operation off the coast of Estonia. Fourteen mines were located and safely disposed of during the two-week operation.

Operation Mainsail At the end of October, when Hurricane 'Mitch' struck in the West Indies, the frigate *Sheffield* and the tanker RFA *Black Rover* proceeded to the Honduran offshore islands to provide emergency disaster relief under Operation Mainsail. Having restored essential services and completed emergency relief work, the ships sailed on 3 November.

Operation Tellar Three days later *Sheffield* and RFA *Black Rover* joined the major international disaster relief operation, codenamed Operation Tellar, in Honduras and Nicaragua, which had been utterly devastated by Hurricane 'Mitch'. Also taking part in the relief operations were the new helicopter carrier *Ocean* and the LSL RFA *Sir Tristram* with 45 Commando Royal Marines. *Ocean* happened to be in the area on trials prior to joining operational service in 1999. The relief work went on for nine days, by the end of which essential services had been restored and many lives had been saved.

Wilkinson Sword of Peace In 1996 the aircraft carriers *Invincible* and *Illustrious* were jointly awarded the Wilkinson Sword of Peace for their valuable work in peace-keeping operations in the Adriatic. HRH the Prince of Wales formally presented the sword to *Invincible* on 9 January 1997.

The Second International Festival of the Sea (IFOS), 28–31 August 1998 The second International Festival of the Sea was held at Portsmouth over the August bank holiday weekend of 1998. This time the Royal Navy assisted with organising the event, which included the Historic Dockyard and was a great success. *Invincible*, *Ark Royal*, *Fearless*, *Nottingham*, *Liverpool*, *Iron Duke*, *Endurance* and *Bridport* took part and were open to crowds of visitors. Other ships, units and Royal Marines provided a range of displays, events, activities, parades and concerts. It was the most significant maritime event of the decade, attracting thousands of visitors.

SHIPS, SUBMARINES, WEAPONS AND AIRCRAFT

New Assault Ships On 18 July 1996 Michael Portillo, the Secretary of State for Defence, announced, 'The Royal Marine ability to mount amphibious operations is critically dependent on the landing platform docks, currently *Fearless* and *Intrepid*. Both vessels have given long and distinguished service including in the Falklands Campaign, but will soon be approaching the end of their operational lives. I am pleased therefore to be able to announce that I am today placing a contract with GEC to design and build two new replacement ships, *Albion* and *Bulwark*.'

The New Merlin Helicopter In 1998 the new EH 101 Merlin HAS Mk 1 helicopter entered service with the Royal Navy. Forty-four were ordered, to be delivered by 2001, with the aim of replacing the ASW Sea King and some of the ASW Lynx helicopters within four years. The helicopters were equipped to operate Stingray torpedoes, Mk 11 depth bombs and anti-ship missiles.

Tomahawk cruise missile (RNSM)

TLAMS In 1998 the new Tomahawk land attack missile (TLAM) was introduced for trials and assessment with the Royal Navy. Sixty-five Tomahawk Block III missiles were ordered from the USA for fitting in two *Swiftsure* class and five *Trafalgar* class submarines. The missile, which could be fired from a submarine's torpedo tubes, had a range of over 1,000 miles and could engage even small targets at extreme range with great precision.

On 10 November 1998 the submarine *Splendid* fired the first British trial TLAM with a dummy warhead on a US trials range off the western seaboard of the USA. The trials continued, and two days later she fired a third TLAM with a live warhead. The TLAM hit the target with pinpoint accuracy, and completely destroyed a communications bunker.

Astute Class Submarines In June 1997 GEC-Marconi was awarded a contract to build three of a new 6,000-ton class of SSN, submarines designed to replace the *Swiftsure* class submarines. The new class, originally known as Batch 2 *Trafalgar* class, was later named the *Astute* class. The new submarines were designed to be faster and quieter than those of the *Trafalgar* class.

PERSONNEL MATTERS

Personnel Strategy Following on from the 'Independent Review of the Armed Forces Manpower, Career and Remunerations Structures' by Sir Michael Bett and known as the Bett Report, a complete review of service personnel covering career and rank structures, pay, allowances, career management and conditions of service was carried out. The review resulted in the publication in February 1997 of a paper setting out the findings, titled 'The Armed Forces of the Future – A Personnel Strategy'. One of the results of

the review was the decision to align the three services more closely in terms of personnel policy and conditions of service.

Ratings For ratings, career progression was in the future to be based more on selective promotion depending on merit and qualifications, rather than depending on time-serving advancement by roster. There was to be much more emphasis on rewarding skill, experience and performance, and a new pay structure was being devised to implement the new policy.

Officers The major change for officers was the introduction of a new three-tier flexible career structure (see below). The strategy also introduced the substantive rank of Commodore and ended the rank of Admiral of the Fleet.

Investors in People An additional aim arising from the personnel strategy was the commitment by the Second Sea Lord to achieve 'Investors in People' accreditation through Training and Enterprise Councils by 1999.

Naval Manning Agency In July 1996 a Naval Manning Agency was set up under a Director General Naval Manning to ensure that sufficient manpower was available on the trained strength and effectively deployed to meet all demands placed on the Royal Navy. The agency introduced a formal manning strategy, explaining the process for manning the Fleet, and a manning plan, setting out the current deployment of manpower, with a forecast of future changes. The agency also introduced a whole range of initiatives to improve the system and provide the most effective manning standards.

Officers

Introduction of the Three-Tier Commission The basic career structure for officers consisting of a General List core supplemented by a Special Duties List and Supplementary List had remained largely unchanged since 1955 and was overdue for updating to suit modern life-styles. Although the General List had been the mainstay of the officer core for nearly fifty years by 1998, only about a quarter of the officers who joined the Service were on a permanent General List commission. A new flexible career structure was designed, to be introduced on 1 April 1999.

The new structure involved a staged three-tier series of commissions with all officers joining on an 'Initial' twelve-year commission. This would be followed by selection to a 'Career' commission to complete sixteen years and qualify for an immediate pension. The third tier would again be by selection to a 'Full Term Commission' to complete service to the age of fifty-five.

Introduction of the Substantive Rank of Commodore The rank of Commodore had, for many years, been a temporary rank for a particular appointment to give a captain authority over other captains regardless of their seniority. It was decided, however, to introduce a substantive rank of Commodore to bring the Royal Navy into line with the other

The Executive Committee of the White Ensign Association on board *Invincible* with CINCFLEET, Admiral Sir Peter Abbott (front row, centre), and FOSF, Vice Admiral John Brigstocke (front row, second from left)
(WEA)

The White Ensign Association at the Royal Naval Air Station at Yeovilton
(WEA)

services and with NATO allies. This was particularly important to enable the Royal Navy to compete with the other services when nominating candidates for an increasing number of 'one star' tri-service rotational appointments (Commodore, Brigadier and Air Commodore). Promotion to the rank of Commodore would be by selection, with promotion boards making the first selections in 2001. It would bring to an end the system whereby captains of over six years' seniority were ranked with, and paid the same as, brigadiers and air commodores.

The Rank of Admiral of the Fleet As mentioned above, the Bett Report brought about the end of the 'five star' rank of Admiral of the Fleet. The historic rank dated back several centuries and had been held by many famous and distinguished admirals. The report found that the 'five star' military ranks were unnecessary because of the reduced size of the armed services and also because those ranks were not used by the allies of the UK. Consequently the long-standing tradition of promoting the First Sea Lord to Admiral of the Fleet on retirement was discontinued.

The White Ensign Association In 1996 Admiral Sir Michael Layard took over as Chairman of the Association, and during the year the Association arranged for a number of senior and influential people to go to sea with the Royal Navy in fourteen different warships. The Association also organised receptions on board the Type 22 frigate *London* and a reception hosted by HRH Prince Andrew on board the Royal Yacht *Britannia*. The receptions were attended by a good cross-section of people from the City, commerce and industry, as well as friends and supporters.

The following year, the Association devoted considerable effort to assisting the last of those leaving the Service under the redundancy scheme to settle in civilian life. During the course of the year it arranged for eleven visits to HM ships,

including those at sea in the Indian Ocean and the Pacific. CINCFLEET, Admiral Sir Peter Abbott, kindly hosted the Executive Committee of the Association on board his flagship, *Invincible* (Captain Roy Clare), during its visit to Portsmouth naval base.

In 1998 the Association celebrated its fortieth anniversary and was privileged to be able to mark the event with a reception held at Buckingham Palace by gracious permission of HM the Queen. HRH Admiral of the Fleet the Duke of Edinburgh hosted the occasion and welcomed over 200 guests of the Association. During the year the Association developed strong links with the Services Career Transition Partnership and with the newly formed Veterans Advice Cell, set up within the MoD following a recommendation in the new 'Policy for People' established in support of the Strategic Defence Review. Over the course of the year the Association also arranged for thirty-two people to go to sea in twelve different warships to experience life in the Royal Navy.

The Committee of the Association also enjoyed a very interesting visit to the Royal Naval air station HMS *Heron* at Yeovilton.

CHAPTER 12

Operations Bolton, Palliser and Anaconda 1999–2001

'9/11' ATTACK – OPERATION BOLTON II (GULF) – OPERATION ALLIED FORCE (KOSOVO) – ARGONAUT 99 AND AURORA 2000 DEPLOYMENTS – OPERATIONS PALLISER AND SILKMAN (SIERRA LEONE) – ARGONAUT 2001 AND SAIF SAREEA II – OPERATION ANACONDA (AFGHANISTAN)

The defining event at the turn of the millennium, which brutally marked the dawning of the twenty-first century, was the series of infamous terrorist attacks on the 'Twin Towers' of the World Trade Center in New York and the Pentagon in Washington on 11 September 2001, immediately dubbed '9/11'. The terrorists who flew their hijacked aircraft into their targets were responsible for the slaughter of some 3,000 on that day and for unleashing an international war on terror which would cause the deaths of many thousands more.

NATO In 1999 NATO forces were deeply engaged in security operations in the former Yugoslavia, whilst at the same time Poland, Hungary and the Czech Republic joined NATO.

Russia In Russia a bloody uprising was provoked when Russian forces invaded Chechnya, and in 2000 Vladimir Putin, an ex-KGB officer, was elected President.

The Middle East Problems continued throughout the Middle East with bombs, murders and terrorist attacks. General Pervez Musharraf seized power in Pakistan in a military coup, and India and Pakistan came perilously close to war after a terrorist attack on the Indian Parliament. In Aden suicide bombers attacked the US destroyer USS *Cole*, which left seventeen of the crew dead and forty-two wounded. In Afghanistan the USA commenced operations against the Taliban, launching air strikes and destroying Osama Bin Laden's terrorist training camps in October 2001. The following month the Taliban agreed to peace talks conducted under the aegis of the UN.

The UK In the UK, problems persisted in Northern Ireland following continued murders, which impeded the peace process in 1998. Although David Trimble and John Hume had been awarded the Nobel Peace Prize at the end of 1998, there was still no acceptance of the Good Friday Agreement. In 2001 the Labour Party, under Tony Blair, won the General Election and maintained close relations with the USA.

UK Defence Policy

Implementation of the 1998 SDR (Strategic Defence Review) formed the key to defence policy in 1999 and set the reductions to be achieved across the armed services. One of the key elements of SDR was the importance of the Maritime Contribution to Joint Operations (MCJO).

FIRST SEA LORDS
Admirals Boyce and Essenhigh

SECOND SEA LORDS
Admirals Brigstocke and Spencer

MANPOWER
43,747

MERCANTILE MARINE
1,449 merchant ships

The Strategic Plan From the SDR the Navy developed its own Strategic Plan to cover the period up to 2015. Published in October 1999, the plan set out a clear doctrine outlining the MCJO as well as various other elements including plans for the management of change within the Navy, and covered the five main pillars of activity: People, Equipment, Readiness for Operations, Partnerships and Resource Management.

Project Capital To improve efficiency, Project Capital was introduced to implement full resource accounting and budgeting across the MoD.

THE FLEET

At the end of the twentieth century the Royal Navy possessed a Fleet of thirty-eight major warships with a number of new ships under construction. It was still a powerful navy, and as Admiral Sir Alan West was to point out as First Sea Lord in 2002, 'The Royal Navy is still the second most powerful Navy in the world and certainly the best.'[1]

Major Units The core of the fleet consisted of the three 20,000-ton *Invincible* class light (anti-submarine warfare)/Command aircraft carriers, *Invincible*, *Illustrious* and *Ark Royal*. *Invincible* was nearly twenty years old, and was undergoing conversion work in drydock at Portsmouth to enable her to operate the GR7 Harriers as well as the FA2 Sea Harriers. *Ark Royal* was shortly to commence a major refit at Rosyth in 2000, with *Invincible* having hers in 2001 and *Illustrious*, the fleet flagship, due to go for her major two-year refit, also at Rosyth, in 2002.

Amphibious Ships The new 20,500-ton helicopter carrier *Ocean*, the biggest ship in the Fleet, had just entered service, having been delivered in 1999.

The aged assault ship *Fearless* was still in commission but due to be replaced by the two new 19,500-ton assault ships, *Albion* and *Bulwark*, with *Albion* due to be in service by the beginning of 2003.

Destroyers and Frigates The escort fleet comprised twelve Type 42 destroyers, eight Type 22 frigates, and thirteen new Type 23 frigates, with three more building.

Mine Counter-Measures Vessels (MCMVs) The MCMVs included thirteen of the Hunt class, nine of the new *Sandown*

The new helicopter
carrier *Ocean* sails
from Plymouth
(NN)

class and the one remaining vessel of the River class, *Orwell*, serving as the Dartmouth training vessel. In addition there were seven main patrol vessels and sixteen more of the small *Archer* class patrol boats.

Submarines The submarine fleet consisted of the four SSBNs, the *Vanguard* Trident missile nuclear submarines, seven *Trafalgar* class fleet submarines and five of the older fleet submarines of the *Swiftsure* class.

Support The Fleet also had five survey vessels and an ice patrol ship, *Endurance*, and was supported by the RFA (Royal Fleet Auxiliary) of twenty ships. The RFA was made up of two fleet tankers, *Olwen* and *Olna*, four Leaf class support tankers and three small fleet tankers of the Rover class. In addition there were two oiler replenishment ships, two fleet support ships, five landing ships (logistic), a 28,000-ton aviation training ship, RFA *Argus*, and a forward repair ship, RFA *Diligence*.

Aircraft and Helicopters The Fleet Air Arm had twenty-four Sea Harriers, seventy of the dependable workhorse Sea King helicopters (deployed in ASW, AEW (airborne early warning) and commando roles), fifty Lynx helicopters and twelve of the planned forty-four new Merlin helicopters,

New assault ship on trials flying the blue ensign and BAE Systems banner (NN)

as well as various training helicopters and fixed-wing aircraft.

The Royal Marines 3 Commando Brigade, Royal Marines, included 40, 42, and 45 Commandos plus supporting logistics regiment, artillery, engineers and signals, and a Commando Brigade Air Squadron. In addition the Royal Marines included Commacchio Group for the defence of key strategic areas (including the national deterrent), the SBS (Special Boat Service) Group and 539 Assault Squadron.

Command The Fleet was commanded by CINCFLEET (the Commander in Chief Fleet) Admiral Nigel Essenhigh, who was relieved by Admiral Alan West at the end of 2000. Rear Admiral Peter Franklin was FOSF (Flag Officer Surface Flotilla), and he was relieved in 2000 by Rear Admiral Ian Forbes.

Flag Officer Submarines (FOSM) was Rear Admiral Stevens, Flag Officer Naval Aviation (FONA) was Rear Admiral Henderson, and the Commandant General Royal Marines was Major General Fulton.

PJHQ (Permanent Joint Headquarters) Joint operations were planned and staffed by the permanent Joint Staff established at PJHQ at Northwood, north-west of London, and collocated with the HQ of the Commander in Chief Fleet. The PJHQ was commanded by the Chief of Joint

Operations (CJO), Vice Admiral Sir Ian Garnett. A key task of CJO was to develop the new JRRF (Joint Rapid Reaction Force) concept set up under the SDR and due to be fully operational by 2001. Joint operations were key to the modern expeditionary warfare strategy, in which the MCJO was the essential element provided by the Royal Navy.

FIRST SEA LORDS

Admiral Sir Michael Boyce Admiral Boyce relieved Admiral Slater as First Sea Lord in October 1998. Michael Boyce was born in 1943 and joined the Royal Navy in 1961. He qualified as a submariner and commanded two conventional diesel-electric submarines, a nuclear attack submarine and the Submarine Training Squadron. Away from the underwater world, he commanded the frigate *Brilliant*, was Director of the Naval Staff Division and had the role of Senior Naval Officer Middle East.

He was promoted Rear Admiral in 1991 and was subsequently Flag Officer Sea Training, Flag Officer Surface Flotilla, Commander in Chief Naval Home Command and Second Sea Lord, and Commander in Chief Fleet. During this period he was knighted and also held a variety of senior NATO commands.

He was First Sea Lord from 1998 until Admiral Essenhigh relieved him on 16 January 2001. Admiral Boyce then went on to become Chief of the Defence Staff at the beginning of 2001 and finally retired in May 2003. He was elevated to the peerage in June 2003, and was elected to the Council of the White Ensign Association in the same year. He became Chairman of the Association in November 2007.

A new Type 23 frigate
(NP)

The Merlin helicopter
(NN)

Admiral Sir Nigel Essenhigh Nigel Essenhigh was born in 1944 and joined the Royal Navy in 1963, qualifying as a Principal Warfare Officer in 1972. After spending much of his early career at sea he was promoted Commander in 1980 and joined the MoD in the Manpower and Training Division. Two years later he commanded the destroyer *Nottingham*, and he was then promoted to Captain in 1985. After graduating from the Royal College of Defence Studies he was appointed to the Naval Plans Division, and then in 1989 he took command of the destroyer *Exeter*.

He was appointed Hydrographer of the Navy as a rear admiral in 1994 and then Assistant Chief of the Defence Staff (Programmes) in 1996. Two years later he was appointed Commander in Chief Fleet as a full admiral, and in 2001 he became First Sea Lord.

OPERATIONS AND DEPLOYMENTS, 1999–2001

In 1999 the Royal Navy continued to maintain ships, vessels and units on station abroad and to deploy ships to key areas in support of overseas interests, territories and commitments in fulfilment of UK defence and foreign policy.

Gibraltar In Gibraltar two patrol craft, *Ranger* and *Trumpeter*, provided a continuous naval presence to deter Spanish incursions and carry out anti-smuggling operations. In addition a destroyer or frigate was kept on stand-by, as Gibraltar Guardship, ready to deploy at short notice.

Cyprus A small squadron of patrol boats was maintained in Cyprus to assist in the protection of the Sovereign Base Area on the south coast. These boats were due to be replaced by two adapted patrol craft, *Pursuer* and *Dasher*, in 2002.

Falkland Islands and Antarctica A destroyer or frigate, supported by an offshore patrol vessel and an RFA tanker, was maintained on station in and around the Falkland Islands to protect British interests in the region. In addition the ice patrol ship *Endurance* was deployed to the area during the Antarctic summer. In April 1999 the destroyer or frigate and supporting tanker were reclassified as 'Atlantic Patrol Task (South)' with wider commitments.

Fishery Protection Squadron The Fishery Protection Squadron of eleven vessels, a mix of Island, Hunt and Castle classes, maintained the 600-year-old task of patrolling the waters around the UK. The fishery protection duty involved policing the British Fishery Limits (BFLs) out to 200 miles from the west coast of the UK and out to the median lines elsewhere. An important element of the squadron's task was the protection of oil and gas installations in the North Sea.

Northern Ireland The three Hunt class MCM (mine counter-measures) ships of the Northern Ireland Squadron, supported by Royal Marine detachments and naval helicopters, conducted counter-terrorist operations under

Admiral the Lord Boyce (WEA)

The frigate *Northumberland* in the Caribbean (NP)

The ice patrol ship *Endurance* (known as the 'Red Plum') (RH)

Operations Sealion and Lifespan. The squadron maintained patrols around coastal waters as well as inshore and on inland waterways. In February 1999, following progress since the signing of the Good Friday Agreement in the previous year, the three Hunt class ships of the Northern Ireland Squadron were finally withdrawn, as well as the Sea King helicopters. 42 Commando continued its deployment in the difficult area of south Armagh for internal security operations as part of the ongoing Operation Banner and then, having completed its tour of duty on 16 March 1999, was withdrawn.

The West Indies A destroyer or frigate, supported by an RFA tanker, was deployed to the Caribbean as the WIGS (West Indies Guardship). The guardship maintained a British presence in the islands and conducted anti-drug smuggling operations. In April 1999, following a review of the WIGS, tasking the guardship was reclassified Atlantic Patrol Task (North) with wider-ranging commitments.

'Drug Busts' In May the Type 23 frigate *Marlborough* carried out an important interception of a drug smuggler in the

Caribbean, and in early November the frigate *Northumberland* intercepted and boarded the MV *Adriatik* off the north coast of Venezuela and seized two tonnes of cocaine with a street value of over £135m.

Sierra Leone The Royal Navy continued to provide support to the troubled government of Sierra Leone in its fight against rebel forces by providing the frigate *Norfolk* and an RFA tanker in and around Freetown. The ships provided back-up to UK forces deployed to the area ashore and also assisted reconnaissance teams in conducting Operation Basilica in Freetown. Teams assisting with the operation included 539 Assault Squadron Royal Marines.

On 3 February 1999 the Atlantic Patrol Ship (South), the frigate *Westminster*, relieved *Norfolk*. When the situation improved it was decided to withdraw *Westminster* and she sailed from the area on 18 March. On shore, land-based operations with a military aid package continued.

On 2 November the frigate *Somerset* returned briefly to Sierra Leone to stand by for a possible evacuation of British nationals during a breakdown in the fragile peace talks,

though after several days the talks resumed and *Somerset* was withdrawn.

Nuclear Deterrent Patrols Throughout the time the *Vanguard* class SSBNs of the 1st Submarine Squadron, armed with Trident missiles, maintained their constant deterrent patrols at sea, operating from their base at Faslane. In April 1999 the squadron achieved thirty years of continuous and undetected deterrent patrols.

Vengeance, the fourth and final *Vanguard* class submarine, completed its sea trials in 1999 and joined the deterrent cycle the following year.

Sub-Strategic Role The Strategic Defence Review allocated the SST (sub-strategic tactical) limited strike role, previously the responsibility of the RAF operating Tornado aircraft armed with WE-177 free-fall nuclear bombs, to the Royal Navy. The *Vanguard* submarines, operating in a sub-strategic Trident role, carried out the task.

Standing NATO Naval Forces NATO remained one of the cornerstones of defence policy under SDR, and the Royal Navy continued to assign ships to the four standing NATO naval forces:

STANAVFORLANT (Atlantic)

STANAVFORMED (Mediterranean)

MCMFORNORTH (MCM Force North-West)

MCMFORMED (MCM Force Mediterranean)

MCMFORMED was a newly formed MCM force for the Mediterranean, and the Royal Navy contributed the Hunt class MCMV *Atherstone* for the first deployment of the squadron. The Royal Navy ships assigned to the standing

NATO forces provided important contributions to the squadrons deployed in various exercises and also on operations in the Mediterranean and Middle East.

Operation Bolton II: Task Force 347.01 At the beginning of 1999, following the commencement of hostilities in the Gulf under Operation Desert Fox, it had been decided to send the aircraft carrier *Invincible*, escorted by the destroyer *Newcastle*, to the Gulf region to reinforce the ships deployed on Operation Bolton II. The ships of Operation Bolton were heavily committed in the Gulf in maritime interdiction operations and air surveillance patrols over Iraq. They were also positioned as a precautionary measure to counter continuing Iraqi intransigence over compliance with UN Security Council resolutions concerning weapons of mass destruction.

On 9 January 1999 *Invincible*, with her escort *Newcastle* and supported by the tanker RFA *Bayleaf* and the auxiliary fleet replenishment ship RFA *Fort Austin*, sailed from Portsmouth bound for the Arabian Sea and the Gulf. She steamed down the Channel and embarked the FA2 Sea Harriers of 800 NAS en route, but sadly none of the hoped-for RAF GR7 Harriers. The group made a fast passage south and headed into the Mediterranean, making only a brief logistic stop at Cyprus before transiting through the Suez Canal on 21 January. The group conducted weapon training as they proceeded down the Red Sea and into the Gulf of Aden.

Invincible then sailed through the Straits of Hormuz and arrived in the theatre of operations on 29 January. She rendezvoused with the ships of the Armilla Patrol, the frigates *Boxer* and *Cumberland*, supported by the tanker RFA *Brambleleaf*, all of which had been subsumed into Operation Bolton II. The *Invincible* group headed up into the northern Gulf and, following a day's briefing with US staffs, commenced operating the Sea Harriers.

The Sea Harriers joined US aircraft flying missions over southern Iraq as part of Operation Southern Watch. To maximise the time on task for the Sea Harriers, *Invincible* had to operate up-threat, well to the north of the force and within close range of Iraqi air and surface threats. Her escorts, *Newcastle* and *Cumberland*, maintained a close vigilance, constantly at alert, whilst her helicopters flew AEW and 'surface picture' compilation missions.

Interdiction operations and flying missions in support of Operations Bolton II and Southern Watch, were maintained throughout February and March. On 1 April *Invincible* was due to return to the UK and so together with *Newcastle* sailed from the Gulf, bound for home.

NATO Operation Allied Force (RN Operation Magellan): Operations over Kosovo

On passage back to Portsmouth the *Invincible* group was ordered on 10 April to divert to the Ionian Sea, to join the NATO forces deployed on Operation Allied Force. The operation was being undertaken in Kosovo to deter Serbian ethnic cleansing following the failure of peace talks in Rambouillet, France. The UK component of the

NATO operation was Operation Kingower, and the UK maritime element was codenamed Operation Magellan. The UK contributed the Type 23 frigate *Iron Duke* to STANAVFORMED, which was part of Operation Allied Force. *Iron Duke* spent six months on the operation, often deployed close in to the coast, well inside Serbian missile range.

Task Force 470 The Type 23 frigate *Somerset* was already in the Adriatic, having been seconded to the French Task Force 470 for a three-month Agapanthe 99 deployment at the beginning of the year. The French Carrier Group, Task Force 470, based on the French aircraft carrier FNS *Foch*, had been sailed from Toulon at speed for the Adriatic in response to the situation in Kosovo. *Somerset*, en route from the UK, arrived in Toulon after the Task Force had sailed and immediately proceeded in company with the French destroyer FNS *Cassard* to join the rest of the Task Force in the Adriatic. On joining the French Task Force, *Somerset* acted as EW Picket and was stationed up-threat, some fifteen miles off the Montenegran coast, to give advance warning of any incoming aircraft or missiles.

First firing of TLAMs The NATO forces in the area embarked on an aerial bombing campaign over Kosovo on 24 March. The first phase of the operation consisted of strikes by cruise missiles to knock out the Serbian air defences, and the nuclear submarine *Splendid* fired the opening salvos. Moments before the first firing of her Tomahawk land attack cruise missiles (TLAMs), the Commanding Officer of *Splendid* sent a signal to the Commanding Officer of the nuclear submarine *Turbulent*, operating closer inshore; it simply said 'DUCK!'[2] It was the first time the Royal Navy had launched TLAMs for an operational strike.

After a brief visit to Cyprus for resupply en route, the *Invincible* Task Group entered the Ionian Sea on 14 April. Shortly after arriving in the area and joining the NATO Task Force, *Invincible* was operating her Sea Harriers, flying integrated operational missions over Kosovo.

On 23 April the Type 23 frigate *Grafton* arrived in the Adriatic and relieved *Somerset* at Trieste. *Somerset* returned to the UK whilst *Grafton* operated with the French Carrier Group, Task Force 470. *Grafton* acted as close escort to FNS *Foch*, which was operating close to the coast to enable her aircraft to spend more time on task over land.

The destroyer *Glasgow* at speed in a heavy sea
(RH)

Operation Kingower The *Invincible* Task Group, supported by RFA *Bayleaf*, remained to the south-east in the Ionian Sea operating with the US Carrier Battle Group based on the US nuclear carrier USS *Theodore Roosevelt*. The FA2 Sea Harriers from *Invincible* were employed in the defensive counter-air role throughout, operating over Albanian territory on combat air patrols covering the enemy airfields at Pristina and Podgorica.

The FA2s were regularly 'locked-on' by Serbian fire control radars and engaged by anti-aircraft fire, but fortunately they were not engaged by SAMs (surface-to-air missiles). The nuclear submarine *Turbulent* was also attached to the Task Group for a short period of operations prior to 'chopping' (transferring) to NATO control for operations off the coast of Montenegro. By the middle of May the number of NATO aircraft deployed in the area was sufficient to conduct all missions, and it was decided that *Invincible* could be released to return to the UK. The Sea Harriers of 800 NAS (Naval Air Squadron) had flown over 300 hours on missions in the area. On 21 May the *Invincible* group withdrew from Operation Magellan and sailed from the Ionian Sea for the UK. The group made a swift passage back and arrived in Portsmouth on 27 May. The bombing campaign of Operation Allied Force meanwhile continued until 10 June.

Operation Allied Harvest On completion of the bombing campaign it was deemed necessary to arrange for the clearance of ordnance jettisoned by aircraft during bombing missions. On 12 June the MCMVs *Sandown* and *Atherstone* were deployed to the area to assist in the clearance operations. *Sandown* was attached to the NATO MCMFORNORTH whilst *Atherstone* formed part of the new NATO MCMFORMED. The operation lasted until 24 August, during which time ninety-three bombs, from a total of 100 jettisoned, had been located. *Atherstone* and *Sandown* destroyed over 20 per cent of the bombs and missiles found.

Argonaut 99 Deployment: Exercise Bright Star In August 1999 an amphibious task group (ATG) sailed from Plymouth for a four-month deployment to the Mediterranean. The codename for the deployment was Argonaut 99, and the Commander Amphibious Task Group (COMATG) was Commodore Kilgour. The Amphibious Ready Group (ARG) included the brand new amphibious ship *Ocean* and the old assault ship *Fearless* as well as the five RFA landing ships (logistic) (LSLs). The deployment included 3,000 personnel in seventeen ships.

The ARG took part in the major exercise Bright Star in the eastern Mediterranean, which was designed to test the new amphibious doctrine and tactics. The concept of operations was based on the overall strategy flowing from the SDR and the concept of the MCJO.

Operation Langar, 18 September – 3 October 1999 In September the UK was requested to assist with the troubles that had erupted in East Timor following moves to independence. The destroyer *Glasgow*, which was in Indonesian waters, was ordered to join the UN forces, under Australian command, off East Timor on 18 September. Other UK forces, forming part of Operation Langar, were sent to the area, including a Royal Marine support team. *Glasgow* remained in the area operating with HMAS *Adelaide* and HMAS *Tobruk*. The ships conducted escort duties and patrols, helping to restore peace and security during the period of transition to independence. On 3 October *Glasgow* was withdrawn from the operation and departed from the area, though army and RAF air transport units remained in East Timor until it was completed on 15 December.

Exercise Sarex 99, November 1999 Following a disaster at sea in the South Atlantic in 1997, some 200 miles east of the Falkland Islands, the UK and Argentinean governments agreed a set of procedures for their two navies to operate together. The procedures were tested over four days in November 1999 during exercise Sarex 99, which was led by the frigate *Somerset*, the Atlantic Patrol Task (South) ship. The exercise involved the Argentinean ships ARA *Parker* and *Gurruchaga* as well as the Falklands patrol ship *Dumbarton Castle*. The exercise also involved an Argentinean P-3 Orion MPA as well as RAF C-130 Hercules and Sea King helicopters from RAF Mount Pleasant airfield in the Falkland Islands.

Aurora 2000 Deployment and Operation Palliser, May 2000

In May 2000 a powerful task group, codenamed Aurora 2000, was deployed to conduct a major amphibious exercise off the coast of Portugal. Central to the group was the new amphibious helicopter carrier *Ocean* with 42 Commando Royal Marines embarked as well as an air group of Sea King, Lynx and Gazelle helicopters from the new Joint Helicopter Command.

The ARG The key element of the Task Group was the ARG, which included the frigate *Chatham*, the LSLs RFA *Sir Bedivere* and RFA *Sir Tristram* and the auxiliary fleet support ship RFA *Fort Austin*.

Operation Palliser: Sierra Leone The Task Group was then suddenly diverted south at full speed to join the joint force in support of Operation Palliser to intervene in the crisis in Sierra Leone. It was the largest UK maritime group since the Falklands Campaign and included 3,000 personnel, who assembled for the emergency in just eight days and sailed over 3,000 miles to appear off the coast of west Africa.

Illustrious, with both RN FA2 and RAF GR7 Harriers embarked and with RFA *Fort George* supporting, were diverted from exercise Linked Seas in the Bay of Biscay to support the Task Group off Sierra Leone.

On arrival the Task Group carried out swift action, inserting a powerful force ashore backed up by a very potent force lying just off the coast. The forces protected and evacuated British nationals and took rapid action to stabilise the dangerous situation ashore. It was a combined operation

Ocean with her air group from the Joint Helicopter Command (NN)

and also involved British troops including the 1st Battalion of the Parachute Regiment, which was subsequently relieved by 42 Commando Royal Marines.

Joint Rapid Reaction Force The success of Operation Palliser provided an excellent example of the new MCJO policy set out in the SDR, as well exercising, for real, the newly established Joint Rapid Reaction Force.

Eastern Adventure, alias Maritime Endeavour Deployment: Task Group 2000, May–November 2000

At the beginning of 2000 an out-of-area group deployment to the Far East was planned. The deployment was to be the first task group circumnavigation for over ten years and was officially codenamed Eastern Adventure but was also known as Maritime Endeavour.

Rear Admiral Stephen Meyer as Commander UK Task Group (COMUKTG), flying his flag in the Type 22 frigate *Cornwall*, commanded the Task Group (TG 2000). The rest of the group consisted of the destroyer *Newcastle*, the frigate *Sutherland* and the nuclear submarine *Tireless*, to be relieved later by *Triumph*. The RFAs *Bayleaf*, *Diligence* and *Fort Victoria* supported the group, with two Sea King helicopters from 819 NAS embarked, as well as several Royal Marine specialist units.

The Task Group sailed from the UK on 2 May 2000 and set course south for Gibraltar. Once in the Mediterranean it steamed east, and as the ships passed south of Toulon they were joined by the French frigate FNS *Aconit*. The group transited through the Suez Canal and continued east for Singapore.

Exercise Flying Fish 2000 One of the principal tasks of the group was to participate in exercise Flying Fish 2000 off the coast of Singapore, to honour the UK's commitment to the Five-Power Defence Arrangement (FPDA), set up nearly thirty years earlier. The purpose of the combined maritime exercise was to defend Malaysia and Singapore against any attack or threatened invasion. Ships and aircraft conducted exercise assaults, and amphibious incursions on the coast were also part of the scenario. On completion of the exercise the ships of the group made a series of visits to the FPDA countries in the Far East, Australia, New Zealand, Malaysia and Singapore.

Defence Export Sales Ships of the group visited many ports including Shanghai, Qingdao and Vladivostock and some in Indonesia and Korea, as well as ports in Australia, Malaysia and New Zealand. Very successful UK defence and export sales days were arranged in many of the places visited, and these paid a significant economic dividend.

Support of Foreign Policy The Task Group had an important political dimension in clearly demonstrating the presence and influence of Britain abroad. It carried out the first ever combined exercises with the Chinese People's Liberation

Army (Navy), and despite communication difficulties the exercises were a marked success.

The group was approaching eastern Russia at the time of the loss of the Russian *Oscar II* class nuclear submarine *Kursk* and just happened to be in the South China Sea at a time when difficulties were being experienced between the British and Chinese governments. It was also in the offing at the time of the Korean summit.

Return to the UK After some six months in the Far East it was time for the Task Group to return to the UK via the Pacific Ocean and the Panama Canal. The passage home was uneventful and finally, at the end of November, the group arrived back, having visited twenty-seven countries and exercised with twenty different navies. The deployment strengthened the links between the Royal Navy and the French Navy. TG 2000 was by all accounts a most successful group deployment.

———— • ————

Operation Silkman: Sierra Leone, November 2000 In November 2000 the five ships of the ARG were diverted to Sierra Leone from the Mediterranean on completion of the NATO exercise Destined Glory. The government of Sierra Leone was being opposed by the rebel Revolutionary United Front (RUF). On 12 November the ARG, led by the helicopter assault ship *Ocean*, and supported by RFA *Argus*, arrived off the coast of Sierra Leone. The ships then sailed into Freetown harbour and anchored in the roads, making an overt show of force as a clear demonstration of Britain's strong support for the government of Sierra Leone.

Sea King helicopters flew over the capital as the Royal Marines of 42 Commando stormed ashore, securing a beachhead on the Aberdeen peninsula some three kilometres to the west of Freetown as part of Operation Silkman. Chinook battlefield support helicopters transported 105mm artillery guns and all-terrain vehicles as underslung loads, landing them with 42 Commando. A convoy of military vehicles then proceeded through the centre of Freetown. A cease-fire had, in fact, been negotiated between the government and the RUF the day before the Royal Marines stormed ashore, but the operation was nevertheless a high-visibility demonstration of the UK's commitment to Sierra Leone.

Argonaut 2001 Deployment:
Exercise Saif Sareea II ('Swift Sword 2')

Towards the end of August 2001 a very powerful task group, the Argonaut 2001 Group (TG 342.01), gathered in the UK under the command of COMUKMARFOR (Commander UK Maritime Force), Rear Admiral James Burnell-Nugent, in his flagship, the carrier *Illustrious*. Various elements of the Task Force departed ahead of the main group, which was due to sail from the UK at the beginning of September bound for the Middle East and Exercise Saif Sareea II. The total group, consisting of twenty-six ships and submarines, was the largest task group assembled since the Falklands War and included *Illustrious*, *Ocean* and the assault ship *Fearless*

escorted by six frigates and destroyers, two fleet submarines and four MCMVs. A survey vessel and ten RFA support ships and tankers supported the group. Embarked were 40 and 45 Commando Royal Marines, and the total number of people to be deployed was 22,500.

The MCMV Squadron The first element of the Task Group, the MCMV squadron, consisting of *Quorn*, *Inverness*, *Walney* and *Cattistock*, supported by RFA *Diligence* and the coastal survey ship *Roebuck*, sailed out of Portsmouth in mid-August and headed west down the Channel. After passing into the Mediterranean the ships headed for a port visit to Mallorca and then sailed east. In the eastern Mediterranean the squadron embarked staff from the Flag Officer Sea Training (FOST) and conducted a series of intensive training and work-up exercises. When the FOST staff departed in early September, the squadron transited through the Suez Canal and sailed down the Red Sea, through the Gulf of Aden and into the Indian Ocean, en route to the Gulf.

The Amphibious Task Group The second element of the Argonaut Task Group to sail was the Amphibious Group led by the assault ship *Fearless*. The group included the helicopter carrier *Ocean*, the landing ships (logistic) *Sir Tristram*, *Sir Bedivere* and *Sir Galahad* and the support ships RFA *Fort Rosalie* and RFA *Fort Austin* as well as the tanker RFA *Oakleaf*. On sailing, the Amphibious Group spent a week off north Devon conducting shake-down exercises with the Royal Marines as part of exercise Channel Wader before heading south for Lisbon and Cadiz, then on into the Mediterranean. In the Mediterranean, helicopters from 845 NAS, embarked in RFA *Fort Austin*, responded to a distress call and rescued twenty men from a sinking vessel 100 miles south-east of Gibraltar. The group then went on to visit Cartagena and Malaga before steaming further east for Cyprus.

The Carrier Group The carrier group, led by the flagship *Illustrious*, sailed from Portsmouth on 3 September and headed down the Channel, embarking the rest of the Carrier Air Group, including Harriers, both FA2s and GR7s, on the way. The destroyers *Nottingham* and *Southampton* and the frigates *Cornwall*, *Kent*, *Marlborough* and *Monmouth*, with the tanker RFA *Bayleaf*, escorted the flagship. The carrier group headed south for the Mediterranean and after passing through the Straits of Gibraltar visited several Mediterranean ports, with *Illustrious* visiting Valletta, Malta, on 10 September for three days. It was whilst *Illustrious* was in Valletta that the attention of the world was focused on the terrorist attacks on the 'Twin Towers' of the World Trade Center in New York.

Meanwhile the Amphibious Group in the eastern Mediterranean divided in to two task units, one of which exercised off the coast of Cyprus whilst the second Task Unit with *Fearless* exercised with Turkish forces further to the north. After *Fearless* had spent a seven-day maintenance period in Marmaris the group formed up and transited through the Suez Canal on 23 September.

Royal Marines storm ashore during an amphibious assault exercise
(NN)

Ocean and *Illustrious* taking part in exercise Saif Sareea II off Oman
(NN)

Royal Marines land on the beaches on the coast of Sierra Leone
(NN)

Exercise Saif Sareea II The various elements of the Task Group converged on Oman and then from 3 to 29 October conducted a series of joint operations, amphibious assault exercises and live firings as part of the overall joint UK–Omani exercise Saif Sareea II.

The total number of people involved was 22,500, with 13,000 Omani troops participating in the major assault exercises. Forty-two RAF fixed-wing aircraft took part as well as forty-four helicopters from the newly formed JHC (Joint Helicopter Command), half of which were naval helicopters. The main purpose of the exercise was a joint task force demonstration of the MCJO under the JRRF concept.

Not only did the exercise build close relations with Oman, but also it was a powerful demonstration that the USA was not the only nation capable of projecting large-scale force over strategic distances, showing the capabilities the UK could bring to the Gulf region.

The shocking events of '9/11' immediately prior to the exercises added much impetus to the operations. The exercises were conducted in the harsh conditions of searing heat in the desert and provided invaluable experience for what was to come later in the Gulf.

'In the Right Place' Exercise Saif Sareea II was a great success, and CINCFLEET, Admiral Sir Jonathan Band, was well pleased with the outcome. He stated: 'No less impressive was the fact that the exercise took place against a backdrop of concurrent operations, particularly as Saif Sareea continued after the terrorist attacks of September 11 and afterwards the British Task Force found itself very well placed to make an immediate contribution to the ensuing War against Terrorism.'[3]

In October, as the Task Force was held in the Arabian Gulf for operations in support of the campaign ashore in Afghanistan, the nuclear fleet submarines were able to provide direct support. On 7 October the nuclear submarines *Trafalgar* and *Triumph* launched Tomahawk cruise missiles against Taliban targets at a great distance inland.

———— • ————

NATO Operation Active Endeavour: The Protection of Shipping in the Mediterranean Following the '9/11' terrorist attacks, NATO instituted various maritime security operations. In the Mediterranean in October 2001 NATO activated the On Call Naval Force and established Operation Active Endeavour, the purpose of which was to monitor all ships in the Mediterranean. A comprehensive plot was compiled, and ships were escorted as they passed through the narrow waters of the Straits of Gibraltar. The Royal Navy assigned frigates and destroyers to the NATO squadron and took its turn to direct the operation on a rotational basis.

Operation Anaconda: The Attack on Terrorist Training Bases in Afghanistan, September 2001 – May 2002

Shortly after the '9/11' terrorist attacks the USA began Operation Anaconda to hunt for Al Qaeda and destroy its training bases in southern Afghanistan. The Americans

Illustrious with coalition ships in the Middle East – a powerful demonstration of 'allied sea power' (NN)

The Task Force in the Arabian Gulf (NN)

requested help from the UK, and 3 Commando Brigade, Royal Marines was selected to assist the US forces deployed ashore in Afghanistan. A Royal Marine reconnaissance unit was sent out to join the US forces in March, and they were forward-deployed, by RAF C-130 Hercules, to Kabul and Bagram. The following month two companies from 45 Commando disembarked from *Ocean* to join the Royal Marines already in theatre, and the combined force was codenamed Task Force Jacana.

Operation Ptarmigan The Royal Marines moved up into the mountains and instigated Operation Ptarmigan to adapt to the altitude, heat and harsh conditions. When they were sufficiently acclimatised they were assessed to have achieved full operational capability on 28 April.

Operation Snipe Task Force Jacana then combined with the US forces, which launched Operation Snipe, sweeping the mountains with their Apache helicopter gunships. This was followed up by inserting the Royal Marines, under the protection of air cover provided by US aircraft, on to mountains and ridge tops to provide FOBs (forward operating bases).

With 450 men in the mountains, the Royal Marines of 45 Commando carried out an arduous two-week operation combing the mountains and sweeping hide-outs and caves. Their finds included a complex of mountain caves housing tanks, artillery, guns and vast quantities of ammunition. Brigadier Lane, in command, described the efforts of his men as being 'of supreme human endeavour'.[4] The captured

arms and ammunition were destroyed in the caves in what was described as the largest controlled explosion by British forces since World War II. The operation was considered a great success in the war on terrorism and helped bring peace and stability to the area.

Operation Buzzard Following the success of Operation Snipe, the next operation launched, codenamed Operation Buzzard, was much closer to the Pakistan border. Soon the Royal Marines were in combat with insurgents, killing a number of them on 23 May before the terrorists fled the area. The Royal Marines then continued to mount their effective patrols in the region. Throughout the period the Royal Marines were fully supported by the RAF with transport aircraft and Chinook helicopters as well as artillery support from the army, all backed up by sea-based logistics.

Operation Oracle From September 2001 the UK contribution (codenamed Operation Oracle) to the US-led war on terrorism, codenamed Operation Enduring Freedom, was significantly increased, with over forty ships, submarines and RFA support ships and tankers deployed to the Gulf region. Nineteen units from exercise Saif Sareea II, including over 7,000 people, were retained in the area and changed from exercise status to full operational readiness. Units from ten other nations including Australia and Japan reinforced the Royal Navy Task Group.

By the end of 2001 the Oracle Task Group in the Middle East included the flagship *Illustrious*, the assault ship *Fearless*, the destroyer *Southampton*, the frigate *Cornwall* and the

TLAM-armed fleet submarine *Trafalgar*, supported by RFAS *Fort George, Fort Rosalie, Brambleleaf, Diligence, Sir Tristram* and *Sir Percival*.

Other Activities

Earthquake in Turkey On 17 November 1999 *Ocean* was returning to UK on completion of exercise Bright Star when she was diverted to the Turkish coast to conduct emergency relief operations following the major earthquake centred on Duzce. The Sea King helicopters played an important part in distributing emergency supplies and transporting rescue teams and repair parties.

Hurricane 'Lenny' In the Caribbean the frigate *Northumberland* was ordered to Anguilla on 18 November 1999 to provide humanitarian assistance in the wake of Hurricane 'Lenny'. The following day she broke off relief work and sailed to rescue the MV *Pride de la Dominique* and towed her into Road Bay, Anguilla, before resuming emergency relief work for a further three days.

Mozambique Floods At the beginning of 2000 the auxiliary oiler replenishment ship RFA *Fort George* was deployed to Mozambique to provide emergency relief aid following major flooding. On arrival she joined the international humanitarian operation, and with her five Sea King helicopters she was able to play an important role in transporting rescue teams and distributing emergency supplies. RFA *Fort George* received praise from many countries for the important contribution she made to the rescue mission.

Greek Ferry Disaster On 26 September 2000 the Greek-registered ferry MV *Express Samina* ran aground off the island of Paros. The frigate *Cumberland* quickly arrived on the scene and assisted in the rescue operation, managing to save many people.

Loss of the *Kursk* Later in 2000 the Russian nuclear submarine *Kursk* sank in a tragic accident in the Barents Sea. On 12 August she was taking part in an exercise and was preparing to fire two dummy torpedoes at the battlecruiser *Peter the Great*, flagship of the Northern Fleet. There appeared to be an explosion when the torpedo propellant ignited, which triggered a chain reaction leading to more violent explosions and the submarine sank. As soon as news of the accident became known Britain offered full support to the Russian Navy, but by the time the offer was accepted and the Royal Navy rescue submersible 'LR 5' deployed to the area in a support ship it was too late to save any of the crew.

Operation Peninsula At the beginning of April 2001 the Royal Navy was called in to assist in controlling the outbreak and spread of foot and mouth disease in Britain as part of Operation Peninsula. The Navy contributed two teams, totalling 170 personnel, in Devon and South Wales, each team working continuously for periods of fourteen days at

The nuclear submarine *Triumph*, with the frigate *Northumberland*, after firing her TLAMs against terrorist targets in Afghanistan
(NN)

The Type 22 frigate *Cumberland*
(NP)

a time. The operation lasted for two months, and during that time a total of 550 naval personnel took part.

Operation Fresco No sooner had personnel stood down from Operation Peninsular than the fire-fighters of Merseyside went on strike on 13 July 2001. As Army personnel were still engaged with foot and mouth operations, the Navy and RAF were required to provide all emergency fire-fighting cover during the period of the strike. The Navy set up fire and rescue teams and manned the 'Green Goddess' fire engines. The Operation Fresco teams responded to 856 call-outs, many more than usual due to hoax calls, and put out some serious fires with no loss of life. The strike ended on 26 July, and service personnel returned to their normal work the following day.

Although the army was not involved, it was interesting that much of the press referred to the 'army' as providing the assistance during the strike.

Submarine Service Centennial In 2001 the Submarine Service celebrated its 100th anniversary with a wide range of events. These included parades by the Barrow branch and the London branch of the Submariners' Association and the Submarine Service Colour in Faslane, as well as a lunch in the Mansion House hosted by the Corporation of the City of London. The Royal Navy Submarine Museum in Gosport, established as the regimental focus for the Submarine Service, was the centrepiece of the centennial celebrations.

International Festival of the Sea 2001 The International Festival of the Sea held at Portsmouth naval base at the end of August 2001 was the largest maritime celebration ever held up to that time. With contributions from both the army and the RAF, it was also the first tri-service event held outside London, and replaced the Royal Tournament.

Life at Sea in the Royal Navy, 1958–2008

In 1958, most ratings onboard ship lived in large messes. The After Mess in frigates, Type 12s – and in the later *Leander*s – was for 55 men, most of whom slept in hammocks; there were a few bunks round the bulkheads. The Ton Class sweepers were all bunks. Kit was stowed in a locker, and basic training taught how to use every bit of space. Few ships had cafeteria messing, and food was brought down to the Mess individually, and eaten in a mess square – the small living area. It was not always easy to transfer the meal from the galley, to your sometimes distant mess. Washing up was done most unhygienically in buckets. The introduction of a dedicated ship's cafeteria Mess also allowed for briefing space, church services, and films, educational and entertaining. Senior Rates had a sleeping area, with double or triple bunks, and a very small living space. In Type 12s, and *Leander*s, the Forward POs Mess was ahead of the 4.5" turret, which meant that in any seaway the mess was distinctly lively, with slamming and regular pitching. Officers had single cabins, roughly 6' by 6' by 7', which for most was also their office and Divisional space: bunks had drawers and a small bureau, a small combination classified document safe, and a key safe. Heating was by 'black' radiator.

Messes in more modern ships became smaller but slightly more spacious. More and more electronic equipment – computers, communication sets, radars – required to be air-conditioned, and eventually the designers decided it was easier to air condition the whole ship rather than having individual plants. This made a dramatic difference, especially in the humid tropics. Up until then, when weather permitted, many sailors had slept on the upper deck.

Ship movement could be severe. Regular rolling in storms could be up to 55 degrees. When ships started to operate helicopters stabilisers had to be fitted, which reduced rolling dramatically.

The RN Film Corporation provided rental copies of reel-to-reel films. Perhaps weekly these would be shown in the Mess, on a sheet hung from the deck head. Eventually tapes and DVDs mostly replaced films, and Messes acquired TVs. There was also the SRE (Ships Radio Equipment), which provided constant music, quizzes, news and general information during the day interrupted by the Main Broadcast when necessary. Card and board games were normal, Uckers being the favourite board game, played on a Ludo board, but much more complex. By the

'Hands to bathe': members of the ship's company from the aircraft carrier *Eagle* swim close alongside
(NN)

1970s some ships had tiny TV studios, producing their own programmes, and ship's one or two sheet newspapers would appear regularly. Occasionally each mess would produce an act for a SOD's Opera – originally the Ship's Operatic and Dramatic Society – basically a Concert.

There were various ways of keeping fit. The ship's PTI, Physical Training Instructor would run keep fit sessions and on the Flight Deck, when the ship's programme permitted, there was Deck Hockey. Later ships had their own keep fit spaces, with various pieces of training equipment.

If the ship's programme permitted there would be Hands to Bathe, usually in the First Dog Watch; the seaboat would be launched, lookouts posted against sharks, jumping ladders rigged, and the ship stopped. Ashore the ship would have

football, rugby and cricket teams, and both inter-ship and inter mess games were normal.

Waste at sea was at first basic: eventually International Laws meant that ships had sewage treatment plants, where the end result was pure water, and rubbish ('gash') had to be processed onboard. Drinking Water except in nuclear submarines was always in limited supply. If one of the ship's evaporators became unserviceable, especially in the tropics, life became unpleasant.

The ship was kept spotlessly clean. Every evening there would be Rounds (an inspection) of living spaces, including heads and showers. Usually each month the Captain would carry out more formal Rounds of the ship.

Lieut Commander Ken Napier MBE, RN

SHIPS, AIRCRAFT AND WEAPONS

Joint Force 2000 Major changes in naval aviation occurred on 1 April 2000 with the demise of the Flag Officer Naval Aviation. A Joint Force 2000 (JF 2000) was created by combining the air defence strike RN Sea Harrier FA2 with the ground attack RAF Harrier GR7 as a part of RAF Strike Command. The aircraft of 800 and 801 NAS were to be collocated at RAF Cottesmore with RAF No 1(F), 3(F) and IV(AC) Squadrons by 2003. JF 2000, commanded by a rear admiral, increased the operational capability within the sphere of maritime operations.

JHC In roughly the same time frame a new JHC was created to combine all the battlefield helicopters. The JHC was formed at Wilton on 1 October 1999 and included the Navy's Sea King commando helicopters together with the Royal Marines' Lynx and Gazelle helicopters as well as army and Air Force battlefield helicopters. The total JHC force included 12,000 sailors, soldiers and airmen with control over some 350 helicopters.

PERSONNEL MATTERS

Defence Training Review A defence training review was established in September 1999 as part of Lord Robertson's study of education and training in the armed forces and the Civil Service. The fundamental review resulted in the introduction of a number of reforms and improvements and established a defence-wide training policy.

Pay 2000 Following detailed study of armed forces' pay by the independent review as well as the Armed Forces' Pay Review Body, recommendations were made for a new pay structure. It was the first major change to the pay of the armed forces since the introduction of the Military Salary nearly thirty years earlier. The aim of Pay 2000 was to introduce a system which was flexible, and more closely linked to actual job content and weight rather than just rank and seniority. It achieved greater accuracy in terms of comparability with pay levels in civilian life.

It was a complex and fundamental change which took over a year to implement. Because it incorporated differentials for job loadings within the same rank, there were inevitably those whose pay was not increased as much as that of others with the same rank or rate and seniority, which caused a certain amount of disappointment. It was to be a few years before the new system was fully understood and accepted by all.

Project TopMast A new system for manning ships and managing people, known as 'TopMast' (Tomorrow's Personnel Management System), was introduced in 2001 to improve the deployment of naval service personnel. TopMast followed through an SDR requirement to move people closer to the centre of defence business. The aim was to adopt a more flexible and responsive strategy for manning ships, in particular roles for specific operations, rather than just

attempting to man all ships for all roles at all times. One of the key elements was a concept called 'Swing' which enabled personnel to be moved around to meet specific requirements.

OWP (Operational Welfare Package) Following a major review in 1999, a tri-service Operational Welfare Package was introduced in April 2001 to provide support for personnel deployed on operations. The package provided a range of communication facilities, including free phone calls, e-mails, letter and parcel facilities, newspapers and television access as well as fitness equipment, all designed to maintain morale for personnel deployed on difficult operations.

Executive Committee of the White Ensign Association at HMS *Dryad* (WEA)

The White Ensign Association In 1999 Sir Michael Bett relieved Admiral Sir Michael Layard as Chairman of the White Ensign Association, and Admiral Sir Jock Slater joined the Council shortly after being relieved as First Sea Lord. Lord Younger, recent Secretary of State for Defence, also joined the Council.

The Association continued to work with the Commander in Chief Fleet in arranging for senior influential people to go to sea with the Royal Navy, and for the first time it was able to arrange for a few important people to go to sea in a submarine, *Sovereign*. One of the most popular visits was to the frigate *Marlborough*, deployed as guardship to the Caribbean. A total of twenty-eight senior business people went to sea to meet personnel and to have the opportunity to observe the high quality, experience and dedication of those serving.

In 2000 the Association arranged for a range of senior people to go to sea with the Royal Navy in a variety of visits from aircraft carriers to nuclear submarines. It also hosted a reception and presentation by the RNPT (Royal Navy Presentation Team) at the Royal Marines Museum at Eastney.

In 2001 the Association visited the School of Maritime Operations at HMS *Dryad* and was greatly impressed with the standards of training and the quality of the simulators, in the case of both operations team training and the 'Amethyst' bridge simulator. Over the year the Association was able to arrange for a series of visits from captains of industry to eleven ships of the Fleet including *Ark Royal* and *Ocean*, which proved very popular.

CHAPTER 13

The Second Gulf War – Operation Telic 2002–2004

OPERATIONS ENDURING FREEDOM AND ORACLE – IRAQ AND THE SECOND GULF WAR –
OPERATIONS TELIC AND JAMES – NTG 03 AND AURORA 04 DEPLOYMENTS

The early years of the twenty-first century were completely overshadowed by the audacious attacks on the World Trade Center in New York and the Pentagon on 11 September 2001 ('9/11'). The moment the hijacked aircraft crashed into their targets, slaughtering some 3,000 people, the scene was set for subsequent military operations in the Middle East. In the following year the Security Council of the United Nations passed Resolution 1441, demanding that Saddam Hussein disarm or face 'serious consequences', and the United States Congress authorised the President to use the US armed forces as 'he' considered necessary and appropriate against Iraq. Although Saddam Hussein accepted the UN resolution, he gave every appearance of continuing to defy the international community, and events were then in train for the Second Gulf War. The USA subsequently launched Operation Enduring Freedom in its fight against international terrorism.

In the UK the Labour government of Tony Blair had been re-elected in 2001 and close political and military links with the USA were maintained. The USA, in great need of firm loyal allies in its fight against terrorism in the West, was keen to maintain the 'special relationship' with the UK.

UK Defence Policy

Following the '9/11' terrorist attacks the basic UK defence policy as set out originally in the 1998 Strategic Defence Review, with its range of missions and tasks, needed to be revised and adapted to meet the new emerging threats. A fresh strategic guidance set out in 2003 developed a revised framework of military tasks, with a wide and flexible range of options. For the Royal Navy this involved several basic elements.

Joint Operations and Amphibious Capability The Royal Navy had to develop a range of plans and tactical concepts to enhance the prime requirements of swift strategic deployability with 'effects based operations' and 'network enabled capability'. Rapid and flexible reaction capability, including MCJO (the Maritime Contribution to Joint Operations), was an important element, and much emphasis was put on joint operations and amphibious warfare capability.

Power Projection Also important was power projection, and the fleet submarines were being equipped with cruise missiles, the TLAMS (Tomahawk Land Attack Missile System). The nuclear submarines *Trafalgar*, *Triumph* and *Splendid* were the first to be fitted for TLAMS. *Splendid* had fired TLAMs in anger for the first time in the Adriatic against

FIRST SEA LORDS
*Admirals
Essenhigh and
West*

SECOND SEA LORDS
*Admirals Spencer
and
Burnell-Nugent*

MANPOWER
41,550

MERCANTILE MARINE
*1,945
merchant ships*

targets in Kosovo in March 1999; *Triumph* and *Trafalgar* had fired TLAMs in anger in November 2001, when they launched missiles against Taliban and Al Qaeda targets in Afghanistan at a range of 950 miles. These were the opening salvos in the coalition's 'war against terror'.

The 2004 Defence Review Unfortunately the 2004 defence review, announced by Geoff Hoon, the Defence Secretary, in July of that year resulted in a further series of cuts to Britain's armed forces. The cuts to the Royal Navy included the axing of 1,500 personnel by 2008 and the paying-off early of twelve ships. The ships to go included three Type 42 destroyers, *Newcastle*, *Cardiff* and *Glasgow*, and three Type 23 frigates, *Norfolk*, *Marlborough* and *Grafton* (*Grafton* was only seven years old but was facing an expensive refit). Three Hunt class minehunters, *Brecon*, *Cottesmore* and *Dulverton*, were to go as also were three *Sandown* class MCMVs (mine counter-measures vessels), *Sandown*, *Inverness* and *Bridport*. The fleet submarines were to be reduced from eleven to eight by 2008, and the number of Nimrod maritime reconnaissance aircraft was to be reduced from twenty-one to sixteen. On the plus side, two more Type 45 destroyers were to be ordered, taking the total to eight, and the strength of the Royal Marines was to be increased.

THE FLEET

Carriers and Amphibious Ships In 2002 the Fleet consisted of the three aircraft carriers of the *Invincible* class. *Invincible*, by then well over twenty years old, was undergoing a refit in Rosyth and was due to rejoin the Fleet the following year though it had been announced that it was planned for her to be placed in reserve in 2006. *Illustrious* was due to start her refit at the end of 2003. The Fleet had a powerful amphibious component, which included the new 20,500-ton amphibious helicopter carrier *Ocean* (the biggest ship in the Fleet). The veteran amphibious ship *Fearless* was about to be paid off, and two new 19,500-ton *Albion* class assault ships were nearing completion, with *Albion* due in 2003 and *Bulwark* in 2004.

The Escort Fleet, MCMVs and Support Ships The escort fleet consisted of eleven Type 42 air defence destroyers, four Type 22 ASW (anti-submarine warfare) frigates and sixteen new Type 23 general purpose frigates. The MCM (mine counter-measures) force was made up of twenty-two MCMVs of the

Hunt and *Sandown* classes, and there were twenty-three patrol vessels, one ice patrol vessel, three hydrographic vessels and twenty-two auxiliaries, tankers and replenishment ships, manned by the RFA (Royal Fleet Auxiliary).

The Submarine Fleet The powerful submarine fleet consisted of the four Trident SSBNs (ballistic missile-carrying nuclear submarines) of the *Vanguard* class, operating the nation's nuclear deterrent, and twelve conventionally armed SSNs (nuclear-powered fleet submarines) of the *Trafalgar* and *Swiftsure* classes. As mentioned above, submarines of both the *Trafalgar* and *Swiftsure* classes were being armed with TLAMS. Unfortunately the fleet submarines were to be reduced to a total of eight by 2008.

The Fleet Air Arm and Royal Marines The Royal Navy operated a Fleet Air Arm of twenty-four FA2 Sea Harriers and 131 helicopters, as well as various training aircraft. It also had an amphibious brigade, 3 Commando Brigade, Royal Marines, which included 40, 42 and 45 Commandos, with full supporting arms.

Command The Fleet was commanded in 2002 by CINCFLEET (the Commander in Chief, Fleet) Admiral Sir Jonathan Band, being relieved by Admiral Sir James Burnell-Nugent in 2004. Rear Admiral David Snelson was COMUKMARFOR (Commander UK Maritime Force) and he was relieved later by Rear Admiral Charles Style.

Rear Admiral Submarines was Rear Admiral Niall Kilgour, Flag Officer Maritime Air was Rear Admiral Scott Lidbetter and the Commandant General Royal Marines (CGRM) was Major General Tony Milton.

New Fleet Headquarters On 2 April 2002 a new 'single headquarters' concept for the Royal Navy was launched in Portsmouth. The concept combined the staff necessary for the three separate functions of Force Generation, Force Deployment and Resource Management in a single head-quarters to achieve much greater efficiency as well as cost savings. The headquarters took several years to complete in its new purpose-built complex, named the Leach Building, at Whale Island on the outskirts of Portsmouth.

The Princess Royal finally dedicated the Leach Building on 21 October 2004. Admiral of the Fleet Sir Henry Leach was the guest of honour at the ceremony, and the Princess Royal unveiled a painting of him briefing Margaret Thatcher on a task force to retake the Falklands in 1982.

FIRST SEA LORD

Admiral Sir Alan West Alan West was born in 1948 and joined the Royal Navy in 1965. After a succession of sea appointments he was promoted Commander in 1980 and took command of the frigate *Ardent*, which sailed with the Falklands Task Force in 1982 and on 21 May was bombed in Falkland Sound and sunk. He was awarded a DSC for his leadership during the campaign.

HMS *Albion*
Albion Class Landing Platform Dock

The *Albion* class of two amphibious assault ships (officially landing platform docks) was designed to replace the veteran *Fearless* class of two smaller assault ships, which had provided such great service with the Fleet for nearly forty years. Like their predecessors, the ships have a floodable well dock aft which can accommodate four landing craft, and although they do not have a hangar they can operate heavy-lift helicopters and up to three Merlin EH 101 helicopters. They can carry thirty armoured vehicles or six Challenger main battle tanks and up to a maximum of 710 troops in austere conditions.

Launched:	9 March 2001
Commissioned:	19 June 2003
Displacement:	19,560 tonnes
Length:	176m
Propulsion:	2 shaft integrated full electric propulsion,
	2 Wartsila 16V 32E 6.25 MW and
	2 Wartsila 4R 32E 1.56 MW diesel generators
	2 AC motors bow thruster unit
Armament:	Guns 2-20mm (twin),
	2 Goalkeeper close-in weapon system,
	4 7.62mm machine guns,
	platform for 3 Merlin EH 101, Chinook capable
Complement:	325, up to 305 troops (710 overload)
No. in class:	2 *Albion* and *Bulwark*

He commanded the guided missile destroyer *Bristol* and served in the Plans Division at MoD. The press made much of an incident in 1986 when he misplaced classified documents concerning cuts in the Fleet; a freelance journalist subsequently found the papers on a towpath. He was promoted Rear Admiral in 1994 and appointed Naval Secretary. Two years later he became Commander UK Task Group (COMUKTG), and he commanded the Ocean Wave 97 Task Group to the Far East. In 1997 he was appointed Chief of Defence Intelligence, and in 2000 Commander in Chief Fleet. He relieved Admiral Essenhigh as First Sea Lord in September 2002 and served for three and a half years in the appointment. Subsequently he was made Baron West of Spithead and appointed as a Parliamentary Under-Secretary of State with responsibility for security.

OPERATIONS AND DEPLOYMENTS, 2002–2004

Standing Commitments

Although the focus of operations was very much on the Middle East, including the eastern Mediterranean, the Royal Navy continued to maintain standing commitments and deployments in other parts of the world.

Atlantic Patrol Task (South) The Type 23 frigate *Monmouth* was on Atlantic Patrol Task (South) and, together with the offshore patrol vessel *Leeds Castle*, was deployed to the Falkland Islands and Antarctica. *Leeds Castle* was permanently on station for three to four years and regularly visited South Georgia and other British dependencies in the far South Atlantic. She was finally withdrawn from the South Atlantic in October 2004 to be replaced by her sister ship *Dumbarton Castle*. The ice patrol vessel *Endurance* was also in the area and was midway through a seasonal deployment in Antarctica for the austral summer.

Atlantic Patrol Task (North) RFA *Oakleaf* was on station in the Caribbean supporting the destroyer or frigate assigned to the Atlantic Patrol Task (North). At the beginning of March the destroyer *Newcastle* arrived in the Caribbean and started a busy six-month deployment in the area. The Royal Navy ships provided major support to the counter-drugs operations in the Caribbean. Subsequent deployments were provided by the frigates *Grafton* and *Iron Duke*, though *Iron Duke* had to deploy, with RFA *Black Rover*, across the Atlantic to Freetown in January 2003 for several months in support of operations in Sierra Leone.

Fishery Protection The Fishery Protection Squadron, operating its eleven vessels of the Hunt, Island and Castle classes, kept up its important task of policing and enforcing EEC fishery policies under the direction of DEFRA (Department for the Environment, Food and Rural Affairs), as well as protecting the vital offshore oil and gas platforms.

Northern Ireland Patrols and ongoing security operations

Admiral Sir Alan West
(WEA)

The frigate *Iron Duke* on Atlantic Patrol Task (North) duties
(NP)

in, and around, Northern Ireland were maintained, with specialist Royal Marine boarding teams supporting Operation Lifespan off the coast of Northern Ireland. 42 Commando Royal Marines carried out a six-month tour of duty on Operation Banner in support of the civil authorities in south Armagh, returning to the mainland in September 2002. The Royal Marines completed their last tour of duty in Northern Ireland in 2004, by which time they had carried out over forty tours of duty in the Province. During the course of their tours they had lost sixteen killed, plus a further eleven killed on the mainland and ninety-five wounded.

Gibraltar The coastal patrol craft *Ranger* and *Trumpeter*, which had been stationed in Gibraltar since 1991, were armed with GPMGs (general purpose machine guns) in 2002. At the end of that year two former Northern Ireland patrol craft, *Greyfox* and *Greywolf*, were deployed to Gibraltar and in the following January they were commissioned as *Scimitar* and *Sabre*. They were smaller and faster than *Ranger* and *Trumpeter*. Later in 2003 *Trumpeter* returned to the UK

but *Ranger* remained with the Gibraltar Squadron until the following year.

Cyprus The armed patrol craft *Pursuer* and *Dasher* were deployed to Cyprus. Together with a detachment of Royal Marines and two fast inshore patrol boats, they provided force protection patrols for the Sovereign Base Area.

Armilla Patrol The Royal Navy continued to maintain the important Armilla Patrol in the Gulf and the Straits of Hormuz, carrying out MIOPs (maritime interdiction operations).

At the beginning of the year the Type 23 frigate *Kent* was on patrol and made an important interception. *Kent* tracked a sanction-breaking ship, the MV *Dana*, which was carrying 4,000 tons of oil, and when the ship finally entered international waters after two days the *Kent*'s Royal Marine boarding party swiftly boarded her. The *Dana* immobilised her engines but, undaunted, *Kent* took her in tow, taking her to the United Nations holding area in the northern Gulf.

The Type 23 frigate *Kent*
(NN)

Kent then returned to her patrol area, going on to intercept over ten more sanction-breakers. In the course of a five-month patrol *Kent* seized 40,000 tons of illegal cargo, worth over £4 million.

NATO Assignments At the end of 2001 the Royal Navy was continuing to assign ships to NATO standing naval forces.

STANAVFORLANT The frigate *Norfolk* was assigned to STANAVFORLANT (the Standing Naval Force Atlantic), operating in the eastern Mediterranean on Operation Active Endeavour and deployed on interdiction tasks along the Syrian and Lebanese coasts. Later the frigate *Cornwall*, which acted as the flagship of the force, relieved her.

STANAVFORMED Also operating in the eastern Mediterranean was the frigate *Chatham*, assigned to STANAVFORMED (the Standing Naval Force Mediterranean) as command ship to directing operations as part of Operation Direct Endeavour. The frigate *Sheffield* sailed from

Portsmouth on 5 February to relieve *Chatham* for a six-month tour as the flagship, and *Chatham* returned home to Devonport at the end of February. The frigate *Northumberland* later relieved *Sheffield*.

NATO MCMFOR (N) The offshore patrol vessel *Dumbarton Castle* (known affectionately as the 'DC') was flagship of the NATO MCMFOR (N) (NATO Mine Counter-Measures Force North). She served from May 2002 for a year, providing command and support facilities. The force was also supported by the roulement of the MCMVs *Walney* and *Inverness*. The British ships led the very successful multi-national exercise Blue Game in the Baltic Sea. Later the MCMFOR (N) joined the major naval exercise JMC (Joint Maritime Course) 032.

Nuclear Deterrent Patrols Throughout the period the Trident nuclear deterrent submarines *Victorious*, *Vigilant* and *Vengeance* of the SSBN Squadron, with their Trident D5 ballistic nuclear missiles, continued to maintain their ceaseless deterrent patrols, hidden in the depths of the world's oceans. By 2003 the *Vanguard* class Trident sub-

The Type 23 frigate
Portland
(RH)

marines had completed forty-five operational patrols, bringing the total number of deterrent patrols carried out by the Royal Navy, since taking over full responsibility for the UK's strategic deterrent in 1969, to 280. The first Trident submarine, *Vanguard*, was taken out of the patrol cycle in February 2002 to start the first Trident submarine refit in the new SSBN 'D154' refit facility in Devonport.

The Ongoing Operation Enduring Freedom

In 2002 the Royal Navy was contributing ships to the MIF (Maritime Interdiction Force) in the Gulf, whilst Royal Marines were fighting the Taliban and Al Qaeda and hunting Osama Bin Laden in the Tora Bora range of mountains in southern Afghanistan. At the same time British and US ships maintained a cordon off the coast to ensure that Osama Bin Laden did not escape from the region by sea. All such operations were conducted as part of the overall Operation Enduring Freedom, the worldwide campaign against international terrorism.

Operation Oracle In early 2002 *Illustrious*, in the LPH (landing platform helicopter) role, was in the Arabian Sea operating with the US Navy carrier battle groups based on the nuclear carriers USS *Theodore Roosevelt* and USS *J C Stennis*. She was leading the British Task Group as part of Operation Oracle.

The Task Group included the assault ship *Fearless*, the destroyer *Southampton*, the frigate *Cornwall*, the submarine *Trafalgar* and RFAS *Fort George*, *Fort Rosalie*, *Brambleleaf*, *Diligence*, *Sir Tristram* and *Sir Percivale*. It had completed the very successful exercise Saif Sareea II and was well placed to play a prominent role in the developing war against terrorism. The Task Force had already assisted with the establishment of the UK-led ISAF (International Security and Assistance Force) by deploying the Royal Marines of 40 Commando to Bagram in Afghanistan. Ships from other countries including Australia and Japan, as well as NATO countries, soon joined the ISAF.

Amphibious Ready Group On 11 February 2002 a task group led by the helicopter assault ship *Ocean*, with 45 Commando Royal Marines embarked, escorted by the destroyer *York*, forming the Amphibious Ready Group, sailed from Portsmouth bound for the Indian Ocean. The frigate *Campbeltown* sailed later from Devonport to join the group. The group made a fast passage, transiting across the Mediterranean and on through the Suez Canal. At the beginning of March the Amphibious Ready Group, which also included the TLAM-capable submarine, *Superb*, arrived in the Gulf and rendezvoused with the *Illustrious* group to return to the UK after its prolonged deployment.

In addition the ships of the Armilla Patrol were active in the area and included the frigates *Portland* and *Argyll*, carrying out MIOPS. The Armilla ships had specially trained RN and RM (Royal Marine) boarding parties on board, which were inserted on non-compliant ships and tankers by fast boat or rapid roping from helicopters. In early April, 45

Ocean returns to Plymouth (NN)

Commando was disembarked from *Ocean* and flown to south-east Afghanistan to join Operation Jacana in hunting Al Qaeda and the terrorist training bases.

At the end of May the decision was taken for the flagship of the Amphibious Ready Group, *Ocean*, escorted by *York* and supported by RFA *Fort George*, to return to the UK. With the Royal Marines of 45 Commando well established ashore in Afghanistan and operating from their staging base at Bagram airfield, the *Ocean* Group sailed from the area, returning to the UK in June.

In the meantime RFAS *Sir Tristram*, *Sir Percivale* and *Fort Austin* remained in the Indian Ocean to support the Royal Marines deployed in southern Afghanistan as part of Task Force Jacana on Operations Ptarmigan and Snipe.

Operations Veritas and Jacana The main campaigns against the Taliban and the Al Qaeda training bases in Afghanistan, codenamed Operations Jacana and Veritas, continued in 2002. The Royal Marines, who had been the first of the coalition forces to enter Kabul, spearheaded the ongoing operations, working very closely with US forces.

Attack on the Tanker MV *Limburg* A timely reminder of the need for vigilance at sea happened on 6 October 2002. The undefended French oil tanker MV *Limburg* was approaching the oil terminal at Minah al Dabah in the Gulf of Aden at slow speed when terrorists in fast speedboats attacked her. The terrorists took the ship completely by surprise and severely damaged her. The attack took place just two years after the destroyer USS *Cole* was rammed by terrorists in a speedboat packed with explosives in the port of Aden and was badly damaged.

THE SECOND GULF WAR, 19 MARCH – 1 MAY 2003

Operation Telic

Throughout 2002 Britain, the USA and their main Western allies undertook intensive military planning and preparations for military intervention in Iraq, to enforce United Nations security resolutions. The planning was to result in Operation Telic and a great build-up of Western forces in the Gulf Area. On 29 November the plan for the deployment of NTG 03 (Naval Task Group 03) was announced, and intense detailed planning could proceed. It was not long before naval personnel started to refer to Operation Telic as 'Tell Everyone Leave Is Cancelled!'[1]

Task Force NTG 03 The UK's main naval contribution to Operation Telic consisted of Task Force NTG 03, headed by the flagship *Ark Royal*, with the Amphibious Task Group, comprising primarily fifteen warships, two submarines, fourteen RFA support ships and tankers and 3 Commando Brigade, Royal Marines. It was the biggest amphibious deployment since the Falklands War and totalled over 5,500 personnel. Rear Admiral David Snelson, COMUKTG, commanded the Task Force, and Commodore Jamie Miller was COMATG (Commander Amphibious Task Group). Admiral Snelson was to be based ashore in Bahrain with the US Navy Central Command.

Original Planned Deployment The original planning in early 2002 was for NTG 03, combined with the Amphibious Task Group, to sail from the UK in January 2003 for a major out-of-area group deployment to the Far East. The Task Group would take part in exercise Flying Fish 03, which was the main annual FPDA (the Five-Power Defence Arrangement) naval and air exercise in the Pacific. NTG 03 was a powerful force consisting of *Ark Royal, Ocean, York, Edinburgh, Liverpool* and *Marlborough* supported by RFAs *Sir Galahad, Sir Tristram, Sir Percivale, Fort Victoria, Fort Austin, Fort Rosalie, Argus* and *Orangeleaf* plus several chartered commercial support ships. The force was intended to deploy to the Gulf, en route to the Pacific Ocean.

All Change In the latter half of 2002, as Saddam Hussein continued to obstruct the UN, it became clear that action in the Gulf would be required to demonstrate the will and authority of the international community as manifest in the UN. The Security Council of the United Nations unanimously passed Resolution 1441 in November, but although Saddam Hussein agreed to admit UN arms inspectors, his regime continued to obstruct them in every way it possibly could. Accordingly the programme for the deployment was modified.

Ark Royal was re-roled from fixed-wing carrier to helicopter carrier for operations in the Gulf. The Defence Secretary stated on 7 January 2003 that Saddam Hussein needed to be presented with a clear and credible threat of force and went on to announce the deployment of the naval Task Force to the region. On 20 January the land forces to be deployed were announced, though it took until 6 February before the make-up of the air component was announced.

Operation Iraqi Freedom From the beginning of January various ships and units started to deploy to the Gulf region as part of the coalition build-up for the US-led Operation Iraqi Freedom.

Ark Royal **Sails** The main Task Force, NTG 03, consisting of the flagship *Ark Royal* in her LPH (helicopter assault) role and her escorts, *York, Edinburgh, Liverpool* and *Marlborough*, sailed out of Portsmouth in the afternoon of Friday 10 January. It was a bright cloudless day but very cold; nevertheless thousands of people thronged the shores of old Portsmouth and lined the walls of Southsea Castle to watch and wave farewell. There had been a great deal of press

interest in the event, which encouraged crowds of people to turn up and wave the fleet off to war, as had happened many times before at important moments of history. On emerging from the Solent the Task Force increased speed and headed west down the Channel.

Royal Fleet Auxiliaries On 15 January many of the RFA vessels supporting the Task Group sailed from various UK ports. The RFAs included the fleet replenishment ships *Fort Rosalie, Fort Austin* and *Fort Victoria*, the LSL (landing ships, logistic) *Sir Galahad, Sir Tristram* and *Sir Percivale* and the aviation support ship *Argus* in her role as a primary casualty reception ship. Other RFA vessels, including the tanker *Bayleaf*, the LSL *Sir Bedivere* and the forward repair ship *Diligence*, were already in the Gulf region, whilst the tankers *Orangeleaf* and *Oakleaf* were in the Mediterranean. A number of civilian charter ships also sailed to support the Task Force.

HMS *Ocean* On the morning of Thursday 16 January *Ocean*, with 40 Commando Royal Marines and the twelve Lynx and Gazelle helicopters of 847 NAS (Naval Air Squadron) embarked, put to sea, sailing out of Devonport with her decks lined in full ceremonial 'Procedure Alpha'. The Type 23 frigate *Northumberland* escorted her. It was a clear, bitterly cold day but thousands of people as well as large numbers of the press lined the shores to wave good-bye and send off *Ocean* in style, with a Royal Marine band playing and thousands of Union Jacks waving. Once out of Plymouth Sound *Ocean* altered course to starboard and increased speed to eighteen knots, heading down the Channel. As she steamed west she embarked the ten Sea King helicopters of 845 NAS. On emerging into the Atlantic the ships altered course south-west to cross the Bay of Biscay in very heavy seas. On 20 January *Ocean* headed east, passing through the Straits of Gibraltar en route to Cyprus.

Other Elements Other ships such as the frigates *Cornwall* and *Chatham* and other support ships sailed independently, whilst the minehunters of the 1st MCM Squadron, *Bangor, Blyth, Brocklesby* and *Sandown* and their support ship, RFA *Sir Bedivere*, had already deployed to the Mediterranean. The minehunters transited through the Suez Canal in December and sailed on to Jebel Ali. Once in the Gulf they were able to acclimatise and gain valuable experience working up in the area of operations. The destroyer *Cardiff* and the frigate *Cumberland* were already in the Gulf along with RFAs *Brambleleaf* and *Grey Rover* and the newly arrived RFA *Orangeleaf*.

Off Cyprus As the various elements of the Task Force reached the Mediterranean they rendezvoused and sailed on to Cyprus. *Ocean* and her group arrived off the coast of Cyprus on 26 January, and 40 Commando conducted four days of amphibious assault rehearsals on the beaches and coastline of the Sovereign Base Area. The rehearsals included a night assault to ensure that they were ready for any eventuality.

On to the Gulf On completion of the exercises ships started to pass through the Suez Canal, with *Ocean* following on 1 February and then sailing on into the Red Sea. As *Ocean* steamed down the Red Sea she was able to conduct acclimatisation exercises and a busy flying programme. Reaching the southern end of the sea and altering course east into the Gulf of Aden, she closed up in 'defence watches'. By 15 February the bulk of the Task Force had assembled in the theatre of operations in the Gulf.

Clandestine Operations Whilst the various elements of the Task Force were en route in January, some ships were already in the northern Gulf. Deployed forward was one of the oldest ships in the Royal Navy, the coastal survey ship *Roebuck*. *Roebuck* operated her survey motor launch, *Bachelor's Delight*, inside Iraqi territorial waters in clandestine missions conducted in the dark. Whilst *Cumberland* acted as guardship off shore, the motor launch bravely surveyed the coastal approaches and the inshore waterway of Khawr' Abd Allah. The valuable accurate surveys, which covered the main shipping channel round Bubiyan Island and up to the port of Umm Qasr, were then distributed to ships of the Task Force as they arrived, including the US forces.

US Naval Task Forces The US Navy was assembling five powerful CBGs (carrier battle groups), two in the eastern Mediterranean with the 6th Fleet and three in the Gulf with the 5th Fleet. The US forces were deploying under Operation Falconer.

The flagship of the US 5th Fleet in the Gulf was the strike carrier USS *Constellation*. The other CBGs in the Gulf theatre of operations were formed on the strike carrier USS *Kitty Hawk* and the nuclear strike carrier USS *Abraham Lincoln*. Meanwhile in the eastern Mediterranean the nuclear strike carriers USS *Harry S Truman* and USS *Theodore Roosevelt* were deployed to conduct flank operations with the 6th Fleet.

Coalition Command General Tommy Franks of the US Army was in overall command of the coalition forces deployed to the Gulf.

UK Command and Control The UK Task Force Commander, Rear Admiral David Snelson, was installed with his key staff ashore, close alongside his US counterparts from the US 5th Fleet in an integrated headquarters. He was in close and constant contact with the British Joint Headquarters in the UK.

3 Commando Brigade The spearhead of the UK land assault force was 3 Commando Brigade Royal Marines, consisting of 40 and 42 Commandos together with the Commando Logistics Regiment, 539 Assault Squadron, 29 Commando Regiment Royal Artillery and 59 Independent Commando Squadron Royal Engineers. The Royal Marines, commanded by Brigadier Jim Dutton, worked very closely with the 3rd Marine Expeditionary Force of the US Marines. On arrival

in the Gulf the Royal Marines continued their preparations, and on 15 February they were assessed as having achieved full operational capability.

The Royal Navy Battle Plan The prime role for the British Task Force was to assault the important Al Faw peninsula. This was a key strategic position covering the approaches and main waterways to Umm Qasr and Basra. It also held the important oil installations on the Shatt al-Arab. Basra, the second city of Iraq, was also the main port, and occupying it was essential to securing southern Iraq, which was the prime objective of the British forces.

The Task Force assembles (NN)

Intensive training and exercises, including rehearsals of beach assaults, were conducted around Kuwait as the massive build-up of US forces continued in the northern Gulf and onshore in Kuwait. The coalition faced a huge Iraqi Army of over 400,000 troops sited in well-prepared defensive positions and dug in to resist any invasion. Although the Iraqi Navy had not recovered from Operation Desert Sword, and was largely ineffective, the Iraqi Air Force had over 100 combat aircraft. The Iraqi forces also possessed a stockpile of Silkworm and Seersucker missiles as well as chemical weapons.

Opening the Offensive,
21 March 2003

Opening Moves Just prior to commencing hostilities the SBS (Special Boat Service) was deployed ashore on the Al Faw peninsula. US SEALS (Special Forces) were also operating ashore in advance of the main assaults.

First Strike On 20 March President Bush authorised a strike against Saddam Hussein's headquarters and the main command and control positions in Baghdad. US warships then launched a series of Tomahawk cruise missiles, which formed the opening round of the war against Saddam Hussein. The Iraqis lost no time in launching a chemical weapons attack against Kuwait.

That night the submarine *Splendid* joined the action, launching Tomahawk cruise missiles against targets in Baghdad. Later the submarine *Turbulent* also launched Tomahawk missiles against targets in the city. The TLAMs were particularly effective as they could hit their targets with pinpoint accuracy and were not affected by the sand storms and anti-aircraft missiles, which curtailed some air strikes over Baghdad.

Delta Company of 40 Commando prepares for the initial assault (NN)

40 Commando on board *Ark Royal* embarks for the initial assault (NN)

Commando Assault At 2200 on 20 March, 40 Commando spearheaded the assault on Iraq by launching a co-ordinated night helicopter assault from *Ark Royal* and from the advanced assembly position 'Viking' in Kuwait. Carried out by Sea King and RAF Chinook helicopters, it was the biggest opposed helicopter assault by British forces since the Suez Campaign in 1956. The prime role of the Royal Marines was to 'kick the door down' and enable the coalition forces to enter Iraq. The initial assault, directed by SBS ashore, was tasked to take three key objectives including the important oil facilities on the Al Faw peninsula. The weather conditions were not favourable, but nevertheless the landing operations went ahead and the primary objectives were quickly achieved with minimum casualties.

The Second Wave The second assault, by 42 Commando, which was due to leapfrog ahead of the first assault and land further inland to the north, was delayed by the crash of a US CH-46 Sea Knight helicopter, which killed the crew and all the personnel from RM Brigade HQ on board. The Sea Knight helicopter belonged to the USMC (United States Marine Corps) and had eight Royal Marines from 3 Brigade 'Recce Group' on board as well as four US marines. Whilst the US Sea Knight helicopters were being given quick safety checks, the second-wave helicopter assault eventually went ahead, utilising UK helicopters, RAF Chinooks and Sea King 4s of 845 NAS from *Ocean*.

The second assault, hastily arranged by the JHC (Joint Helicopter Command), was well over six hours later than planned and was conducted in deteriorating weather conditions. 42 Commando was then inserted into forward positions where it encountered fairly stiff opposition. Nevertheless the landings were a success and secured the flanks of 40 Commando.

Naval Gunfire Support NGS (naval gunfire support) was provided by British and Australian frigates formed on a gun line in the Khawr' Abd Allah waterway. The frigate *Marlborough* was right in close, north of Bubiyan Island, at the head of the gunline, with the frigates *Richmond* and *Chatham* and HMAS *Anzac* to the south-east. It was an exposed position in very shallow water, requiring the utmost skill in navigation and ship handling. The ships on the gun line commenced firing in the early hours of 21 March, bombarding Iraqi bunkers and defensive positions up to eleven miles inland.

It was the first time since the Falklands War that the Royal Navy had carried out NGS for real. The same ships continued to provide NGS during the initial advance stages of the campaign on shore; carrying out a total of seventeen NGS support missions. At one stage *Richmond* was attacked by Iraqi missiles launched from the Al Faw peninsula, which fortunately missed. As the Royal Marines advanced, Lynx and Gazelle helicopters from 847 NAS acted as aerial spotters,

Men on board *Edinburgh* remained closed up at action stations to repel any Iraqi air or missile attacks
(NP)

Richmond's 4.5in gun opens fire
(NN)

detecting Iraqi artillery positions and calling in suppression air strikes.

Iraqi Navy Shortly after the naval bombardment unidentified contacts were detected heading south down the Shatt al-Arab waterway towards the coalition ships forming the SAG (Surface Action Group) engaged in NGS. These were identified as an Iraqi frigate escorted by two patrol craft. *Chatham*, as OTC (officer in tactical command) of the SAG, called in air strikes. RAF Tornados then attacked the Iraqi units, damaging a *Bogomol* class patrol vessel, which was left, crippled and abandoned. The other Iraqi units quickly reversed course and headed back up the Shatt al-Arab. A few days later US aircraft attacked Iraqi naval units close to Basra,

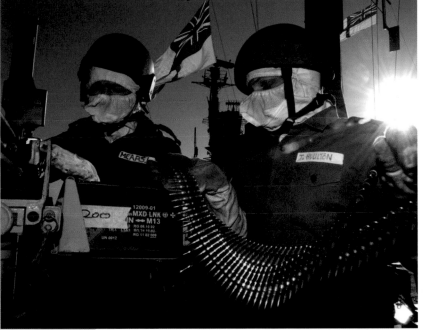

destroying them and effectively neutralising the Iraqi Navy. Ships of the Task Force remained closed up at action stations to repel any Iraqi air or missile attacks.

Sea King Helicopter Collision In the early hours of 22 March at approximately 0430 two Sea King Mk 7s (AEW helicopters) of 'A' Flight 849 NAS, from *Ark Royal*, were involved in a mid-air collision. Both helicopters crashed, killing seven members of their crew, including one US serviceman. One of the helicopters was flying out to commence a mission, whilst the other was inbound having completed its time on task. The Mk 7 AEW Sea Kings were carrying out an important role tracking enemy vehicle movements on shore using their new and amazingly accurate Searchwater 2000 radars.

Operation James and the Assault on Basra
The Commandos Advance on Umm Qasr and Basra Having consolidated their position and secured the oil installations, the Royal Marines of 40 Commando advanced inland. They

were screened by 42 Commando on their flanks and backed up by artillery and air strikes, called in to wipe out pockets of resistance. Attached to the Royal Marines was 'B' Squadron of Scimitar light tanks of the Queen's Dragoon Guards. Also backing up the Royal Marines were air patrols flown by helicopters from *Ocean* as well as *Ark Royal*. Lynx helicopters took on Iraqi tanks with their TOW (tube-launched, optically tracked, wire-guided) missiles. At the same time the US Marines were advancing on the port of Umm Qasr, whilst 42 Commando infiltrated Umm Qasr itself.

This enabled 40 Commando to advance towards Basra, and as it did so a squadron of powerful Challenger II main battle tanks were placed under its command. As the second city of Iraq, Basra was an important strategic objective and was well guarded. Whilst the Royal Marines were taking Umm Qasr, the USA was launching further air strikes on Baghdad.

Operation James As the Royal Marines advanced north they encountered increasing pockets of resistance. By 30 March 40 Commando, supported by a company from 42 Commando, reached Abu Al Khasib, which was on the outskirts of Basra on the approach road from the south. It was here that Iraqi forces, manning heavily fortified positions, halted them. To take Abu Al Khasib the Royal Marines launched Operation James, calling in support by tanks, aircraft and attack helicopters. It was a traditional infantry-style assault, with the marines advancing slowly on foot, in sections, protecting each other and relying on artillery and air support when they became tied down.

The Lynx helicopters of 847 NAS from *Ocean* distinguished themselves, taking on Iraqi tanks with their TOW missiles and achieving quite a number of 'kills'. Lieutenant Commander James Newton, a Lynx pilot with 847 NAS, was awarded the DFC (Distinguished Flying Cross) for his part

Ocean and *Ark Royal* in the Gulf (NN)

Royal Marines of 539 Assault Squadron on the Shatt al-Arab waterway (NN)

in courageously taking out three Iraqi tanks with TOW missiles under heavy fire and at close range.[2]

As they advanced the Royal Marines fired a total of 5,000 mortar rounds. The battle for Abu Al Khasib became a fierce day-and-a-half-long struggle with hard street fighting as the Royal Marines advanced into the town and flushed the Iraqis out of houses and defensive positions. Many tanks and armoured vehicles were either destroyed or captured, and over 300 Iraqi troops were captured with many more dead. It had been a most successful operation and opened the way for the final assault on Basra itself.

Basra: Operation Sinbad With the approaches from the south well secured, Operation Sinbad, the main assault on Basra was the next phase. This time it was the turn of the Royal Marines of 42 Commando to advance with the 7th Armoured Brigade, passing through the lines secured by 40 Commando and on into the south of the city. The Royal Marines attacked from the south-east whilst the 7th Armoured Brigade with their heavy armour advanced from the south-west. After fairly heavy fighting 42 Commando took 'Basra Palace', the presidential palace in southern Basra. On 7 April the British advance arrived in the centre of Basra, and it did not take much longer to complete the taking of the city. With the securing of Basra the initial phase was completed in the south.

All Credit to the Royal Marines The fact that all was achieved so swiftly and with the absolute minimum of casualties reflected great credit on the Royal Marines for their courage, determination and sheer professionalism. Their considerable experience of street fighting gained in Northern Ireland and other trouble spots around the world helped to prepare them to carry out their vital task so effectively.[3]

Follow-Up Operations

Mine Clearance Operations With the Al Faw peninsula rendered safe and Umm Qasr secured the next move was to open up the Khawr' Abd Allah waterway and clear a main supply route for the support and reinforcement of coalition forces advancing north in Iraq. Re-supply had been carried out valiantly by helicopters, but they could not lift the vast amounts of ammunition, fuel and stores needed to supply the growing numbers of coalition forces on shore.

The Royal Navy Minehunters of 1st MCMV Squadron carried out the mine clearance operations, some with UK, US or Australian bomb disposal teams embarked.

The MCMVs *Ledbury* and *Grimsby* had arrived in the Gulf and reinforced the 1st MCMV Squadron. Many potential mines and explosive devices were discovered, and although only three turned out to be live mines all had to be thoroughly investigated and disposed of.

Opening Umm Qasr Port After the waterway was cleared the jetties and port facilities at Umm Qasr Port had to be surveyed and rendered safe before the port could be opened.

Bangor and 1st MCMV Squadron clear the Khawr' Abd Allah waterway (NN)

RFA *Sir Galahad* on her way to the port of Umm Qasr (NN)

The LSL RFA *Sir Galahad* had been loaded with 650 tons of much needed humanitarian aid, including food, blankets and medical supplies; much of this had been provided by the UK, but she had also loaded humanitarian aid kindly donated from Kuwait. She sailed from Kuwait and was escorted by patrol boats and helicopter gunships. With *Sandown* leading ahead, RFA *Sir Galahad* bravely made her way up the Khawr' Abd Allah channel to Umm Qasr.

It took seven and a half hours, but her arrival in the port of Umm Qasr on 27 March showed that a safe route by water to Iraq was now open. It also demonstrated to the world that the coalition forces were following up their operations by providing humanitarian aid to the Iraqis. The coalition forces continued to work hard to restore Umm Qasr as the main route for trade in and out of southern Iraq. On 7 April RFA *Sir Percivale* arrived in the port of Umm Qasr with over 300 tons of humanitarian aid from Kuwait.

US Advance on Baghdad Whilst British forces had been taking over southern Iraq, US forces had been steadily advancing on Baghdad. On 23 March armoured units had pushed across the Euphrates at Nasiriyah and pressed on towards Baghdad. As before the Iraqis tried to widen the conflict, launching Scud missiles at Kuwait, but fortunately with little effect. On 30 March US forces opened a second offensive from north of Baghdad, whilst taking Karbala and Najaf in the south. After taking Nasiriyah the USA went on to take Saddam International Airport on the edge of Baghdad on 3 April. Two days later US tanks advanced deep into Baghdad, steadily taking over the city, which finally fell on 9 April. The capitulation of Baghdad was celebrated by iconic pictures of liberated Iraqis toppling the large statue of Saddam Hussein in the centre of the city. The pictures of Iraqis dancing on the fallen statue were flashed around the world to herald the success of the coalition forces. On 13 April US forces advanced on Tikrit, and two days later when the town was secured the war was declared to be over.

Reduction of the Task Force – 'Job Done!'
By early April the war in Iraq had moved deep inland and become very much a land campaign, with ground forces operating from well-established bases. The maritime element of the campaign was of reducing importance, its primary role being the support of operations on shore by providing the main logistic supply chain and air support as required. The land campaign progressed well, and it was considered that the situation had stabilised sufficiently to start reducing elements of the Task Force.

Return of *Ark Royal* The Royal Marines and their support aircraft were firmly based on shore, and so it was decided to transfer the command from *Ark Royal* to *Ocean*, and for *Ark Royal* to return to the UK. When the command had been embarked in *Ocean*, *Ark Royal* headed south-east to transit through the Straits of Hormuz and out of the Gulf, escorted by the destroyer *York* and supported by the fleet replenishment ship RFA *Fort Victoria*. On her way home *Ark Royal*

rendezvoused with MY *Leander* in the Western Mediterranean and was congratulated on 'a job well done' by Commodore Sir Donald Gosling, President of the White Ensign Association.

At the same time a much reduced task group, comprising the destroyer *Liverpool* and the frigate *Marlborough*, supported by RFA *Grey Rover*, was being detached from the Task Force to fulfil the original plan for NTG 03. These ships were being released to head south-east for the Straits of Hormuz and the Indian Ocean (see below under 'Far East Deployment'). Meanwhile *Ark Royal* and her escorts sailed back up through the Suez Canal and on through the Straits of Gibraltar to return to a rapturous welcome in Portsmouth at the beginning of May.

Return of *Ocean* Three weeks later it was decided to withdraw *Ocean* and most of the rest of the Task Group. On 19 April the majority of the Royal Marines of 40 Commando began re-embarking on board *Ocean*. At the same time, stores, supplies and equipment for those remaining behind were disembarked and set up in secure bases on shore. On completion the Amphibious Task Group gathered together and sailed south to commence the passage home.

The ships returning with *Ocean* included *Edinburgh* and the RFAS *Argus*, *Sir Percivale*, *Sir Galahad*, *Fort Austin*, *Fort Rosalie* and *Orangeleaf*. As the ships sailed they left behind the frigates *Richmond* on Armilla Patrol and *Chatham* on

Ark Royal, on her way home from the Gulf, rendezvoused with MY *Leander* in the Mediterranean (DG)

Operation Oracle duties. Also remaining in the Gulf were the MCMVs *Ledbury*, *Grimsby*, *Shoreham* and *Ramsey* to continue their important work of keeping the sea lanes open for international shipping.

The Task Force sailed through the Suez Canal at a heightened state of alert in case of any revenge attacks and then on through the Mediterranean. After only a brief two-day stop at Gibraltar the ships headed for the Channel and home – 'Job done!' Approaching Plymouth the twenty-four helicopters of 847 and 845 NAS took off from *Ocean*, conducting a formation 'fly off'. Despite the poor weather and bad visibility the helicopters of the ship's TAG (Tailored Air Group) made an impressive display as they headed for land to fly over RNAS (Royal Naval Air Station) Culdrose and on to Plymouth, where they would fly over the crowds waiting to welcome *Ocean* and her escorts back from the war.

USS *Harry S Truman* The USA also started to reduce its carrier battle groups in the area. The US nuclear strike carrier USS *Harry S Truman*, operating with the 6th Fleet in the Mediterranean, departed from the eastern Mediterranean on 18 April. The group, which included a guided missile cruiser, five destroyers, a frigate and two oilers, then headed to Portsmouth to make their first port call as guests of the Royal Navy after three months' continuous time at sea.

———————— • ————————

End of the War ('Mission Accomplished') After the fall of Tikrit and the defeat of Saddam Hussein and his murderous regime, the war had come to an end. On 1 May President George W Bush, Commander in Chief of the US armed forces, flew out to the nuclear strike carrier USS *Abraham Lincoln* to pay tribute to the men and women who had fought and won the 'Second Gulf War'. As President Bush said, 'the tyrant has fallen and Iraq is free'. The people of Iraq had indeed been liberated but the restoration of law

and order and the rebuilding of the shattered country were going to be extremely difficult challenges for the coalition forces. As Admiral Boyce, the outgoing Chief of the Defence Staff, said: 'Though the main combat phase in Iraq was intense and complex, the emerging peace will draw heavily upon our renowned expertise in peace keeping.' Few may have realised quite how prophetic his words would prove to be.

Far East Deployment: Task Group 03, 19 April – August 2003

NTG 03 With the main combat phase of the Gulf War over it had been decided to detach elements of the original Task Group NTG 03 from the Task Force and release them from the Gulf in early April to continue with the scheduled deployment to the Far East. Accordingly *Liverpool* and *Marlborough*, with the nuclear fleet submarine *Splendid* and supported by the light fleet tanker RFA *Grey Rover*, departed from the Gulf on 19 April and after transiting through the Straits of Hormuz sailed into the Arabian Sea bound for the Far East.

The *Liverpool* Group *Liverpool* and *Splendid* together with RFA *Grey Rover* then headed east for Singapore. In Singapore the ships were able to take part in exercise Lionheart with the Singaporean Navy.

Ark Royal returns to a rapturous welcome in Portsmouth
(NN)

Exercise Lionheart was designed to work up anti-submarine and anti-surface warfare tactics in preparation for the major FPDA exercise Flying Fish off the coast of Malaysia. The ships first visited China and Japan, and in Singapore *Liverpool* was able to carry out a mid-deployment maintenance period prior to sailing for the exercise.

Piracy A strong naval presence in the area was becoming of increasing importance at that time. Whilst piracy was rising worldwide, with the International Maritime Bureau reporting an increase from eighty-seven incidents in the first three months of 2002 to 103 in the first quarter of 2003, the greatest rise was in Indonesia. There had been twenty-eight separate attacks on shipping by pirates in the region in the first three months of 2003. Naval exercises and the close co-ordination of naval and air assets in the area were important elements in the ongoing struggle against piracy.

Marlborough Meanwhile, on sailing from the Gulf *Marlborough* had detached from the group and headed south for the Seychelles. Five days later her ship's company were enjoying a well-earned rest at Port Victoria on Mahe Island. On completion *Marlborough* sailed for Cairns, with just a brief stop at Diego Garcia to break the 6,000-mile passage across the Indian Ocean.

Exercise Flying Fish 03 After visits to New Zealand and Australian ports *Marlborough* arrived in the South China Sea to join the rest of NTG 03 and take part in exercise Flying Fish 03. This was the most ambitious of the FPDA exercises since they were first started in 1971, and it was therefore important that units of the Royal Navy were able to take part. The exercise involved twenty-seven ships, seventy aircraft and over 4,000 personnel from five nations. Six FA2 Sea Harriers from 800 NAS flew out to the Royal Malaysian Air Force base Butterworth to take part and were joined by a Nimrod maritime reconnaissance aircraft from 206 Squadron RAF.

Return to the UK On completion of the exercise and the remaining port visits in the Far East, the ships of NTG 03 headed back to the UK, finally arriving in their home base of Portsmouth in the middle of a heat wave in August. It had been an action-packed seven month deployment.

———— • ————

Ongoing Security Duties in the Gulf After the various elements of the Task Force had departed from the Gulf region the Armilla Patrol continued its important task of protecting shipping and policing the waters of the Gulf and the Straits of Hormuz. The frigate *Richmond* had resumed patrol duties when the Amphibious Task Group and NTG 03 departed. The first duty was to protect the crucial logistic chain supplying the coalition forces ashore in Iraq, particularly the British forces in Basra and southern Iraq. The frigate *Kent* later relieved *Richmond*. *Kent* was heavily involved in anti-smuggling patrols, and many vessels were

arrested and then impounded. She was also heavily committed in keeping the port of Basra open. Eventually the frigate *St Albans* released *Kent* to return to the UK at the end of the year.

Ongoing Security Duties in the Mediterranean: Operation Active Endeavour In the Mediterranean, Operation Active Endeavour, which had been set up in October 2001 as a NATO maritime security measure to monitor shipping, was continued, with Royal Navy frigates being regularly deployed to the NATO squadron. In April 2003 the rules of engagement were broadened and boarding operations began to be conducted on suspicious ships.

By March the following year the remit of the NATO Squadron had been expanded to cover the whole of the Mediterranean Sea, and three months later NATO decided to invite other nations to contribute naval forces. The British frigates deployed to the Standing NATO Squadron had embarked specialist teams of Royal Marines from the Fleet Protection Group.

Aurora 04 Deployment,
7 May – 16 July 2004

In May 2004 a powerful naval task group was formed for the Aurora 04 Deployment to take part in the international maritime exercise Rapid Alliance. This was a combined Joint Task Force exercise, planned and directed by the USA, and included ships from Canada, France and Germany as well as the UK.

Carrier Task Group The carrier *Invincible* sailed from Portsmouth on 7 May, and her escort, the frigate *Marlborough*, left Portsmouth a week later. *Invincible* set course west across the Atlantic, arriving in Charleston on 20 May for a five-day visit. On sailing from Charleston she headed for Norfolk, Virginia, to meet up with the rest of the Task Group in order to prepare for exercise Rapid Alliance.

The Amphibious Task Group On 13 May the ATG (Amphibious Task Group), led by *Ocean*, sailed from Devonport together with the brand new amphibious assault ship *Albion* with 42 Commando Royal Marines embarked. The Amphibious Task Group included the frigates *Sutherland* and *Cornwall*, the RFAs *Argus*, *Fort Rosalie*, *Fort George*, *Sir Galahad* and *Sir Tristram* and the tanker RFA *Oakleaf*. It was the biggest deployment since Operation Telic a year earlier and involved 6,000 personnel, including 2,000 Royal Marines from 3 Commando Brigade. The group sailed across the Atlantic to the rendezvous at the US naval base in Norfolk, Virginia, arriving on 28 May.

Mine Counter-Measures Element The 2nd MCM Squadron, which included the MCMVs *Walney*, *Pembroke*, *Sandown* and *Middleton* with the survey ship *Roebuck*, supported by the LSL RFA *Sir Bedivere*, formed the MCM element of the exercise. The tanker RFA *Brambleleaf* supported the MCM Squadron for its passage across the Atlantic.

The frigate *Campbeltown* on Operation Active Endeavour
(NN)

The new amphibious assault ship *Albion* sails
(RH)

The frigate *Sutherland* refuelling (NP)

Exercise Rapid Alliance The Aurora Task Force sailed from Norfolk, Virginia, on 1 June for exercise Rapid Alliance and headed south for North Carolina. On arrival off the US Marine Corps base of Camp Lejeune on the coast of North Carolina, the Amphibious Task Group carried out a series of amphibious landings using helicopter and landing craft.

1,800 Royal Marines were landed with Challenger 2 main battle tanks from the Royal Tank Regiment. When all amphibious assets had arrived in the area the intensive part of the exercise was carried out with opposed landings in Onslow Bay, involving a total of some 30,000 personnel. The carriers, including the *Invincible* group, operated further out to sea with the US Carrier Battle Group formed on the strike carrier USS *John F Kennedy* fending off surface, sub-surface

and air attacks. The exercises were very successful and enhanced operational capability as well as inter-operability with US forces for the ongoing war on terrorism.

Completion of Aurora 04 Exercise Rapid Alliance was completed on 22 June and the ships dispersed to various ports on the US east coast, with *Invincible* sailing to Port Canaveral before heading back up north for a five-day visit to New York with *Cornwall* and RFA *Fort George*.

Ocean sailed for Mayport whilst *Albion*, escorted by *Sutherland*, headed for Fort Lauderdale. Other ships visited Baltimore, Boston, Wilmington, Key West and New Orleans. The various elements of the Task Group then returned across the Atlantic, with *Invincible* and *Marlborough* arriving home

Ocean and *Albion* during exercise Rapid Alliance
(NN)

The MCMV *Middleton*
(RH)

Invincible passes the Statue of Liberty (NN)

Southampton guards *Invincible* during exercise Destined Glory (NN)

in Portsmouth on 16 July and *Ocean* arriving back in Devonport with *Cornwall* on the same day. *Albion*, which had sailed on to New Orleans after Fort Lauderdale, did not arrive back in Devonport until 29 July.

Exercise Destined Glory, September 2004 Rear Admiral Charles Style, the UK Maritime Force Commander, flying his flag in *Invincible*, led a task group into the Mediterranean in September to take part in the important NATO exercise Destined Glory. The exercise, which included an invasion of southern Sardinia, was designed to test NATO's new Response Force. NATO had established the Response Force concept in 2002 to respond to the changing threats to the alliance.

The UK Task Group included the Type 42 destroyers *Southampton* and *Manchester* and the Type 23 frigate *Kent*, supported by the fleet replenishment ship RFA *Fort George*. The Sea Harriers of 801 NAS, embarked in *Invincible*, provided an important element of the air component of the exercise. The Sea King helicopters of 771 and 849 NAS also played an important part. Involving forty-seven ships, fifty aircraft and nearly 10,000 personnel, the exercise was a great success: Admiral Style said that it demonstrated NATO's resolve and credibility and added that the exercise provided an excellent display of 'an expeditionary force which does not rely on having a fixed operating base in a host country'. It was a clear example of the flexibility and reach of naval forces.

Operation Garron: Tsunami Relief, December 2004 The Asian Tsunami struck on 26 December 2004, wreaking havoc on the shores of south-east Asia. The swift response by the UK government was to launch Operation Garron on 30 December. The frigate *Chatham* and the forward repair ship RFA *Diligence* were ordered to the area at speed, arriving off the coast of Sri Lanka early in the New Year and commencing humanitarian relief work in the coastal towns of Kallar and Batticaloa. The ships were able to provide a great deal of emergency relief work in the region over an extended period.

taken out to *Ocean*, which was lying more than a mile off the Hoe. The assembled flotilla of ships with *Ocean* included *Norfolk*, *Albion* and *Grafton*, the RFAS *Argus*, *Sir Bedivere* and *Wave Knight*, HMML *Gleaner* and the six patrol boats *Blazer*, *Tracker*, *Raider*, *Puncher*, *Explorer* and *Express*.

The old colour, presented by Her Majesty thirty-four years earlier on board the aircraft carrier *Eagle* (see Chapter 3), was marched off. As Her Majesty arrived *Norfolk* fired a twenty-one-gun royal salute. After presenting the new colour the Queen, as Lord High Admiral, said that she 'took great pride in this link between the Sovereign and the Royal Navy which stretched back to King Alfred'.[4] The presentation was followed by a sail-past by the destroyer *Newcastle*, the frigate *Portland*, the minehunter *Walney* and the River class patrol ship *Severn*.

Operation Fresco During 2003 the Royal Navy contributed over 6,000 sailors and Royal Marines to man emergency fire appliances during the national strike by the fire-fighters. In 2004 the Royal Navy again trained up personnel to take over emergency duties, though fortunately a strike was averted at the last moment in September.

Umm Qasr Incident, June 2004 The UK forces in Iraq were reminded of the fragile situation on the borders with Iran when three small Royal Navy patrol craft were seized by powerful Iranian forces. The patrol craft were making their way from the port of Umm Qasr to Basra when the Iranians,

Other Activities

HMS *Nottingham* On 7 July 2002 the Type 42 destroyer *Nottingham* gained notoriety when she struck Wolfe Rock off Howe Island in Australian waters. The ship was badly holed below the waterline but was saved by swift and determined damage-control actions carried out by her ship's company. In the end she was brought back to the UK for repair on a heavy ship lift, arriving in Portsmouth in December. *Nottingham* was repaired by FSL (Fleet Support Ltd) and rejoined the Fleet in the summer of 2004.

Sixtieth Anniversary of the Battle of the Atlantic Eleven ships from eight nations joined *Invincible* in Liverpool in May 2003 to mark the sixtieth anniversary of the Battle of the Atlantic. Over 160,000 people congregated in Liverpool to watch the various events held to commemorate the Allied victory in the longest-running battle in World War II. *Invincible* was moored on the Mersey in the centre of Liverpool, and with her were *Walney*, *Biter* and *Charger*. Events included displays by the Royal Marines, veterans' parades, church services and fly-pasts by Nimrod maritime patrol aircraft.

Presentation of the New Queen's Colour, 23 July 2003 A moment of proud pageantry took place at Plymouth on 23 July 2003 when HM the Queen presented a new colour to the Fleet on board *Ocean*. It was a wet and blustery day but, undaunted, the Queen and the Duke of Edinburgh were

RN and RFA sailors working in Batticaloa (NN)

The Queen presents a new colour to the Fleet (NN)

who claimed they had strayed into Iranian territory, forcibly detained them. The eight Royal Naval personnel were arrested and then became the subject of high-level diplomacy between the UK and Iran, with very strong representations by the British government. Fortunately they were released unharmed shortly afterwards.

The Boscastle Disaster After torrential rains in northern Cornwall in August 2004, hundreds of people were trapped in the village of Boscastle when the rivers burst their banks. A Fleet Air Arm Sea King helicopter was scrambled from Culdrose and played a key role in the rescue operation. The Sea King managed to save a dozen people before RAF helicopters arrived to assist in the rescue operations.

Wilkinson Sword of Peace, 23 September 2004 The Wilkinson Sword of Peace for 2004 was awarded to the LSL RFA *Sir Galahad* for the humanitarian relief work that she carried out in Iraq. RFA *Sir Galahad* was the first ship to berth in the port of Umm Qasr, where her cargo of relief aid of food, blankets and medical supplies was unloaded. The sword was presented at the ship's base port of Marchwood on 23 September 2004.

SHIPS, AIRCRAFT AND WEAPONS

RFA Wave Class In 2003 the two new Auxiliary Replenishment Oilers, RFAs *Wave Ruler* and *Wave Knight*, built by BAE Systems, entered service as replacements for the tankers RFAS *Olna* and *Olwen*. The 31,000-ton fast fleet tankers of the Wave class also provided a platform for operating helicopters.

Future Carrier Aircraft In late 2002 it was announced that the Royal Navy and the RAF would operate the short take off and vertical landing (STOVL) variant of the F-35 Joint Strike Fighter under a programme named Future Joint Combat Aircraft. The F-35 is an all-weather all-role aircraft, and the UK aims to procure 150, with the first deliveries planned for 2010 and an in-service date of 2012.

MANPOWER MATTERS

Personnel Change Programme The Navy Board introduced a Personnel Change Programme (PCP) to create sustainable manpower structures for the future Navy and improve job satisfaction. The aim of the programme was to reduce multi-skilling and increase specialist skills to make personnel more efficient.

Branch Development A major part of the PCP was the development of the Warfare, Engineering and Air Engineering Branches. The project was designed to adjust branch training to meet the future manning requirements.

Personnel Focus Following studies set up in 2002, initiatives were taken to re-emphasise and improve the divisional system and also to enhance the value of the leading hands.

The *Navy News* In August 2004 the newspaper of the Royal Navy, the *Navy News*, celebrated its fiftieth anniversary with a banquet held in the Banqueting Hall in Whitehall. Guests of honour included the former Chief of the Defence Staff Admiral the Lord Boyce and the Commander in Chief, Admiral Sir Jonathan Band.

THE WHITE ENSIGN ASSOCIATION

Windsor Castle Banquet On 23 May 2002 the Association was honoured to be guests of HRH the Prince of Wales, Royal Patron of the Association, at a banquet in Windsor Castle. The banquet, which was held in the magnificent setting of the St George's Hall, was a glittering occasion attended by many of the members and supporters of the Association.

Chairman The former First Sea Lord Admiral Sir Jock Slater relieved Mr John Andrewes as Chairman of the Association at the AGM, held at Lloyds of London, in November 2002. At the same time Captain John Roberts relieved Captain David Wixon as the Chief Executive of the Association.

***Collingwood* visit** In 2003 the Association visited the major shore training establishment HMS *Collingwood* at Fareham and spent the day visiting the various training facilities, including the simulators and bridge training complex.

HMS *Belfast* The following year HRH the Prince of Wales visited the Association's headquarters on board HMS *Belfast*. The Prince was briefed on the many activities of the Association and met the Council.

Commodore Sir Donald Gosling introduces Mrs Wixon, wife of the Chief Executive, to the Royal Patron, HRH the Prince of Wales at the Association Banquet in Windsor Castle in 2002 (WEA)

Lord Boyce, former Chief of the Defence Staff, talks to sea cadet Sophie Andrews at the fiftieth anniversary banquet of the *Navy News* (NN)

CHAPTER 14

Operations Telic and Herrick
and the Fleet Review 2005–2006

Operations Highbrow (Lebanon Evacuation), Herrick V (Afghanistan) and Vela (Sierra Leone) –
Marstrike 05 and Aquila 06 Deployments – International Fleet Review

Whilst in 2005 the '9/11' terrorist attacks and ongoing conflict in Iraq and Afghanistan continued to overshadow political affairs in the West, serious problems continued to beset progress in other parts of the world. In south-east Asia the shock waves of the Tsunami had devastated many of the coastal areas in the region, and the Royal Navy was needed to help in the relief work. Later, the USA suffered its own disaster, when Hurricane Katrina struck in the Gulf of Mexico. It was a devastating hurricane which caused widespread damage, and the US government needed the assistance of the Royal Navy in opening the shipping lanes in the Mississippi.

In the Middle East tension increased in the Lebanon with the murder of the Prime Minister, Rafik Hariri, by a suicide bomber, whilst the last Syrian troops were withdrawn from the Lebanon, helping to create a power vacuum. Following the death of Yasser Arafat, Mahmoud Abbas became President of the Palestinian Authority. In Bali, a suicide bomber, linked to Al Qaeda, slaughtered twenty-six people.

In Iraq the first free elections for over fifty years were held in early 2005, with a very encouraging turnout to vote. Eventually Saddam Hussein was apprehended by US forces and handed over to the new Iraqi authorities. Subsequently an Iraqi court tried him, and in 2006, after being found guilty of crimes against the people of Iraq, he was executed.

In the UK the Labour government of Tony Blair was re-elected in 2005, but with a reduced majority. In July, following the success and enjoyment of the International Fleet Review at Spithead, the country was shocked by the terrorist attacks committed by suicide bombers in London on 7 July, soon referred to as the UK's '7/7'.

UK Defence Policy: The Nuclear Deterrent In 2006 the government faced the difficult question of the future of the national strategic nuclear deterrent. In view of the very long lead-time for such weapon systems, decisions had to be faced in sufficient time before the Trident system came to the end of its operational life. The four *Vanguard* class SSBNs (ballistic missile-carrying nuclear submarines) were due to complete their service and be decommissioned in the early 2020s, and it would take seventeen years to design and build a replacement submarine. The Trident missile system would also last until 2020, and the American government planned to extend its life to 2042. Britain possessed fifty Trident missiles and 200 nuclear warheads, though it was planned to reduce the stockpile of warheads to 160.

FIRST SEA LORDS
*Admirals West
and Band*

SECOND SEA LORD
Admiral Johns

MANPOWER
38,000

MERCANTILE MARINE
*1,450
merchant ships*[1]

In view of the increasingly uncertain and unsafe world, the government decided it was prudent to plan on maintaining a minimum viable nuclear deterrent for the foreseeable future. Four basic systems were considered at length, a land-based silo system, an air-launched missile from manned bombers, a ship-launched missile and a submarine-launched system. It was found that the submarine-launched ballistic missile system provided the cheapest and by far the most effective strategic nuclear deterrent. Contributory to the argument was the fact that for thirty-six years no submarine deterrent patrol had ever been detected.

The plan to maintain the strategic nuclear deterrent and proceed with a replacement submarine-launched nuclear missile system was therefore announced by the government. Furthermore, it was announced that the replacement nuclear submarines would be built in the UK. The Prime Minister stated: 'The risk of giving up something that has been one of the mainstays of our security since the War, and doing so when the one certain thing about our world today is its uncertainty, is not a risk I feel we can responsibly take. Our independent nuclear deterrent is the ultimate insurance.'[2] Thus the decision was taken that the Royal Navy would continue to hold the 'right of the line' as far as defence of the realm was concerned until at least 2050.

THE FLEET

Aircraft Carriers In 2005 the core of the Fleet was still based on the three *Invincible* class light aircraft carriers, now well over twenty years old. *Illustrious* had just rejoined the fleet after a major £120 million refit in Rosyth and became the Fleet flagship in June, whilst *Invincible* was put in to reserve at the end of the year in a ninety-day-notice state of readiness, officially classified as 'Extended Readiness'. At the beginning of 2006 *Ark Royal* was taken in hand at Rosyth for a refit, to be converted for her role as a strike carrier and also for the helicopter assault role.

The *Invincibles* were due to be replaced by two new large carriers (CVF), *Queen Elizabeth* and *Prince of Wales*, planned in the 1998 Strategic Defence Review to join the Fleet in 2012 and 2015, though delays had made those in-service dates very ambitious. In December 2005 the new carrier project proceeded to the demonstration phase, as part of the two-phase approach to the next stage of commitment to the programme.

The Amphibious Task Group The amphibious fleet consisted of the LPH (landing platform helicopter) *Ocean*, the biggest ship in the Royal Navy, and the two new LPDs (landing platform, docks), *Albion* and *Bulwark*. The brand new 16,000-ton RFA (Royal Fleet Auxiliary) ships of the Bay class, officially designated landing ship dock (auxiliary), were reinforcing the amphibious fleet, with RFAS *Largs Bay* and *Mounts Bay* being completed in 2006 and *Lyme Bay* and *Cardigan Bay* in the following year. Three other LSLs (landing ships, logistic) of the RFA remained in service to provide cover until all the Bay class were in service.

Submarines The submarine fleet consisted of the four *Vanguard* class SSBN Trident missile deterrent submarines, the seven fleet submarines of the *Trafalgar* class and the three remaining elderly fleet submarines of the *Swiftsure* class. A new class of four fleet submarines, the *Astute* class, had been ordered, to start joining the fleet towards the end of the decade.

The Escort Ships The escort fleet of twenty-five frigates and destroyers consisted of the eight remaining Batch 2 and Batch 3 Type 42 destroyers, the last four of the Batch 3 Type 22 frigates and thirteen Type 23 Duke class frigates. Work had

started on the new generation Type 45 *Daring* class destroyers, which were designed with the primary role of defending the new aircraft carriers.

Mine Counter-Measures and Patrol Vessels The MCMVs (mine counter-measures vessels) were being reorganised. The eight Hunt class were to form the 1st MCMV Squadron, to be based at Portsmouth, and the eight remaining *Sandown* class were to form the 2nd MCMV Squadron, to be based north in Faslane. The three Hunt class MCMVs, which had been converted for Northern Ireland patrol duties, were to

be withdrawn and decommissioned by the end of 2005, owing to the stable security situation in the Province.

The fine Castle class patrol vessels were coming to the end of their time, *Leeds Castle* being withdrawn in 2005 and *Dumbarton Castle* being deployed to the Falklands for her final commission. The new River class patrol vessels were joining the Fleet, with three in service with the Fishery Protection Squadron. A fourth, *Clyde*, was building and due to be completed by 2007 for ultimate service in the Falklands in place of *Dumbarton Castle*. There were eighteen P2000 *Archer* class patrol boats, of which two had been specially adapted for Northern Ireland but withdrawn and redeployed to Gibraltar.

The new amphibious ships *Albion* and *Bulwark*
(NN)

The new fleet flagship *Illustrious*
(NP)

Royal Marines The Corps of Royal Marines consisted of 3 Commando Brigade, with 40, 42 and 45 Commandos, with artillery, engineering and logistic support. There were a number of other specialist Royal Marine units, including 539 Assault Squadron, the SBS (Special Boat Service) and the Fleet Protection Group.

Fleet Air Arm The fixed-wing aircraft of the Fleet Air Arm included the GR7/A Harriers of 800 and 801 NAS (Naval Air Squadron). The faithful Sea Harrier was finally decommissioned in March 2006. The helicopters included the long-serving Sea Kings, the Mk 4s (assault role) of 845, 846, and 848 NAS, the Mk 5s (search and rescue task) of 771 NAS and the Mk 7s (airborne surveillance and control role) of 849 NAS. The rest of the helicopters included the Merlin (anti-submarine and anti-surface role) of 814, 820, 824 and 829 NAS, the Lynx Mk 3 and Mk 8 (anti-submarine and anti-surface role) of 702 and 815 NAS and the Lynx Mk 7 (anti-tank role) of 847 NAS.

Royal Fleet Auxiliary The Fleet was supported by the RFA, which consisted of two Wave class fleet tankers, four Leaf class support tankers and three Rover class small fleet tankers. In addition there were four fleet replenishment ships, two of the modern Fort class and two of the older Fort class, as well as the aviation training ship RFA *Argus* and the forward repair ship RFA *Diligence*.

Command of the Fleet Admiral Sir James Burnell-Nugent was appointed Commander in Chief Fleet in November 2005, with Rear Admiral Charles Style as the sea-going Commander UK Maritime Forces, later to be relieved by Rear Admiral Morisetti, and Commodore Tony Rix was the Commander UK Task Group, later to be relieved by Commodore Williams. Major General James Dutton was the Commander UK Amphibious Forces, and Brigadier Rose was the Commander of 3 Commando Brigade.

The Fleet Bases The surface fleet was divided into two flotillas and based in the two main south coast naval bases at Portsmouth and Devonport. The Portsmouth flotilla consisted of the carriers and destroyers, with some Type 23 frigates and the 1st MCMV Squadron, whilst the Devonport flotilla was made up of the amphibious ships, Type 22 and Type 23 frigates, a squadron of fleet submarines and the survey ships. The third naval base was in Faslane, Scotland, and was home to the nuclear deterrent *Vanguard* class Trident submarines, a squadron of fleet submarines and the 2nd MCMV Squadron.

Future of the Naval Bases In 2006 an investigation was set up to consider the future requirement and optimum structure for the three naval bases in view of the reduced size of the fleet. If the result of the investigation was to reduce the naval bases to just two, then painful decisions would be needed as to which naval base to axe, with all the attendant political problems that would result from such an important consequence for a local economy. There was much fear in Portsmouth and Devonport that their naval bases might be up for the 'chop'. The fear was not only in the local communities with regard to their economic future, but also amongst naval personnel as to where they should buy houses, educate their children and seek jobs for their partners.

FIRST SEA LORD

At the beginning of 2005 Admiral Sir Alan West continued as First Sea Lord, and he remained in post for the bicentennial Trafalgar celebrations in the summer. He was relieved on 7 February of the following year by Admiral Sir Jonathan Band, and retired from the Service. Later he was created Baron West of Spithead and brought into the Cabinet with responsibility for advising on national security.

Admiral Sir Jonathan Band Jonathan Band was born in 1950 and joined the Royal Navy in 1967. After graduating from Exeter University he went to sea in *Lewiston*, *Rothesay* and *Eskimo*; he also had an exchange with the US Navy, serving in the guided missile destroyer USS *Belknap*. He served in

Admiral Sir
Jonathan Band
(RN)

The destroyer
Liverpool on
Atlantic Patrol Task
(North)
(NN)

the Fishery Protection Squadron in command of the minesweeper *Soberton* and then, in 1981, was appointed Flag Lieutenant to the Commander in Chief Fleet, serving Admiral Fieldhouse during the Falklands War.

In 1983 he was promoted Commander and took command of the Batch 2 (Exocet-armed) *Leander* class frigate *Phoebe*, operating in the NATO area with the new towed array sonar system. Following the Joint Services Defence College, he was appointed to the Defence Policy Staff in the Ministry of Defence. He commanded the Type 23 frigate *Norfolk* and, after further appointments in the MoD as the Assistant Director Naval Plans and Programmes and the Defence Costs Study ('Front Line First'), he commanded the carrier *Illustrious* from 1995 to 1997, taking part in Ocean Wave 97.

Jonathan Band was promoted Rear Admiral in May 1997 and appointed Assistant Chief of the Naval Staff. After serving as the Deputy Commander in Chief Fleet and subsequently carrying out the Defence Training Review in the rank of Vice Admiral, he was appointed Commander in Chief Fleet in the rank of Admiral in August 2002. He relieved Admiral West as First Sea Lord in February 2006.

OPERATIONS AND DEPLOYMENTS, 2005–2006

Standing Commitments

Although the focus of activity was very much on operations in the Middle East, including the eastern Mediterranean, the Royal Navy continued to maintain standing commitments and deployments in other parts of the world.

Atlantic Patrol Task (North): Task Group 326.01 At the beginning of February 2005 the Type 42 destroyer *Liverpool*, supported by the fleet tanker RFA *Wave Knight*, was assigned to the duties of the North Atlantic Patrol Area, covering the Caribbean. The Royal Navy ships provide major support to the counter-drugs operations in the Caribbean as well as contributing to stability and protecting British interests in the area.

Atlantic Patrol Task (South): Task Group 326.02 The Type 42 destroyer *Gloucester* was on Atlantic Patrol Task (South)

The Type 22 frigate *Chatham* off South Georgia
(DCG)
(RC)

and was relieved by the Type 23 frigate *Portland* in March 2005. The OPV (offshore patrol vessel) *Dumbarton Castle* was deployed to the Falkland Islands and Antarctica to protect British interests in the area. *Dumbarton Castle* was permanently on station for several years, not due to be relieved before 2007, and regularly visited South Georgia and other British dependencies in the far South Atlantic. The ice patrol vessel *Endurance* was also in the area and was midway through a seasonal deployment in Antarctica for the austral summer. Other destroyers and frigates visited the area from time to time.

The Gulf: Task Group 330.01 The Type 23 frigate *Marlborough* was on duty in the Gulf and Straits of Hormuz as the Operation Telic guardship. Her task was protecting international shipping on the main tanker routes in and out of the Gulf. *Marlborough* was also protecting British interests in the area and helping to police the waters against smuggling and drug running. At the end of March she was relieved by another Type 23 frigate, *Argyll*. Also in the Gulf was the Type 22 frigate *Chatham* as part of the ongoing US Operation Enduring Freedom, though at the beginning of the year she was detached to Sri Lanka with the forward repair ship RFA *Diligence* to render humanitarian aid in the wake of the Tsunami disaster at the end of 2004. After nearly two months of vital work, *Chatham* returned to the Gulf to continue with Operation Enduring Freedom.

Iraq Ashore in Iraq the Royal Navy had an important part to play in ongoing security operations as well as the commitment to train Iraqi maritime forces. It was a dangerous environment, with casualties being sustained as personnel operated under constant threat and attack.

In May 2006 a Lynx helicopter of 847 NAS was shot down over Basra by a surface-to-air missile. The missile struck the tail section, and the helicopter was engulfed in a fireball killing all five servicemen on board. When troops and accident investigators went into Basra to recover the bodies and the burned-out wreck they were attacked by a violent mob. In November several Royal Marines were amongst those killed when their river patrol was bombed as it passed a pontoon bridge on the Shatt al-Arab.

Fishery Protection The three River class OPVs operating with vessels of the Hunt class MCMVs formed the Fishery Protection Squadron. The squadron carried out its important tasks patrolling the coastline of the UK and working under the direction of DEFRA (the Department for the Environment, Food and Rural Affairs), policing and enforcing EEC fishery policies and protecting the dwindling fish stocks in the North Sea.

The squadron also protected the vital oil and gas platforms. *Chiddingfold*, *Hurworth* and *Middleton* exercised with Special Forces, as well as HM Revenue and Customs, the Coastguard and the RNLI.

The destroyer
Nottingham in the
Mediterranean
(NN)

Northern Ireland Although some patrols and ongoing security measures had been maintained in and around Northern Ireland, they had been greatly scaled back. The Northern Ireland Squadron, *Cottesmore*, *Dulverton* and *Brecon*, completed their last Northern Ireland patrol in March 2005 and were withdrawn from the area. The squadron was then finally decommissioned in the summer of 2005.

Gibraltar The fast coastal patrol craft *Scimitar* and *Sabre*, originally built for security duties in Northern Ireland, were stationed in Gibraltar with responsibility for protection of

the vital naval base and escorting allied warships transiting through the Straits of Gibraltar.

Cyprus The *Archer* class patrol craft *Pursuer* and *Dasher* were deployed to Cyprus. Together with a detachment of Royal Marines and two fast inshore patrol boats, they provided force protection patrols for the Sovereign Base Area. As well as carrying out counter-terrorist activities, they had an important task in protecting allied shipping, using Cyprus as a key strategic staging post before transiting through the Canal en route to the Gulf.

NATO MCM Group 1: The MCMV *Bangor* was assigned to NATO MCM (Mine Counter-Measures) Group 1 to take part in allied naval exercises such as Brilliant Mariner and Cold Response.

Operation Garron At the very beginning of January 2005 the frigate *Chatham* and the forward repair ship RFA *Diligence* had been sent to Sri Lanka as part of Operation Garron to provide emergency relief work in the wake of the Tsunami which had struck in southeast Asia.

The ships, which had just arrived off the coast, commenced relief work immediately in Batticaloa, Kurundi and Kalmadu. Engineers from RFA *Diligence* were flown to the Maldive Islands to help repair electrical power supplies and water desalination plants. The Royal Marines from the Fleet Protection Group were also sent out to assist in the relief work. The support tanker RFA *Bayleaf*, which was serving in the Gulf, was alerted to stand by to proceed east and join Operation Garron.

Marstrike 05 Deployment, 17 January–March 2005

A major task group, designated Marstrike 05, was planned for deployment to the Middle East at the beginning of 2005.

The Task Group Sails The Marstrike 05 Task Group, led by Rear Admiral Charles Style, COMUKMARFOR (Commander UK Maritime Force), in his flagship *Invincible*, sailed from Portsmouth on 17 January 2005. The Task Group consisted of the carrier *Invincible*, escorted by the Type 42 destroyer *Nottingham* and the Type 23 frigate *Grafton*. The fleet replenishment ship RFA *Fort George* supported the group. *Invincible*'s TAG (Tailored Air Group) included FA2 Sea Harriers of 801 NAS, and Sea King AEW (airborne early warning) helicopters of 849 NAS. The TAG was reinforced by GR7 Harriers deployed from 4 Squadron RAF, and RFA *Fort George* embarked four Merlin helicopters. As the ships of the Task Group steamed west down the Channel, the Type 23 frigate *Montrose* sailed from Devonport and joined them.

In the Mediterranean The Task Group entered Gibraltar on 21 January for a brief three-day visit before heading out into the Mediterranean. The French *Lafayette* class frigate FNS *Guepratte* joined the Task Group from Marseilles, and intensive integration training was conducted as the ships continued their way east across the Mediterranean. On passage *Nottingham* was detached on a rescue mission to aid a stricken ship, the MV *Vigla*, which had caught fire and was sinking off the coast of Malta. Although *Nottingham* ploughed through very heavy seas at a speed of twenty-four knots, by the time she arrived the ship had sunk and she was only able to recover bodies from the sea. The bodies were landed at Limassol.

After a few days of rough weather the Task Group arrived off the coast of Cyprus. The very rough weather continued, which made the job of embarking stores and supplies

NATO Assignments In 2005 the Royal Navy was continuing to assign ships to NATO Standing Naval Forces as required.

STANDING NATO MARITIME GROUP: OPERATION ACTIVE ENDEAVOUR: The Type 42 destroyer *Cardiff* was assigned to the Standing NATO Maritime Group deploying to the Mediterranean in March 2005 for a three-month tour of duty. The group was conducting Operation Active Endeavour monitoring all ships and vessels in the Mediterranean, a vital task in the war on terrorism. By the end of 2006 the NATO Squadron had monitored some three quarters of a million vessels in the Mediterranean.

hazardous; nevertheless, the essential stores were finally embarked, enabling the group to sail for the Suez Canal after only a short delay.[3]

East of Suez On 1 February the Task Group transited through the Suez Canal and headed down the Red Sea. After transiting the Gulf of Aden, the group arrived in the port of Salalah in Oman on 7 February for a three-day visit. The fleet submarine *Sceptre* also passed through the canal and, after a short visit to Aqaba, joined the Task Group. On sailing from Salalah the group conducted an intensive work-up schedule with a very busy flying programme to prepare for exercise Magic Carpet en route to Bahrain.

Launching GR7 Harriers from *Invincible* during exercise Magic Carpet
(NN)

Exercise Magic Carpet The major exercise Magic Carpet was held off the coast of Oman from 18 February to 2 March. American, Omani and French forces joined the exercise, which was designed to test the ability of the Royal Navy to deploy, operate and maintain a potent maritime strike force. A whole range of scenarios was used, including opposed landings and defence against surface, underwater and air attacks. Use was also made of the Omani live bombing ranges, which included the first successful sortie for a GR7 Harrier with an enhanced Paveway 2 laser-guided bomb deploying from *Invincible* forty miles out at sea.

The Merlin helicopters performed particularly well, fulfilling all expectations in availability and reliability on task. The exercise, which was a most encouraging success, also demonstrated the commitment of the UK to the maintenance of security and stability in the Middle East, especially as it coincided with the sensitive period of elections in Iraq. The GR7 Harriers also deployed from *Invincible* to Kandahar air base to support Operation Herrick in Afghanistan.

Exercise Noble Javelin On completion of exercise Magic Carpet, the Task Group arrived in Muscat on 8 March for a well-earned four-day break.

After a week of maritime security patrols in the Gulf of Aden the Task Group then made a fairly swift passage back to the Mediterranean, transiting through the Suez Canal on 27 March to participate in the NATO exercise Noble Javelin. The exercise was designed to test the new 'Ready Force' concept to an out-of-area location, which was provided by the Canary Islands. It was commanded by COMDJTF (NATO Commander Deployable Joint Task Force) with *Invincible* as the command ship. On completion of the

Invincible sails into Muscat
(NN)

Ships gather in Glasgow for exercise Neptune Warrior (JMC 052)
(NN)

exercise, towards the end of March, the ships of the Task Group returned to their bases in the UK.

Final JMC Exercise In November the Amphibious Task Group sailed north for the last JMC (Joint Maritime Course) exercise. The JMC exercises had been an important part of the maritime exercise programme for over fifty years, having been set up in the dark days of the Cold War. To reflect the changing pattern of defence and maritime warfare, they were now being revised and updated to include elements designed to test new tactics and weapon systems. The new-style exercises would be codenamed Neptune Warrior in future.

Leading the Task Group was the brand new amphibious assault ship *Bulwark*, and she was accompanied by the LSL RFA *Sir Bedivere* with Royal Marines from 45 Commando

Illustrious arrives in Malta (NN)

embarked. The MCMVs *Blyth* and *Ramsey* supported the Task Group. Joining the group off western Scotland was *Ocean*, straight from exercises off the coast of Devon. *Ocean* had been exercising her new digital Bowman communications system as well as the Apache attack helicopters, which were flown by RAF crews.

The Amphibious Task Force carried out a range of joint exercises under dark menacing skies, with opposed landings conducted through swept channels. Other elements of the JMC included ASW (anti-submarine warfare) exercises and an air warfare component, based on the weapon ranges off Cape Wrath. Amphibious raids were also carried out against the islands of Scalpay and Raasay.

The success of these exercises marked a fitting end to the long run of JMC exercises. On completion of the JMC, *Ocean* headed south for a brief visit to Devonport before sailing north to test her operational capability under the extreme weather conditions off northern Norway.

Malta Conference Towards the end of 2005 the fleet flagship, *Illustrious*, sailed from Portsmouth and headed for the Mediterranean. After sailing through the Straits of Gibraltar she steamed east to Malta, where she prepared to enter harbour with full ceremonial. She then sailed into Grand Harbour in procedure Alpha, exchanging twenty-one-gun salutes with the Maltese saluting battery on the ramparts of Valletta. At Malta *Illustrious* hosted a reception attended by HM the Queen and assisted with the meeting of Commonwealth heads of state.

Task Force 58
At the beginning of 2006 *Bulwark* and the destroyer *Nottingham* departed from the UK en route for the Mediterranean.

Operation Active Endeavour After a brief visit to Gibraltar, *Nottingham* continued on her way to relieve the destroyer

Nottingham with the Russian missile cruiser *Moskva* on Operation Active Endeavour
(NN)

Manchester and join the NATO Standing Response Force. The force was deployed to the Mediterranean on anti-terrorist duties as part of the international Operation Active Endeavour, primarily in the eastern Mediterranean. *Nottingham* was to serve for three months before being relieved by the destroyer *York*.

Task Force 58 *Bulwark* meanwhile sailed on through the Mediterranean and transited through the Suez Canal on her way to the Gulf. Once in the Gulf she joined the allied naval force, Task Force 58, which was conducting maritime security operations in the region and guarding the two huge oil platforms through which most of Iraq's oil was being piped to waiting tankers. Command of Task Force 58 was being exercised by the Royal Navy, with Commodore Bruce Williams and his staff embarked on board the US *Ticonderoga* class missile cruiser USS *Cape St George*, waiting for the arrival of *Bulwark*. The frigate *Montrose* and the

forward repair ship RFA *Diligence* also formed part of Task Force 58. Whilst in the Gulf, *Bulwark* carried out maritime security operations policing predominently the waters in the north.

Exercise Sea Dagger After a spell on patrol, *Bulwark* stood down from her security operations in the northern Gulf and sailed south with 4 Assault Squadron and Alpha Company of 40 Commando to conduct exercise Sea Dagger with the United Arab Emirates (UAE). This was a combined amphibious assault exercise including three UAE landing ships and a company of UAE marines. The final assaults included a night landing and a cliff assault.

On completion of exercise Sea Dagger, *Bulwark* returned on station to protect the oil platforms and police the dangerous waters in the north of the Gulf. Also on station was the frigate *St Albans*, which had just arrived in the area to relieve *Montrose*. *Bulwark* had a successful time during

Lancaster astern of the French nuclear carrier FS *Charles de Gaulle* on the Agapanthe 06 Deployment (NN)

her second and final spell operating with the multi-national coalition Task Force 150. She intercepted an oil-smuggling tanker and assisted a stricken merchant ship which was on fire and drifting. Having completed her time on task, *Bulwark* sailed from the Gulf and began the passage back to the UK, where she was due back on 21 July, in time to clean up for Plymouth Navy Days in August. In fact, dramatic events in the Mediterranean were to prevent her from arriving home on schedule.

French Carrier Task Group: Agapanthe 06 Deployment Also deployed in the Middle East was the Type 23 frigate *Lancaster*, which was acting as an escort to the French nuclear carrier FS *Charles de Gaulle*. The French Carrier Task Group, which was on an anti-terrorist deployment to the Middle East, codenamed Agapanthe 06, also included the French frigates FS *Montcalm* and FS *Cassard*, the submarine FS *Saphir* and the auxiliary support ship FS *Somme*, and formed part of the allied maritime force conducting security

operations in the Arabian Sea and Indian Ocean. The Dutch destroyer HMNLS *De Zeven Provincien* was also operating with the group.

In March, *Lancaster* and FS *Montcalm* were detached from the group and sent 250 miles at full speed to aid a stricken container ship in the Gulf of Aden. The bulk container ship *Hyundai Fortune* had sent out a 'Mayday' distress call after suffering a huge explosion, caused by a container of fireworks, which had ignited blazing fires, engulfing the whole after-section of the ship and tearing the superstructure apart. *Lancaster* took charge of rescue operations and established a safety zone around the stricken ship, whilst HMNLS *De Zeven Provincien* rescued the crew, and FS *Montcalm* took casualties back to FS *Charles de Gaulle*. The damage, in excess of £150m, was assessed as one of the most expensive maritime disasters on record.

Exercises with the Indian Navy On completion of the rescue, the French Carrier Task Group proceeded east across the India Ocean for a short period of rest and recreation in

Mumbai. The Task Group then sailed for exercises with the Indian Navy, including the Indian Navy aircraft carrier INS *Viraat* (ex HMS *Hermes*).

Return to the UK After a further spell of patrol duties in the Gulf, *Lancaster* departed from the area for passage back to the UK. On her way back, in the Mediterranean, she stopped in Corfu for a visit and whilst there cleaned up the special naval war grave and memorial for the dead of the Corfu Incident. Forty-four men of the destroyers *Saumarez* and *Volage* had lost their lives in the incident in 1946, and twelve of them were buried in the cemetery. The work was not wasted as, later in the year, on 22 October, a special ceremony was held to mark the sixtieth anniversary of the incident.

The ceremony was attended by members of the ship's company of *Sutherland*, the former First Sea Lord, Admiral Sir Jock Slater, and the President of the White Ensign Association, Commodore Sir Donald Gosling, who had been present at the time of the incident, serving in the cruiser *Leander*.

At last, in the middle of July, *Lancaster* arrived back in Portsmouth to a rousing welcome home and a fly-past, which included a veteran World War II Lancaster bomber.

———•———

Peace-Keeping in Afghanistan At the beginning of the year, 150 Royal Marines from 42 Commando were deployed to Helmand Province in the south of Afghanistan. They formed the advance guard of a force of up to 3,300 British troops to be sent to Afghanistan for peace-keeping duties. The task of the Royal Marines was to protect army and RAF personnel from Taliban attacks as they prepared an operating base at Lashkar Gar, capital of the province. The rest of the Commando was due to be sent to Afghanistan later in the

Illustrious sails out of Portsmouth on a grey day, bound for the Middle East (NN)

year. Earlier, Royal Marine Engineers returned from the mountains of Kashmir, where they had built thirty temporary schools and seventeen health centres.

The Aquila 06 Deployment: March–July 2006

In 2006 a further task group was planned for a deployment to the Middle East, designated Aquila 06.

The Aquila 06 Task Group At the end of March, the Aquila 06 Task Group was formed up for deployment to the Indian Ocean and the Arabian Sea. *Illustrious*, in her new role as a strike carrier, was the flagship of Rear Admiral Neil Morisetti, COMUKMARFOR. The carrier's TAG consisted of GR7 Harriers of 800 NAS, Merlin helicopters of 814 NAS and 'A' Flight of 849 NAS.

Illustrious was escorted by the Type 42 destroyer *Gloucester*, and supported by the fleet replenishment ship RFA *Fort Victoria*, the support tanker RFA *Brambleleaf* and the forward repair ship RFA *Diligence*. The fleet submarine *Sovereign* was assigned to the Task Group, and the French frigate FS *Surcouf* was also to join the group as it transited across the Mediterranean.

The Task Group Sails *Illustrious* and the group sailed from Portsmouth on the 29 March with Lady Sarah Chatto as the ship's friend on board the flagship. It was a dark grey day when the group sailed out of the Solent and, after disembarking visitors, turned west, exiting the Channel before setting course south-west across the Bay of Biscay. The Task Group headed on south past Gibraltar for a short visit to Santa Cruz in Tenerife. *Gloucester* sailed from Portsmouth a few days later and made passage through a rough sea in the Bay of Biscay to refuel from RFA *Brambleleaf*.

After enjoying three days in the Canaries the group sailed north-east on 5 April to rendezvous with *Gloucester* and then head for the Straits of Gibraltar. Following a brief visit to Gibraltar, the group put to sea on 8 April and headed east across the Mediterranean. As the ships sailed east they were joined by the French frigate FS *Surcouf*. They then exercised together as they steamed across the Mediterranean before transiting through the Suez Canal on 18 April.

Exercise Magic Carpet After passing through the Suez Canal the Task Group headed for Oman and on into the Arabian Sea. *Gloucester* detached from the group and proceeded into the Gulf to Dubai for a ten-day visit. The Task Group then carried out exercise Magic Carpet.

Exercise Konkan 06 After recovering from exercise Magic Carpet the Task Group sailed east on 29 April through the Arabian Sea to rendezvous with the Indian Navy for exercise Konkan 06 in the Indian Ocean. *Illustrious* carried out a port visit to Mumbai whilst *Gloucester*, which had rejoined the group, visited Karachi. The ships then took part in the ten-day exercise Konkan 06. It was the first bilateral maritime exercise with the Indian Navy for almost forty years.

Task Force 150 (Operation Calash) After the exercises, the Aquila 06 Task Group continued working with the multi-national coalition Task Force 150 patrolling the waters of the Arabian Sea and Indian Ocean. The codename for this operation was Calash. The coalition forces were carrying out essential security work, enabling the world's shipping to pass through the vital sea lanes from east to west with some degree of protection.

As well as continuing the campaign against terrorism, the coalition forces were apprehending smugglers and drug traffickers. Vast quantities of heroin were being shipped through the western Indian Ocean, earning it the nickname of the 'Hashish Highway'. The coalition forces were also maintaining the campaign against the many pirates in the area. Small high-speed vessels from the coasts of the Yemen and Somalia regularly attack international shipping, and Task Force 150 was working hard to deter and suppress as many raids as possible.

Return Voyage At the end of June the Carrier Task Group completed its time in the Middle East and set course to return to the UK in order to be home by the end of July. It transited back through the Suez Canal on 28 June and

Illustrious in the Indian Ocean
(NN)

headed for a visit to Athens before going on to Algiers and Gibraltar. On arrival in Gibraltar on 14 July, *Illustrious* had been looking forward to embarking families for the last leg of the deployment back to Portsmouth. Sadly, however, the situation in the Lebanon had become serious and *Illustrious* was required for emergency evacuation operations. She was ordered to put to sea and sail back across the Mediterranean at full speed for Beirut, to take part in Operation Highbrow.

Exercise Joint Venture 06, May 2006 In May 2006 Rear Admiral Neil Morisetti, as the UK Maritime Component Commander, directed exercise Joint Venture 06. The exercise, codenamed Operation Saltation, was designed to test the maritime battle staff's ability to deploy and operate effectively in any emergency. The battle staff of 120 deployed to South Cerney, north-west of Swindon, and altogether some 1,300 military and civilian personnel were involved in the exercise.

Operation Highbrow: The Evacuation of Lebanon, July 2006

At the beginning of July 2006 the security situation in the Lebanon, following the Israeli invasion of the south of the country and the ongoing aerial attacks against Hezbollah,

was assessed as dangerous. As the situation deteriorated further it was decided to evacuate foreign nationals, and on 16 July the UK launched Operation Highbrow. Between 10,000 and 20,000 British passport holders were estimated to be in the Lebanon at the time, and it was not possible to fly them out as Beirut's international airport had been knocked out by Israeli air strikes on 13 July.

Illustrious, Bulwark, Gloucester, York and *St Albans* and the fleet replenishment ship RFA *Fort Victoria* were assigned to the operation and tasked to close the coast of Lebanon as quickly as possible. *Illustrious* and *Bulwark* had already sailed through the eastern Mediterranean, with *Bulwark* on a visit to Barcelona and *Illustrious* having arrived in Gibraltar, when they were ordered to head back east at best possible speed. *Illustrious* made the 2,000-mile passage back across the Mediterranean at an average speed of nearly thirty knots. RAF Chinook helicopters and six Sea King Mk 4 helicopters from 845 and 846 NAS were also assigned to the operation and flew the 1,800 miles from RNAS (Royal Naval Air Station) Yeovilton to Cyprus. Even the fleet submarine *Superb* was diverted to the area to assist with the evacuation task. Chinook helicopters flew in troops from Cyprus, and the whole operation was co-ordinated by the PJHQ (Permanent Joint Headquarters).

On 16 July a British team, led by a naval commander, was inserted into Beirut by Chinook helicopter to establish communications with PJHQ and make preparations for the mass evacuation of British citizens. The city at the time was under aerial attack. The first ship to arrive off the Lebanon was *Gloucester*; she had transited through the Suez Canal just seventeen hours earlier as a nuclear submarine escort, and put into the port of Beirut straight away on 17 July to commence evacuation operations. Parts of the port were under continuous air attack from Israeli aircraft and extreme caution was needed. She was followed a very short time later by the destroyer *York*, which had detached from the NATO maritime force deployed in the Mediterranean on Operation Active Endeavour. The frigate *St Albans* and RFA *Fort Victoria* had been in the Red Sea and did not take long to reach Beirut. Other ships arrived soon afterwards, and the biggest evacuation operation since World War II was well underway. It was a dangerous environment, with air engagements taking place and Hezbollah missile attacks on Israeli warships off the coast. An Israeli corvette, the *Hanit*, which had been firing her main armament at Beirut airport, was struck and almost destroyed by a Hezbollah missile. An Egyptian ship was sunk in another missile strike. All ships engaged in the evacuation had to be fully alert and on the lookout for missile attacks.

Some 4,400 refugees were evacuated from the waterfront in an efficient and orderly manner under the full gaze of the world's press. In typical fashion, the ships' companies showed great compassion for the evacuees, making them as comfortable as possible. The evacuees were transported to Cyprus, where they were landed and then flown back to the UK by the RAF. As soon as they had landed their evacuees the ships immediately headed back to Beirut to take off more. The last embarkation of refugees took place on 22 July, and

after that time the Royal Navy ships moved further out to sea but maintained an 'over the horizon presence' in case of further trouble. As the situation gradually eased ships were withdrawn, leaving just *York* in the vicinity as she continued to operate with the NATO Task Force, which was then being led by the Italian carrier IS *Giuseppe Garibaldi*. Its primary task was to maintain security operations until an international peace-keeping force, the UN Interim Force of 15,000, could be assembled and deployed to the Lebanon. The Task Force also worked hard to prevent illegal arms being shipped in, and more than 1,000 vessels were challenged and searched. Those discovered with weapons were handed over to the Lebanese Navy.

Royal Navy ships involved in the Evacuation of Lebanon	
Aircraft carrier:	*Illustrious*
Assault ship:	*Bulwark*
Destroyers:	*Gloucester, York*
Frigate:	*St Albans*
Submarine:	*Superb*
RFA fleet replenishment ship:	*Fort Victoria*
Sea King helicopters of 846, 848 and 849 NAS also took part.	

Operation Herrick 5,
October 2006–April 2007

42 Commando In October 2006, 42 Commando Royal Marines, with HQ 3 Commando Brigade, deployed to Afghanistan to relieve 3 Para in the dangerous Helmand Province area of southern Afghanistan for Operation Herrick 5. Elements of 45 Commando were in Kabul. Prior to deployment the Royal Marines underwent an intensive period of specialist training to prepare them for the tactics and procedures employed in operations fighting the Taliban in that hostile region. They were trained to operate with the new Viking armoured vehicle and also the AH-64 Apache attack helicopter. On arrival on station they relieved 3 Para and formed the 'primary manoeuvre element' of the Helmand Task Force for their six-month deployment to Afghanistan.

'Relief In Place' Operations The Royal Marines carried out a series of unfortunately nicknamed 'RIP' (relief in place) operations, which enabled the troops they were relieving to fall back from the front line with no loss of secured territory, even in remote areas such as Now Zad in northern Helmand, where the Royal Regiment of Fusiliers was based and had been attacked 150 times by the Taliban. 'Kilo' Company of 42 Commando was flown in close to the edge of Now Zad by Chinook helicopters, and the Royal Marines came under immediate fire from the Taliban as they commenced relief operations. When the Taliban had been repulsed the handover continued.

800 NAS Also in theatre was 800 NAS flying Harrier GR7s, based at Kandahar. Sadly, on 2 September, just before the Royal Marines of 42 Commando arrived in theatre, a Nimrod maritime reconnaissance patrol aircraft crashed near Kandahar, killing all fourteen servicemen (army, RAF and Royal Marines) on board. The Harriers were conducting vital ground attack suppression missions in support of ground operations, and those flown by 800 NAS fired more weapons in two weeks' operations against the Taliban than they had fired in any previous air deployment.

In a dangerous mission in September, a Royal Marine officer attached to the RAF and serving with No18 (B) Squadron distinguished himself. Major Mark Hammond led a helicopter mission to evacuate wounded men from a compound in Sangin under fire. He courageously made three runs against heavy gunfire and rocket-propelled grenades, with his helicopter taking severe damage, but undaunted he managed to complete the evacuation of the wounded. He was awarded the Distinguished Flying Cross.

Total Naval Personnel in Afghanistan With both the Royal Marines and 800 NAS, the total number of Royal Navy personnel in southern Afghanistan came to over 3,000. The total, which included Naval medical services, logistics, language and intelligence experts and engineers, amounted to more than half the total British forces deployed in Afghanistan and hence far more than either of the other two services. Although Afghanistan is many miles from the sea, few in UK were aware that the Royal Navy was so heavily committed on the front line in that very dangerous area.

Visit of the Prime Minister The Prime Minister, Tony Blair, paid a flying visit to the base at Camp Bastion in Lashkar Gah. He praised the services for the work they were carrying out in the dangerous region and said they were helping to decide the fate of world security in the early twenty-first century. He added that they should know that the work they were doing was on behalf of not just the people of Afghanistan, but also the people of Britain and the wider world, and was greatly appreciated.

Action against the Taliban Shortly after arriving in Helmand, the Royal Marines were in action against the Taliban.

42 Commando in action at Musa Qal'eh
(NN)

After checking weapons on the ranges, a detachment of Royal Marines was flown to man a FOB (forward operating base) close to Gereshk in central Helmand. The Royal Marines suffered their first casualties in the first few days and were involved in hostile action almost daily. In Lashkar Gah, capital of Helmand Province, the Royal Marines were busy training the Afghan National Army. At times the fighting was intense, and it was at Lashkar Gah that the first Royal Marine was killed when a NATO convoy was attacked as it left the compound. The Royal Marines were engaging the Taliban several times a day in actions ranging from skirmishes on patrols to mortar attacks on bases.

Operation Slate The Royal Marines mounted their first armoured operation, Operation Slate, at the beginning of November to relieve the town of Gereshk. A column of thirty-three armoured Viking vehicles, with 500 men, left the base at Camp Bastion and set off for the Taliban-surrounded town in central Helmand Province. As they approached their objective, the column came under heavy fire from the Taliban. The Taliban were using RPGs (rocket-propelled grenades) as well as machine guns and mortars. A direct hit from an RPG knocked out a Viking but, undeterred, the Royal Marines pressed on, forcing the Taliban to retreat. 42 Field Squadron Royal Engineers were then able to construct fortified checkpoints for the local Afghan police force to man on the approaches to Gereshk.

Operation Zina An armoured column of Royal Marine Vikings progressed along the main highway across open plains from the air base at Kandahar and through Gereshk to Camp Bastion as Operation Zina. The column took ten hours to cover the distance and was watched the whole way by Taliban insurgents. Overhead the Harriers of 800 NAS constantly flew support missions ready to suppress any attacks from the insurgents.

Operation Vela: Sierra Leone, 2006

Major Amphibious Exercises In the autumn of 2006 the Amphibious Task Group was fully engaged in a series of amphibious exercises as part of the major exercise Operation Vela off the coast of west Africa. The Commander of the group was Commodore Philip Jones, and the landing force was commanded by Colonel David Hook. It was the biggest amphibious operation since the major exercise Saif Sareea in 2001.

Exercise Grey Cormorant The schedule started with a work-up phase in the UK codenamed exercise Grey Cormorant, which incorporated various practice amphibious landings on the north coast of Cornwall. On completion of the initial stage the Amphibious Task Group sailed south for the next phase, off the coast of west Africa.

A GR7 Harrier of 800 NAS in action against the Taliban, firing flares as a defensive measure to deflect any heat-seeking surface-to-air missiles
(NN)

The Operation Vela Task Group heading for Sierra Leone
(NN)

The Amphibious Task Group The Vela Task Group comprised the flagship, *Ocean*, the assault ship *Albion* and RFAS *Mounts Bay* and *Sir Bedivere*, escorted by the destroyer *Southampton*, the frigate *Argyll*, the ocean survey ship *Enterprise* and the 1st MCM Squadron. RFAS *Wave Knight*, *Fort Austin*, *Diligence* and *Oakleaf* supported the Task Group, and the helicopters of the Commando Helicopter Force, including Sea Kings and Lynx of 845, 846 and 847 NAS, were embarked. 40 Commando Royal Marines, 539 Assault Squadron, 29 Commando Regiment Royal Artillery and 59 Commando Engineering Squadron were also embarked in the ships of the Task Group. The total number of personnel involved was just over 3,000. The battle staffs were embarked in *Albion* with her state-of-the-art command and control facilities.

Exercise Green Eagle The serious phase of Operation Vela started when the Task Group arrived off the coast of Sierra Leone and embarked on exercise Green Eagle. This consisted of a month's intensive programme of amphibious assaults, beach landings and jungle warfare training.

Hearts and Minds The exercises also included periods of working with the people of Sierra Leone on 'hearts and minds' projects. Engineers from 59 Commando Squadron Engineers rebuilt three bridges; a team from *Ocean* rebuilt a school at Tokeh, and a team from RFA *Diligence* worked at the Milton Morgai School for the blind. Various teams helped rebuild and paint damaged hospitals and houses. Toys, including footballs, were given to local children, and time was taken out to play with them, which they appreciated enormously.

Exercise Green Eagle (NN)

OTHER FLEET ACTIVITIES

Trafalgar 200 Fleet Review
The International Fleet Review The Royal Navy commemorated the bicentenary of the Battle of Trafalgar and the life of Admiral Lord Nelson with an impressive International Fleet Review at Spithead and a number of other events and ceremonies at the end of June 2005.

Fleet Review, 28 June 2005 Some 170 ships gathered together in the Solent over the days leading up to the review and were anchored in precise lines by ship type and nation. On 27 June a dress rehearsal was held, and on the morning of 28 June, the ice patrol ship *Endurance* acting as a Royal Yacht, led by the Trinity House vessel *Patricia*, sailed out of Portsmouth harbour. On board *Endurance* were HM the Queen and a host of senior international dignitaries and VIPs.

In the Solent the reviewing ships, MV *Patricia*, *Endurance*, *Chatham*, *Scott*, RFA *Sir Bedivere*, *Enterprise*, MY *Leander* (private yacht of Commodore Sir Donald Gosling, President of the White Ensign Association) and the tall ship *Grand Turk*, formed up in two divisions. The two divisions then proceeded to steam up and down the lines of ships in the Solent. On completion, a fly-past was carried out by aircraft of the Fleet Air Arm, followed by a high-speed steam-past of destroyers and frigates.

Son et Lumière In the evening a spectacular *son et lumière* representing a mock sea battle was held using tall ships. The finale was a massive firework display and illumination of the review fleet.

The French nuclear strike carrier FS *Charles de Gaulle* in the Solent for the Fleet Review to commemorate Nelson and Trafalgar
(MH)

The fleet flagship *Invincible*, dressed overall and with her sides manned to cheer HM the Queen
(MH)

International Drumhead Ceremony On Wednesday 29 June 2005 maritime veterans from many nations and conflicts gathered together on Southsea Common at Portsmouth for a special Drumhead Ceremony to commemorate those fallen in conflict. The moving service was held round an altar of drums, stacked in a pyramid shape and draped with regimental colours.

International Festival of the Sea The following day, a four-day International Festival of the Sea began at Portsmouth Historic Dockyard and Royal Naval Base. Many of the ships which had taken part in the International Fleet Review, as well as the tall ships, were open to visitors. Static and dynamic displays were held on shore and afloat, as well as band recitals, concerts and parades.

The Royal Fleet Auxiliary Centenary, 3 August 2005 Ships of the RFA embarked on a centenary tour of the UK in July and August to commemorate the 100 years of excellent service provided by the RFA in support of the Royal Navy. The RFA carried out a series of popular port visits by the fleet tanker RFA *Wave Ruler*, the 28,000-ton aviation training ship RFA *Argus* and the LSL RFA *Sir Galahad*. The ships visited London, Newcastle, Rosyth, Scarborough, Glasgow, Liverpool, Portsmouth, Cardiff, Belfast, Dartmouth and Falmouth.

The RFA celebrated its 100th birthday on 3 August 2005. It was a very proud moment for a Service that had served the Royal Navy so faithfully and well, accompanying it loyally and bravely on nearly every operation, deployment and campaign. Over that time the RFA had suffered many casualties and gained a great many decorations, battle honours, and bravery and gallantry awards.

Kidnap Rescue Earlier in the year in February *Invincible* and *Montrose* carried out a dramatic rescue. Somali pirates had seized a Thai fishing vessel and kidnapped the crew of twenty-three fishermen. Helicopters from both warships searched the area and managed to track down the pirates. A boarding party from *Montrose*, assisted by the USS *Munro*, then arrested the pirates and released the kidnapped crew.

Russian Submarine Rescue On 5 August 2005, a flash 'Submiss' appeal was received by the Royal Navy following the disappearance of a small Russian submarine, the *Priz AS-28*, in the Pacific Ocean. Immediately a Royal Navy rescue team, led by Commander Ian Riches and equipped with a Scorpio 45 remotely operated submersible robot, set off for Russia. The Russian submarine was snagged on cables and wires more than 600 feet deep, and it took the Royal Navy rescue team over six hours to free it, but the submarine came to the surface with the entire crew exhausted but still alive. It was a tremendous achievement, and the Russian President, Mr Putin, telephoned Prime Minister Tony Blair saying that the rescue mission by the Royal Navy had been of utmost value to Russia.

Operation Maturin Following the earthquake in Pakistan in October 2005, the Royal Marines were deployed to the lower Himalayas on Operation Maturin, assisting in the major relief operations.

Wilkinson Sword of Peace At the end of 2005 the frigate *Richmond* was awarded the Wilkinson Sword of Peace for the great work done by the ship's company in the Caribbean following the devastation wrought by Hurricane 'Ivan'. The disaster relief work included the provision of emergency water supplies, treating over 200 of the sick, repairing and opening Grenada's hospital, restoring electrical power and opening the airport for delivery of relief supplies.

The steam-past of destroyers and frigates at the Fleet Review (Geoff Hunt RSMA) (GH)

SHIPS, WEAPONS AND AIRCRAFT

New Type 45 *Daring* Class Destroyers Construction of the new 7,530-ton Type 45 *Daring* class destroyers was well underway. The destroyers were being built in sections, with the 1,100-ton bow sections being built by Vosper Thornycroft in Portsmouth and then transported by barge to BAE Systems shipyard at Govan on the Clyde for completion.

The Viking All-Terrain Armoured Vehicle In 2005 the Royal Marines took delivery of their new all-terrain armoured vehicle, the Viking. The initial outfit was for 108 Vikings. The armoured fighting vehicle is fully amphibious, able to operate in up to sea state 2 and transportable by helicopter.

The 50-metre E45 bow section of the destroyer *Daring* being towed out of Portsmouth
(RNM)

Sonar 2087 Towed Array The towed-array sonar S2087 was being developed and fitted as a fully integrated, towed, active and passive ASW sonar system. The system, with its greatly extended range, was developed for the Type 23 frigates to replace the passive 2031 sonar system. By the end of 2006 the frigates *Westminster*, *Northumberland* and *Richmond* had been fitted with S2087.

Farewell the SHAR (the Sea Harrier) On 28 March 2006 the Sea Harriers of 801 NAS took off from their base at RNAS Yeovilton for the very last time. They then dipped their noses in farewell salute to Vice Admiral Adrian Johns, Second Sea Lord and senior serving naval aviator, before landing one by one for the final time. The Sea Harrier was then withdrawn from service, but the men of 801 NAS were reformed to fly Harrier GR7s and 9s with the RAF as part of the Joint Force Harrier based at RAF Cottesmore.

PERSONNEL MATTERS

The Naval Divisional System It was recognised that the naval divisional system, whereby men and women were formed into small divisions under a dedicated divisional officer and senior rate for personal administration and management, was one of the great strengths in promoting the welfare of the men and women. It was also acknowledged as one of the important elements of naval leadership. It was therefore decided to reinvigorate the divisional system, involving the leading hands more and bringing them into the reporting process.

Centenary of Britannia Royal Naval College, Dartmouth In 2005 the Britannia Royal Naval College at Dartmouth celebrated a century of naval officer training. The fine naval college, on the prominent hill overlooking the River Dart at Dartmouth, was designed by Sir Aston Webb and was built to replace the old hulks of *Britannia* and *Hindostan*, moored in the Dart, which had trained generations of naval officers. King Edward VII laid the foundation stone of the new college on 2 March 1902, and the Britannia Royal Naval College was opened on 14 September 1905. The purpose-built college went on to educate generations of naval officers, not just those of the Royal Navy but also significant numbers of officer cadets from Commonwealth navies.

Defence Training Review In order to achieve efficiencies and cost savings, the Defence Training Review investigated the combining of defence training commitments. As a result, tri-service training centres were to be established for much of the specialist training in the armed forces.

The New Pension Scheme (AFPS 05) In 2005 a brand new Armed Forces Pension Scheme, known as the AFPS 05 Pension Scheme, was introduced for all those joining the armed forces after 1 April 2005. It was a radically different pension scheme, aimed to replace the previous pension scheme, known as AFPS 75, which provided an immediate pension, payable after a minimum of twenty-two years'

service over the age of eighteen (sixteen years' service over the age of twenty-one for officers). The new scheme paid a full, enhanced pension at age sixty-five, with a scheme of early departure compensatory payments up to age sixty-five for those with sufficient qualifying service. In other words the old pension scheme was re-profiled to pay more in retirement and less in pre-retirement years.

'Offer to Transfer' (OTT) All those serving in the armed forces prior to April 2005 had preserved rights to remain on the old pension scheme, but they were also given the opportunity to transfer to the new scheme should they wish. This was known as the 'Offer to Transfer', known rather unfortunately as the 'OTT'. Those serving were given one year in which to decide whether they wished to exercise their option and transfer all their service to the new pension scheme.

To assist all those serving with the difficult choice of whether to change to the new scheme or remain on AFPS 75, the White Ensign Association recruited Lieutenant Commander Mike Howell, a naval pensions expert, who spent one year touring ships, units and establishments advising and guiding all those facing the difficult choice.

Joint Personnel Administration (JPA) In 2006 the new fully computerised administration system for personnel in all three armed services, known as JPA (Joint Personnel Administration),

The Britannia Royal Naval College, Dartmouth
(NN)

was introduced. The system was designed to give all serving personnel direct access to a centralised system concerning all pay, allowances, expenses, leave, records, etc.

It was introduced initially in the RAF, and many teething problems were encountered. The 'switch-over' week for the 37,000 personnel in the Royal Navy, including Reserves, was 13–22 October 2006, with individuals phasing in over a two-week period in November.

A 'Tugg' cartoon
(NN)

As expected, the new system did not work entirely smoothly and many people were disappointed with the countless problems that ensued. Some people were left without pay and had mortgages, commitments, direct debits and standing orders not met owing to lack of funds. Where penalty charges were incurred individuals were compensated.

Operational Allowance In October 2006 the MoD announced the introduction of a new Operational Allowance to compensate service personnel for the dangers faced in certain operational areas. The areas specified included Iraqi territorial waters in the northern Gulf, which covered Royal Navy ships attached to allied Task Force 158.

Branch Development A new simplified branch structure was being designed to match the changing needs of the Service. Eight new basic branches covering Seamanship and Warfare, Engineering and Logistics would, in 2007, replace the many sub-branches (see chapter 15).

Tugg Lieutenant Bill Wilson M B E, known to generations of the Navy simply as 'Tugg', sadly died in November 2006. He joined the Royal Navy as a Naval Air Mechanic in 1947 and was promoted to Officer in 1964. He served in the aircraft carrier *Victorious* and was persuaded to run the ship's newspaper, 'Vic News'. He developed a special cartoon style portraying 'Jack' and went on to become the most celebrated cartoonist in naval circles. He mostly illustrated naval magazines and papers, including the *Navy News*, but was also used to liven up official publications, such as *Cockpit* and Naval BRs (Naval Books of Reference). His cartoons appeared in the national press, including *Punch*, *The Times*, *Daily Mirror* and *News of the World*.

THE WHITE ENSIGN ASSOCIATION

Fleet Review Members of the Council of the White Ensign Association were privileged to be invited by the President, Commodore Sir Donald Gosling K C V O, R N R, to witness the International Fleet Review on 22 June 2005, from on board his yacht M Y *Leander*.

M Y *Leander*, flying the White Ensign, took her place in the reviewing line astern of *Enterprise*, and members of the Council and VIP guests were able to see the host of ships and watch the various events, including the fly-past and the steam-past, at close quarters.

Faslane Visit Earlier in the year the Council visited the Trident nuclear submarine base at H M S *Neptune* on the Gare Loch at Faslane. The Commodore of Faslane, Commodore Carolyn Stait, hosted the Association, and visits were arranged to various units and ships as well as the *Vanguard* class nuclear deterrent submarine *Vigilant*.

Reception in *Invincible* In the summer the Council hosted a reception on board the carrier *Invincible* at Greenwich. The reception was a most enjoyable event, helping to raise the profile of the Association, and was attended by several hundred people.

Chairman Mr John Andrewes relieved Admiral Sir Jock Slater as Chairman of the White Ensign Association at the AGM held at Lloyds of London in November 2005. Admiral the Lord Boyce was appointed Vice Chairman.

CTCRM, Lympstone Early in 2006 the Association spent a day at the Commando Training Centre, Royal Marines (CTCRM) at Lympstone. The Council observed the rigorous training regime carried out by the Royal Marines.

The Council and staff of the WEA at CTCRM Lympstone (CTCRM)

Royal Patron H R H the Prince of Wales, Patron of the White Ensign Association, was promoted full Admiral on 14 November 2006.

Ongoing Operations in Iraq and Afghanistan 2007–2009

OPERATION TELIC (IRAQ AND THE GULF) – OPERATIONS HERRICK V AND VII (AFGHANISTAN) –
ORION 07 AND ORION 08 DEPLOYMENTS

The focus of world politics remained firmly centred on the Middle East at the beginning of 2007 with security operations in Iraq, the northern Gulf and Afghanistan dominating US and British foreign policy. Operation Enduring Freedom, the worldwide campaign against terrorism, was maintained. Terrorist bomb attacks around the world continued to kill and maim, with Al-Qaeda bombs in Algiers slaughtering thirty-three people. Executions of high-ranking members of Saddam Hussein's regime continued in Iraq, including those of Saddam Hussein's half-brother, the former Iraq Intelligence Chief and the former Chief Judge of the Revolutionary Court.

In the Far East, following a threatened naval blockade, North Korea agreed to abandon its nuclear programme in exchange for a deal to provide oil supplies. The Royal Navy had not been able to contribute to the naval blockade due to the pressure of other commitments. Iran on the other hand continued, against pressure from the international community, with its nuclear programme, Project 111, which Western intelligence sources believed was designed to produce a nuclear warhead.

In Europe Romania and Bulgaria joined the European Union, whilst in the UK Tony Blair stepped down as Prime

FIRST SEA LORD
Admiral Band

SECOND SEA LORDS
Admirals Johns and Massey

MANPOWER
38,000

MERCANTILE MARINE
1,228 merchant ships

Minister, handing over to his former Chancellor of the Exchequer, Gordon Brown. In Northern Ireland an iconic moment occurred when Ian Paisley, leader of the Ulster Democratic Unionist Party, shook hands with Gerry Adams, President of Sinn Fein, as they met to form a power-sharing executive and assembly in Northern Ireland.

UK Defence Policy At the beginning of 2007 the UK remained fully committed to ongoing operations in Iraq (Operation Telic) and in Afghanistan (Operation Herrick) despite mounting political pressures to withdraw from Iraq and the widening deficit in the defence budget. Considerable military and naval forces were deployed to the area to help build peace and security in such an unstable yet vital part of the world.

THE FLEET

The Royal Navy retained a balanced Fleet in 2007 with a worldwide capability. It was still very powerful even though it had been reduced considerably in size and was heavily stretched in fulfilling all its operational commitments as well as meeting exercise and training requirements. The First Sea Lord stated: 'Despite the rather gloomy portrayal of a shrinking Navy that is all too frequently rehearsed in the press, what is so often misunderstood is the significantly improved capability the Royal Navy may now draw on.'[1]

Aircraft Carriers The core of the Fleet was based on the two remaining old *Invincible* class carriers. *Ark Royal* had rejoined the Fleet in March 2007 after a two-year £20 million refit in Rosyth, which provided her with an improved amphibious assault capability.

Illustrious remained the fleet flagship, whilst the third carrier, *Invincible*, remained in reserve at 'extended readiness' in Portsmouth naval base at ninety days' notice for operational service. The carriers are due to be decommissioned progressively, beginning with *Invincible* in 2010, followed by *Ark Royal* in 2012 and then finally by *Illustrious* in 2015.

The Future Carriers (CVF Programme) The *Invincible* class carriers are due to be replaced by the two new large 64,000-ton aircraft carriers *Queen Elizabeth* and *Prince of Wales*. The in-service dates are planned for 2014 and 2016,

---

HMS *Queen Elizabeth*
Future Aircraft Carriers (CVF)
The planned new 64,000-ton aircraft carriers *Queen Elizabeth* and *Prince of Wales* are designed to replace the three *Invincible* class light aircraft carriers with an in-service date of 2014 and 2016 respectively. The carriers will be conventionally powered and will

operate an air group of forty aircraft, which will include the Lockheed Martin F-35B (short take off and vertical landing, or STOVL) Joint Strike Fighter, the EH 101 Merlin helicopter and maritime surveillance and control (AEW) aircraft. The carriers will be the biggest and most powerful surface warships ever operated by the Royal Navy. An interesting design feature is the inclusion of two separate structures on the flight deck, with flying operations to be conducted from the after tower and the forward tower to be used for navigation, direction and ship handling.

Launched:	
Commissioned:	
Displacement:	65,000 tonnes
Length:	284m
Propulsion:	4 Rolls-Royce Olympus TM3B gas turbines to 2 shafts
Armament:	Total of 40 to include: joint combat aircraft, maritime airborne surveillance and control (MASC) aircraft and Merlin helicopters.
Complement:	1,500 (including air crew)
No. in class:	2 planned: *Queen Elizabeth* and *Prince of Wales*

which could produce a brief capability shortfall between the decommissioning of *Ark Royal* in 2012 and the commissioning of *Queen Elizabeth* two years later, particularly if there should be any slippage in their construction. The new carriers are firmly in the programme, though their future remains by no means guaranteed. The concept was agreed nearly a decade ago, in 1998, though no firm order had been placed by 2007. A welcome step was however taken in July 2007 when the government announced that funding for the carriers had been approved; this injected some £7.7 billion into the defence budget. The Defence Minister, Baroness Taylor, then signed the contract for the two new aircraft carriers on 3 July 2008 on board *Ark Royal* in Portsmouth. The main aircraft intended for the new carriers will be the new JSF (Joint Strike Fighter), the F-35 strike jet, though questions remain over its in-service date. Clearly much remains at stake for the future capability of the Royal Navy.

(Top) The newly refitted *Ark Royal* in Portsmouth (RH)

(Above left) The new landing ship dock (auxiliary) RFA *Largs Bay* (RH)

(Above right) The Type 23 frigate *Westminster* (John Webster RSMA) (JW)

Amphibious Ships The powerful amphibious fleet consisted of the LPH (landing platform helicopter) *Ocean* and the two LPDs (landing platform docks), *Albion* and *Bulwark*. At the end of 2007 *Ocean* undertook a £30 million maintenance and upgrade programme, rejoining the Fleet in September 2008. The four new RFA (Royal Fleet Auxiliary) ships of the Bay class, officially designated landing ship dock (auxiliary), RFAs *Largs Bay*, *Mounts Bay*, *Lyme Bay* and *Cardigan Bay* reinforced the amphibious fleet. Also supporting it was the last of the landing ships (logistic), RFA *Sir Bedivere*.

Escort Fleet The escort fleet consisted of twenty-five frigates and destroyers. The thirteen Type 23 Duke class frigates provided the core of the escort fleet, supported by the aging eight remaining elderly Batch 2 and Batch 3 Type 42 destroyers and the last four of the Batch 3 Type 22 frigates.

The first four of the new 7,230-ton Type 45 *Daring* class destroyers were well under construction, with the bow section of the fourth, *Dragon*, being completed by VT Shipbuilders at Portsmouth in October 2007. *Daring* commenced trials earlier in the year and was intended to join the Fleet at the beginning of 2009. Six of the class were under construction, and it was hoped that further units would be built.

Submarines The submarine fleet consisted of the four Trident missile-equipped *Vanguard* class SSBNs (ballistic missile-carrying nuclear submarines), which continued to be responsible for the UK's strategic nuclear deterrent, the seven *Trafalgar* class SSNs (nuclear fleet submarines) and the last two *Swiftsure* class SSNs.

Mine Counter-Measures Vessels (MCMVs) The MCMV flotilla consisted of the eight ships of the Hunt class, built from glass-reinforced plastic (GRP) and equipped with the latest 2193 sonar, and the eight smaller GRP single-role minehunters of the *Sandown* class.

Patrol Vessels and Survey Ships The patrol vessels consisted of the four River class, two specialist patrol vessels, *Scimitar* and *Sabre*, and sixteen P2000 *Archer* class coastal patrol craft. The surveying fleet comprised the 13,000-ton ocean survey vessel *Scott*, two *Echo* class coastal survey vessels, one old coastal survey vessel, *Roebuck*, and an inshore survey vessel.

RFA The Royal Navy was supported by two modern fleet tankers, two old support tankers and two old small fleet tankers. There were also four fleet replenishment ships, an aviation training ship and a forward repair ship. As mentioned above, the RFA manned the four new amphibious ships (landing ship dock) of the Bay class.

Naval Aviation The aircraft of the Fleet Air Arm consisted of the Harrier GR7s and GR9s of 800 and 801 NAS (Naval Air Squadron), subsumed into the Naval Strike Wing of the JFH (Joint Force Harrier), and the Merlin, Sea King and Lynx helicopters.

Royal Marines The Corps of the Royal Marines consisted of 3 Commando Brigade with 40, 42 and 45 Commandos and 539 Assault Squadron, with logistic, communications, artillery and engineering support. 3 Commando Brigade formed a core component of the UK's Joint Rapid Reaction Force.

Fleet Command Admiral Sir Mark Stanhope, straight from a key NATO appointment with SACLANT (the Supreme Allied Commander Atlantic) in the USA, relieved Admiral Burnell-Nugent as CINCFLEET (Commander in Chief Fleet) in November

The SSBN *Vengeance* returns from patrol (NN)

IMPULSE

2007. The sea-going operational Commander was Rear Admiral Zambellas as COMUKMARFOR (Commander UK Maritime Forces), with Commodore Potts as COMUKTG (Commander UK Task Group) and Commodore Jones as COMATG (Commander Amphibious Task Group). Commodore Cunningham was Commander UK Carrier Strike Group, and Brigadier Capewell was Commander 3 Commando Brigade Royal Marines.

Fleet Bases At the beginning of 2008 the Royal Navy still retained three main naval bases in the UK, with the surface fleet continuing to be divided into two main flotillas based at the two south coast naval bases at Portsmouth and Devonport. The Portsmouth Flotilla consisted of the two operational aircraft carriers, the Type 42 destroyers and half the Type 23 frigates together with the Fishery Protection Squadron, the 2nd MCM (Mine Counter-Measures) Squadron and the 1st Patrol Boat Squadron.

The Devonport Flotilla was based on the ships of the Amphibious Task Group, the Type 22 frigates and the other half of the Type 23 frigates. The survey ships and a squadron of hunter-killer fleet submarines were also part of the flotilla. The third naval base, in the north at Faslane, was home to the nuclear deterrent Trident submarines, a squadron of hunter-killer fleet submarines and the 1st MCM Squadron.

Future of the Naval Bases The study into the future requirements for and structure of the UK naval bases that had been set up in 2006 finally reached a conclusion and reported in February 2008. The sensitive question as to which base might be axed was finally resolved with the decision to retain all three for the time being but with reduced capability in Portsmouth and Devonport. The decision was greeted with much relief, both in the local communities and generally throughout the Navy. There still remained a question mark over the viability of retaining the nuclear deterrent in Scotland if that became politically unacceptable to the people of Scotland.

First Sea Lord In 2008 Admiral Sir Jonathan Band continued as head of the Royal Navy in the appointment of First Sea Lord and Chief of the Naval Staff.

OPERATIONS AND DEPLOYMENTS, 2007–2009

Although the focal point of operations remained the Middle East, including the eastern Mediterranean, the Royal Navy continued to conduct operations in other parts of the world. Although this was not widely known, in January 2007 the Royal Navy and Royal Marines made up more than 50 per cent of the UK forces deployed in southern Afghanistan.

Standing Commitments

In 2007 the Royal Navy maintained its full range of commitments in home waters, abroad and to the standing NATO forces, as follows:

Strategic Nuclear Deterrent The *Vanguard* class SSBNs continued their constant nuclear deterrent patrols undetected in the vast depths of the world's oceans. By 2007 the Royal Navy had carried the burden of providing the nation's strategic nuclear deterrent continuously for almost thirty-nine years. In June 2007 the Trident submarine *Vengeance* returned to Faslane having completed the 300th nuclear deterrent patrol by the Royal Navy. It was a fine achievement, and waiting to greet *Vengeance* as she berthed alongside were the Secretary of State for Defence, Des Browne, and the First Sea Lord, Admiral Sir Jonathan Band. Later in December[2] *Vengeance* completed what she claimed to be a record deterrent deployment of 103 days.[3]

14 June 2008 saw an important milestone, being the fortieth anniversary of the departure of the Polaris-armed SSBN *Resolution* from Faslane on the first strategic nuclear deterrent patrol undertaken by the Royal Navy.

Fishery Protection The Fishery Protection Squadron was reorganised in 2006 after the withdrawal of the Northern Ireland Squadron. The core of the 'Fish Squadron' remained the three River class OPVs (offshore patrol vessels) *Tyne*, *Severn* and *Mersey*, but the MCMVs, which also formed part of the 'Fish Squadron', were divided into two squadrons. The eight *Sandown* class MCMVs formed the 1st MCM Squadron, based at Faslane, whilst the eight Hunt class MCMVs formed the 2nd MCM Squadron, based at Portsmouth.

The ships of the 'Fish Squadron' kept up their important tasks, working under the direction of DEFRA (the Department for the Environment, Food and Rural Affairs) in policing and enforcing EEC fishery policies as well as patrolling the UK's extended fisheries zone. As fishing stocks continued to decrease the task became increasingly important. The squadron also carried out the vital task of protecting the offshore oil rigs and gas installations.

Gibraltar The two armed *Scimitar* class fast patrol boats, *Scimitar* and *Sabre*, together with three Arctic RIBs (rigid inflatable boats), formed the Gibraltar Patrol Boat Squadron and were permanently stationed in Gibraltar. The fast patrol boats worked watch and watch about in weekly shifts. The prime duty of the squadron was protecting the security of the British territorial waters surrounding the Rock of Gibraltar, but it also supported the many NATO ships and vessels passing through the Straits of Gibraltar.

At the beginning of the year the squadron took part in the security exercise Med Gun, which involved the fast insertion of men from 148 Commando Battery Royal Artillery by parachute as a rapid response reinforcement exercise.

Cyprus The small armed *Archer* class patrol craft *Pursuer* and *Dasher* continued to be deployed to Cyprus. Together with a detachment of Royal Marines and two fast inshore patrol boats, they maintained force protection patrols for the Sovereign Base Area. As well as carrying out counter-terrorist activities, they protected allied shipping transiting through the important staging post at Cyprus en route to the Gulf.

Task Group 326.01: Atlantic Patrol Task (North) The Type 42 destroyer *Liverpool*, having relieved the frigate *Portland*, was assigned to the duties of the North Atlantic Patrol Area, which included the Caribbean. The fleet tanker RFA *Wave Ruler* supported her. Ships of the Royal Navy provide major support to the US-led counter-drugs operations in the Caribbean throughout the year. Other ships were deployed to the area, with the helicopter assault ship *Ocean* arriving in March 2007 and the new RFA *Largs Bay* deploying later in the year. In October 2007 *Portland* managed to recover over three tons of cocaine in an interception in the North Atlantic, and two months later RFA *Largs Bay* intercepted a drugs smuggler with over half a ton of cocaine. Other ships provided subsequent deployments to the Caribbean.

Task Group 326.02: Atlantic Patrol Task (South) The Type 42 destroyer *Nottingham* was on Atlantic Patrol Task (South), having relieved her sister ship, the destroyer *Southampton*. The OPV *Dumbarton Castle* (known as 'DC') was still on station in the Falkland Islands and Antarctica, acting as the permanent guardship to protect British interests in the area. Although it had been planned for *Dumbarton Castle* to be relieved earlier, she had to extend her duty by a further four months until eventually she was relieved by the new OPV *Clyde* when she finally arrived on station in September 2007. *Clyde* was due to stay in the Falkland Islands for three to four years. The OPV also visited South Georgia and the other

Campbeltown, Argyll and *Enterprise* with RFA *Sir Bedivere* in the Gulf
(NN)

British dependencies in the far South Atlantic on a regular basis. In November 2007 the ice patrol vessel *Endurance* was en route for the Antarctic, where she was to be deployed for eighteen months.

NATO Assignments The Royal Navy continued to assign ships to the two main standing NATO maritime squadrons, namely Standing NATO Maritime Group Two (SNMG2) and Standing NATO Mine Counter-Measures Group One (SNMCMG1). SNMG2 was deployed in the Mediterranean on maritime security operations, monitoring and protecting international shipping, as part of Operation Active Endeavour.

Ongoing Operations in Iraq and Afghanistan

The main ongoing operations in 2007 were concentrated on Operation Herrick in Afghanistan and Operation Telic in Iraq and the Gulf.

Afghanistan 3 Brigade with 40 Commando Royal Marines was deployed on Operation Herrick V in Helmand Province in the south of Afghanistan. The Royal Marines were supported by 846 NAS.

The Gulf There were five elements of the Royal Navy's commitment in Iraq and the Gulf under Operation Telic. They included forces assigned to CTF (Coalition Task Force) 158 in the northern Gulf, CTF 152 in the southern and central areas of the Gulf, a Naval Assistance and Training

Team (NaTT) ashore in Iraq and a mine counter-measures squadron. The fifth element consisted of the headquarters and staff of the United Kingdom Maritime Component Commander (UKMCC) ashore in Bahrain. In 2007 the UKMCC was Commodore Keith Winstanley.

Task Group 330.01: The Gulf The Type 22 frigate *Campbeltown* had just taken over duty from the frigate *Argyll* in the southern Gulf and Straits of Hormuz in protecting international shipping on the main tanker routes in and out of the Gulf. *Campbeltown* was part of CTF 152 but was also protecting British interests in the area and helping to police the waters against smuggling and drug-running. Also in the Gulf was the survey vessel *Enterprise*, keeping the charts in the vital waterways up to date.

Iraq: Operation Telic The Royal Navy continued to play an important part with the other armed services in the ongoing extensive security operations in the south of Iraq to stabilise the country, and also in the training requirement to prepare the Iraqi forces to take over complete responsibility for security in Iraq. An essential part of the task was to keep the Shatt al-Arab waterway open and protect the oil facilities at Al Faw as well as the oil platforms at the head of the Gulf. The Royal Navy was also contributing forces to CTF 158 in the northern Gulf.

Naval Assistance and Training Team The Royal Navy led the NaTT responsible for much of the training of the Iraqi Navy. The NaTT was based on board RFA *Sir Bedivere* at Umm Qasr in 2007, and RFA *Sir Bedivere* was relieved by RFA *Cardigan Bay* in early 2008.

Exercise Smoking Gun After nearly four years of training the Iraqi Navy was ready to be tested. During June and July 2007 the staff of CTF 158 observed the various elements of exercise Smoking Gun, to test the preparedness and response of the new Iraqi Navy to simulated attacks from US fast patrol craft. When the Iraqis were informed they had passed they cheered wildly and were delighted to take over patrols in the waterways on their own, though the NaTT remained in Umm Qasr to complete the training.[4]

It was assessed that the Iraqi Navy was the most progressive of the Iraqi armed forces, and this reflected much credit on the work of the Royal Navy. It operated Predator class patrol boats as well as rigid inflatable and light aluminium boats and took delivery of the first of its new patrol ships at the end of 2008.

Withdrawal from Basra Towards the end of 2007 the British forces deployed in Basra were pulled back and reduced as the Iraqis continued to take over responsibility for maintaining security. The British troops left their headquarters in Basra Palace, handing over control of Basra to the Iraqi authorities in December. Britain continued to reduce troop numbers in the area towards the target of 2,500 originally set for spring 2008, though in the event that proved too ambitious and troop levels had to be maintained at a higher level. 845 NAS, the longest-serving helicopter squadron on Operation Telic, returned to UK with its Sea King helicopters at the end of November. It had served on Operation Telic for three and a half years. Two months later 847 NAS also returned to the UK with its Lynx helicopters.

Mine Counter-Measures The minehunters *Blyth* and *Ramsey* had arrived in the Gulf at the end of 2006 and were based

The MCMV *Atherstone* followed by the minehunters *Blyth* and *Ramsey* conducting mine clearance operations in the Khawr' Abd Allah waterway in the Gulf
(NN)

at Bahrain. They were deployed in the main shipping lanes, conducting the vital task of keeping the waterways in the Gulf clear of mines. They were reinforced by the Hunt class MCMVs *Atherstone* and *Chiddingfold* in early 2008.

Operation Herrick V

At the beginning of 2007, 3 Commando Brigade, supported by the GR7 Harriers of 800 NAS, was heavily engaged in a series of operations and actions as part of the winter offensive against the Taliban in the Helmand River valley in southern Afghanistan. The Royal Marines formed the core of the forces deployed and conducted offensive sweeps from their headquarters at Camp Bastion in Lashkar Gah, capital of Helmand Province.

(Below) Royal Marines strap themselves to an Apache helicopter for the rescue mission
(NN)

(Bottom) 42 Commando on Operation Volcano
(NN)

(Right) Royal Marines from 42 Commando clear out Taliban forces from Kajaki
(NN)

Operation Clay One of the main Taliban bases in the Garmsir region adjacent to the town of Kajaki was attacked by Royal Marines from the Reconnaissance Force, together with troops from the Light Dragoons, in Operation Clay. In a four-hour battle, assisted by strikes from supporting Apache helicopter gunships, they stormed the base, defeating the Taliban. Having dislodged the Taliban, the Royal Engineers were able to repair the hydro-electric dam on the Helmand River and restore electricity supplies for nearly two million Afghans in the surrounding area.[5]

Further Battles in the Garmsir Region At the same time Royal Marines of 45 Commando attacked other Taliban bases in Garmsir, frequently with the aid of Harrier or

Apache helicopter strikes. The Taliban were driven out of a terrorist training camp in Kajaki Olya, and a battle was fought at Gereshk. After defeating the Taliban in several engagements and driving them off, the Royal Marines captured stockpiles of weapons, AK-47 rifles, grenades and bomb-making equipment. The operations were a success, though the Royal Marines suffered a number of casualties in the fierce fighting.[6]

Recovery Operation at Jugroom Fort In an attack on Jugroom Fort in Garmsir, Lance Corporal Mathew Ford of 45 Commando was shot in the assault, but as the Royal Marines pulled back to regroup they discovered that his body had been left lying in front of the fort. Determined to leave no man behind, they set about mounting a dramatic recovery action using two Apache helicopters. Four volunteers, Captain David Rigg, Warrant Officer Colin Hearn, and Royal Marines Gary Robinson and Chris Fraser-Perry, strapped themselves to the outer sponsons of the Apaches, which then approached the fort flying low at 50mph.

Under heavy fire one Apache engaged the Taliban whilst the second Apache set down in front of the fort, allowing the men to recover the body of Mathew Ford. Amazingly

both Apaches returned with no further casualties. Warrant Officer Hearn said, 'I'm a Royal Marine. I'm RSM of the unit. He's a Royal Marine – the same as me. There was no way we were ever going to leave him, or anyone else, on that battlefield.' Lance Corporal Ford was the fourth Royal Marine killed in the Garmsir offensive.[7]

Training the Afghan National Army Whilst supporting operations Royal Marines from 42 and 45 Commando and the Commando Logistics Regiment were assigned to OMT (the Operational Mentoring Team, known as the 'omelette'), charged with the important task of training the Afghan National Army at Camp Shorabak.

Operation Volcano The Royal Marines followed up their successes, continuing to drive the Taliban further away from the main towns and villages in southern Afghanistan. They drove the Taliban out of the important town of Kajaki in northern Helmand and launched Operation Volcano to push them out of the surrounding countryside, including the stronghold of Barikju to the north of Kajaki. In some areas the Royal Marines encountered fierce resistance; insurgents in the village of Chinah poured in heavy fire and had to be suppressed with air strikes.

Operation Glacier In March the Royal Marines carried out one of the last operations of their deployment, Operation Glacier. Supported by Afghan Army gunners, they carried out an all-night assault on the Taliban headquarters south of Garmsir. Following artillery bombardment and air strikes, 250 Royal Marines, Afghan troops and Light Dragoons attacked the Taliban positions. The attackers cleared the Taliban out of a network of trenches, bunkers and compounds, destroying the defences as they went. It was an important success as the Taliban positions had commanded the strategic approaches to the region. Shortly after Operation Glacier the Royal Marines prepared to hand over to 16 Mechanised Brigade, having completed their deployment to Operation Herrick V.[8]

Achievement Following the completion of Operation Herrick V, thirty-nine Royal Marines were honoured for their gallantry during the campaign. The honours awarded included one Conspicuous Gallantry Cross, two Distinguished Service Orders, ten Military Crosses and two Queen's Gallantry Medals. Sadly the Royal Marines suffered ninety casualties, twelve of them fatal.

Operation Calash: Coalition Task Force 150 In 2007 the UK continued to support CTF 150 under Operation Calash in the Gulf of Aden, and provided the support tanker RFA *Bayleaf* as the 'Arabian Gulf Ready Tanker'. RFA *Bayleaf* was well experienced in the task, having been first assigned to the operation in 2003.

The area was of considerable strategic importance as it contained the main shipping routes from the Middle East and the Far East to Europe and the USA, and CTF 150 had been conducting maritime security operations in the vital waterway at the entrance to the Red Sea since it was formed in 2001. Its ships patrolled the Red Sea, Arabian Sea, Gulf of Oman and Indian Ocean. The area was subject not only to terrorist attacks, with the most notorious being the attacks on the USS *Cole* and the French tanker MV *Limburg*, but also to increasing numbers of attacks by pirates. One of the most dangerous areas was off the Yemeni coast, where progress was being made with the training of the newly established Yemeni coastguard force.[9]

Iraq and the Northern Gulf

Operation Troy, February 2007 Further to the north in Iraq, the Royal Marines of 539 Assault Squadron were part of Operation Troy, a major operation against smuggling and

Royal Marines patrol the Shatt al-Arab waterway (NN)

other illegal activities in Basra carried out in the middle of February 2007. The operation entailed a complete lock-down of Basra and Umm Qasr for three days and was timed to coincide with a similar but larger-scale operation, codenamed Imposing Justice, in Baghdad. Whilst the army closed down Basra, the Royal Marines sealed off the port and waterways into the city. The Royal Marines, together with Iraqi Coast Guards, mounted water patrols with ORC (offshore raiding craft) gunboats on the Shatt al-Arab waterway and the many canals leading to Basra. The border with Iran was closed, and British and Iraqi forces searched the notorious areas of the city, flushing out criminals, terrorists and weapon caches.

The Royal Navy Takes Command of CTF 158 At sea in the northern Gulf, the ships of CTF 158 maintained their vital and ceaseless patrols, protecting the merchant shipping, tankers and major oil platforms as well as the vital oil terminals at Al Basra and Khawr Al Amaya. Command of CTF 158 rotated, and in March it was the turn of the Royal Navy. The Type 22 frigate *Cornwall* had just arrived in the Gulf from the UK with the fleet replenishment ship RFA *Fort Austin*. She took up station off Iraq, joining the

The frigate
Sutherland in
the Gulf with
Task Force 158
(FPU)

Type 23 frigate *Sutherland*, and assumed the duties of flagship of CTF 158. Commodore Nick Lambert, supported by his team from the Maritime Battle Staff, took over from Rear Admiral Garry Hall of the US Navy as the Task Force Commander. *Sutherland* had recently returned to the Gulf following her participation in the multi-national exercise Aman 07 organised by the Pakistani Navy off Karachi in early March.

The ships of CTF 158 monitored and investigated all ships in the area, and as well as keeping a close watch on all shipping movements they were busy assisting in training the Iraqi Navy.

The *Cornwall* Incident, 23 March 2007 Whilst *Cornwall* was conducting stop-and-search operations enforcing UN resolutions close to the Iraqi coast an unfortunate and embarrassing incident occurred. A boarding team of fifteen, including seven Royal Marines, left *Cornwall* on a routine mission in two RIBs to investigate an Indian ship, the *Al Hanin*. The *Cornwall* team had already boarded more than sixty vessels that month. They were operating close to the coast, and because of the shallow water *Cornwall* was patrolling some way out at sea.

Having completed their routine inspection the team left the ship. At that stage they were assessed as being within approximately two miles of Iranian waters, though the exact limits of Iraqi and Iranian territorial waters have since been disputed. As soon as they pulled away from the *Al Hanin* they were surrounded by heavily armed Iranian Revolutionary Guards in fast gunboats, armed with heavy-calibre machine guns and rocket-propelled grenades and attempting to arrest them. Without sufficient arms or the authority to oppose the Iranians there was very little that the Royal Navy team could do other than to submit to capture. It should be remembered that Britain was not at war with Iran and that any armed resistance could well have provoked an extremely serious international incident. The members of the team were held prisoner and humiliated in the full glare of the world's press for twelve days, before considerable political pressure finally secured their release in time for Easter.

On their return to the UK, the media hounded members of the team for their story, and when two were permitted to sell their stories to the popular press, in the hope of redressing the balance of sensational and distorted reports, there was immediate criticism that they had been allowed to do so. It was an unfortunate incident, blown up out of all proportion by the media, which the First Sea Lord said left the Royal Navy 'bruised and angry'.[10]

The *Tireless* Incident, 21 March 2007 At about the same time the Navy suffered another misfortune with a tragic incident on board the nuclear submarine *Tireless*. The *Trafalgar* class fleet submarine had been operating with a US nuclear attack submarine, the USS *Alexandria*, underneath the polar ice cap as part of ICEX-2007 (Anglo-American Ice Exercise 2007). It was an important classified operation testing submarine operability and war-fighting capabilities under the ice. During the course of the operation, when *Tireless* was beneath the Arctic ice, an emergency oxygen device exploded. The fires started were quickly put out but the blast fatally wounded Leading OM Paul McCann and OM Anthony Huntrod. A third man was injured, but when the submarine surfaced he was flown to Alaska for emergency medical treatment and recovered. *Tireless* then continued with her six-day under-ice transit of the North Pole, demonstrating that the submarine and her ship's company remained fully efficient.[11]

Caribbean Deployment, March–July 2007 It was not all bad news in the spring of 2007, for the helicopter assault ship *Ocean* achieved a major coup during her deployment to the Caribbean. A small task group, consisting of the helicopter assault ship *Ocean* escorted by the Type 23 frigate *Portland* and supported by the fleet tanker RFA *Wave Knight*, deployed to the Caribbean and west Africa in March. Embarked in *Ocean* were the Sea King Mk 7 helicopters of 854 NAS and the Merlin helicopters of 700M NAS (700M being the Operational Evaluation Unit for the MH 1 Merlin helicopter). The ships were deployed for four months and worked closely with US authorities as part of the Joint Inter Agency Task Force (South) in the war against drug trafficking in the region.

The nuclear submarine *Tireless* surfaces through the Arctic ice cap
(NN)

Ocean used her Sea King surveillance helicopters of 854 NAS and made several 'drug busts'. In her first patrol she had captured a big haul of drugs, and then on her third anti-drug patrol she intercepted a heavily loaded smuggler and captured another large haul of strong-grade heroin. The value of drugs intercepted was well in excess of £60 million.[12]

After visiting various islands of the Caribbean, including Trinidad, Montserrat and Tortola, the ships headed to Norfolk, Virginia, in order to join in the 400th anniversary celebrations at Jamestown. Once there, they enjoyed a well earned mid-

deployment break and hosted a ten-day defence export sales event. The defence sales exposition was a great success, with much interest being taken in the new Merlin HM1 ASW (anti-submarine warfare) helicopters of 700M NAS.

Ocean enters Martinique in ceremonial procedure 'Alpha' (NN)

Volans 2007 Deployment, February–December 2007 Owing to the very high demands placed on the Fleet it was not possible to send a task group on an out-of-area deployment to the Far East in 2007. Instead the Naval Staff planned for a single frigate, without dedicated tanker support, to embark on a nine-month out-of-area deployment.

Accordingly, in February 2007 the Type 23 frigate *Monmouth* sailed from Devonport for a circumnavigation of the globe. The operational name for the deployment was Volans 2007. On sailing from the UK *Monmouth* headed straight for the Mediterranean and there took part in the NATO Operation Active Endeavour. The operation entailed conducting surveillance and security patrols, monitoring and boarding suspect shipping. Whilst in the eastern Mediterranean the ship's helicopter managed to rescue five crew members from a merchant ship, the ss *Afrodite S*, which was sinking in a gale off the Greek coast.

After Active Endeavour *Monmouth* transited through the Suez Canal and joined CTF 150 for a period of maritime security duties on Operation Calash in the Gulf of Aden. She became the first British or US warship to visit the port of Aden since the terrorist attack on the USS *Cole* seven years earlier.

The frigate then headed east for Singapore, and on sailing

from Singapore she took part in the annual major FPDA (Five-Power Defence Arrangement) exercise with the navies of Australia, New Zealand, Malaysia and Singapore. On completion of the exercise *Monmouth* embarked on a round of port visits, showing the flag and hosting UK export sales exhibitions. Following two months in Australia and New Zealand the frigate sailed for Japan, China and South Korea to exercise with the US, Korean and Chinese navies.

On leaving Tokyo Bay *Monmouth* set course east across the Pacific Ocean, and then, following a visit to San Diego, transited through the Panama Canal. The final foreign visit was to Antigua, and then she had a straight passage east across the Atlantic. She arrived back home in Devonport in late December. It had been a most successful 40,000 mile, nine-month, unsupported circumnavigation.[13]

Exercise Neptune Warrior 071, April–May 2007 At the end of April a powerful naval task force of nineteen ships, twenty helicopters and over fifty aircraft gathered off the north-west coast of Scotland. Naval forces from eight nations joined for Operation Neptune Warrior 071, which was conducted in the sea areas from Campbeltown to Cape Wrath in the north.

The UK Task Force included the carriers *Illustrious* and *Ark Royal*, the amphibious assault ship *Albion*, the frigates *Kent* and *St Albans*, the MCMV *Middleton* and the new Bay class amphibious landing support ships RFAS *Largs Bay* and *Mounts Bay*. The Harrier GR7s and GR9s of the Naval Strike Wing of the Joint Force Harrier were deployed to *Illustrious*. The important UK biennial joint exercise provided the preparatory phase for the major NATO exercise Noble Mariner (see below). On its completion the forces set course east, with *Illustrious* sailing to Oslo and most of the rest of the Task Force heading for Gothenburg.

Orion 07 Deployment,
May–August 2007

A small MCM task group consisting of the Hunt class MCMVs *Atherstone* and *Hurworth* from the 2nd MCM Squadron and the *Sandown* class *Walney* and *Shoreham* from the 1st MCM Squadron, supported by the brand new amphibious landing support ship RFA *Cardigan Bay*, deployed to the Mediterranean and the Black Sea for four and a half months for a deployment codenamed Operation Orion 07. The Task Group sailed from the UK in May 2007 and headed down to Gibraltar for a brief visit before sailing east to La Spezia on the west coast of Italy. After a weekend in La Spezia it sailed for an exercise with RFA *Cardigan Bay* before steaming south for Stromboli and the Straits of Messina. On sailing into the Ionian Sea the group divided, with the MCMVs transiting through the Corinth Canal to Piraeus and RFA *Cardigan Bay* sailing the long way around Cape Matapan.

Exercise Ariadne The Task Group arrived off Patras, Greece, and commenced exercise Ariadne, hunting for mines laid by the Hellenic Navy. It was a large-scale exercise, with naval forces from Belgium, Spain, Germany, Greece and Turkey, and as well as hunting mines the forces involved came under

RFA *Black Rover* refuels the minehunter *Shoreham* during the Orion 07 Deployment (NN)

attack from helicopters and fast jets. On completion of the exercise the ships sailed for a visit to Piraeus whilst *Atherstone* headed for Souda Bay.

The Black Sea The Task Group then transited through the Dardanelles to Erdek in the Sea of Marmara for exercises with the Turkish Navy, followed by a visit to Izmir. The MCMVs then passed through the Bosphorus and conducted exercises with the Romanian and Bulgarian Navies in the Black Sea. On finishing the exercise programme the MCMVs headed back through the Sea of Marmara to join up with RFA *Cardigan Bay* and set course west for Malta.

After a very enjoyable visit to Malta the group put to sea from Valletta for exercises on its way to Cagliari in Sardinia, and thence went on to Gibraltar. Following a brief stay in Gibraltar, the ships steamed south-west to visit Casablanca.

Return Home On completion of a two-day visit to Casablanca, the group set course north-east and sailed for Gibraltar on the homeward leg of the deployment. RFA *Cardigan Bay* was detached from the group, and after a brief call in to Gibraltar the group returned to the UK.

———•———

Exercise Noble Mariner, May–June 2007 In early May 2007 the naval forces of the seventeen allied nations of the Western world gathered together off Esbjerg, Denmark, for the major exercise Noble Mariner. The objective of this important

NATO exercise was to test the NATO Response Force (NRF) in connection with two other NATO exercises, Noble Award (carried out by NATO air components) and Kindred Sword (carried out by NATO land components).

Rear Admiral Neil Morisetti, the UK Maritime Force Commander, commanded the UK contribution from his flagship, the aircraft carrier *Ark Royal*. The powerful UK Task Group included *Illustrious*, *Albion*, *Manchester* and *Roebuck* and the amphibious support landing ships RFAs *Largs Bay* and *Mounts Bay* with 40 Commando Royal Marines embarked. The Harriers from the Naval Strike Wing were deployed to the Task Group and RFAs *Fort George* and *Fort Rosalie* supported it. Admiral Morisetti also acted as the overall NATO Task Force Commander for most of the exercises. Altogether 3,000 UK naval personnel were involved.

The ships operated in the Skagerrak, Kattegat and Baltic. A whole range of exercises was conducted, with shore bombardment and assault operations including landings by Royal Marines and other NATO marine forces on the shores of Pomerania.

On completion of Noble Mariner the ships dispersed, and *Albion* headed for a visit to St Petersburg. She was the largest ship to visit the city, and berthed alongside at Lieutenant Schmidt pier in central St Petersburg. The visit was a great success and she then sailed on for a port visit to Helsinki.[14]

End of Operation Banner, 31 July 2007 Progress on the road to achieving a lasting peace in Northern Ireland was marked on 31 July with the formal ending of Operation Banner after thirty-eight years of security operations in support of the police and civil authorities in the Province. Despite the fact that the general public has tended to assume that peace-keeping duties in Northern Ireland have been the sole responsibility of the army, both the RAF and the Royal Navy, with the Royal Marines, have played very important roles in containing violence and building peace and security. At midnight on 31 July Operation Banner came to an end, and the next day the main British forces deployed on the operation began to leave. The Lynx helicopters of 815 NAS were amongst the last to leave when they departed from their base at Aldergrove Airport on 2 August. Remaining behind in Northern Ireland was a permanent residual garrison of 5,000 as part of Operation Helvetic, ready for rapid deployment anywhere in the world and also available to support the civil authorities in Northern Ireland in the event of any extreme public disorder.

Exercise Noble Mariner: the destroyer *Manchester* follows RFAS *Largs Bay* and *Mounts Bay* under the Great Belt Bridge between Sweden and Denmark
(NN)

Operation Bold Step, 15–31 July 2007

In July the important Joint Task Force exercise Operation Bold Step was held in the North Atlantic off the east coast of the USA. The Royal Navy deployed her flagship, the carrier *Illustrious*, in the strike role, escorted by the Type 42 destroyer *Manchester*. Before the exercise schedule started the ships paid a visit to New York.

Carrier Strike Group 10 The exercise, which included three carrier battle groups, was designed to prepare the US Carrier Battle Group, based on the nuclear strike carrier USS *Harry S Truman*, Carrier Strike Group 10, for deployment to the Middle East. The group consisted of USS *Winston Churchill*, USS *Hue City*, USS *Oscar Austin*, the *Los Angeles* class nuclear submarine USS *Montpelier* and the destroyer *Manchester*. It was an important exercise for *Manchester*, preparing her for her role as escort to USS *Harry S Truman* when Carrier Strike

Group 10 deployed east. The nuclear strike carrier USS *Dwight D Eisenhower* led the second Carrier Battle Group in the exercise, whilst *Illustrious* led the third group, which consisted of the cruisers USS *Monterey* and USS *San Jacinto*, two frigates, USS *Nicholas* and USS *Simpson*, and the destroyer USS *Carney*.

For the two-week period of the exercise *Illustrious* embarked sixteen USMC AV-8B Harriers and 200 marines of US Marine Attack Squadron 542. It was a busy exercise schedule with *Illustrious* conducting strike missions as part of a heavy flying programme as well as carrying out surface and anti-submarine operations and boarding exercises. On completion of the exercises *Illustrious* returned across the Atlantic to Portsmouth to grant pre-deployment summer leave in August.

Operation Grey Heron In September the various units of the Amphibious Task Force assembled in the Solent for exercises codenamed Grey Heron. The powerful Amphibious Task Force included 3 Commando Brigade, with 45 Commando and the Commando Helicopter Force embarked, the assault ship *Albion*, the carrier *Ark Royal*, the support landing ships RFAS *Mounts Bay* and *Largs Bay* and the RFAS *Argus* and *Fort Rosalie*. In cold blustery weather the force mounted landings on the Stokes Bay beach at Browndown. Grey Heron involved testing new concepts of rapid deployment inland, as opposed to previous tactics of establishing a beachhead and preparing to break out before advancing inland.

Operation Herrick VII

Build-Up of Naval Personnel in Afghanistan In the autumn of 2007 the numbers of Royal Navy personnel deployed to

The nuclear strike carriers USS *Harry S Truman* and USS *Dwight D Eisenhower* astern of *Illustrious*
(NN)

Illustrious prepares for 'flying stations'
(NN)

Afghanistan started to build up again for Operation Herrick VII. 40 Commando Royal Marines arrived in September and were deployed to the northern Helmand area, where they relieved the 1st Battalion Royal Anglian Regiment as part of Battle Group North. The Naval Strike Wing returned to the air base at Kandahar flying GR7 and GR9 Harriers in October, to provide air strikes in support of ground missions. On their first day back in theatre the Harrriers were called out to support British troops under heavy fire from the Taliban. The Harriers roaring in overhead were sufficient to drive off the Taliban attack. 846 NAS, flying up-rated Sea King Mk 4 helicopters, was also deployed to Afghanistan as part of the Joint Helicopter Force.

The Battle for Musa Qaleh In November the Royal Marines commenced an offensive in the far north of Helmand Province to retake Musa Qaleh from the Taliban. The town had been built on the River Musa Qaleh and straddled the main strategic route between Baghran and Sangin. Musa Qaleh had been liberated from the Taliban in the previous year and handed back to the local tribal leaders, but when the coalition forces left the Taliban had returned and now dominated the town again. It had become an important base for the Taliban, with an estimated total of over 2,500 Taliban fighters in the area.

A two-pronged attack was launched with the Royal Marines of 40 Commando in their Viking armoured vehicles on the left bank of the river and Scots Guards with their Warrior armoured cars on the other bank. The Royal Marines were able to advance using cover provided by the remains of

The destroyer *Manchester* in the Mediterranean en route to the Gulf (NN)

Delta Company of 40 Commando advances as the sun rises (NN)

trenches left over from the Soviet war in Afghanistan, and after several days of hard fighting were able to force their way into Musa Qaleh. It was an important victory as it effectively removed the Taliban from their last stronghold in the area.

The Kajaki Dam At the end of the year the Royal Marines carried out raids on Taliban positions near the key strategic

position of the Kajaki dam. The Taliban had been ejected from the area in the previous year but had slowly returned and now had to be tackled again. Using RIBs the Royal Marines, supported by troops from the Afghan Army, crossed the artificial lake behind the dam during daring night-time raids, catching the Taliban by surprise and defeating them.

———•———

HMS *Manchester* Escorts Carrier Strike Group 10 Following on from the success of Operation Bold Step 07-02, the Type 42 destroyer *Manchester* sailed from Portsmouth on a bitterly cold November morning and headed for a rendezvous in the Bay of Biscay with the US Carrier Battle Group, Carrier Strike Group 10, led by the nuclear strike carrier USS *Harry S Truman* en route to the Middle East. *Manchester* was assigned to the Carrier Battle Group to act as escort with responsibility for close air defence of the carrier. It was the first time that the Royal Navy had the opportunity to be so closely integrated with a US carrier strike group. The group headed down to Gibraltar and on across the Mediterranean to the Gulf as part of the ongoing US Operation Enduring Freedom. In the Gulf the Carrier Battle Group formed part of the US 5th Fleet, and *Manchester* was put in charge of controlling air defence operations in that area.

On completion of her important assignment *Manchester* detached from the Carrier Battle Group and sailed for home. She departed from the Gulf and finally arrived back in Portsmouth on 28 May 2008.

Orion 08 Deployment, 21 January–30 May 2008

The Orion 08 Task Group At the beginning of January 2008 a task group, codenamed Orion 08, was formed for a four-month out-of-area deployment to the Middle East. The carrier *Illustrious* (Captain Steve Chick) was the flagship, and her TAG (Tailored Air Group) consisted of six Merlin helicopters of 814 NAS (the 'Flying Tigers') and 'A' Flight of 849 NAS. Commodore Tom Cunningham commanded the

Task Group. The Type 42 destroyer *Edinburgh* and the Type 23 frigate *Westminster* escorted *Illustrious*, whilst the fleet replenishment ships RFAS *Wave Knight* and *Fort Austin*, and the support tanker RFA *Bayleaf* supported the group. The nuclear fleet submarine *Trafalgar* was attached to the Task Group, and the French destroyer FS *Surcouf*, the US destroyer USS *Cole* and the Spanish frigate SNS *Mendez Nunez* were also assigned to join it. The USS *Cole* would escort *Illustrious* throughout most of the deployment. The Task Group was planned to involve a total of thirteen ships, one submarine and 2,500 personnel.

The Task Group Sails The Task Group sailed initially from Portsmouth on Monday 21 January, though once out in the Channel the twenty-six-year-old *Illustrious* was beset with several problems and had to return to port to sort out trouble with the refrigerators and also with the propeller shaft. Two days later the MCMVs *Atherstone* and *Chiddingfold* sailed from Portsmouth to support the group.

Ships of the group then put to sea again on a bright sunny morning in early February. The carrier, however, was required to spend a little more time with the expert staff of the Flag Officer Sea Training before they were satisfied that the ship was sufficiently ready to continue with the deployment.

***Illustrious* Catches Up** Finally *Illustrious* was on her way south to catch up with the rest of the Task Group. After passing through the Straits of Gibraltar she set course east across the Mediterranean, heading for a rendezvous with

Orion 08 Task Force sailing in close formation in the Mediterranean (left to right: *Mendez Nunez, Wave Knight, Illustrious, Edinburgh* and *Cole*)
(NN)

the rest of the squadron. *Illustrious*, accompanied by *Edinburgh*, sailed into Malta on 26 February for a popular three-day visit. On sailing from Malta she steamed on east to join the rest of the group, which by this time included *Westminster* and *Edinburgh*, RFA *Wave Knight*, USS *Cole* and SPS *Mendez Nunez*, for 'force integration training' in the eastern Mediterranean. *Illustrious* replenished supplies and stores from Cyprus on 3 March before heading for Port Said and the Suez Canal.

The Red Sea The transit of the Suez Canal took sixteen hours with just a brief anchorage in the Bitter Lakes to enable a northbound convoy to pass. The ships were closed up at an alert state as they passed through, fully prepared in case of any terrorist attack from the nearby banks of the canal. Once they were in the Red Sea extensive exercises were conducted as the group sailed steadily south east en route to the Indian Ocean and the Gulf of Oman. The group transited Bab-al-Mandab and, after embarking stores and passengers by helicopter from Djibouti, headed on east through the Gulf of Aden, arriving in Muscat on 14 March.

Exercise Hajjar Osprey On sailing from Muscat on 19 March four of the Harrier GR7s and GR9s of the Naval Strike Wing of JFH joined *Illustrious*, having flown out from Cottesmore via Cyprus. The group took part in exercise Hajjar Osprey with the Omani Navy. The main element of the exercise consisted of flying Harrier strike missions over inland targets and testing the air defence capability of the Task Force. Two

Falcon jets flew out from the UK to join the Task Group for a week of trials during the air defence serials of the exercise.[15]

The Harriers Depart On 11 April the Harriers of the Naval Strike Wing left *Illustrious* and flew back, via Cyprus, to Cottesmore to prepare for deployment to Operation Herrick in Afghanistan.

Exercise Phoenix After a farewell call at Muscat the Task Group sailed for anti-submarine exercises in the Arabian Sea. During the exercise the Merlins of 814 NAS hunted for the nuclear fleet submarine *Trafalgar* and the Indian diesel submarine INS *Shishumar*.

HMS *Edinburgh* The destroyer *Edinburgh* detached from the Task Group and headed for Karachi for exercises with the Pakistani Navy before sailing for the Far East. She had already been detached earlier in March, for a short period in the Gulf to carry out security operations with CTF 150. This time after leaving Karachi she set course south-east round the southern tip of India for a two-day visit to Colombo in Sri Lanka.

Edinburgh then set course across the Indian Ocean to Singapore for exercise Bersama Shield and a busy programme of port visits. On sailing from Sembawang, Singapore, she took part in the major FPDA exercise Bersama Lima off the coast of Malaysia, with ships and aircraft from Malaysia, Singapore, Australia and New Zealand.

Exercise Konkan Meanwhile on completion of exercise Phoenix the rest of the Task Group sailed for Goa to prepare for the major biannual naval exercise Konkan. The Task Group then headed out into the Indian Ocean and joined in the exercise, which was directed by the Indian Navy. It was a full-scale exercise with surface and submarine warfare elements as well as air defence serials. The Indian Navy ships INS *Mysore*, a powerful 8,000-ton Delhi class missile cruiser, INS *Rajput*, a potent 7,000-ton Kashin II class guided missile destroyer, and INS *Gomati* took part. FRS51 Sea Harriers from the Indian Navy also joined in the simulated air attacks on the Task Group. On completion of the exercise the group returned to Goa for post-exercise debriefing and analysis.

Operation Calash After completing the exercise programme the Task Group departed from the Gulf of Oman for the return leg to the UK. *Illustrious*, escorted by the destroyer USS *Cole*, sailed west for the Gulf of Aden and conducted security patrols in the area with CTF 150 as part of Operation Calash.

Return Home After conducting further exercises with the Saudi Navy, *Illustrious* embarked supplies by helicopter from Djibouti on 6 May. She then transited through the Straits of Bab-al-Mandab into the Red Sea and set course north-west for the Gulf of Suez. The ships transited through the Suez Canal on 10 May and once back in the Mediterranean headed for Cyprus. *Illustrious* anchored briefly off the coast

of Cyprus for a logistic visit, and the ship's company was entertained to a spectacular aerial display performed by the Hawk jets of the RAF Red Arrows display team.

The group then headed for Izmir on 13 May for an official visit to Turkey. The call at Izmir was the finale of the deployment, with a magnificent reception for the visit of HM the Queen to Turkey. On putting to sea from Izmir *Illustrious* headed west through the Mediterranean for a brief call at Gibraltar, after which she steamed north for the UK, finally arriving home in Portsmouth naval base with the USS *Cole* on 30 May.[16]

TV Series A camera team from Granada filmed the deployment of *Illustrious* for Channel Five Television. The series, entitled 'Warship', was screened in six episodes during May and June and proved popular.

The Red Arrows over *Illustrious* off Cyprus
(NN)

Command of CTFs in the Gulf In 2008 the Royal Navy took command of the two main coalition forces in the Gulf. In March, CTF 158, responsible for security in the northern Gulf, came under the command of Commodore Duncan Potts, and then in June, Commodore Peter Hudson took over command of CTF 152, which was responsible for security in the central and southern Gulf.

Other Fleet Activities

Wilkinson Sword of Peace In March 2007 the Wilkinson Sword of Peace was awarded to the Type 22 frigate *Chatham* for its invaluable disaster relief work in 2005 in the wake of the Tsunami in south-east Asia. The ship, together with the forward repair ship RFA *Diligence*, had arrived quickly in the region and achieved a great deal of humanitarian relief work, restoring vital services and repairing hospitals, schools and even fishing vessels around the town of Batticaloa.

Antarctic In January 2007 the ice patrol ship *Endurance* hastened to assist the stricken cruise ship MS *Nordkapp*, which had struck a submerged iceberg in the dangerous waters of the Antarctic Ocean and was sinking. The ship sank quickly but *Endurance* was able to rescue the passengers and no lives were lost.

Mediterranean Two months later the frigate *Monmouth* went to the assistance of a sinking cargo ship, the SS *Afrodite S,* in the eastern Mediterranean. The frigate carried out a dramatic rescue in a raging sea, and with her helicopter managed to save the crew of the stricken ship before it sank.

Abolition of the Slave Trade In March 2007 the Royal Navy helped celebrate the 200th anniversary of the Act for the Abolition of the Slave Trade. It was fitting for the Royal Navy to take part in view of the vital role the service had played in the suppression of the slave trade. The frigate *Northumberland* escorted the replica eighteenth-century slave ship *Zong* up the River Thames to London.

Emergency Flood Relief Tasks The Royal Navy provided emergency aid during the disastrous floods in the UK at the beginning of the summer in 2007. Emergency relief teams were assembled to assist in the flooded towns and villages along the Severn valley. An initial team of a hundred was provided from the ships' companies of *Ocean* and *Northumberland,* and as the situation worsened RNAS (Royal Naval Air Station) Yeovilton provided another team of a hundred. Priority work was given to the protection of the electric substations to maintain power supplies across the Severn valley, and teams, fed by the army from field kitchens, worked through the nights to ensure that the substations remained on line. Teams from *Ark Royal* helped maintain safe water supplies, and further personnel were drafted in from *Cumberland, Campbeltown* and *Gloucester* and the submarines *Tireless* and *Turbulent* as necessary to keep on top of the rising water levels. The Managing Director of the electric company said, 'It's been a tremendous effort and the Armed Forces have done a terrific job in restoring power to thousands of homes in the region under very challenging conditions.'[17]

Hurricane Disaster Relief Tasks At the end of the summer Hurricane 'Dean' struck the north coast of Belize, causing widespread damage in the Corozal district. As the hurricane moved west it had been tracked, and the frigate *Portland* and the fleet replenishment ship RFA *Wave Ruler* in the Caribbean were alerted to follow and be prepared to provide emergency relief. Accordingly it did not take long for them to arrive off the coast of Belize. A British army support unit in Belize was already on the spot and was soon joined by naval relief parties flown in from the ships off shore.

The teams quickly set about restoring electrical and water supplies, sanitation and medical assistance before commencing the task of repairing buildings and clearing blocked roads. Fortunately RFA *Wave Ruler* carried large stocks of emergency relief stores including blankets, medical supplies, tents, tools and equipment. No sooner had much of the essential work been done than Belize was threatened by a second hurricane, Hurricane 'Felix'. Belize lay directly in its path as it moved west, but fortunately at the very last moment it veered away and moved towards Nicaragua. The Deputy Prime Minister of Belize, Vildo Marin, expressed his country's immense gratitude for the relief work carried out in the stricken area.

The War on Drugs The Royal Navy continued to play an important part in the war on drugs, both in the Gulf and in the Caribbean. In the first half of 2008 the Royal Navy seized a record amount of just over twenty-three tons of drugs in the Gulf region, the proceeds from much of which would almost certainly have been used to fund international terrorists and the Taliban in Afghanistan.

SHIPS, WEAPONS AND AIRCRAFT

The New Type 45 Destroyers In 2007 work was well advanced on the six new generation 8,000-ton Type 45 *Daring* class air warfare destroyers *Daring, Dauntless, Diamond, Dragon, Defender* and *Duncan,* with *Daring,* the first of class, already at sea on trials and scheduled to be commissioned at Portsmouth in early 2009. The second of class, *Dauntless,* was fitting out at Scotstoun, whilst the third, *Diamond,* had just recently been launched in Glasgow. The destroyers were originally designed to provide area defence for the new carriers, and it was hoped that at least another

The Type 23 frigate
Portland
(RN)

two would be ordered. The new destroyers, due to replace the elderly Type 42 destroyers, will provide a powerful capability enhancement to the Fleet.

New Aircraft Carriers On 3 July 2008, on board *Ark Royal* in Portsmouth, the Defence Minister, Baroness Taylor, signed the contract for the two new aircraft carriers, *Queen Elizabeth* and *Prince of Wales*. The carriers, at 64,000, tons would be the biggest, most powerful and most expensive warships ever built for the Royal Navy. The in-service dates were planned for 2014 and 2016.

The New *Astute* Class Submarines The new-generation 7,400-ton nuclear attack submarines of the *Astute* class were well advanced. The Duchess of Cornwall launched *Astute*, the first of class, in 2007, and towards the end of the year *Astute* successfully carried out her first dive. She was well on track to be in service in 2009. The rest of class, *Ambush*, *Artful* and *Audacious*, were under construction and were all to be armed with TLAMs (Tomahawk land attack cruise missiles) as well as Spearfish torpedoes.

The Royal Navy has a very high reputation for her great expertise in anti-submarine warfare, though her ability to conduct effective ASW screening had been reducing with the decreasing numbers of ASW escorts available and a changing focus on littoral operations. The *Astute* class would help tackle the problem with their improved sensor suite and highly sophisticated combat system, already being fitted in the existing SSN force. Amongst the available force mix, one of the SSN's main contributions will be in early deployment in the theatre of operations, as well as in being a prime asset to counter the threat of an enemy submarine force. Critically, the *Astute*'s improved communication fit will allow greater co-ordination with other forces. Future ASW strategy with the *Astute* class will concentrate on distant, forward deployment, rather than focusing on close-in task group protection.

HMS *Daring*
Type 45 *Daring* Class Destroyer
Daring, the first of the new generation Type 45 *Daring* class destroyers, currently at sea on trials, is due to be commissioned in Portsmouth naval base in early 2009. The *Daring*s have been designed as powerful state-of-the-art area air-defence ships to replace the very successful and long-serving Type 42 destroyers. A prime task for the *Daring*s will be protection of the new aircraft carriers. They will operate Lynx or Merlin helicopters and with their flexible weapon fit, including cruise missiles, will have a general-purpose role.

Launched:	1 February 2006
Commissioned:	Expected into service 2009
Displacement:	7,350 tonnes
Length:	152.4m
Propulsion:	Integrated electric propulsion: 2 Rolls-Royce/Northrop Grumman/DCN WR-21 gas turbines, 2 Converteam electric motors, 2 shafts
Armament:	SSM 8 Harpoon (2 quad), surface-to-air (SAM), 6 DCN Sylver A 50 VLS PAAMS (principal anti-air missile system), 16 Aster 15 and 32 Aster 30 weapons or combination, 1 Vickers 4.5in (114mm)/55 Mk 8 Mod 1, 2 20mm Vulcan Phalanx close-in weapon systems, Lynx or Merlin helicopter
Complement:	191
No. in class:	6 planned: *Daring, Dauntless, Diamond, Dragon, Defender* and *Duncan*

Future Surface Combatants The Naval Staff had started to design the next-generation frigate to replace the Type 22 and Type 23 frigates with the 'Future Surface Combatant' project. In fact the project envisaged three new classes of warship to replace eight existing classes. The new warships would include a 6,000-ton ASW vessel to replace the frigates, a general-purpose vessel and a 2,000-ton ocean-going patrol vessel with an MCM capability. At the end of 2008 the project was still in its early stages.

MARS Programme A similar project was underway to replace the aging RFA fleet of tankers and support ships. The programme, entitled MARS (Military Afloat Research and Sustainability), was designed to cover the logistic support needs of the Fleet in the future with a new concept mix of fleet tankers and solid support ships.

Tomahawk Block 4 Missile In July 2007 the fleet submarine *Trenchant* fired the new Block IV variant of TLAM, 'TacTom' (Tomahawk long-range tactical land attack cruise missile). The firings, on the naval ranges off the east coast of the USA, were a complete success. The new Block IV TLAM is a much improved missile and will replace the UK's outfit of Block III missiles.[18]

New Maritime Warfare Centre In August 2007 the Commander in Chief Fleet, Admiral Sir James Burnell-Nugent, opened the new Maritime Warfare Centre in HMS *Collingwood*, the shore base at Fareham in Hampshire. This new ultra-modern hi-tech facility replaced the previous sites at Southwick Park and the Portsdown Technology Park.

HMS *Astute*
Astute Class Fleet Submarine
The four *Astute* class nuclear hunter-killer fleet submarines were designed to replace the *Swiftsure* class SSNs, which had given valuable service with the Fleet since the 1970s. At over 7,000 tonnes (7,800 tonnes dived) they are by far the biggest fleet submarines built for the Royal Navy. With Tomahawk cruise missiles, as well as torpedoes and Harpoon anti-ship missiles, they will be able to fulfil a variety of roles capable of operating all over the world and projecting power far inland. *Astute* was launched by the Duchess of Cornwall in 2007 and is due to enter service in 2009.

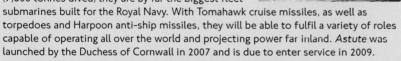

Launched:	8 June 2007
Commissioned:	Expected into service 2009
Displacement:	7,800 tonnes dived
Length:	97m
Propulsion:	Rolls-Royce PWR2 reactor (with full submarine life core), MAN (Paxman) diesel generator, 1 shaft
Armament:	6 21" (533mm) torpedo tubes, Tomahawk land attack missiles
Complement:	98
No. in class:	4 planned: *Astute, Ambush, Artful* and *Audacious*

PERSONNEL MATTERS

'Galaxy' Paper At the beginning of 2007 Vice Admiral Johns, the Second Sea Lord, issued an internal communication to officers and senior ratings briefing them on likely delays in promotion and probable reduced promotion prospects as a consequence of planned changes in manpower levels. The briefing was picked up by the press and turned into a 'gloom and doom' story about a 'promotion freeze', which unsettled and worried some about their future careers in the Royal Navy.

Branch Development Vesting Day, 30 March 2007 The rating structure of the Royal Navy was fundamentally redesigned and modernised to reflect the manning requirements of modern ships, systems and operating patterns. New specialisations were established for training and employment, and to modernise professional development in the most efficient manner. The vesting day for the introduction of the new branches with new titles and new branch badges was 30 March 2007. On that day some 20,000 ratings adopted new branch titles and new branch badges, with ships being phased through onboard organisational changes, enabling ratings to complete the necessary transition training but at the same time maintain full operational capability. The switch to the new branch structure was completed by the end of the year.

Branch Development: The New Ratings Branches

The new ratings structure of the Royal Navy consisted of three principal branches: Warfare, Engineering and Logistics.

Warfare Branch Within the Warfare Branch the maintenance role was removed to enable ratings to concentrate on a narrower field of Warfare, Communications or the newly reinvigorated Seaman specialisation.

Engineering Branch In the Engineering Branch all new entries join as Engineer Technicians to be trained in maintenance and repair, and all have the opportunity to achieve a foundation degree in engineering. The branch was divided between Marine Engineering and Weapon Engineering, corresponding with the other services and facilitating more efficient integrated joint operations.

Logistics Branch With the emphasis on expeditionary warfare, a supply chain specialism had been developed to enable forces to deploy instantly with forward integrated logistics support. The three specialist areas established were Supply Chain, Catering Services and Personnel, the latter carrying out pay and administrative transactions using the newly taken on Joint Personnel Administration System.

———•———

VISP (Valuing and Investing in Service Personnel) At the beginning of 2008 the armed forces launched an extensive personnel survey called VISP (Valuing and Investing in Service Personnel). The tri-service survey was intended to establish how a range of service policies were coping with fast-changing elements of service life including promotion, career development, accommodation and allowances. Essentially it was an updated service attitudes survey. The survey questionnaire was sent to 16,000 naval personnel, and three months were allowed for the first phase of the project. The results were used to feed back into improvements in personnel policies so as to improve recruiting and retention.

Project Fisher In 2007 Project Fisher was set up to examine the most efficient ways of using manpower and manning ships in order to provide greater flexibility and responsiveness to requirements. The work built on the 'TopMast' concept, and an assessment of the new manning thoeries was conducted in early 2008.

HRH Prince William On 2 June 2008 HRH Prince William joined the Royal Navy as a sub lieutenant (Sub Lieutenant W Wales, Royal Navy) for an eight-week acquaint period. He spent three weeks of basic naval training at the Britannia Royal Naval College at Dartmouth and then went to sea for a five-week deployment to the Caribbean on board the Type 23 frigate *Iron Duke*. The assignment was part of the Prince's programme of familiarisation with the armed services.

Iron Duke – Type 23 frigate (PW) (RC)

He was only at sea for four days before he was making headline news when *Iron Duke* intercepted a drug smuggler on 2 July. Sub Lieutenant Wales was on board the ship's Lynx helicopter when he spotted the fifty-foot-long vessel off the coast of Barbados. The vessel was intercepted and discovered to have £40m worth of cocaine on board.

THE WHITE ENSIGN ASSOCIATION

Visit to Devonport Naval Base In April 2007 the Council of the Association went to the West Country for two days and visited HM Naval Base Devonport. The Council toured the base's facilities and also took the opportunity to visit the new amphibious assault ship *Bulwark*, the Type 22 frigate *Campbeltown* and the *Trafalgar* class nuclear submarine *Tireless*. The Association's Patron, Admiral HRH The Prince of Wales, visited the base on the same day as the Commodore

Guests of the White Ensign Association on board the carrier *Ark Royal*
(RH)

in Chief Plymouth. The members of the Council were greatly impressed by all they saw, especially the high calibre of the men and women they met.

Sea Days Later in the year *Ark Royal* hosted a Sea Day for guests of the Association. The guests were taken to sea and had the opportunity to witness exercises in the Channel.

Chairman Admiral the Lord Boyce relieved Mr John Andrewes as Chairman of the White Ensign Association at the Annual General Meeting held at Lloyds of London in November 2007. Sir John Parker was appointed Vice Chairman.

Fiftieth Anniversary The White Ensign Association celebrated its Golden Jubilee with a banquet on 29 January 2008, held at Buckingham Palace and hosted by the Association's Royal Patron, Admiral HRH The Prince of Wales. Guests of honour included the Countess Mountbatten of Burma and the First Sea Lord, Admiral Sir Jonathan Band.

Assistance Provided by the Association By the time the Association celebrated its fiftieth anniversary it had helped well in excess of 37,000 people and briefed over 100,000. Admiral Sir Jonathan Band, the First Sea Lord, stated: 'I am delighted to state, unequivocally, my appreciation and support for the invaluable work of the White Ensign Association. At a time when the Royal Navy is deployed on operations more than at any other period in recent history, including contributing fully to operations in Afghanistan and Iraq, the work of the Association is of ever-growing importance. The Admiralty Board and I join together in commending the vital work of this organisation and in voicing our appreciation for the service the Association provides.'[19]

Visit to RNAS Yeovilton At the end of April 2008 the Council of the Association visited RNAS Yeovilton. The Council was fully briefed on operations, including the Lynx Helicopter Force and the Commando Helicopter Force, and then given a comprehensive tour of the air station's facilities, including the Lynx flight simulators. The members of Council witnessed flying operations and a brief flying display by Lynx helicopters. They also took the opportunity to visit the Fleet Air Arm Museum and see the 'Flight Deck' experience.

Farewell the Artificer

'They are an amazing breed, these quiet, rather pale men, in whose hands lie the strength and power of the ship.' (Rudyard Kipling, *The Fleet in Being*, 1898)

In 2007, Artificers – including women in the surface fleet since the early 1990s – were given the Tri-Service title of Engineering Technician (ET), abandoning a naval title introduced in 1868. All Engineering ratings now enter as ETs and are taught engineering principles, the ability to operate machinery and basic craft skills via hands-on practical work. Further training in engineering skills is provided on promotion to the next higher naval rate and later career opportunities included award of a Foundation Degree as a Senior Rating, and promotion to Warrant or Commissioned Officer. All ETs (Marine Engineering) receive their initial 5 months' training at *Sultan*, Gosport, where all ME training is consolidated: earmarked for transfer to a Tri-Service Defence Training Academy by 2013.

In 1958, when the White Ensign Association was founded, Engine Room Artificers (ERAs) joined the Navy at HMS *Fisgard*, near Devonport, as 16 year-old Apprentices before going on to HMS *Caledonia* at Rosyth to complete their 4-year course of craft skills and engineering theory and practice. These were followed by 2 years' practical training in the Fleet before being rated Chief Petty Officer (CPO) and considered competent to take charge of a ship's Marine Engineering watch. Subsequent experience and training could lead to selection as a Chief Artificer allowing them to take full charge of a small ship's ME Department, such as a Minesweeper, and was an essential step for selection and commissioning as a Special Duties List ME officer. As Air, Marine and Weapon engineering were harmonized in the 'Big E' Branch, ERAs were renamed Marine Engineering Artificers (Propulsion), without significant changes to their operator and craft training. After introduction of the "Fleet Chief" (later to be Warrant Officer (WO) 1st Class) in 1970 in all Branches, Charge Chief Artificers were accepted in 2004 as WOs 2nd Class.

Shipwright Artificers – known as 'Chippies' since Nelson's days – entered the *Fisgard/Caledonia* stream alongside ERAs, but trained only in wood- and metal-working craft skills, not in machinery operation and maintenance and when re-named MEAs (Hull), they remained non-watchkeepers. The proposed abolition of the MEA (Hull) specialist stream in 1981 was cancelled after experience of damage repair needs in the Falklands Campaign and a new specialist MEA (Metalworker) introduced, but now part of the watchkeeping team.

By 1958 the much shorter Branch training of Mechanics (E) s, a separate stream of semi-skilled ratings with origins in the Stokers of coal-fired ships, was well established at HMS *Sultan*, where they returned for further Career training if 'advanced' (promoted), or if selected for 2-years' training as ME Mechanicians (MEMNs): increasingly regarded as equivalent to MEAs for drafting purposes and for ME officer selection. All Artificers and Mechanicians could be selected as Special Duties ME officers, these at one stage making up half the ME Officer total. Mechanician training provided the only route for a Mechanic to become a commissioned officer.

Engineering Branch Development (EBD) in 1979 re-introduced electrical skills to the ME sub-Branch along with new titles, linking naval rate to sub-specialism as well as indicating level of electrical competence: for example, CPOMEA (ML) for a CPO ME Artificer with mainly mechanical and some electrical competence, and POMEM (EL) for a PO ME Mechanic with deeper electrical competence and skills.

All craft skill and engineering training for ME Mechanicians had been concentrated at *Sultan* from the outset, and in 1985 all Artificer training was moved to *Sultan* to be fully integrated with Mechanician courses. Since the 1960s, *Sultan* also had developed ADditional QUALification courses (ADQUALs) providing Artificers with specialised maintenance skills, such as in refrigeration plant, before being 'drafted' to nominated 'billets' in ships' ME complements.

Tubal Cain, First Artificer
(Genesis 4:22)

Epilogue

'The Future – the ongoing need to strive for peace and security'

Even the briefest of glances back over the last fifty years shows clearly just how dangerous, unjust and unstable is the world we live in. It is also clear that events are unpredictable, and therefore difficult to plan and prepare for.

Britain is a small island nation, with a relatively large population, and has for many years not been able to provide for all its needs. To survive the country has to import all the raw materials it lacks, and export products to earn the wealth to pay for those imported materials. Britain cannot therefore cut itself off from the dangerous world and live in isolation. The country has no choice but to compete for resources and be fully involved in the world scene.

For trade to take place efficiently a basic level of security is essential. If resources and materials cannot be harvested, transported and distributed in relative safety then the system breaks down. All trading nations therefore have a strong vested interest in ensuring at least minimum levels of stability and security. For the time being peace and security are underwritten ultimately by military force, for that is the basic order of the world. This is not the place to discuss the wisdom or morality of such a means of preserving peace and security but merely to recognise the realities of survival in the way mankind runs the earth.

Britain was for many years the world's greatest trading nation, and it was on that trade that Britain built the biggest empire ever. That empire has gone and passed into history, but Britain remains a major trading nation and must continue to trade on a worldwide scale. As much as 95 per cent of Britain's visible trade is reliant on shipping, with 586 million tonnes of freight passing through British ports in 2005 (in comparison two million tonnes were carried by air freight)[1], and sea transport is Britain's third largest service sector. The country must protect that trade by all means to ensure survival. As stated above, protection of our trade entails stability and security in those parts of the world where we do business as well as keeping the sea lanes, through which our trade flows, open and safe. It is in both those tasks that the Royal Navy will continue to have a vital role to play. Guarding the vital oil tankers from the Gulf as they pass through the dangerous Straits of Hormuz provides a classic example of the requirement for close naval protection. At the same time the Navy is heavily involved in power projection, through expeditionary warfare in the key trouble spots such as Iraq and Afghanistan. The amphibious warfare capability enables Britain to intervene where necessary, and the escort fleet provides the backbone of local sea control and trade protection at sea.

Those fundamental requirements will continue into the foreseeable future. In fact competition for resources will intensify as pressures from Asia and the Far East grow at an exponential rate. International terrorism shows no sign of decreasing: in fact quite the opposite as terrorists become more experienced and sophisticated in their attacks on the international community. Their aims appear to be simply to cause the maximum mayhem and destruction, with total disregard for human life, even at the cost of their own lives. Piracy is becoming a much more dangerous threat at sea, particularly in the trade choke points such as the Gulf of Aden and the Malacca Straits. The audacious capture of the supertanker *Sirius Star* by pirates off east Africa in November 2008 illustrated the growing menace.

The USA leads the struggle on international terrorism through Operation Enduring Freedom and tends to be the prime focus for attacks. Nevertheless it would be extremely foolhardy to rely entirely on the USA for our survival. Whilst we have a common cause and operate together we derive considerable advantages from their military power, but history has repeatedly demonstrated that we cannot depend on allies always being on our side. In many major conflicts, apart from the Cold War and the Gulf Wars, the UK has usually been on its own, despite its common bond with the USA, and in all probability will continue to be in that position. It would be irresponsible and extremely dangerous to act otherwise.

Defence of the homeland and national security is often overlooked, as there has been no evident, direct threat to the UK mainland since the end of the Cold War nearly twenty years ago. Nevertheless, the UK has been repeatedly attacked throughout its history and may well be again at some time in the future. It is in maintaining credible defence of the homeland that the role of the Navy will continue to be key, from providing deterrence at the strategic international level through the spectrum of threats down to the protection of ports and offshore oil and gas assets.

All of these tasks are likely to get harder in the future as the competition for finite resources increases inexorably and the fragile international framework of law and order is subject to ever-greater strains and stresses. To guarantee our future safety, wealth and welfare the country needs the will and determination to provide the means to safeguard the nation. With the necessary investment the Royal Navy can continue to provide that safeguard.

AREAS OF NAVAL OPERATIONS WORLDWIDE 1957–2009

Brunei and Borneo 1962–1966

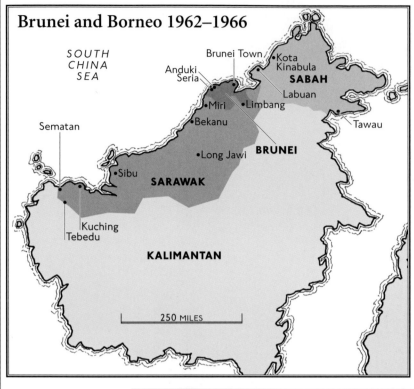

SOUTH CHINA SEA

Brunei Town
Kota Kinabula
Anduki
Seria
SABAH
Labuan
Miri
Limbang
Bekanu
Tawau
Sematan
BRUNEI
Long Jawi
Sibu
SARAWAK
Kuching
Tebedu
KALIMANTAN

250 MILES

East African Mutinies 1964

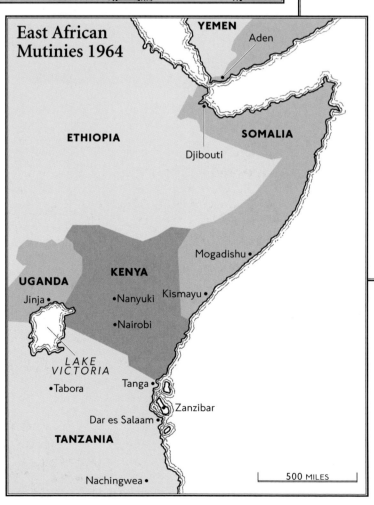

YEMEN
Aden
ETHIOPIA
SOMALIA
Djibouti
Mogadishu
UGANDA
KENYA
Jinja
Nanyuki
Kismayu
Nairobi
LAKE VICTORIA
Tanga
Tabora
Zanzibar
Dar es Salaam
TANZANIA
Nachingwea

500 MILES

BELIZE
GUATEMALA

Falklands Conflict

SOUTH GEORGIA

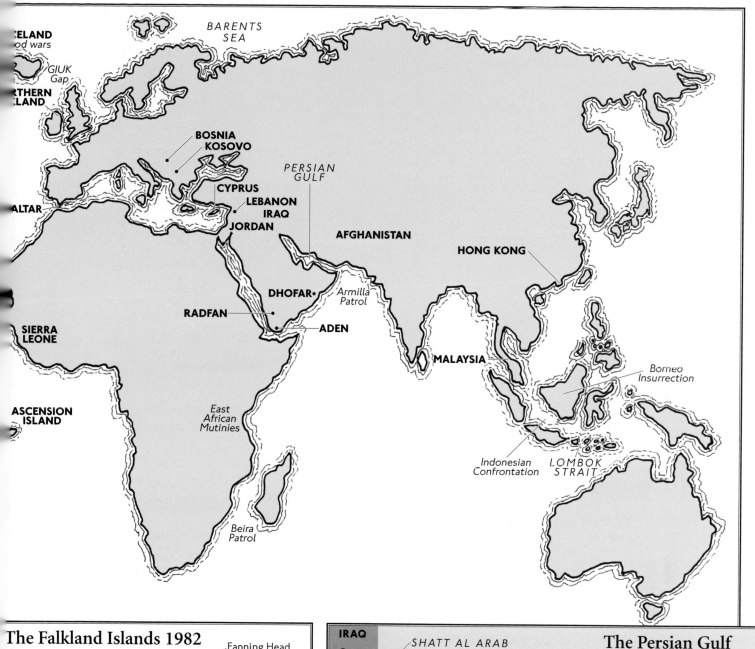

ICELAND
Cod wars

*GIUK
Gap*

NORTHERN
IRELAND

GIBRALTAR

SIERRA
LEONE

ASCENSION
ISLAND

*BARENTS
SEA*

**BOSNIA
KOSOVO**

CYPRUS
LEBANON
IRAQ
JORDAN

*PERSIAN
GULF*

AFGHANISTAN

HONG KONG

DHOFAR

*Armilla
Patrol*

RADFAN

ADEN

MALAYSIA

*Borneo
Insurrection*

*East
African
Mutinies*

*Indonesian
Confrontation*

*LOMBOK
STRAIT*

*Beira
Patrol*

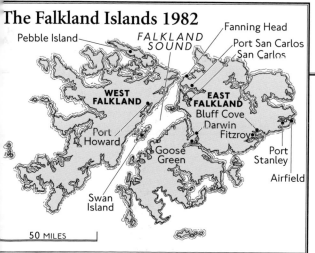

The Falkland Islands 1982

Pebble Island

*FALKLAND
SOUND*

Fanning Head

Port San Carlos
San Carlos

**WEST
FALKLAND**

**EAST
FALKLAND**

Bluff Cove
Darwin
Fitzroy

Port
Stanley

Airfield

Port
Howard

Goose
Green

Swan
Island

50 MILES

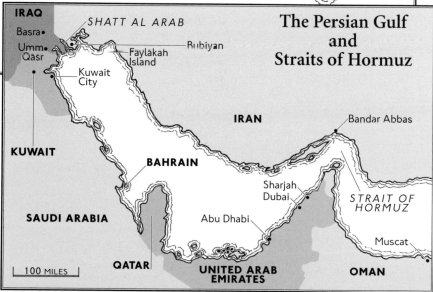

The Persian Gulf
and
Straits of Hormuz

IRAQ

SHATT AL ARAB

Basra

Umm
Qasr

Faylakah
Island

Bubiyan

Kuwait
City

KUWAIT

IRAN

Bandar Abbas

BAHRAIN

Sharjah
Dubai

Abu Dhabi

*STRAIT
OF
HORMUZ*

SAUDI ARABIA

Muscat

100 MILES

QATAR

**UNITED ARAB
EMIRATES**

OMAN

337

NOTES

* denotes that full details of the publication quoted appear in the list of sources on page 340.

Chapter 1 (1957–1959)

1. *Lloyd's Register of Shipping* (20 million tons gross, registered).
2. An apocryphal story, but it was very widespread and popular within naval circles.
3. Eric Grove, *Vanguard to Trident**.
4. Admiral Sir Alan West, introduction to *Broadsheet 2001/2002**.
5. Desmond Wettern, *The Decline of British Seapower**.
6. Stanley Begg, member of the ship's company of the Loch class frigate *Loch Alvie*.
7. Desmond Wettern, *The Decline of British Seapower**.
8. The other pilot, Lieutenant de Vaisseau Nicola, was never found. Tragically his widow had just given birth to a daughter, whom he had not seen. The writer met the daughter, Anne-Christine, many years later when she married his wife's first cousin. The daughter was well aware that the Royal Navy had searched for her father.
9. The USS *Nautilus*, commanded by Commander Bill Anderson, reached the North Pole on 3 August 1958 and sent a historic signal: 'For the world, our country and the Navy – the North Pole.'
10. North European and MEDiterranean Route Instructions give details of danger areas, swept routes and buoyage in the North, Baltic, Mediterranean and Black Seas. They are published by the MoD (Navy), Hydrographic Department.
11. The Sea Cadet Corps encouraged many youngsters to join the Royal Navy, and still does today.
12. Admiralty Fleet Order 1510/58 (June 1958) stated: 'Through the initiative of distinguished gentlemen who hold responsible financial, industrial and commercial positions, and who have a personal regard for the Royal Navy a new Association called the White Ensign Association Ltd has been formed under the Chairmanship of Admiral Sir John Eccles, for the purpose of assisting and promoting the interests of men and women who are now serving or who have at any time served in the Royal Navy, the Royal Marines, any Naval or Royal Marine Reserve or in the Women's Royal Naval Service or Queen Alexandra's Royal Naval Nursing Service, especially those leaving the Service during the current period of reduction in Service manpower.'
13. Admiralty Fleet Order 1510/58 (June 1958).

Chapter 2 (1960–1964)

1. Denis Healey in the House of Commons on 27 November 1967, referring to the satisfactory conclusion of the campaign in Indonesia and Borneo: 'When the House thinks of the tragedy that could have fallen on a whole corner of a Continent if we had not been able to hold the situation and bring it to a successful termination, it will appreciate that in history books it will be recorded as one of the most efficient uses of military force in the history of the world.'
2. Andrew Marr, *A History of Modern Britain**.
3. General Sir William Jackson GBE, KCB, MC, official military historian to the Cabinet Office, *Withdrawal from Empire**.
4. Naval Historical Branch; Captain Andrew Welch RN, *The Royal Navy in the Cod Wars**.
5. Major General Julian Thompson, *The Royal Marines**.
6. Captain J A Finnigan RN, closed up at action stations as a junior officer on board the destroyer *Caesar* in the Lombok Strait in September 1964.
7. Denis Healey, House of Commons, 27 November 1967.

8. Vice Admiral Harold Hickling, *Postscript to Voyager**.
9. Lieutenant Commander Ken Napier MBE, RN.
10. General Sir William Jackson, *Withdrawal from Empire**.
11. Major General Julian Thompson, *The Royal Marines**.

Chapter 3 (1965–1969)

1. NATO Information Service, Brussels, *NATO Facts and Figures* (NATO Publications, January 1976).
2. Statement of Defence Estimates, 1965 (Cmnd 2592).
3. Statement of Defence Estimates, 1966 (Cmnd 2901).
4. Vice Admiral Sir Hugh Mackenzie KCB, DSO*, DSC stated: 'Polaris submarines on QRA (Quick Readiness Alert) were indeed at war with no coming home, and everything that the submarine did on patrol was geared towards the achievement of three clearly defined aims
   Remaining undetected
   Maintaining constant communications
   Being at short notice to fire
   Maintenance of the deterrent was the primary aim of the Royal Navy.'
   Submitted by Commander Jeff Tall OBE, RN, Director of the Submarine Museum.
5. Lieutenant Commander Ken Napier MBE, RN.
6. Ibid.
7. The Commission Book of *Albion*'s second commission, as a commando carrier, report of 848 Naval Air Commando Squadron RN.
8. Captain Doug Littlejohns CBE, RN, serving as a junior officer on board *Albion* during her second commission, as a commando carrier, off the coast of Indonesia.
9. Lieutenant Commander Ken Napier MBE, RN, serving as a junior officer on board *Maryton* during the Indonesian Confrontation.
10. Ibid.
11. Ibid.
12. Desmond Wettern, *The Decline of British Seapower**.
13. Ibid.
14. Lieutenant Colonel John Owen, commanding 45 Commando Royal Marines in Aden in June 1967. From Robin Neillands, *A Fighting Retreat – The British Empire 1947–97**.
15. Stephen Harper, in Major General Julian Thompson (ed), *The Imperial War Museum Book of Modern Warfare**.
16. *The Times*, 2 December 1965.
17. The Commission Book of the assault ship *Fearless*.
18. Randolph and Winston Churchill, *The Six Day War**.
19. Stephen Harper, *The Imperial War Musuem Book of Modern Warfare**.

Chapter 4 (1970–1974)

1. Statement of Defence Estimates, 1970.
2. 'The Royal Navy Task Group' 9/74 (O/N 4303785), the official MoD (Navy) press release for the September 1974 Group Deployment.
3. Lieutenant Commander Ken Napier MBE, RN.
4. Commander Jeff Tall OBE, RN, Director of the Royal Naval Submarine Museum.
5. Captain Andrew Welch RN, *The Royal Navy in the Cod Wars**.
6. SOSUS is an acronym for **SO**und **SU**rveillance **S**ystem, which consisted of bottom-mounted hydrophone arrays connected by underwater cables to facilities ashore. The individual arrays were installed primarily on continental slopes and seamounts at locations optimised for undistorted long-range submarine generated acoustic propagation. The combination of location within the ocean and the sensitivity of arrays allowed the system to detect acoustic power of less than a watt at

ranges of several hundred kilometres. At the shore-based facilities (NAVFAC) frequency analysis was carried out on the signals from the arrays and paper outputs of lofargrams produced, which were used to detect and classify contacts. This information was disseminated to units at sea and used to protect SSBN anonymity (evasion), and SSN cuing (prosecution), and was a vital tool during the Cold War.
(Commander Jeff Tall OBE, RN, Director of the Royal Naval Submarine Museum.)
7. Jim Ring, *We Come Unseen**.
8. The September 1974 press release (O/N 4303785) stated: 'Gone is the traditional method of operating single ships over a wide area, and in its place is the Task Force idea – exemplified by the present group of six ships and, normally, a submarine.'
9. General Sir John Akehurst 'The Unknown War', in Major General Julian Thompson (ed), *The Imperial War Museum Book of Modern Warfare**.
10. Commander Jeff Tall OBE, RN, Director of the Royal Naval Submarine Museum.

Chapter 5 (1975–1979)

1. Chris Bishop and Chris Chant, *Aircraft Carriers**.
2. Alex Hook, *Modern War Day by Day**.
3. Statement of Defence Estimates, 1976 (Cmnd 6432).
4. Margaret Thatcher in her 'Britain Awake' speech at Kensington Town Hall on 19 January 1976.
5. Rear Admiral Richard Hill, *Lewin of Greenwich**.
6. Captain Basil Watson RN, *Commander in Chief**.
7. The account of incidents at sea is based on reports from some of the ships involved, and research by Captain Andrew Welch. For a detailed account of all incidents see Andrew Welch, *The Royal Navy in the Cod Wars**.
8. David Miller, *Commanding Officers**.
9. Peter Elliott, *The Cross and the Ensign**.
10. Iain Ballantyne, *HMS London**.
11. Ibid. (Able Seaman Eddie Cowling).
12. James D Ladd, *SBS: The Invisible Raiders**.
13. Lieutenant Commander Ken Napier MBE, RN (SNONI staff).

Chapter 6 (1980–1982)

1. Statement of Defence Estimates, April 1980 (Cmnd 7826-1)
2. *Board Bulletin* 1981
3. There are a great many good books on the Falklands Campaign but the prime source used is *The Royal Navy and the Falklands War** by the late David Brown, Head of the Naval Historical Branch during the Campaign. Max Hastings and Simon Jenkins, *The Battle for the Falklands* (Michael Joseph, 1983) and Admiral Sandy Woodward, *One Hundred Days** also provide first-class accounts from people who were down there at the time.
4. Admiral Sir James Perowne KBE.
5. On 23 April the British had already delivered a statement to the Argentineans stating: 'In announcing the establishment of a Maritime Exclusion Zone around the Falkland Islands, Her Majesty's Government made it clear that this measure was without prejudice to the right of the United Kingdom to take whatever additional measures may be needed in the exercise of its right of self-defence under Article 51 of the United Nations Charter. In this connection, Her Majesty's Government now wishes to make clear that any approach on the part of Argentine warships, including submarines, naval auxiliaries or military aircraft, which could amount to a threat to interfere with the mission of British Forces in the South Atlantic will encounter the appropriate response.'
Contributed by Commander Jeff Tall OBE, RN, Director of the Submarine Museum.

6. Commander Jeff Tall OBE, RN, Director of the Submarine Museum.
7. Legal or not legal? 'The sinking of *Belgrano* was justified under international law, as the heading of a belligerent naval vessel has no bearing on its status. Furthermore, Hector Bonzo, the captain of *Belgrano*, has himself testified that the attack was legitimate for this reason. The fact that the ship was outside the British declared Total Exclusion Zone does not affect this analysis, especially since the British had informed Argentina on 23 April that Argentine ships and aircraft outside the Exclusion Zone could be attacked if they posed a threat to the British Task Force, and senior figures in the Argentine Navy have made clear that they understood this message; for example, Argentine Rear-Admiral Allara who commanded the *Belgrano*'s task group said "After that message of 23 April, the entire South Atlantic was an operational theatre for both sides. We, as professionals, said it was just too bad that we lost *Belgrano*.' Finally, in 1994, the Argentine government conceded that the sinking of *Belgrano* was a "legal act of war".' Contributed by Commander Jeff Tall OBE, RN, Director of the Submarine Museum.
8. Admiral Sir Michael Layard KC KCB, CBE.
9. David Brown, *The Royal Navy and the Falklands War**.
10. The pilot killed was Vice Commodore de la Colina, the most senior Argentine Air Force officer to be killed during the conflict.

Chapter 7 (1983–1985)
1. The Franks Report, 1983 (Cmnd 8787).
2. MoD, *The Falklands Campaign: The Lessons* (Cmnd 8758).
3. *Broadsheet 1983*.
4. Ibid.
5. Jim Ring, *We Come Unseen**.
6. Neil McCart, *Harrier Carriers Volume 1: HMS Invincible* (Fan Publications 2004), page 55.
7. Captain Dan Conley OBE, RN.
8. John Lehman, Former Secretary of the US Navy.

Chapter 8 (1986–89)
1. 'The Maritime Strategy', unclassified edition issued by the US Naval Institute in January 1986 and précis by Admiral James D Watkins US Navy.
2. John Lehman, Former Secretary of the US Navy, *Seas of Glory**.
3. Statement of Defence Estimates, 1986 (Cmnd 9763).
4. Gary Weir and Walter Boyne, *Rising Tide**.
5. Desmond Wettern in 'The Royal Navy in Transition' (*Journal of Defence and Diplomacy*, 1988, page 59) stated that Britain provided 70 per cent of the NATO maritime forces for the eastern Atlantic area. He went on to point out 'There is little doubt that some of the of the new frigates currently joining the fleet are among the most powerful and best equipped of their kind in the world, especially as submarine hunters. But achieving such a level of qualitative excellence in antisubmarine warfare has to be paid for, and with a contracting defence budget over the past three years, the maritime element of local defence of the British Isles has suffered in an either/or situation created by lack of funds.'
6. Lieutenant Commander Ken Napier MBE, RN.
7. Richard Johnstone-Bryden, *The Royal Yacht Britannia**.
8. Ibid.
9. John Lehman, Former Secretary of the US Navy.
10. Ivan Rendall, *Splash One**.
11. John Lehman, Former Secretary of the US Navy.
12. Ibid.

13. Richard Johnstone-Bryden, *The Royal Yacht Britannia**.
14. Gary Weir and Walter Boyne *Rising Tide**.
15. Lieutenant Commander Ken Napier MBE, RN; Iain Ballantyne, *Strike from the Sea**.
16. Captain Dan Conley OBE, RN.
17. Lieutenant Commander Ken Napier MBE, RN.
18. Time-Life Books, *Carrier Warfare**..
19. Lieutenant Commander Ken Napier MBE, RN.
20. Ibid.
21. Sun Tzu, *The Art of War*, translated by Ralph D Sawyer (Barnes and Noble Inc by arrangement with West View Press, 1994),
22. John Pina Craven, former Chief Scientist, US Navy Special Projects Office, *The Silent War**.
23. Rear Admiral Robert R Fountain US Navy, in Kenneth Sewell and Jerome Preisler, *All Hands Down: The True Story of the Soviet Attack on the USS Scorpion* (Simon & Schuster, 2008).
24. Gary Weir and Walter Boyne, *Rising Tide**.

Chapter 9 (1990–1992)
1. Statement of Defence Estimates, 1991 (Cmnd 1559).
2. Captain T D Elliott RN, *A Gulf Record**, Iain Ballantyne, *Strike from the Sea**, and General Sir Peter De La Billiere, *Storm Command**.
3. Iain Ballantyne, *HMS London**.
4. 'Conventional' refers to patrol submarines with diesel-electric power units instead of nuclear power.
5. Statement of Defence Estimates 1981 (Cmnd. 8288).
6. The CFS *Chicoutimi*, sold to Canada, came to prominence in 2004 when she suffered a fire caused by seawater, which appeared to leak through the conning tower hatch. Tragically it resulted in loss of life and a timely reminder of the risk carried by all submariners.

Chapter 10 (1993–1995)
1. 'Naval Forces in British Defence Policy', *Broadsheet 1994/5**, page 9.
2. 'Report of Proceedings', *Broadsheet 1994/5**, page 19.
3. Captain Terry Loughran RN.
4. Lieutenant Nick Richardson RN, *No Escape Zone**.
5. Lieutenant Commander Ken Napier MBE, RN.
6. The Naval Staff (Staff of Rear Admiral Submarines)
7. From the Naval Prayer.

Chapter 11 (1996–1998)
1. *Broadsheet 1995/6**.
2. The Strategic Defence Review, July 1998 (Cmnd 3999).
3. Ibid.
4. Lieutenant Commander Ken Napier MBE, RN.
5. Admiral Sir Jock Slater GCB, LVO.
6. *Broadsheet 1997/8**.

Chapter 12 (1999–2001)
1. Admiral Sir Alan West, introduction to *Broadsheet 2001/2002*.
2. Commander Piers Barker RN, Staff of Rear Admiral Submarines.
3. Admiral Sir Jonathan Band KCB, Commander in Chief Fleet, 'The Front Line', *Broadsheet 2001/2002**.
4. Ibid.

Chapter 13 (2002–2004)
1. Iain Ballantyne, *Strike from the Sea**.
2. James Newton, *Armed Action**.
3. Robert Fox, *Iraq Campaign 2003**.
4. *Navy News*, August 2003.

Chapter 14 (2005–2006)
1. An approximate figure based on extrapolation and general information available at that time.
2. *Navy News*, January 2007, page 2.

3. *Navy News*, March 2005, page 12, and April 2005, page 15.

Chapter 15 (2007–2008)
1. Admiral Sir Jonathan Band, First Sea Lord, in the Introduction to Paul Beaver (ed), *Royal Navy – a Global Force**.
2. 'Diary of Events – December', *Broadsheet 2007*, page 11.
3. In fact the record claimed by the nuclear submarine *Vengeance* had already been achieved by *Resolution*, commanded by Commander Jeff Tall OBE, RN, when she completed 108 days in 1991 (confirmed by Commander Tall in 2008).
4. *Navy News*, August 2007.
5. Ibid.
6. Ibid.
7. Ibid.
8. Ibid.
9. *Broadsheet 2007**.
10. *Navy News*, May 2007, page 10.
11. Ibid, page 17.
12. 'Ocean tackles the Drugs Trade' *Broadsheet 2007**, page 26.
13. 'Black Duke Goes Global' *Broadsheet 2007**, page 28.
14. *Navy News*, August 2007.
15. *Navy News*, May 2008.
16. Commander L Notley RN, Logistics Commander *Illustrious*.
17. *Navy News*, September 2007.
18. 'Changing, but Ever Steady – The Royal Navy Submarine Service in 2007', *Broadsheet 2007**, page 20.
19. Admiral Sir Jonathan Band in a speech at Buckingham Palace on 29 January 2008.

Epilogue
1. Department for Transport, *Maritime Statistics*, 2005.

SOURCES

This tribute has been compiled from primary and secondary sources as well as personal records and also from experience recalled some time after the events occurred. Some of the chapters have been vetted by the First Sea Lords of the day, and the Association is very grateful to them for that assistance.

Frustratingly, even primary sources have at times proved contradictory and in such cases lack of time has forced us to resort to the time-honoured method of 'best guess'. There will inevitably be those who dispute some detail or other as well as those disappointed that we have failed to include their details; we can only apologise in advance, pointing out that we have attempted to act in good faith throughout the production of this book.

The Association is extremely grateful to all the many people who have helped in their different ways to ensure the accuracy and coverage of the last fifty years of the Royal Navy.

Admiralty Archives	Kate Tildesley
Admiralty Library	Jenny Wraith
Admiralty Manuals of Seamanship (vols I–III)	Her Majesty's Stationery Office
Brassey's Annual	
British Maritime Doctrine (BR 1806)	Royal Navy
Broadsheet (1976–2007)	Royal Navy
Board *Bulletin* (1968–1975)	Royal Navy
Commission Books (various)	Individual ships, including *Albion, Ark Royal, Blake, Britannia, Bulwark, Centaur, Eagle, Falmouth, Fearless, Invincible, London, Lynx, Tartar, Tiger, Victorious*
Fleet Air Arm Museum	Catherine Cooper
Fleet Operations Programmes (FOPs)	Royal Navy (NHB)
Fleet Operations Schedules	Royal Navy (NHB)
Flight Deck	DNAW, MoD
Jane's Fighting Ships	Jane's
Jane's Weapons Systems	Jane's
Naval Books of Reference (BRs)	Various, published by Her Majesty's Stationery Office
Naval Historical Branch (NHB)	Captain Chris Page (Director)
Naval Review	Richard Hill (editor)
The Navy List	Her Majesty's Stationery Office
Navy News	Sarah Fletcher (editor)
Proceedings	United States Naval Institute
Reports of Proceedings	Official reports by commanding officers of ships and submarines, copies filed with the NHB (by courtesy of Captain Page, Director of the NHB)
Royal Marines Historical Society	
Royal Naval Museum	Dr Colin White
Royal United Services Institute for Defence Studies	
Statements of Defence Estimates	HM Government
Submarine Museum	Commander Jeff Tall
Warships International Fleet Review	Iain Ballantyne (editor)

Bibliography

Adams, T and J Smith — *The Royal Fleet Auxiliary* (Chatham Publishing 2005)

Ballantyne, Iain — *Strike from the Sea: The Royal Navy and US Navy at War in the Middle East, 1949–2003* (Pen & Sword 2004)
HMS London (Leo Cooper 2003)

Beaver, Paul — *The Royal Navy in the 1980s* (Arms & Armour 1985)
(cd), *Royal Navy – a Global Force* (Newsdesk Communications Ltd 2007)

Billiere, General Sir Peter De La — *Storm Command* (Harper Collins 1992)

Bishop, Chris — *Aircraft Carriers* (Silverdale Books 2004)

Brogan, Patrick — *World Conflicts* (Bloomsbury 1992)

Brown, David (NHB) — *The Royal Navy and The Falklands* (Leo Cooper 1987)

Brown, Neville — *British Arms & Strategy 1970~80* (RUSI 1969)

Carver, Field Marshal Lord — *Tightrope Walking: Defence Policy since 1945* (Hutchinson 1992)

Chant, Chris — *Warships Today* (Summertime Publishing 2004)
History of the World's Warships (Regency House 2001)

Churchill, R S and W S — *The Six Day War* (Heinemann 1967)

Clancy, Tom — *Submarine* (Harper Collins 1993)

Clapp, M and E Southby-Tailyour — *Amphibious Assault Falklands* (Orion 1996)

Compton-Hall, Richard — *Submarine Versus Submarine* (David & Charles 1988)

Cornwell, E L — *Warships in Action Today* (Ian Allan 1980)

Crane, Jonathan — *Submarine* (BBC Publications 1984)

Craven, John Pina — *The Silent War: The Cold War Battle beneath the Sea* (Simon & Schuster 2002)

Critchley, Mike — *British Warships and Auxiliaries* (Maritime Books)

Croft, Stuart — *British Security Policy* (Harper Collins 1991)

Elliot, Peter — *The Cross and the Ensign: A Naval History of Malta 1798–1979* (Granada 1980)

Elliott, Toby D — *A Gulf Record: RN Task Force 321.1* (Connexions 1991)

Fox, Robert — *Iraq Campaign 2003* (Agenda Publishing 2003)

Francis, Clare — *The Commanding Sea* (BBC Pelham 1981)

Friedman, Norman — *Sea Power and Space* (Chatham Publishing 2000)

Garbutt, P E — *Naval Challenge* (Macdonald & Co. 1961)

Gilbert, Martin — *History of the Twentieth Century* (Harper Collins 1999)

Grenville, J A S — *Collins History of the World* (Harper Collins 1994)

Grove, Eric — *Vanguard to Trident* (The Bodley Head Ltd 1987)
Maritime Strategy and European Security (Brassey's 1990)
Various articles in defence journals

Hastings, Max and Simon Jenkins — *Battle for the Falklands* (Michael Joseph 1983)

Heathcote, T A — *British Admirals of the Fleet* (Leo Cooper 2002)

Hickling, Vice Admiral Harold — *Postscript to Voyager* (A H & A W Reed 1969)

Hill, Richard — *Lewin of Greenwich: The Authorised Biography of Admiral of the Fleet Lord Lewin* (Cassell & Co 2000)
The Oxford Illustrated History of the Royal Navy (Oxford University Press 1995)

Hook, Alex — *Modern War Day by Day* (Grange Books 2004)

Jackson, Gen Sir William — *Withdrawal from Empire* (Batsford 1986)

Johnstone-Brydon, Richard — *The Royal Yacht Britannia: The Official History* (Conway Maritime Press 2003)

Ladd, James D — *SBS: The Invisible Raiders* (Arms & Armour Press 1983)

Lehman, John — *On Seas of Glory* (Touchstone 2002)

Lovering, Tristan — *Amphibious Assault* (Seafarer 2007)

Maclean, Malcolm — *Naval Accidents since 1945* (Maritime Books 2008)

Marr, Andrew — *A History of Modern Britain* (Macmillan 2007)

McGuire, Paul and Margaret — *The Price of Admiralty* (Oxford University Press 1944)

McInnes, Colin — *Trident – The Only Option* (Brassey's Defence Publishers 1986)

Miller, David — *Illustrated Directory of Warships* (Salamander 2002)
The Cold War (John Murray 1998)
Commanding Officers (John Murray 2001)

Neillands, Robin — *Fighting Retreat: The British Empire 1947–97* (Hodder & Stoughton 1996)

McCart, Neil — *Harrier Carriers – HMS Invincible* (Fan 2004)
Three Ark Royals (Fan Publications 1999)

Newton, Lt Commander James — *Armed Action* (Headline Review 2007)

Owen, David — *Anti-Submarine Warfare* (Seaforth 2007)

Parker, John — *Illustrated World Guide to Submarines* (Hermes 2007)

Pimlott, John (Ed) — *British Military Operations 1945–1985* (Bison Books 1986)

Preston, Antony — *World's Great Aircraft Carriers* (Chancellor Press 1999)

Rendall, Ivan — *Splash One* (Weidenfeld & Nicolson 1998)

Richardson, Nick	*No Escape Zone* (Warner 2000)
Ring, Jim	*We Come Unseen* (John Murray 2001)
Roberts, Prof F	*Sixty Years of Nuclear History* (Carpenter 1999)
Sontag, Sherry and Christopher Drew with Annette Lawrence Drew	*Blind Man's Bluff* (Hutchinson 1999)
Southby-Tailyour, Ewen	*Reasons in Writing – A Commando's View of the Falklands War* (Leo Cooper 1993)
Speed, Keith	*Sea Change* (Ashgrove 1982)
	'The Royal Navy in NATO', *NATO's Fifteen Nations*, August–September 1981, page 64
Terraine, John	*Life and Times of Lord Mountbatten* (Arrow 1980)
Terrill, C	HMS *Brilliant* (BBC Books 1995)
Tew, Captain Ian	*Salvage: A Personal Odyssey* (Seafarer Books 2007)
Thompson, Major General Julian	*The Royal Marines: From Sea Soldiers to a Special Force* (Sidgwick & Jackson 2000) (ed), *The Imperial War Museum Book of Modern Warfare* (Sidgwick & Jackson 2002)
Time-Life	*Carrier Warfare* (Caxton Publishing 1991)
Tute, Warren	*The True Glory* (Macdonald & Co 1983)
Van der Vat, Dan	*Standards of Power* (Hutchinson 2000) *Stealth at Sea* (Weidenfeld & Nicolson, 1994)
Varner, Roy and Wayne Collier	*A Matter of Risk* (Hodder & Stoughton 1979)
Ward, Commander 'Sharkey'	*Sea Harrier over the Falklands* (Orion 1992)
Watson, Captain Basil	*Commander in Chief: The Life of Admiral of the Fleet the Lord Fieldhouse* (RN Submarine Museum 2005)
Watts, Anthony	*Warships & Navies 1973* (Ian Allan 1972)
Weir, Gary and Walter Boyne	*Rising Tide: The Untold Story of the Russian Submarines that Fought the Cold War* (Basic Books 2003)
Welch, Captain Andrew	*The Royal Navy in the Cod Wars* (Maritime Books, 2006)
Wells, John	*The Royal Navy: An Illustrated Social History* (Alan Sutton, 1994)
West, Nigel	*The Secret War for the Falklands* (Time Warner 1997)
Wettern, Desmond	'The Royal Navy in Transition', *Journal of Defence and Diplomacy*, 1988 'Britain's Forgotten Lessons', *United States Naval Institute Proceedings*, March 1987 *The Decline of British Seapower* (Jane's 1982) Various articles in defence journals
Wixon, Captain David	*Bravo Zulu – Bravo Alpha* (The Gosling Foundation 2004)
Woodward, Admiral Sir Sandy	*One Hundred Days* (Harper Collins 1992)
Wragg, David	*Carrier Combat* (Sutton Publishing 1997)

Recommended Sources

Early period:	Eric Grove, *Vanguard to Trident* Desmond Wettern, *The Decline of British Seapower* Robin Neillands, *Fighting Retreat*
Cod Wars:	Andrew Welch, *The Royal Navy in the Cod Wars*
Falklands War:	David Brown, *The Royal Navy and the Falklands* Max Hastings, *Battle for the Falklands*
The Cold War:	David Miller, *The Cold War*
Cold War submarine operations:	Jim Ring, *We Come Unseen*
Gulf operations:	Iain Ballantyne, *Strike from the Sea* Captain Toby Elliott, *A Gulf Record: RN Task Force 321.1* Robert Fox, *Iraq Campaign 2003*

Ship, Submarine and Aircraft Data Boxes
Technical data compiled by Commander Mike Howell.

MAJOR SHIPS OF THE ROYAL NAVY 1958–2009

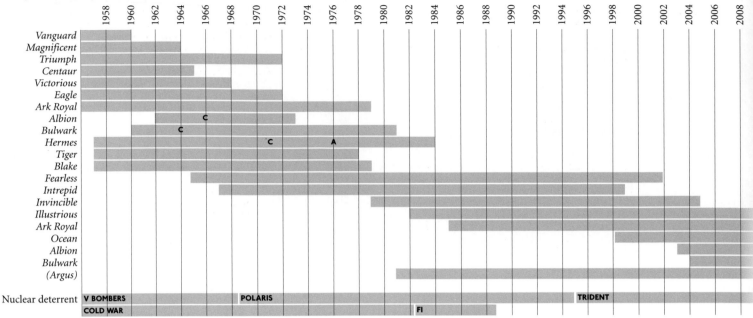

The table reflects changing strategy, showing the transition from fixed-wing carriers to the CVS, then growing emphasis on amphibious capability. It also highlights the critical situation in the early 1980s.

(Nuclear deterent RN from June 1968)

A=Conversion to VSTOL aircraft carrier   C=Conversion to commando carrier   FI=Falkland Islands Campaign

THE ROYAL NAVY 2009

SURFACE FLEET
Aircraft Carriers
2 + 1 reserve (20,000t): *Illustrious* and *Ark Royal* (and *Invincible* in reserve)
Amphibious Assault Ships
3   *Ocean* (20,500t), *Albion* and *Bulwark* (19,500t)
Destroyers
3 (+ 3 building) Type 45s (7,350t): *Daring, Dauntless, Diamond* (*Dragon, Defender* and *Duncan* building)
4   Type 42s Batch 2 (3,560t): *Exeter, Southampton, Nottingham, Liverpool*
4   Type 42s Batch 3 (3,880t): *Manchester, Gloucester, York, Edinburgh*
Frigates
4   Type 22s (5,300t): *Cornwall, Cumberland, Campbeltown, Chatham*
13   Type 23s (4,900t): *Argyll, Lancaster, Iron Duke, Monmouth, Montrose, Westminster, Northumberland, Richmond, Somerset, Sutherland, Kent, Portland, St Albans*
Mine Counter-Measures Vessels (MCMVs)
8   Hunt class (685t): *Ledbury, Cattistock, Brocklesby, Middleton, Chiddingfold, Atherstone, Hurworth, Quorn*
8   Sandown class (450t): *Walney, Penzance, Pembroke, Grimsby, Bangor, Blyth, Ramsey, Shoreham*
Patrol Ships and Vessels
1   Antarctic patrol ship (7,500t): *Endurance*
4   River class (1,677t): *Tyne, Severn, Mersey, Clyde*
18   Archer class (40t)
Survey Vessels
1   ocean survey vessel (13,500t): *Scott*
2   coastal survey vessels (3,470t): *Echo* and *Enterprise*
2   multi-role: *Roebuck* (1,300t) *Gleaner* (26t)

SUBMARINE SERVICE
Ballistic Missile Submarines (SSBNs)
4   (16,000t): *Vanguard, Victorious, Vigilant, Vengeance*
Fleet Submarines (SSNs)
7   Trafalgar class (5,000t): *Trafalgar, Turbulent, Tireless, Torbay, Trenchant, Talent, Triumph*
2   Swiftsure class (5,000t): *Superb, Sceptre*
1 (+ 3 building) Astute class (7,800t): *Astute* (*Ambush, Artful, Audacious* building)

ROYAL FLEET AUXILIARY
Landing Ships (Dock)
4   Bay class (16,160t): *Largs Bay, Lyme Bay, Mounts Bay, Cardigan Bay*
Tankers
2   Wave class fleet tankers (31,000t): *Wave Knight, Wave Ruler*
2   Leaf class support tankers (40,870t): *Bayleaf, Orangeleaf*
2   Rover class small fleet tankers (11,522t): *Gold Rover, Black Rover*
Fleet Replenishment Ships
2   *Fort Victoria* class (36,580t): *Fort Victoria, Fort George*
2   *Fort Rosalie* class (23,482t): *Fort Rosalie, Fort Austin*
Other Auxiliaries
1   landing ship (logistic) (6,700t): *Sir Bedivere*
1   aviation training ship (28,080t): *Argus*
1   forward repair ship (10,765t): *Diligence*

ROYAL MARINES
HQ 3 Commando Brigade, UK Landing Force Command Support Group, 40, 42 and 45 Commandos, 539 Assault Squadron, 29 Commando Regiment Royal Artillery, 59 Commando Squadron Royal Engineers, Commando Logistics Regiment 1 Assault Group RM, Fleet Protection Group, RM Band Service Special Boat Service

FLEET AIR ARM
Fixed Wing
Naval Strike Wing of Joint Force Harrier (GR7, GR9 and GR9A Harriers): 800 and 801 Squadrons,
Training and Transport (T2 and T3 Jetstreams): 750 Squadron, (Grob Gs) 727 Squadron
Merlin Helicopter Force (Mk 1 ASW and AS): 700M, 814, 820, 824 and 829 Squadrons
Sea King Helicopter Force (Mk 5 and Mk 7): 771, 849, 854 and 857 Squadrons, Gannet SAR Flight
Sea King Commando Helicopter Force (Mk 4): 845, 846 and 848 Squadrons
Lynx Squadrons (Mk 3 and Mk 8 ASW and AS): 702 and 815 Squadrons, 847 Squadron (Mk 7)

ROYAL NAVY OPERATIONS 1957–2009

Active Endeavour	2001 Mediterranean (maritime surveillance and security)
Agila	11–13.12.1979 Rhodesia (monitor cease-fire)
Alleviate	23.6–8.7.1997 Adriatic (evacuation from Albania)
Allied Force	12.6–24.8.1999 Adriatic (NATO clearance of ordnance off Kosovo)
Allied Harvest	12.6–24.8.1999 Adriatic (NATO–UN security/clearance)
Armilla	7.10.1980 Persian Gulf (naval security patrols)
Armilla Accomplice	26.3–31.12.1984 Gulf (mine counter-measures)
Balsac	15-28.1.1986 Aden (service assisted evacuation of PDRY)
Banner	7.6–20.10.1989 Northern Ireland (security operations)
Basilica	12.1–18.3.1999 West Africa (support to civil power, Sierra Leone)
Bold Step	7.2007 North Atlantic (joint RN–US Navy security exercises)
Bolton	14.11.1997 Gulf (preparations to enforce UN Resolutions)
Bracken	1–31.12.1971 Persian Gulf (evacuation protection)
Burlap	19.11–11.12.1970 East Pakistan (disaster relief)
Buzzard	7.2002 Afghanistan (operations against the Taliban)
Calash	2003 Gulf of Aden (maritime surveillance and security)
Calendar II	1.7.1988 Gulf of Oman (exercise Cimnel, mine clearance)
Care	27.9–8.10.1987 Bermuda (hurricane relief)
Caspar	23–27.10.1997 Firth of Forth (support to civil power)
Caxton	17–29.8.1997 Caribbean (disaster relief)
Celia	22.11.91–8.1992 Adriatic (Yugoslavian Civil War)
Cert	21–25.4.1986 Mediterranean (protection of Royal Yacht *Britannia*)
Chantress	6.4–21.8.1995 Angola (UN Stabilisation Force)
Cimnel	12.8–31.12.1987 (exercise Armilla Accomplice)
Citation	4.10.91–3.1992 West Indies (evacuation preparations)
Claret	1964–5 Indonesian Confrontation (pre-emptive cross-border raids)
Clay	2007 Afghanistan (operation against Taliban base)
Clover	17.4–12.1986 Gibraltar (defensive patrols)
Corporate	2.2–14.6.1982 Falkland Islands (recovery operation)
Cosmo	10–20.2.1986 Haiti (internal security/evacuation)
Culex	7–12.1979 Hong Kong (security patrols)
Cutter	5.5–10.12.1988 (prison accommodation during industrial action)
Decisive Enhancement	12–30.10.1996 Adriatic (patrols off Croatia)
Deliberate Guard	8–10.12.1997 Adriatic (support of SFOR/former Yugoslavia)
Deny Flight	1995 Adriatic (air operations against Bosnian Serbs)
Determinant	20.3–29.5.1997 Zaire (security/evacuation operations)
Determined Force	1998 Adriatic (support of NATO SFOR)
Determined Guard	1997 Adriatic (support of UN Stabilisation Force)
Diligent Force	1996 Adriatic (maritime support for Implementation Force)
Driver	9.10–15.11.1994 Persian Gulf (deter threat to Kuwait)
Eldorado	1.6–18.7.1990 Liberia (security/evacuation operation)
Enduring Freedom	2002 worldwide (US-led war on international terrorism)
Eschew	22.1–30.6.1986 Turks and Caicos (civil unrest)
Estimate	11.10.1967–25.6.1968 Aden (protection of evacuation)
Estimate II	27–31.3.1969 Lagos (UK–Rhodesia–UDI talks)
Faldage	10–11.3.1975 Cambodia (evacuation operation)
Farinha	6.1997 UK waters (counter-drugs operations)
Fate	25–30.10.1966 East Aden (cordon and search against rebels)
Fortitude	7.1958 eastern Mediterranean (support to Jordan)
Fresco	13–26.7.2001 UK (cover during strike by firemen)
Fuzecap	18.5.1972 and 15.4–14.5.1973 (search for explosives in *QEII*)
Garrick	21.5–20.9.1998 Indonesia (evacuation preparations)
Garron	2004 south-east Asia (Tsunami emergency relief work)
Glacier	3.2007 Afghanistan (operation against Taliban HQ)
Glasscutter	27–31.7.1972 Northern Ireland (security operations)
Goblet	13–16.12.1985 Leeds (provision of water supplies)
Granby	9.8.1990–11.4.1991 Persian Gulf (liberation of Kuwait)
Grapple	10–12.1992 Adriatic (support to UN Protection Forces)
Grenada	20.1.1972–1985 Northern Ireland (security operations)
Grey Heron	9.2007 UK (amphibious security exercise in the Solent)
Hamden	1993 Adriatic (support of UN Protection Force)
Harlech	9–31.8.1995 West Indies (standby volcano relief)
Harling	15.8–14.10.1984 Gulf of Suez (mine clearance)
Haven	20.4–15.7.1991 Turkey and Iraq (assistance to Kurdish refugees)
Helvin	14–17.3.1997 Adriatic (Albanian evacuation)
Hermicarp I and II	3.2–21.3.1977 and 16.8–13.10.1977 Pacific (explosive clearance)
Herrick	2003 Afghanistan (security operations against the Taliban)
Highbrow	7.2006 Lebanon (evacuation during civil war)
Holystone	Cold War (covert submarine intelligence-gathering missions)
Hound	10.1988 and 11.1990 UK waters (assistance to customs operations)
Interknit	11.1972 Northern Ireland (security in Carlingford Lough)
Jacana	2002 Afghanistan (operations against the Taliban)
James	2003 Iraq (Royal Marine advance on Basra)
Joint Endeavour	1996 Adriatic (maritime support for Implementation Force)
Journeyman	25.11–19.12.1977 South Atlantic (deterrent operation)
Jubilee	9.6.1986 Jamaica (flood relief operations)
Jural	1997 Persian Gulf (UN 'no fly' zone over Iraq)
Keyhole	19–20.6.1982 Antarctic (recapture of South Thule)
Ketone	5–8.10.1987 West Glamorgan (Fire Service industrial action)
Kingfisher	14–30.10.1997 West Africa (protected evacuation preparations)
Kingower	24.3–20.5.1999 Adriatic (UN security operations)
Kingpin	28.1.1987 Gibraltar (exercise Clover security patrols)
Langar	1.9–3.10.1999 Indonesia (restore peace and security in East Timor)
Lecturer	1.1992–11.1993 Cambodia (security operations)
Lesser	14–22.6.1982 Lebanon (evacuation from Jounich)
Lifespan	1997–2006 Northern Ireland (counter-terrorist operations)
Lodestar	1998 Adriatic (support of NATO SFOR/former Yugoslavia)
Lodestone	8–10.12.1997 Adriatic (support of SFOR/former Yugoslavia)
Magellan	13–28.10.1998 Adriatic (demonstration of NATO resolve)
Magister	12.10–29.11.1967 Aden (evacuation)
Mainsail	31.10–3.11.1987 West Indies (hurricane disaster relief)
Manna	8.5–3.6.1991 Bangladesh (disaster relief)
Maritime Guard	1997 Adriatic (monitoring UN embargo)
Maritime Monitor	6–12.1992 Adriatic (monitoring UN embargo)
Maturin	10.2005 Pakistan (disaster relief work in lower Himalayas)
Motorman	31.7.1972 Northern Ireland (internal security)
Nutcracker	1.1964 Aden (Radfan operation in the Yemen)
Offcut	18.11.1983–31.3.1984 Lebanon (peace-keeping)
Okehampton	1.11.1984–21.2.1985 South Georgia (salvage operation)
Oracle	2002 Gulf (maritime security operations, UK contribution to US-led international war on terrorism, Operation Enduring Freedom)
Orderly	7.11.1989–31.3.1990 UK (ambulance assistance)
Palatine	1998 Adriatic (with NATO SFOR in the former Yugoslavia)
Palliser	5.2000 Sierra Leone (security operations)
Peninsula	4–6.2001 UK (controlling foot and mouth disease)
Proximity	6.11.1986 SW Approaches (anti-smuggling operation)
Radcot	10–14.10.1988 English Channel (seaward defence patrols)
Resilient	11.2–20.3.1998 West Africa (humanitarian aid in Sierra Leone)
Rheostat I	7.4–31.10.1974 Suez Canal (mine clearance)
Rheostat II	4.4–1.6.1975 Suez Canal (mine clearance)
Sealion	19.5.1997 Northern Ireland (combines Grenada and Interknit)
Sharp Edge	1.6–18.7.1990 Liberian Civil War – evacuation)
Sharp Fence	1992 Adriatic (monitoring UN sanctions)
Sharp Guard	6.1993 Adriatic (enforcing blockade)
Sharp Vigilance	6–12.1992 Adriatic (monitoring UN sanctions)
Sheepskin	14.3–5.5.1969 Anguilla (restoration of sovereignty)
Shoveller	16.6.1976– Northern Ireland (river security)
Sibling	4–9.10.1987 Irish Sea (seaward defence patrols)
Silkman	11.2000 Sierra Leone (security operations)
Sinbad	2003 Iraq (liberation of Basra)
Slate	2005 Afghanistan (operation against Taliban units)
Snipe	5.2002 Afghanistan (mountain operations against the Taliban)
Snowdon	23.9–9.12.1993 West Indies (maritime interdiction)
Southern Watch	1.1–17.4.1998 Gulf (enforcement of 'no fly' zone, Iraq)
Spartan	17–30.9.1994 West Indies (UN maritime interdiction)
Stella	29.3–26.4.1975 Vietnam (evacuation of refugees)
Swanston	15–28.9.1998 Adriatic (evacuation from Albania)
Tellar	6–15.11.1998 West Indies (hurricane disaster relief)
Telic	2003 Iraq (Second Gulf War)
Tiller	2–10.6.1997 West Africa (security in Sierra Leone)
Titan	14.6–19.8.1980 New Hebrides (restore order over independence)
Triad	1.2–3.3.1995 Mogadishu (protection of withdrawal)
Troy	2.2007 Iraq (Basra security operation)
Vantage	30.6–16.8.1961 Kuwait (reinforcement against Iraq)
Vasco	23.9–3.10.1985 Mexico (disaster relief)
Vela	2006 West Africa (security and stability in Sierra Leone)
Veritas	2002 Afghanistan (operations against the Taliban)
Victor Search	20–31.8.1959 Irish Sea (search for RAF Victor II)
Volcano	2007 Afghanistan (operation against Taliban base)
Warden	15.7–1.10.1991 Turkey (exercise Haven – Kurdish refugees)
Whippet	9.1958 Arctic waters (Cod War operations)
Yammer	5.3–5.8.1985 Turks and Caicos (security operation)
Zealous	10–12.1972 East Africa (security operation)
Zina	2005 Afghanistan (operation against Taliban units)

MAIN NAVAL TASK GROUP DEPLOYMENTS 1973–2008

Royal Navy Task Groups (TGs)

In 1974 the MoD announced the group deployment (GD) policy as follows:

The Royal Navy is now meeting its commitments east of the Cape of Good Hope, in a different way. Gone is the traditional method of operating single ships over a wide area, and in its place is the Task Force idea. This system provides a much more economical and flexible method of operating in distant waters, and also allows the Navy to work with groups of ships from other navies.

An example of greater efficiency is the much higher level of training, which can be achieved during a nine-month deployment. Since they are in almost constant company, the ships can exercise with one another, taking turns to act the hunter or the hunted, the tracker or the target, in realistic simulations of battle conditions. Sailors are kept constantly at peak efficiency, and do not need the re-training that might otherwise be necessary after long solo voyages.

As an additional advantage, the group concept offers the public of many nations improved opportunities of meeting a greater number of the men and a wider variety of the ships that make up today's Royal Navy.

(MoD, O/N 4301875, September 1974)

* – Flagship

1971–2	GD concept formulated (VCNS, Admiral Lewin)
1973	TG 317.1, 1st GD (R Ad Clayton FOF2 in HMS *Tiger**) to the Pacific
1974	TG 317.1 (R Ad Clayton FOF2 in HMS *Fife*) to Australia and the Far East
1974	TG 317.2, 2nd GD (R Ad Leach FOF1 in HMS *Blake*) to the Far East
1975	TG 317.3, 3rd GD (R Ad Fieldhouse FOF2 in HMS *Glamorgan*) to the Pacific
1976	TG 317.4, (R Ad Morton FOF1 in HMS *Antrim*) to the Middle East
1977	TG 317.5, (R Ad Wemyss FOF2 in HMS *Tiger*) to the North and South Atlantic
1978	TG 317.6, (R Ad Wemyss FOF2 in HMS *Tiger*) to the Far East
1978	TG 317.7, (R Ad Squires FOF1 in HMS *Blake*) to the Pacific
1979	TG 317.8, (R Ad Stanford FOF2 in HMS *Norfolk*) to the Far East
1980	TG 318.0, (R Ad Jenkins FOF1 in HMS *Antrim*) (TG 317.9 cancelled)
1981	(No group deployment, to save fuel)
1982	(Falklands War TF 317)
1983	TG 318.3, Orient Express (R Ad Gerken FOF2 in HMS *Invincible*) to the Far East
1984	TG 323.4, Orient Express contd (R Ad Black FOF2 in HMS *Illustrious*)
1986	TG 318.4, Global 86 (R Ad Hogg FOF1 in HMS *Beaver* initially, then HMS *Illustrious*) to South America, Australia and the Far East
1988	TG 318.1, Outback 88 (R Ad Woodhead FOF2 in HMS *Ark Royal*) to the Far East

1989	(End of the Cold War: no group deployment)
1990	TG 316.1, Endeavour 90 (Capt Franklyn in HMS *Bristol* (DTS)) around the world
1990	TG 318.5 (R Ad Hill-Norton FOF3 in HMS *Ark Royal*) to the USA and Canada for Westlant 90 and Marcot 90
1991	(First Gulf War: no group deployment)
1992	TG 318.1, Orient 92 (R Ad Brigstocke COMUKTG in HMS *Invincible*) to the Far East
1993	TG 612.02 (R Ad Brigstocke COMUKTG in HMS *Ark Royal*) to the Adriatic for Operation Grapple (later relieved by R Ad Gretton COMUKTG in HMS *Invincible*)
1994	TG 612.02, HMS *Ark Royal* and HMS *Invincible* in turns to the Adriatic for Operation Grapple
1995	TG 612.02, HMS *Ark Royal* and HMS *Invincible* in turns to the Adriatic for Operation Grapple; Australasia 95 deployment scaled down to small NTG frigates and RFA vessels to the Far East
1995–6	TG 612.02 (R Ad Franklyn COMUKTG in HMS *Illustrious*) to the Adriatic
1996	TG 331.01 (R Ad West COMUKTG in HMS *Illustrious*) to the USA
1997	TG 327.01, Ocean Wave 97 (R Ad West COMUKTG in HMS *Illustrious*) to the Far East
1998	TG 347.01 (R Ad Forbes COMUKTG in HMS *Invincible*) to the Gulf for Operations Jural and Bolton
1999	TG 347.01 (Capt Burnell-Nugent in HMS *Invincible*) to the Gulf for Operation Bolton II and to the Adriatic for Operation Magellan
1999	Argonaut 99 (Cdre Kilgour COMATG in HMS *Ocean*) to the Mediterranean
2000	TG 2000, Eastern Adventure/Maritime Endeavour (R Ad Meyer COMUKTG in HMS *Cornwall*): circumnavigation of the globe
2000	Aurora 2000 ATG to Sierra Leone for Operation Palliser
2001	TG 342.01, Argonaut 01 (R Ad Burnell-Nugent COMUKMARFOR in HMS *Illustrious*), with HMS *Fearless* and HMS *Ocean* to the Middle East
2003	(NTG 03: Operation Telic - Second Gulf War: no group deployment)
2004	Aurora 04: HMS *Invincible*, HMS *Ocean* and HMS *Albion* across the North Atlantic for Rapid Alliance
2005	Marstrike 05 (R Ad Style COMUKMARFOR in HMS *Invincible*) to the Middle East
2006	Aquila 06 (R Ad Morisetti COMUKMARFOR in HMS *Illustrious*) to the Middle East
2007	Orion 07 MCMV Group (Cdr Davies MCM1 in RFA *Cardigan Bay*) to the Mediterranean, the Black Sea and the South Atlantic
2008	Orion 08 (Cdre Cunningham in HMS *Illustrious*) to the Middle East

BASIC ROYAL NAVY TASK FORCE ORGANISATION

The following demonstrates the pyramid structure of an illustrative Royal Navy Task Force (TF 314) formed as a naval component of national force. It shows the breakdown of the different echelons or levels of the organisation formed for specific tasks and the way they are numbered.

The various components are made up of the necessary assets for the specific task allocated to them.

1. The Task Force '314': (TF 314)

2. Task Groups: ('314.1' *et seq*)	(TG 314.1)	(TG 314.2)

3. Task Units: ('314.1.1' *et seq*)	(TU 314.1.1)	(TU 314.1.2),	(TU 314.2.1)	(TU 314.2.2)

4. Task Elements: ('314.1.1.1' *et seq*)	(TE 314.1.1.1)	(TE 314.1.2.1)	(TE 314.2.1.1)	(TU 314.2.2.1)
	(TE 314.1.1.2)	(TE 314.1.2.2)	(TE 314.2.1.2)	(TU 314.2.2.2)
	(TE 314.1.1.3)	(TE 314.1.2.3)	(TE 314.2.1.3)	(TU 314.2.2.3)

Source: Based on structures set out by the Naval Staff in *British Maritime Doctrine*, BR 1806, third edition 2004.

THE BRITISH EMPIRE AND THE ROYAL NAVY

The British Empire was the largest empire in the history of the world and at its peak, in 1921, it covered 14.4 million square miles, over a quarter of the surface of the earth's landmass. It included a population of 458 million people, which was nearly a quarter of the population of the world at that time. It was referred to as the empire on which 'the sun never set'.

The build-up of the empire had been a gradual process and there are various claims as to when that actually started. The sixteenth century was an age of exploration, trade, expansion and colonisation. In 1583 Sir Humphrey Gilbert claimed the island of Newfoundland, and in the following year Sir Walter Raleigh founded the colony of Roanoke, North Carolina. The Seven Years War (1756–63) was an important milestone as Britain gained mastery of the sea after the Battle of Quiberon Bay (1759). As a result of the war Britain emerged as the dominant colonial power having gained India, America and Canada.

As a small island race, Britain possessed a great maritime prowess that enabled it to build and sustain such a vast empire throughout the world. That widespread empire was supported, protected and defended by the Royal Navy. Britain claimed, with considerable justification, to 'rule the waves', and her warships patrolled the world's oceans, which covered almost three-quarters of the earth's surface. The Royal Navy was certainly a major player on the world scene in the eighteenth and nineteenth centuries. It was an enormously powerful force with huge global reach, described in the *Oxford Illustrated History of the Royal Navy* as 'the biggest centrally directed organisation in the world'. The size and importance of the Royal Navy seemed to be inextricably linked to that of the British Empire. As the Navy had played such a key role in founding and sustaining that empire it was fitting that the Navy should play an important part in its final chapter.

By the 1960s, with the decline of the empire, and the withdrawal from east of Suez, the Royal Navy was undergoing a fundamental change in role, adjusting from defending the empire to its long-standing primary role of safeguarding the nation. At the same time it was overseeing and protecting the retreat from empire as Britain steadily withdrew from its many remaining overseas possessions.

Before its peak in 1921 Britain had already lost Canada, Australia, New Zealand and South Africa, but after the Second World War the rest of the empire steadily broke up. Although the majority of colonies became independent, a lot of them chose to remain within the British Commonwealth. Territories of the empire gained their independence, even if remaining within the Commonwealth, as follows:

1947	India and Pakistan
1948	Ceylon, Burma and Palestine
1956	Sudan
1957	Malaya and Ghana
1960	Nigeria, Somalia and Cyprus
1961	Sierra Leone, Tanganyika, Northern and Southern Cameroon
1962	Uganda, Western Samoa, Jamaica, Trinidad and Tobago
1963	Singapore, North Borneo, Sarawak, Kenya and Zanzibar
1964	Malta, Malawi, and Northern Rhodesia
1965	The Gambia and the Maldives
1966	Barbados, Guyana, Botswana and Lesotho
1967	Aden
1968	Mauritius, Swaziland and Nauru
1970	Fiji and Tonga
1973	The Bahamas
1974	Grenada
1975	Papua New Guinea
1976	The Seychelles
1978	Solomon and Ellice Islands and Dominica
1979	Gilbert Islands, St Lucia, St Vincent and the Grenadines
1980	Southern Rhodesia (Zimbabwe) and New Hebrides
1981	Belize, Antigua and Barbuda
1983	St Kitts-Nevis
1984	Brunei
1997	Hong Kong

SECRETARIES FOR DEFENCE AND FIRST SEA LORDS

First Lords of the Admiralty were appointed up until 1 April 1964, when the Cabinet post of First Lord was abolished. Thereafter the post of Secretary of State for Defence was introduced, with responsibility for all three armed services.

C – Conservative
L – Labour
* – designate

Prime Minister	First Lord	First Sea Lord
57–63 Harold Macmillan (C)	57–59 George Douglas Home	55–59 Lord Mountbatten
	59–63 Peter Carrington	59–60 Adm Lambe
		60–63 Adm John
63–64 Alec Douglas-Home (C)	63–64 George Jellicoe	63–66 Adm Luce
Prime Minister	**Defence Secretary**	**First Sea Lord**
64–70 Harold Wilson (L)	64–70 Denis Healey	66–68 Adm Begg
		68–70 Adm Le Fanu
70–74 Edward Heath (C)	70–74 Peter Carrington	70–71 Adm Hill-Norton
	74 Iain Gilmour	71–74 Adm Pollock
74–76 Harold Wilson (L)	74–76 Roy Mason	74–77 Adm Ashmore
76–79 James Callaghan (L)	76–79 Frederick Mulley	77–79 Adm Lewin
79–90 Margaret Thatcher (C)	79–81 Francis Pym	79–82 Adm Leach
	81–83 John Nott	82–85 Adm Fieldhouse
	83–86 Michael Heseltine	85–89 Adm Staveley
	86–89 George Younger	
	89–92 Tom King	89–93 Adm Oswald
90–97 John Major (C)	92–95 Malcolm Rifkind	93–95 Adm Bathurst
	95–97 Michael Portillo	95–98 Adm Slater
97–07 Tony Blair (L)	97–99 George Robertson	98–01 Adm Boyce
	99–05 Geoff Hoon	01–02 Adm Essenhigh
	05–06 John Reid	02–06 Adm West
	06–08 Des Browne	06– Adm Band
07– Gordon Brown (L)	08– John Hutton	[09– Adm Stanhope*]

PRESIDENTS AND CHAIRMEN OF THE WHITE ENSIGN ASSOCIATION, 1958–2009

Presidents
David ROBARTS
Sir John PRIDEAUX
LORD KINGSDOWN
LORD BOARDMAN (Vice President Sir Donald GOSLING)
LORD ALEXANDER (Vice President Sir Donald GOSLING)
Commodore Sir Donald GOSLING KCVO, RNR

Chairmen
Admiral Sir John ECCLES GCB, KCVO, CBE, DL
Admiral Sir Deric HOLLAND-MARTIN GCB, DSO, DSC
Admiral Sir Andrew LEWIS KCB
Sir Donald GOSLING
Admiral of the Fleet Lord LEWIN KG, GCB, MVO, DSC
Sir Derrick HOLDEN-BROWN
Admiral of the Fleet Lord FIELDHOUSE GCB, GBE
Henry LAMBERT
Admiral Sir Michael LAYARD KCB, CBE
Sir Michael BETT CBE
Admiral Sir Jock SLATER GCB, LVO, DL (Vice Chair: J D Andrewes)
John Andrewes (Vice Chair: Admiral the Lord Boyce)
Admiral the Lord Boyce GCB, OBE, DL (Vice Chair: Sir John Parker)

GLOSSARY OF TERMS AND ABBREVIATIONS

The exact definitions of some abbreviations have been amended slightly to make their meanings clearer.

AA	anti-aircraft
AAA	anti-aircraft artillery
AAW	anti-air warfare
ABM	anti-ballistic missile
ACNS (P)	Assistant Chief of Naval Staff (Policy)
ACR	Admiral Commanding Reserves
AD	(1) Air Defence; (2) aircraft-direction, describing ships fitted with highly developed electronic equipment for the direction of carrier-borne and shore-based aircraft
ADEX	air defence exercise
AEGIS	sophisticated naval air defence system developed by the US Navy. The automatic fire control system co-ordinates missile defences against incoming threats from surface, sub-surface and air threats
AEW	airborne early warning
AFO	Admiralty Fleet Order (administrative instructions)
AFPRB	Armed Forces Pay Review Body (independent body which recommends levels of service pay in the armed forces)
AFS (H)	auxiliary forward support ship operating helicopters
AIM-9	Sidewinder air-to-air missile (carried by SHAR and A-4Q)
AMP	Assisted Maintenance Period (routine period of ship maintenance with assistance from external engineering staff)
AMRAAM	advanced medium-range air-to-air missile
ANZUK	Australia New Zealand United Kingdom (FPDA)
APLIS	Applied Physics Laboratory Ice Station (submarine ops evaluation)
ARG	Amphibious Ready Group (UK amphibious force)
AS.12	air-to-surface missile (carried by Wasp helicopter)
ASW	anti-submarine warfare
ATG	Amphibious Task Group
AUTEC	Atlantic Underwater Test and Evaluation Centre in the Bahamas
AWRE	Atomic Weapons Research Establishment at Aldermaston, in the Thames Valley
A-4Q	Skyhawk attack aircraft
BFL	British Fishery Limit
BOST	basic operational sea training
BRITFOLEB	British Force Lebanon
BRNC	Britannia Royal Naval College at Dartmouth, Devon, for the education and general naval training of junior officers
CACS	Computer Assisted Command System (ship's computerised operations command and control system)
CAG	Carrier Air Group
CAP	Combat Air Patrol
CASEVAC	casualty evacuation (frequently by helicopter)
CBFFI	Commander British Forces Falkland Islands
CBG	Carrier Battle Group (US self-contained naval squadron based on a major aircraft carrier with escorts and full support)
CCIS	command and control information systems
Cdo	Royal Marine Commando ('battalion' size unit)
CDS	Chief of the Defence Staff
CENTO	Central Treaty Organisation, set up in 1955 between UK, Iran, Iraq, Turkey and Pakistan
CINCHAN	NATO Commander in Chief Channel (normally held by the UK CINCFLEET)
CINCEASTLANT	NATO Commander in Chief Eastern Atlantic Area (normally held by the UK CINCFLEET)
CINCFLEET	Commander in Chief Fleet
CIWS	close-in weapon system (inner layer of defence against incoming anti-ship missiles, normally a rapid firing gun)
CJO	Chief of Joint Operations
Cmnd	Government Command Document (SDE etc)
CMS	coastal minesweeper
CODLAG	combined diesel, electric and gas turbine propulsion system
COMATG	Commander Amphibious Task Group
COMAW	Commodore Amphibious Warfare
COMDJTF	NATO Commander Deployable Joint Task Force
COMPHIBRON	Commander Amphibious Squadron (USN/USMC squadron)
COMUKMARFOR	Commander UK Maritime Force
COMUKTG	Commander UK Task Group
COSAG	combined steam and gas (dual-propulsion system for ships)
COST	Committee on Officer Structure and Training
CTCRM	Commando Training Centre Royal Marines, at Lympstone in Devon
CTF	(1) Commander Task Force; (2) Coalition Task Force (followed by the Task Force number)
CTG	Commander Task Group
CTU	Commander Task Unit
CVF	Carrier Vessel Future (the Future Aircraft Carrier)
CVS	small carrier operating STOVL aircraft (the *Invincible* class anti-submarine warfare carriers, built as command ships of ASW forces)
DC	Defence Council Document (NATO)
DCI	Defence Council Instructions (replaced AFOs)
DD	Destroyer (large escort ship, usually air-defence)
DED	docking and essential defect repair
DEFCON	Defence Readiness State (US forces)
DESO	Defence Export Sales Organisation
DF	direction finding
DLG	destroyer leader guided missile (the County class guided missile destroyers)
DTS	Dartmouth Training Squadron/Ship (dedicated to training junior officers)
ECM	electronic counter measures (radar jamming)
EEC	European Economic Community
Elint	electronic intelligence gathering (usually by Soviet spy ships)
EOD	explosive ordnance disposal (team)
EOKA	Ethniki Organosis Kuprion Agoniston (a right-wing Greek Cypriot terrorist group)
ESM	electronic support/surveillance measures (passive electronic interception of radio and radar, tactics)
EW	electronic warfare
EXOCET	air-to-surface (AM.39) and surface-to-surface (MM.39) missiles
FAA	Fleet Air Arm
FF	frigate (medium-size escort ship)
FFO	furnace fuel oil (fuel used by older ships)
FLS	forward logistic site (NATO naval logistic base)
FMU	fleet maintenance unit (available to deploy to ships)
FOB	forward operating base
FOCAS	Flag Officer Carriers and Amphibious Ships
FOF1	Flag Officer 1st Flotilla
FONA	Flag Officer Naval Aviation
FOP	fleet operational programme (ship deployment plans)
FOS	fleet operational schedule
FOSF	Flag Officer Surface Flotilla
FOSM	Flag Officer Submarines
FOST	Flag Officer Sea Training
FPB	fast patrol boat
FPC	fast pursuit craft (operated by Royal Marines)
FPDA	Five-Power Defence Arrangement (defensive treaty signed by the UK, Australia, New Zealand, Singapore and Malaysia in 1971)
FPS	Fishery Protection Squadron (the 'Fish' Squadron)
FRADU	Fleet Requirements and Aircraft Direction Unit, at RNAS Culdrose (a squadron of jet aircraft, usually Hawks, for fleet training and exercises)
GMD	guided missile destroyer (usually the County class)
GPMG	general purpose machine gun
GR3	Ground Attack Harrier
GRIUK	Greenland–Iceland–Faeroes–UK
HDML	harbour defence motor launch
ICBM	intercontinental ballistic missile
IED	improvised explosive device (usually home-made terrorist bomb)
IFOR	Implementation Force (UN enforcement operations)
IS	internal security
ISAF	International Security and Assistance Force
JFH	Joint Force Harrier
JHC	Joint Helicopter Command
JHQ	Joint Headquarters (for conduct of combined operations)
JIC	Joint Intelligence Committee
JMC	Joint Maritime Course (advanced naval and maritime air training exercises held annually off the coast of Scotland)
JRRF	Joint Rapid Reaction Force (concept established by SDR)
JSF	Joint Strike Fighter (the F-35 strike jet for the new-generation aircraft carriers for the Royal Navy)
JTF	Joint Task Force
LCT	landing craft (tanks)

LPD	landing platform (dock) (a large amphibious ship with an open stern which floods down to enable it to operate landing craft)
LPH	landing platform helicopter
LSL	landing ship (logistic)
LST	landing ship (tanks)
LTC	long-term costing (MoD budget planning)
MARS	Military Afloat Research and Sustainability
MC	military committee (NATO)
MCJO	Maritime Contribution to Joint Operations
MCM	mine counter-measures
MCMFORMED	Mine Counter-Measures Force Mediterranean
MCMFORNORTH	Mine Counter-Measures Force North-West
MCMV	mine counter-measures vessel
MEZ	Maritime Exclusion Zone
MGRM	Major General Royal Marines
MHC	mine hunting craft
MIDLINK	Middle East maritime exercise
MIOPS	maritime interdiction operations
MLF	multilateral force
MLU	mid-life update (major ship refit to modernise equipment fit)
MNC	Major NATO Commander (one of the three top NATO military commanders)
MoD	Ministry of Defence
MPA	maritime patrol aircraft
MRLS	multiple rocket launcher system
MSC	coastal minesweeper
MSS	minesweeping squadron
MV	Motor Vessel
MY	Motor Yacht
NAS	Naval Air Squadron
NATO	North Atlantic Treaty Organisation
NaTT	Naval Assistance and Training Team (naval team training the Iraqi Navy)
NAVOCFORCHAN	NATO Naval On Call Force Channel (MCMV under CINCHAN)
NAVOCFORMED	NATO Naval On Call Force Mediterranean (multi-national)
NBCD	defensive measures against the threat of nuclear, biological and chemical weapons
NGS	naval gunfire support (shore bombardment by naval guns)
NHB	Naval Historical Branch
NLF	National Liberation Front (Aden)
NP	Naval Party (small group of naval personnel on detached duty)
NRF	NATO Response Force
NTG	Naval Task Group
OM	operator-mechanic
OPV	offshore patrol vessel
OTC	Officer in Tactical Command
PAAMS	principal anti-air missile system
PC	patrol craft
PDRY	People's Democratic Republic of Yemen
PJHQ	Permanent Joint Headquarters (for the planning and directing of joint operations)
PWO	Principal Warfare Officer
RA	Royal Artillery
RAF	Royal Air Force
RAS	replenishment at sea (refuelling or receiving stores whilst steaming alongside or close to a tanker or supply ship)

RFA	Royal Fleet Auxiliary (logistic support ships, tankers, replenishment and specialist ships operated in support of the RN)
RIB	rigid inflatable boat
RIMPAC	Naval exercise for Pacific Rim countries
RM	Royal Marines
RMAS	Royal Maritime Auxiliary Service (craft, tugs, salvage and mooring vessels, and small coastal and harbour craft operated in support of the RN)
RNAS	Royal Naval Air Station
RNEC	Royal Naval Engineering College (HMS *Thunderer*) at Manadon, Plymouth
RNLN	Royal Netherlands Navy
RNPT	Royal Naval Presentation Team
RNR	Royal Naval Reserve
RNZN	Royal New Zealand Navy
ROE	rules of engagement
RoP	Report of Proceedings (Commanding Officer's official report)
RPG	rocket propelled grenade
RRF	Rapid Reaction Force (established by SDR)
RSRM	Raiding Squadron Royal Marines (using RIBs or FPCs)
SACEUR	Supreme Allied Commander Europe (one of the top three NATO military commanders)
SACLANT	Supreme Allied Commander Atlantic (one of the top three military commanders of NATO)
SAF	Sultan of Oman's Armed Forces
SAG	Surface Action Group
SALT	Strategic Arms Limitations Talks
SAM	surface-to-air missile
SAS	Special Air Service (army)
SBA	Sovereign Base Area (Cyprus)
SBS	Special Boat Squadron (Royal Marines), similar to army 'SAS'
SD	Special Duties List (denotes officers promoted from the ranks for specialised duties)
SDE	Statement of Defence Estimates
SDR	Strategic Defence Review (fundamental review in 1998)
SEATO	South-East Asia Treaty Organisation
SF	Special Forces (includes SAS and SBS)
SHAR	Sea Harrier (naval VSTOL aircraft)
SINS	Ship Inertial Navigation System
SL	Supplementary List (denotes officers selected to supplement the mainstream officer corps)
SLOCs	sea lines of communication
SMOPS	School of Maritime Operations
SMP	self maintenance period (maintenance using ship's resources)
SNMCMG1	Standing NATO Mine Counter-Measures Group 1
SNMG2	Standing NATO Maritime Group 2
SNOFI	Senior Naval Officer Falkland Islands
SNOME	Senior Naval Officer Middle East
SNONI	Senior Naval Officer Northern Ireland
SNOWI	Senior Naval Officer West Indies
SON	Sultan of Oman's Navy
SOSUS	sound surveillance system (linked network of listening devices on the sea bed to detect submarines in the area)
SPF	Special Forces (elite troops trained for special operations)

SSBN	ballistic missile-carrying nuclear submarine
SSK	hunter-killer (diesel electric submarine)
SSKN	hunter-killer (nuclear submarine)
SSM	surface-to-surface missile
SSN	nuclear fleet submarine
SSGN	cruise or guided missile armed nuclear submarine
STANAVFORCHAN	Standing Naval Force Channel (MCMV)
STANAVFORLANT	Standing Naval Force Atlantic
STANAVFORMED	Standing Naval Force Mediterranean
START	Strategic Arms Reduction Treaty (1980s)
STOVL	short take off and vertical landing
STUFT	ships taken up from trade (chartered merchant ships)
SWAPS	South-Western Approaches (west of the end of the English Channel)
TA	towed array (series of sonar transducers towed astern of a submarine or ship)
TacTom	latest variant of the Tomahawk land attack missile
TAG	Tailored Air Group (air group for CVS mission)
TAS	torpedo and anti-submarine warfare (specialisation for officers and ratings)
TEZ	Total Exclusion Zone
TF	Task Force (force formed for specific task)
TG	Task Group (group formed for specific deployment or operation)
TLAM	Tomahawk land attack cruise missile
TMA	target motion analysis (the study of submarine sonar and acoustic information)
TopMast	Total Personnel Management System (flexible manning of ships)
TOW	tube-launched, optically tracked, wire-guided missiles
UDI	Unilateral Declaration of Independence
UKMCC	UK Maritime Component Commander
UKTG	United Kingdom On Call Task Group
UN	United Nations
UNFICYP	United Nations Force in Cyprus
UNSCOM	United Nations Special Commission (set up to cover Iraq)
UNSCR	United Nations Security Council Resolution
UNSFOR	United Nations Stabilisation Force (in the former Republic of Yugoslavia)
USS	United States Ship
UVF	Ulster Volunteer Force
VCDS	Vice Chief of the Defence Staff
VCNS	Vice Chief of the Naval Staff
VDS	variable depth sonar
VERTREPS	vertical transfers by helicopter, known as vertical replenishment
VSTOL	vertical short take off and landing
VTOL	vertical take off and landing
WESTLANT	Westlant Deployment, generally used to describe major annual spring deployments for exercises with the US Navy 2nd Fleet in the north-west Atlantic, including the US Navy's fleet weapon ranges off Puerto Rico
WEU	Western European Union
WEUCONMARFOR	Western European Maritime Contingency Force
WIGS	West Indies Guardship
WRNS	Women's Royal Naval Service

INDEX

ACKNOWLEDGEMENTS

The White Ensign Association wishes to thank the following for their invaluable help in the production of this book:

Stuart Baines, Iain Ballantyne, Commander Piers Barker RN, General Sir Henry Beverley KCB, OBE, Harvey Burwin, Lieutenant Commander Clive Chaney RN, David Cobb, Captain Dan Conley RN, Catherine Cooper, Captain Rick Cosby LVO, RN, Lieutenant Commander Mike Critchley RN, Commander Philip Doyne-Ditmas OBE RN, Sarah Fletcher, Moira Gittos, Lieutenant Commander D C Graham RD, RNR, Roger Hancock, David Hardstaff, Lieutenant Commander Mike Howell RN, Commander Charles Howeson RN, Geoff Hunt, Pippa Johnson, Admiral Sir Michael Layard KCB, CBE, Captain Doug Littlejohns CBE, RN, Karen Maxwell, Captain Jock Morrison RN, Trevor Muston, Lieutenant Commander Ken Napier MBE, RN, Captain Chris Page RN, James Quibell, Captain Keith Ridland RN, Odile Roberts, Becky Saxe-Falstein, Matthew Sheldon, Alec Simpson, Captain John Speller OBE, RN, Commander Geoff Tall OBE, RN, Kate Tildesley, Vice Admiral Sir John Webster KCB, Captain Andrew Welch RN, Dr Colin White, Vice Admiral Peter Wilkinson CVO, Commander Alistair Wilson RN, as well as many others.